THE ART OF
CRITICISM

THE ART OF CRITICISM

HENRY JAMES ON THE
THEORY AND THE PRACTICE
OF FICTION

EDITED BY
WILLIAM VEEDER
AND
SUSAN M. GRIFFIN

THE UNIVERSITY OF CHICAGO PRESS   CHICAGO AND LONDON

WILLIAM VEEDER is professor of English at the University of Chicago and the author of *Henry James—The Lessons of the Master* and *Mary Shelley & Frankenstein*, both published by the University of Chicago Press.

SUSAN M. GRIFFIN is assistant professor of English at the University of Louisville.

THE UNIVERSITY OF CHICAGO PRESS, CHICAGO 60637
THE UNIVERSITY OF CHICAGO PRESS, LTD., LONDON

LIBRARY OF CONGRESS CATALOGING-IN-PUBLICATION DATA
James, Henry, 1843–1916.
    The art of criticism.

    Bibliography: p.
    Includes index.
    1. Fiction—Authorship—Addresses, essays, lectures.
2. Fiction—History and criticism—Addresses, essays,
lectures.   I. Veeder, William R.   II. Griffin, Susan M.,
1953–   .   III. Title.
PS2112.V4   1986   801'.953   85-24544
ISBN 0-226-39196-5
ISBN 0-226-39197-3 (pbk.)

C O N T E N T S

Introduction   1

PART ONE: PRACTICING NOVELIST AS PRACTICAL CRITIC

1 Matthew Arnold's *Essays in Criticism* (1865)   11
2 Sainte-Beuve (1880, 1904)   24
3 *Middlemarch* (1873)   48
4 Honoré de Balzac (1875, 1878)   59
5 From *Hawthorne* (1879)   101
6 Ivan Turgénieff (1884, 1888)   132

PART TWO: THE THEORIST ON FICTION AND CULTURE

7 The Art of Fiction (1884, 1888)   165
8 Guy de Maupassant (1888)   197
9 Criticism (1891, 1893)   232
10 The Future of the Novel (1899)   242

PART THREE: THE MASTER AND HIS PREFACES

11 *Roderick Hudson* (1907)   259
12 *The American* (1907)   271
13 *The Portrait of a Lady* (1908)   286
14 *The Awkward Age* (1908)   300
15 *What Maisie Knew* (1908)   316
16 *The Aspern Papers* (1908)   330
17 *The Wings of the Dove* (1909)   346
18 *The Ambassadors* (1909)   361
19 *The Golden Bowl* (1909)   376

PART FOUR: GENIUS IN OLD AGE

20 Emile Zola (1903, 1914)   425
21 The Novel in *The Ring and the Book* (1912, 1914)   460
   Bibliography   491
   Index   503

. . . to wonder is to live back gratefully into the finer reasons of things.

Preface to *The Princess Casamassima*

INTRODUCTION

In a now famous letter of September 20, 1867, Henry James told T. S. Perry

> When I say that I should like to do as Ste.-Beuve has done, I don't mean that I should like to imitate him, or reproduce him in English: but only that I should like to acquire something of his intelligence and his patience and vigour. One feels—I feel at least, that he is a man of the past, of a dead generation; and that we young Americans are (without cant) men of the future. I feel that my only chance for success as a critic is to let all the breezes of the west blow through me at their will. We are Americans born—*il faut en prendre son parti.* I look upon it as a great blessing; and I think that to be an American is an excellent preparation for culture. We have exquisite qualities as a race, and it seems to me that we are ahead of the European races in the fact that more than either of them we can deal freely with forms of civilization not our own, can pick and choose and assimilate and in short (aesthetically etc) claim our property wherever we find it. To have no national stamp has hitherto been a defect and a drawback, but I think it not unlikely that American writers may yet indicate that a vast intellectual fusion and synthesis of the various National tendencies of the world is the condition of more important achievements than any we have seen.

James was prescient in envisioning himself the man of the future whose freedom of mind could transcend the boundaries of nationality. For half a century he dealt with forms of civilization not his own. Or rather he made those forms his own. Able to "pick and choose and assimilate," he spoke foreign languages fluently, studied cultures freely, and produced masterpieces in virtually every prose genre. This "intellectual fusion and synthesis" helped make Henry James the premier critic of fiction in the nineteenth century.

1

That the first condition of good criticism is intellectual freedom became clear to James in his youth. Recalling his boyhood pleasure at comparing stage versions of *Uncle Tom's Cabin,* he describes his "great initiation" into "ironic detachment," into that freedom which is the precondition of criticism. "One small spectator . . . got his first glimpse of that possibility of a 'free play of mind' over a subject which was to throw him with force at a later stage of culture, when subjects had considerably multiplied, into the critical arms of Matthew Arnold" (*A,* 94). "Free play of mind," or disinterestedness, is the critical ideal which James derived from civilizations not his own, from England and the continent, from Arnold and Sainte-Beuve and ultimately from Goethe. What James defines as disinterestedness in "The Art of Fiction"—"we must grant the artist his subject . . . our criticism is applied only to what he makes of it"—is what Sainte-Beuve admired in "le grand Goethe, le maître de la critique, [qui] a établi ce principe souverain qu'il faut surtout s'attacher à l'exécution dans les oeuvres de l'artiste et voir s'il a fait, et comment il a fait, ce qu'il a voulu."*

For James, disinterestedness is the state of being *in-between,* in at least three senses. The good critic is "a compromise between the philosopher and the historian" ("A French Critic" [1865]). This difficult synthesis James finds best exemplified in Sainte-Beuve.

> He is a philosopher in so far as that he deals with ideas. He counts, weighs, measures, appraises them. But he is not a philosopher in so far as that he works with no supreme object. There results from his work no deliberate theory of life, of nature, of the universe. He is not, as the philosopher must ever be more or less, a partizan. . . . The philosopher's function is to compare a work with an abstract principle of truth; the critic's is to compare a work with itself, with its own concrete standard of truth. The critic deals, therefore, with parts, the philosopher with wholes. In M. Sainte-Beuve, however, it is the historian who is most generously represented. As a critic, he bears the same relation to facts that he does to ideas. As the metaphysician handles ideas with a preconceived theory, so the historian handles facts with a preconcerted plan. But with this theory or this plan, the critic has nothing to do. (1865)

* "The great Goethe, the master of criticism, [who] has established this sovereign principle, that it is necessary above all to focus on execution in the works of the artist and to see if he has accomplished and how he has accomplished what he set out to do." Quoted from Sainte-Beuve's *La Morale et L'Art,* by John Goode, in his excellent "The art of fiction: Walter Besant and Henry James," *Tradition and tolerance in nineteenth-century fiction,* ed. David Howard et al. (London: Routledge and Kegan Paul, 1966), p. 264.

2

The alternative to being between philosopher and historian is to be like Taine, "*alternately* a philosopher and a historian" (1865; our italics). The consequence is that "M. Taine is not pre-eminently a critic [at all] . . . he is perpetually sacrificing shades to broad lines . . . he is too passionate, too partial, too eloquent."

James also locates the critic between the scholar and the man of the world. Again the ideal is Sainte-Beuve.

> The great critic had as much of what is called human nature as of erudition, and the proof of his genius was the fashion in which he made them go hand-in-hand. He was a man of books, and yet in perception, in divination, in sympathy, in taste, he was consummately a man of the world. It is a marvel to see the way in which he effects this subtle interfusion of science and experience. He appeals to the cultured man, to the highly civilized and finished social unit, but he appeals to him in behalf of something which demands no sacrifice of points of contact with the world, but an increase and a higher sensibility in each. ("Sainte-Beuve's English Portraits" [1875])

Finally, James sees the good critic combining "masculine" and "feminine" traits androgynously:

> there is something feminine in his [Sainte-Beuve's] tact, his penetration, his subtlety and pliability, his rapidity of transition, his magical divinations, his sympathies and antipathies, his marvelous art of insinuation, of expressing himself by fine touches and of adding touch to touch. But all this side of the feminine genius was re-enforced by faculties of quite another order—faculties of the masculine stamp; the completeness, the solid sense, the constant reason, the moderation, the copious knowledge, the passion for exactitude and for general considerations. In attempting to appreciate him, it is impossible to keep these things apart; they melt into each other like the elements of the atmosphere. . . . ("Sainte-Beuve" [1904])

That Henry James himself combined the feminine and the masculine, the scholarly and the worldly, the contemplative and the analytic, is readily documented. What must be added is that James was also in-between both psychologically and culturally. Psychologically he was an outsider—from the time that his brother William distinguished him from the "boys who curse and swear" (*A*, 147), to his own later recognition that the men's world was downtown whereas he remained uptown with the women, to his still later absence from the battlefields of the Civil War. The outsider as onlooker was, however, an insider—once he looked on with an interest as passionate and an attention as intense as James'. From his early stories about Civil War veterans, to his long participation in the social and intellectual life of America and Europe, to his late examination of wealth and corruption in *The Ivory Tower*, Henry James was preeminently the student of culture.

His stance was culturally in-between by the very fact that his role was necessarily *critical*. He began writing as the heir of Boston Brahmin editors who sought resolutely to raise the standards of American cultural life. James was particularly well equipped for this critical task because he was doubly an outsider: not only did he share the Brahmin's distate for American vulgarity, he escaped their parochial focus upon New England. James was self-consciously *a New Yorker*. Scholars have repeatedly overlooked this distinction, but the James family felt it so keenly that they had their New York origins inscribed upon their Cambridge tombstones. That Henry James could also recognize and satirize the limitations of New York in a masterpiece like *Washington Square* means he could criticize American limitations as America itself was largely unable to do. He provided the same service, moreover, for the other world which he lived in but was never really part of, England.

> It is from American critics like James and Eliot that we Europeans have learned to understand our social and literary traditions in a way we could never have learned by ourselves, for they, with natural ease, look at our past, as it is extremely difficult for us to look, with contemporary eyes. (W. H. Auden, Introduction, *The American Scene* [New York: Charles Scribner's Sons, 1946], p. xx)

Henry James thus came to embody for his culture the ideal of free play of mind which he had described to T. S. Perry. He became the good critic as citizen of the world.

This ideal of criticism James lived out for half a century, producing a critical oeuvre remarkable for the number and variety of its masterpieces. His commentaries upon theater and painting were long ago collected. But copyright restrictions have until recently prevented a comparable effort with James' greatest critical achievement, his commentaries upon fiction. Leon Edel and Mark Wilson have now collected all of the literary criticism into two volumes (New York: The Library of America, 1984). In *The Art of Criticism* we attempt to bring together the best of James' Prefaces with the best of his other essays.

4

Confronted with hundreds of texts, we have selected those which both represent James' best work and reveal the range of his critical talent. In studying the fiction of five nations, he became the master of various critical genres: the review, the overview of a career, the biography, the appreciation, as well as explorations of method and theory. Finally, in the Prefaces, James applies his critical skills to himself. In effect reviewing his own best productions, James provides his career with an overview rooted in biography, and creates a body of theory unprecedented in the criticism of fiction.

We have attempted to suggest the shape of James' critical career, as well as the magnitude of his achievement, by selecting essays from all four phases of his half-century endeavor. (These phases are not of course watertight; James continues, for example, to do practical criticism during the years of his major essays in theory.) James begins as a practical critic. We present his response to the two critics and four novelists who influenced him most. The review of Arnold and the overview of Sainte-Beuve establish James' critical standards and illuminate his practical criticism in this and later phases. That the subjects of his best essays on fiction are not only major novelists but major influences upon his own novels indicates the depth and intimacy of James' involvement with his culture. As an exile from America, he writes acutely on Hawthorne for the same reason that as an American in exile he writes sensitively about Eliot, Balzac, and Turgenev: James the outsider-insider is already using his free play of mind to engage with forms of civilization made intensely his own.

James continues this critical engagement when he turns to what may seem a more rarefied endeavor—writing the great theoretical essays of his second phase. Theory for James is fundamentally social because criticism for him is part of the moral life of the culture. In the early 1880s, he uses his authority as a major novelist (one reviewer had called him "the first of English-writing novelists") to exhort Anglo-American society to examine its standards for fiction. How, James asks, can a culture which equates the moral with what is fit for the ears of the Young Person ever begin to understand moral reality? How can that culture even discuss with probity and daring what reality is? As James' practical criticism involved him with the major figures of the era, his efforts in theory join him with the major novelists—Hardy, Gissing, Moore—whose dissatisfactions with their reading public begin the period's attack upon Mrs. Grundy.

"The Art of Fiction" is of course the premier text of James' theoretical phase, but he told Robert Louis Stevenson only four months after completing the essay that it expressed "only half of what I had to say" (December 5, 1884). James spoke out several more times in this second phase, producing "Criticism" and "The Future of the Novel" in the 1890s. (We include "Guy de Maupassant" among the theory pieces because throughout this essay James uses his detailed analysis of Maupassant's fiction to raise larger questions of method and principle.)

The New York Edition provided James with the opportunity to bring together theory and practice in the analysis of his own writing. In the Prefaces, James interweaves his speculations about the natures of writer, text, reader, and critic with discussion of the practical revision of his fiction. "Revision" for James entails not only rewriting, but re-seeing, re-reading. This imaginative interaction is meant to create, by example, a community of fellow readers for his fiction. As with our selections for the edition as a whole, we have tried to reprint James' best Prefaces and to include those which address each of his major critical concerns. In some instances this ideal combination was impossible; James' comments on the short story, for example, are scattered throughout his weaker Prefaces. We have therefore used our notes to include important passages from such Prefaces.

James' last phase is largely retrospective. His one projective effort, "The New Novel," has moments of power, but is too long and too often devoted to talents ultimately minor to be included among his best work. We have chosen instead essays on Zola and Browning which reflect James' continuing range—his concern with French and English writers of two generations. The essays also demonstrate the extraordinary endurance of James' critical energy. "Emile Zola" shows him still attempting to perfect "disinterestedness," because Zola confronts James again with one of the paramount moral issues: how to do justice to a writer whose integrity impresses and whose vision repels. "The Novel in 'The Ring and the Book'" shows vitality in a different way. For James, Browning was at once a Victorian and a modern writer. Reading *The Ring and the Book* in 1912, therefore, James, whose own novels span two centuries, confronts both Browning as poet and himself as novelist. James combines the roles of reader and writer, as he reenacts Browning's narrative transformation of historical materials. James also shows himself both Victorian and modern as a critic: he encounters freshly the questions of fictional form raised in his 1873 review of *Middlemarch*, actively theorizing about the very nature of narrative.

As a life-long effort, James' criticism achieves the goal which Sainte-Beuve set for the critic and which James made his own—to produce "an honorable witness to one's time" ("Sainte-Beuve's First Articles" [1875]).

The Art of Criticism presents each James essay in entirety (the book-length *Hawthorne* being the inevitable exception). We have attempted to provide the reader with what James himself emphasized in his literary criticism: the text's context. Each essay is therefore followed by a commentary and notes which provide biographical, bibliographical, and critical backgrounds. We have also tried to place each essay in the context of James' criticism as a whole, including in the notes important passages from essays that could not be included in a selected edition. James' range of allusions and diversity of readers force editors to walk a fine line between over- and under-annotating. We identify, for example, Charles Reade, but not Charles Dickens. Similarly, since James often follows a French phrase with its English equivalent, we have provided translations only when James' context does not. With each essay we have used James' final version (and title). For those essays which James revised, variants between the first and last versions are listed following the notes (changes in punctuation and spelling are not cited). Reference to the essays in the notes sections and the lists of variants is by page and line number; thus 88:6 refers to page 88, line 6. This sequence of James essay, commentary, notes, and textual variants, is altered slightly for the Prefaces. Since James often discusses a given critical topic in a number of Prefaces, we have, to avoid repetition, given one editorial commentary for the Prefaces as a whole. It follows the Preface to *The Golden Bowl* and is followed, in turn, by the notes to each of the Prefaces.

James' ongoing concern with a variety of critical topics makes cross-referencing a crucial and formidable task. Major discussions of a topic are cited in the notes; for minor ones, see the Index. James essays which are not included in this edition but are listed in our bibliography, are cited initially by title and date and subsequently by date only. For cross-references to essays within this edition, we direct the reader to the appropriate chapter (in the case of general discussions) or page (when the reference is specific).

When quoting James' fiction, we have used, whenever possible, the New York Edition, citing volume, book, and chapter. The fullest collection of James' letters is Edel's four-volume selection (Cambridge: Harvard University Press, 1974–84), cited by correspondent and date. References to *The Notebooks of Henry James*, ed. Matthiesen and Murdock (New York: Oxford University Press, 1947), abbreviated as *N*, are given by date when available, by page when entries are undated. In referring to James' autobiographical writings, we cite Dupee's one-volume edition, *Autobiography* (1956; rpt., Princeton: Princeton University Press, 1983), abbreviated as *A*.

Because good bibliographies of secondary criticism on James exist, we list critics selectively, omitting "Notes" and dissertations. Interested readers may consult, as we have, Budd, *Henry James: A Bibliography of Criticism, 1975–1981* (Westport, Conn.: Greenwood Press, 1983); McColgan, *Henry James, 1917–1959: A Reference Guide* (Boston: G. K. Hall, 1979); Ricks, *Henry James: A Bibliography of Secondary Works* (Metuchen, N.J.: Scarecrow Press, 1975); Scura, *Henry James, 1960–1974: A Reference Guide* (Boston: G. K. Hall, 1979); and Taylor, *Henry James, 1866–1916: A Reference Guide* (Boston: G. K. Hall, 1982). Secondary sources that we refer to often—Daugherty, *The Literary Criticism of Henry James* (Athens: Ohio University Press, 1981); Kelley, *The Early Development of Henry James* (1930; rpt., Urbana: University of Illinois Press, 1965); Miller, *Theory of Fiction: Henry James* (Lincoln: University of Nebraska Press, 1972); Roberts, *Henry James's Criticism* (1929; rpt., New York: Haskell House, 1965)—are identified by the author's name only; page numbers are given for substantive discussions. Unless otherwise noted, all references to Edel are to his *The Life of Henry James*, 5 vols. (Philadelphia: J. B. Lippincott, 1953–72), cited by volume and page number. Like all students of James, we are indebted to Edel and Laurence, *A Bibliography of Henry James*, 3d ed. (New York: Oxford University Press, 1982); Gard, *Henry James: The Critical Heritage* (London: Routledge & Kegan Paul, 1968); and Stafford, *A Name, Title, and Place Index to the Critical Writings of Henry James* (Englewood, Col.: Microcard Editions Books, 1975). We have also used profitably Foley's dissertation, "Criticism in American Periodicals of the Works of Henry James from 1866 to 1916" (The Catholic University of America, 1944). We would like to express our debt and gratitude to James E. Miller, Jr., and to Robert E. Streeter, for their encouragement in this project; to Professor Priscilla Clark for generous assistance with James' French; to John Wright, Lukass Franklin, Heather Blair, Timothy Child, and Karen Rosenthal for their help throughout; to the A & S and Graduate Dean's offices of the University of Louisville, and to the Dean of the Division of the Humanities of the University of Chicago, for research funds; and to the University of Chicago Press, for its sustained reasonableness.

PART ONE

PRACTICING NOVELIST AS PRACTICAL CRITIC

O N E

MATTHEW ARNOLD'S
Essays in Criticism

M R. ARNOLD'S ESSAYS IN CRITICISM COME TO AMERI-
can readers with a reputation already made,—the reputation
of a charming style, a great deal of excellent feeling, and an almost
equal amount of questionable reasoning. It is for us either to confirm
the verdict passed in the author's own country, or to judge his work
afresh. It is often the fortune of English writers to find mitigation of
sentence in the United States.

The Essays contained in this volume are on purely literary subjects; which is for us, by itself, a strong recommendation. English
literature, especially contemporary literature, is, compared with that
of France and Germany, very poor in collections of this sort. A great
deal of criticism is written, but little of it is kept; little of it is deemed to
contain any permanent application. Mr. Arnold will doubtless find in
this fact—if indeed he has not already signalized it—but another
proof of the inferiority of the English to the Continental school of
criticism, and point to it as a baleful effect of the narrow practical
spirit which animates, or, as he would probably say, paralyzes, the
former. But not only is his book attractive as a whole, from its exclusively literary character; the subject of each essay is moreover particularly interesting. The first paper is on the function of Criticism at
the present time; a question, if not more important, perhaps more
directly pertinent here than in England. The second, discussing the
literary influence of Academies, contains a great deal of valuable observation and reflection in a small compass and under an inadequate
title. The other essays are upon the two De Guérins, Heinrich Heine,
Pagan and Mediæval Religious Sentiment, Joubert, Spinoza, and
Marcus Aurelius. The first two articles are, to our mind, much the
best; the next in order of excellence is the paper on Joubert; while the
others, with the exception, perhaps, of that on Spinoza, are of about
equal merit.

Mr. Arnold's style has been praised at once too much and too little. Its resources are decidedly limited; but if the word had not become so cheap, we should nevertheless call it fascinating. This quality implies no especial force; it rests in this case on the fact that, whether or not you agree with the matter beneath it, the manner inspires you with a personal affection for the author. It expresses great sensibility, and at the same time great good-nature; it indicates a mind both susceptible and healthy. With the former element alone it would savor of affectation; with the latter, it would be coarse. As it stands, it represents a spirit both sensitive and generous. We can best describe it, perhaps, by the word sympathetic. It exhibits frankly, and without detriment to its national character, a decided French influence. Mr. Arnold is too wise to attempt to write French English; he probably knows that a language can only be indirectly enriched; but as nationality is eminently a matter of form, he knows too that he can really violate nothing so long as he adheres to the English letter.

His Preface is a striking example of the intelligent amiability which animates his style. His two leading Essays were, on their first appearance, made the subject of much violent contention, their moral being deemed little else than a wholesale schooling of the English press by the French programme. Nothing could have better proved the justice of Mr. Arnold's remarks upon the "provincial" character of the English critical method, than the reception which they provoked. He now acknowledges this reception in a short introduction, which admirably reconciles smoothness of temper with sharpness of wit. The taste of this performance has been questioned; but wherever it may err, it is assuredly not in being provincial; it is essentially civil. Mr. Arnold's amiability is, in our eye, a strong proof of his wisdom. If he were a few degrees more short-sighted, he might have less equanimity at his command. Those who sympathize with him warmly will probably like him best as he is; but with such as are only half his friends, this freedom from party passion, from what is after all but a lawful professional emotion, will argue against his sincerity. For ourselves, we doubt not that Mr. Arnold possesses thoroughly what the French call the courage of his opinions. When you lay down a proposition which is forthwith controverted, it is of course optional with you to take up the cudgels in its defence. If you are deeply convinced of its truth, you will perhaps be content to leave it to take care of itself; or, at all events, you will not go out of your way to push its fortunes; for you will reflect that in the long run an opinion often borrows credit from the forbearance of its patrons. In the long run, we say; it will meanwhile cost you an occasional pang to see your cherished theory turned into a football by the critics. A football is not, as such, a very respectable object, and the more numerous the players, the more ridiculous it becomes. Unless, therefore, you are very confident of your ability to rescue it from the chaos of kicks, you will best consult its interests by not mingling in the game. Such has been Mr. Arnold's choice. His opponents say that he is too much of a poet to be a critic; he is certainly too much of a poet to be a disputant. In the Preface in question he has abstained from reiterating any of the views put forth in the two offensive Essays; he has simply taken a delicate literary vengeance upon his adversaries.

For Mr. Arnold's critical feeling and observation, used independently of his judgment, we profess a keen relish. He has these qualities, at any rate, of a good critic, whether or not he have the others,—the science and the logic. It is hard to say whether the literary critic is more called upon to understand or to feel. It is certain that he will accomplish little unless he can feel acutely; although it is perhaps equally certain that he will become weak the moment that he begins to "work," as we may say, his natural sensibilities. The best critic is probably he who leaves his feelings out of account, and relies upon reason for success. If he actually possesses delicacy of feeling, his work will be delicate without detriment to its solidity. The complaint of Mr. Arnold's critics is that his arguments are too sentimental. Whether this complaint is well founded, we shall hereafter inquire; let us determine first what sentiment has done for him. It has given him, in our opinion, his greatest charm and his greatest worth. Hundreds of other critics have stronger heads; few, in England at least, have more delicate perceptions. We regret that we have not the space to confirm this assertion by extracts. We must refer the reader to the book itself, where he will find on every page an illustration of our meaning. He will find one, first of all, in the apostrophe to the University of Oxford, at the close of the Preface,—"home of lost causes and forsaken beliefs and unpopular names and impossible loyalties." This is doubtless nothing but sentiment, but it seizes a shade of truth, and conveys it with a directness which is not at the command of logical demonstration. Such a process might readily prove, with the aid of a host of facts, that the University is actually the abode of much retarding conservatism; a fine critical instinct alone, and the measure of audacity which accompanies such an instinct, could succeed in placing her on the side of progress by boldly saluting her as the Queen of Romance: romance being the deadly enemy of the commonplace; the commonplace being the fast ally of Philistinism, and

Philistinism the heaviest drag upon the march of civilization. Mr. Arnold is very fond of quoting Goethe's eulogy upon Schiller, to the effect that his friend's greatest glory was to have left so far behind him *was uns alle bändigt, das Gemeine*, that bane of mankind, the common. Exactly how much the inscrutable Goethe made of this fact, it is hard at this day to determine; but it will seem to many readers that Mr. Arnold makes too much of it. Perhaps he does, for himself; but for the public in general he decidedly does not. One of the chief duties of criticism is to exalt the importance of the ideal; and Goethe's speech has a long career in prospect before we can say with the vulgar that it is "played out." Its repeated occurrence in Mr. Arnold's pages is but another instance of poetic feeling subserving the ends of criticism. The famous comment upon the girl Wragg, over which the author's opponents made so merry, we likewise owe—we do not hesitate to declare it—to this same poetic feeling. Why cast discredit upon so valuable an instrument of truth? Why not wait at least until it is used in the service of error? The worst that can be said of the paragraph in question is, that it is a great ado about nothing. All thanks, say we, to the critic who will pick up such nothings as these; for if he neglects them, they are blindly trodden under foot. They may not be especially valuable, but they are for that very reason the critic's particular care. Great truths take care of themselves; great truths are carried aloft by philosophers and poets; the critic deals in contributions to truth. Another illustration of the nicety of Mr. Arnold's feeling is furnished by his remarks upon the quality of *distinction* as exhibited in Maurice and Eugénie de Guérin, "that quality which at last inexorably corrects the world's blunders and fixes the world's ideals, [which] procures that the popular poet shall not pass for a Pindar, the popular historian for a Tacitus, nor the popular preacher for a Bossuet." Another is offered by his incidental remarks upon Coleridge, in the article on Joubert; another, by the remarkable felicity with which he has translated Maurice de Guérin's *Centaur*; and another, by the whole body of citations with which, in his second Essay, he fortifies his proposition that the establishment in England of an authority answering to the French Academy would have arrested certain evil tendencies of English literature,—for to nothing more offensive than this, as far as we can see, does his argument amount.

In the first and most important of his Essays Mr. Arnold puts forth his views upon the actual duty of criticism. They may be summed up as follows. Criticism has no concern with the practical; its function is simply to get at the best thought which is current,—to see things in themselves as they are,—to be disinterested. Criticism can be disinterested, says Mr. Arnold,

> "by keeping from practice; by resolutely following the law of its own nature, which is to be a free play of the mind on all subjects which it touches, by steadily refusing to lend itself to any of those ulterior political, practical considerations about ideas which plenty of people will be sure to attach to them, which perhaps ought often to be attached to them, which in this country, at any rate, are certain to be attached to them, but which criticism has really nothing to do with. Its business is simply to know the best that is known and thought in the world, and, by in its turn making this known, to create a current of true and fresh ideas. Its business is to do this with inflexible honesty, with due ability; but its business is to do no more, and to leave alone all questions of practical consequences and applications,— questions which will never fail to have due prominence given to them."

We used just now a word of which Mr. Arnold is very fond,—a word of which the general reader may require an explanation, but which, when explained, he will be likely to find indispensable; we mean the word *Philistine*. The term is of German origin, and has no English synonyme. "At Soli," remarks Mr. Arnold, "I imagined they did not talk of solecisms; and here, at the very head-quarters of Goliath, nobody talks of Philistinism." The word *épicier*, used by Mr. Arnold as a French synonyme, is not so good as *bourgeois*, and to those who know that *bourgeois* means a citizen, and who reflect that a citizen is a person seriously interested in the maintenance of order, the German term may now assume a more special significance. An English review briefly defines it by saying that "it applies to the fatheaded respectable public in general." This definition must satisfy us here. The Philistine portion of the English press, by which we mean the considerably larger portion, received Mr. Arnold's novel programme of criticism with the uncompromising disapprobation which was to be expected from a literary body, the principle of whose influence, or indeed of whose being, is its subservience, through its various members, to certain political and religious interests. Mr. Arnold's general theory was offensive enough; but the conclusions drawn by him from the fact that English practice has been so long and so directly at variance with it, were such as to excite the strongest animosity. Chief among these was the conclusion that this fact has retarded the development and vulgarized the character of the English mind, as compared with the French and the German mind. This rational inference may be nothing but a poet's flight; but for ourselves, we assent to it. It reaches us too. The facts collected by Mr. Arnold on this point have long wanted a voice. It has long seemed to us that, as a nation, the English are singularly incapable of large, of high, of general views. They are indifferent to pure truth, to *la verité vraie*. Their views are almost exclusively practical, and it is in the nature of practical views to be narrow. They seldom indeed admit a fact but on compulsion; they demand of an idea some better recommendation, some longer pedigree, than that it is true. That this lack of spontaneity in the English intellect is caused by the tendency of English criticism, or that it is to be corrected by a diversion, or even by a complete reversion, of this tendency, neither Mr. Arnold nor ourselves suppose, nor do we look upon such a result as desirable. The part which Mr. Arnold assigns to his reformed method of criticism is a purely tributary part. Its indirect result will be to quicken the naturally irrational action of the English mind; its direct result will be to furnish that mind with a larger stock of ideas than it has enjoyed under the time-honored *régime* of Whig and Tory, High-Church and Low-Church organs.

We may here remark, that Mr. Arnold's statement of his principles is open to some misinterpretation,—an accident against which he has, perhaps, not sufficiently guarded it. For many persons the word *practical* is almost identical with the word *useful*, against which, on the other hand, they erect the word *ornamental*. Persons who are fond of regarding these two terms as irreconcilable, will have little patience with Mr. Arnold's scheme of criticism. They will look upon it as an organized preference of unprofitable speculation to common sense. But the great beauty of the critical movement advocated by Mr. Arnold is that in either direction its range of action is unlimited. It deals with plain facts as well as with the most exalted fancies; but it deals with them only for the sake of the truth which is in them, and not for *your* sake, reader, and that of your party. It takes *high ground*, which is the ground of theory. It does not busy itself with consequences, which are all in all to you. Do not suppose that it for this reason pretends to ignore or to undervalue consequences; on the contrary, it is because it knows that consequences are inevitable that it leaves them alone. It cannot do two things at once; it cannot serve two masters. Its business is to make truth generally accessible, and not to apply it. It is only on condition of having its hands free, that it can make truth generally accessible. We said just now that its duty was, among other things, to exalt, if possible, the importance of the ideal. We should perhaps have said the intellectual; that is, of the principle of understanding things. Its business is to urge the claims of all things to be understood. If this is its function in England, as Mr. Arnold represents, it seems to us that it is doubly its function in this country. Here is no lack of votaries of the practical, of experimentalists, of empirics. The tendencies of our civilization are certainly not such as foster a preponderance of morbid speculation. Our national genius inclines yearly more and more to resolve itself into a vast machine for sifting, in all things, the wheat from the chaff. American society is so shrewd, that we may safely allow it to make application of the truths of the study. Only let us keep it supplied with the truths of the study, and not with the half-truths of the forum. Let criticism take the stream of truth at its source, and then practice can take it half-way down. When criticism takes it halfway down, practice will come poorly off.

If we have not touched upon the faults of Mr. Arnold's volume, it is because they are faults of detail, and because, when, as a whole, a book commands our assent, we do not incline to quarrel with its parts. Some of the parts in these Essays are weak, others are strong; but the impression which they all combine to leave is one of such beauty as to make us forget, not only their particular faults, but their particular merits. If we were asked what is the particular merit of a given essay, we should reply that it is a merit much less common at the present day than is generally supposed,—the merit which preeminently characterizes Mr. Arnold's poems, the merit, namely, of having a *subject*. Each essay is *about* something. If a literary work now-a-days start with a certain topic, that is all that is required of it; and yet it is a work of art only on condition of ending with that topic, on condition of being written, not from it, but to it. If the average modern essay or poem were to wear its title at the close, and not at the beginning, we wonder in how many cases the reader would fail to be surprised by it. A book or an article is looked upon as a kind of Staubbach waterfall, discharging itself into infinite space. If we were questioned as to the merit of Mr. Arnold's book as a whole, we should say that it lay in the fact that the author takes high ground. The manner of his Essays is a model of what criticisms should be. The foremost English critical journal, the Saturday Review, recently disposed of a famous writer by saying, in a parenthesis, that he had done nothing but write nonsense all his life. Mr. Arnold does not pass judgment in parenthesis. He is too much of an artist to use leading propositions

17

for merely literary purposes. The consequence is, that he says a few things in such a way as that almost in spite of ourselves we remember them, instead of a number of things which we cannot for the life of us remember. There are many things which we wish he had said better. It is to be regretted, for instance, that, when Heine is for once in a way seriously spoken of, he should not be spoken of more as the great poet which he is, and which even in New England he will one day be admitted to be, than with reference to the great moralist which he is not, and which he never claimed to be. But here, as in other places, Mr. Arnold's excellent spirit reconciles us with his short-comings. If he has not spoken of Heine exhaustively, he has at all events spoken of him seriously, which for an Englishman is a good deal. Mr. Arnold's supreme virtue is that he speaks of all things seriously, or, in other words, that he is not offensively clever. The writers who are willing to resign themselves to this obscure distinction are in our opinion the only writers who understand their time. That Mr. Arnold thoroughly understands his time we do not mean to say, for this is the privilege of a very select few; but he is, at any rate, profoundly conscious of his time. This fact was clearly apparent in his poems, and it is even more apparent in these Essays. It gives them a peculiar character of melancholy,—that melancholy which arises from the spectacle of the old-fashioned instinct of enthusiasm in conflict (or at all events in contact) with the modern desire to be fair,—the melancholy of an age which not only has lost its *naïveté,* but which knows it has lost it.

The American publishers have enriched this volume with the author's Lectures on Homer, and with his French Eton. The Lectures demand a notice apart; we can only say here that they possess all the habitual charm of Mr. Arnold's style. This same charm will also lend an interest to his discussion of a question which bears but remotely upon the subject of education in this country.

18

The first of James' two essays on Matthew Arnold was written for the *North American Review* in the late spring of 1865 when he was living at 13 Ashburton Place, his parents' home in Boston. James was at the beginning of his literary career. He was reviewing for the *North American*, had just published a short story in the *Atlantic Monthly*, and was soon to be invited by Godkin to contribute to the just-founded *Nation*. One of the anomalies of James' career is that, unlike most young writers, he began at the top; and unlike most writers of any era, he remained there for half a century.

James knew *Essays in Criticism* from its birth when he read the page proofs "honourably smirched by the American compositor's fingers" ("Mr. and Mrs. James T. Fields" [1915]). What James did not know, at least immediately, was Arnold's pleasure at his review "which I like as well as anything I have seen." James and Arnold were to meet and become friends in the years ahead. Arnold, who rarely read and less rarely praised novels, saluted James handsomely for *Roderick Hudson* in 1875. Six years later James told T. S. Perry, "I was pleased to hear that he [Arnold] told a friend of mine the other day that 'Henry James is a de-ah!'" (February 16, 1881).

The ideal of disinterestedness, of free play of mind, which James learned from Arnold and Sainte-Beuve (see Introduction) is already evident in his 1865 essay on Arnold. James locates himself in-between culturally and intellectually. He sees that contemporary English criticism is poor in its purely literary volumes "compared with that of France and Germany"; he believes that criticism's function is a question even "more directly pertinent" in America than in England. Intellectually, he rejects any opposition between the *"practical"* and the *"ornamental"* in criticism, insisting synthetically that "in either direction its range of action is unlimited."

James' disinterested stance in-between allows him to recognize and to celebrate Arnold's comparable role as a synthesizing figure. Arnold has created a prose style which "expresses great sensibility, and at the same time great good-nature; it indicates a mind both susceptible and healthy . . . a spirit both sensitive and generous." In 1884, James expands upon this sense of Arnold as a man in-between. "Mr. Arnold touches M. Renan on one side, as he touches Sainte-Beuve on the other" ("Matthew Arnold"). Arnold also stands between England and the rest of the world. "He discharges an office so valuable, a function so delicate, he interprets, explains, illuminates so many of the obscure problems presented by English life to the gaze of the alien . . . he meets him halfway" (1884). What this means is that the true critic has enough distance upon his culture to recognize eccentricities and limitations which other countrymen remain unconscious or enamored of. But he is not so far outside that he, like the actual alien, is baffled by the eccentricities. On the contrary, he can explain them to the alien precisely because the true critic remains, as Arnold does, essentially part of his culture. "[Matthew Arnold] is *en fin de compte* (as the foreigner might say) English of the English" (1884).

Disinterestedness allows James to see Arnold's limitations as well as strengths, and to grow to a still more just, less a priori appreciation of him. In 1865, James refers repeatedly to "the complaint of Mr. Arnold's critics . . . that his arguments are too sentimental." Does Arnold have "the science and the logic" of the true critic? Is he guilty of "questionable reasoning"? James never expressly answers these questions. They seem to arise almost obligatorily, as though French rationalism has so captivated him that he feels required to valorize the role of cerebration in critical practice. But the role of sentiment, the priority of feeling, in *Arnold's* practice is already beckoning James toward the beautiful realization that "in the arts feeling is always meaning" ("The Letters of Eugène Delacroix," *International Review* 8[1880]:359). Thus James in 1865 makes one more nod to cerebration—"whether this complaint [about Arnold's questionable reasoning] is well-founded, we shall hereafter inquire"—and then goes on to what concerns him primarily, to "determine first what sentiment has done for" Matthew Arnold. Admitting that Arnold's paean to Oxford as the Queen of Romance is "nothing but sentiment," James insists that "it seizes a shade of truth, and conveys it with a directness which is not at the command of logical demonstration." Likewise Arnold's conclusion that Philistinism has vulgarized the English mind is, James admits, "nothing but a poet's flight," yet "we assent to it. It reaches us too." James may bow to rationalism enough to assert the unlikely view that "the best critic is probably he who leaves his feelings out of account, and relies upon reason for success," but he goes on to articulate the belief that will increasingly inform his critical practice. "If he [the best critic] actually possesses delicacy of feeling, his work will be delicate without detriment to its [intellectual] solidity."

The final indication of disinterestedness in James' view of Arnold appears when he goes beyond comparing strengths with weaknesses and compares the British critic with Sainte-Beuve. "Melancholy" is the touchstone in 1865. Sainte-Beuve could use more of it ("A French Critic" [1865]), whereas Arnold's capacity to be "profoundly conscious of his time" endows his poetry and criticism with "a peculiar character of melancholy . . . the melancholy of an age which not only has lost its *naïveté*, but which knows it has lost it" (1865). Arnold's deeper contact with the age derives from a range of emotional sympathy, "a largeness of horizon which Sainte-Beuve never reached. The horizon of Sainte-Beuve was French . . . that of Matthew Arnold, as I have hinted, is European, more than European, inasmuch as it includes America" (1884). And so, after "confess[ing] that the measure of my enjoyment of a critic is the degree to which he resembles Sainte-Beuve," James does more than establish that "this resemblance exists in Matthew Arnold." He establishes that amid Arnold's "many disparities and differences" from Sainte-Beuve is the precious one of the role which Arnold fashioned for himself. He is "the *general* critic." The intensity of feeling which characterizes James' admiration for this achievement marks the depths of his personal response to Matthew Arnold. "It is Mr. Arnold, therefore, that we think of when we figure to ourselves the best knowledge of what is being done in the world, the best appreciation of literature and life. . . . more than anyone else, the happily-proportioned, the truly distinguished man of letters."

For modern discussions of James' relationship with Arnold and Sainte-Beuve see Berland's *Culture and Conduct in the Novels of Henry James* (Cambridge: Cambridge University Press, 1981), Coulling's *Matthew Arnold and His Critics* (Athens: Ohio University Press, 1974), Daugherty (3–8, 127), Edel (2: 122–25), Kelley (39–41), Raleigh's *Matthew Arnold and American Culture* (Berkeley: University of California Press, 1957), and Ruggiero's "Henry James as a Critic: Some Early French Influences," *Rivista di Letteratura Moderne e Comparate* 26 (1973): 285–306.

For the relationship between Arnold and Sainte-Beuve see Arnold's 1869 eulogy on the French critic's death in volume 5 of *The Complete Prose Works of Matthew Arnold*, ed. R. H. Super (Ann Arbor: University of Michigan Press, 1965). The personal relations between the critics are discussed by Super (especially in volume 3 of *The Complete Prose Works*), and by Honan in *Matthew Arnold, A Life* (New York: McGraw-Hill, 1981). For the critics' intellectual exchange see Major, "Matthew Arnold and Attic Prose Style," *PMLA* 59 (1944): 1086–1103; Smart, "Matthew Arnold and Sainte-Beuve," *Athenaeum* (September 3, 1898), p. 325; Super, "Documents in the Matthew Arnold—Sainte-Beuve Relationship," *Modern Philology* 60 (1962): 206–10; Whitridge, "Matthew Arnold and Sainte-Beuve," *PMLA* 53 (1938): 303–13.

NOTES

11:5. the verdict passed in the author's own country. James shows throughout this review a thorough familiarity with the controversy over Arnold's style and ideas (especially in "The Function of Criticism at the Present Time" and "The Literary Influence of Academies"). The readiest guide to this controversy is Coulling. See also the excellent notes to Super's edition of *Essays in Criticism* in volume 3 of *The Complete Prose Works* and to Hoctor's *Matthew Arnold's Essays in Criticism* (Chicago: University of Chicago Press, 1964). The distinction which James makes in this paragraph between British and American readers is repeated in his review of *Middlemarch* and his biography of Hawthorne, Chapters 3 and 5.

11:25. Maurice de Guérin (1810–39), French author of the posthumously published prose poem *Le Centaur;* Eugénie de Guérin (1805–48), his devoted sister whose *Journal intime* was appreciated by Sainte-Beuve as well as Arnold.

Joseph Joubert (1754–1824), French author on diverse subjects including literature and philosophy.

Heinrich Heine (1797–1856), German poet and satirist. Besides the essay on Heine in *Essays in Criticism,* Arnold also wrote the poem "Heine's Grave" (1867) which James mentions in his 1884 essay.

Benedict de Spinoza (1632–77), Dutch rationalist philosopher. Marcus Aurelius (121–80), Roman emperor and Stoic philosopher.

13:31. the close of the Preface. It is symptomatic of James' sensitivity that he focuses immediately upon lines which have become among the most famous in Arnold.

14:2. Goethe's eulogy upon Schiller. "Epilog zu Schillers Glocke," l. 162.

14:13. the girl Wragg. Elizabeth Wragg murdered her infant son on September 10, 1864. On March 13, 1865, she was sentenced to twenty years of penal servitude. Arnold used as a leitmotif throughout this section of the essay "Wragg is in custody."

14:13. the author's opponents made so merry. See Fitz-James Stephens' stinging paragraph on Wragg and his subsequent parody of Arnold's leitmotif in "Mr. Matthew Arnold and his Countrymen" *Saturday Review* 18 (1864): 684.

14:29. Cornelius Tacitus (56–120), Roman orator and historian. Jacques-Bénigne Bossuet (1627–1704), French bishop, orator, and polemicist.

15:26. *épicier.* Grocer.

16:2. the English mind, as compared with the French and the German. This is the first of many times that James, like Arnold, uses the Continent to criticize Anglo-Saxon practices.

16:22. organs. The *Edinburgh Review* spoke for the Whigs; the *Quarterly*

Review and *Blackwood's* for the Tories; the *Westminster Review* for the radicals. In terms of denominations, High Church publications included the *Church and State Review,* the *Guardian,* and the *Examiner;* Low Church, the *Record,* the *Nonconformist,* and the *Morning Star.*

16:40. serve two masters. In echoing the Bible (Matt. 6:24), James is following the Arnoldian practice of bolstering an argument with the implicit sanction of Scripture.

17:34. Staubbach is a falls in the Bernese Alps, Switzerland, famous for immense plumes of spray.

18:27. Lectures on Homer. In 1861 Arnold published his Oxford lectures as *On Translating Homer: Three Lectures.* Francis Newman, who was roundly attacked in the lectures, responded immediately with *Homeric Translation in Theory and Practice.* Arnold replied with "Last Words" on the controversy in November 1861. French Eton. Arnold's *A French Eton* (1864) shows the influence of his visit to Lacordaire at Sorèze College in 1859.

T W O
SAINTE-BEUVE

W HEN, IN PUBLISHING SOME YEARS SINCE THE SMALL
collection of letters which Sainte-Beuve had addressed to his
gracious and appreciative friend the Princess Mathilde, his last secre-
tary, M. Troubat, announced his intention of getting together and
bringing to the light the general correspondence of the great critic, the
thing seemed a capital piece of literary good news. After a considerable interval the editor has redeemed his promise, and we have two
substantial volumes of Sainte-Beuve's letters. The result may be said,
on the whole, to be very interesting—our prospect of high entertainment was not illusory. The letters extend from the year 1822 to the
autumn of 1869, the moment of the writer's death, and are naturally
most abundant during the closing years of his career—the second
volume occupying entirely the period from 1865. The editor mentions
that during the passage of the second volume through the press a
number of letters of whose existence he had not been aware came into
his hands. These he has reserved for a supplementary volume; the
reader will have to interpolate them at their proper dates. I do not
longer await the appearance of this volume—it was promised several
months ago—in order to speak of its predecessors, for these are complete in themselves, and are so rich in interesting matter that I shall be
able to do them but scanty justice.

Sainte-Beuve's letters do nothing but complete a picture which
was already a very vivid one. He had already painted his own portrait, painted it in a myriad fine, unerring, cumulative touches; no
writer was ever more personal, more certain, in the long run, to in-
fuse into his judgments of people and things those elements out of
which an image of himself might be constructed. The whole of the
man was in the special work—he was *all* a writer, a critic, an appreciator. He was literary in every pulsation of his being, and he expressed himself totally in his literary life. No character and no career
were ever more homogeneous. He had no disturbing, perverting

tastes; he suffered no retarding, embarrassing accidents. He lost no time, and he never wasted any. He was not even married; his literary consciousness was never complicated with the sense of an unliterary condition. His mind was never diverted or distracted from its natural exercise—that of looking in literature for illustrations of life, and of looking in life for aids to literature. Therefore it is, as I say, that his work offers a singularly complete image of his character, his tastes, his temper, his idiosyncrasies. It was from himself always that he spoke—from his own personal and intimate point of view. He wrote himself down in his published pages, and what was left for his letters was simply to fill in the details, to supply a few missing touches, a few inflections and shades. As a matter of course he was not an elaborate letter-writer. He had always his pen in his hand, but it had little time for long excursions. His career was an intensely laborious one— his time, attention and interest, his imagination and sympathies were unceasingly mortgaged. The volumes before us contain almost no general letters, pages purely sociable and human. The human and sociable touch is frequent, is perpetual; to use his own inveterate expression, he "slips it in" wherever there is an opening. But his occasions are mostly those of rapid notes dictated by some professional or technical pretext. There is very little overflow of his personal situation, of his movements and adventures, of the incidents of his life. Sainte-Beuve's adventures, indeed, were not numerous, and the incidents in his life were all intellectual, moral, professional incidents— the publication of his works, the changes, the phases, the development of his opinions. He never traveled; he had no changes of place, of scenery, of society, to chronicle. He once went to Liège, in Flanders, to deliver a course of lectures, and he spent a year at Lausanne for the same purpose; but, apart from this, his life was spent uninterruptedly in Paris.

Of course, when one makes the remark that a man's work is in a peculiar degree the record of a mind, the history of a series of convictions and feelings, the reflection of a group of idiosyncrasies, one does not of necessity by that fact praise it to the skies. Everything depends on what the mind may have been. It so happened that Sainte-Beuve's was extraordinary, was so rich and fine and flexible, that this personal accent, which sounds everywhere in his writings, acquired a superior value and an exquisite rarity. He had indeed a remarkable combination of qualities, and there is something wondrous in his way of reconciling certain faculties which are usually held to be in the nature of things opposed to each other. He had, to begin with, two passions, which are commonly assumed to exclude each other—the passion for scholarship and the passion for life. He was essentially a creature of books, a *literatus;* and yet to his intensely bookish and acquisitive mind nothing human, nothing social or mundane was alien. The simplest way to express his particular felicity is to say that, putting aside the poets and novelists, the purely imaginative and inventive authors, he is the student who has brought into the study the largest element of reflected life. No scholar was ever so much of an observer, of a moralist, a psychologist; and no such regular and beguiled *abonné* to the general spectacle was ever so much of a scholar. He valued life and literature equally for the light they threw upon each other; to his mind one implied the other; he was unable to conceive of them apart. He made use in literature, in an extraordinary manner, of the qualities that are peculiarly social. Some one said of him that he had the organization of a nervous woman and the powers of acquisition of a Benedictine. Sainte-Beuve had nerves assuredly; there is something feminine in his tact, his penetration, his subtlety and pliability, his rapidity of transition, his magical divinations, his sympathies and antipathies, his marvelous art of insinuation, of expressing himself by fine touches and of adding touch to touch. But all this side of the feminine genius was re-enforced by faculties of quite another order—faculties of the masculine stamp; the completeness, the solid sense, the constant reason, the moderation, the copious knowledge, the passion for exactitude and for general considerations. In attempting to appreciate him it is impossible to keep these things apart; they melt into each other like the elements of the atmosphere; there is scarcely a stroke of his pen that does not contain a little of each of them. He had ended by becoming master of a style of which the polished complexity was a complete expression of his nature—a style which always reminds one of some precious stone that has been filed into a hundred facets by the skill of a consummate lapidary. The facets are always all there; the stone revolves and exhibits them in the course of a single paragraph. When I speak of attempting to appreciate him I know it is not an easy matter, and I have no intention of undertaking a task for which his own resources would have been no more than sufficient. He might have drawn himself, intendingly, from head to foot, but no other artist holds in his hand the fine-tipped, flexible brushes with which such a likeness should be pointed and emphasized.

Various attempts, nevertheless, have been made to appraise him, as was eminently natural and inevitable. He spent his life in analyzing and pondering other people, and it was a matter of course that he also should be put into the scales. But, as a general thing, on

these occasions they were not held with a very even hand; as too
often happens in France, the result was disfigured by party passion.
This is especially the case with the judgments of hostility, of which
the number, as may well be imagined, is not small. Sainte-Beuve had
wounded too many susceptibilities and vanities—had taken upon
himself functions too thankless and invidious—to find the critic's
couch a bed of roses. And he not only offended individuals, he offended societies and "sets," who, as a general thing, never forgave
him, and who took their revenge according to their lights and their
means. The very pivot of his intellectual existence was what he would
have called the liberty of appreciation; it was upon this he took his
stand—it was in the exercise of this privilege that his career unfolded
itself. Of course he did not claim a monopoly of the privilege, and he
would never have denied that the world was at liberty to appreciate
Sainte-Beuve. The greater wisdom, to my mind, was on his side; his
great qualities—his intense interest in the truth of any matter, his
desire to arrive at the most just and comprehensive perception of it,
his delight in the labor involved in such attempts, and his exquisite
skill in presenting the results of such labor—these things have never
been impugned. Into the innumerable hostilities and jealousies of
which he was the object—the resentments more or less just, the reproaches more or less valid, the calumnies more or less impudent—
no stranger, fortunately, need pretend to penetrate. These are matters of detail, and here the details are altogether too numerous.
Sainte-Beuve's greatest admirers are not obliged to accept him uncon-
ditionally. Like every one else he had the defects of his qualities. He
had a very large dose of what the French call "malice"—an element
which was the counterpart of his subtlety, his feminine fineness of
perception. This subtlety served him not only as a magical clew to
valuable results, but it led him sometimes into small deviations that
were like the lapses, slightly unholy, of the tempted. It led him to
analyze motives with a minuteness which was often fatal to their apparent purity; it led him to slip in—to *glisser*, as he always says—the
grain of corrosive censure with the little parcel of amenities. For feats
of this kind his art was instinctive; he strikes the reader as more than
feminine—as positively feline. It is beyond question that he has at
times the feline scratch. The truth is, that his instrument itself—his
art of expression—puts almost a premium upon the abuse of innuen-
do. The knowledge that he could leave the impression without having said the thing must frequently have been an intellectual temptation. Besides, it may be said that his scratch was really, on the whole,
defensive, or, at the worst, retributive; it was, to my belief, never

wanton or aggressive. We each have our defensive weapon, and I am unable to see why Sainte-Beuve's was not a legitimate one. He had the feline agility and pliancy; nothing was more natural than that he should have had the feline claw. But he apprehended the personality, the moral physiognomy of the people to whom he turned his attention—Victor Cousin, for instance, Lamartine, Villemain, Balzac, Victor Hugo, Chateaubriand—with an extraordinary clearness and sharpness; he took intellectual possession of it and never relaxed his grasp. The image was always there, with all its features, for familiar reference; it illuminated and colored every allusion he had occasion to make to the original. "What will you have?" he would have said; "I am so intensely impressible, and my impressions are so vivid, so permanent. One can go but by one's impressions; those are mine. Heaven knows how the plate has been polished to take them!" He was very apt to remember people's faults in considering their merits. He says in one of his letters that he is more sensitive to certain great faults than to certain great merits. And then, with his passion for detail, for exactitude and completeness, for facts and examples, he thought nothing unimportant. To be vague was the last thing possible to him, and the deformities or misdemeanors of people he had studied remained in his eyes as definite as the numbers of a "sum" in addition or subtraction.

His great justification, however, it seems to me, is, that the cause he upheld was the most important, for it was simply the cause of liberty, in which we are all so much interested. This, in essence, is what I mean by saying that certain of those habits of mind which made many people dislike him were defensive weapons. It was doubtless not always a question of defending his own character, but it was almost always a question of defending his position as a free observer and appreciator. This is the fine thing about him, and the only thing with which, as strangers, happily detached from that imbroglio of rival interests and ambitions in which his lot was cast, we need greatly concern ourselves. In a society that swarmed with camps and coteries, with partisans and advocates, he was more than any one else the independent individual, pinning his faith to no emblazoned standard and selling his vote to no exclusive group. The literary atmosphere in France has always been full of watchwords and catchwords, the emblems and tokens of irreconcilable factions and of what may be called vested literary interests. His instinct, from the beginning of his career, was to mistrust any way of looking at things which should connect the observer with a party pledged to take the point of view most likely to minister to its prosperity. He cared nothing for the prosperity of parties; he cared only for the ascertainment of the reality and for hitting the nail on the head. He only cared to look freely—to look all round. The part he desired to play was that of the vividly intelligent, brightly enlightened mind, acting in the interest of literature, knowledge, taste, and spending itself on everything human and historic. He was frankly and explicitly a critic; he attributed the highest importance to the critical function, and he understood it in so large a way that it gives us a lift to agree with him. The critic, in his conception, was not the narrow lawgiver or the rigid censor that he is often assumed to be; he was the student, the inquirer, the interpreter, the taker of notes, the active, restless commentator, whose constant aim was to arrive at justness of characterization. Sainte-Beuve's own faculty of characterization was of the rarest and most remarkable; he held it himself in the highest esteem; his impression was the thing in the world he most valued. There is something admirable in his gravity, consistency and dignity on this point. I know nothing more finely characteristic of him than a phrase which occurs in one of the volumes before me in the course of his correspondence with Madame Christine de Fontanes on the subject of the biographical notice he had undertaken to supply for a new edition of her father's works. The whole correspondence is most interesting and shows him at his best—full of urbanity and tact, but full also of firmness and reason, knowing exactly what he wishes and means and adhering to it absolutely. M. de Fontanes, whose reputation has sensibly faded now, was a critic and poet of eminence under the First Empire and the Restoration; his daughter was editing a "definitive" collection of his writings, and Sainte-Beuve had sent her his own article to read before insertion. The tone of the article was respectful and sympathetic (it is included at present among his "Portraits Littéraires"), but to certain points in his judgment of her father the Comtesse de Fontanes had taken exception. He offered to withdraw the article altogether, but he refused to alter a word. "Upon anything else in the world I would yield," he says; "*pas sur les choses de la plume quand une fois je crois avoir DIT*" (not on things of the pen when once I think I have hit it) ". . . That's my weakness," he adds; "can you forgive me?" For my own part, I can forgive him easily; I should have found it hard to forgive him if he had acted otherwise. All Sainte-Beuve is in those few words—all his famous "method," which has been so much talked about, and, one may almost say, all his philosophy. His method was to "hit it"—to "say it," as he says—to express it, to put his fingers on the point; his philosophy was to accept and make the best of truths so discriminated. He goes on to give Madame Christine de Fontanes several examples of what he means. "I wrote a biographical notice of M. Ampère the elder, from private documents supplied by the son, my friend. I didn't read him the notice. He only saw it printed, and he was content, save with a word that I had slipped in upon something that I believed to be a weakness of character in M. Ampère with regard to great people. He said to me, 'I was pleased with it all, except that word, which I would have begged you to leave out if I had seen it beforehand.' It was just for that that I had not submitted my article to him. *If I had not been free to write that word I would not have written the notice. . . .* When I wrote upon Madame de Staël," he goes on, "Madame de Broglie [her daughter] sent for me, and, with all that authority of grace and virtue which was hers, prescribed to me certain limits; she desired me to communicate my article in advance; I was unwilling to do so. When she came to read it she was pleased, except with regard to a page which nothing in the world would have induced me to withdraw, for it consisted of my reserves and my insinuations (with regard to the 'romantic' life at Coppet)." Nothing could be more characteristic and delightful than this frank allusion to his insinuations. To "insinuate" was a part of his manner, and was to his sense a perfectly legitimate way of dealing with a subject. Granting certain other of the conditions, he was assuredly right. And indeed there is nothing intrinsically unlawful in an insinuation; everything depends on the rest of the tone, and also on the thing insinuated. "From all this," he pursues, after various other remarks upon the points at issue with Madame de Fontanes, "I conclude that it is impossible that the notice should go into the edition. On your side is your duty; on mine is a feeling which I don't know how to name, *mais qui est ma nature même.*" It was in fact Sainte-Beuve's "very nature" to trust his perception and to abide by what he considered his last analysis of a matter. He knew with what quality of intelligence he had aimed at the point—he knew the light, the taste, the zeal, the experience he had brought to bear upon it. A certain side of his feeling about criticism is strikingly expressed in one of the later letters (in date) of this collection. The page is so excellent, so full of a sense of the realities of life as distinguished from the shadows, that I quote the greater part of it. It contains an allusion, by the way, which helps to understand the little discussion of which I have just partly given an account. He is writing to M. Ernest Bersot:

"Is it not necessary," he asks, "to break with that false conventionality, that system of cant, which declares that we shall judge a writer not only by his intentions, but by his pretensions? It is time that this should come to an end. I will take the critics as instances. What! am I to see nothing of M. de Fontanes but the great master, polished, noble, elegant, trimmed with fur, religious—not the quick, impetuous, abrupt, sensual man that he was? What! La Harpe shall be but a man of taste, eloquent in his academic chair, and I shall not see him of whom Voltaire used to say, *'Le petit se fâche!'* And for the present, come now—I talk to you without circumlocution—I have no animosity at heart, and I appreciate those who have been, in whatever degree, my masters; but here are five-and-thirty years, and more, that I live before Villemain, the great talent, the fine mind, so draped and decorated with generous, liberal, philanthropic, Christian, civilizing sentiments, etc., and in fact the most sordid soul—*le plus méchant singe qui existe.* What must one do, in definitive—how must one conclude with respect to him? Must one go on praising his noble, lofty sentiments, as is done invariably all round him? And, as this is the reverse of the truth, must one be a dupe and continue to dupe others? Are men of letters, historians and moralistic preachers nothing more than comedians, whom one has no right to take outside of the *rôle* that they have arranged for themselves? Must one see them only on the stage and look at them only while they are there? Or else is it permitted, when the subject is known, to come boldly, though at the same time discreetly, and slip in the scalpel and show the weak point of the breastplate—show the *seam*, as it were, between the talent and the soul; to praise the one, but to mark also the defect of the other, perceptible even in the talent itself and in the effect that it produces in the long run? Will literature lose by this? It is possible; but moral science will gain. That's where we are going, fatally. *There is no longer such a thing as an isolated question of taste.* When I know the man, then only can I explain to myself the talker, and especially that species of talker who is the most artful of all—the one who prides himself on having nothing of the mere talker left. And the great men (you will say), and the respect one owes them, and the reputation that must be so dearly paid for? Very true; every man who competes for praise and celebrity is devoted to every infamy by that very fact. It is the law. Molière is insulted by Bossuet, Goethe by the first rowdy that comes along; only yesterday Renan and Littré by Dupanloup—and insulted in his character, in his morality. What is to be done about it? It isn't by cuddling one's self that one can escape from it. One must *be* something or some one; and in that case one resists— one has one's army—one counts in spite of one's detractors. As soon as you penetrate a little under the veil of society, as in nature, you see nothing but wars, struggles, destructions and recompositions. This

Lucretian view of criticism isn't a cheerful one; but, once we attain to it, it seems preferable, even with its high sadness, to the worship of idols."

If it be needful to admit that the harsher side of Sainte-Beuve's temperament comes out in such a passage as I have just quoted, it may be added that these volumes are by no means without testimony to the extreme acuteness with which he could feel irritation and the inimitable neatness and lucidity with which he could express it. The letter to M. Villemain, of the date of September, 1839, and that to Victor Cousin, of July, 1843, are highly remarkable in this respect, and remarkable, too, for the manner in which they appeal to the sympathy of a reader who is totally unacquainted with the merits of the quarrel. The delicate acerbity of the tone, the absence of passion, of violence, of confusion, produce an impression of beauty, and our intellectual relish of the perfection with which he says what he desires suffices by itself to place us on his side. There are various examples of his skill in that process known to the French as telling a person *son fait*. "I only ask of you one thing," he writes to Madame Louise Colet, who had pestered him to publish a critical appreciation of her literary productions, "to admire you in silence, without being obliged to point out to the public just where I cease to admire you." In the letters to the Princess Mathilde there occurs a very entertaining episode, related by Sainte-Beuve to his sympathetic correspondent. A lady had sent him her manuscript commonplace-book to read, with the request that he would give an opinion upon the literary value of its contents. Turning it over, Sainte-Beuve encountered a passage relating to himself and not present to the lady's mind when she sent him the volume—a passage of a highly calumnious character, attributing to him the most unattractive qualities and accusing him of gross immorality. He copies out for the Princess the letter with which he has returned the manuscript of his imprudent friend and in which, after administering a rebuke of the most ingeniously urbane character, he concludes by begging her "to receive the assurance of an esteem which he shall never again have occasion to express." The whole letter should be read. Even in perfectly friendly letters his irrepressible "malice" crops out—it has here and there even a slightly diabolical turn. A most interesting letter to Charles Baudelaire, of the year 1858, is full of this quality, especially in the closing lines: ". . . It isn't a question of compliments. I am much more disposed to scold [Baudelaire had just sent him "Les Fleurs du Mal"], and if I were walking with you on the edge of the sea, along a cliff, without pretending to play the Mentor, I would try and trip you up, my dear friend, and throw you suddenly into the water, so that, as you know how to swim, you should henceforth take your course out there in the sunshine and the tide." The most interesting parts of the contents of these volumes, however, I have found to be the graver and more closely personal ones. In the history of such a mind every autobiographical touch has a high interest. There are a number of autobiographical touches bearing on his material life and illustrating his extreme frugality and the modesty—the more than modesty—of his literary income. "From 1830 to 1840," he says, "I lived in a student's room (in the Cour du Commerce) on a fourth floor, and at the rate of *twenty-three francs* a month, my breakfasts included." In 1840 he was appointed titular librarian at the Bibliothèque Mazarine, and then "I found myself rich, or at my ease, for the first time in my life. I began to study again, I learned Greek; my work contains indications of this increase of leisure and of my being able to do it as I chose. Then came the Academy, towards 1843; I became a member of the committee of the Dictionary, and really I had hard work to spend my income. To do so, I had to buy rare books, for which the taste came to me little by little . . . I have *never* had a debt in my life . . . they attack me there on my strong side. I have my weaknesses, I have told you so: they are those which gave to King Solomon the disgust of everything and the satiety of life. I may have regretted feeling sometimes that they quenched my ardor—but they never perverted my heart."

Of autobiographical touches of the other sort—those that bear upon his character and his opinions—there are a considerable number—a number which, however, would be a good deal larger if the letters written before the year 1860 had been more carefully preserved by his correspondents. I have marked a great many of these passages, but I must content myself with a few extracts. There was an element of philosophic stoicism in Sainte-Beuve, which is indicated in his earliest letters; the note is struck at intervals throughout the correspondence. "Take care of yourself," he says to one of his friends, in a letter written at the age of twenty-four; "pass the least time possible in regrets; resign yourself to having had no youth, no past, no future; I don't tell you not to suffer from it, not to die of it even, at the end; but I tell you not to lose your temper over it, nor to let it make you stand still and stamp." This is quite the same man who found himself impelled to write in 1864: "The more I go on the more indifferent I become; only, judgments take form within me, and, once established, after being shaken and tested two or three times, they never leave me. I believe, moreover, that I have no animosity. Observe that I have no time for that; animosities themselves need to be cultivated. Ob-

33

liged as I am to change so often the direction of my mind and my interest, to fasten and make them sink into writings and authors so different, trying to find in each of these the greatest possible amount of truth, I grow case-hardened to pricks and irritations, and after a little while I don't even know what they are meant for. But, I repeat to you—and it is the misfortune and also a little the honor of the critical spirit—my judgments abide with me." That is the Sainte-Beuve of my predilection—I may almost say of my faith—the Sainte-Beuve whose voice was incapable of the note of vulgarity, whose vision was always touched with light. I see no element of narrowness or obstinacy in the declaration I have just quoted; I only see the perceptive mind, the ripe intelligence. There is an expression of this ripe intelligence, this faculty of perception resting upon a sense of experience, in a letter of 1863 to a female friend. "We are getting ready for a great battle, in which philosophic minds will be known by true marks. I am one of them, after all. I went in for a little Christian mythology in my day, but that has evaporated. It was like the swan of Leda, a means of getting at the fair and wooing them in a more tender fashion. Youth has time and makes use of everything. Now I am old and I have chased away all the clouds. I mortify myself less, and I see *plus juste*. It is a pity that all this can not last, and that the moment when one is most master of one's self and one's thoughts should be that at which they are nearest faltering and finishing." I don't know at what period Sainte-Beuve disentangled himself from the "Christian mythology," but already in 1845 he makes a striking allusion to what he deems to be the collapse of his power to feel at the seat of feeling. "Your letter touched me, honored me; but I always find myself without words before your praise, feeling so little worthy of it, passed as I have into the state of a pure critical intelligence, and assisting as I do with a melancholy eye at the death of my heart. I judge myself, and I rest calm, cold, indifferent. I am dead, and I see myself dead—but without emotion or confusion. Whence comes this strange state? Alas! there are causes old and deep. Here I am talking to you suddenly as to a confessor; but I know you are so friendly, so *charitable*—and it is this, this last point, which is everything, and which the world calls the heart, that is dead in me. The intellect shines over the graveyard like a dead moon." This is strongly stated; apparently Sainte-Beuve is speaking of a certain special function of the heart which, after forty, is supposed to have seen its best days. Of a certain intellectual cordiality, the power of tender, of sympathetic understanding, he gave full proof during the remainder of his long career. If his heart was dead its ghost at least very restlessly walked. Moreover, the heart can hardly be said to die. In some cases it has never existed, and in these it is not likely to spring into being. But when it has once existed the imagination, in spite of what surgeons call the removal, does some of the work. The house may be closed, but the garden still goes on.

It was to be expected that the letters of a great critic should contain a great deal of good criticism, and in this respect these volumes will not be found disappointing. They contain a great variety of fragmentary judgments and of characteristic revelations and sidelights. With his great breadth of view, his general intelligence and his love of seeing "juste," Sainte-Beuve was nevertheless a man of strong predispositions, of vigorous natural preferences. He never repudiated the charge of having strong "bents" of taste. This indeed would have been most absurd; for one's taste is an effect, more than a cause, of one's preferences; it is indeed the result of a series of particular tastes. With Sainte-Beuve, as with every one else, it grew more and more flexible with time; it adapted itself and opened new windows and doors. He achieved in his last years feats that may fairly be called extraordinary in the way of doing justice to writers and works of an intensely "modern" stamp—to Baudelaire and Flaubert, to Feydeau and the brothers Goncourt. There is even in the second of these volumes a letter, on the whole appreciative, to the young writer whose vigorous brain, in later years, was to give birth to the monstrous "Assommoir." But originally Sainte-Beuve's was not a mind that appeared likely, even at a late stage of its evolution, to offer hospitality to M. Émile Zola. He was always a man of his time; he played his part in the romantic movement; Joseph Delorme and the novel of "Volupté" are creations eminently characteristic of that fermentation of opinion, that newer, younger genius which produced the great modern works of French literature. Sainte-Beuve, in other words, was essentially of the generation of Lamartine and Victor Hugo, of Balzac and George Sand. But he was, if not more weighted, more anchored than some of his companions; he was incapable of moving in a mass; he never was a violent radical. He had a high tenderness for tradition, for the old models, for classic ideas. In 1845 he was open to the charge of "reactionary" taste; it must be remembered that the critics and commentators cannot, in the nature of things, afford to run the risks and make the bold experiments of the poets and producers. "I have *never* liked the modern drama as Hugo and Dumas have made it, and I have never recognized in it, the least in the world, the ideal that I conceive in this respect. . . . I should be unable to express to you what I feel with regard to the enormities which have partly defeated our hopes, but there are points on which I hold my ground, and I flatter myself that I have never deserted my early convictions. It is all the same to me that Madame de Girardin should come and tell me that I am going in for reaction pure and simple, and I don't give myself the trouble even of heeding it; but, if you say it, I permit myself to answer *no*, and to tell you that you are completely mistaken, which is the result, perhaps, of your not attaching the same importance as I to purely literary points—points on which I have remained very much the same." Sainte-Beuve here defends himself against the charge of having dropped out of the line; he intimates that it is he who has adhered to the pure "romantic" tradition, and that the eccentric movement refers itself to the two writers he mentions. They were not the only ones of whom he failed to approve; it is unfortunately a substantial fact that he never rendered half justice to Balzac, and that to George Sand he rendered but half at the most. There is an interesting passage bearing upon this in a letter of 1866, written to a critic who had published an appreciative notice of Sainte-Beuve's long and delightful article upon Gavarni. "You have indeed put your finger upon the two delicate points. At bottom, I know, Musset had *passion* and Théo [Théophile Gautier] didn't have it; and one warms people up only by having a flame one's self. And then Balzac, I know too, with defects that I feel too much (being of quite another family), had *power*, and Gavarni only had an infinitude of wit, elegance and observation. But Gavarni had taste and *le trait juste*—things I greatly value. That being said, I have my private idea, not as an advocate, but as a critic of conviction, which is, namely, that in our day there is too much water carried to the river, too much admiration *quand même*, too little real judging. Once the word genius is pronounced, everything is accepted and proclaimed. Musset's worst verses are quoted as proverbs; they are admired on trust. So for the great novelist. It would seem that there had been no observer but he; that Eugène Sue, Frédéric Soulié—all those big fellows—have ceased to exist, have been absorbed by him. But it is, above all, when it is a question of the great men of the past, that I am unable to accept the high figure at which they put his genius. This is the bottom of my thought, and it doubtless judges me myself. . . ." And it is here that he goes on to add the remark I have quoted, to the effect that he is more sensitive to certain great defects than to a certain order of qualities. He had, in his latter years, an occasional caprice or slight perversity of judgment; he took two or three very incongruous literary fancies. Such was the high relish which, for a certain period, he professed for the few first productions of M. Ernest Feydeau, and such the serious attention that he appears to have bestowed upon the literary activity of Charles

Baudelaire. Both of these writers had their merits, but one would have said that Sainte-Beuve, who discriminated so closely, would not have found his account in them. He writes to M. Feydeau, in 1860, on the occasion of this gentleman having put the finishing touches to a novel on a peculiarly repulsive theme, which was a very light literary matter into the bargain: "It will be very nice of you to tell me when 'Sylvie' will be worthy in your eyes to make her début in my faubourg; I shall be all eyes, all ears, to receive her."

But he paid so many tributes of a different kind that it is out of place to do more than touch upon that one. Here is quite another note. "If you knew English," he writes to a clerical friend who had sent him some poetic attempts, "you would have a treasure-house upon which you could draw. They have a poetic literature very superior to ours— and, above all, more healthy, more full. Wordsworth is not translated; one doesn't translate those things; one goes and drinks them at the fount. Let me enjoin upon you to learn English. . . . In a year or two you would be master of it, and you would have a private poetic treasure for your own use. Be a poet—I was only a little rivulet from those beautiful poetic lakes, with all their gentleness and melancholy." What I have found most interesting in these pages is the mark of the expert, as I may call it—the definiteness and clearness, the ripe sagacity, of the writer's critical sense. When it is a case of giving advice, of praising or of blaming, of replying to a question or an appeal, there is something delightful in our impression of the perfect competence. He always knows so well the weak point, always touches in passing upon the remedy. "The day on which you shall be willing to sacrifice a little to that French taste which you know so well, to our need of a frame and a border, you will have the value of all your essential qualities." He writes that to his distinguished fellow critic M. Schérer, whose culture he deemed a little too Germanic; and it would have been impossible to give him in a single sentence better practical advice. There is an admirable letter to M. Taine, on the appearance of the latter's rather infelicitous attempt at satire—the volume of impressions of M. Graindorge. This letter should be read by every one who has read the book— it is impossible to express more felicitously the feeling of discomfort produced by seeing a superior man make a great mistake. I have spoken of Sainte-Beuve's letter to Émile Zola: it is full of exquisite good sense (the writer's great quality), and the closing lines are worth quoting as an illustration of the definite and practical character of the critical reflections that he offered his correspondents. The allusion is to M. Zola's first novel, "Thérèse Raquin." "You have done a bold act; you have, in your work, braved both the public and the critics. Don't be surprised at certain indignations—the battle has begun; your name has been sounded. Such struggles terminate, when an author of talent is so minded, by another work equally bold, but a little less on the stretch, in which the public and the critics fancy they see a concession to their own sense; and the affair is wound up by one of those treaties of peace which consecrate one more reputation." It must be added that this was not the advice that M. Émile Zola took. He has never, that I know of, signed a treaty of peace; and, though his reputation is great, it can hardly be said to have been "consecrated." But I must make no more quotations; I must do no more than recommend these two volumes to all those readers for whom our author may have been at any time a valued companion. They will find a complete reflection of the man and the writer—the materials for a living image. They will find too a large confirmation of their confidence. Sainte-Beuve's was a mind of a thousand sides, and it is possible sometimes to meet it at a disconcerting or displeasing angle. But as regards the whole value I should never for an instant hesitate. If it is a question of taking the critic or leaving him—of being on his "side" or not—I take him, definitively, and on the added evidence of these letters, as the very genius of observation, discretion and taste.

James wrote the last of his four essays on Sainte-Beuve at his Paris hotel in the Rue Neuve St. Augustin during the snowy winter of 1879–80. The essay was published in the *North American Review* in 1880 and was revised in 1904 for William M. Payne's *American Literary Criticism*. In 1880 James was within sight of the greatness which he had sought throughout his apprentice years. He had won international acclaim with "Daisy Miller," and was completing his first major novel, *The Portrait of a Lady*. As critic, he had recently published two books (*French Poets and Novelists* and *Hawthorne*), and in 1880 he had at last an occasion which allowed full expression of his feelings for "the great critic." The texts which occasioned James' earlier reviews— Sainte-Beuve's less important French portraits, his first articles, and his English portraits—were minor. Sainte-Beuve's letters portrayed the man himself.

What James' review of the letters portrays is the extent to which he has—and has not—grown in disinterestedness.

> It is very well for him [Sainte-Beuve] to ask his correspon-
> dent to excuse his levity [about female sexuality]; his En-
> glish reader will probably not do so. But in this particular
> matter we must almost always make allowance for a de-
> gree of levity which we ourselves are not prepared to emu-
> late; and I refer to Sainte-Beuve's conformity of tone only
> because it helps to explain his incongruous appreciation of
> MM. Baudelaire and Feydeau. It is a tribute to the Gallic
> imagination.

This passage is a touchstone for Jamesian disinterestedness because it appears in 1880 and is deleted from the revised version of the essay. James evidently feels sufficiently easy with the Gallic imagination by 1904, and assumes a sufficient ease in his readers, that he need make no apology for Sainte-Beuve. But that James could make even this much apology for the Gallic imagination in 1880 is a tribute to the growth of his own imagaination by then. It is, moreover, a tribute hard-won. James' early reviews of Sainte-Beuve stress the "moral" issue, the Anglo-American discomfort with the Gallic imagination. Singling out Sainte-Beuve's portrait of an eighteenth-century woman who sustained a lifelong passion amid "a faithless and licentious society," James notes moralistically: "that he [Sainte-Beuve] should relate such a story in such a manner is conclusive evidence that he is very little of a moralist" ("Sainte-Beuve's Portraits" [1868]). That James goes on—apparently contradictorily—to wish the translator had "ventured to retain the sketch" for the English edition under review indicates how free James' play of mind is even this early, how ready he is to be satisfied by Sainte-Beuve's aesthetic qualities. This tension between aesthetics and morality leaves James' 1868 review sounding indecisive, even baffled.

> He is a little of a poet, a little of a moralist, a little of a historian, a little of a philosopher, a little of a romancer. But successively, with patience and care, you detect each of these characters in its littleness—you detect the wonderful man in flagrant default of imagination, of depth, of sagacity, of constructive skill, and you feel that he is reduced to logical proportions. At the same time you feel that there is another element of his mind which looks small from no point of view, but which remains immeasurable, original, and delightful. This is his passion for literature . . . his style.

The early tension in James between moral and aesthetic even prompts him to deny to Sainte-Beuve preeminence among French critics.

> For ourselves, we prefer M. Scherer. He has not M. Sainte-Beuve's unrivalled power of reproducing the physiognomy of a particular moment or of a particular figure of the past . . . But we prefer him because his morality is positive without being obtrusive; and because, besides the distinction of beauty and ugliness, the aesthetic distinction of right and wrong, there constantly occurs in his pages the moral distinction between good and evil. ("A French Critic" [1865])

By the mid-seventies, however, James has dismissed Scherer, who "lacks imagination" and "is subject to odd lapses and perversities of taste" ("Schérer's Literary Studies" [1876]). More important, James' bafflement before Sainte-Beuve has now turned to wonder. "We feel as if we could never learn enough about him. His intellectual fecundity was so unbounded that one imagines that the history of his individual opinions would throw a preternaturally brilliant light upon the laws of the human mind at large" ("Sainte-Beuve's First Articles" [1875]). James' increasing ease with the Gallic imagination does not mean that he loses sight of Sainte-Beuve's limitations. Unlike Arnold who even under fire "never . . . ceased to play fair" ("Matthew Arnold" [1884]), Sainte-Beuve allows himself "many a thrust and scratch, quite out of the rules of the game" ("Sainte-Beuve's English Portraits" [1875]). Syntax now reveals James' balanced view of Sainte-Beuve's strengths and weaknesses. Along with "his patience, his religious exactitude, his marvelous memory, his exquisite fancy," there are "limitations of temper, of morality, of generosity, and they would also now and then be limitations of taste" ("Sainte-Beuve's English Portraits").

By 1880 James has achieved a comparably balanced view of Sainte-Beuve's most problematic aspect, his Gallic imagination. James stands now in-between—explaining Gallic morality to Anglo-American readers rather than simply joining them in criticism of it. James insists both that Feydeau's *Sylvie* is "peculiarly repulsive" and that Sainte-Beuve's enthusiasm for Feydeau must be understood in context. "It must be remembered that Sainte-Beuve was absolutely destitute of prudery; his attitude in regard to that great group of considerations which we of English speech have so conveniently labeled the 'proprieties' was eminently Gallic." That James was correct about Feydeau's limitations—but was still undervaluing Sainte-Beuve's other favorite, Baudelaire—indicates that he has increased considerably in suppleness but has not reached the flexibility of the essays on Maupassant (1888) and Zola (1903). Overall, what is most impressive about James in 1880 is the extent to which he participates in the range, the "remarkable combination of qualities," which characterized "the great critic." James is demonstrating his capacity to practice what he would preach in "The Art of Fiction"—that the reader must grant the writer's donnée. What James said so eloquently about Sainte-Beuve can be applied with Beuvian "justness" to the American master himself. "His great justification, however, it seems to me, is, that the cause that he upheld was the most important, for it was simply the cause of liberty."

For modern discussions of Sainte-Beuve in relation to Henry James and Matthew Arnold see the last two paragraphs of the Commentary for Chapter 1.

NOTES

24:2. *Lettres à la Princesse* appeared in 1873 and went through five editions that year.

24:8. *Correspondances de C. A. Sainte-Beuve* (1877–78).

24:16. *Nouvelle Correspondance de C. A. Sainte-Beuve* appeared later in 1880.

25:42. passions . . . exclude each other. More than a quarter-century later, James in the Prefaces to *The Portrait of a Lady* and *The Golden Bowl*, Chapters 13 and 19, reaffirms his belief that art and life do not, cannot, stand in opposition.

27:7. offended individuals . . . societies and "sets." For a detailed summary of Sainte-Beuve's tangled relations with groups and individuals see Giese's chapter "Sainte-Beuve and His Contemporaries" in *Sainte-Beuve: A*

Literary Portrait (Madison: University of Wisconsin Studies, no. 31, 1931). See also Lehman's *Sainte-Beuve* (Oxford: Clarendon Press, 1962) and Nicholson's *Sainte-Beuve* (London: Constable, 1957).

28:6. Victor Cousin (1792–1867), French philosopher.

Alphonse-Marie-Louis de Prat de Lamartine (1790–1869), French poet and politician.

Abel-François Villemain (1790–1870), French literary historian, critic, politician, and professor.

François-René de Chateaubriand, Vicomte (1768–1848), French author and politician.

29:24. Louis de Fontanes (1757–1821), French politician and author.

29:29. "Portraits Littéraires." Sainte-Beuve first collected his early periodical essays in *Critiques et Portraits littéraires* between 1832 and 1839; then in the 1840s he divided them into *Portraits littéraires, Portraits de femmes,* and *Portraits contemporains.* The essay on de Fontanes appears in volume 2 of *Portraits littéraires.*

30:2. André-Marie Ampère (1775–1836), French mathematician and scientist. His son, Jean-Jacques (1800–1864), was a historian and man of letters.

30:38. Pierre-Aimé-Ernest Bersot (1816–1880), French writer on morals, literature, and philosophy.

31:4. Jean-François de la Harpe (1739–1803), French dramatist and critic.

31:6. *le petit se fâche.* The poor guy gets upset.

31:12. *le plus méchant singe qui existe.* The vilest beast alive.

31:34. Jacques-Bénigne Bossuet (1627–1704), French bishop, orator, and polemicist, attacked French theater in *Maximes et Réflections sur la Comédie* (1694).

Félix-Antoine-Philibert Dupanloup (1802–78), French bishop, theologian, and polemicist, criticized Renan's depiction of Jesus as an ordinary mortal and resigned from the French Academy rather than accept the membership of the positivist Émile Littré (1801–81) whom he had opposed for more than a decade on the grounds of materialism and atheism.

32:1. Lucretian view. Carus T. Lucretius (99?–55?), Roman poet and philosopher, condemned the artificiality, luxuriance, and violence of society in Book V of *De Rerum Natura.*

32:17. *son fait. "Dire son fait à quelqu' un"* means to tell someone what you think of him.

32:18. Louise Colet (1808–76), French writer, and lover of Flaubert and de Musset.

32:37. For James' reservations about Baudelaire see Bibliography, part 3.

35:19. Ernest Feydeau (1821–73), French novelist. James mentions later in the essay Feydeau's *Sylvie* (1861) which Sainte-Beuve was so optimistic about but which, like all of Feydeau's novels after the successfully scandalous *Fanny* (1858), received little popular or critical attention.

35:20. Edmond (1822–96) and Jules (1830–70) de Goncourt, French novelists and men of letters.

35:26. Delorme. In 1829 Sainte-Beuve published the first of his two collections of reflective verse, *Vie, Poésies et Pensées de Joseph Delorme*. Sainte-Beuve presents himself in the volume as the editor of poems supposedly written by his friend Delorme whom he describes as the archetypical romantic—melancholy, misunderstood, ill-fated. In 1834 Sainte-Beuve published his long, somewhat biographical novel *Volupté*.

36:2. Madame Émile de Girardin (née Delphine Gay, 1804–55), French writer of fiction, verse, and journalism, was a central figure in the romantic movement.

36:13. For Sainte-Beuve's increasingly antagonistic relationship with Balzac see note for p. 59, 1. 23, to "Honoré de Balzac."

36:17. "Gavarni" is the pseudonym of Sulpice-Guillaume Chevalier (1804–66), French lithographer and caricaturist.

36:26. *Quand même.* No matter what the reality.

36:30. Eugène Sue (1804–75), French author of many romances. Frédéric Soulié (1800–47), French author of sensational popular novels.

37:29. Edmond Scherer (1815–89), French critic. See Bibliography, part 3.

37:32. Hippolyte Adolphe Taine (1828–93), French critic and writer on diverse topics. For James' review of Taine's *Notes on Paris: The Life and Opinions of M. Frédéric-Thomas Graindorge*, see Bibliography, part 3.

Textual Variants

24:9. very interesting. 1880: a very interesting one.

24:22. picture. 1880: portrait.

24:23. He. 1880: Sainte-Beuve.

24:23. portrait. 1880: likeness.

24:27. constructed . . . man. 1880: constructed. In Sainte-Beuve the whole man.

24:30. life. 1880: activity.

25:4. condition. 1880: function.

25:9. and intimate. 1880: and, as they say in France, intimate.

25:12. shades. 1880: *nuances.*

25:13. He. 1880: Sainte-Beuve.

25:14. long excursions. 1880: set epistles.

25:14. His career. 1880: His literary career.

25:17. pages. 1880: letters.

25:19. his . . . notes. 1880: his letters are almost always rather brief notes.

25:21. There . . . of. 1880: There are very few letters devoted to giving an account of.

25:24. professional. 1880: literary.

25:35. depends . . . It. 1880: depends upon the value of the mind in question. It.

25:36. was . . . so. 1880: was a wonderful one—a mind so.

25:38. value. 1880: savor.

25:38. a remarkable. 1880: a most remarkable.

25:39. something . . . certain. 1880: something marvelous in the manner in which he reconciles certain.

26:3. or mundane. Added 1904.

26:4. express . . . to. 1880: express Sainte-Beuve's high plan is perhaps to.

26:6. student. 1880: writer.

26:6. brought. 1880: imported.

26:7. study. 1880: literature.

26:7. reflected. Added 1904.

26:8. no . . . was. 1880: no observer, surely, was.

26:20. was re-enforced. 1880: was in Sainte-Beuve reinforced.

26:30. lapidary. The. 1880: lapidary. In Sainte-Beuve the.

26:31. always. Added 1904.

26:31. them in. 1880: them all in.

26:35. drawn. 1880: painted his portrait.

26:35. intendingly, from head to foot. Added 1904.

26:38. emphasized. [par.] Various. Paragraph break added 1904.

26:39. appraise him. 1880: appreciate Sainte-Beuve.

27:2. the . . . by. 1880: the process was invalidated by.

27:3. the . . . as. 1880: the hostile judgements that have been passed upon the great critic—of which the number, as.

27:10. his. 1880: Sainte-Beuve's.

27:29. him . . . It. 1880: him to play tricks of a sometimes unprofitable kind. It.

27:34. For. 1880: In.

27:35. kind . . . he. 1880: kind, Sainte-Beuve was really wonderful; he.

27:41. his. 1880: Sainte-Beuve.

27:42. retributive. 1880: indicative.

28:4. claw, But. 1880: claw. There is nothing surprising in the tone in which he was usually alluded to by those of his contemporaries who were not fond of him—in the charges of "perfidity" and malignity; only we must not allow these things too much weight. Sainte-Beuve defended himself, as I have said, in his own manner; he was extremely susceptible and sensitive; he was even a trifle rancorous; he rarely forgave an injury. I spoke just now of his being "personal," and there is no doubt that he was sometimes so in the invidious sense of the word, as well as in the honorable sense in which I then used it. I do not mean that he sinned in this respect after the fashion of certain American newspapers—that he was coarsely abusive and intrusive, that he exercised himself upon the private and domestic affairs and idiosyncrasies of the objects of his criticism. But.

28:10. he. 1880: Sainte-Beuve.

28:14. He. 1880: Sainte-Beuve.

28:16. sensitive to certain great. 1880: sensible of a certain order of.

28:21. the . . . . [par.] His. 1880: the figures in a table of arithmetical factors. [par.] His.

28:24. cause . . . for. 1880: cause that Sainte-Beuve defended was the largest of all, for.

28:30. him. 1880: Sainte-Beuve.

28:34. he. 1880: Sainte-Beuve.

28:39. His. 1880: Sainte-Beuve's.

28:42. He. 1880: Sainte-Beuve.

29:8. that . . . agree. 1880: that we can easily agree.

29:11. restless. 1880: indefatigable.

29:14. esteem. . . . There. 1880: esteem; he valued immensely his *impression*. There.

29:17. him. 1880: Sainte-Beuve.

29:21. him. 1880: Sainte-Beuve.

29:31. He. 1880: Sainte-Beuve.

29:41. so. 1880: thus.

30:18. and delightful. 1880: of Sainte-Beuve.

30:21. conditions . . . right. 1880: conditions of his activity, I hold he was quite right.

30:23. on the rest of. 1880: upon.

30:23. tone. . . . "From. 1880: tone, the manner, the spirit, the cause in which it is made. "From.

30:29. perception. 1880: impressions.

30:31. aimed at. 1880: regarded.

30:34. The . . . so. 1880: The epistle seems to me so good, so.

30:35. quote. 1880: shall take the liberty of quoting.

30:38. He. 1880: Sainte-Beuve.

32:3. idols." [par.] If. 1880: idols." [par.] There are many things to be said about such a dissertation as that, and among them it may be said that there is something harsh and invidious in tone, and that, in whatever degree it may testify to that love of ascertaining the reality which I have spoken of as Sainte-Beuve's great merit, it indicates a good deal of skill in placing the reality in an unbecoming light. This is not the effect, however, that it produces upon my own mind; I take it as the expression of a wholesome impatience of that dull and unintelligent vision of things which so often passes in literature as adequate and decorous, and which, in fact, is poor sentiment quite as truly as it is poor criticism. Sainte-Beuve was a man of imagination and, as our ancestors used to say, of sensibility; as a critic, he had lively sympathies. But he was not a sentimentalist; he was incapable of preferring a contemplation of the surface to a knowledge of the internal spring. [par.] If.

32:16. side. There are. 1880: side. There is something essentially French in the tone of Sainte-Beuve's excited susceptibilities; it is hard to imagine an Englishman addressing to a friend, whose conduct he holds to have absolved him from further friendly allegiance, quite the same sort of reproaches as those which Sainte-Beuve conveys in so remarkably tidy a packet to his distinguished fellow critics. These are quarrels of literary—of intensely literary—men; and even an Englishman who rejoices in the questionable privilege of possessing what is called the artistic temperament would hardly measure so explicitly the injuries offered to his "personality." An Englishman's disposition is simpler and less expressive—his dignity is less vigilant, more confident. There are.

32:17. his. 1880: Sainte-Beuve's.

32:32. concludes. 1880: terminates.

32:35. irrepressible. 1880: famous.

32:37. turn. 1880: savor.

33:5. such a mind. 1880: a mind like Sainte-Beuve's.

33:28. have. Added 1904.

33:40. leave me. 1880: take their departure.

34:3. these. 1880: them.

34:7. with. 1880: within.

34:8. whose . . . of. 1880: whose judgments had no element of.

34:9. vulgarity . . . touched. 1880: vulgarity, but were always serious, comprehensive, touched.

34:11. ripe. Added 1904.

34:26. his. . . . "Your. 1880: his sentimental faculty: "Your.

34:38. is. . . . Of. 1880: is not very active in any one. Of.

34:41. full. 1880: very frequent.

34:42. dead. . . . Moreover. 1880: dead, he had at least what may be called the imagination of the heart. Moreover.

35:2. But. . . . [par.] It was. 1880: But, if it has existed, it is never distinctly got rid of. It changes its terms of manifesting itself, but there is always a savor of it in the conduct. [par.] It was.

35:12. "bents". 1880: idiosyncrasies.

35:17 doors. . . . feats. 1880: doors. Indeed, in his last years, he achieved feats.

35:31 was . . . of. 1880: was much more on his guard than most of.

35:32 was . . . he. 1880: was a conservative as well as a liberal; he.

35:33. high. 1880: great.

36:33. accept. . . . This. 1880: accept that number of genius under which they place him. This.

36:39. very incongruous. 1880: rather unaccountable.

36:39. fancies. Such. 1880: fancies. [par.] Such.

37:2. who . . . would. 1880: who was so sensitive to faults, would.

37:5. on. 1880: of.

37:5. theme. 1880: character.

37:5. light literary matter. 1880: flimsy piece of work.

37:8. her." [par.] But. 1880: her." It must be remembered that Sainte-Beuve was absolutely destitute of prudery; his attitude in regard to that great group of considerations which we of English speech have so conveniently labeled the "proprieties" was eminently Gallic. There is a curious example of this fact in a letter written in 1868, and given in the second of these volumes, in which (alluding conjecturally to a question as to which the French are always so alert in conjecture—the character of the relations between Benjamin Constant and Madame de Charrière) he makes light to an extraordinary degree of the whole matter of modesty and purity. He lays it down as highly probable that the lady just mentioned was conspicuously deficient in these qualities, and then adds: "Excuse my levity, but be so good as to observe that this does not in any way diminish the esteem that I have for Madame de Charrière. I will say the same for Madame de Staël, equally facile on this point." Sainte-Beuve had, as a matter of course, the Gallic imagination. It is very well for him to ask his correspondent to excuse his levity; his English reader will probably not do so. But in this particular matter we must almost always make allowance for a degree of levity which we ourselves are not prepared to emulate; and I refer to Sainte-Beuve's conformity of tone only because it helps to explain his incongruous appreciation of MM. Baudelaire and Feydeau. It is a tribute to the Gallic imagination. [par.] But.

37:9. he. 1880: Sainte-Beuve.

37:10. that. 1880: this.

37:10. quite another. 1880: a very different.

37:24. the. 1880: Sainte-Beuve's.

37:36. superior. 1880: clever.

38:1. battle has begun. 1880: combat is opened.

38:11. our author. 1880: Sainte-Beuve.

38:13. image. 1880: portrait.

38:15. sides. 1880: details.

38:15. possible. . . . But. 1880: possible to pick out certain points before which an admirer may falter and hesitate. But.

38:16. value. Added 1904.

38:17. the critic. 1880: Sainte-Beuve.

38:18. of . . . I. 1880: of giving in our adhesion or withholding it—I.

T H R E E
Middlemarch

"MIDDLEMARCH" IS AT ONCE ONE OF THE STRONG-est and one of the weakest of English novels. Its predecessors as they appeared might have been described in the same terms; "Romola," is especially a rare masterpiece, but the least *entraînant* of masterpieces. "Romola" sins by excess of analysis; there is too much description and too little drama; too much reflection (all certainly of a highly imaginative sort) and too little creation. Movement lingers in the story, and with it attention stands still in the reader. The error in "Middlemarch" is not precisely of a similar kind, but it is equally detrimental to the total aspect of the work. We can well remember how keenly we wondered, while its earlier chapters unfolded themselves, what turn in the way of form the story would take—that of an organized, moulded, balanced composition, gratifying the reader with a sense of design and construction, or a mere chain of episodes, broken into accidental lengths and unconscious of the influence of a plan. We expected the actual result, but for the sake of English imaginative literature which, in this line is rarely in need of examples, we hoped for the other. If it had come we should have had the pleasure of reading, what certainly would have seemed to us in the immediate glow of attention, the first of English novels. But that pleasure has still to hover between prospect and retrospect. "Middlemarch" is a treasure-house of details, but it is an indifferent whole.

Our objection may seem shallow and pedantic, and may even be represented as a complaint that we have had the less given us rather than the more. Certainly the greatest minds have the defects of their qualities, and as George Eliot's mind is preëminently contemplative and analytic, nothing is more natural than that her manner should be discursive and expansive. "Concentration" would doubtless have deprived us of many of the best things in the book—of Peter Featherstone's grotesquely expectant legatees, of Lydgate's medical rivals, and of Mary Garth's delightful family. The author's purpose was to

48

be a generous rural historian, and this very redundancy of touch, born of abundant reminiscence, is one of the greatest charms of her work. It is as if her memory was crowded with antique figures, to whom for very tenderness she must grant an appearance. Her novel is a picture—vast, swarming, deep-colored, crowded with episodes, with vivid images, with lurking master-strokes, with brilliant passages of expression; and as such we may freely accept it and enjoy it. It is not compact, doubtless; but when was a panorama compact? And yet, nominally, "Middlemarch" has a definite subject—the subject indicated in the eloquent preface. An ardent young girl was to have been the central figure, a young girl framed for a larger moral life than circumstance often affords, yearning for a motive for sustained spiritual effort and only wasting her ardor and soiling her wings against the meanness of opportunity. The author, in other words, proposed to depict the career of an obscure St. Theresa. Her success has been great, in spite of serious drawbacks. Dorothea Brooke is a genuine creation, and a most remarkable one when we consider the delicate material in which she is wrought. George Eliot's men are generally so much better than the usual trowsered offspring of the female fancy, that their merits have perhaps overshadowed those of her women. Yet her heroines have always been of an exquisite quality, and Dorothea is only that perfect flower of conception of which her predecessors were the less unfolded blossoms. An indefinable moral elevation is the sign of these admirable creatures; and of the representation of this quality in its superior degrees the author seems to have in English fiction a monopoly. To render the expression of a soul requires a cunning hand; but we seem to look straight into the unfathomable eyes of the beautiful spirit of Dorothea Brooke. She exhales a sort of aroma of spiritual sweetness, and we believe in her as in a woman we might providentially meet some fine day when we should find ourselves doubting of the immortality of the soul. By what unerring mechanism this effect is produced—whether by fine strokes or broad ones, by description or by narration, we can hardly say; it is certainly the great achievement of the book. Dorothea's career is, however, but an episode, and though doubtless in intention, not distinctly enough in fact, the central one. The history of Lydgate's *menage,* which shares honors with it, seems rather to the reader to carry off the lion's share. This is certainly a very interesting story, but on the whole it yields in dignity to the record of Dorothea's unresonant woes. The "love-problem," as the author calls it, of Mary Garth, is placed on a rather higher level than the reader willingly grants it. To the end we care less about Fred Vincy than appears to be expected of us. In so far as the writer's design has been to reproduce the total sum of life in an English village forty years ago, this common-place young gentleman, with his somewhat meagre tribulations and his rather neutral egotism, has his proper place in the picture; but the author narrates his fortunes with a fulness of detail which the reader often finds irritating. The reader indeed is sometimes tempted to complain of a tendency which we are at loss exactly to express—a tendency to make light of the serious elements of the story and to sacrifice them to the more trivial ones. Is it an unconscious instinct or is it a deliberate plan? With its abundant and massive ingredients "Middlemarch" ought somehow to have depicted a weightier drama. Dorothea was altogether too superb a heroine to be wasted; yet she plays a narrower part than the imagination of the reader demands. She is of more consequence than the action of which she is the nominal centre. She marries enthusiastically a man whom she fancies a great thinker, and who turns out to be but an arid pedant. Here, indeed, is a disappointment with much of the dignity of tragedy; but the situation seems to us never to expand to its full capacity. It is analyzed with extraordinary penetration, but one may say of it, as of most of the situations in the book, that it is treated with too much refinement and too little breadth. It revolves too constantly on the same pivot; it abounds in fine shades, but it lacks, we think, the great dramatic *chiaroscuro*. Mr. Casaubon, Dorothea's husband (of whom more anon) embittered, on his side, by matrimonial disappointment, takes refuge in vain jealousy of his wife's relations with an interesting young cousin of his own and registers this sentiment in a codicil to his will, making the forfeiture of his property the penalty of his widow's marriage with this gentleman. Mr. Casaubon's death befalls about the middle of the story, and from this point to the close our interest in Dorothea is restricted to the question, will she or will not marry Will Ladislaw? The question is relatively trivial and the implied struggle slightly factitious. The author has depicted the struggle with a sort of elaborate solemnity which in the interviews related in the two last books tends to become almost ludicrously excessive.

The dramatic current stagnates; it runs between hero and heroine almost a game of hair-splitting. Our dissatisfaction here is provoked in a great measure by the insubstantial character of the hero. The figure of Will Ladislaw is a beautiful attempt, with many finely-completed points; but on the whole it seems to us a failure. It is the only eminent failure in the book, and its defects are therefore the more striking. It lacks sharpness of outline and depth of color; we have not found ourselves believing in Ladislaw as we believe in Dorothea, in Mary Garth, in Rosamond, in Lydgate, in Mr. Brooke and

Mr. Casaubon. He is meant, indeed, to be a light creature (with a large capacity for gravity, for he finally gets into Parliament), and a light creature certainly should not be heavily drawn. The author, who is evidently very fond of him, has found for him here and there some charming and eloquent touches; but in spite of these he remains vague and impalpable to the end. He is, we may say, the one figure which a masculine intellect of the same power as George Eliot's would not have conceived with the same complacency; he is, in short, roughly speaking, a woman's man. It strikes us as an oddity in the author's scheme that she should have chosen just this figure of Ladislaw as the creature in whom Dorothea was to find her spiritual compensations. He is really, after all, not the ideal foil to Mr. Casaubon which her soul must have imperiously demanded, and if the author of the "Key to all Mythologies" sinned by lack of order, Ladislaw too has not the concentrated fervor essential in the man chosen by so nobly strenuous a heroine. The impression once given that he is a *dilettante* is never properly removed, and there is slender poetic justice in Dorothea's marrying a *dilettante*. We are doubtless less content with Ladislaw, on account of the noble, almost sculptural, relief of the neighboring figure of Lydgate, the real hero of the story. It is an illustration of the generous scale of the author's picture and of the conscious power of her imagination that she has given us a hero and heroine of broadly distinct interests—erected, as it were, two suns in her firmament, each with its independent solar system. Lydgate is so richly successful a figure that we have regretted strongly at moments, for immediate interests' sake, that the current of his fortunes should not mingle more freely with the occasionally thin-flowing stream of Dorothea's. Toward the close, these two fine characters are brought into momentary contact so effectively as to suggest a wealth of dramatic possibility between them; but if this train had been followed we should have lost Rosamond Vincy—a rare psychological study. Lydgate is a really complete portrait of a *man,* which seems to us high praise. It is striking evidence of the altogether superior quality of George Eliot's imagination that, though elaborately represented, Lydgate should be treated so little from what we may roughly (and we trust without offence) call the sexual point of view. Perception charged with feeling has constantly guided the author's hand, and yet her strokes remain as firm, her curves as free, her whole manner as serenely impersonal, as if, on a small scale, she were emulating the creative wisdom itself. Several English romancers—notably Fielding, Thackeray, and Charles Reade—have won great praise for their figures of women: but they owe it, in reversed conditions, to a meaner sort of art, it seems to us, than George Eliot has used in the case of Lydgate; to an indefinable appeal to masculine prejudice—to a sort of titillation of the masculine sense of difference. George Eliot's manner is more philosophic—more broadly intelligent, and yet her result is as concrete or, if you please, as picturesque. We have no space to dwell on Lydgate's character; we can but repeat that he is a vividly consistent, manly figure—powerful, ambitious, sagacious, with the maximum rather than the mimimum of egotism, strenuous, generous, fallible, and altogether human. A work of the liberal scope of "Middlemarch" contains a multitude of artistic intentions, some of the finest of which become clear only in the meditative after-taste of perusal. This is the case with the balanced contrast between the two histories of Lydgate and Dorothea. Each is a tale of matrimonial infelicity, but the conditions in each are so different and the circumstances so broadly opposed that the mind passes from one to the other with that supreme sense of the vastness and variety of human life, under aspects apparently similar, which it belongs only to the greatest novels to produce. The most perfectly successful passages in the book are perhaps those painful fireside scenes between Lydgate and his miserable little wife. The author's rare psychological penetration is lavished upon this veritably mulish domestic flower. There is nothing more powerfully real than these scenes in all English fiction, and nothing certainly more *intelligent*. Their impressiveness, and (as regards Lydgate) their pathos, is deepened by the constantly low key in which they are pitched. It is a tragedy based on unpaid butchers' bills, and the urgent need for small economies. The author has desired to be strictly real and to adhere to the facts of the common lot, and she has given us a powerful version of that typical human drama, the struggles of an ambitious soul with sordid disappointments and vulgar embarrassments. As to her catastrophe we hesitate to pronounce (for Lydgate's ultimate assent to his wife's worldly programme is nothing less than a catastrophe). We almost believe that some terrific explosion would have been more probable than his twenty years of smothered aspiration. Rosamond deserves almost to rank with Tito in "Romola" as a study of a gracefully vicious, or at least of a practically baleful nature. There is one point, however, of which we question the consistency. The author insists on her instincts of coquetry, which seems to us a discordant note. They would have made her better or worse—more generous or more reckless; in either case more manageable. As it is, Rosamond represents, in a measure, the fatality of British decorum.

In reading, we have marked innumerable passages for quotation and comment; but we lack space and the work is so ample that half a dozen extracts would be an ineffective illustration. There would be a great deal to say on the broad array of secondary figures, Mr. Casaubon, Mr. Brooke, Mr. Bulstrode, Mr. Farebrother, Caleb Garth, Mrs. Cadwallader, Celia Brooke. Mr. Casaubon is an excellent invention; as a dusky *repoussoir* to the luminous figure of his wife he could not have been better imagined. There is indeed something very noble in the way in which the author has apprehended his character. To depict hollow pretentiousness and mouldy egotism with so little of narrow sarcasm and so much of philosophic sympathy, is to be a rare moralist as well as a rare story-teller. The whole portrait of Mr. Casaubon has an admirably sustained greyness of tone in which the shadows are never carried to the vulgar black of coarser artists. Every stroke contributes to the unwholesome, helplessly sinister expression. Here and there perhaps (as in his habitual diction), there is a hint of exaggeration; but we confess we like fancy to be fanciful. Mr. Brooke and Mr. Garth are in their different lines supremely genial creations; they are drawn with the touch of a Dickens chastened and intellectualized. Mrs. Cadwallader is, in another walk of life, a match for Mrs. Poyser, and Celia Brooke is as pretty a fool as any of Miss Austen's. Mr. Farebrother and his delightful "womankind" belong to a large group of figures begotten of the superabundance of the author's creative instinct. At times they seem to encumber the stage and to produce a rather ponderous mass of dialogue; but they add to the reader's impression of having walked in the Middlemarch lanes and listened to the Middlemarch accent. To but one of these accessory episodes—that of Mr. Bulstrode, with its multiplex ramifications—do we take exception. It has a slightly artificial cast, a melodramatic tinge, unfriendly to the richly natural coloring of the whole. Bulstrode himself—with the history of whose troubled conscience the author has taken great pains—is, to our sense, too diffusely treated; he never grasps the reader's attention. But the touch of genius is never idle or vain. The obscure figure of Bulstrode's comely wife emerges at the needful moment, under a few light strokes, into the happiest reality.

All these people, solid and vivid in their varying degrees, are members of a deeply human little world, the full reflection of whose antique image is the great merit of these volumes. How bravely rounded a little world the author has made it—with how dense an atmosphere of interests and passions and loves and enmities and strivings and failings, and how motley a group of great folk and small, all after their kind, she has filled it, the reader must learn for himself. No writer seems to us to have drawn from a richer stock of those long-cherished memories which one's later philosophy makes doubly tender. There are few figures in the book which do not seem to have grown mellow in the author's mind. English readers may fancy they enjoy the "atmosphere" of "Middlemarch;" but we maintain that to relish its inner essence we must—for reasons too numerous to detail—be an American. The author has commissioned herself to be real, her native tendency being that of an idealist, and the intellectual result is a very fertilizing mixture. The constant presence of thought, of generalizing instinct, of *brain*, in a word, behind her observation, gives the latter its great value and her whole manner its high superiority. It denotes a mind in which imagination is illumined by faculties rarely found in fellowship with it. In this respect—in that broad reach of vision which would make the worthy historian of solemn fact as well as wanton fiction—George Eliot seems to us among English romancers to stand alone. Fielding approaches her, but to our mind, she surpasses Fielding. Fielding was didactic—the author of "Middlemarch" is really philosophic. These great qualities imply corresponding perils. The first is the loss of simplicity. George Eliot lost hers some time since; it lies buried (in a splendid mausoleum) in "Romola." Many of the discursive portions of "Middlemarch" are, as we may say, too clever by half. The author wishes to say too many things, and to say them too well; to recommend herself to a scientific audience. Her style, rich and flexible as it is, is apt to betray her on these transcendental flights; we find, in our copy, a dozen passages marked "obscure." "Silas Marner" has a delightful tinge of Goldsmith—we may almost call it: "Middlemarch" is too often an echo of Messrs. Darwin and Huxley. In spite of these faults—which it seems graceless to indicate with this crude rapidity— it remains a very splendid performance. It sets a limit, we think, to the development of the old-fashioned English novel. Its diffuseness, on which we have touched, makes it too copious a dose of pure fiction. If we write novels so, how shall we write History? But it is nevertheless a contribution of the first importance to the rich imaginative department of our literature.

James wrote his unsigned review of *Middlemarch* after reading the newly published novel at the Hôtel Rastadt in Paris in 1872. He was supporting himself at the time with his stories, reviews, and travel pieces. Between 1866 and 1885, James wrote ten articles on Eliot, six on her fiction. His first signed piece of literary criticism was the 1866 "The Novels of George Eliot." He visited Eliot several times; two of these visits are described in detail in *The Middle Years*.

James' apprenticeship as a writer was served, in part, as a reader of George Eliot. Late in life he described *The Mill on the Floss* as "the all-engulfing . . . incomparably privileged production, which shone for young persons of that contemporaneity with a nobleness that nothing under our actual star begins in like case to match" (*A*, 518). Eliot's importance is also indicated by the variety of correspondents with whom he discusses her work. (The letters on *Daniel Deronda* in volume 2 of the *Letters* are especially rich.) James' critics have, since the earliest notices, connected the two writers. Contemporary reviewers described both as serious, "metaphysical" novelists, noting their use of similar character types and shared tendency towards psychological portraiture. (See, for example, the unsigned reviews of *The Portrait of a Lady* in *Literary World*, 12 (December 1881): 473–74; *Saturday Review*, 52 (December 1881): 703–4; *Nation*, 34 (February 1882): 102–3; and Howells, "Henry James Jr.," *Century*, 3 (November 1882): 25–29.) Later F. R. Leavis argued in *The Great Tradition* (London: Chatto and Windus, 1948) that "it can be shown, with a conclusiveness rarely possible in these matters, that James did actually go to school to George Eliot." Leon Edel calls *The Portrait of a Lady* "a 'George Eliot novel' written by James in the way he believed she *should* have written" (2: 371). James himself pointed out several novelistic traits he shared with Eliot, most notably, the central use of "frail vessels" of female consciousness (Preface to *The Portrait of a Lady*, p. 292).

James judges Eliot's individual works variously over the years. In 1873, *Middlemarch* is not "the first of English novels," but by 1914 he concludes: "I find it idle even to wonder what 'place' the author of *Silas Marner* and *Middlemarch* may be conceived to have in the pride of our literature . . ." (*A*, 573). What matters to James is his "living and recorded *relation*" with Eliot and her work: Readers of Eliot "simply sit with our enjoyed gain, our residual rounded possession in our lap; a safe old treasure" (*A*, 573–74).

On the nature of that treasure James does not vary. He reviews *Middlemarch* as an English novel because George Eliot was, for James, above all an *English* novelist. Writing to Alice James on February 22, 1876, he criticizes *Daniel Deronda* but goes on to say: "But I enjoyed it more than anything of hers—or any other novelist's almost—I have ever read. Partly for reading it in this beastly Paris, and realizing the superiority of English culture and the English mind to the French. The English richness of George Eliot beggars everything else, everywhere, that one might compare with her." James' essays on Eliot describe that national richness: her ability to represent the England that he loves, her contribution to the English novel as a literary form, and the English traits of mind evidenced in her work.

The *Middlemarch* review is also representative because it begins and ends with references to what James sees throughout his life as the two central tensions in Eliot's work. The first can be seen in his judgment that: " 'Middlemarch' is a treasurehouse of details, but it is an indifferent whole." From his earliest review of Eliot ("*Felix Holt, the Radical,*" 1866), where he notes her powers of "microscopic observation," James treasures her warmly detailed pictures of humble life, yet finds that Eliot, like so many English novelists, fails to recognize the importance of form. Eliot focuses on minutiae at the expense of composition. Her most minor characters are full and vital, but she loses sight of her heroes and heroines. Because the whole is subordinate to its parts in Eliot's novels, her plots are contrived, and dramatic development remains weak.

James' emphasis on the presence of Eliot's "*brain*" in *Middlemarch* points to a second tension in her fiction, between what he calls in his review of *The Life of George Eliot* (1885) "reflection" and "perception." He praises Eliot consistently over the years for her "reflection": the seriousness with which she treats fiction, the fund of ideas and knowledge which she brings to her writing. Because a reflective English novelist is untypical, Eliot is a particularly important example for the writer who, in "The Art of Fiction," deplores the English public's demand that all fiction should "more or less admit that it is only a joke" (p. 166). On the other hand, Eliot's "perception"—the human sympathy that results from her experience and memory of life—is, for James, typically English. Balzac "grudges and hates and despises" his bourgeosie; whereas Eliot treats her most absurd characters "humanly" and "generously," never grudging them their freedom ("Honoré de Balzac," p. 81). Eliot's fiction is great when reflection and perception are held in balance. However, James fears that, beginning with what he calls in 1873 the "splendid mausoleum" of *Romola,* Eliot often loses this balance. Romola "is overladen with learning, it smells of the lamp, it tastes just perceptibly of pedantry" (1885). When reflection weighs heavy, Eliot's work leans to the abstract and the didactic.

Yet Eliot's faults are less significant than her persistent ability to create, as she does in *Middlemarch*, "a deeply human little world," a world that offers to James, future English citizen, reader of English novels, and writer of fiction in English, profound historical and aesthetic satisfactions. "It was by George Eliot's name that I was to go on knowing, was never to cease to know, a great treasure of beauty and humanity, of applied and achieved art, a testimony, historic as well as aesthetic, to the deeper interest of the intricate English aspects" (*A*, 574).

Among James studies that treat his work on Eliot, see Edel, (2: 368–72, and 1–4, passim); Daugherty (chaps. 2 and 6); Kelley (chaps. 2 and 14); Roberts. For two examples of Eliot scholars' criticisms of James' writings on the novelist, see Hardy, *The Novels of George Eliot: A Study in Form* (London: The Athlone Press, 1959), and Harvey, *The Art of George Eliot* (London: Chatto and Windus, 1961). A large number of both the books on James and those on Eliot mention in passing her influence on him. Examples of studies devoted specifically to that influence include Byrd, "The Fractured Crystal in *Middlemarch* and *The Golden Bowl*," *Modern Fiction Studies* 18 (Winter 1972–73): 551–54; Hochman, "From *Middlemarch* to *The Portrait of a Lady*: Some Reflections on Henry James and the Traditions of the Novel," *Hebrew University Studies in Literature* 5 (1977): 102–6; Lainoff, "James and Eliot: The Two Gwendolens," *Victorian Newsletter* 21 (Spring 1962): 23–24; Q. D. Leavis, "A Note on Literary Indebtedness: Dickens, George Eliot, Henry James," *Hudson Review* 8 (Autumn 1955): 423–28; Levine, "Isabel, Gwendolen, and Dorothea," *Journal of English Literary History* 30 (September 1963): 244–57; Selig, "The Red Haired Lady Orator: Parallel Passages in *The Bostonians* and *Adam Bede*," *Nineteenth Century Fiction* 16 (September 1961): 164–69.

NOTES

48:2. Its predecessors. *Scenes of Clerical Life* (1858), *Adam Bede* (1859), *The Mill on the Floss* (1860), *Silas Marner* (1861), *Romola* (1863), *Felix Holt* (1866).

48:4. *entraînant.* inspiriting, stirring.

48:15. unconscious of the influence of a plan. James frequently criticizes what he calls in the Preface to *The Tragic Muse* the "large loose baggy monsters" of nineteenth-century fiction. On March 5, 1873, he wrote to Grace Norton that "To produce some little exemplary works of art is my narrow and lowly dream. They are to have less 'brain' than *Middlemarch*; but (I boldly proclaim it) they are to have more *form*."

49:5. "Picture" is used here to refer to literary pictorialism. James also employs the term to designate a narrative segment, as opposed to a dramatic "scene." See the Preface to *The Wings of the Dove,* Chapter 17, and index.

51:41. Charles Reade (1814–84), English novelist. James never reviewed his work, but in the 1866 review of *Felix Holt,* he compared Eliot unfavorably with Reade whom he called "the most readable of living English novelists, and . . . a distant kinsman of Shakespeare."

53:6. *repoussoir.* A painting term, meaning that which foils, sets off, or contrasts.

53:18. a Dickens chastened and intellectualized. In his review of *Our Mutual Friend* James argues that the writing of the un-"chastened" Dickens is no longer based on real types: "there is no humanity here" (see below, Bibliography, part 4).

53:19. Mrs. Poyser is a farm wife in Eliot's *Adam Bede.*

53:20. Miss Austen's. In his review of *Felix Holt,* James describes George Eliot as of a "kind" with Jane Austen.

54:5. be an American. In "The Novels of George Eliot" (1866), James argues that, while Americans will not be able to judge the accuracy of Eliot's details, they can sense the truth of her novels. In his review of Arnold's *Essays in Criticism* (p. 11), he states that "It is often the fortune of English writers to find mitigation of sentence in the United States."

54:26. Thomas Henry Huxley (1825–95), British scientist and humanist.

54:31. how shall we write History? On the novel as history, see "Honoré de Balzac" and "The Art of Fiction," Chapters 4 and 7. On the distinction between literature and history, see the Preface to *The Aspern Papers* and "The Novel in *The Ring and the Book,*" Chapters 16 and 21.

F O U R
HONORÉ DE BALZAC

THE FRENCH IN GENERAL DO THEIR DUTY BY THEIR great men; they render them a liberal tribute of criticism, commentary, annotation, biographical analysis. They do not, indeed, make them the subject of "memoirs" in the English sense; there are few French examples of that class of literature to which Boswell's "Johnson" and Lockhart's "Scott" belong. But there usually clusters about the image of a conspicuous writer an infinite number of *travaux*, as the French say, of every degree of importance. Many of these are very solid and serious; their authors are generally to be charged with attaching too absolute a value to their heroes. The departed genius is patiently weighed and measured; his works are minutely analysed; the various episodes of his life are made the object of exhaustive research; his letters are published, and his whole personality, physical, moral, intellectual, passes solemnly into literature. He is always in order as a "subject"; it is admitted that the last word can never be said about him. From this usual fate of eminent Frenchmen, one of the greatest has been strikingly exempted. Honoré de Balzac is weighted neither with the honours nor with the taxes of an accumulated commentary. The critic who proposes to study him, and who looks for extrinsic assistance in his task, perceives such aid to be very meagre. Balzac has been discussed with first-rate ability only by one writer. M. Taine's essay, incomplete as it is, may be said at any rate to be essentially worthy of its subject. Sainte-Beuve wrote upon Balzac two or three times, but always with striking and inexplicable inadequacy. There is a long article on the author of the "Comédie Humaine" by Théophile Gautier, which is admirably picturesque but not at all critical. M. Edmond Schérer, a writer upon whom an ample fold of Sainte-Beuve's mantle has fallen, lately published a few pages which are suggestive, but in which he affirms that Balzac is neither an artist, a master, nor a writer. The great novelist's countrymen, in a word, have taken him less seriously than was to be expected. If we desire

59

biographical details we are reduced to consulting the very flimsy gossip of M. Léon Gozlan. Balzac has indeed what is called his *légende*, but it has been chiefly in the keeping of the mere tattlers of literature. The critic is forced to look for the man almost exclusively in his works; and it must be confessed that in the case of a writer so voluminous as Balzac such a field is ample. We should rather rejoice than regret that there are not more pages to turn. Balzac's complete works occupy twenty-three huge octavo volumes in the stately but inconvenient "édition définitive," lately published. There is a prospect of his letters being given to the world in a complementary volume.

I

Honoré de Balzac was born at Tours in 1799; he died at Paris in 1850. Most first-rate men at fifty-one have still a good deal of work in them, and there is no reason to believe that, enormous as had been the demands he made upon it, Balzac's productive force was fully spent. His prefaces are filled with confident promises to publish novels that never appeared. Nevertheless it is impossible altogether to regret that Balzac died with work still in him. He had written enough; he had written too much. His novels, in spite of their extraordinary closeness of tissue, all betray the want of leisure in the author. It is true that shortly before his death he had encountered a change of fortune; he had married a rich woman and he was in a position to drive his pen no faster than his fancy prompted. It is interesting to wonder whether Balzac at leisure—Balzac with that great money-question which was at once the supreme inspiration and the aesthetic alloy of his life, placed on a relatively ideal basis—would have done anything essentially finer than "Les Parents Pauvres" or "Le Père Goriot." We can hardly help doubting it. M. Taine, looking as usual for formulas and labels, says that the most complete description of Balzac is that he was a man of business—a man of business in debt. The formula here is on the whole satisfactory; it expresses not only what he was by circumstances, but what he was by inclination. We cannot say how much Balzac liked being in debt, but we are very sure he liked, for itself, the process of manufacture and sale, and that even when all his debts had been paid he would have continued to keep his shop.

Before he was thirty years old he had published, under a variety of pseudonyms, some twenty long novels, veritable Grub Street productions, written in sordid Paris attics, in poverty, in perfect obscurity. Several of these "œuvres de jeunesse" have lately been republished, but the best of them are unreadable. No writer ever served a harder apprenticeship to his art, or lingered more hopelessly at the base of the ladder of fame. This early incompetence seems at first an anomaly, but it is only partially an anomaly. That so vigorous a genius should have learned his trade so largely by experiment and so little by divination; that in order to discover what he could do he should have had to make specific trial of each of the things he could not do—this is something which needs explanation. The explanation is found, it seems to us, simply in the folly of his attempting, at that age, to produce such novels as he aspired to produce. It was not that he could not use his wings; it was simply that his wings had not grown. The wings of great poets generally sprout very early; the wings of great artists in prose, great explorers of the sources of prose, begin to spread themselves only after the man is tolerably formed. Good observers, we believe, will confess to a general mistrust of novels written before thirty.. Byron, Shelley, Keats, Lamartine, Victor Hugo, Alfred de Musset, were hardly in their twenties before they struck their fully resonant notes. Walter Scott, Thackeray, George Eliot, Madame Sand, waited till they were at least turned thirty, and then without prelude, or with brief prelude, produced a novel that was a masterpiece. If it was well for them to wait, it would have been infinitely better for Balzac. Balzac was to be preëminently a social novelist; his strength was to lie in representing the innumerable actual facts of the French civilization of his day—things only to be learned by patient experience. Balzac's inspiration, his stock, his *fonds*, was outside of him,. in the complex French world of the nineteenth century. If, instead of committing to paper impossible imaginary tales, he could have stood for a while in some other relation to the society about him than that of a scribbler, it would have been a very great gain. The great general defect of his manner, as we shall see, is the absence of fresh air, of the trace of disinterested observation; he had from his earliest years, to carry out our metaphor, an eye to the shop. In every great artist who possesses taste there is a little—a very little—of the amateur; but in Balzac there is absolutely nothing of the amateur, and nothing is less to be depended upon than Balzac's taste. But he was forced to write; his family wished to make a lawyer of him, and he preferred to be a romancer. He mastered enough law to be able to incorporate the mysteries of legal procedure in the "Comédie Humaine," and then embarked upon the most prolific literary career, perhaps, that the world has seen. His family cut down his supplies and tried to starve him out; but he held firm, and in 1830 made his first step into success. Meanwhile he had engaged in several commercial ventures, each one of which failed, leaving him a ponderous legacy of debt. To the end of his life he was haunted with undischarged obligations and was constantly trying new speculations and investments. It is true, we believe, that he amused himself with representing this pecuniary incubus as far more mysteriously and heroically huge than it was. His incessant labour brought him a remuneration which at this day and in this country would be considered contemptible. M. Gozlan affirms that his annual income, in his successful years, rarely exceeded 12,000 francs. This appears incredible until we find the editor of the "Revue de Paris" crying out against his demand of 3,000 francs for the MS. of "Eugénie Grandet." There is something pitiful in the contrast between this meagre personal budget and his lifelong visions of wealth and of the ways of amassing wealth, his jovial, sensual, colossal enjoyment of luxury, and the great monetary architecture as it were of the "Comédie Humaine." Money is the most general element of Balzac's novels; other things come and go, but money is always there. His great ambition and his great pretension as a social chronicler was to be complete, and he was more complete in this direction than in any other. He rarely introduces a person without telling us in detail how his property is invested, and the fluctuations of his *rentes* impartially divide the writer's attention with the emotions of his heart. Balzac never mentions an object without telling us what it cost, and on every occasion he mentions an enormous number of objects. His women, too, talk about money quite as much as his men, and not only his ignoble and mercenary women (of whom there are so many) but his charming women, his heroines, his great ladies. Madame de Mortsauf is intended as a perfect example of feminine elevation, and yet Madame de Mortsauf has the whole of her husband's agricultural economy at her fingers' ends; she strikes us at moments as an attorney in petticoats. Each particular episode of the "Comédie Humaine" has its own hero and heroine, but the great general protagonist is the twenty-franc piece.

One thing at any rate Balzac achieved during these early years of effort and obscurity; he had laid the foundations of that intimate knowledge of Paris which was to serve as the basis—the vast mosaic pavement—of the "Comédie Humaine." Paris became his world, his universe; his passion for the great city deserves to rank in literature beside Dr. Johnson's affection for London. Wherever in his novels Paris is not directly presented she is even more vividly implied; the great negative to this brilliant positive, that *vie de province* of which he produced such elaborate pictures, is always observed from the standpoint of the Boulevard. If Balzac had represented any other country than France, if his imagination had ever left a footprint in England or

Germany, it is a matter of course for those who know him that his fathomless Parisian cockneyism would have had on these occasions a still sharper emphasis. But there is nothing to prove that he in the least "realized," as we say, the existence of England and Germany. That he had of course a complete theory of the British constitution and the German intellect makes little difference; for Balzac's theories were often in direct proportion to his ignorance. He never perceived with any especial directness that the civilized world was made up of something else than Paris and the provinces; and as he is said to have been able to persuade himself, by repeating it a few times, that he had done various things which he had not done—made a present of a white horse, for instance, to his publisher—so he would have had only to say often enough to himself that England was a mythic country to believe imperturbably that there was in fact, three hundred miles away, no magnificent far-spreading London to invalidate his constant assumption that Paris is the pivot of human history. Never was a great genius more essentially local. Shakespeare, Scott, Goethe, savour of their native soil; but they have a glance that has only to fix itself a moment to call up easily other horizons. Balzac's power of creation gains perhaps in intensity what it loses in reach; it is certain at any rate that his conception of the stage on which the "Comédie Humaine" is perpetually being acted is surrounded by a Chinese wall. Never was an imagination more in sympathy with the French theory of centralization.

When his letters are published it will be interesting to learn from them, in so far as we may, how his life was spent during these first ten years of his manhood. He began very early to write about countesses and duchesses; and even after he had become famous, the manner in which he usually portrays the denizens of the Faubourg St. Germain obliges us to believe that the place they occupy in his books is larger than any that they occupied in his experience. Did he go into society? did he observe manners from a standpoint that commanded the field? It was not till he became famous that he began to use the aristocratic prefix; in his earlier years he was plain M. Balzac. I believe it is more than suspected that the pedigree represented by this *de* was as fabulous (and quite as ingenious) as any that he invented for his heroes. Balzac was profoundly and essentially *roturier*; we shall see that the intrinsic evidence of his plebeian origin is abundant. He may very well, like his own Eugène de Rastignac, have lived at a Maison Vauquer; but did he, like Rastignac, call upon a Madame de Beauséant and see her receive him as a kinsman? We said just now that we had to look for Balzac almost altogether in his books; and yet his books are singularly void of personal revelations. They tell us a vast deal about his mind, but they suggest to us very little about his life. It is hard to imagine a writer less autobiographic. This is certainly a proof of the immense sweep of his genius—of the incomparable vividness of his imagination. The things he invented were as real to him as the things he knew, and his actual experience is overlaid with a thousand thicknesses, as it were, of imaginary experience. The person is irrecoverably lost in the artist. There is sufficient evidence, however, that the person led a rather hungry and predatory life during these early years, and that he was more familiar with what went on in the streets than with what occurred in the *salons*. Whatever he encountered, however, he observed. In one of his tales he describes a young man who follows people in the street to overhear what they say. This at least is autobiographic, and the young man is Honoré de Balzac, "devoured by his genius and by the consciousness of his genius," as M. Taine says—with all the unwritten "Comédie Humaine" within him. "In listening to these people I could espouse their life. I felt their rags upon my back; I walked with my feet in their tattered shoes; their desires, their wants—everything passed into my soul, and my soul passed into theirs; it was the dream of a waking man." This glimpse of Balzac laying up data is especially interesting because it is singularly rare. It must be that for years he spent many an hour in silent, instinctive contemplation, for his novels imply a period of preparatory research, of social botanizing, geologizing, palaeontologizing, just as Humboldt's "Cosmos" implies a large amount of travel. It happens that most of the anecdotes about Balzac pertain to his productive period, and present him to us in his white friar's dress, getting out of bed at midnight to work, in a darkened room, three weeks at a sitting. The open-air Balzac, as we may call it, has been little commemorated. White Dominican robes, darkened rooms, deep potations of coffee, form the staple of M. Gozlan's reminiscences. Every man works as he can and as he must; and if, in order to write the "Parents Pauvres," Balzac had had to dress himself in a bearskin, we trust he would not have hesitated. But it is nevertheless true that between the lines of the "Comédie Humaine" the reader too often catches a glimpse of the Dominican robe and the darkened room, and longs for an open window and a costume somewhat less capricious. A realistic novelist, he remembers, is not an astrologer or an alchemist.

In 1830 Balzac published the "Peau de Chagrin"—the first work of the series on which his reputation rests. After this, for twenty years, he produced without cessation. The quantity of his work, when we consider the quality, seems truly amazing. There are writers in the same line who have published an absolutely greater number of volumes. Alexandre Dumas, Madame Sand, Anthony Trollope, have all been immensely prolific; but they all weave a loose web, as it were, and Balzac weaves a dense one. The tissue of his tales is always extraordinarily firm and hard; it may not at every point be cloth of gold, but it has always a metallic rigidity. It has been worked over a dozen times, and the work can never be said to belong to light literature. You have only to turn the pages of a volume of Balzac to see that, whatever may be the purity of the current, it at least never runs thin. There is none of that wholesale dialogue, chopped into fragments, which Alexandre Dumas manufactures by the yard, and which bears the same relation to real narrative architecture as a chain of stepping-stones tossed across a stream does to a granite bridge. Balzac is always definite; you can say Yes or No to him as you go on; the story bristles with references that must be verified, and if sometimes it taxes the attention more than is thought becoming in a novel, we must admit that, being as hard reading in the way of entertainment as Hallam or Guizot, it may also have been very hard writing. This it is that makes Balzac's fertility so amazing—the fact that, whether we relish its results or not, we at least perceive that the process is not superficial. His great time was from 1830 to 1840; it was during these ten years that he published his most perfect works. "Eugénie Grandet," "La Recherche de l'Absolu," "Le Père Goriot," "Un Ménage de Garçon," "Le Cabinet des Antiques," belong to the earlier period. "Béatrix," "Modeste Mignon," "Une Ténébreuse Affaire," "Les Illusions Perdues," the "Mémoires de deux Jeunes Mariées," "La Muse du Département," "Le Député d'Arcis," belong to the latter. Balzac is never simple, and in a sense which it will be interesting to attempt to explain, he is always corrupt; but "La Recherche de l'Absolu" and "Le Père Goriot"—we will not mention "Eugénie Grandet," which was so praised for its innocence that the author found himself detesting it—have a certain relative simplicity and purity; whereas in the "Jeunes Mariées," "Béatrix," and "Modeste Mignon," we are up to our necks in sophistication. If, however, the works of the first half of Balzac's eminent period are, generally speaking, superior to those of the second half, it must be added that there are two or three incongruous transpositions. "Le Lys dans la Vallée," published in 1835, is bad enough to be coupled with "Béatrix"; and "Les Parents Pauvres" and "Les Paysans," finished shortly before the author's death, are in many respects his most powerful achievements. Most of Balzac's shorter tales are antecedent to 1840, and his readers know how many masterpieces the list contains. "Le Colonel Chabert" and "L'Interdiction" are found in it, as well as "La Femme Abandonnée," "La Grenadière" and "Le Message," and the admirable little stories grouped together (in the common duodecimo edition) with "Les Marana." The duration of Balzac's works will certainly not be in proportion to their length. "Le Curé de Tours," for all its brevity, will be read when "Le Député d'Arcis" lies unopened; and more than one literary adventurer will turn, outwearied, from "La Peau de Chagrin" and find consolation in "Un Début dans la Vie."

We know not how early Balzac formed the plan of the "Comédie Humaine"; but the general preface, in which he explains the unity of his work and sets forth that each of his tales is a block in a single immense edifice and that this edifice aims to be a complete portrait of the civilization of his time—this remarkable manifesto dates from 1842. (If we call it remarkable, it is not that we understand it; though so much as we have just expressed may easily be gathered from it. From the moment that Balzac attempts to philosophize, readers in the least sensible of the difference between words and things must part company with him.) He complains, very properly, that the official historians have given us no information about manners that is worth speaking of; that this omission is unpardonable; and that future ages will care much more for the testimony of the novel, properly executed, than for that of the writers who "set in order facts which are about the same in all nations, look up the spirit of laws which have fallen into disuse, elaborate theories which lead nations astray, or, like certain metaphysicians, endeavour to explain what is." Inspired by this conviction, Balzac proposed to himself to illustrate by a tale or a group of tales every phase of French life and manners during the first half of the nineteenth century. To be colossally and exhaustively complete—complete not only in the generals but in the particulars—to touch upon every salient point, to illuminate every typical feature, to reproduce every sentiment, every idea, every person, every place, every object, that has played a part, however minute, however obscure, in the life of the French people—nothing less than this was his programme. The undertaking was enormous, but it will not seem at first that Balzac underestimated the needful equipment. He was conscious of the necessary talent and he deemed it possible to acquire the necessary knowledge. This knowledge was almost encyclopaedic, and yet, after the vividness of his imagination, Balzac's strongest side is his grasp of actual facts. Behind our contemporary civilization is an immense and complicated machinery—the machinery of government, of police, of the arts, the professions, the trades. Among these things Balzac moved easily and joyously; they form the rough skeleton of his great edifice. There is not a little pedantry in his pretension to universal and infallible accuracy; but his accuracy, so far as we can measure it, is extraordinary, and in dealing with Balzac we must, in every direction, make our account with pedantry. He made his *cadres*, as the French say; he laid out his field in a number of broad divisions; he subdivided these, and then he filled up his moulds, pressing the contents down and packing it tight. You may read the categories on the back of the cover of the little common edition. There are the "Scènes de la Vie Privée"—"de la Vie de Province"—"de la Vie Parisienne"—"de la Vie Politique"—"de la Vie Militaire"—"de la Vie de Campagne"; and in a complementary way there are the "Études Philosophiques"—(this portentous category contains the picturesque "Recherche de l'Absolu")—and the "Études Analytiques." Then, in the way of subdivisions, there are "Les Célibataires," "Les Parisiens en Province," "Les Rivalités," "Les Illusions Perdues," the "Splendeurs et Misères des Courtisanes," the "Parents Pauvres," the "Envers de l'Histoire Contemporaine." This goodly nomenclature had a retroactive effect; the idea of the "Comédie Humaine," having developed itself when the author was midway in his career, a number of its component parts are what we may call accomplices after the fact. They are pieces that dovetail into the vast mosaic as they best can. But even if the occasional disparities were more striking they would signify little, for what is most interesting in Balzac is not the achievement but the attempt. The attempt was, as he himself has happily expressed it, to "faire concurrence à l'état civil"—to start an opposition, as we should say in America, to the civil registers. He created a complete social system—an hierarchy of ranks and professions which should correspond with that of which the officers of the census have cognizance. Everything is there, as we find it in his pages—the king (in "Le Député d'Arcis" Louis XVIII. is introduced and makes witticisms quite *inédits*) the administration, the church, the army, the judicature, the aristocracy, the bourgeoisie, the prolétariat, the peasantry, the artists, the journalists, the men of letters, the actors, the children (a little girl is the heroine of "Pierrette," and an urchin the hero of "Un Début dans la Vie") the shopkeepers of every degree, the criminals, the thousand irregular and unclassified members of society. All this in Balzac's hands becomes an organic whole; it moves together; it has a pervasive life; the blood circulates through it; its parts are connected by sinuous arteries. We have seen in English literature, in two cases, a limited attempt to create a permanent stock, a standing fund, of characters. Thackeray has led a few of his admirable figures from one novel to another, and Mr. Trollope has deepened illusion for us by his repeated evocations of Bishop Proudie and Archdeacon Grantley. But these things are faint shadows of Balzac's extravagant thoroughness—his fantastic cohesiveness. A French brain alone could have persisted in making a system of all this. Balzac's "Comédie Humaine" is on the imaginative line very much what Comte's "Positive Philosophy" is on the scientific. These great enterprises are equally characteristic of the French passion for completeness, for symmetry, for making a system as neat as an epigram—of its intolerance of the indefinite, the unformulated. The French mind likes better to squeeze things into a formula that mutilates them, if need be, than to leave them in the frigid vague. The farther limit of its power of arrangement (so beautiful as it generally is) is the limit of the knowable. Consequently we often see in the visions and systems of Frenchmen what may be called a conventional infinite. The civilization of the nineteenth century is of course not infinite, but to us of English speech, as we survey it, it appears so multitudinous, so complex, so far-spreading, so suggestive, so portentous—it has such misty edges and far reverberations—that the imagination, oppressed and overwhelmed, shrinks from any attempt to grasp it as a whole. The French imagination, in the person of Balzac, easily dominates it, as he would say, and, without admitting that the problem is any the less vast, regards it as practically soluble. He would be an incautious spirit who should propose hereupon to decide whether the French imagination or the English is the more potent. The one sees a vast number of obstacles and the other a vast number of remedies—the one beholds a great many shadows and the other a great many lights. If the human comedy, as Balzac pours it, condensed and solidified, out of his mould, is a very reduced copy of its original, we may nevertheless admit that the mould is of enormous dimensions. "Very good," the English imagination says; "call it large, but don't call it universal." The impartial critic may assent; but he privately remembers that it was in the convenient faculty of persuading himself that he could do everything that Balzac found the inspiration to do so much.

In addition to possessing an immense knowledge of his field, he was conscious that he needed a philosophy—a system of opinions. On this side too he equipped himself; so far as quantity goes no man was ever better provided with opinions. Balzac has an opinion on everything in heaven and on earth, and a complete, consistent theory of the universe, which was always ready for service. "The signs of a superior mind," says M. Taine, in speaking of him, "are *vues d'ensemble*—general views"; and judged by its wealth in this direction Balzac's should be the greatest mind the world has seen. We can think of no other mind that has stood ready to deliver itself on quite so many subjects. We doubt whether, on the whole, Aristotle had so many *vues d'ensemble* as Balzac. In Plato, in Bacon, in Shakespeare, in Goethe, in Hegel, there are shameful intermissions and lapses, ugly blank spots, ungraceful liabilities to be taken by surprise. But Balzac, as the showman of the human comedy, had measured his responsibilities unerringly and concluded that he must not only know what everything is, but what everything should be. He is thus *par excellence* the philosophic novelist; his pages bristle with axioms, moral, political, ethical, aesthetical; his narrative groans beneath the weight of metaphysical and scientific digression. The value of his philosophy and his science is a question to be properly treated apart; we mean simply to indicate that, formally, in this direction he is as complete as in the others. In the front rank, of course, stand his political and religious opinions. These are anchored to "the two eternal truths—the monarchy and the Catholic Church." Balzac is, in other words, an elaborate conservative—a Tory of the deepest dye. How well, as a picturesque romancer, he knew what he was about in adopting this profession of faith will be plain to the most superficial reader. His philosophy, his morality, his religious opinions have a certain picturesque correspondence with his political views. Speaking generally, it may be said that he had little belief in virtue and still less admiration for it. He is so large and various that you find all kinds of contradictory things in him; he has that sign of the few supreme geniuses that, if you look long enough he offers you a specimen of every possible mode of feeling. He has represented virtue, innocence and purity in the most vivid forms. César Birotteau, Eugénie Grandet, Mlle. Cormon, Mme. Graslin, Mme. Claës, Mme. de Mortsauf, Popinot, Genestas, the Cousin Pons, Schmucke, Chesnel, Joseph Bridau, Mme. Hulot—these and many others are not only admirably good people, but they are admirably successful figures. They live and move, they produce an illusion, for all their goodness, quite as much as their baser companions—Mme. Vauquer, Mme. Marneffe, Vautrin, Philippe Bridau, Mme. de Rochefide. Balzac had evidently an immense kindliness, a salubrious good nature which enabled him to feel the charm of all artless and helpless manifestations of life. That robustness of temperament and those high animal spirits which carried him into such fantastic explorations of man's carnal nature as the "Physiologie du Mariage" and the "Contes Drôlatiques"—that lusty natural humour which was not humour in our English sense, but a relish, sentimentally more dry but intellectually more keen, of all grotesqueness and quaintness and uncleanness, and which, when it felt itself flagging, had still the vigour to keep itself up a while as what the French call the "humoristic"—to emulate Rabelais, to torture words, to string together names, to be pedantically jovial and archaically hilarious—all this helped Balzac to appreciate the simple and the primitive with an intensity subordinate only to his enjoyment of corruption and sophistication. We do wrong indeed to say subordinate; Balzac was here as strong and as frank as he was anywhere. We are almost inclined to say that his profoundly simple people are his best—that in proportion to the labour expended upon them they are most lifelike. Such a figure as "big Nanon," the great, strapping, devoted maidservant in "Eugénie Grandet," may stand as an example. (Balzac is full, by the way, of good servants; from Silvie and Christophe in "Le Père Goriot" to Chesnel the notary, whose absolutely canine fidelity deprives him even of the independence of a domestic, in "Le Cabinet des Antiques.") What he represents best is extremely simple virtue, and vice simple or complex, as you please. In superior virtue, intellectual virtue, he fails; when his superior people begin to reason they are lost—they become prigs and hypocrites, or worse. Madame de Mortsauf, who is intended to be at once the purest and cleverest of his good women, is a kind of fantastic monster; she is perhaps only equalled by the exemplary Madame de l'Estorade, who (in "Le Député d'Arcis") writes to a lady with whom she is but scantily acquainted a series of *pros* and *cons* on the question whether "it will be given" (as she phrases it) to a certain gentleman to make her "manquer à ses devoirs." This gentleman has snatched her little girl from under a horse's hoofs, and for a while afterward has greatly annoyed her by his importunate presence on her walks and drives. She immediately assumes that he has an eye to her "devoirs." Suddenly, however, he disappears, and it occurs to her that he is "sacrificing his fancy to the fear of spoiling his fine action." At this attractive thought her "devoirs" begin to totter, and she ingenuously exclaims, "But on this footing he would really be a man to reckon with, and, my dear M. de l'Estorade, you would have decidedly to look out!" And yet Madame de l'Estorade is given us as a model of the all-gracious wife and mother; she figures in the "Deux Jeunes Mariées" as the foil of the luxurious, passionate and pedantic Louise de Chaulieu—the young lady who, on issuing from the convent where she has got her education, writes to her friend that she is the possessor of a "virginité savante."

There are two writers in Balzac—the spontaneous one and the reflective one—the former of which is much the more delightful, while the latter is the more extraordinary. It was the reflective observer that aimed at colossal completeness and equipped himself with a universal philosophy: and it was of this one we spoke when we said just now that Balzac had little belief in virtue. Balzac's beliefs, it must be confessed, are delicate ground; from certain points of view, perhaps, the less said about them the better. His sincere, personal beliefs may be reduced to a very compact formula; he believed that it was possible to write magnificent novels, and that he was the man to do it. He believed, otherwise stated, that human life was infinitely dramatic and picturesque, and that he possessed an incomparable analytic perception of the fact. His other convictions were all derived from this and humbly danced attendance upon it; for if being a man of genius means being identical with one's productive faculty, never was there such a genius as Balzac's. A monarchical society is unquestionably more picturesque, more available for the novelist than any other, as the others have as yet exhibited themselves; and therefore Balzac was with glee, with gusto, with imagination, a monarchist. Of what is to be properly called religious feeling we do not remember a suggestion in all his many pages; on the other hand, the reader constantly encounters the handsomest compliments to the Catholic Church as a social *régime*. A hierarchy is as much more picturesque than a "congregational society" as a mountain is than a plain. Bishops, abbés, priests, Jesuits, are invaluable figures in fiction, and the morality of the Catholic Church allows of an infinite *chiaroscuro*. In "La Fille aux Yeux d'Or" there is a portrait of a priest who becomes preceptor to the youthful hero. "This priest, vicious but politic, sceptical but learned, perfidious but amiable, feeble in aspect, but as strong in body as in head, was so truly useful to his pupil, so complaisant to his vices, so good a calculator of every sort of force, so deep when it was necessary to play some human trick, so young at table, at the gaming house, at—I don't know where—that the only thing the grateful Henry de Marsay could feel soft-hearted over in 1814 was the portrait of his dear bishop—the single object of personal property he was able to inherit from this prelate, an admirable type of the men whose genius will save the Catholic Apostolic and Roman Church." It is hardly an exaggeration to say that we here come as near as we do at any point to Balzac's religious feeling. The reader will see that it is simply a lively assent to that great worldly force of the Catholic Church, the art of using all sorts of servants and all sorts of means. Balzac was willing to accept any morality that was curious and unexpected, and he found himself as a matter of course more in sympathy with a theory of conduct which takes account of circumstances and recognises the merits of duplicity, than with the comparatively colourless idea that virtue is nothing if not uncompromising. Like all persons who have looked a great deal at human life, he had been greatly struck with most people's selfishness, and this quality seemed to him the most general in mankind. Selfishness may go to dangerous lengths, but Balzac believed that it may somehow be regulated and even chastened by a strong throne and a brilliant court, with MM. de Rastignac and de Trailles as supports of the one and Mesdames de Maufrigneuse and d'Espard as ornaments of the other, and by a clever and impressive Church, with plenty of bishops of the pattern of the one from whose history a leaf has just been given. If we add to this that he had a great fancy for "electricity" and animal magnetism, we have touched upon the most salient points of Balzac's philosophy. This makes, it is true, rather a bald statement of a matter which at times seems much more considerable; but it may be maintained that an exact analysis of his heterogeneous opinions will leave no more palpable deposit. His imagination was so fertile, the movement of his mind so constant, his curiosity and ingenuity so unlimited, the energy of his phrase so striking, he raises such a cloud of dust about him as he goes, that the reader to whom he is new has a sense of his opening up gulfs and vistas of thought and pouring forth flashes and volleys of wisdom. But from the moment he ceases to be a simple dramatist Balzac is an arrant charlatan. It is probable that no equally vigorous mind was ever at pains to concoct such elaborate messes of folly. They spread themselves over page after page, in a close, dense verbal tissue, which the reader scans in vain for some little flower of available truth. It all rings false—it is all mere flatulent pretension. It may be said that from the moment he attempts to deal with an abstraction the presumption is always dead against him. About what the discriminating reader thus brutally dubs his charlatanism, as about everything else in Balzac, there would be very much more to say than this small compass admits of. (Let not the discriminating reader, by the way, repent of his brutality; Balzac himself was brutal, and must be handled with his own weapons. It would be absurd to write of him in semi-tones and innuendoes; he never used them himself.) The chief point is that he himself was his most perfect dupe; he believed in his own magnificent rubbish, and if he made it up, as the phrase is, as he went along, his credulity kept pace with his invention. This was, briefly speaking, because he was morally and intellectually so superficial. He paid himself, as the French say, with shallower conceits than ever before passed muster with a strong man. The moral, the intellectual atmosphere of his genius is extraordinarily gross and turbid; it is no wonder that the flower of truth does not bloom in it, nor any natural flower whatever. The difference in this respect between Balzac and the other great novelists is extremely striking. When we approach Thackeray and George Eliot, George Sand and Turgénieff, it is into the conscience and the mind that we enter, and we think of these writers primarily as great consciences and great minds. When we approach Balzac we seem to enter into a great temperament—a prodigious nature. He strikes us half the time as an extraordinary physical phenomenon. His robust imagination seems a sort of physical faculty and impresses us more with its sensible mass and quantity than with its lightness or fineness.

This brings us back to what was said just now touching his disbelief in virtue and his homage to the selfish passions. He had no natural sense of morality, and this we cannot help thinking a serious fault in a novelist. Be the morality false or true, the writer's deference to it greets us as a kind of essential perfume. We find such a perfume in Shakespeare; we find it, in spite of his so-called cynicism, in Thackeray; we find it, potently, in George Eliot, in George Sand, in Turgénieff. They care for moral questions; they are haunted by a moral ideal. This southern slope of the mind, as we may call it, was very barren in Balzac, and it is partly possible to account for its barrenness. Large as Balzac is, he is all of one piece and he hangs perfectly together. He pays for his merits and he sanctifies his defects. He had a sense of this present terrestrial life which has never been surpassed, and which in his genius overshadowed everything else. There are many men who are not especially occupied with the idea of another world, but we believe there has never been a man so completely detached from it as Balzac. This world of our senses, of our purse, of our name, of our *blason* (or the absence of it)—this palpable world of houses and clothes, of seven per cents and multiform human faces, pressed upon his imagination with an unprecedented urgency. It certainly is real enough to most of us, but to Balzac it was ideally real—charmingly, absorbingly, absolutely real. There is nothing in all imaginative literature that in the least resembles his mighty passion for *things*—for material objects, for furniture, upholstery, bricks and mortar. The world that contained these things filled his consciousness, and *being*, at its intensest, meant simply being thoroughly at home among them. Balzac possessed indeed a lively interest in the supernatural: "La Peau de Chagrin," "Louis Lambert," "Séraphita," are a powerful expression of it. But it was a matter of adventurous fancy, like the same quality in Edgar Poe; it was perfectly cold, and had nothing to do with his moral life. To get on in this world, to succeed, to live greatly in all one's senses, to have plenty of *things*— this was Balzac's infinite; it was here that his heart expanded. It was natural, therefore, that the life of mankind should seem to him above all an eager striving along this line—a multitudinous greed for personal enjoyment. The master-passion among these passions—the passion of the miser—he has depicted as no one else has begun to do. Wherever we look, in the "Comédie Humaine," we see a miser, and he—or she—is sure to be a marvel of portraiture. In the struggle and the scramble it is not the sweetest qualities that come uppermost, and Balzac, watching the spectacle, takes little account of these. It is strength and cunning that are most visible—the power to climb the ladder, to wriggle to the top of the heap, to clutch the money-bag. In human nature, viewed in relation to this end, it is force only that is desirable, and a feeling is fine only in so far as it is a profitable practical force. Strength of purpose seems the supremely admirable thing, and the spectator lingers over all eminent exhibitions of it. It may show itself in two great ways—in vehemence and in astuteness, in eagerness and in patience. Balzac has a vast relish for both, but on the whole he prefers the latter form as being the more dramatic. It admits of duplicity, and there are few human accomplishments that Balzac professes so explicit a respect for as this. He scatters it freely among his dear "gens d'église," and his women are all compounded of it. If he had been asked what was, for human purposes, the faculty he valued most highly, he would have said the power of dissimulation. He regards it as a sign of all superior people, and he says somewhere that nothing forms the character so finely as having had to exercise it in one's youth, in the bosom of one's family. In this attitude of Balzac's there is an element of affectation and of pedantry; he praises duplicity because it is original and audacious to do so. But he praises it also because it has for him the highest recommendation that anything can have—it is picturesque. Duplicity is more picturesque than honesty—just as the line of beauty is the curve and not the straight line. In place of a moral judgment of conduct, accordingly, Balzac usually gives us an aesthetic judgment. A magnificent action with him is not an action which is remarkable for its high motive, but an action with a great force of will or of desire behind it, which throws it into striking and monumental relief. It may be a magnificent sacrifice, a magnificent devotion, a magnificent act of faith; but the presumption is that it will be a magnificent lie, a magnificent murder, or a magnificent adultery.

II

This overmastering sense of the present world was of course a superb foundation for the work of a realistic romancer, and it did so much for Balzac that one is puzzled to know where to begin to enumerate the things he owed to it. It gave him in the first place his background—his *mise en scéne*. This part of his story had with Balzac an importance—his rendering of it a solidity—which it had never enjoyed before, and which the most vigorous talents in the school of which Balzac was founder have never been able to restore to it. The place in which an event occurred was in his view of equal moment with the event itself; it was part of the action; it was not a thing to take or to leave, or to be vaguely and gracefully indicated; it imposed itself; it had a part to play; it needed to be made as definite as anything else. There is accordingly a very much greater amount of description in Balzac than in any other writer, and the description is mainly of towns, houses and rooms. Descriptions of scenery, properly so called, are rare, though when they occur they are often admirable. Almost all of his tales "de la vie de province" are laid in different towns, and a more or less minute portrait of the town is always attempted. How far in these cases Balzac's general pretension to be exact and complete was sustained we are unable to say; we know not what the natives of Limoges, of Saumur, of Angoulême, of Alençon, of Issoudun, of Guérande, thought of his presentation of these localities; but if the picture is not veracious, it is at least always definite and masterly. And Balzac did what he could, we believe, to be exact; he often made a romancer's pilgrimage to a town that he wished to introduce into a story. Here he picked out a certain number of houses to his purpose, lodged the persons of his drama in them, and reproduced them even to their local odours. Many readers find all this very wearisome, and it is certain that it offers one a liberal chance to be bored. We, for our part, have always found Balzac's houses and rooms extremely interesting; we often prefer his places to his people. He was a profound connoisseur in these matters; he had a passion for bric-à-brac, and his tables and chairs are always in character. It must be admitted that in this matter as in every other he had his right and his wrong, and that in his enumerations of inanimate objects he often sins by extravagance. He has his necessary houses and his superfluous houses: often when in a story the action is running thin he stops up your mouth against complaint, as it were, by a choking dose of brick and mortar. The power of his memory, his representative vision, as regards these things is something amazing; the reader never ceases to wonder at the promptness with which he can "get up" a furnished house—at the immense supply of this material that he carries about in his mind. He expends it with a royal liberality; where another writer makes an allusion Balzac gives you a Dutch picture. In "Le Cabinet des Antiques," on the verge of its close, Madame Camusot makes a momentary appearance. She has only twenty lines to speak, but immediately we are confronted with her domicile. "Leaning against the next house, so as to present its front to the court, it had on each floor but one window on the street. The court, confined in its width by two walls ornamented by rose-bushes and privet, had at its bottom, opposite the house, a shed supported upon two brick arches. A little half-door admitted you into this dusky house, made duskier still by a great walnut-tree planted in the middle of the court." We are told furthermore about the dining-room and the kitchen, about the staircase and the rooms on the first floor. We learn that the second floor was an attic, and that it had one room for the cook and another for the femme de chambre, who kept the children with her. We are informed that the woodwork, painted a dirty grey, was of the most melancholy aspect, and that Madame Camusot's bedroom had a carpet and blue and white ornaments. All this is entirely out of the current of the story, which pretends to be short and simple, and which is ostensibly hurrying towards its dénoûment. Some readers will always remember the two brick arches of Madame Camusot's shed, the dirty grey of her walls and the blue and white upholstery of her room; others will say that they care nothing about them, and these are not to be gainsaid.

Three or four descriptions of this kind stand out in the reader's memory. One is the picture of the dark and chill abode in which poor Eugénie Grandet blooms and fades; another is the elaborate and elegant portrait of the beautiful old house at Douai, half Flemish, half Spanish, in which the delusions of Balthazar Claës bring his family to ruin; the best of all is the magnificent account of the "pension bourgeoise des deux sexes et autres," kept by Madame Vauquer, née de Conflans, preceded by a glass door armed with a shrill alarm-bell, through which you see an arcade in green marble painted on a wall and a statue of Cupid with the varnish coming off in scales. In this musty and mouldy little boarding-house the Père Goriot is the senior resident. Certain students in law and medicine, from the Quartier Latin, hard by, subscribe to the dinner, where Maman Vauquer glares at them when she watches them cut their slice from the loaf. When the Père Goriot dies horribly, at the end of the tragedy, the kindest thing said of him, as the other boarders unfold their much-crumpled napkins, is, "Well, he won't sit and sniff his bread any more!" and the speaker imitates the old man's favourite gesture. The portrait of the Maison Vauquer and its inmates is one of the most portentous settings of the scene in all the literature of fiction. In this case there is nothing superfluous; there is a profound correspondence between the background and the action. It is a pity not to be able to quote the whole description, or even that of the greasy, dusky dining-room in which so much of the story goes forward. "This apartment is in all its lustre at the moment when, toward seven o'clock in the morning, Madame Vauquer's cat precedes his mistress, jumping on the sideboards, smelling at the milk contained in several basins covered with plates, and giving forth his matutinal purr. Presently the widow appears, decked out in her tulle cap, under which hangs a crooked band of false hair; as she walks she drags along her wrinkled slippers. Her little plump elderly face, from the middle of which protrudes a nose like a parrot's beak; her little fat dimpled hands, her whole person, rounded like a church-rat, the waist of her gown, too tight for its contents, which flaps over it, are all in harmony with this room, where misfortune seems to ooze, where speculation lurks in corners, and of which Madame Vauquer inhales the warm, fetid air without being nauseated. Her countenance, fresh as a first autumn frost, her wrinkled eyes, whose expression passes from the smile prescribed to *danseuses* to the acrid scowl of the discounter—her whole person, in short, is an explanation of the boarding-house, as the boarding-house is an implication of her person. . . . Her worsted petticoat, which falls below her outer skirt, made of an old dress, and with the wadding coming out of the slits in the stuff, which is full of them, resumes the parlour, the dining-room, the yard, announces the kitchen, and gives a presentiment of the boarders." But we must pause, for we are passing from the portraiture of places to that of people.

This latter is Balzac's strongest gift, and it is so strong that it easily distances all competition. Two other writers in this line have gone very far, but they suffer by comparison with him. Dickens often sets a figure before us with extraordinary vividness; but the outline is fantastic and arbitrary; we but half believe in it, and feel as if we were expected but half to believe in it. It is like a silhouette in cut paper, in which the artist has allowed great license to his scissors. If Balzac had a rival, the most dangerous rival would be Turgénieff. With the Russian novelist the person represented is equally definite—or meant to be equally definite; and the author's perception of idiosyncrasies is sometimes even more subtle. With Turgénieff as with Balzac the whole person springs into being at once; the character is never left shivering for its fleshly envelope, its face, its figure, its gestures, its tone, its costume, its name, its bundle of antecedents. But behind Balzac's figures we feel a certain heroic pressure that drives them home to our credence—a contagious illusion on the author's own part. The imagination that produced them is working at a greater heat; they seem to proceed from a sort of creative infinite and they help each other to be believed in. It is pictorially a larger, sturdier, more systematic style of portraiture than Turgénieff's. This is altogether the most valuable element in Balzac's novels; it is hard to see how the power of physical evocation can go farther. In future years, if people find his tales, as a whole, too rugged and too charmless, let them take one up occasionally and, turning the leaves, read simply the portraits. In Balzac every one who is introduced is minutely described; if the individual is to say but three words he has the honours of a complete portrait. Portraits shape themselves under his pen as if in obedience to an irresistible force; while the effort with most writers it to collect the material—to secure the model—the effort with Balzac is to disintegrate his visions, to accept only one candidate in the dozen. And it is not only that his figures are so definite, but that they are so plausible, so real, so characteristic, so recognisable. The fertility of his imagination in this respect was something marvellous. When we think of the many hundred complete human creatures (he calls the number at least two thousand) whom he set in motion, with their sharp differences, their histories, their money-matters, their allotted place in his great machine, we give up the attempt to gauge such a lusty energy of fancy. In reading over Balzac, we have marked a great many portraits for quotation, but it is hard to know what to choose or where to begin. The appreciative reader may safely begin at hazard. He opens the little tale of "L'Interdiction," and finds the physiognomy of the excellent Judge Popinot thus depicted: "If nature, therefore, had endowed M. Popinot with an exterior but scantily agreeable, the magistracy had not embellished him. His frame was full of angular lines. His big knees, his large feet, his broad hands, contrasted with a sacerdotal face, which resembled vaguely the head of a calf, soft to insipidity, feebly lighted by two lateral eyes, altogether bloodless, divided by a straight flat nose, surmounted by a forehead without protuberance, decorated by two huge ears, which bent awkwardly forward. His hair, thin in quantity and quality, exposed his skull in several irregular furrows. A single feature recommended this countenance to the study of physiognomy. The man had a mouth on whose lips a divine goodness hovered. These were good big red lips, sinuous, moving, with a thousand folds, through which nature had never expressed any but high feelings—lips which spoke to the heart," &c.

That is certainly admirable for energy and vividness—closeness to the individual. But, after all, Popinot plays a part; he appears in several tales; he is the type of the upright judge, and there is a fitness in his figure being strongly lighted. Here is Madame de Kergarouet, who merely crosses the stage in "Béatrix," who rises in answer to a momentary need, and yet who is as ripe and complete, as thoroughly seen, felt and understood, as if she had been soaked, as it were, for years in the author's consciousness: "As for the Vicomtesse de Kergarouet, she was the perfect *provinciale*. Tall, dry, faded, full of hidden pretensions which showed themselves after they had been wounded; talking much and, by dint of talking, catching a few ideas, as one cannons at billiards, and which gave her a reputation for cleverness; trying to humiliate the Parisians by the pretended *bonhomie* of departmental wisdom, and by a make-believe happiness which she was always putting forward; stooping to get herself picked up and furious at being left on her knees; fishing for compliments, and not always taking them; dressing herself at once strikingly and carelessly; taking the want of affability for impertinence, and thinking to embarrass people greatly by paying them no attention; refusing what she wanted in order to have it offered to her twice, and to seem to be urged beyond resistance; occupied with the things that people have ceased to talk about and greatly astonished at not being in the current of fashion; finally, keeping quiet with difficulty an hour without bringing up Nantes, and the tigers of Nantes, and the affairs of the high society of Nantes, and complaining of Nantes, and criticising Nantes, and making a personal application of the phrases extracted from the people whose attention wandered, and who agreed with her to get rid of her. Her manners, her language, her ideas, had all more or less rubbed off on her four daughters." Here also, to prove that Balzac's best portraits are not always his harshest, is an admirably friendly portrait of an old rustic gentlewoman, taken from the same novel: "Mademoiselle Zephirine, deprived of her sight, was ignorant of the changes which her eighty years had made in her physiognomy. Her pale, hollow face, which the immobility of her white, sightless eyes caused to look like that of a dead person, which three or four protruding teeth rendered almost threatening, in which the deep orbit of the eyes was circled with red tones, in which a few signs of virility, already white, cropped up about the mouth and chin—this cold, calm face was framed in a little nun-like cap of brown calico, pricked like a counterpane, garnished with a cambric frill, and tied under the chin by two strings which were always a trifle rusty. She wore a short gown of coarse cloth, over a petticoat of *piqué,* a real mattress which contained forty-franc pieces—as also a pair of pockets sewed to a belt which she put on and took off morning and night like a garment. Her body was fastened into the common jacket of Brittany, in stuff matching with that of her skirt, ornamented with a little collar of a thousand folds, the washing of which was the subject of the only dispute she ever had with her sister-in-law—she herself wishing to change it but once a week. From the great wadded sleeves of this jacket issued two desiccated but nervous arms, at the end of which moved two hands of a ruddy hue, which made her arms appear as white as the wood of the poplar. Her hands, with the fingers hooked and contracted by knitting, were like a stocking-loom for ever wound up; the phenomenon would have been to see them stop. From time to time she took a long knitting-needle that was planted in her bosom, and thrust it in between her cap and her head, while she rummaged in her white hair. A stranger would have laughed at the carelessness with which she stuck the needle back again, without the least fear of wounding herself. She was as straight as a belfry. This columnar rectitude might have passed for one of those egotisms practised by old people, which prove that pride is a passion necessary to life. Her smile was gay."

One of the most striking examples of Balzac's energy and facility of conception and execution in this line is the great gallery of portraits of the people who come to the party given by Madame de Bargeton, in "Les Illusions Perdues." These people are all mere supernumeraries; they appear but on this occasion, and having been marshalled forth in their living grotesqueness, they stand there simply to deepen the local colour about the central figure of Madame de Bargeton. When it lets itself loose among the strange social types that vegetate in silent corners of provincial towns, and of which an old and complex civilization, passing from phase to phase, leaves everywhere so thick a deposit, Balzac's imagination expands and revels and rejoices in its strength. In these cases it is sometimes kindly and tender and sympathetic; but as a general thing it is merciless in its irony and contempt. There is almost always, to us English readers, something cruel and wounding in French irony—something almost sanguinary in French caricature. To be ridiculous is made to appear like a crime and to deprive the unhappy victim of any right that an acute observer is bound to respect. The Dodson family, in George Eliot's "Mill on the Floss"—the illustrious stock from which Mrs. Glegg and Mrs. Pullet issue—are apparently a scantily mitigated mixture of the ridiculous and the disagreeable; and yet every reader of that admirable novel will remember how humanly, how generously these ladies are exhibited, and how in the author's treatment of them the highest sense of their absurdities never leads her to grudge them a particle of their freedom. In a single word, the picture is not invidious. Balzac, on the other hand, in corresponding pictures—pictures of small middle-class ignorance, narrowness, penury, poverty, dreariness, ugliness physical and mental—is always invidious. He grudges and hates and despises. These sentiments certainly often give a masterly force to his touch; but they deepen that sense, which he can so ill afford to have deepened, of the meagreness of his philosophy. It is very true that the "vie de province" of the "Comédie Humaine" is a terribly dreary and sordid affair; but, making every concession to the ignorant and self-complacent stupidity of the small French bourgeoisie during the Restoration and the reign of Louis Philippe, it is impossible to believe that a chronicler with a scent a little less rabidly suspicious of Philistinism would not have shown us this field in a somewhat rosier light. Like all French artists and men of letters, Balzac hated the bourgeoisie with an immitigable hatred, and more than most of his class he hated the provincial. All the reasons for this general attitude it would take us too far to seek; two of them, we think, are near the surface. Balzac and his comrades hate the bourgeois, in the first place, because the bourgeois hates them, and in the second place, because they are almost always fugitives from the bourgeoisie. They have escaped with their lives, and once in the opposite camp they turn and shake their fists and hurl defiance. Provincial life, as Balzac represents it, is a tissue of sordid economies and ignoble jealousies and fatuous tittle-tattle, in cold, musty, unlovely houses, in towns where the grass grows in the streets, where the passage of a stranger brings grotesquely eager faces to the window, where one or two impotently pretentious salons, night after night, exhibit a collection of human fossils. Here and there a brighter thread runs through the dusky web—we remember Véronique Tascheron, Eugénie Grandet, Marguerite Claës, Ursule Mirouët, David and Eve Séchard. White has a high picturesque value when properly distributed, and Balzac's innocent people, who are always more or less tragical dupes and victims, serve admirably to deepen the general effect of dreariness, stinginess and ferocious venality. With what a grasp of the baser social realities, with what energy and pathos and pictorial irony he has moulded these miseries and vices into living figures, it would be interesting to be able to exhibit in detail. It is grim economy that is always in the foreground—it is the clutch of the five-franc piece that is the essence of every gesture. It is the miser Grandet, doling out the sugar lump by lump for the coffee of the household; it is that hideous she-wolf of thrift, Silvie Rogron, pinching and persecuting and starving little Pierrette Lorrain; it is the heirs male and female of Doctor Mirouët flocking to the reading of his will like vultures and hyenas.

Balzac's figures, as a general thing, are better than the use he makes of them; his touch, so unerring in portraiture and description, often goes wofully astray in narrative, in the conduct of a tale. Of all the great novelists, he is the weakest in talk; his conversations, if they are at all prolonged, become unnatural, impossible. One of his pupils, as they say in French, Charles de Bernard (who had, however, taken most justly the measure of his own talent, and never indiscreetly challenged comparison with the master)—this charming writer, with but a tenth of Balzac's weight and genius, very decidedly excels him in making his figures converse. It is not meant by this, however, that the story in Balzac is not generally powerfully conceived and full of dramatic stuff. Afraid of nothing as he was, he attacked all the deepest things in life and laid his hand upon every human passion. He has even—to be complete—described one or two passions that are usually deemed unmentionable. He always deals with a strong feeling in preference to a superficial one, and his great glory is that he pretended to take cognizance of man's moral nature to its deepest, most unillumined and, as the French say, most *scabreux* depths—that he maintained that for a writer who proposes seriously to illustrate the human soul there is absolutely no forbidden ground. He has never, that we remember, described what we call in English a flirtation, but he has described ardent love in a thousand forms (sometimes very well, sometimes horribly ill), with its clustering attributes of sensuality and jealousy, exaltation and despair, good and evil. It is hard to think of a virtue or a vice of which he has not given some eminent embodiment. The subject, in other words, is always solid and interesting; through his innumerable fallacies of form and style, of taste and art, that is always valuable. Some of his novels rise much above the others in this dignity and pregnancy of theme; M. Taine, in his essay, enumerates the most striking cases, and his sonorous echo of Balzac's tragic note is a tribute to our author's power. Balzac's masterpiece, to our own sense, if we must choose, is "Le Père Goriot." In this tale there is most of his characteristic felicity and least of his characteristic infelicity. Shakespeare had been before him, but there is excellent reason to believe that beyond knowing that "King Lear" was the history of a doting old man, buffeted and betrayed by cruel daughters, Balzac had not placed himself in a position to be accused of plagiarism. He had certainly not read the play in English, and nothing is more possible than that he had not read it in such French translations as existed in 1835. It would please him to have his reader believe that he has read everything in the world; but there are limits to the reader's good nature. "Le Père Goriot" holds so much, and in proportion to what it holds is, in comparison with its companions, so simple and compact, that it easily ranks among the few greatest novels we possess. Nowhere else is there such a picture of distracted paternal love, and of the battle between the voice of nature and the constant threat of society that you shall be left to rot by the roadside if you drop out of the ranks. In every novel of Balzac's, on the artistic line, there are the great intentions that fructify and the great intentions that fail. In "Le Père Goriot" the latter element, though perceptible, comes nearest to escaping notice. Balzac has painted a great number of "careers"; they begin in one story and are unfolded in a dozen others. He has a host of young men whom he takes up on the threshold of life, entangles conspicuously in the events of their time, makes the pivots of contemporaneous history. Some of them are soldiers, some men of letters, some artists; those he handles with most complacency are young men predestined by high birth to politics. These latter are, as a class, Balzac's most conspicuous failures, but they are also his most heroic attempts. The reader will remember De Marsay, De Trailles, Rastignac, the two Vandenesses, D'Esgrignon, Baudenord, Des Lupeaulx, Tillet, Blondet, Bridau, Nathan, Bixiou, Rubempré, Lousteau, D'Arthez. The man whose career is most distinctly traced is perhaps Eugène de Rastignac, whose first steps in life we witness in "Le Père Goriot." The picture is to some extent injured by Balzac's incurable fatuity and snobbishness; but the situation of the young man, well born, clever, and proud, who comes up to Paris, equipped by his family's savings, to seek his fortune and find it at any cost, and who moves from the edge of one social abyss to the edge of another (finding abysses in every shaded place he looks into) until at last his nerves are steeled, his head steadied, his conscience cased in cynicism and his pockets filled—all this bears a deep imaginative stamp. The donnée of "Le Père Goriot" is typical; the shabby Maison Vauquer, becoming the stage of vast dramas, is a sort of concentrated focus of human life, with sensitive nerves radiating out into the infinite. Then there is Madame d'Espard's attempt to prove that her excellent husband is insane and to have him sequestrated; and the Countess Ferraud, who repudiates her husband, when he reappears, crippled and penniless, after having been counted among the slain at the battle of Eylau; and Philippe

Bridau, who bullies, sponges, swindles, bleeds his family to death to pay for his iniquities; Madame Marneffe, who drags an honourable family into desolation and ruin by the rapacity of her licentiousness, and the Baron Hulot d'Ervy, who sees his wife and children beggared and disgraced, and yet cannot give up Madame Marneffe; Victurnien d'Esgrignon, who comes up from Alençon to see the world, and sees it with a vengeance, so that he has to forge a note to pay for his curiosity, and his doting family have to beggar themselves to pay for his note; Madame de La Baudraye, who leaves her husband, burns her ships, and comes to live in Paris with an ignoble journalist, partly for the love of letters and partly for the love of the journalist himself; Lucien de Rubempré, who tries to be a great poet, and to give an airing, in the highest places, to the poetic temperament, and who, after irrecordable alternations of delight and of misery, hangs himself in a debtors' prison; Marguerite Claës, who finds her father turning monomaniac and melting down her patrimony, and her motherless brother's and sister's, in the crucible of alchemy, and who fights for years a hand-to-hand duel with him, at great cost to her natural tenderness and her reputation; Madame de Mortsauf, who, after years of mysterious anguish, dies broken-hearted, between a brutal husband and a passionate lover, without ever having said a word to offend the one or, as she regards it, to encourage the other; poor Cousin Pons, the kindly virtuoso, who has made with years of patient labour a precious collection of pictures, and who is plundered, bullied, and morally murdered by rapacious relatives, and left without a penny to bury him.

It is the opinion of many of Balzac's admirers, and it was the general verdict of his day, that in all this the greatest triumphs are the characters of women. Every French critic tells us that his immense success came to him through women—that they constituted his first, his last, his fondest public. "Who rendered more deliciously than he," asks Sainte-Beuve, "the duchesses and viscountesses of the end of the Restoration—those women of thirty who, already on the stage, awaited their painter with a vague anxiety, so that when he and they stood face to face there was a sort of electric movement of recognition?" Balzac is supposed to have understood the feminine organism as no one had done before him—to have had the feminine heart, the feminine temperament, feminine nerves, at his fingers' ends—to have turned the feminine puppet, as it were, completely inside out. He has placed an immense number of women on the stage, and even those critics who are least satisfied with his most elaborate female portraits must at least admit that he has paid the originals the compli-

84

ment to hold that they play an immense part in the world. It may be said, indeed, that women are the keystone of the "Comédie Humaine." If the men were taken out, there would be great gaps and fissures; if the women were taken out, the whole fabric would collapse. Balzac's superior handling of women seems to us to be both a truth and a fallacy; but his strength and weakness so intermingle and overlap that it is hard to keep a separate account with each.

His reader very soon perceives, to begin with, that he does not take that view of the sex that would commend him to the "female sympathizers" of the day. There is not a line in him that would not be received with hisses at any convention for giving women the suffrage, for introducing them into Harvard College, or for trimming the exuberances of their apparel. His restrictive remarks would be considered odious; his flattering remarks would be considered infamous. He takes the old-fashioned view—he recognises none but the old-fashioned categories. Woman is the female of man and in all respects his subordinate; she is pretty and ugly, virtuous and vicious, stupid and cunning. There is the great *métier de femme*—the most difficult perhaps in the world, so that to see it thoroughly mastered is peculiarly exhilarating. The *métier de femme* includes a great many branches, but they may be all summed up in the art of titillating in one way or another the senses of man. Woman has a "mission" certainly, and this is it. Man's capacity for entertainment fortunately is large, and he may be gratified along a far-stretching line; so that woman in this way has a very long rope and no reason to complain of want of liberty. Balzac's conception of what a woman may be and do is very comprehensive; there is no limit to her cleverness, her energy, her courage, her devotion; or, on the other hand, to her vices, her falsity, her meanness, her cruelty, her rapacity. But the great sign of Balzac's women is that in all these things the sexual quality is inordinately emphasized and the conscience on the whole inordinately sacrificed to it. It is an idea familiar to all novelists—it is indeed half their stock in trade—that women in good and in evil act almost exclusively from personal motives. Men do so often, the romancer says; women do so always. Balzac carries this idea infinitely farther than any other novelist, and imparts to the personal motive a peculiar narrowness and tenacity. It suggests the agility and the undulations, the claws and the venom, of the cat and the serpent. That perfectly immoral view of what people do, which we spoke of as one of his great characteristics, is supremely conspicuous in Balzac's dealings with his heroines. "Leur gros libertin de père," M. Taine calls him in relation to certain of them; and the phrase really applies to him in relation to all, even the purest and most elevated. It is their personal, physical quality that he relishes—their attitudes, their picturesqueness, the sense that they give him of playing always, sooner or later, into the hands of man—*gros libertin* that he naturally and inevitably is. He has drawn a great many women's figures that are nobly pure in intention; he has even attempted three or four absolute saints. But purity in Balzac's hands is apt to play us the strangest tricks. Madame Graslin is a saint who has been privy to the murder of her lover and who allows an innocent man to suffer the penalty of the law; Madame Hulot is a saint who at fifty (being very well preserved) offers herself to a man she loathes in order to procure money for her daughter's marriage portion; Madame de Mortsauf is a saint familiar with the most cynical views of life (*vide* her letter of advice to Félix de Vandenesse on his entering upon his career, in which the tone is that of a politician and shrewd man of the world) who drives about with her lover late at night, kissing his head and otherwise fondling him. Balzac's women—and indeed his characters in general—are best divided into the rich and the poor, the Parisians and the rustics. His most ambitious female portraits are in the former class—his most agreeable, and on the whole his most successful, in the latter. Here the women, young and old, are more or less grotesque, but the absence of the desire to assimilate them to the type of the indescribable monster whom Balzac enshrines in the most sacred altitudes of his imagination as the Parisienne, has allowed them to be more human and more consonant to what we, at least, of the Anglo-Saxon race, consider the comfortable social qualities in the gentler sex. Madame Bridau, Madame Grandet, Mademoiselle Cormon, Madame Séchard—these, in Balzac, are the most natural figures of good women. His imagination has easily comprehended them; they are homely and pious and *naïves*, and their horizon is bounded by the walls of their quiet houses. It is when Balzac enters the field of the great ladies and the courtesans that he is supposed to have won his greatest triumphs, the triumphs that placed all the women on his side and made them confess that they had found their prophet and their master. To this view of the matter the writer of these lines is far from assenting. He finds it impossible to understand that the painter of Louise de Chaulieu and Madame d'Espard, of Madame de La Baudraye and Madame de Bargeton, of Lady Dudley and Madame de Maufrigneuse, should not have made all the clever women of his time his enemies.

It is not however, certainly, that here his energy, his force of colour, his unapproached power of what the French call in analytic portrayal "rummaging"—to *fouiller*—are not at their highest. Never is he more himself than among his coquettes and courtesans, among Madame Schontz and Josépha, Madame Marneffe and Madame de Rochefide. "Balzac loves his Valérie," says M. Taine, speaking of his attitude toward the horrible Madame Marneffe, the depths of whose depravity he is so actively sounding; and paradoxical as it sounds it is perfectly true. She is, according to Balzac's theory of the matter, a consummate Parisienne, and the depravity of a Parisienne is to his sense a more remunerative spectacle than the virtue of any *provinciale,* whether her province be Normandy or Gascony, England or Germany. Never does he so let himself go as in these cases—never does his imagination work so at a heat. Feminine nerves, feminine furbelows, feminine luxury and subtlety, intoxicate and inspire him; he revels among his innumerable heroines like Mahomet in his paradise of houris. In saying just now that women could not complain of Balzac's restrictions upon their liberty, we had in mind especially the liberty of telling lies. This exquisite and elaborate mendacity he considers the great characteristic of the finished woman of the world, of Mesdames d'Espard, de Sérisy, de Langeais, de Maufrigneuse. The ladies just enumerated have all a great many lovers, a great many intrigues, a great many jealousies, a terrible entanglement of life behind the scenes. They are described as irresistibly charming, as *grandes dames* in the supreme sense of the word; clever, cold, self-possessed, ineffably elegant, holding salons, influencing politics and letting nothing interfere with their ambition, their coquetry, their need for money. Above all they are at swords' points with each other; society for them is a deadly battle for lovers, disguised in a tissue of caresses. To our own sense this whole series of figures is fit only to have a line drawn through it as a laborious and extravagant failure—a failure on which treasures of ingenuity have been expended, but which is perhaps on that account only the more provocative of smiles. These ladies altogether miss the mark; they are vitiated by that familiar foible which Thackeray commemorated in so many inimitable pages. Allusion was made in the earlier part of these remarks to Balzac's strong plebeian strain. It is no reproach to him; if he was of the "people," he was magnificently so; and if the people never produced anything less solid and sturdy it would need to fear no invidious comparisons. But there is something ineffably snobbish in his tone when he deals with the aristocracy, and in the tone which those members of it who circulate through his pages take from him. They are so conscious, so fatuous, so *poseurs,* so perpetually alluding to their grandeurs and their quarterings, so determined to be impertinent, so afraid they shall not be impertinent enough, so addicted to reminding you that they are not bourgeois, that they do not pay their debts or practise the vulgar virtues, that they really seem at times to be the creatures of the dreams of an ambitious hairdresser who should have been plying his curling-irons all day and reading fashionable novels all the evening. The refinement of purpose in Balzac, in everything that relates to the emphasis of the aristocratic tone, is often extraordinary; and to see such heroic ingenuity so squandered and dissipated gives us an alarming sense of what a man of genius may sometimes do in the way of not seeing himself as others see him. Madame d'Espard, when she has decided to "take up" her provincial *cousine*, Madame de Bargeton, conveys her one night to the opera. Lucien de Rubempré comes into the box and, by his provincial dandyism and ingenuous indiscretions, attracts some attention. A rival who is acquainted with the skeleton in his closet goes and tells Madame d'Espard's friends and enemies that he is not properly a De Rubempré (this being only his mother's name), and that his father was M. Chardon, a country apothecary. Then the traitor comes and announces this fact to Madame d'Espard and intimates that her neighbours know it. This great lady hereupon finds the situation intolerable, and informs her companion that it will never do to be seen at the opera with the son of an apothecary. The ladies, accordingly, beat a precipitate retreat, leaving Lucien the master of the field. The caste of Vere de Vere in this case certainly quite forgot its repose. But its conduct is quite of a piece with that of the young men of high fashion who, after Madame de Bargeton has been a fortnight in Paris (having come very ill-dressed from Angoulême) are seen to compliment her on the "metamorphosis of her appearance." What is one to say about Madame de Rochefide, a person of the highest condition, who has by way of decoration of her drawing-room a series of ten water-colour pictures representing the different bedrooms she has successively slept in? What Balzac says is that this performance "gave the measure of a superior impertinence"; and he evidently thinks that he has bestowed the crowning touch upon a very crushing physiognomy. What is here indicated of Balzac's great ladies is equally true of his young dandies and lions—his De Marsays and De Trailles. The truly initiated reader of the "Comédie Humaine" will always feel that he can afford to skip the page when he sees the name of De Marsay. Balzac's dandies are tremendous fellows from a picturesque point of view; the account of De Marsay in "La Fille aux Yeux d'Or" is an example of the "sumptuous" gone mad. Balzac leaves nothing vague in the destinies he shapes for these transcendant fops. Rastignac is prime minister of France, and yet Rastignac in his impecunious youth has been on those terms with Madame de Nücingen which characterized the relations of Tom Jones with Lady Bellaston. Fielding was careful not to make his hero a rival of Sir Robert Walpole. Balzac's young *gentilshommes,* as possible historical figures, are completely out of the question. They represent, perhaps, more than anything else, the author's extraordinary union of vigour and shallowness. In this, however, they have much in common with several other classes of characters that we lack space to consider. There are the young girls (chiefly of the upper class) like Modeste Mignon and Louise de Chaulieu; there are the women of literary talent, like Mademoiselle des Touches and Madame de La Baudraye; there are the journalists, like Lousteau and Emile Blondet. In all these cases Balzac "rummages" with extraordinary ardour; but his faults of taste reach their maximum and offer us an incredible imbroglio of the superb and the ignoble. Mademoiselle de Chaulieu talks about her arms, her bosom, her hips, in a way to make a trooper blush. Lousteau, when a lady says a clever thing, tells her he will steal it from her for his newspaper and get two dollars. As regards Rubempré and Canalis, we have specimens of their poetry, but we have on the whole more information about their coats and trousers, their gloves and shirts and cosmetics.

In all this it may seem that there has been more talk about faults than about merits, and that if it is claimed that Balzac did a great work we should have plucked more flowers and fewer thistles. But the greatest thing in Balzac cannot be exhibited by specimens. It is Balzac himself—it is the whole attempt—it is the method. This last is his unsurpassed, his incomparable merit. That huge, all-compassing, all-desiring, all-devouring love of reality which was the source of so many of his fallacies and stains, of so much dead-weight in his work, was also the foundation of his extraordinary power. The real, for his imagination, had an authority that it has never had for any other. When he looks for it in the things in which we all feel it, he finds it with a marvellous certainty of eye, and proves himself the great novelist that he pretends to be. When he tries to make it prevail everywhere, explain everything and serve as a full measure of our imagination—then he becomes simply the greatest of dupes. He is an extraordinary tissue of contradictions. He is at once one of the most corrupt of writers and one of the most naïf, the most mechanical and pedantic, and the fullest of *bonhomie* and natural impulse. He is one of the finest of artists and one of the coarsest. Viewed in one way, his novels are ponderous, shapeless, overloaded; his touch is graceless, violent, barbarous. Viewed in another, his tales have more colour, more composition, more grasp of the reader's attention than any others. Balzac's style would demand a chapter apart. It is the least simple style, probably, that ever was written; it bristles, it cracks, it swells and swaggers; but it is a perfect expression of the man's genius. Like his genius, it contains a certain quantity of everything, from immaculate gold to flagrant dross. He was a very bad writer, and yet unquestionably he was a very great writer. We may say briefly, that in so far as his method was an instinct it was successful, and that in so far as it was a theory it was a failure. But both in instinct and in theory he had the aid of an immense force of conviction. His imagination warmed to its work so intensely that there was nothing his volition could not impose upon it. Hallucination settled upon him, and he believed anything that was necessary in the circumstances. This accounts for all his grotesque philosophies, his heroic attempts to furnish specimens of things of which he was profoundly ignorant. He believed that he was about as creative as the Deity, and that if mankind and human history were swept away the "Comédie Humaine" would be a perfectly adequate substitute for them. M. Taine says of him very happily that, after Shakespeare, he is our great magazine of documents on human nature. When Shakespeare is suggested we feel rather his differences from Shakespeare—feel how Shakespeare's characters stand out in the open air of the universe, while Balzac's are enclosed in a peculiar artificial atmosphere, musty in quality and limited in amount, which persuades itself with a sublime sincerity that it is a very sufficient infinite. But it is very true that Balzac may, like Shakespeare, be treated as a final authority upon human nature; and it is very probable that as time goes on he will be resorted to much less for entertainment, and more for instruction. He has against him that he lacks that slight but needful thing—charm. To feel how much he lacked it, you must read his prefaces, with their vanity, avidity, and garrulity, their gross revelation of his processes, of his squabbles with his publishers, their culinary atmosphere. But our last word about him is that he had incomparable power.

"Honoré de Balzac," the first of James' five essays on the French master, was written in the summer of 1875 when James was living at 111 East Twenty-Fifth Street in New York City. 1875 was a crucial time for the young writer. He published in this year with a prodigiousness equal to anything achieved by Balzac and the great Victorians. Seventy-five titles appeared, including James' first full-length novel, *Roderick Hudson*. Moreover, James left America in the fall of 1875 for what became his permanent residence in Europe. This geographical reorientation is reflected in James' literary criticism. The success of *Transatlantic Sketches* prompted him to plan a counterpart volume on European writers. Though most of the essays were written in Paris after James reached there in the fall of 1875, he began work on Balzac while still in New York, partly because the twenty-three volume definitive edition of Balzac had just appeared. "Honoré de Balzac" was published in *Galaxy* in 1875 and was revised for *French Poets and Novelists* in 1878.

In the general context of James' more than ninety essays on French literature, "Honoré de Balzac" expresses his admiration for French rendering of sense impressions. He pays homage to Balzac's profuse, weighted presentation of physical detail. Another aspect of French practice—its sensuality and "amorality"—evokes from James a response which marks "Honoré de Balzac" as early work. In keeping with his stringent criticism of Baudelaire and Zola in the 1870s, James faults Balzac for sensualism, particularly in his presentation of women.

In the particular context of James' five essays on Balzac, "Honoré de Balzac" sets forth the questions which James will answer variously between 1875 and 1913. What he praises early, he never wavers on. "Complete," "hard," and "powerful" are recurrent adjectives which celebrate Balzac for his combined "vividness of . . . imagination" and "grasp of actual facts." They result in unprecedented power of portrayal—settings, accoutrements, and above all, individualized characters, "a sense of this present terrestrial life which has never been surpassed."

What James faults Balzac for in 1875, he reacts less stringently to after 1900. James' emphasis as critic varies with his expertise as novelist. The young American whose early fiction borrows most directly from Balzac takes most seriously the French writer's failures of execution. The experienced James who by 1900 has fashioned his own, unique style owes little now to Balzac formally and concentrates critically upon the *spirit*, the integrity of his fellow master. "Let me say, definitely, that I hold several of his faults to be grave . . . but let me add, as promptly, that they are faults, on the whole, of execution . . . they never come back to that fault in the artist, in the novelist, that

91

amounts most completely to a failure of dignity, the absence of saturation with his idea" ("The Lesson of Balzac" [1905]). The result of this shift of emphasis is *not*, as James attests, that he becomes uncritical in the later essays. Balzac's lack of "disinterested observation" which James faults in 1875 is reexamined, for example, in the "Honoré de Balzac" essays of both 1902 ("that odd want of elbow-room") and 1913 ("there was thus left over for him less of . . . any curiosity, whatever, that didn't 'pay'"). The weakness in portraying aristocrats which James details in 1875 is called in 1902 "one of the strangest deviations of taste that the literary critic is in an important connection likely to encounter." James eventually softens his 1875 contention that Balzac was "morally and intellectually so superficial," but he still maintains in 1913 that Balzac's "sense . . . of the real . . . fails to take in whatever fine truth experience may have vouchsafed to us about the highest kind of temper, the inward life of the mind, the *cultivated* consciousness." Likewise softened but still insisted upon in 1913 are James' criticisms of Balzac's philosophizing and theorizing. "His generalising remains throughout so markedly inferior to his particularising."

The change of emphasis which causes these softenings of James' early strictures operates still more benignly with other issues raised in 1875. To his early, repeated charge that Balzac lacks "charm," the James of 1902 replies "if charm . . . is what he lacks, how comes it that he so touches and holds us?" James acknowledges the accuracy of his early belief that Balzac's materialism suffuses every aspect of life with the financial, but he adds in 1902 that "to say these things, however, is after all to come out where we want, to suggest his extraordinary scale and his terrible completeness." In 1905 James catalogues virtually all his early objections, in the act of subordinating them.

> With all his faults of pedantry, ponderosity, pretentiousness, bad taste and charmless form, his spirit has somehow paid for its knowledge. His subject is again and again the completed human creature or human condition; and it is with these complications, as if he knew them, as Shakespeare knew them . . . by the history of his soul.

Here is the key: Balzac the man, "a figure more extraordinary than any he drew" (1905). James is thus giving priority in his late essays to a recognition sounded in 1875. "What is most interesting in Balzac is not the achievement but the attempt." Edel is correct that by daring to be the Napoleon of novelists, Balzac inspired James in his own assault upon the fortress of fortune and fame (1: 72). "One really knows in all imaginative literature," James says in 1902 of *La Comédie humaine*, "no undertaking to compare with it." Balzac is peerless, "the only member of his order really monumental . . . . the father of us all" (1902, 1905).

The contemporary reception of *French Poets and Novelists* was generally favorable, and "Honoré de Balzac" was singled out for praise. In England, the *Athenaeum* (March 16, 1878: 339–40) and the *Spectator* (51 [1878]: 1076–77) agree that "there has of late years appeared nothing upon French literature so intelligent as this book" (339); "we have not often met with a volume of brighter, fresher, and juster criticism" (1076). Focusing on specific essays, the *London Quarterly* (50 [1878]: 526–27) and the *Saturday Review* (45 [1878]: 504–5) second the *Spectator*'s belief that "the essay on Balzac is . . . the best" (1077). George Saintsbury goes on to explain why. James' methodological preference for the sympathetically objective stance, as opposed to schematic, dogmatic, or partisan attitudes, allows him to praise and to criticize judiciously. "His essays on Sand and Balzac are really admirable . . . his matter-of-fact, external way of looking at it [his subject] has its advantage. As an instance of this we make mention that while his admiration for Balzac is unstinted . . . he fully admits the 'lack of charm' which is the great fault of the *Comédie Humaine*, and which most of its admirers deny so lustily" (*Academy* 13 [1878]: 338).

In America, Brander Matthews is prescient in placing James among the premier critics of the period. "It is not too much to say that with the exception of Mr. Lowell and Mr. Matthew Arnold, Mr. James is the foremost literary critic of our language" (*Literary Table* 4[March 30, 1878]: 197). For other American responses to *French Poets and Novelists*, see: William Dean Howells in the *Atlantic Monthly* 42 (1878): 118–19, and anonymous reviews in *Harper's* 56 (1878): 939–40, the *Penn Monthly* 9 (1878): 402–3, the *Churchman* 38 (July 6, 1878): 14, and the *Independent* 30 (July 25, 1878): 13.

Modern critics of James' work on French literature have tended to devote themselves to three tasks: defining James' major points about Balzac; establishing where and how James' fiction reflects Balzac's influence; and debating to what extent James reacts prudishly to French "nastiness" and to what extent he courageously demands an adult fiction free to present what The Young Person does not and should not understand. For early summaries of James' major points about Balzac see Pacey's "Henry James and his French Contemporaries," *American Literature* 13 (1941): 240–56, and Fay's "Balzac and

Henry James," *French Review* 24 (1951): 325–30. For specific comparison of "Honoré de Balzac" and James' attitude toward Balzac *before* 1875 see Kelley (208–15). On the question of Balzac's influence on James' fiction see Adams' argument and bibliography ("Young Henry James and the Lesson of His Master Balzac," *Revue de littérature comparée* 35 [1961]: 458–67), plus Powers (*Henry James and the Naturalist Movement* [East Lansing: Michigan State University Press, 1971]), Grover (*Henry James and the French Novel* [London: Paul Elek, 1973]), and Brooks (*The Melodramatic Imagination* [New Haven: Yale University Press, 1976]). For the prudery/courage controversy see Field's "'Nervous Anglo-Saxon Apprehensions': Henry James and the French," *The French-American Review* 5 (1981): 1–13, Miller (8), Roberts (36–38), and Wellek's "Henry James's Literary Theory and Criticism," *American Literature* 30 (1958–59): 305–7. See also Ruggiero's "Henry James as a Critic: Some Early French Influences," *Rivista di Letterature Moderne e Comparate* 26 (1973): 285–306, and Stowe's *Balzac, James, and the Realistic Novel* (Princeton: Princeton University Press, 1983).

NOTES

For particular incidents in Balzac's life see André Maurois' biography, *Prometheus*, trans. Norman Denny (London: Bodley Head, 1965). For bibliographical details of Balzac works mentioned by James, and for details about Balzac characters discussed by him see volume 12 of the Pléiade edition of *La Comédie humaine*, ed. Pierre-George Castex (Paris: Gallimard, 1976–81).

59:7. *travaux*. Literary works.

59:22. Hippolyte Adolphe Taine (1828–93), French critic. Between February 3d and March 3d, 1858, Taine wrote six essays on Balzac for *Débats*. He collected these essays in 1865 in *Nouveaux Essais de critique et d'histoire*. Taine's famous comparison of Balzac and Thackeray which James refers to several times appeared in 1870 in volume 4 of *History of English Literature*. For James on Taine see, Bibliography, part 3.

59:23. Charles Augustin Sainte-Beuve (1804–69), French critic. James mentions "two or three" essays because the second of Sainte-Beuve's three essays on Balzac is in fact a version of the first. In the November 15, 1834, number of *Revue des Deux Mondes*, Sainte-Beuve gave Balzac a mixed review. Then after twelve years of increasingly hostile exchanges (Sainte-Beuve's *Revue des Deux Mondes* essays for October 15, 1838, November 1, 1838, September 1, 1839, and March 1, 1840, are not expressly devoted to reviewing Balzac novels but they do introduce attacks upon him for materialism, egotism, and making literature into an industry), Sainte-Beuve in 1846 republished his 1834 review, substantially increasing its virulence (*Portraits contemporains*, vol. 1). After Balzac's death, Sainte-Beuve praised him (though with lingering reservations) in a eulogy which appeared in *Le Constitutionnel* (September 2, 1850) and was reprinted in volume 2 of Sainte-Beuve's *Causeries du Lundi* (1850).

59:26. Théophile Gautier (1811–72), French author of fiction, poetry, travel books. Gautier wrote a long essay for *Le Moniteur* on Balzac which he then expanded slightly and published as *Honoré de Balzac* (1859).

59:27. Edmond Henri Adolphe Scherer (1815–89), French critic. Scherer's short essay on Balzac appeared in *Le Temps* (March 1870) and was collected in volume 4 of his *Études sur la littérature contemporaine* (1886).

60:2. Léon Gozlan (1803–66), French writer. *Balzac en pantoufles* appeared in 1856, *Balzac chez lui* in 1862.

60:9. "édition définitive." The *Oeuvres complètes de Honoré de Balzac* appeared between 1869 and 1873. Edel argues convincingly that James based his New York edition upon this twenty-three volume collection.

60:9. a prospect of his letters. The two volume *Correspondance de H. de Balzac, 1819–1850* appeared in 1876. James reviewed it for *Galaxy* (1877) and included the review in *French Poets and Novelists*.

60:38. these "oeuvres de jeunesse." The *Oeuvres de jeunesse de Balzac* had appeared in 1868.

61:15. Alphonse-Marie-Louis de Prat de Lamartine (1790–1869), French poet and politician.

61:16. Alfred de Musset (1810–67), French poet, novelist, and dramatist.

61:24. *fonds.* Funds, resources.

62:20. *rentes.* Investment income.

62:37. Dr. Johnson's affection for London. Among Johnson's many paeans, James may have in mind here the memorable sentence from the *Life*, "when a man is tired of London, he is tired of Life" (Saturday, September 20, 1777).

63:18. savour of their native soil. Despite the many differences which James sees between Balzac and Hawthorne, he describes the French master here in terms similar to those applied to Hawthorne in 1879. "Hawthorne's work savours thoroughly of the local soil . . ." ("From *Hawthorne*" p.103)

63:37. *roturier.* A commoner.

64:25. Alexander von Humboldt (1769–1859), German statesman, scientist, traveler. *Cosmos* (1845–62), one of the most ambitious works of science ever undertaken, describes the universe from the stars down to organic life on earth.

65:19. Henry Hallam (1777–1859), British historian.
   François-Pierre-Guillaume Guizot (1787–1874), French statesman and historian. Among Guizot's many volumes, James expressly mentions in 1878 the *General History of Civilization in Europe* (*Atlantic Monthly*, 41: 72).

67:5. *cadres.* Borders (of a map).

67:32. *inédits.* Fresh, original.

68:1. figures from one novel to another. George Savage Fitz-Boodle who appears in Thackeray's early "Fitz-Boodle Papers" (*Fraser's* [1842–43]) reappears as a character in "Men's Wives" (*Fraser's* [1843]) and as editor of "The Luck of Barry Lyndon" (*Fraser's* [1844]; subsequently published in novel form as *The Memoir of Barry Lyndon, Esq., by Himself*). In *The Adventures of Philip* (1861–62), characters from "The Shabby Genteel Story" (1840) reappear. Most famous of Thackeray's recurring characters is Arthur Pendennis who is the protagonist of *The History of Pendennis* (1848–50) and then the narrator of *The Newcomes* (1853–55).

68:2. repeated evocations. "Reverend" Grantly (not "Grantley") appears in *The Warden* (1855), the first of Trollope's Barsetshire novels. He is joined by Bishop Proudie in *Barchester Towers* (1857) where he is now Archdeacon. Both men reappear in *Framley Parsonage* (1861) and *The Last Chronicle of Barset* (1867).

68:7. Auguste Comte (1798–1857), French philosopher. In his *Course of Positive Philosophy* (1830–42), Comte divided knowledge into three stages (theological, metaphysical, and positive), and classified the sciences according to their decreasing generality and increasing complexity.

70:25. "manquer à ses devoirs." Fail in one's duties.

72:11. animal magnetism. This term refers to a mysterious force which influences human behavior. Friedrich Anton Mesmer (1734–1815), an Austrian physician, claimed to draw upon this force in his hypnotic treatment of patients. Balzac was much taken with Mesmer.

73:29. *blason*. Coat of arms.

74:23. "gens d'église." Clergy.

74:33. the line of beauty is the curve. This is a tenet of Hogarth (*The Analysis of Beauty*) whose work James knew from childhood.

76:4. a Dutch picture. Literary critics in the nineteenth century frequently borrowed from the visual arts the distinction between "dutch" (common, homey, intricately detailed) and "classical" (elegant, Italianate or French). In *The Ambassadors* James contrasts Maria Gostrey's "Dutch" apartment in Paris with Marie de Vionnet's empire one.

80:40. *The Mill on the Floss* (1860). For Eliot and Balzac, see our commentary on *Middlemarch*, Chapter 3.

81:8. always invidious. That Anglo-Saxon novelists are more generous to their flawed characters than French novelists is a contention which James repeats with one of the literary grandsons of Balzac, Guy de Maupassant, Chapter 8.

81:16. Philistinism. Matthew Arnold (1822–88) in *Essays in Criticism* (1865) and *Culture and Anarchy* (1869) characterized as Philistines those deficient in liberal culture and enlightenment. (James' first essay on Arnold, see Chapter 1; see also Bibliography, part 3).

82:11. Charles de Bernard (1804–50), French novelist. In 1876 James wrote an essay on de Bernard and Flaubert for the *Galaxy* and included it in *French Poets and Novelists*.

82:23. *scabreux*. Indelicate, scabrous.

85:11. suffrage . . . Harvard College . . . apparel. James' examples here refer to three major controversies of the woman question in the nineteenth century—women's rights to vote, to study, and to dress as they choose.

85:18. *métier de femme*. Woman's calling.

85:22. Woman has a "mission" certainly. James is wittily contrasting here woman's traditional mission (to use her supposed moral purity to elevate human relations and redeem society) and woman's role in Balzac's fiction (to use her sexuality to please and manipulate men).

88:22. the caste . . . repose. In volume 2 of his Library of America edition of James' criticism, Edel refers readers of this sentence to the second stanza of Tennyson's "Lady Clara Vere de Vere" (1833): "Her manners had not that repose/Which stamps the caste of Vere-de-Vere."

89:3. Robert Walpole, first earl of Orford (1676–1745), British prime minister 1715–17, 1721–42.

TEXTUAL VARIANTS

60:7. pages. 1875: leaves.

60:10. complementary volume. 1875: two complementary volumes.

60:12. fifty-one . . . and. 1875: fifty-one retain a large productive force, and.

60:14. Balzac's productive force. 1875: that of Balzac.

60:15. that. 1875: which.

60:31. We cannot say. 1875: I do not know.

60:32. We are. 1875: I am.

61:8. us. 1875: me.

61:14. we believe. 1875: I think.

61:18. Madame. 1875: Mme.

61:19. that. 1875: which.

61:27. have . . . a. 1875: have incorporated himself in this society about him as something else than a.

61:37. incorporate the. 1875: incorporate unerringly the.

62:3. we. 1875: I.

62:20. the . . . impartially. 1875: the viscissitudes of his fortune impartially. . .

62:35. pavement—of. 1875: pavement as it were—of.

63:18. that. 1875: which.

63:24. theory. 1875: mania.

63:31. they occupied. 1875: they ever occupied.

63:32. that. 1875: which.

63:41. see. 1875: have.

63:41. we. 1875: I.

64:16. M. Added 1878.

64:25. large. 1875: vast.

64:33. we. 1875: I.

65:12. Alexandre Dumas manufactures. 1875: Dumas and Trollope manufacture.

66:15. we. 1875: I.

66:15. we. 1875: I.

66:16. we. 1875: I.

67:12. Philosophiques" . . . and. 1875: Philosophiques"—portentous name! (the picturesque "Recherche de l'Absolu" is one of these)—and.

67:22. that. 1875: which.

67:27. in America. 1875: here.

67:29. correspond with. 1875: mirror.

68:1. Mr. Added 1878.

68:1. deepened illusion for. 1875: mildly bewildered.

68:2. repeated. . . . But. 1875: repeated reappearances of his Bishop Proudies and his Archdeacon Grantleys. But.

68:9. a . . . of. 1875: a subject *totus teres atque rotundus*—of.

68:15. conventional. 1875: miniature.

68:23. would be. 1875: is.

68:24. should propose. 1875: proposes.

68:39. consistent. . . . "The. 1875: consistent, ever available theory of the universe. "The.

69:1. We. 1875: I.

69:3. We. 1875: I.

69:13. we. 1875: I.

69:18. dye. How. 1875: dye (as we should say in English). How.

69:24. large. 1875: vast.

69:37. artless. 1875: naif.

70:7. We. 1875: I.

70:8. We. 1875: I.

70:36. luxurious, passionate. 1875: luxurious and passionate.

71:2. we. 1875: I.

71:2. we. 1875: I.

71:12. identical with. 1875: all in.

71:17. we. 1875: I.

71:25. sceptical. 1875: disbelieving.

72:4. Selfishness. 1875: It.

72:14. considerable. 1875: redundant and far-reaching.

72:22. is. 1875: was.

73:3. extremely. 1875: most.

73:6. these writers. 1875: them.

73:11. fineness. 1875: firmness.

73:12. us. 1875: me.

73:14. sense. 1875: fancy.

73:14. we. 1875: I.

73:15. deference to. 1875: preoccupation with.

73:23. defects. He. 1875: defects. [par.] He.

74:3. expanded. 1875: came in.
74:10. scramble. 1875: race.
74:13. ladder, to. 1875: ladder, to scramble, to.
75:3. begin . . . he. 1875: begin the recital of what he.
75:11. part to play. 1875: role to fill.
75:13. very much. 1875: vastly.
75:19. we are. 1875: I am.
75:23. we. 1875: I.
75:29. We, for our. 1875: I, for my.
75:30. we. 1875: I.
75:35. extravagance. 1875: excess and indiscretion.
76:1. "get up". 1875: turn out.
76:2. immense supply. 1875: huge stock.
76:2. this material. 1875: this sort of material.
77:1. and sniff. 1875: there sniffing.
77:29. we. 1875: I.
77:29. we. 1875: I.
78:22. we think. 1875: one thinks.
78:25. we give. 1875: one gives.
78:26. we. 1875: I.
79:2. &c. 1875: etc.
79:13. talking. 1875: talk.
79:22. to. Added 1878.
79:28. Nantes. Added 1878.
81:21. we. 1875: I.
82:15. figures converse. 1875: characters talk.
82:20. deemed. 1875: considered.
82:33. valuable. 1875: secure.
82:37. our. 1875: my.
83:15. great. 1875: vast.
83:16. host. 1875: number.
83:21. conspicuous. 1875: colossal.
84:12. give an airing. 1875: ventilate.
85:5. us. 1875: me.
85:27. very comprehensive. 1875: enormous.
85:39. we. 1875: I.
86:2. attitudes. 1875: attributes.
86:27. Séchard. 1875: Lechard.
87:1. coquettes and courtesans. 1875: duchesses and countesses.
87:15. we. 1875: I.
87:27. our own. 1875: my.
87:40. *poseurs*. 1875: *paseuss*.
87:41. quarterings. 1875: *blasons*.
88:1. do not. 1875: don't.
88:2. to. 1875: as if they might.
88:6. extraordinary. 1875: most prodigious.

88:8. us. 1875: one.
88:17. traitor. 1875: betrayer.
88:21. apothecary . . . beat. 1875: apothecary, whereupon they beat.
88:28. by way of. 1875: as a.
88:39. d'Or''. . . . Balzac. 1875: d'Or'' is worth reading, to enable one to give a truly adequate soul to Mr. Squeer's famous formula—"There's richness!" Balzac.
88:41. transcendant fops. 1875: heroic dandies.
89:4. completely. 1875: ineffably.
89:8. that. 1875: which.
89:13. extraordinary. 1875: tremendous.
89:17. newspaper. 1875: paper.
89:23. we. 1875: I.
89:35. greatest. 1875: hugest.
90:6. We. 1875: One.
90:7. instinct. 1875: impulse.
90:20. Shakespeare—feel. 1875: Shakespeare—I feel.
90:31. culinary. 1875: kitchen.

F I V E

FROM
Hawthorne

CHAPTER I

IT WILL BE NECESSARY, FOR SEVERAL REASONS, TO GIVE
this short sketch the form rather of a critical essay than of a biography. The data for a life of Nathaniel Hawthorne are the reverse of
copious, and even if they were abundant they would serve but in a
limited measure the purpose of the biographer. Hawthorne's career
was probably as tranquil and uneventful a one as ever fell to the lot of
a man of letters; it was almost strikingly deficient in incident, in what
may be called the dramatic quality. Few men of equal genius and of
equal eminence can have led on the whole a simpler life. His six volumes of Note-Books illustrate this simplicity; they are a sort of monument to an unagitated fortune. Hawthorne's career had few
vicissitudes or variations; it was passed for the most part in a small
and homogeneous society, in a provincial, rural community; it had
few perceptible points of contact with what is called the world, with
public events, with the manners of his time, even with the life of his
neighbours. Its literary incidents are not numerous. He produced, in
quantity, but little. His works consist of four novels and the fragment
of another, five volumes of short tales, a collection of sketches, and a
couple of story-books for children. And yet some account of the man
and the writer is well worth giving. Whatever may have been Hawthorne's private lot, he has the importance of being the most beautiful
and most eminent representative of a literature. The importance of
the literature may be questioned, but at any rate, in the field of letters,
Hawthorne is the most valuable example of the American genius.
That genius has not, as a whole, been literary; but Hawthorne was on
his limited scale a master of expression. He is the writer to whom his
countrymen most confidently point when they wish to make a claim
to have enriched the mother-tongue, and, judging from present ap-

pearances, he will long occupy this honourable position. If there is something very fortunate for him in the way that he borrows an added relief from the absence of competitors in his own line and from the general flatness of the literary field that surrounds him, there is also, to a spectator, something almost touching in his situation. He was so modest and delicate a genius that we may fancy him appealing from the lonely honour of a representative attitude—perceiving a painful incongruity between his imponderable literary baggage and the large conditions of American life. Hawthorne on the one side is so subtle and slender and unpretending, and the American world on the other is so vast and various and substantial, that it might seem to the author of *The Scarlet Letter* and the *Mosses from an Old Manse*, that we render him a poor service in contrasting his proportions with those of a great civilization. But our author must accept the awkward as well as the graceful side of his fame; for he has the advantage of pointing a valuable moral. This moral is that the flower of art blooms only where the soil is deep, that it takes a great deal of history to produce a little literature, that it needs a complex social machinery to set a writer in motion. American civilization has hitherto had other things to do than to produce flowers, and before giving birth to writers it has wisely occupied itself with providing something for them to write about. Three or four beautiful talents of trans-Atlantic growth are the sum of what the world usually recognises, and in this modest nosegay the genius of Hawthorne is admitted to have the rarest and sweetest fragrance.

His very simplicity has been in his favour; it has helped him to appear complete and homogeneous. To talk of his being national would be to force the note and make a mistake of proportion; but he is, in spite of the absence of the realistic quality, intensely and vividly local. Out of the soil of New England he sprang—in a crevice of that immitigable granite he sprouted and bloomed. Half of the interest that he possesses for an American reader with any turn for analysis must reside in his latent New England savour; and I think it no more than just to say that whatever entertainment he may yield to those who know him at a distance, it is an almost indispensable condition of properly appreciating him to have received a personal impression of the manners, the morals, indeed of the very climate, of the great region of which the remarkable city of Boston is the metropolis. The cold, bright air of New England seems to blow through his pages, and these, in the opinion of many people, are the medium in which it is most agreeable to make the acquaintance of that tonic atmosphere. As to whether it is worth while to seek to know something of New England in order to extract a more intimate quality from *The House of Seven Gables* and *The Blithedale Romance*, I need not pronounce; but it is certain that a considerable observation of the society to which these productions were more directly addressed is a capital preparation for enjoying them. I have alluded to the absence in Hawthorne of that quality of realism which is now so much in fashion, an absence in regard to which there will of course be more to say; and yet I think I am not fanciful in saying that he testifies to the sentiments of the society in which he flourished almost as pertinently (proportions observed) as Balzac and some of his descendants—M.M. Flaubert and Zola—testify to the manners and morals of the French people. He was not a man with a literary theory; he was guiltless of a system, and I am not sure that he had ever heard of Realism, this remarkable compound having (although it was invented some time earlier) come into general use only since his death. He had certainly not proposed to himself to give an account of the social idiosyncrasies of his fellow-citizens, for his touch on such points is always light and vague, he has none of the apparatus of an historian, and his shadowy style of portraiture never suggests a rigid standard of accuracy. Nevertheless he virtually offers the most vivid reflection of New England life that has found its way into literature. His value in this respect is not diminished by the fact that he has not attempted to portray the usual Yankee of comedy, and that he has been almost culpably indifferent to his opportunities for commemorating the variations of colloquial English that may be observed in the New World. His characters do not express themselves in the dialect of the *Biglow Papers*—their language indeed is apt to be too elegant, too delicate. They are not portraits of actual types, and in their phraseology there is nothing imitative. But none the less, Hawthorne's work savours thoroughly of the local soil—it is redolent of the social system in which he had his being. . . .

CHAPTER II

The twelve years that followed were not the happiest or most brilliant phase of Hawthorne's life; they strike me indeed as having had an altogether peculiar dreariness. They had their uses; they were the period of incubation of the admirable compositions which eventually brought him reputation and prosperity. But of their actual aridity the young man must have had a painful consciousness; he never lost the impression of it. Mr. Lathrop quotes a phrase to this effect from one of his letters, late in life. "I am disposed to thank God for the gloom and chill of my early life, in the hope that my share of adversity came then, when I bore it alone." And the same writer alludes to a touching passage in the English Note-Books, which I shall quote entire:—

> "I think I have been happier this Christmas (1854) than ever before—by my own fireside, and with my wife and children about me—more content to enjoy what I have, less anxious for anything beyond it, in this life. My early life was perhaps a good preparation for the declining half of life; it having been such a blank that any thereafter would compare favourably with it. For a long, long while, I have occasionally been visited with a singular dream; and I have an impression that I have dreamed it ever since I have been in England. It is, that I am still at college, or, sometimes, even, at school—and there is a sense that I have been there unconscionably long, and have quite failed to make such progress as my contemporaries have done; and I seem to meet some of them with a feeling of shame and depression that broods over me as I think of it, even when awake. This dream, recurring all through these twenty or thirty years, must be one of the effects of that heavy seclusion in which I shut myself up for twelve years after leaving college, when everybody moved onward and left me behind. How strange that it should come now, when I may call myself famous and prosperous!—when I am happy too."

The allusion here is to a state of solitude which was the young man's positive choice at the time—or into which he drifted at least under the pressure of his natural shyness and reserve. He was not expansive, he was not addicted to experiments and adventures of intercourse, he was not, personally, in a word, what is called sociable. . . .

It seems to me then that it was possibly a blessing for Hawthorne that he was not expansive and inquisitive, that he lived much to himself and asked but little of his *milieu*. If he had been exacting and ambitious, if his appetite had been large and his knowledge various, he would probably have found the bounds of Salem intolerably narrow. But his culture had been of a simple sort—there was little of any other sort to be obtained in America in those days, and though he was doubtless haunted by visions of more suggestive opportunities, we may safely assume that he was not to his own perception the object of compassion that he appears to a critic who judges him after half a century's civilization has filtered into the twilight of that earlier time. If New England was socially a very small place in those days,

Salem was a still smaller one; and if the American tone at large was intensely provincial, that of New England was not greatly helped by having the best of it. The state of things was extremely natural, and there could be now no greater mistake than to speak of it with a redundancy of irony. American life had begun to constitute itself from the foundations; it had begun to *be,* simply; it was at an immeasurable distance from having begun to enjoy. I imagine there was no appreciable group of people in New England at that time proposing to itself to enjoy life; this was not an undertaking for which any provision had been made, or to which any encouragement was offered. Hawthorne must have vaguely entertained some such design upon destiny; but he must have felt that his success would have to depend wholly upon his own ingenuity. I say he must have proposed to himself to enjoy, simply because he proposed to be an artist, and because this enters inevitably into the artist's scheme. There are a thousand ways of enjoying life, and that of the artist is one of the most innocent. But for all that, it connects itself with the idea of pleasure. He proposes to give pleasure, and to give it he must first get it. Where he gets it will depend upon circumstances, and circumstances were not encouraging to Hawthorne.

He was poor, he was solitary, and he undertook to devote himself to literature in a community in which the interest in literature was as yet of the smallest. It is not too much to say that even to the present day it is a considerable discomfort in the United States not to be "in business." The young man who attempts to launch himself in a career that does not belong to the so-called practical order; the young man who has not, in a word, an office in the business-quarter of the town, with his name painted on the door, has but a limited place in the social system, finds no particular bough to perch upon. He is not looked at askance, he is not regarded as an idler; literature and the arts have always been held in extreme honour in the American world, and those who practise them are received on easier terms than in other countries. If the tone of the American world is in some respects provincial, it is in none more so than in this matter of the exaggerated homage rendered to authorship. The gentleman or the lady who has written a book is in many circles the object of an admiration too indiscriminating to operate as an encouragement to good writing. There is no reason to suppose that this was less the case fifty years ago; but fifty years ago, greatly more than now, the literary man must have lacked the comfort and inspiration of belonging to a class. The best things come, as a general thing, from the talents that are members of a group; every man works better when he has companions working in the same line, and yielding the stimulus of suggestion, comparison, emulation. Great things of course have been done by solitary workers; but they have usually been done with double the pains they would have cost if they had been produced in more genial circumstances. The solitary worker loses the profit of example and discussion; he is apt to make awkward experiments; he is in the nature of the case more or less of an empiric. The empiric may, as I say, be treated by the world as an expert; but the drawbacks and discomforts of empiricism remain to him, and are in fact increased by the suspicion that is mingled with his gratitude, of a want in the public taste of a sense of the proportions of things. Poor Hawthorne, beginning to write subtle short tales at Salem, was empirical enough; he was one of, at most, some dozen Americans who had taken up literature as a profession. The profession in the United States is still very young, and of diminutive stature; but in the year 1830 its head could hardly have been seen above ground. It strikes the observer of to-day that Hawthorne showed great courage in entering a field in which the honours and emoluments were so scanty as the profits of authorship must have been at that time. I have said that in the United States at present authorship is a pedestal, and literature is the fashion; but Hawthorne's history is a proof that it was possible, fifty years ago, to write a great many little masterpieces without becoming known. He begins the preface to the *Twice-Told Tales* by remarking that he was "for many years the obscurest man of letters in America." When once this work obtained recognition, the recognition left little to be desired. Hawthorne never, I believe, made large sums of money by his writings, and the early profits of these charming sketches could not have been considerable; for many of them, indeed, as they appeared in journals and magazines, he had never been paid at all; but the honour, when once it dawned—and it dawned tolerably early in the author's career—was never thereafter wanting. Hawthorne's countrymen are solidly proud of him, and the tone of Mr. Lathrop's *Study* is in itself sufficient evidence of the manner in which an American story-teller may in some cases look to have his eulogy pronounced.

Hawthorne's early attempt to support himself by his pen appears to have been deliberate; we hear nothing of those experiments in counting-houses or lawyers' offices, of which a permanent invocation to the Muse is often the inconsequent sequel. He began to write, and to try and dispose of his writings; and he remained at Salem apparently only because his family, his mother and his two sisters, lived there. His mother had a house, of which during the twelve years that elapsed until 1838, he appears to have been an inmate. Mr.

Lathrop learned from his surviving sister that after publishing *Fanshawe* he produced a group of short stories entitled *Seven Tales of my Native Land,* and that this lady retained a very favourable recollection of the work, which her brother had given her to read. But it never saw the light; his attempts to get it published were unsuccessful, and at last, in a fit of irritation and despair, the young author burned the manuscript. . . .

I have said that Hawthorne was an observer of small things, and indeed he appears to have thought nothing too trivial to be suggestive. His Note-Books give us the measure of his perception of common and casual things, and of his habit of converting them into *memoranda.* These Note-Books, by the way—this seems as good a place as any other to say it—are a very singular series of volumes; I doubt whether there is anything exactly corresponding to them in the whole body of literature. They were published—in six volumes, issued at intervals—some years after Hawthorne's death, and no person attempting to write an account of the romancer could afford to regret that they should have been given to the world. There is a point of view from which this may be regretted; but the attitude of the biographer is to desire as many documents as possible. I am thankful, then, as a biographer, for the Note-Books, but I am obliged to confess that, though I have just re-read them carefully, I am still at a loss to perceive how they came to be written—what was Hawthorne's purpose in carrying on for so many years this minute and often trivial chronicle. For a person desiring information about him at any cost, it is valuable; it sheds a vivid light upon his character, his habits, the nature of his mind. But we find ourselves wondering what was its value to Hawthorne himself. It is in a very partial degree a register of impressions, and in a still smaller sense a record of emotions. Outward objects play much the larger part in it; opinions, convictions, ideas pure and simple, are almost absent. He rarely takes his Note-Book into his confidence or commits to its pages any reflections that might be adapted for publicity; the simplest way to describe the tone of these extremely objective journals is to say that they read like a series of very pleasant, though rather dullish and decidedly formal, letters, addressed to himself by a man who, having suspicions that they might be opened in the post, should have determined to insert nothing compromising. They contain much that is too futile for things intended for publicity; whereas, on the other hand, as a receptacle of private impressions and opinions, they are curiously cold and empty. They widen, as I have said, our glimpse of Hawthorne's mind (I do not say that they elevate our estimate of it), but they do so by what they fail to contain, as much as by what we find in them. Our business for the moment, however, is not with the light that they throw upon his intellect, but with the information they offer about his habits and his social circumstances.

I know not at what age he began to keep a diary; the first entries in the American volumes are of the summer of 1835. There is a phrase in the preface to his novel of *Transformation*, which must have lingered in the minds of many Americans who have tried to write novels and to lay the scene of them in the western world. "No author, without a trial, can conceive of the difficulty of writing a romance about a country where there is no shadow, no antiquity, no mystery, no picturesque and gloomy wrong, nor anything but a commonplace prosperity, in broad and simple daylight, as is happily the case with my dear native land." The perusal of Hawthorne's American Note-Books operates as a practical commentary upon this somewhat ominous text. It does so at least to my own mind; it would be too much perhaps to say that the effect would be the same for the usual English reader. An American reads between the lines—he completes the suggestions—he constructs a picture. I think I am not guilty of any gross injustice in saying that the picture he constructs from Hawthorne's American diaries, though by no means without charms of its own, is not, on the whole, an interesting one. It is characterised by an extraordinary blankness—a curious paleness of colour and paucity of detail. Hawthorne, as I have said, has a large and healthy appetite for detail, and one is therefore the more struck with the lightness of the diet to which his observation was condemned. For myself, as I turn the pages of his journals, I seem to see the image of the crude and simple society in which he lived. I use these epithets, of course, not invidiously, but descriptively; if one desire to enter as closely as possible into Hawthorne's situation, one must endeavour to reproduce his circumstances. We are struck with the large number of elements that were absent from them, and the coldness, the thinness, the blankness, to repeat my epithet, present themselves so vividly that our foremost feeling is that of compassion for a romancer looking for subjects in such a field. It takes so many things, as Hawthorne must have felt later in life, when he made the acquaintance of the denser, richer, warmer European spectacle—it takes such an accumulation of history and custom, such a complexity of manners and types, to form a fund of suggestion for a novelist. If Hawthorne had been a young Englishman, or a young Frenchman of the same degree of genius, the same cast of mind, the same habits, his consciousness of the world around him would have been a very different affair; however obscure, however reserved, his own personal life, his sense of the life of his fellow-mortals would have been almost infinitely more various. The negative side of the spectacle on which Hawthorne looked out, in his contemplative saunterings and reveries, might, indeed, with a little ingenuity, be made almost ludicrous; one might enumerate the items of high civilization, as it exists in other countries, which are absent from the texture of American life, until it should become a wonder to know what was left. No State, in the European sense of the word, and indeed barely a specific national name. No sovereign, no court, no personal loyalty, no aristocracy, no church, no clergy, no army, no diplomatic service, no country gentlemen, no palaces, no castles, nor manors, nor old country-houses, nor parsonages, nor thatched cottages nor ivied ruins; no cathedrals, nor abbeys, nor little Norman churches; no great Universities nor public schools—no Oxford, nor Eton, nor Harrow; no literature, no novels, no museums, no pictures, no political society, no sporting class—no Epsom nor Ascot! Some such list as that might be drawn up of the absent things in American life—especially in the American life of forty years ago, the effect of which, upon an English or a French imagination, would probably as a general thing be appalling. The natural remark, in the almost lurid light of such an indictment, would be that if these things are left out, everything is left out. The American knows that a good deal remains; what it is that remains—that is his secret, his joke, as one may say. It would be cruel, in this terrible denudation, to deny him the consolation of his national gift, that "American humour" of which of late years we have heard so much. . . .

. . . Like almost all people who possess in a strong degree the story-telling faculty, Hawthorne had a democratic strain in his composition and a relish for the commoner stuff of human nature. Thoroughly American in all ways, he was in none more so than in the vagueness of his sense of social distinctions and his readiness to forget them if a moral or intellectual sensation were to be gained by it. He liked to fraternise with plain people, to take them on their own terms, and put himself if possible into their shoes. His Note-Books, and even his tales, are full of evidence of this easy and natural feeling about all his unconventional fellow-mortals—this imaginative interest and contemplative curiosity—and it sometimes takes the most charming and graceful forms. Commingled as it is with his own subtlety and delicacy, his complete exemption from vulgarity, it is one of the points in his character which his reader comes most to appreciate—that reader I mean for whom he is not as for some few, a dusky and malarious genius.

But even if he had had, personally, as many pretensions as he had few, he must in the nature of things have been more or less of a consenting democrat, for democracy was the very key-stone of the simple social structure in which he played his part. The air of his journals and his tales alike are full of the genuine democratic feeling. . . .

. . . I have said that there was less psychology in Hawthorne's Journals than might have been looked for; but there is nevertheless a certain amount of it, and nowhere more than in a number of pages relating to this remarkable "Monsieur S." (Hawthorne, intimate as he apparently became with him, always calls him "Monsieur," just as throughout all his Diaries he invariably speaks of all his friends, even the most familiar, as "Mr." He confers the prefix upon the unconventional Thoreau, his fellow-woodsman at Concord, and upon the emancipated brethren at Brook Farm.) These pages are completely occupied with Monsieur S., who was evidently a man of character, with the full complement of his national vivacity. There is an elaborate effort to analyse the poor young Frenchman's disposition, something conscientious and painstaking, respectful, explicit, almost solemn. These passages are very curious as a reminder of the absence of the off-hand element in the manner in which many Americans, and many New Englanders especially, make up their minds about people whom they meet. This, in turn, is a reminder of something that may be called the importance of the individual in the American world; which is a result of the newness and youthfulness of society and of the absence of keen competition. The individual counts for more, as it were, and, thanks to the absence of a variety of social types and of settled heads under which he may be easily and conveniently pigeonholed, he is to a certain extent a wonder and a mystery. An Englishman, a Frenchman—a Frenchman above all—judges quickly, easily, from his own social standpoint, and makes an end of it. He has not that rather chilly and isolated sense of moral responsibility which is apt to visit a New Englander in such processes; and he has the advantage that his standards are fixed by the general consent of the society in which he lives. A Frenchman, in this respect, is particularly happy and comfortable, happy and comfortable to a degree which I think is hardly to be over-estimated; his standards being the most definite in the world, the most easily and promptly appealed to, and the most identical with what happens to be the practice of the French genius itself. The Englishman is not quite so well off, but he is better off than his poor interrogative and tentative cousin beyond the seas. He is blessed with a healthy mistrust of analysis, and hair-splitting is

110

the occupation he most despises. There is always a little of the Dr. Johnson in him, and Dr. Johnson would have had wofully little patience with that tendency to weigh moonbeams which in Hawthorne was almost as much a quality of race as of genius; albeit that Hawthorne has paid to Boswell's hero (in the chapter on "Lichfield and Uttoxeter," in his volume on England), a tribute of the finest appreciation. American intellectual standards are vague, and Hawthorne's countrymen are apt to hold the scales with a rather uncertain hand and a somewhat agitated conscience.

CHAPTER III

. . . This is the real charm of Hawthorne's writing—this purity and spontaneity and naturalness of fancy. For the rest, it is interesting to see how it borrowed a particular colour from the other faculties that lay near it—how the imagination, in this capital son of the old Puritans, reflected the hue of the more purely moral part, of the dusky, overshadowed conscience. The conscience, by no fault of its own, in every genuine offshoot of that sombre lineage, lay under the shadow of the sense of *sin*. This darkening cloud was no essential part of the nature of the individual; it stood fixed in the general moral heaven under which he grew up and looked at life. It projected from above, from outside, a black patch over his spirit, and it was for him to do what he could with the black patch. There were all sorts of possible ways of dealing with it; they depended upon the personal temperament. Some natures would let it lie as it fell, and contrive to be tolerably comfortable beneath it. Others would groan and sweat and suffer; but the dusky blight would remain, and their lives would be lives of misery. Here and there an individual, irritated beyond endurance, would throw it off in anger, plunging probably into what would be deemed deeper abysses of depravity. Hawthorne's way was the best, for he contrived, by an exquisite process, best known to himself, to transmute this heavy moral burden into the very substance of the imagination, to make it evaporate in the light and charming fumes of artistic production. But Hawthorne, of course, was exceptionally fortunate; he had his genius to help him. Nothing is more curious and interesting than this almost exclusively *imported* character of the sense of sin in Hawthorne's mind; it seems to exist there merely for an artistic or literary purpose. He had ample cognizance of the Puritan conscience; it was his natural heritage; it was reproduced in him; looking into his soul, he found it there. But his relation to it was only, as one may say, intellectual; it was not moral and theological. He played with it and used it as a pigment; he treated it, as the metaphysicians say, objectively. He was not discomposed, disturbed, haunted by it, in the manner of its usual and regular victims, who had not the little postern door of fancy to slip through, to the other side of the wall. It was, indeed, to his imaginative vision, the great fact of man's nature; the light element that had been mingled with his own composition always clung to this rugged prominence of moral responsibility, like the mist that hovers about the mountain. It was a necessary condition for a man of Hawthorne's stock that if his imagination should take licence to amuse itself, it should at least select this grim precinct of the Puritan morality for its play-ground. He speaks of the dark disapproval with which his old ancestors, in the case of their coming to life, would see him trifling himself away as a story-teller. But how far more darkly would they have frowned could they have understood that he had converted the very principle of their own being into one of his toys!

It will be seen that I am far from being struck with the justice of that view of the author of the *Twice-Told Tales*, which is so happily expressed by the French critic to whom I alluded at an earlier stage of this essay. To speak of Hawthorne, as M. Emile Montégut does, as a *romancier pessimiste,* seems to me very much beside the mark. He is no more a pessimist than an optimist, though he is certainly not much of either. He does not pretend to conclude, or to have a philosophy of human nature; indeed, I should even say that at bottom he does not take human nature as hard as he may seem to do. "His bitterness," says M. Montégut, "is without abatement, and his bad opinion of man is without compensation. . . . His little tales have the air of confessions which the soul makes to itself; they are so many little slaps which the author applies to our face." This, it seems to me, is to exaggerate almost immeasurably the reach of Hawthorne's relish of gloomy subjects. What pleased him in such subjects was their picturesqueness, their rich duskiness of colour, their chiaroscuro; but they were not the expression of a hopeless, or even of a predominantly melancholy, feeling about the human soul. Such at least is my own impression. He is to a considerable degree ironical—this is part of his charm—part even, one may say, of his brightness; but he is neither bitter nor cynical—he is rarely even what I should call tragical. There have certainly been story-tellers of a gayer and lighter spirit; there have been observers more humorous, more hilarious—though on the whole Hawthorne's observation has a smile in it oftener than may at first appear; but there has rarely been an observer more serene, less agitated by what he sees and less disposed to call things deeply into question. As I have already intimated, his Note-Books are full of this

112

simple and almost childlike serenity. That dusky pre-occupation with the misery of human life and the wickedness of the human heart which such a critic as M. Emile Montégut talks about, is totally absent from them; and if we may suppose a person to have read these Diaries before looking into the tales, we may be sure that such a reader would be greatly surprised to hear the author described as a disappointed, disdainful genius. "This marked love of cases of conscience," says M. Montégut, "this tactiturn, scornful cast of mind, this habit of seeing sin everywhere and hell always gaping open, this dusky gaze bent always upon a damned world and a nature draped in mourning, these lonely conversations of the imagination with the conscience, this pitiless analysis resulting from a perpetual examination of one's self, and from the tortures of a heart closed before men and open to God—all these elements of the Puritan character have passed into Mr. Hawthorne, or to speak more justly, have *filtered* into him, through a long succession of generations." This is a very pretty and very vivid account of Hawthorne, superficially considered; and it is just such a view of the case as would commend itself most easily and most naturally to a hasty critic. It is all true indeed, with a difference; Hawthorne was all that M. Montégut says, *minus* the conviction. The old Puritan moral sense, the consciousness of sin and hell, of the fearful nature of our responsibilities and the savage character of our Taskmaster—these things had been lodged in the mind of a man of Fancy, whose fancy had straightway begun to take liberties and play tricks with them—to judge them (Heaven forgive him!) from the poetic and aesthetic point of view, the point of view of entertainment and irony. This absence of conviction makes the difference; but the difference is great.

Hawthorne was a man of fancy, and I suppose that in speaking of him it is inevitable that we should feel ourselves confronted with the familiar problem of the difference between the fancy and the imagination. Of the larger and more potent faculty he certainly possessed a liberal share; no one can read *The House of the Seven Gables* without feeling it to be a deeply imaginative work. But I am often struck, especially in the shorter tales, of which I am now chiefly speaking, with a kind of small ingenuity, a taste for conceits and analogies, which bears more particularly what is called the fanciful stamp. The finer of the shorter tales are redolent of a rich imagination.

> "Had Goodman Brown fallen asleep in the forest and only dreamed a wild dream of witch-meeting? Be it so, if you will; but, alas, it was a dream of evil omen for young Goodman Brown! a stern, a sad, a darkly meditative, a distrustful, if not a desperate, man, did he become from the

night of that fearful dream. On the Sabbath-day, when the congregation were singing a holy psalm, he could not listen, because an anthem of sin rushed loudly upon his ear and drowned all the blessed strain. When the minister spoke from the pulpit, with power and fervid eloquence, and with his hand on the open Bible of the sacred truth of our religion, and of saint-like lives and triumphant deaths, and of future bliss or misery unutterable, then did Goodman Brown grow pale, dreading lest the roof should thunder down upon the gray blasphemer and his hearers. Often, awaking suddenly at midnight, he shrank from the bosom of Faith; and at morning or eventide, when the family knelt down at prayer, he scowled and muttered to himself, and gazed sternly at his wife, and turned away. And when he had lived long, and was borne to his grave a hoary corpse, followed by Faith, an aged woman, and children, and grandchildren, a goodly procession, besides neighbours not a few, they carved no hopeful verse upon his tombstone, for his dying hour was gloom."

There is imagination in that, and in many another passage that I might quote; but as a general thing I should characterise the more metaphysical of our author's short stories as graceful and felicitous conceits. They seem to me to be qualified in this manner by the very fact that they belong to the province of allegory. Hawthorne, in his metaphysical moods, is nothing if not allegorical, and allegory, to my sense, is quite one of the lighter exercises of the imagination. Many excellent judges, I know, have a great stomach for it; they delight in symbols and correspondences, in seeing a story told as if it were another and a very different story. I frankly confess that I have as a general thing but little enjoyment of it and that it has never seemed to me to be, as it were, a first-rate literary form. It has produced assuredly some first-rate works; and Hawthorne in his younger years had been a great reader and devotee of Bunyan and Spenser, the great masters of allegory. But it is apt to spoil two good things—a story and a moral, a meaning and a form; and the taste for it is responsible for a large part of the forcible-feeble writing that has been inflicted upon the world. The only cases in which it is endurable is when it is extremely spontaneous, when the analogy presents itself with eager promptitude. When it shows signs of having been groped and fumbled for, the needful illusion is of course absent and the failure complete. Then the machinery alone is visible, and the end to which it operates becomes a matter of indifference. There was but little literary criticism in the United States at the time Hawthorne's earlier works were published; but among the reviewers Edgar Poe perhaps held the scales the highest. He at any rate rattled them loudest, and pretended, more than any one else, to conduct the weighing-process on scientific principles. Very remarkable was this process of Edgar Poe's, and very extraordinary were his principles; but he had the advantage of being a man of genius, and his intelligence was frequently great. His collection of critical sketches of the American writers flourishing in what M. Taine would call his *milieu* and *moment,* is very curious and interesting reading, and it has one quality which ought to keep it from ever being completely forgotten. It is probably the most complete and exquisite specimen of *provincialism* ever prepared for the edification of men. Poe's judgments are pretentious, spiteful, vulgar; but they contain a great deal of sense and discrimination as well, and here and there, sometimes at frequent intervals, we find a phrase of happy insight imbedded in a patch of the most fatuous pedantry. He wrote a chapter upon Hawthorne, and spoke of him on the whole very kindly; and his estimate is of sufficient value to make it noticeable that he should express lively disapproval of the large part allotted to allegory in his tales—in defence of which, he says, "however, or for whatever object employed, there is scarcely one respectable word to be said. . . . The deepest emotion," he goes on, "aroused within us by the happiest allegory *as* allegory, is a very, *very* imperfectly satisfied sense of the writer's ingenuity in overcoming a difficulty we should have preferred his not having attempted to overcome. . . . One thing is clear, that if allegory ever establishes a fact, it is by dint of overturning a fiction;" and Poe has furthermore the courage to remark that the *Pilgrim's Progress* is a "ludicrously overrated book." Certainly, as a general thing, we are struck with the ingenuity and felicity of Hawthorne's analogies and correspondences; the idea appears to have made itself at home in them easily. Nothing could be better in this respect than *The Snow-Image* (a little masterpiece), or *The Great Carbuncle,* or *Doctor Heidegger's Experiment,* or *Rappaccini's Daughter.* But in such things as *The Birth Mark* and *The Bosom-Serpent,* we are struck with something stiff and mechanical, slightly incongruous, as if the kernel had not assimilated its envelope. But these are matters of light impression, and there would be a want of tact in pretending to discriminate too closely among things which all, in one way or another, have a charm. The charm—the great charm—is that they are glimpses of a great field, of the whole deep mystery of man's soul and conscience. They are moral, and their interest is moral; they deal with something more than the mere accidents and conventionalities, the surface occurrences of life. The fine thing in Hawthorne is that he cared for the deeper psychology, and that, in his way, he tried to become familiar with it. This natural, yet fanciful familiarity with it, this air, on the author's part, of being a confirmed *habitué* of a region of mysteries and subtleties, constitutes the originality of his tales. And then they have the further merit of seeming, for what they are, to spring up so freely and lightly. The author has all the ease, indeed, of a regular dweller in the moral, psychological realm; he goes to and fro in it, as a man who knows his way. His tread is a light and modest one, but he keeps the key in his pocket. . . .

CHAPTER V

. . . The work has the tone of the circumstances in which it was produced. If Hawthorne was in a sombre mood, and if his future was painfully vague, *The Scarlet Letter* contains little enough of gaiety or of hopefulness. It is densely dark, with a single spot of vivid colour in it; and it will probably long remain the most consistently gloomy of English novels of the first order. But I just now called it the author's masterpiece, and I imagine it will continue to be, for other generations than ours, his most substantial title to fame. The subject had probably lain a long time in his mind, as his subjects were apt to do; so that he appears completely to possess it, to know it and feel it. It is simpler and more complete than his other novels; it achieves more perfectly what it attempts, and it has about it that charm, very hard to express, which we find in an artist's work the first time he has touched his highest mark—a sort of straightness and naturalness of execution, an unconsciousness of his public, and freshness of interest in his theme. It was a great success, and he immediately found himself famous. The writer of these lines, who was a child at the time, remembers dimly the sensation the book produced, and the little shudder with which people alluded to it, as if a peculiar horror were mixed with its attractions. He was too young to read it himself, but its title, upon which he fixed his eyes as the book lay upon the table, had a mysterious charm. He had a vague belief indeed that the "letter" in question was one of the documents that come by the post, and it was a source of perpetual wonderment to him that it should be of such an unaccustomed hue. Of course it was difficult to explain to a child the significance of poor Hester Prynne's blood-coloured *A*. But the mystery was at last partly dispelled by his being taken to see a collection of pictures (the annual exhibition of the National Academy), where he encountered a representation of a pale, handsome woman, in a quaint black dress and a

white coif, holding between her knees an elfish-looking little girl, fan-
tastically dressed and crowned with flowers. Embroidered on the
woman's breast was a great crimson *A*, over which the child's fingers,
as she glanced strangely out of the picture, were maliciously playing. I
was told that this was Hester Prynne and little Pearl, and that when I
grew older I might read their interesting history. But the picture remained vividly imprinted on my mind; I had been vaguely frightened
and made uneasy by it; and when, years afterwards, I first read the
novel, I seemed to myself to have read it before, and to be familiar with
its two strange heroines. I mention this incident simply as an indication of the degree to which the success of *The Scarlet Letter* had made
the book what is called an actuality. Hawthorne himself was very
modest about it; he wrote to his publisher, when there was a question
of his undertaking another novel, that what had given the history of
Hester Prynne its "vogue" was simply the introductory chapter. In
fact, the publication of *The Scarlet Letter* was in the United States a
literary event of the first importance. The book was the finest piece of
imaginative writing yet put forth in the country. There was a consciousness of this in the welcome that was given it—a satisfaction in
the idea of America having produced a novel that belonged to literature, and to the forefront of it. Something might at last be sent to
Europe as exquisite in quality as anything that had been received, and
the best of it was that the thing was absolutely American; it belonged to
the soil, to the air; it came out of the very heart of New England.

It is beautiful, admirable, extraordinary; it has in the highest
degree that merit which I have spoken of as the mark of Hawthorne's
best things—an indefinable purity and lightness of conception, a quality which in a work of art affects one in the same way as the absence of
grossness does in a human being. His fancy, as I just now said, had
evidently brooded over the subject for a long time; the situation to be
represented had disclosed itself to him in all its phases. When I say in
all its phases, the sentence demands modification; for it is to be remembered that if Hawthorne laid his hand upon the well-worn theme,
upon the familiar combination of the wife, the lover, and the husband,
it was after all but to one period of the history of these three persons
that he attached himself. The situation is the situation after the woman's fault has been committed, and the current of expiation and repen-
tance has set in. In spite of the relation between Hester Prynne and
Arthur Dimmesdale, no story of love was surely ever less of a "love
story." To Hawthorne's imagination the fact that these two persons
had loved each other too well was of an interest comparatively vulgar;
what appealed to him was the idea of their moral situation in the long

years that were to follow. The story indeed is in a secondary degree that of Hester Prynne; she becomes, really, after the first scene, an accessory figure; it is not upon her the *dénoûment* depends. It is upon her guilty lover that the author projects most frequently the cold, thin rays of his fitfully-moving lantern, which makes here and there a little luminous circle, on the edge of which hovers the livid and sinister figure of the injured and retributive husband. The story goes on for the most part between the lover and the husband—the tormented young Puritan minister, who carries the secret of his own lapse from pastoral purity locked up beneath an exterior that commends itself to the reverence of his flock, while he sees the softer partner of his guilt standing in the full glare of exposure and humbling herself to the misery of atonement—between this more wretched and pitiable culprit, to whom dishonour would come as a comfort and the pillory as a relief, and the older, keener, wiser man, who, to obtain satisfaction for the wrong he has suffered, devises the infernally ingenious plan of conjoining himself with his wronger, living with him, living upon him, and while he pretends to minister to his hidden ailment and to sympathise with his pain, revels in his unsuspected knowledge of these things and stimulates them by malignant arts. The attitude of Roger Chillingworth, and the means he takes to compensate himself—these are the highly original elements in the situation that Hawthorne so ingeniously treats. None of his works are so impregnated with the after-sense of the old Puritan consciousness of life to which allusion has so often been made. If, as M. Montégut says, the qualities of his ancestors *filtered* down through generations into his composition, *The Scarlet Letter* was, as it were, the vessel that gathered up the last of the precious drops. And I say this not because the story happens to be of so-called historical cast, to be told of the early days of Massachusetts and of people in steeple-crowned hats and sad-coloured garments. The historical colouring is rather weak than otherwise; there is little elaboration of detail, of the modern realism of research; and the author has made no great point of causing his figures to speak the English of their period. Nevertheless, the book is full of the moral presence of the race that invented Hester's penance—diluted and complicated with other things, but still perfectly recognisable. Puritanism, in a word, is there, not only objectively, as Hawthorne tried to place it there, but subjectively as well. Not, I mean, in his judgment of his characters, in any harshness of prejudice, or in the obtrusion of a moral lesson; but in the very quality of his own vision, in the tone of the picture, in a certain coldness and exclusiveness of treatment.

The faults of the book are, to my sense, a want of reality and an abuse of the fanciful element—of a certain superficial symbolism. The people strike me not as characters, but as representatives, very picturesquely arranged, of a single state of mind; and the interest of the story lies, not in them, but in the situation, which is insistently kept before us, with little progression, though with a great deal, as I have said, of a certain stable variation; and to which they, out of their reality, contribute little that helps it to live and move. I was made to feel this want of reality, this over-ingenuity, of *The Scarlet Letter*, by chancing not long since upon a novel which was read fifty years ago much more than today, but which is still worth reading—the story of *Adam Blair*, by John Gibson Lockhart. This interesting and powerful little tale has a great deal of analogy with Hawthorne's novel—quite enough, at least, to suggest a comparison between them; and the comparison is a very interesting one to make, for it speedily leads us to larger considerations than simple resemblances and divergences of plot.

Adam Blair, like Arthur Dimmesdale, is a Calvinistic minister who becomes the lover of a married woman, is overwhelmed with remorse at his misdeed, and makes a public confession of it; then expiates it by resigning his pastoral office and becoming a humble tiller of the soil, as his father had been. The two stories are of about the same length, and each is the masterpiece (putting aside of course, as far as Lockhart is concerned, the *Life of Scott*) of the author. They deal alike with the manners of a rigidly theological society, and even in certain details they correspond. In each of them, between the guilty pair, there is a charming little girl; though I hasten to say that Sarah Blair (who is not the daughter of the heroine but the legitimate offspring of the hero, a widower) is far from being as brilliant and graceful an apparition as the admirable little Pearl of *The Scarlet Letter*. The main difference between the two tales is the fact that in the American story the husband plays an all-important part, and in the Scottish plays almost none at all. *Adam Blair* is the history of the passion, and *The Scarlet Letter* the history of its sequel; but nevertheless, if one has read the two books at a short interval, it is impossible to avoid confronting them. I confess that a large portion of the interest of *Adam Blair*, to my mind, when once I had perceived that it would repeat in a great measure the situation of *The Scarlet Letter*, lay in noting its difference of tone. It threw into relief the passionless quality of Hawthorne's novel, its element of cold and ingenious fantasy, its elaborate imaginative delicacy. These things do not precisely constitute a weakness in *The Scarlet Letter*; indeed, in a certain way they constitute a great strength; but the absence of a certain something warm and straightforward, a trifle more grossly human and vulgarly natural,

119

which one finds in *Adam Blair*, will always make Hawthorne's tale less touching to a large number of even very intelligent readers, than a love-story told with the robust, synthetic pathos which served Lockhart so well. His novel is not of the first rank (I should call it an excellent second-rate one), but it borrows a charm from the fact that his vigorous, but not strongly imaginative, mind was impregnated with the reality of his subject. He did not always succeed in rendering this reality; the expression is sometimes awkward and poor. But the reader feels that his vision was clear, and his feeling about the matter very strong and rich. Hawthorne's imagination, on the other hand, plays with his theme so incessantly, leads it such a dance through the moon-lighted air of his intellect, that the thing cools off, as it were, hardens and stiffens, and, producing effects much more exquisite, leaves the reader with a sense of having handled a splendid piece of silversmith's work. Lockhart, by means much more vulgar, produces at moments a greater illusion, and satisfies our inevitable desire for something, in the people in whom it is sought to interest us, that shall be of the same pitch and the same continuity with ourselves. Above all, it is interesting to see how the same subject appears to two men of a thoroughly different cast of mind and of a different race. Lockhart was struck with the warmth of the subject that offered itself to him, and Hawthorne with its coldness; the one with its glow, its sentimental interest—the other with its shadow, its moral interest. Lockhart's story is as decent, as severely draped, as *The Scarlet Letter;* but the author has a more vivid sense than appears to have imposed itself upon Hawthorne, of some of the incidents of the situation he describes; his tempted man and tempting woman are more actual and personal; his heroine in especial, though not in the least a delicate or a subtle conception, has a sort of credible, visible, palpable property, a vulgar roundness and relief, which are lacking to the dim and chastened image of Hester Prynne. But I am going too far; I am comparing simplicity with subtlety, the usual with the refined. Each man wrote as his turn of mind impelled him, but each expressed something more than himself. Lockhart was a dense, substantial Briton, with a taste for the concrete, and Hawthorne was a thin New Englander, with a miasmatic conscience.

In *The Scarlet Letter* there is a great deal of symbolism; there is, I think, too much. It is overdone at times, and becomes mechanical; it ceases to be impressive, and grazes triviality. The idea of the mystic *A* which the young minister finds imprinted upon his breast and eating into his flesh, in sympathy with the embroidered badge that Hester is condemned to wear, appears to me to be a case in point. This suggestion should, I think, have been just made and dropped; to insist upon it and return to it, is to exaggerate the weak side of the subject. Hawthorne returns to it constantly, plays with it, and seems charmed by it; until at last the reader feels tempted to declare that his enjoyment of it is puerile. In the admirable scene, so superbly conceived and beautifully executed, in which Mr. Dimmesdale, in the stillness of the night, in the middle of the sleeping town, feels impelled to go and stand upon the scaffold where his mistress had formerly enacted her dreadful penance, and then, seeing Hester pass along the street, from watching at a sick-bed, with little Pearl at her side, calls them both to come and stand there beside him—in this masterly episode the effect is almost spoiled by the introduction of one of these superficial conceits. What leads up to it is very fine—so fine that I cannot do better than quote it as a specimen of one of the striking pages of the book.

> "But before Mr. Dimmesdale had done speaking, a light gleamed far and wide over all the muffled sky. It was doubtless caused by one of those meteors which the night-watcher may so often observe burning out to waste in the vacant regions of the atmosphere. So powerful was its radiance that it thoroughly illuminated the dense medium of cloud, betwixt the sky and earth. The great vault brightened, like the dome of an immense lamp. It showed the familiar scene of the street with the distinctness of mid-day, but also with the awfulness that is always imparted to familiar objects by an unaccustomed light. The wooden houses, with their jutting stories and quaint gable-peaks; the doorsteps and thresholds, with the early grass springing up about them; the garden-plots, black with freshly-turned earth; the wheel-track, little worn, and, even in the market-place, margined with green on either side;—all were visible, but with a singularity of aspect that seemed to give another moral interpretation to the things of this world than they had ever borne before. And there stood the minister, with his hand over his heart; and Hester Prynne, with the embroidered letter glimmering on her bosom; and little Pearl, herself a symbol, and the connecting-link between these two. They stood in the noon of that strange and solemn splendour, as if it were the light that is to reveal all secrets, and the daybreak that shall unite all that belong to one another."

That is imaginative, impressive, poetic; but when, almost immediately afterwards, the author goes on to say that "the minister looking upward to the zenith, beheld there the appearance of an immense letter—the letter *A*—marked out in lines of dull red light," we feel that he goes too far and is in danger of crossing the line that separates the sublime from its intimate neighbour. We are tempted to say that this is not moral tragedy, but physical comedy. In the same way, too much is made of the intimation that Hester's badge had a scorching property, and that if one touched it one would immediately withdraw one's hand. Hawthorne is perpetually looking for images which shall place themselves in picturesque correspondence with the spiritual facts with which he is concerned, and of course the search is of the very essence of poetry. But in such a process discretion is everything, and when the image becomes importunate it is in danger of seeming to stand for nothing more serious than itself. When Hester meets the minister by appointment in the forest, and sits talking with him while little Pearl wanders away and plays by the edge of the brook, the child is represented as at last making her way over to the other side of the woodland stream, and disporting herself there in a manner which makes her mother feel herself "in some indistinct and tantalising manner, estranged from Pearl; as if the child, in her lonely ramble through the forest, had strayed out of the sphere in which she and her mother dwelt together, and was now vainly seeking to return to it." And Hawthorne devotes a chapter to this idea of the child's having, by putting the brook between Hester and herself, established a kind of spiritual gulf, on the verge of which her little fantastic person innocently mocks at her mother's sense of bereavement. This conception belongs, one would say, quite to the lighter order of a storyteller's devices, and the reader hardly goes with Hawthorne in the large development he gives to it. He hardly goes with him either, I think, in his extreme predilection for a small number of vague ideas which are represented by such terms as "sphere" and "sympathies." Hawthorne makes too liberal a use of these two substantives; it is the solitary defect of his style; and it counts as a defect partly because the words in question are a sort of specialty with certain writers immeasurably inferior to himself.

I had not meant, however, to expatiate upon his defects, which are of the slenderest and most venial kind. *The Scarlet Letter* has the beauty and harmony of all original and complete conceptions, and its weaker spots, whatever they are, are not of its essence; they are mere light flaws and inequalities of surface. One can often return to it; it supports familiarity and has the inexhaustible charm and mystery of great works of art. It is admirably written. Hawthorne afterwards polished his style to a still higher degree, but in his later productions—it is almost always the case in a writer's later productions—there is a touch of mannerism. In *The Scarlet Letter* there is a high degree of polish, and at the same time a charming freshness; his phrase is less conscious of itself. His biographer very justly calls attention to the fact that his style was excellent from the beginning; that he appeared to have passed through no phase of learning how to write, but was in possession of his means from the first of his handling a pen. His early tales, perhaps, were not of a character to subject his faculty of expression to a very severe test, but a man who had not Hawthorne's natural sense of language would certainly have contrived to write them less well. This natural sense of language—this turn for saying things lightly and yet touchingly, picturesquely yet simply, and for infusing a gently colloquial tone into matter of the most unfamiliar import, he had evidently cultivated with great assiduity. I have spoken of the anomalous character of his Note-Books—of his going to such pains often to make a record of incidents which either were not worth remembering or could be easily remembered without its aid. But it helps us to understand the Note-Books if we regard them as a literary exercise. They were compositions, as school boys say, in which the subject was only the pretext, and the main point was to write a certain amount of excellent English. Hawthorne must at least have written a great many of these things for practice, and he must often have said to himself that it was better practice to write about trifles, because it was a greater tax upon one's skill to make them interesting. And his theory was just, for he has almost always made his trifles interesting. In his novels his art of saying things well is very positively tested, for here he treats of those matters among which it is very easy for a blundering writer to go wrong—the subtleties and mysteries of life, the moral and spiritual maze. In such a passage as one I have marked for quotation from *The Scarlet Letter* there is the stamp of the genius of style.

> "Hester Prynne, gazing steadfastly at the clergyman, felt a dreary influence come over her, but wherefore or whence she knew not, unless that he seemed so remote from her own sphere and utterly beyond her reach. One glance of recognition she had imagined must needs pass between them. She thought of the dim forest with its little dell of solitude, and love, and anguish, and the mossy tree-trunk, where, sitting hand in hand, they had mingled their sad and passionate talk with the melancholy murmur of the brook. How deeply had they known each other then! And was this the man? She hardly knew him now! He, moving

123

proudly past, enveloped as it were in the rich music, with the procession of majestic and venerable fathers; he, so unattainable in his worldly position, and still more so in that far vista in his unsympathising thoughts, through which she now beheld him! Her spirit sank with the idea that all must have been a delusion, and that vividly as she had dreamed it, there could be no real bond betwixt the clergyman and herself. And thus much of woman there was in Hester, that she could scarcely forgive him—least of all now, when the heavy footstep of their approaching fate might be heard, nearer, nearer, nearer!—for being able to withdraw himself so completely from their mutual world, while she groped darkly, and stretched forth her cold hands, and found him not!"

CHAPTER VII

. . . He was a beautiful, natural, original genius, and his life had been singularly exempt from worldly preoccupations and vulgar efforts. It had been as pure, as simple, as unsophisticated, as his work. He had lived primarily in his domestic affections, which were of the tenderest kind; and then—without eagerness, without pretension, but with a great deal of quiet devotion—in his charming art. His work will remain; it is too original and exquisite to pass away; among the men of imagination he will always have his niche. No one has had just that vision of life, and no one has had a literary form that more successfully expressed his vision. He was not a moralist, and he was not simply a poet. The moralists are weightier, denser, richer, in a sense; the poets are more purely inconclusive and irresponsible. He combined in a singular degree the spontaneity of the imagination with a haunting care for moral problems. Man's conscience was his theme, but he saw it in the light of a creative fancy which added, out of its own substance, an interest, and, I may almost say, an importance.

In October of 1878, John Morley invited James to contribute a book on either Irving or Hawthorne to the distinguished English Men of Letters Series (other contributors included Anthony Trollope, Leslie Stephen, Edmund Gosse, and J. A. Symonds). *Hawthorne* was begun during the summer of 1879 in London at 3 Bolton Street and finished that September in Paris at 42 Rue de Luxembourg.

Edel calls 1879 one of "the two great years of Henry James's descent upon and conquest of London" (2:328). This conquest was both social and literary. Winter 1878-79 was the season in which, notoriously, James dined out 140 times. Yet his literary production was substantial. In 1879, James wrote "The Pension Beaurepas," "The Diary of a Man of Fifty," "A Bundle of Letters," *Confidence,* and *Hawthorne.* After "An International Episode" was published in America, James collected this and a number of his other tales for publication in England, as well as bringing out English editions of *The American* and, after a full revision, *Roderick Hudson.*

In a letter honoring Hawthorne's centenary in 1904, James pronounced the American novelist "a Classic." This made Hawthorne a unique literary example for James, one which proved "that an American could be an artist, one of the finest, without 'going outside' about it, as I liked to say; quite in fact as if Hawthorne had become one just by being American *enough,* by the felicity of how the artist in him missed nothing, suspected nothing, that the ambient air didn't affect him as containing" (*A,* 480). Although Hawthorne's was an example that James, who did go "outside," could not wholeheartedly follow, its importance to James' writing was recognized early. On January 19, 1870, William James wrote to Henry of the "resemblance of Hawthorne's style to yours and Howells's." Henry replied on February 13, "I'm glad you've been liking Hawthorne. But I mean to write as good a novel one of these days (perhaps) as the House of the Seven Gables." In an article on "Henry James, Jr.," *Century* 3 (November 1882): 25–29, Howells, praising the "new school" of fiction of which James was the "chief exemplar," traced its origins to Hawthorne and George Eliot. Critics have continued to discover Hawthorne's presence in James' work, not only when James remains "inside" and describes New England or New Englanders, but also when he employs elements of romance and the supernatural in his early tales and intricate symbolism in his late novels. (It is generally agreed that, with the exception of *The Bostonians,* and, for some, *The Portrait of a Lady,* Hawthorne's influence is weakest in James' middle period.) Further, T. S. Eliot's 1918 list of the Hawthornian concerns that James shared—"The interest in the 'deeper psychology,' the observation, and the sense for situation"—was a program for many of the studies that followed ("On Henry James," *The Little Review* 5 [August 1918], rpt. in *The Question of Henry James*, ed. Dupee, [New York: Henry Holt, 1945]). On Hawthorne and James see Babiiha's bibliography, *The James-Hawthorne Relation* (Boston: G. K. Hall, 1980), which covers the scholarship through 1975. Studies since then include: Long, *The Great Succession: Henry James and the Legacy of Hawthorne* (Pittsburgh: University of Pittsburgh Press, 1979); Rowe, "What the Thunder Said: James's *Hawthorne* and the American Anxiety of Influence: A Centennial Essay," *Henry James Review* 4 (1983): 81–119; Waggoner, *The Presence of Hawthorne* (Baton Rouge: Louisiana State University Press, 1979).

Hawthorne, the only full-length literary biography that James wrote, is the most substantial of his four pieces on the American novelist. Although James says explicitly that the book is in "the form rather of a critical essay than of a biography," its implicit argument is that Hawthorne's work must be read in the context of his milieu. This is an argument that James makes again in his article for the *Library of the World's Best Literature* in 1896, when he calls Hawthorne's stories "products of the dry New England air," and in the 1904 letter, which identifies Hawthorne throughout as a product of Salem (where the centenary proceedings took place).

Hawthorne's fiction mirrors his world, not by recreating it in a novel of manners, but by the way it "savours thoroughly of the local soil—it is redolent of the social system in which he had his being." James relishes this New England flavor, yet his tone is often condescending. Hawthorne, the product of a "small and homogeneous society, in a provincial, rural community" is himself labeled "provincial," "childlike," "natural," and "poor" throughout the book. As James' own distance from the American soil becomes more firmly established, these belittling labels disappear from his descriptions of his American predecessor. Late in life James recalls that, despite the fact that he had read Hawthorne since childhood, it was only on the day of the earlier writer's death that he took in "for the first time and at one straight draught the full sweet sense of our one fine romancer's work" (*A*, 478).

Hawthorne also examines how the writer reflects his environment by reacting to it. In the absence of a rich history and social hierarchy, Hawthorne discovered that "[T]he individual counts for more" and focused on "the deeper psychology. . . ." James explores this psychological penetration further in 1896 when he argues that Hawthorne pierced beneath the surface of the "common tasks and small conditions" of New England and saw "the pressing moral anxiety, the restless individual conscience . . . taking for granted, on the part of the society about him, a life of the spirit more complex than anything that met the mere eye of sense." And in the centenary letter, James says that, faced with "the blissfully homogeneous community" of Salem, "[W]hat was admirable and instinctive in Hawthorne was that he saw the quaintness or the weirdness, the interest *behind* the interest . . . saw it as something deeply within us. . . ."

Not only does Hawthorne go behind and beneath the thin surface of American life, but he also goes above it, to romance and allegory. James' judgment of this imaginative ascent changes with time. In 1879, when the French Realists are his literary models, he is critical of Hawthorne's departures from their program for the novel. "The historical colouring [in *The Scarlet Letter*] is rather weak than otherwise; there is little elaboration of detail, of the modern realism of research; and the author has made no great point of causing his figures to speak the English of their period." By 1896 James is an experienced novelist who feels free to praise "Hawthorne's distinguished mark,— that feeling for the latent romance of New England. . . ." And in 1904 he can say that the very value of *The Blithedale Romance* comes from Hawthorne's ability to make the real romantic: "The book takes up the parti-colored, angular, audible, traceable Real, the New England earnest, aspiring reforming Real, scattered in a few frame houses over a few stony fields, and so invests and colors it, makes it rich and strange—and simply by finding a felicitous *tone* for it—that its characters and images remain for us curious winged creatures preserved in the purest amber of the imagination." (On realism vs. romance, see the Preface to *The American*, Chapter 12).

Hawthorne's imaginative reaction to his environment also explains why he is not a *"romancier pessimiste."* Although James describes Hawthorne repeatedly as "dusky," he insists that Hawthorne is not a gloomy, guilt-ridden Puritan. Hawthorne's fancy transmutes his Puritan heritage: "Nothing is more curious and interesting than this almost exclusively *imported* character of the sense of sin in Hawthorne's mind; it seems to exist there merely for an artistic or literary purpose." The argument that Hawthorne's darkness was artistic rather than personal receives less emphasis in James' later writings, yet he continues to describe Hawthorne as aloof and lighthearted. "But of all cynics he was the brightest and kindest, and the subtleties he spun are mere silken threads for stringing polished beads. His collection of moral mysteries is the cabinet of a dilettante" (1896).

James' mixture of praise and condescension has been the major topic for *Hawthorne's* critics. Most have accounted for James' ambivalence by pointing to his own ambiguous position at the time: an American writer, just in the process of establishing himself in England, introducing his American literary predecessor to the British public. James' contemporary reviewers reflected this split. Favorably, if not enthusiastically, received in England, *Hawthorne,* following so closely upon "Daisy Miller," convinced some American critics that James had forsaken and betrayed his native land. There was American praise for *Hawthorne,* but Howells' protest (*Atlantic* 4–5 [February 1880]: 282–85) at James' characterization of Hawthorne as "provincial" and culturally deprived was a mild example of the common indignation. In writing to Howells on January 31, 1880, James admitted he had overused the word "provincial," but maintained that America lacked the conditions conducive to great fiction: "I sympathize even less with your protest against the idea that it takes an old civilization to set a novelist in motion—a proposition that strikes me so true as to be a truism. It is on manners, customs, usages, habits, forms, upon all these things matured and established, that a novelist lives—they are the very stuff his work is made of. . . ." (See Vol. 2 of the *Letters* for other correspondence on *Hawthorne.*) For reviews of *Hawthorne* by James' British contemporaries, see: *Athenaeum* (January 3, 1880): 14; "Mr. James's Life of Hawthorne," *Spectator* 53 (January 3, 1880), 18; "James's Hawthorne," *Saturday Review,* 49 (January 10, 1880): 59–61; Saintsbury, *Academy* 17 (January 17, 1880): 40–41; *National Repository* 7 (March 1880): 283. American reviews include: *Nation* 30 (January 29, 1880): 80–81; Howells, "James's *Hawthorne,*" *Atlantic* 4–5 (February 1880): 282–85; *Christian Union* 21 (February 11, 1880): 133–34; Foxcroft, *Literary World* 11 (February 14, 1880): 51–53; *Independent* 32 (February 26, 1880): 12; *Appleton's,* n.s., 8 (March 1880): 282–84; *Eclectic,* n.s., 31 (March 1880): 378–79; *Harper's* 60 (March 1880): 633; *Lippincott's* 25 (March 1880): 388–91; Perry, *International Review* 8 (April 1880): 447–50; *Scribner's* 19 (April 1880): 943–44; *Churchman* 41 (April 24, 1880): 462.

Although few go so far as Waggoner, who claims that "the book . . . tells us . . . rather more about James than it does about Hawthorne," many twentieth-century critics have studied James through *Hawthorne,* reading it as James' attempt to outline a program for himself as an American writer. Twentieth-century critics have also addressed what Trilling called the difference between "James's ironical entertainer . . . a graceful and charming figure" and "our modern Hawthorne, our dark poet, charged with chthonic knowledge." For later commentary, again, see Babiiha, as well as Daugherty, pp.

94–101; Edel (2:386–91); Trilling, "Hawthorne in Our Time," in *Beyond Culture* (New York: Viking Press, 1965) (originally "Our Hawthorne," in *Hawthorne Centenary Essays,* ed. Roy Harvey Pearce [Columbus: Ohio State University Press, 1964]).

For information on Hawthorne's life, see Turner, *Nathaniel Hawthorne: A Biography* (New York: Oxford University Press, 1980). For information on the Hawthorne works discussed by James, see *The Centenary Edition of the Works of Nathaniel Hawthorne,* 14 vols. to date, ed. Charvat, Pearce, Simpson (Columbus: Ohio State University Press) and *English Notebooks,* ed. Steward (1941; rpt., New York: Russell and Russell, 1962).

NOTES

101:3. the data for a life of Nathaniel Hawthorne. James took virtually all of his information about Hawthorne's life from George Parson Lathrop's recently published *A Study of Hawthorne* (1876). Though he acknowledges Lathrop's work in a note, saying "without the help afforded by his elaborate essay the present little volume could not have been prepared," in a letter to Thomas Sargent Perry on September 14, 1879, James calls Lathrop's book a "singularly foolish pretentious little volume" and goes on to say "The amount of a certain sort of emasculate twaddle produced in the United States is not encouraging."

101:9. six volumes of Note-Books. *Passages from the American Notebooks of Nathaniel Hawthorne* 2 vols. (1868), *Passages from the English Notebooks of Nathaniel Hawthorne* 2 vols. (1870), *Passages from the French and Italian Notebooks of Nathaniel Hawthorne* 2 vols. (1872). James reviewed the last of these for the *Nation* (See Bibliography, part 4).

101:17. four novels . . . a couple of story-books. James either miscounts Hawthorne's novels or discounts *Fanshawe* (1828). The others are *The Scarlet Letter* (1850), *The House of the Seven Gables* (1851), *The Blithedale Romance* (1852), *The Marble Faun* (1860). There are four major fragments: *Septimius Felton: or, The Elixir of Life* (1872), *The Dolliver Romance and Other Pieces* (1876), *Doctor Grimshawe's Secret* (1883), *The Ancestral Footstep* (1883). James apparently knew of the first two. Hawthorne's tales were collected as *Twice-Told Tales* (1837 and 1842), *Mosses from an Old Manse* (1846), *The Snow Image and Other Thrice-Told Tales* (1851). His sketches of England appeared as *Our Old Home* (1863). The books for children are *Grandfather's Chair* (1841), *Famous Old People* (1841), *Liberty Tree* (1841), *Biographical Stories for Children* (1842), *True Stories from History and Biography* (1851), *A Wonder Book for Boys and Girls* (1851), *Tanglewood Tales for Boys and Girls* (1853).

103:10. Balzac and some of his descendants testify. On "the manners and morals of the French people, see "Honoré de Balzac," "Guy de Maupassant," and "Emile Zola," Chapters 4, 8, and 20.

103:12. guiltless of a system. For James' comparable praise of Saint-Beuve as a distinctly literary—as opposed to a philosophical—talent, see our commentary to "Saint-Beuve."

103:26. *The Biglow Papers* (1848, first series; 1867, second series) by James Russell Lowell (1819–91) were topical, political satires written in New England dialect. Lowell used the voice of the "Yankee of comedy" that James refers to above, a stock figure in American humorous writing, originating with Seba Smith's *Letters of Major Jack Downing,* which began appearing in the *Portland Courier* in 1830.

103:29. savours thoroughly of the local soil. Despite the distinction James draws between Hawthorne and Balzac, he uses similar language to describe the French writer in "Honoré de Balzac," p. 63. In addition, James' praise of the way Hawthorne seems "completely to possess" the subject of *The Scarlet Letter* is echoed in 1905 when James says of Balzac: "They [failures of execution] never come back to that fault in the artist, in the novelist, that amounts most completely to a failure of dignity, the absence of saturation with his idea. . . . There is never in Balzac that damning interference which consists of the painter's not seeing, not possessing, his image" ("The Lesson of Balzac").

103:32. The twelve years that followed. The preceding chapter ends: "On leaving college Hawthorne had gone back to live at Salem."

105:24. "in business." In *Washington Square* (chap. 1) James describes America as "a country in which, to play a social part, you must either earn your income or make believe that you earn it. . . ." Also see note for 272:23, Preface to *The American.*

106:2. solitary workers. For James' concern with creating a community of writers and readers, see our commentaries to "The Art of Fiction," the Prefaces, and "The Novel in *The Ring and the Book,*" Chapters 7, 19, and 21.

106:37. lawyers' offices. For the close connection of legal and literary careers in America, see Ferguson, *Law and Letters in American Culture* (Cambridge: Harvard University Press, 1984).

108:7. The 1860 Hawthorne novel published in America as *The Marble Faun: A Romance of Monte Beni* was titled *Transformation; or the Romance of Monte Beni* in the English edition.

108:18. an American reads. On the differences between British and American readers, see James' reviews of Matthew Arnold's *Essays in Criticism* (p. 11) and George Eliot's *Middlemarch* (p. 54).

108:36. later in life. Hawthorne held the American consulship at Liverpool from July 1853 to February 1857. He remained in Europe until June 1860.

109:8. No State . . . Ascot!. This famous passage appears nearly verbatim in the February 21, 1879, entry in James' *Notebooks* as part of an idea for a story. As Edel (2: 388) has noted, the *Hawthorne* lines are a variation on the passage from Hawthorne's own preface to *The Marble Faun* that James quotes above. On the artistic thinness of America, see also the Prefaces to *Roderick Hudson* and *The Aspern Papers,* Chapters 11 and 16.

110:29. An Englishman, a Frenchman . . . judges quickly. In *The Europeans* (chap. 7), James characterizes the difference between how the "European" Felix and the American Mr. Wentworth judge others: "Felix had a confident, gaily trenchant way of judging human actions which Mr. Wentworth grew little by little to envy; it seemed like criticism made easy. Forming an opinion—say on a person's conduct—was with Mr. Wentworth a good deal like fumbling in a lock with a key chosen at hazard."

111:6. his volume on England. *Our Old Home: A Series of Sketches* (1863). This was a collection of previously published essays, but Hawthorne thoroughly rewrote his 1857 "Uttoxeter" into "Lichfield and Uttoxeter" for the volume.

112:20. *"Un Romancier Pessimiste en Amerique,"* which appeared in the August 1, 1860, issue of *Revue des Deux Mondes,* was a review of *Transformation.* In a letter to his sister on February 22, 1876, James described the critic and translator, Emile Montégut (1825–95), as "a Frenchman of the intense, unhumorous type, *abondant dans son propre sens* and spinning out his shallow ingeniosities with a complacency to make the angels howl. He is a case of the writer in the flesh killing one's mental image of him." James' insistence throughout the biography that Hawthorne is not a "romancier pessimiste" is somewhat balanced by his recognition of darkness as a *topic* in the fiction, a recognition that informs his famous observation that "Emerson, as a sort of spiritual sun-worshipper, could have attached but a moderate value to Hawthorne's cat-like faculty of seeing in the dark."

115:1. Edgar Allan Poe's review of *Twice-Told Tales,* from which James quotes below, first appeared in *Graham's Magazine,* May 1842.

115:8. Hippolyte Adolphe Taine (1828–93), French critic. See Bibliography, part 3.

116:11. The work. *The Scarlet Letter.*

116:38. The National Academy of Design, founded in 1825 as the New York Drawing Society and located in Manhattan, showed primarily works by living American painters.

119:10. *Some Passages in the Life of Mr. Adam Blair, Minister at the Gospel of Cross-Meikle* (1822) by John Gibson Lockhart (1794–1854), British man of letters. James rates his biography of Scott (alluded to below) with Boswell's *Life of Johnson,* in "Honoré de Balzac," p. 59.

S I X
Ivan Turgénieff

WHEN THE MORTAL REMAINS OF IVAN TURGÉNIEFF
were about to be transported from Paris for interment in his
own country, a short commemorative service was held at the Gare du
Nord. Ernest Renan and Edmond About, standing beside the train in
which his coffin had been placed, bade farewell in the name of the
French people to the illustrious stranger who for so many years had
been their honoured and grateful guest. M. Renan made a beautiful
speech, and M. About a very clever one, and each of them characterised, with ingenuity, the genius and the moral nature of the most
touching of writers, the most lovable of men. "Turgénieff," said M.
Renan, "received by the mysterious decree which marks out human
vocations the gift which is noble beyond all others: he was born essentially impersonal." The passage is so eloquent that one must repeat the whole of it. "His conscience was not that of an individual to
whom nature had been more or less generous: it was in some sort the
conscience of a people. Before he was born he had lived for thousands of years; infinite successions of reveries had amassed themselves in the depths of his heart. No man has been as much as he the
incarnation of a whole race: generations of ancestors, lost in the sleep
of centuries, speechless, came through him to life and utterance."

I quote these lines for the pleasure of quoting them; for while I
see what M. Renan means by calling Turgénieff impersonal, it has
been my wish to devote to his delightful memory a few pages written
under the impression of contact and intercourse. He seems to us impersonal, because it is from his writings almost alone that we of English, French and German speech have derived our notions—even
yet, I fear, rather meagre and erroneous—of the Russian people. His
genius for us is the Slav genius; his voice the voice of those vaguely-
imagined multitudes whom we think of more and more to-day as
waiting their turn, in the arena of civilisation, in the grey expanses of
the North. There is much in his writings to encourage this view, and

132

it is certain that he interpreted with wonderful vividness the temperament of his fellow-countrymen. Cosmopolite that he had become by the force of circumstances, his roots had never been loosened in his native soil. The ignorance with regard to Russia and the Russians which he found in abundance in the rest of Europe—and not least in the country he inhabited for ten years before his death—had indeed the effect, to a certain degree, to throw him back upon the deep feelings which so many of his companions were unable to share with him, the memories of his early years, the sense of wide Russian horizons, the joy and pride of his mother-tongue. In the collection of short pieces, so deeply interesting, written during the last few years of his life, and translated into German under the name of *Senilia*, I find a passage—it is the last in the little book—which illustrates perfectly this reactionary impulse: "In days of doubt, in days of anxious thought on the destiny of my native land, thou alone art my support and my staff, O great powerful Russian tongue, truthful and free! If it were not for thee how should man not despair at the sight of what is going on at home? But it is inconceivable that such a language has not been given to a great people." This Muscovite, home-loving note pervades his productions, though it is between the lines, as it were, that we must listen for it. None the less does it remain true that he was not a simple conduit or mouthpiece; the inspiration was his own as well as the voice. He was an individual, in other words, of the most unmistakable kind, and those who had the happiness to know him have no difficulty to-day in thinking of him as an eminent, responsible figure. This pleasure, for the writer of these lines, was as great as the pleasure of reading the admirable tales into which he put such a world of life and feeling: it was perhaps even greater, for it was not only with the pen that nature had given Turgénieff the power to express himself. He was the richest, the most delightful, of talkers, and his face, his person, his temper, the thoroughness with which he had been equipped for human intercourse, make in the memory of his friends an image which is completed, but not thrown into the shade, by his literary distinction. The whole image is tinted with sadness: partly because the element of melancholy in his nature was deep and constant—readers of his novels have no need to be told of that; and partly because, during the last years of his life, he had been condemned to suffer atrociously. Intolerable pain had been his portion for too many months before he died; his end was not a soft decline, but a deepening distress. But of brightness, of the faculty of enjoyment, he had also the large allowance usually made to first-rate men, and he was a singularly complete human being. The author of these pages had greatly admired his writings before having the fortune to make his acquaintance, and this privilege, when it presented itself, was highly illuminating. The man and the writer together occupied from that moment a very high place in his affection. Some time before knowing him I committed to print certain reflections which his tales had led me to make; and I may perhaps, therefore, without impropriety give them a supplement which shall have a more vivifying reference. It is almost irresistible to attempt to say, from one's own point of view, what manner of man he was.

It was in consequence of the article I just mentioned that I found reason to meet him, in Paris, where he was then living, in 1875. I shall never forget the impression he made upon me at that first interview. I found him adorable; I could scarcely believe that he would prove—that any man could prove—on nearer acquaintance so delightful as that. Nearer acquaintance only confirmed my hope, and he remained the most approachable, the most practicable, the least unsafe man of genius it has been my fortune to meet. He was so simple, so natural, so modest, so destitute of personal pretension and of what is called the consciousness of powers, that one almost doubted at moments whether he were a man of genius after all. Everything good and fruitful lay near to him; he was interested in everything; and he was absolutely without that eagerness of self-reference which sometimes accompanies great, and even small, reputations. He had not a particle of vanity; nothing whatever of the air of having a part to play or a reputation to keep up. His humour exercised itself as freely upon himself as upon other subjects, and he told stories at his own expense with a sweetness of hilarity which made his peculiarities really sacred in the eyes of a friend. I remember vividly the smile and tone of voice with which he once repeated to me a figurative epithet which Gustave Flaubert (of whom he was extremely fond) had applied to him— an epithet intended to characterise a certain expansive softness, a comprehensive indecision, which pervaded his nature, just as it pervades so many of the characters he has painted. He enjoyed Flaubert's use of this term, good-naturedly opprobrious, more even than Flaubert himself, and recognised perfectly the element of truth in it. He was natural to an extraordinary degree; I do not think I have ever seen his match in this respect, certainly not among people who bear, as he did, at the same time, the stamp of the highest cultivation. Like all men of a large pattern, he was composed of many different pieces; and what was always striking in him was the mixture of simplicity with the fruit of the most various observation. In the little article in which I had attempted to express my admiration for his works, I had been moved to say of him that he had the aristocratic temperament: a remark which in the light of further knowledge seemed to me singularly inane. He was not subject to any definition of that sort, and to say that he was democratic would be (though his political ideal was a democracy), to give an equally superficial account of him. He felt and understood the opposite sides of life; he was imaginative, speculative, anything but literal. He had not in his mind a grain of prejudice as large as the point of a needle, and people (there are many) who think this a defect would have missed it immensely in Ivan Serguéitch. (I give his name, without attempting the Russian orthography, as it was uttered by his friends when they addressed him in French.) Our Anglo-Saxon, Protestant, moralistic, conventional standards were far away from him, and he judged things with a freedom and spontaneity in which I found a perpetual refreshment. His sense of beauty, his love of truth and right, were the foundation of his nature; but half the charm of conversation with him was that one breathed an air in which cant phrases and arbitrary measurements simply sounded ridiculous.

I may add that it was not because I had written a laudatory article about his books that he gave me a friendly welcome; for in the first place my article could have very little importance for him, and in the second it had never been either his habit or his hope to bask in the light of criticism. Supremely modest as he was, I think he attached no great weight to what might happen to be said about him; for he felt that he was destined to encounter a very small amount of intelligent appreciation, especially in foreign countries. I never heard him even allude to any judgment which might have been passed upon his productions in England. In France he knew that he was read very moderately; the "demand" for his volumes was small, and he had no illusions whatever on the subject of his popularity. He had heard with pleasure that many intelligent persons in the United States were impatient for everything that might come from his pen; but I think he was never convinced, as one or two of the more zealous of these persons had endeavoured to convince him, that he could boast of a "public" in America. He gave me the impression of thinking of criticism as most serious workers think of it—that it is the amusement, the exercise, the subsistence of the critic (and, so far as this goes, of immense use); but that though it may often concern other readers, it does not much concern the artist himself. In comparison with all those things which the production of a considered work forces the artist little by little to say to himself, the remarks of the critic are vague and of the moment; and yet, owing to the large publicity of the proceeding, they have a power to irritate or discourage which is quite out of proportion to their use to the person criticised. It was not, moreover (if this explanation be not more gross than the spectre it is meant to conjure away), on account of any esteem which he accorded to my own productions (I used regularly to send them to him) that I found him so agreeable, for to the best of my belief he was unable to read them. As regards one of the first that I had offered him he wrote me a little note to tell me that a distinguished friend, who was his constant companion, had read three or four chapters aloud to him the evening before and that one of them was written *de main de maître!* This gave me great pleasure, but it was my first and last pleasure of the kind. I continued, as I say, to send him my fictions, because they were the only thing I had to give; but he never alluded to the rest of the work in question, which he evidently did not finish, and never gave any sign of having read its successors. Presently I quite ceased to expect this, and saw why it was (it interested me much), that my writings could not appeal to him. He cared, more than anything else, for the air of reality, and my reality was not to the purpose. I do not think my stories struck him as quite meat for men. The manner was more apparent than the matter; they were too *tarabiscoté,* as I once heard him say of the style of a book—had on the surface too many little flowers and knots of ribbon. He had read a great deal of English, and knew the language remarkably well—too well, I used often to think, for he liked to speak it with those to whom it was native, and, successful as the effort always was, it deprived him of the facility and raciness with which he expressed himself in French.

I have said that he had no prejudices, but perhaps after all he had one. I think he imagined it to be impossible to a person of English speech to converse in French with complete correctness. He knew Shakespeare thoroughly, and at one time had wandered far and wide in English literature. His opportunities for speaking English were not at all frequent, so that when the necessity (or at least the occasion) presented itself, he remembered the phrases he had encountered in books. This often gave a charming quaintness and an unexpected literary turn to what he said. "In Russia, in spring, if you enter a beechen grove"—those words come back to me from the last time I saw him. He continued to read English books and was not incapable of attacking the usual Tauchnitz novel. The English writer (of our day) of whom I remember to have heard him speak with most admiration was Dickens, of whose faults he was conscious, but whose power of presenting to the eye a vivid, salient figure he rated very high. In the young French school he was much interested; I mean, in the new votaries of realism, the grandsons of Balzac. He was a good friend of most of them, and with Gustave Flaubert, the most singular and most original of the group, he was altogether intimate. He had his reservations and discriminations, and he had, above all, the great back-garden of his Slav imagination and his Germanic culture, into which the door constantly stood open, and the grandsons of Balzac were not, I think, particularly free to accompany him. But he had much sympathy with their experiment, their general movement, and it was on the side of the careful study of life as the best line of the novelist that, as may easily be supposed, he ranged himself. For some of the manifestations of the opposite tradition he had a great contempt. This was a kind of emotion he rarely expressed, save in regard to certain public wrongs and iniquities; bitterness and denunciation seldom passed his mild lips. But I remember well the little flush of conviction, the seriousness, with which he once said, in allusion to a novel which had just been running through the *Revue des Deux Mondes*, "If I had written anything so bad as that, I should blush for it all my life."

His was not, I should say, predominantly, or even in a high degree, the artistic nature, though it was deeply, if I may make the distinction, the poetic. But during the last twelve years of his life he lived much with artists and men of letters, and he was eminently capable of kindling in the glow of discussion. He cared for questions of form, though not in the degree in which Flaubert and Edmond de Goncourt cared for them, and he had very lively sympathies. He had a great regard for Madame George Sand, the head and front of the old romantic tradition; but this was on general grounds, quite independent of her novels, which he never read, and which she never expected him, or apparently any one else, to read. He thought her character remarkably noble and sincere. He had, as I have said, a great affection for Gustave Flaubert, who returned it; and he was much interested in Flaubert's extraordinary attempts at bravery of form and of matter, knowing perfectly well when they failed. During those months which it was Flaubert's habit to spend in Paris, Turgénieff went almost regularly to see him on Sunday afternoon, and was so good as to introduce me to the author of *Madame Bovary*, in whom I saw many reasons for Turgénieff's regard. It was on these Sundays, in Flaubert's little salon, which, at the top of a house at the end of the Faubourg Saint-Honoré, looked rather bare and provisional, that, in the company of the other familiars of the spot, more than one of whom[1] have commemorated these occasions, Turgénieff's beautiful faculty of talk showed at its best. He was easy, natural, abundant, more than I can describe, and everything that he said was touched with the exquisite quality of his imagination. What was discussed in that little smoke-clouded room was chiefly questions of taste, questions of art and form; and the speakers, for the most part, were in aesthetic matters, radicals of the deepest dye. It would have been late in the day to propose among them any discussion of the relation of art to morality, any question as to the degree in which a novel might or might not concern itself with the teaching of a lesson. They had settled these preliminaries long ago, and it would have been primitive and incongruous to recur to them. The conviction that held them together was the conviction that art and morality are two perfectly different things, and that the former has no more to do with the latter than it has with astronomy or embryology. The only duty of a novel was to be well written; that merit included every other of which it was capable. This state of mind was never more apparent than one afternoon when *ces messieurs* delivered themselves on the subject of an incident which had just befallen one of them. *L'Assommoir* of Emile Zola had been discontinued in the journal through which it was running as a serial, in consequence of repeated protests from the subscribers. The subscriber, as a type of human imbecility, received a wonderful dressing, and the Philistine in general was roughly handled. There were gulfs of difference between Turgénieff and Zola, but Turgénieff, who, as I say, understood everything, understood Zola too, and rendered perfect justice to the high solidity of much of his work. His attitude, at such times, was admirable, and I could imagine nothing more genial or more fitted to give an idea of light, easy, human intelligence. No one could desire more than he that art should be art; always, ever, incorruptibly, art. To him this proposition would have seemed as little in need of proof, or susceptible of refutation, as the axiom that law should always be law or medicine always medicine. As much as any one he was prepared to take note of the fact that the demand for abdications and concessions never comes from artists themselves, but always from purchasers, editors, subscribers. I am pretty sure that his word about all this would have been that he could not quite see what was meant by the talk about novels being moral or the reverse; that a novel could no more propose to itself to be moral than a painting or a symphony, and that it was arbitrary to lay down a distinction between the numerous forms of art. He was the last man

1. Maxime Du Camp, Alphonse Daudet, Emile Zola.

to be blind to their unity. I suspect that he would have said, in short, that distinctions were demanded in the interest of the moralists, and that the demand was indelicate, owing to their want of jurisdiction. Yet at the same time that I make this suggestion as to his state of mind I remember how little he struck me as bound by mere neatness of formula, how little there was in him of the partisan or the pleader. What he thought of the relation of art to life his stories, after all, show better than anything else. The immense variety of life was ever present to his mind, and he would never have argued the question I have just hinted at in the interest of particular liberties—the liberties that were apparently the dearest to his French *confrères*. It was this air that he carried about with him of feeling all the variety of life, of knowing strange and far-off things, of having an horizon in which the Parisian horizon—so familiar, so wanting in mystery, so perpetually *exploité*—easily lost itself, that distinguished him from these companions. He was not all there, as the phrase is; he had something behind, in reserve. It was Russia, of course, in a large measure; and, especially before the spectacle of what is going on there to-day, that was a large quantity. But so far as he was on the spot, he was an element of pure sociability.

I did not intend to go into these details immediately, for I had only begun to say what an impression of magnificent manhood he made upon me when I first knew him. That impression, indeed, always remained with me, even after it had been brought home to me how much there was in him of the quality of genius. He was a beautiful intellect, of course, but above all he was a delightful, mild, masculine figure. The combination of his deep, soft, lovable spirit, in which one felt all the tender parts of genius, with his immense, fair Russian physique, was one of the most attractive things conceivable. He had a frame which would have made it perfectly lawful, and even becoming, for him to be brutal; but there was not a grain of brutality in his composition. He had always been a passionate sportsman; to wander in the woods or the steppes, with his dog and gun, was the pleasure of his heart. Late in life he continued to shoot, and he had a friend in Cambridgeshire for the sake of whose partridges, which were famous, he used sometimes to cross the Channel. It would have been impossible to imagine a better representation of a Nimrod of the north. He was exceedingly tall, and broad and robust in proportion. His head was one of the finest, and though the line of his features was irregular, there was a great deal of beauty in his face. It was eminently of the Russian type—almost everything in it was wide. His expression had a singular sweetness, with a touch of Slav languor, and his eye, the kindest of eyes, was deep and melancholy. His hair, abundant and straight, was as white as silver, and his beard, which he wore trimmed rather short, was of the colour of his hair. In all his tall person, which was very striking wherever it appeared, there was an air of neglected strength, as if it had been a part of his modesty never to remind himself that he was strong. He used sometimes to blush like a boy of sixteen. He had very few forms and ceremonies, and almost as little manner as was possible to a man of his natural *prestance*. His noble appearance was in itself a manner; but whatever he did he did very simply, and he had not the slightest pretension to not being subject to rectification. I never saw any one receive it with less irritation. Friendly, candid, unaffectedly benignant, the impression that he produced most strongly and most generally was, I think, simply that of goodness.

When I made his acquaintance he had been living, since his removal from Baden-Baden, which took place in consequence of the Franco-Prussian war, in a large detached house on the hill of Montmartre, with his friends of many years, Madame Pauline Viardot and her husband, as his fellow-tenants. He occupied the upper floor, and I like to recall, for the sake of certain delightful talks, the aspect of his little green sitting-room, which has, in memory, the consecration of irrecoverable hours. It was almost entirely green, and the walls were not covered with paper, but draped in stuff. The *portières* were green, and there was one of those immense divans, so indispensable to Russians, which had apparently been fashioned for the great person of the master, so that smaller folk had to lie upon it rather than sit. I remember the white light of the Paris street, which came in through windows more or less blinded in their lower part, like those of a studio. It rested, during the first years that I went to see Turgénieff, upon several choice pictures of the modern French school, especially upon a very fine specimen of Théodore Rousseau, which he valued exceedingly. He had a great love of painting, and was an excellent critic of a picture. The last time I saw him—it was at his house in the country—he showed me half a dozen large copies of Italian works, made by a young Russian in whom he was interested, which he had, with characteristic kindness, taken into his own apartments in order that he might bring them to the knowledge of his friends. He thought them, as copies, remarkable; and they were so, indeed, especially when one perceived that the original work of the artist had little value. Turgénieff warmed to the work of praising them, as he was very apt to do; like all men of imagination he had frequent and zealous admirations. As a matter of course there was almost always some young Russian in whom he was interested, and refugees and pilgrims of both sexes were his natural clients. I have heard it said by persons who had known him long and well that these enthusiasms sometimes led him into error, that he was apt to *se monter la tête* on behalf of his protégés. He was prone to believe that he had discovered the coming Russian genius; he talked about his discovery for a month, and then suddenly one heard no more of it. I remember his once telling me of a young woman who had come to see him on her return from America, where she had been studying obstetrics at some medical college, and who, without means and without friends, was in want of help and of work. He accidentally learned that she had written something, and asked her to let him see it. She sent it to him, and it proved to be a tale in which certain phases of rural life were described with striking truthfulness. He perceived in the young lady a great natural talent; he sent her story off to Russia to be printed, with the conviction that it would make a great impression, and he expressed the hope of being able to introduce her to French readers. When I mentioned this to an old friend of Turgénieff he smiled, and said that we should not hear of her again, that Ivan Serguéitch had already discovered a great many surprising talents, which, as a general thing, had not borne the test. There was apparently some truth in this, and Turgénieff's liability to be deceived was too generous a weakness for me to hesitate to allude to it, even after I have insisted on the usual certainty of his taste. He was deeply interested in his young Russians; they were what interested him most in the world. They were almost always unhappy, in want and in rebellion against an order of things which he himself detested. The study of the Russian character absorbed and fascinated him, as all readers of his stories know. Rich, unformed, undeveloped, with all sorts of adumbrations, of qualities in a state of fusion, it stretched itself out as a mysterious expanse in which it was impossible as yet to perceive the relation between gifts and weaknesses. Of its weaknesses he was keenly conscious, and I once heard him express himself with an energy that did him honour and a frankness that even surprised me (considering that it was of his countrymen that he spoke), in regard to a weakness which he deemed the greatest of all—a weakness for which a man whose love of veracity was his strongest feeling would have least toleration. His young compatriots, seeking their fortune in foreign lands, touched his imagination and his pity, and it is easy to conceive that under the circumstances the impression they often made upon him may have had great intensity. The Parisian background, with its brilliant sameness, its absence of surprises (for those who have known it long), threw them into relief and made him see them as he saw the figures in his tales, in relations, in situations which brought them out. There passed before him in the course of time many wonderful Russian types. He told me once of his having been visited by a religious sect. The sect consisted of but two persons, one of whom was the object of worship and the other the worshipper. The divinity apparently was travelling about Europe in company with his prophet. They were intensely serious but it was very handy, as the term is, for each. The god had always his altar and the altar had (unlike some altars) always its god.

In his little green salon nothing was out of place; there were none of the odds and ends of the usual man of letters, which indeed Turgénieff was not; and the case was the same in his library at Bougival, of which I shall presently speak. Few books even were visible; it was as if everything had been put away. The traces of work had been carefully removed. An air of great comfort, an immeasurable divan and several valuable pictures—that was the effect of the place. I know not exactly at what hours Turgénieff did his work; I think he had no regular times and seasons, being in this respect as different as possible from Anthony Trollope, whose autobiography, with its candid revelation of intellectual economies, is so curious. It is my impression that in Paris Turgénieff wrote little; his times of production being rather those weeks of the summer that he spent at Bougival, and the period of that visit to Russia which he supposed himself to make every year. I say "supposed himself," because it was impossible to see much of him without discovering that he was a man of delays. As on the part of some other Russians whom I have known, there was something Asiatic in his faculty of procrastination. But even if one suffered from it a little one thought of it with kindness, as a part of his general mildness and want of rigidity. He went to Russia, at any rate, at intervals not infrequent, and he spoke of these visits as his best time for production. He had an estate far in the interior, and here, amid the stillness of the country and the scenes and figures which give such a charm to the *Memoirs of a Sportsman*, he drove his pen without interruption.

It is not out of place to allude to the fact that he possessed considerable fortune; this is too important in the life of a man of letters. It had been of great value to Turgénieff, and I think that much of the fine quality of his work is owing to it. He could write according to his taste and his mood; he was never pressed nor checked (putting the Russian censorship aside) by considerations foreign to his plan, and never was in danger of becoming a hack. Indeed, taking into consideration the absence of a pecuniary spur and that complicated indolence from which he was not exempt, his industry is surprising, for his tales are a long list. In Paris, at all events, he was always open to proposals for the midday breakfast. He liked to breakfast *au cabaret*, and freely consented to an appointment. It is not unkind to add that, at first, he never kept it. I may mention without reserve this idiosyncrasy of Turgénieff's, because in the first place it was so inveterate as to be very amusing—it amused not only his friends but himself; and in the second, he was as sure to come in the end as he was sure not to come in the beginning. After the appointment had been made or the invitation accepted, when the occasion was at hand, there arrived a note or a telegram in which Ivan Serguéitch excused himself, and begged that the meeting might be deferred to another date, which he usually himself proposed. For this second date still another was sometimes substituted; but if I remember no appointment that he exactly kept, I remember none that he completely missed. His friends waited for him frequently, but they never lost him. He was very fond of that wonderful Parisian *déjeûner*—fond of it I mean as a feast of reason. He was extremely temperate, and often ate no breakfast at all; but he found it a good hour for talk, and little, on general grounds, as one might be prepared to agree with him, if he was at the table one was speedily convinced. I call it wonderful, the *déjeûner* of Paris, on account of the assurance with which it plants itself in the very middle of the morning. It divides the day between rising and dinner so unequally, and opposes such barriers. of repletion to any prospect of ulterior labours, that the unacclimated stranger wonders when the fertile French people do their work. Not the least wonderful part of it is that the stranger himself likes it, at last, and manages to piece together his day with the shattered fragments that survive. It was not, at any rate, when one had the good fortune to breakfast at twelve o'clock with Turgénieff that one was struck with its being an inconvenient hour. Any hour was convenient for meeting a human being who conformed so completely to one's idea of the best that human nature is capable of. There are places in Paris which I can think of only in relation to some occasion on which he was present, and when I pass them the particular things I heard him say there come back to me. There is a café in the Avenue de l'Opéra—a new, sumptuous establishment, with very deep settees, on the right as you leave the Boulevard—where I once had a talk with him, over an order singularly moderate, which was prolonged far into the afternoon, and in the course of which he was extraordinarily suggestive and interesting, so that my memory now reverts affectionately to all the circumstances. It evokes the grey damp of a Parisian December, which made the dark interior of the café look more and more rich and hospitable, while the light faded, the lamps were lit, the habitués came in to drink absinthe and play their afternoon game of dominoes, and we still lingered over our morning meal. Turgénieff talked almost exclusively about Russia, the nihilists, the remarkable figures that came to light among them, the curious visits he received, the dark prospects of his native land. When he was in the vein, no man could speak more to the imagination of his auditor. For myself, at least, at such times, there was something extraordinarily vivifying and stimulating in his talk, and I always left him in a state of "intimate" excitement, with a feeling that all sorts of valuable things had been suggested to me; the condition in which a man swings his cane as he walks, leaps lightly over gutters, and then stops, for no reason at all, to look, with an air of being struck, into a shop window where he sees nothing. I remember another symposium, at a restaurant on one of the corners of the little *place* in front of the Opéra Comique, where we were four, including Ivan Serguéitch, and the two other guests were also Russian, one of them uniting to the charm of this nationality the merit of a sex that makes the combination irresistible. The establishment had been a discovery of Turgénieff's—a discovery, at least, as far as our particular needs were concerned—and I remember that we hardly congratulated him on it. The dinner, in a low entresol, was not what it had been intended to be, but the talk was better even than our expectations. It was not about nihilism but about some more agreeable features of life, and I have no recollection of Turgénieff in a mood more spontaneous and charming. One of our friends had, when he spoke French, a peculiar way of sounding the word *adorable*, which was frequently on his lips, and I remember well his expressive prolongation of the *a* when, in speaking of the occasion afterwards, he applied this term to Ivan Serguéitch. I scarcely know, however, why I should drop into the detail of such reminiscences, and my excuse is but the desire that we all have, when a human relationship is closed, to save a little of it from the past—to make a mark which may stand for some of the happy moments of it.

Nothing that Turgénieff had to say could be more interesting than his talk about his own work, his manner of writing. What I have heard him tell of these things was worthy of the beautiful results he produced; of the deep purpose, pervading them all, to show us life itself. The germ of a story, with him, was never an affair of plot—that was the last thing he thought of: it was the representation of certain persons. The first form in which a tale appeared to him was as the figure of an individual, or a combination of individuals, whom he

wished to see in action, being sure that such people must do something very special and interesting. They stood before him definite,
vivid, and he wished to know, and to show, as much as possible of
their nature. The first thing was to make clear to himself what he did
know, to begin with; and to this end, he wrote out a sort of biography
of each of his characters, and everything that they had done and that
had happened to them up to the opening of the story. He had their
dossier, as the French say, and as the police has of that of every conspicuous criminal. With this material in his hand he was able to proceed; the story all lay in the question, What shall I make them do? He
always made them do things that showed them completely; but, as he
said, the defect of his manner and the reproach that was made him
was his want of "architecture"—in other words, of composition. The
great thing, of course, is to have architecture as well as precious material, as Walter Scott had them, as Balzac had them. If one reads
Turgénieff's stories with the knowledge that they were composed—
or rather that they came into being—in this way, one can trace the
process in every line. Story, in the conventional sense of the word—a
fable constructed, like Wordsworth's phantom, "to startle and waylay"—there is as little as possible. The thing consists of the motions of
a group of selected creatures, which are not the result of a precon-
ceived action, but a consequence of the qualities of the actors. Works
of art are produced from every possible point of view, and stories,
and very good ones, will continue to be written in which the evolution is that of a dance—a series of steps the more complicated and
lively the better, of course, determined from without and forming a
figure. This figure will always, probably, find favour with many readers, because it reminds them enough, without reminding them too
much, of life. On this opposition many young talents in France are
ready to rend each other, for there is a numerous school on either
side. We have not yet in England and America arrived at the point of
treating such questions with passion, for we have not yet arrived at
the point of feeling them intensely, or indeed, for that matter, of understanding them very well. It is not open to us as yet to discuss
whether a novel had better be an excision from life or a structure built
up of picture-cards, for we have not made up our mind as to whether
life in general may be described. There is evidence of a good deal of
shyness on this point—a tendency rather to put up fences than to
jump over them. Among us, therefore, even a certain ridicule attaches to the consideration of such alternatives. But individuals may
feel their way, and perhaps even pass unchallenged, if they remark
that for them the manner in which Turgénieff worked will always

seem the most fruitful. It has the immense recommendation that in relation to any human occurrence it begins, as it were, further back. It lies in its power to tell us the most about men and women. Of course it will but slenderly satisfy those numerous readers among whom the answer to this would be, "Hang it, we don't care a straw about men and women: we want a good story!"

And yet, after all, *Elena* is a good story, and *Lisa* and *Virgin Soil* are good stories. Reading over lately several of Turgénieff's novels and tales, I was struck afresh with their combination of beauty and reality. One must never forget, in speaking of him, that he was both an observer and a poet. The poetic element was constant, and it had great strangeness and power. It inspired most of the short things that he wrote during the last few years of his life, since the publication of *Virgin Soil,* things that are in the highest degree fanciful and exotic. It pervades the frequent little reveries, visions, epigrams of the *Senilia.* It was no part of my intention, here, to criticise his writings, having said my say about them, so far as possible, some years ago. But I may mention that in re-reading them I find in them all that I formerly found of two other elements—their richness and their sadness. They give one the impression of life itself, and not of an arrangement, a *réchauffé* of life. I remember Turgénieff's once saying in regard to Homais, the little Norman country apothecary, with his pedantry of "enlightened opinions," in *Madame Bovary,* that the great strength of such a portrait consisted in its being at once an individual, of the most concrete sort, and a type. This is the great strength of his own representations of character; they are so strangely, fascinatingly particular, and yet they are so recognisably general. Such a remark as that about Homais makes me wonder why it was that Turgénieff should have rated Dickens so high, the weakness of Dickens being in regard to just that point. If Dickens fail to live long, it will be because his figures are particular without being general; because they are individuals without being types; because we do not feel their continuity with the rest of humanity—see the matching of the pattern with the piece out of which all the creations of the novelist and the dramatist are cut. I often meant, but accidentally neglected, to put Turgénieff on the subject of Dickens again, and ask him to explain his opinion. I suspect that his opinion was in a large measure merely that Dickens diverted him, as well he might. That complexity of the pattern was in itself fascinating. I have mentioned Flaubert, and I will return to him simply to say that there was something very touching in the nature of the friendship that united these two men. It is much to the honour of Flaubert, to my sense, that he appreciated Ivan Turgénieff. There was a partial similarity between them. Both were large, massive men, though the Russian reached to a greater height than the Norman; both were completely honest and sincere, and both had the pessimistic element in their composition. Each had a tender regard for the other, and I think that I am neither incorrect nor indiscreet in saying that on Turgénieff's part this regard had in it a strain of compassion. There was something in Gustave Flaubert that appealed to such a feeling. He had failed, on the whole, more than he had succeeded, and the great machinery of erudition,—the great polishing process,—which he brought to bear upon his productions, was not accompanied with proportionate results. He had talent without having cleverness, and imagination without having fancy. His effort was heroic, but except in the case of *Madame Bovary*, a masterpiece, he imparted something to his works (it was as if he had covered them with metallic plates) which made them sink rather than sail. He had a passion for perfection of form and for a certain splendid suggestiveness of style. He wished to produce perfect phrases, perfectly interrelated, and as closely woven together as a suit of chain-mail. He looked at life altogether as an artist, and took his work with a seriousness that never belied itself. To write an admirable page—and his idea of what constituted an admirable page was transcendent—seemed to him something to live for. He tried it again and again, and he came very near it; more than once he touched it, for *Madame Bovary* surely will live. But there was something ungenerous in his genius. He was cold, and he would have given everything he had to be able to glow. There is nothing in his novels like the passion of Elena for Inssaroff, like the purity of Lisa, like the anguish of the parents of Bazaroff, like the hidden wound of Tatiana; and yet Flaubert yearned, with all the accumulations of his vocabulary, to touch the chord of pathos. There were some parts of his mind that did not "give," that did not render a sound. He had had too much of some sorts of experience and not enough of others. And yet this failure of an organ, as I may call it, inspired those who knew him with a kindness. If Flaubert was powerful and limited, there is something human, after all, and even rather august in a strong man who has not been able completely to express himself.

After the first year of my acquaintance with Turgénieff I saw him much less often. I was seldom in Paris, and sometimes when I was there he was absent. But I neglected no opportunity of seeing him, and fortune frequently assisted me. He came two or three times to London, for visits provokingly brief. He went to shoot in Cambridgeshire, and he passed through town in arriving and departing. He liked the English, but I am not sure that he liked London, where he had passed a lugubrious winter in 1870–71. I remember some of his impressions of that period, especially a visit that he had paid to a "bishopess" surrounded by her daughters, and a description of the cookery at the lodgings which he occupied. After 1876 I frequently saw him as an invalid. He was tormented by gout, and sometimes terribly besieged; but his account of what he suffered was as charming—I can apply no other word to it—as his description of everything else. He had so the habit of observation, that he perceived in excruciating sensations all sorts of curious images and analogies, and analysed them to an extraordinary fineness. Several times I found him at Bougival, above the Seine, in a very spacious and handsome chalet—a little unsunned, it is true—which he had built alongside of the villa occupied by the family to which, for years, his life had been devoted. The place is delightful; the two houses are midway up a long slope, which descends, with the softest inclination, to the river, and behind them the hill rises to a wooded crest. On the left, in the distance, high up and above an horizon of woods, stretches the romantic aqueduct of Marly. It is a very pretty domain. The last time I saw him, in November 1882, it was at Bougival. He had been very ill, with strange, intolerable symptoms, but he was better, and he had good hopes. They were not justified by the event. He got worse again, and the months that followed were cruel. His beautiful serene mind should not have been darkened and made acquainted with violence; it should have been able to the last to take part, as it had always done, in the decrees and mysteries of fate. At the moment I saw him, however, he was, as they say in London, in very good form, and my last impression of him was almost bright. He was to drive into Paris, not being able to bear the railway, and he gave me a seat in the carriage. For an hour and a half he constantly talked, and never better. When we got into the city I alighted on the boulevard extérieur, as we were to go in different directions. I bade him goodbye at the carriage window, and never saw him again. There was a kind of fair going on, near by, in the chill November air, beneath the denuded little trees of the Boulevard, and a Punch and Judy show, from which nasal sounds proceeded. I almost regret having accidentally to mix up so much of Paris with this perhaps too complacent enumeration of occasions, for the effect of it may be to suggest that Ivan Turgénieff had been Gallicised. But this was not the case; the French capital was an accident for him, not a necessity. It touched him at many points, but it let him alone at many others, and he had, with that great tradition of ventilation of the Russian mind, windows open into distances which stretched far beyond the *banlieue*. I have spoken of him from the limited point of view of my own acquaintance with him, and unfortunately left myself little space to allude to a matter which filled his existence a good deal more than the consideration of how a story should be written— his hopes and fears on behalf of his native land. He wrote fictions and dramas, but the great drama of his life was the struggle for a better state of things in Russia. In this drama he played a distinguished part, and the splendid obsequies that, simple and modest as he was, have unfolded themselves over his grave, sufficiently attest the recognition of it by his countrymen. His funeral, restricted and officialised, was none the less a magnificent "manifestation." I have read the accounts of it, however, with a kind of chill, a feeling in which assent to the honours paid him bore less part than it ought. All this pomp and ceremony seemed to lift him out of the range of familiar recollection, of valued reciprocity, into the majestic position of a national glory. And yet it is in the presence of this obstacle to social contact that those who knew and loved him must address their farewell to him now. After all, it is difficult to see how the obstacle can be removed. He was the most generous, the most tender, the most delightful, of men; his large nature overflowed with the love of justice: but he also was of the stuff of which glories are made.

Twice in 1882 Henry James was summoned to Boston where a parent lay dying. Each time he arrived too late. Then, on September 3, 1883, only two days after returning to Bolton Street, James received word that death had struck down another loved one. Ivan Turgenev had succumbed to his cancer. James had met Turgenev in 1875, when the two expatriates became warm friends in Paris. Turgenev introduced James to Flaubert's circle and maintained contact after the American expatriate moved to London. In October of 1883 James responded to Turgenev's death by writing the fourth of his five essays on the Russian master. It appeared in the *Atlantic Monthly* in 1884 and was revised for *Partial Portraits* in 1888. To commemorate his friend, mentor, and idol, James chose a genre hallowed in the history of criticism but little practiced today, the appreciation.

James self-consciously sets "Ivan Turgénieff" off against its 1874 predecessor. In the earlier essay he had analyzed texts, now he appreciates a man. Death has upped the ante. Moments in the random flux of experience have been given value by Turgenev, and James' task is to preserve that value. Entering "into the detail of . . . reminiscences," the critic resolute before death produces "a more vivifying reference" than any textual analysis because of "the desire we all have, when a human relationship is closed . . . to make a mark which may stand for some of the happy moments of it." This very process finds its source in Turgenev who vivified not only charming cafés but dying itself. "His account of what he suffered was as charming—I can apply no other word to it—as his description of everything else." In his last meeting with James, when death was upon Turgenev, "he was, as they say in London, in very good form. . . . For an hour and a half he constantly talked, and never better." As his bodily form deteriorates, Turgenev persists in that form of spiritual excellence which death cannot mar and which James accepts as his ideal and challenge. His essay must be an exercise in good form, a proper expression of the implacable spirit, a perfect example of the right genre. As Turgenev did not hide the fact of his disease, James faces the "intolerable pain" of one "condemned to suffer atrociously." But as Turgenev managed to transform his "account" into something charming, James repeatedly transforms human limitation into something attractive. Like comedy, the appreciation laughs idiosyncrasy away. Turgenev often stood up fellow diners, for example, but James "mention[s] without reserve this idiosyncrasy because . . . it was . . . very amusing—it amused not only his friends but himself."

"Friends" is the key term. It echoes throughout the appreciation, as the laughter of these friends charmed by Turgenev, despite and partly because of his idiosyncrasies, resounds as their fondest appreciation of him. This community of friends is, in turn, Turgenev's supreme feat of vivification. When James says "I found him adorable," he may sound slightly gushy, but he is leading up to the dinner party where

> one of our friends had, when he spoke French, a peculiar way of sounding the word *adorable* . . . and I remember well his expressive prolongation of the *a* when, in speaking of the occasion afterwards, he applied the term to Ivan Serguéitch.

A community of adorers created by the adorable man will preserve his memory "afterwards" because they are vivified by that memory. James escapes gushiness by including in his appreciation the story of the ludicrous "divinity . . . travelling about Europe in company with his prophet . . . it was very handy. . . . The god had always his altar and the altar had (unlike some altars) always its god." Only with a wryly Turgenevian distance upon every action can James consecrate his act of appreciation.

A second, potentially less attractive type of distancing also surfaces in James' definition of community. He preserves Turgenev not only from oblivion but also from other mourners. Appreciation threatens to become appropriation. On the one hand, James undermines other English-speaking friends of Turgenev. American devotees too "zealous" to appreciate Turgenev's essential modesty "never convinced . . . him, that he could boast of a 'public' in America." Britain as well as America is involved in the dismissal when James contends that "our Anglo-Saxon, Protestant, moralistic, conventional standards were far away from him." James is technically included in the "our," but the whole thrust of his appreciation is to confirm his sympathy with Turgenev's suppler vision. And so, when James laments that Turgenev's speaking English "with those to whom it was native . . . deprived him of the facility and raciness with which he expressed himself in French," we may infer that Ivan Serguéitch should confine himself to the one Anglo-American friend whose beautiful French allowed Turgenev to remain at the top of his expressive form.

We might, on the other hand, conclude that Turgenev should simply dispense with Anglo-Americans altogether and speak French with the French. This graver threat to James' possession of his idol is addressed throughout the essay.

I almost regret having accidentally to mix up so much of Paris with [Turgenev] . . . for the effect of it may be to suggest that Ivan Turgénieff had been Gallicised. But this was not the case; the French capital was an accident for him.

There is no serious chance of Turgenev seeming Gallicized because James has been undermining France since the first paragraph. Renan and About produce eulogies which—unlike James'—are characterized by "ingenuity" rather than deep feeling because the French suffer from too little heart and too much head. "Feelings which so many of his [Parisian] companions were unable to share" are just what James shares with Turgenev and what James' essay shares with us. Even Turgenev's closest French friend, Gustave Flaubert, suffers, according to James, from an overbalance of "erudition" which leaves him essentially "ungenerous." The too cerebral orientation of Flaubert's circle inclines them to overemphasize formal issues, whereas Turgenev, like James, "cared for questions of form, though not in the degree in which" they did. Instead of any balancing interest in sentiment, the fiction of Flaubert's circle indulged in "liberties" (of a presumably sexual nature) which Turgenev shunned in favor of "freedom" of vision (James' paramount ideal). Turgenev even, in James' account of him, shares the younger novelist's ambivalence about two French *bêtes noires*—Flaubert, whose "extraordinary attempts at bravery of form and of matter" Turgenev acknowledged while "knowing perfectly well when they failed," and Zola, whom Turgenev "understood" across "gulfs of difference."

James further distinguishes himself from both French and Anglo-American extremes when he takes up literary criticism. On the question of highly structured versus spontaneously evolved fiction, "many young talents in France are ready to rend each other," whereas "in England and America . . . even a certain ridicule attaches to the consideration of such alternatives." James shares the French passion for literary discussion without either losing his Anglo-American perspective on violent passions or sinking into the complacency which vitiates English-language practice. This stance between the French who rend and the Anglo-Americans who ridicule is the ideal of the good critic, the disinterested place in-between which James learned from both his French and his British mentors in criticism, Sainte-Beuve and Matthew Arnold. Disinterestedness, in turn, enables us to see that, although there is unquestionably an element of possessiveness in James' exclusion of French and Anglo-American rivals for Turgenev's friendship, much more is involved than jealousy. James must take up a position in-between because that is where Turgenev himself abides.

Turgenev, combining heart and head, "felt and understood the opposite sides of life. . . . [He] understood everything" while "feeling all." He recognized both the "faults" and the "power" of Dickens, the "gifts and weaknesses" of Russia, the "defect of his [own literary] manner" as well as its strengths. As the ideal critic for James achieves an androgynous balancing of traits conventionally considered male and female (see Introduction), Turgenev combines a manly "immense . . . Russian physique" with an inclination toward the "soft, tender." He is both "masculine" and "mild."

James' very capacity to recognize and to celebrate Turgenev's completeness indicates a comparable capacity to be in-between. Both "the pleasure of reading" Turgenev and "the happiness to know him" are available to James who appreciates the "combination of beauty and reality" in Turgenev's fiction and the blend of "observer and . . . poet" in the man. James also recognizes the limitations as well as the strengths of Turgenev. James goes out of his way to qualify what would otherwise be facile. "I have said that he had no prejudices, but perhaps after all he had one." Likewise, "the usual certainty of his taste" is sometimes offset by a "liability to be deceived."

This determination to introduce the complicating reality is James' paramount similarity to Turgenev. Scholars have noticed how many of James' characterizations of the Russian apply to himself—each author is a "cosmopolite . . . by the force of circumstances," each considers fiction a "careful study of life," each "could not quite see what was meant by the talk of novels being moral or the reverse," both find their inspiration in "the figure of an individual." James' insistence upon complication is, however, of a more general importance. Its growth between 1874 and 1884 signals his maturation as a critic and as a person.

> In the little article [of 1874] . . . I had been moved to say of him that he had the aristocratic temperament: a remark which in light of future knowledge seemed to me singularly inane. He was not subject to any definition of that sort, and to say that he was democratic would be (though his political ideal was a democracy), to give an equally superficial account of him.

To fix in a formulated phrase becomes impossible in the face of Turgenev. "Cant phrases and arbitrary measurements simply sounded ridiculous" in conversation with him, and in writing about him James finds that Turgenev cannot be "bound by mere neatness of formula." James had known the dangers of neat formulation in 1874. He had expressly defined his critical function as "not to impose a conclusion, but to help well-disposed readers to a larger enjoyment." Impose he did, however. Sometimes his formulae were neat, as when he said that Turgenev wrote "more for love than for lucre" or that *A Sportsman's Notebook* exemplified "moral meaning giving a sense to form and form giving relief to moral meaning." But particularly as the 1874 essay drew to a close, James seemed to have felt impelled to counter any heterodoxy in Turgenev by imposing orthodox conclusions. "We hold to the good old belief that the presumption, in life, is in favor of the brighter side, and we deem it, in art, an indispensable condition of our interest in a depressed observer that he should have at least tried his best to be cheerful." It is unthinkable in 1884 to say that Turgenev's "sadness has its element of error." Guided by the principle enunciated in "The Art of Fiction" (1884)—that an author must be granted his donnée—James takes Turgenev's pessimism not as a failing to be judged but as a fact to be recognized.

More generally, instead of polishing formulae, James in 1884 believes that critics had best "feel their way." His sentences now seek to conform to the shape of the subject, as increased complexity of perception necessitates increased intricacy of style. Compare his brittle aristocrat-democrat dichotomy of 1874 with his careful distinction in 1884: "his was not, I should say, predominantly, or even in a high degree, the artistic nature, though it was deeply, if I may make the distinction, the poetic." Feeling one's way means more than careful distinguishing, it means liberating feeling from head-dominated structures of argument. When James says "I did not intend to go into these details immediately," we see the power of emotional reminiscence overriding any logic of presentation. This same liberation frees James from the arbitrarily limited controversy over form and content. "The great thing, of course, is to have architecture as well as precious material." He likewise eschews any a priori restriction upon composition and insists that "works of art are produced from every possible point of view."

The ultimate proof of James' new suppleness appears at the end of the essay when he must put the very genre of the appreciation into perspective. To understand this gesture, we must trace the circular structure of "Ivan Turgénieff." The essay opens with James meditating upon the ceremony at the Gard du Nord where the train waits to carry Turgenev's remains to Russia. On this journey James cannot go,

154

so he in effect turns the other way and journeys where he can go with Turgenev, back in time to their meetings and pleasures. This journey through the essay brings James eventually to his final ride with Turgenev. Alighting, as he inevitably must, from their carriage, James can only watch his friend proceed on that journey to death which will pause at the Gard du Nord and then continue east to the "official" funeral in St. Petersburg. James' whole spirit inclines him to disparage the state occasion so different from the personal farewell of his appreciation. Such a disparagement, however, would be a failure in Turgenevian terms, not because the Russian would in any way value the hollow eulogies of politicians whom he opposed, but because he would recognize in national mourning another type of emotion which deserves respect. James recognizes this too—at the very cost of his genre. The truest mark of his ability to appreciate Turgenev is that he perceives the limitations of the appreciation. Turgenev is beyond the simply personal, however much James may resent the pomp and circumstance of state occasions. "All this pomp and ceremony seemed to lift him out of the range of familiar recollection."

This very act of appreciation is, of course, eminently appropriate to an appreciation. Turgenev has not so much destroyed the form as expanded it. As the huge Russian is capable of the national as well as the personal, James' very surrendering of his friend to a national destiny allows him to celebrate the personal as well. The final words of the essay were achieved only upon revision in 1888, as though only an expanse of time could do full justice to a nature as expansive as Turgenev's. At last James gets it right. In the human sense which counts most, he is again speaking as much of himself as of Turgenev when his appreciation finds the transforming words, "he also was of the stuff of which glories are made."

The power of James' essay was recognized immediately by reviewers of *Partial Portraits*. The *Atlantic* called it "the gem of the volume" (62 [1888]: 567); the *Nation*, "a truly exquisite essay" (47 [July 26, 1888]: 76). See also the *Literary World* 19 (July 7, 1888): 212, and the *Critic* 12 (June 9, 1888): 279. Early reviewers noted James' literary debt to Turgenev, particularly in the decade after his first essay on the Russian and before his naturalistic novels of 1886. See *North American Review* 122 (1876): 421, *Atlantic* 39 (1877): 742, *Academy* 14 (1878): 354, *Atlantic* 43 (1879): 107, *Spectator* 53 (1880): 48, *Californian* 5 (1882): 86–87, *Nation* 34 (1882): 102, *Princeton Review* 13 (1884): 1–15. For a book-length study of and bibliography on James and Turgenev see Peterson's *The Clement Vision* (Port Washington, N.Y.: Kennikat, 1975). See also Daugherty (80–85) and Kelley (176–81, 225–28). For bibliographical references to the many Turgenev tales and novels mentioned by James see Magarshack's *Turgenev: A Life* (New York: Grove, 1954), Pritchett's *The Gentle Barbarian* (New York: Random House, 1977), and Schapiro's *Turgenev: His Life and Times* (New York: Random House, 1978).

NOTES

132:7. Ernest Renan (1823–92), French historian, biblical scholar, philologist, and critic.

Edmond About (1828–85), French journalist and novelist.

133:12. *Senilia.* Published originally in 1883 with the title *Senilia. Dichtungen in Prosa*, Turgenev's last volume, appeared later in an English version titled *Senilia: Poems in Prose* (Bristol 1890).

134:10. in consequence. James sent his 1874 essay ("Frühlingsfluthen . . .") to Turgenev and received a warm reply inviting him to call in Paris.

134:29. figurative epithet. Flaubert's image for Turgenev, *poire molle*, soft pear, is as one-sided as Renan's characterization of the Russian as "essentially impersonal." As James devotes most of his essay to correcting Renan by providing the other, personal side, to Turgenev, so his repeated insistence upon Turgenev's masculinity is an implicit corrective to Flaubert's overemphasis upon softness.

135:3. inane. Prompted by "an indefinable sense of his [Turgenev's] being of a so-called 'aristocratic' temperament," James in 1874 envisions "very shapely hands and feet" on the Russian whom he later found to be an ungainly giant, and concludes that "much of the charm of M. Turgénieff's manner resides in this impalpable union of an aristocratic temperament with a democratic intellect."

135:30. had heard. On June 19, 1874, Henry James, Sr., wrote to Turgenev that "it seems a pity that you should be ignorant of the immense appreciation your books have in this region. . . . the verdict of the large circle of admirers you have in this place is, that the novel owns a new power in your hands."

136:7. unable to read them. Edel argues that James is substantially undervaluing Turgenev's response to his fiction. The Russian characterized James to W. R. S. Ralston as "having much ability." Moreover, Turgenev's letters, Edel notes, "do not suggest that he thought Henry's tales were not 'meat for men.' . . . he assures him that he will read *The American* and give an honest opinion 'as one must where a person possessing ability such as yours is concerned.' When we recall that earlier Turgenev had praised the 'manliness' and the 'psychological sagacity' of Henry's style, we begin to wonder whether Henry was not offering his subjective view of what Turgenev thought of his work. . . . One possible reason for Henry's self-abasement suggests itself. William James had often reproached Henry for his 'fancy' writing—the 'knots of ribbon'— . . . [and] his father praised his criticism at the expense of his fiction. Henry may have unconsciously transferred to Turgenev the reservations of Quincy Street" (2: 213).

136:11. *de main de maître.* The hand of a master.

136:21. *tarabiscoté.* Elaborate, finicky.

138:10. the teaching of a lesson. For James on the issue of art and morality, see "The Art of Fiction," "Guy de Maupassant," and "Emile Zola," Chapters 7, 8, and 20. The ability to see the novel as a work of art is one thing which, for James, distinguishes the French literary community from the Anglo-Saxon. He makes this distinction later in "Ivan Turgénieff" and throughout his criticism.

138:19. *L'Assommoir* (1877). The journal which discontinued Zola's novel was *La République des Lettres.*

139:14. horizon. James indicts the limited horizons of French provincialism elsewhere in this essay and in his contrast of the "horizons" of Sainte-Beuve and Arnold (see the Commentary to Chapter 1).

139:14. *exploité.* Worked, as a mine.

140:9. *prestance.* Imposing presence.

140:17. house. Turgenev settled in Paris in October of 1871, moving permanently into 50 rue de Douai three years later. He had met the great singer, Pauline Viardot-Garcia, at St. Petersburg during the 1843–44 season of the Italian Opera. Instantly enthralled by her voice and her person, Turgenev became part of the Viardots' life for the next forty years, following the singer and her accommodating husband to Baden-Baden, then to London, and eventually to Paris. He and Viardot became lovers in 1848, and the ill-fated liaison rekindled briefly in 1856, but Pauline was never deeply attracted to Turgenev, and her numerous affairs tortured him. He wrote: "love is not even a feeling; it is a disease. . . . There is no equality in love . . . one partner is a slave and the other an absolute master" (Magarshack p. 78). Viardot retained her mastery to the end.

140:23. *portières.* Curtains hung across a doorway, either as decoration or to replace the door.

141:4. *se monter la tête.* To get excited.

142:19. Trollope. In his *Autobiography* (written in 1875–76 but published posthumously in 1883), Trollope defined the art of fiction very mechanistically; the novelist is a mere workman unaffected by "inspiration." Trollope himself rose at 5:30 and produced 2,500 words before breakfast, allowing neither vacations nor travel to disturb his schedule. The revelation of this mechanistic bent disconcerted many of Trollope's readers.

142:33. *Memoirs of a Sportsman* (1852; titled in other translations *A Hunter's Sketchbook, A Sportsman's Notebook, Annals of a Sportsman*).

144:17. two other guests. Paul Zhukovsky, son of the famous poet-translator Vassili Zhukovsky; the Princess Durousov, whose salon was frequented by Turgenev, and later by Maupassant and Gide.

144:39. never . . . plot. For further attacks upon the primacy of plot and "story," see "The Art of Fiction," Chapter 7.

144:41. the figure of an individual. James elaborates upon the source of Turgenev's inspiration and shows his strong affinity with him in the Preface to *The Portrait of a Lady*, Chapter 13.

145:19. Wordsworth's phantom. "She was a Phantom of Delight," l. 10.

146:21. *réchauffé*. Rehash.

146:29. Dickens. James' review of *Our Mutual Friend* (see Bibliography, part 4) presents many of his strictures against Dickens. For the role of Dickens in the 1884 controversy over the art of fiction, and its aftermath, see our commentary on "The Art of Fiction," Chapter 7, and the notes to pp. 165:22, 169:3, and 181:35 of that chapter.

147:40. came . . . to London. Turgenev visited James in London in 1879 and 1881. On June 20, 1879, after the Russian's reception of an honorary D.C.L. from Oxford, James hosted a dinner for him at the Reform Club.

147:41. Cambridgeshire. At George Eliot's home, Turgenev met William Henry Bullock who hosted the Russian several times at Six Mile Bottom, the estate which Turgenev said featured the finest pheasant shooting in England.

148:2. lugubrious winter. The Franco-Prussian War had seriously curtailed Pauline Viardot's income at Baden-Baden, so she struck out for London where concerts and lessons beckoned. Turgenev followed dutifully, living from November 1870 to February 1871 at 4 Bentinck Street in Manchester Square. He wrote to Flaubert that the English "lead a very hard life. You have to get used to it as to their climate" (Magarshack p. 265).

148:13. villa. Turgenev with the Viardots purchased the *Villa des Frenês* in 1875.

148:19. the last time. Magarshack dates this ride November 17, Schapiro November 18, 1882.

148:42. *banlieue*. Suburbs.

TEXTUAL VARIANTS

132:13. one must. 1884: I shall.

132:18. depths. 1884: bottom.

132:24. contact and intercourse. 1884: his personal character.

133:8. which. 1884: that.

133:14. reactionary. 1884: reversionary.

133:19. Muscovite. 1884: national.

133:21. was not. 1884: was a very definite individual. He was not.

133:23. an individual. 1884: a *person*.

133:23. unmistakable. 1884: substantial.

133:25. eminent. 1884: detached.

133:34. tinted. 1884: touched.

133:39. too. Added 1888.

133:39. not. . . . But. 1884: not serene and propitious, but dark and almost violent. But.

133:42. being. . . . had. 1884: being. I had.

134:4. his affection. 1884: my affections.

134:14. so. 1884: as.

134:16. unsafe. 1884: precarious.

134:33. painted. 1884: described.

134:39. pieces. 1884: elements.

135:6. speculative, anything but literal. 1884: humorous, ironical.

135:10. (I give his name, without attempting the Russian orthography, as it was uttered by his friends when they addressed him in French.) Added 1888.

135:31. many intelligent. 1884: several different.

136:3. moreover . . . on. 1884: moreover (this is a very frank allusion), on.

136:13. fictions. 1884: stories.

136:19. not to the purpose. 1884: a good deal too thin.

136:37. the last. 1884: the very last.

137:1. salient. 1884: definite.

137:2. high. In. 1884: high. George Eliot he also greatly admired. He had made her acquaintance during the sorrowful winter of the Franco-Prussian war, which he spent in London, and I have heard her express a high appreciation of his own genius. In.

137:32. sincere. He. 1884: sincere. His opinion of Victor Hugo could not have been expressed in a few words, but admiration, of course, was a considerable part of it. I remember (on Turgénieff's lips) a brilliant description of Victor Hugo's transcendent state of mind with regard to himself (Victor Hugo), and as a corollary with regard to others. If it was deliberate and discriminating, it was also pictorial and humorous. He.

137:34. bravery. 1884: refinement.

137:34. and of. 1884: and irony of.

138:26. high. 1884: extraordinary.

138:40. the numerous. 1884: such.

139:3. jurisdiction. Yet. 1884: jurisdiction. It was not for art to be moral, any more than for chemistry; it was for morality, since it cared so much about the matter, to be artful. Yet.

139:4. his. 1884: Turgénieff's.

139:20. sociability. [par.] I. 1884: sociability. He was with everything that was said, and the simplicity, naturalness, *bonhomie*, of his talk made it as charming as it was just. His contribution to every discussion always touched the essential part of it. [par.] I.

139:29. conceivable. 1884: known.

140:10. to. 1884: of.

141:36. veracity. 1884: the truth.

142:9. god. [par.] In. 1884: god. [par.] On the first floor of the house in the Rue de Douai was a gallery of pictures (where later, I remember, one evening, I saw him take part with delightful comicality in an extemporized charade), into which, one of the first times I saw him, he took me to look at a portrait just painted of him by a Russian artist working in Paris. This, perhaps, was one of his premature admirations, for the picture, though respectable, could not long satisfy any one who carried well in his eye the admirable head and the deep physiognomy of the original; and I remember that in the Salon of that year it produced little effect. To paint Turgénieff at all properly would have required a painter of style. I may appear to gossip too much; but it seems to me that if with the more irresponsible method of the pen one attempts a sketch of so interesting a man, every trifle is of value as an item of resemblance. I will venture to say, then, that in his personal arrangements there was an almost exaggerated neatness, a love of order which resulted sometimes in angularity. In.

142:19. its. . . . It. 1884: its extraordinary record of fixed habits, I have just been reading. It.

142:36. fortune. . . . It. 1884: fortune; for such an accident in the life of a man of letters has the highest importance. It.

143:2. a long list. 1884: very numerous.

143:24. prospect. 1884: view.

143:41. reverts. . . . It. 1884: reverts to all the circumstances with a tenderness that I cannot express. It.

144:4. morning meal. 1884: "breakfast."

144:14. being struck. 1884: brightness.

144:34. happy. Added 1888.

145:24. in . . . them. 1884: in order to illustrate a plot. Such stories will always, probably, find most favor with many readers, because they remind them.

145:37. There . . . them. Added 1888.

146:7. *Lisa*. 1884: A Nest of Noblemen.

146:12. things that. 1884: which.

146:19. richness. 1884: depth.

146:37. diverted. 1884: entertained.

146:38. complexity. 1884: curiosity.

146:39. fascinating. I. 1884: fascinating. [par.] I.

146:40. touching in. 1884: touching to me in.

147:1. large. 1884: tall.

147:3. had. . . . Each. 1884: had in their composition the element of irony and sadness. Each.

147:9. erudition . . . which. 1884: erudition and labor which.

147:14. (it . . . plates). Added 1888.

147:15. which. . . . He. 1884: which sunk them rather than floated them. He.

147:24. ungenerous. 1884: unfaithful.

147:30. "give," that. 1884: "give," as the French say, that.

147:32. failure of an organ. 1884: local dumbness.

147:34. something . . . in. 1884: something impressive in.

147:40. assisted. 1884: favored.

148:37. Turgénieff. 1884: Serguéitch.

148:38. case . . . touched. 1884: case; no sojourner in Paris was less French than he. Paris touched.

149:19. he. . . . 1884: he was also a rare genius.

PART TWO

THE THEORIST ON
FICTION AND CULTURE

SEVEN

THE ART OF FICTION

I SHOULD NOT HAVE AFFIXED SO COMPREHENSIVE A TITLE to these few remarks, necessarily wanting in any completeness upon a subject the full consideration of which would carry us far, did I not seem to discover a pretext for my temerity in the interesting pamphlet lately published under this name by Mr. Walter Besant. Mr. Besant's lecture at the Royal Institution—the original form of his pamphlet—appears to indicate that many persons are interested in the art of fiction, and are not indifferent to such remarks, as those who practise it may attempt to make about it. I am therefore anxious not to lose the benefit of this favourable association, and to edge in a few words under cover of the attention which Mr. Besant is sure to have excited. There is something very encouraging in his having put into form certain of his ideas on the mystery of story-telling.

It is a proof of life and curiosity—curiosity on the part of the brotherhood of novelists as well as on the part of their readers. Only a short time ago it might have been supposed that the English novel was not what the French call *discutable*. It had no air of having a theory, a conviction, a consciousness of itself behind it—of being the expression of an artistic faith, the result of choice and comparison. I do not say it was necessarily the worse for that: it would take much more courage than I possess to intimate that the form of the novel as Dickens and Thackeray (for instance) saw it had any taint of incompleteness. It was, however, *naïf* (if I may help myself out with another French word); and evidently if it be destined to suffer in any way for having lost its *naïveté* it has now an idea of making sure of the corresponding advantages. During the period I have alluded to there was a comfortable, good-humoured feeling abroad that a novel is a novel, as a pudding is a pudding, and that our only business with it could be to swallow it. But within a year or two, for some reason or other, there have been signs of returning animation—the era of discussion would appear to have been to a certain extent opened. Art

165

lives upon discussion, upon experiment, upon curiosity, upon variety of attempt, upon the exchange of views and the comparison of standpoints; and there is a presumption that those times when no one has anything particular to say about it, and has no reason to give for practice or preference, though they may be times of honour, are not times of development—are times, possibly even, a little of dulness. The successful application of any art is a delightful spectacle, but the theory too is interesting; and though there is a great deal of the latter without the former I suspect there has never been a genuine success that has not had a latent core of conviction. Discussion, suggestion, formulation, these things are fertilising when they are frank and sincere. Mr. Besant has set an excellent example in saying what he thinks, for his part, about the way in which fiction should be written, as well as about the way in which it should be published; for his view of the "art," carried on into an appendix, covers that too. Other labourers in the same field will doubtless take up the argument, they will give it the light of their experience, and the effect will surely be to make our interest in the novel a little more what it had for some time threatened to fail to be—a serious, active, inquiring interest, under protection of which this delightful study may, in moments of confidence, venture to say a little more what it thinks of itself.

It must take itself seriously for the public to take it so. The old superstition about fiction being "wicked" has doubtless died out in England; but the spirit of it lingers in a certain oblique regard directed toward any story which does not more or less admit that it is only a joke. Even the most jocular novel feels in some degree the weight of the proscription that was formerly directed against literary levity: the jocularity does not always succeed in passing for orthodoxy. It is still expected, though perhaps people are ashamed to say it, that a production which is after all only a "make-believe" (for what else is a "story"?) shall be in some degree apologetic—shall renounce the pretension of attempting really to represent life. This, of course, any sensible, wide-awake story declines to do, for it quickly perceives that the tolerance granted to it on such a condition is only an attempt to stifle it disguised in the form of generosity. The old evangelical hostility to the novel, which was as explicit as it was narrow, and which regarded it as little less favourable to our immortal part than a stage-play, was in reality far less insulting. The only reason for the existence of a novel is that it does attempt to represent life. When it relinquishes this attempt, the same attempt that we see on the canvas of the painter, it will have arrived at a very strange pass. It is not expected of the picture that it will make itself humble in order to be forgiven; and the analogy between the art of the painter and the art of the novelist is, so far as I am able to see, complete. Their inspiration is the same, their process (allowing for the different quality of the vehicle), is the same, their success is the same. They may learn from each other, they may explain and sustain each other. Their cause is the same, and the honour of one is the honour of another. The Mahometans think a picture an unholy thing, but it is a long time since any Christian did, and it is therefore the more odd that in the Christian mind the traces (dissimulated though they may be) of a suspicion of the sister art should linger to this day. The only effectual way to lay it to rest is to emphasise the analogy to which I just alluded—to insist on the fact that as the picture is reality, so the novel is history. That is the only general description (which does it justice) that we may give of the novel. But history also is allowed to represent life; it is not, any more than painting, expected to apologise. The subject-matter of fiction is stored up likewise in documents and records, and if it will not give itself away, as they say in California, it must speak with assurance, with the tone of the historian. Certain accomplished novelists have a habit of giving themselves away which must often bring tears to the eyes of people who take their fiction seriously. I was lately struck, in reading over many pages of Anthony Trollope, with his want of discretion in this particular. In a digression, a parenthesis or an aside, he concedes to the reader that he and this trusting friend are only "making believe." He admits that the events he narrates have not really happened, and that he can give his narrative any turn the reader may like best. Such a betrayal of a sacred office seems to me, I confess, a terrible crime; it is what I mean by the attitude of apology, and it shocks me every whit as much in Trollope as it would have shocked me in Gibbon or Macaulay. It implies that the novelist is less occupied in looking for the truth (the truth, of course I mean, that he assumes, the premises that we must grant him, whatever they may be), than the historian, and in doing so it deprives him at a stroke of all his standing-room. To represent and illustrate the past, the actions of men, is the task of either writer, and the only difference that I can see is, in proportion as he succeeds, to the honour of the novelist, consisting as it does in his having more difficulty in collecting his evidence, which is so far from being purely literary. It seems to me to give him a great character, the fact that he has at once so much in common with the philosopher and the painter; this double analogy is a magnificent heritage.

It is of all this evidently that Mr. Besant is full when he insists upon the fact that fiction is one of the *fine* arts, deserving in its turn of all the honours and emoluments that have hitherto been reserved for the successful profession of music, poetry, painting, architecture. It is impossible to insist too much on so important a truth, and the place that Mr. Besant demands for the work of the novelist may be represented, a trifle less abstractly, by saying that he demands not only that it shall be reputed artistic, but that it shall be reputed very artistic indeed. It is excellent that he should have struck this note, for his doing so indicates that there was need of it, that his proposition may be to many people a novelty. One rubs one's eyes at the thought; but the rest of Mr. Besant's essay confirms the revelation. I suspect in truth that it would be possible to confirm it still further, and that one would not be far wrong in saying that in addition to the people to whom it has never occurred that a novel ought to be artistic, there are a great many others who, if this principle were urged upon them, would be filled with an indefinable mistrust. They would find it difficult to explain their repugnance, but it would operate strongly to put them on their guard. "Art," in our Protestant communities, where so many things have got so strangely twisted about, is supposed in certain circles to have some vaguely injurious effect upon those who make it an important consideration, who let it weigh in the balance. It is assumed to be opposed in some mysterious manner to morality, to amusement, to instruction. When it is embodied in the work of the painter (the sculptor is another affair!) you know what it is: it stands there before you, in the honesty of pink and green and a gilt frame; you can see the worst of it at a glance, and you can be on your guard. But when it is introduced into literature it becomes more insidious—there is danger of its hurting you before you know it. Literature should be either instructive or amusing, and there is in many minds an impression that these artistic preoccupations, the search for form, contribute to neither end, interfere indeed with both. They are too frivolous to be edifying, and too serious to be diverting; and they are moreover priggish and paradoxical and superfluous. That, I think, represents the manner in which the latent thought of many people who read novels as an exercise in skipping would explain itself if it were to become articulate. They would argue, of course, that a novel ought to be "good," but they would interpret this term in a fashion of their own, which indeed would vary considerably from one critic to another. One would say that being good means representing virtuous and aspiring characters, placed in prominent positions; another would say that it depends on a "happy ending," on a distribution at the last of prizes, pensions, husbands, wives, babies, millions, appended paragraphs, and cheerful remarks. Another still would say that it means being full of incident and movement, so that we shall wish to jump ahead, to see who was the mysterious stranger, and if the stolen will was ever found, and shall not be distracted from this pleasure by any tiresome analysis or "description." But they would all agree that the "artistic" idea would spoil some of their fun. One would hold it accountable for all the description, another would see it revealed in the absence of sympathy. Its hostility to a happy ending would be evident, and it might even in some cases render any ending at all impossible. The "ending" of a novel is, for many persons, like that of a good dinner, a course of dessert and ices, and the artist in fiction is regarded as a sort of meddlesome doctor who forbids agreeable aftertastes. It is therefore true that this conception of Mr. Besant's of the novel as a superior form encounters not only a negative but a positive indifference. It matters little that as a work of art it should really be as little or as much of its essence to supply happy endings, sympathetic characters, and an objective tone, as if it were a work of mechanics: the association of ideas, however incongruous, might easily be too much for it if an eloquent voice were not sometimes raised to call attention to the fact that it is at once as free and as serious a branch of literature as any other.

Certainly this might sometimes be doubted in presence of the enormous number of works of fiction that appeal to the credulity of our generation, for it might easily seem that there could be no great character in a commodity so quickly and easily produced. It must be admitted that good novels are much compromised by bad ones, and that the field at large suffers discredit from overcrowding. I think, however, that this injury is only superficial, and that the superabundance of written fiction proves nothing against the principle itself. It has been vulgarised, like all other kinds of literature, like everything else to-day, and it has proved more than some kinds accessible to vulgarisation. But there is as much difference as there ever was between a good novel and a bad one: the bad is swept with all the daubed canvases and spoiled marble into some unvisited limbo, or infinite rubbish-yard beneath the back-windows of the world, and the good subsists and emits its light and stimulates our desire for perfection. As I shall take the liberty of making but a single criticism of Mr. Besant, whose tone is so full of the love of his art, I may as well have done with it at once. He seems to me to mistake in attempting to say so definitely beforehand what sort of an affair the good novel will be. To indicate the danger of such an error as that has been the purpose of these few pages; to suggest that certain traditions on the subject, applied *a priori*, have already had much to answer for, and that the good health of an art which undertakes so immediately to reproduce

169

life must demand that it be perfectly free. It lives upon exercise, and the very meaning of exercise is freedom. The only obligation to which in advance we may hold a novel, without incurring the accusation of being arbitrary, is that it be interesting. That general responsibility rests upon it, but it is the only one I can think of. The ways in which it is at liberty to accomplish this result (of interesting us) strike me as innumerable, and such as can only suffer from being marked out or fenced in by prescription. They are as various as the temperament of man, and they are successful in proportion as they reveal a particular mind, different from others. A novel is in its broadest definition a personal, a direct impression of life: that, to begin with, constitutes its value, which is greater or less according to the intensity of the impression. But there will be no intensity at all, and therefore no value, unless there is freedom to feel and say. The tracing of a line to be followed, of a tone to be taken, of a form to be filled out, is a limitation of that freedom and a suppression of the very thing that we are most curious about. The form, it seems to me, is to be appreciated after the fact: then the author's choice has been made, his standard has been indicated; then we can follow lines and directions and compare tones and resemblances. Then in a word we can enjoy one of the most charming of pleasures, we can estimate quality, we can apply the test of execution. The execution belongs to the author alone; it is what is most personal to him, and we measure him by that. The advantage, the luxury, as well as the torment and responsibility of the novelist, is that there is no limit to what he may attempt as an executant—no limit to his possible experiments, efforts, discoveries, successes. Here it is especially that he works, step by step, like his brother of the brush, of whom we may always say that he has painted his picture in a manner best known to himself. His manner is his secret, not necessarily a jealous one. He cannot disclose it as a general thing if he would; he would be at a loss to teach it to others. I say this with a due recollection of having insisted on the community of method of the artist who paints a picture and the artist who writes a novel. The painter *is* able to teach the rudiments of his practice, and it is possible, from the study of good work (granted the aptitude), both to learn how to paint and to learn how to write. Yet it remains true, without injury to the *rapprochement,* that the literary artist would be obliged to say to his pupil much more than the other, "Ah, well, you must do it as you can!" It is a question of degree, a matter of delicacy. If there are exact sciences, there are also exact arts, and the grammar of painting is so much more definite that it makes the difference.

I ought to add, however, that if Mr. Besant says at the beginning of his essay that the "laws of fiction may be laid down and taught with as much precision and exactness as the laws of harmony, perspective, and proportion," he mitigates what might appear to be an extravagance by applying his remark to "general" laws, and by expressing most of these rules in a manner with which it would certainly be unaccommodating to disagree. That the novelist must write from his experience, that his "characters must be real and such as might be met with in actual life;" that "a young lady brought up in a quiet country village should avoid descriptions of garrison life," and "a writer whose friends and personal experiences belong to the lower middle-class should carefully avoid introducing his characters into society;" that one should enter one's notes in a common-place book; that one's figures should be clear in outline; that making them clear by some trick of speech or of carriage is a bad method, and "describing them at length" is a worse one; that English Fiction should have a "conscious moral purpose;" that "it is almost impossible to estimate too highly the value of careful workmanship—that is, of style;" that "the most important point of all is the story," that "the story is everything": these are principles with most of which it is surely impossible not to sympathise. That remark about the lower middle-class writer and his knowing his place is perhaps rather chilling; but for the rest I should find it difficult to dissent from any one of these recommendations. At the same time, I should find it difficult positively to assent to them, with the exception, perhaps, of the injunction as to entering one's notes in a common-place book. They scarcely seem to me to have the quality that Mr. Besant attributes to the rules of the novelist—the "precision and exactness" of "the laws of harmony, perspective, and proportion." They are suggestive, they are even inspiring, but they are not exact, though they are doubtless as much so as the case admits of: which is a proof of that liberty of interpretation for which I just contended. For the value of these different injunctions— so beautiful and so vague—is wholly in the meaning one attaches to them. The characters, the situation, which strike one as real will be those that touch and interest one most, but the measure of reality is very difficult to fix. The reality of Don Quixote or of Mr. Micawber is a very delicate shade; it is a reality so coloured by the author's vision that, vivid as it may be, one would hesitate to propose it as a model: one would expose one's self to some very embarrassing questions on the part of a pupil. It goes without saying that you will not write a good novel unless you possess the sense of reality; but it will be difficult to give you a recipe for calling that sense into being. Humanity is immense, and reality has a myriad forms; the most one can affirm is that some of the flowers of fiction have the odour of it, and others have not; as for telling you in advance how your nosegay should be composed, that is another affair. It is equally excellent and inconclusive to say that one must write from experience; to our supposititious aspirant such a declaration might savour of mockery. What kind of experience is intended, and where does it begin and end? Experience is never limited, and it is never complete; it is an immense sensibility, a kind of huge spiderweb of the finest silken threads suspended in the chamber of consciousness, and catching every airborne particle in its tissue. It is the very atmosphere of the mind; and when the mind is imaginative—much more when it happens to be that of a man of genius—it takes to itself the faintest hints of life, it converts the very pulses of the air into revelations. The young lady living in a village has only to be a damsel upon whom nothing is lost to make it quite unfair (as it seems to me) to declare to her that she shall have nothing to say about the military. Greater miracles have been seen than that, imagination assisting, she should speak the truth about some of these gentlemen. I remember an English novelist, a woman of genius, telling me that she was much commended for the impression she had managed to give in one of her tales of the nature and way of life of the French Protestant youth. She had been asked where she learned so much about this recondite being, she had been congratulated on her peculiar opportunities. These opportunities consisted in her having once, in Paris, as she ascended a staircase, passed an open door where, in the household of a *pasteur,* some of the young Protestants were seated at table round a finished meal. The glimpse made a picture; it lasted only a moment, but that moment was experience. She had got her direct personal impression, and she turned out her type. She knew what youth was, and what Protestantism; she also had the advantage of having seen what it was to be French, so that she converted these ideas into a concrete image and produced a reality. Above all, however, she was blessed with the faculty which when you give it an inch takes an ell, and which for the artist is a much greater source of strength than any accident of residence or of place in the social scale. The power to guess the unseen from the seen, to trace the implication of things, to judge the whole piece by the pattern, the condition of feeling life in general so completely that you are well on your way to knowing any particular corner of it—this cluster of gifts may almost be said to constitute experience, and they occur in country and in town, and in the most differing stages of education. If experience consists of impressions, it may be said that impressions *are* experience, just as (have we not seen it?) they are the very air we

172

breathe. Therefore, if I should certainly say to a novice, "Write from experience and experience only," I should feel that this was rather a tantalising monition if I were not careful immediately to add, "Try to be one of the people on whom nothing is lost!"

I am far from intending by this to minimise the importance of exactness—of truth of detail. One can speak best fron one's own taste, and I may therefore venture to say that the air of reality (solidity of specification) seems to me to be the supreme virtue of a novel—the merit on which all its other merits (including that conscious moral purpose of which Mr. Besant speaks) helplessly and submissively depend. If it be not there they are all as nothing, and if these be there, they owe their effect to the success with which the author has produced the illusion of life. The cultivation of this success, the study of this exquisite process, form, to my taste, the beginning and the end of the art of the novelist. They are his inspiration, his despair, his reward, his torment, his delight. It is here in very truth that he competes with life; it is here that he competes with his brother the painter in *his* attempt to render the look of things, the look that conveys their meaning, to catch the colour, the relief, the expression, the surface, the substance of the human spectacle. It is in regard to this that Mr. Besant is well inspired when he bids him take notes. He cannot possibly take too many, he cannot possibly take enough. All life solicits him, and to "render" the simplest surface, to produce the most momentary illusion, is a very complicated business. His case would be easier, and the rule would be more exact, if Mr. Besant had been able to tell him what notes to take. But this, I fear, he can never learn in any manual; it is the business of his life. He has to take a great many in order to select a few, he has to work them up as he can, and even the guides and philosophers who might have most to say to him must leave him alone when it comes to the application of precepts, as we leave the painter in communion with his palette. That his characters "must be clear in outline," as Mr. Besant says—he feels that down to his boots; but how he shall make them so is a secret between his good angel and himself. It would be absurdly simple if he could be taught that a great deal of "description" would make them so, or that on the contrary the absence of description and the cultivation of dialogue, or the absence of dialogue and the multiplication of "incident," would rescue him from his difficulties. Nothing, for instance, is more possible than that he be of a turn of mind for which this odd, literal opposition of description and dialogue, incident and description, has little meaning and light. People often talk of these things as if they had a kind of internecine distinctness, instead of melting into each other at every breath, and being intimately associated parts of one general effort of expression. I cannot imagine composition existing in a series of blocks, nor conceive, in any novel worth discussing at all, of a passage of description that is not in its intention narrative, a passage of dialogue that is not in its intention descriptive, a touch of truth of any sort that does not partake of the nature of incident, or an incident that derives its interest from any other source than the general and only source of the success of a work of art—that of being illustrative. A novel is a living thing, all one and continuous, like any other organism, and in proportion as it lives will it be found, I think, that in each of the parts there is something of each of the other parts. The critic who over the close texture of a finished work shall pretend to trace a geography of items will mark some frontiers as artificial, I fear, as any that have been known to history. There is an old-fashioned distinction between the novel of character and the novel of incident which must have cost many a smile to the intending fabulist who was keen about his work. It appears to me as little to the point as the equally celebrated distinction between the novel and the romance—to answer as little to any reality. There are bad novels and good novels, as there are bad pictures and good pictures; but that is the only distinction in which I see any meaning, and I can as little imagine speaking of a novel of character as I can imagine speaking of a picture of character. When one says picture one says of character, when one says novel one says of incident, and the terms may be transposed at will. What is character but the determination of incident? What is incident but the illustration of character? What is either a picture or a novel that is *not* of character? What else do we seek in it and find in it? It is an incident for a woman to stand up with her hand resting on a table and look out at you in a certain way; or if it be not an incident I think it will be hard to say what it is. At the same time it is an expression of character. If you say you don't see it (character in *that—allons donc!*), this is exactly what the artist who has reasons of his own for thinking he *does* see it undertakes to show you. When a young man makes up his mind that he has not faith enough after all to enter the church as he intended, that is an incident, though you may not hurry to the end of the chapter to see whether perhaps he doesn't change once more. I do not say that these are extraordinary or startling incidents. I do not pretend to estimate the degree of interest proceeding from them, for this will depend upon the skill of the painter. It sounds almost puerile to say that some incidents are intrinsically much more important than others, and I need not take this precaution after having professed my sympathy for the major ones in remarking that the only classification

174

of the novel that I can understand is into that which has life and that which has it not.

The novel and the romance, the novel of incident and that of character—these clumsy separations appear to me to have been made by critics and readers for their own convenience, and to help them out of some of their occasional queer predicaments, but to have little reality or interest for the producer, from whose point of view it is of course that we are attempting to consider the art of fiction. The case is the same with another shadowy category which Mr. Besant apparently is disposed to set up—that of the "modern English novel"; unless indeed it be that in this matter he has fallen into an accidental confusion of standpoints. It is not quite clear whether he intends the remarks in which he alludes to it to be didactic or historical. It is as difficult to suppose a person intending to write a modern English as to suppose him writing an ancient English novel: that is a label which begs the question. One writes the novel, one paints the picture, of one's language and of one's time, and calling it modern English will not, alas! make the difficult task any easier. No more, unfortunately, will calling this or that work of one's fellow-artist a romance—unless it be, of course, simply for the pleasantness of the thing, as for instance when Hawthorne gave this heading to his story of *Blithedale*. The French, who have brought the theory of fiction to remarkable completeness, have but one name for the novel, and have not attempted smaller things in it, that I can see, for that. I can think of no obligation to which the "romancer" would not be held equally with the novelist; the standard of execution is equally high for each. Of course it is of execution that we are talking—that being the only point of a novel that is open to contention. This is perhaps too often lost sight of, only to produce interminable confusions and cross-purposes. We must grant the artist his subject, his idea, his *donnée*: our criticism is applied only to what he makes of it. Naturally I do not mean that we are bound to like it or find it interesting: in case we do not our course is perfectly simple—to let it alone. We may believe that of a certain idea even the most sincere novelist can make nothing at all, and the event may perfectly justify our belief; but the failure will have been a failure to execute, and it is in the execution that the fatal weakness is recorded. If we pretend to respect the artist at all, we must allow him his freedom of choice, in the face, in particular cases, of innumerable presumptions that the choice will not fructify. Art derives a considerable part of its beneficial exercise from flying in the face of presumptions, and some of the most interesting experiments of which it is capable are hidden in the bosom of common things. Gustave Flaubert has written a story about the devotion of a servant-girl to a parrot, and the production, highly finished as it is, cannot on the whole be called a success. We are perfectly free to find it flat, but I think it might have been interesting; and I, for my part, am extremely glad he should have written it; it is a contribution to our knowledge of what can be done—or what cannot. Ivan Turgénieff has written a tale about a deaf and dumb serf and a lap-dog, and the thing is touching, loving, a little masterpiece. He struck the note of life where Gustave Flaubert missed it—he flew in the face of a presumption and achieved a victory.

Nothing, of course, will ever take the place of the good old fashion of "liking" a work of art or not liking it: the most improved criticism will not abolish that primitive, that ultimate test. I mention this to guard myself from the accusation of intimating that the idea, the subject, of a novel or a picture, does not matter. It matters, to my sense, in the highest degree, and if I might put up a prayer it would be that artists should select none but the richest. Some, as I have already hastened to admit, are much more remunerative than others, and it would be a world happily arranged in which persons intending to treat them should be exempt from confusions and mistakes. This fortunate condition will arrive only, I fear, on the same day that critics become purged from error. Meanwhile, I repeat, we do not judge the artist with fairness unless we say to him, "Oh, I grant you your starting-point, because if I did not I should seem to prescribe to you, and heaven forbid I should take that responsibility. If I pretend to tell you what you must not take, you will call upon me to tell you then what you must take; in which case I shall be prettily caught. Moreover, it isn't till I have accepted your data that I can begin to measure you. I have the standard, the pitch; I have no right to tamper with your flute and then criticise your music. Of course I may not care for your idea at all; I may think it silly, or stale, or unclean; in which case I wash my hands of you altogether. I may content myself with believing that you will not have succeeded in being interesting, but I shall, of course, not attempt to demonstrate it, and you will be as indifferent to me as I am to you. I needn't remind you that there are all sorts of tastes: who can know it better? Some people, for excellent reasons, don't like to read about carpenters; others, for reasons even better, don't like to read about courtesans. Many object to Americans. Others (I believe they are mainly editors and publishers) won't look at Italians. Some readers don't like quiet subjects; others don't like bustling ones. Some enjoy a complete illusion, others the consciousness of large concessions. They choose their novels accordingly, and if they don't care about your idea they won't, *a fortiori*, care about your treatment."

So that it comes back very quickly, as I have said, to the liking: in spite of M. Zola, who reasons less powerfully than he represents, and who will not reconcile himself to this absoluteness of taste, thinking that there are certain things that people ought to like, and that they can be made to like. I am quite at a loss to imagine anything (at any rate in this matter of fiction) that people *ought* to like or to dislike. Selection will be sure to take care of itself, for it has a constant motive behind it. That motive is simply experience. As people feel life, so they will feel the art that is most closely related to it. This closeness of relation is what we should never forget in talking of the effort of the novel. Many people speak of it as a factitious, artificial form, a product of ingenuity, the business of which is to alter and arrange the things that surround us, to translate them into conventional, traditional moulds. This, however, is a view of the matter which carries us but a very short way, condemns the art to an eternal repetition of a few familiar *clichés*, cuts short its development, and leads us straight up to a dead wall. Catching the very note and trick, the strange irregular rhythm of life, that is the attempt whose strenuous force keeps Fiction upon her feet. In proportion as in what she offers us we see life *without* rearrangement do we feel that we are touching the truth; in proportion as we see it *with* rearrangement do we feel that we are being put off with a substitute, a compromise and convention. It is not uncommon to hear an extraordinary assurance of remark in regard to this matter of rearranging, which is often spoken of as if it were the last word of art. Mr. Besant seems to me in danger of falling into the great error with his rather unguarded talk about "selection." Art is essentially selection, but it is a selection whose main care is to be typical, to be inclusive. For many people art means rose-coloured window-panes, and selection means picking a bouquet for Mrs. Grundy. They will tell you glibly that artistic considerations have nothing to do with the disagreeable, with the ugly; they will rattle off shallow commonplaces about the province of art and the limits of art till you are moved to some wonder in return as to the province and the limits of ignorance. It appears to me that no one can ever have made a seriously artistic attempt without becoming conscious of an immense increase—a kind of revelation—of freedom. One perceives in that case—by the light of a heavenly ray—that the province of art is all life, all feeling, all observation, all vision. As Mr. Besant so justly intimates, it is all experience. That is a sufficient answer to those who maintain that it must not touch the sad things of life, who stick into its divine unconscious bosom little prohibitory inscriptions on the end of sticks, such as we see in public gardens—"It is forbidden to walk on the grass; it is forbidden to touch the flowers; it is not allowed to introduce dogs or to remain after dark; it is requested to keep to the right." The young aspirant in the line of fiction whom we continue to imagine will do nothing without taste, for in that case his freedom would be of little use to him; but the first advantage of his taste will be to reveal to him the absurdity of the little sticks and tickets. If he have taste, I must add, of course he will have ingenuity, and my dis-respectful reference to that quality just now was not meant to imply that it is useless in fiction. But it is only a secondary aid; the first is a capacity for receiving straight impressions.

Mr. Besant has some remarks on the question of "the story" which I shall not attempt to criticise, though they seem to me to con-tain a singular ambiguity, because I do not think I understand them. I cannot see what is meant by talking as if there were a part of a novel which is the story and part of it which for mystical reasons is not—unless indeed the distinction be made in a sense in which it is difficult to suppose that any one should attempt to convey anything. "The story," if it represents anything, represents the subject, the idea, the *donnée* of the novel; and there is surely no "school"—Mr. Besant speaks of a school—which urges that a novel should be all treatment and no subject. There must assuredly be something to treat; every school is intimately conscious of that. This sense of the story being the idea, the starting-point, of the novel, is the only one that I see in which it can be spoken of as something different from its organic whole; and since in proportion as the work is successful the idea per-meates and penetrates it, informs and animates it, so that every word and every punctuation-point contribute directly to the expression, in that proportion do we lose our sense of the story being a blade which may be drawn more or less out of its sheath. The story and the novel, the idea and the form, are the needle and thread, and I never heard of a guild of tailors who recommended the use of the thread without the needle, or the needle without the thread. Mr. Besant is not the only critic who may be observed to have spoken as if there were certain things in life which constitute stories, and certain others which do not. I find the same odd implication in an entertaining article in the *Pall Mall Gazette*, devoted, as it happens, to Mr. Besant's lecture. "The story is the thing!" says this graceful writer, as if with a tone of op-position to some other idea. I should think it was, as every painter who, as the time for "sending in" his picture looms in the distance, finds himself still in quest of a subject—as every belated artist not fixed about his theme will heartily agree. There are some subjects which speak to us and others which do not, but he would be a clever man who should undertake to give a rule—an index expurgatorius— by which the story and the no-story should be known apart. It is impossible (to me at least) to imagine any such rule which shall not be altogether arbitrary. The writer in the *Pall Mall* opposes the delightful (as I suppose) novel of *Margot la Balafrée* to certain tales in which "Bostonian nymphs" appear to have "rejected English dukes for psychological reasons." I am not acquainted with the romance just designated, and can scarcely forgive the *Pall Mall* critic for not mentioning the name of the author, but the title appears to refer to a lady who may have received a scar in some heroic adventure. I am inconsolable at not being acquainted with this episode, but am utterly at a loss to see why it is a story when the rejection (or acceptance) of a duke is not, and why a reason, psychological or other, is not a subject when a cicatrix is. They are all particles of the multitudinous life with which the novel deals, and surely no dogma which pretends to make it lawful to touch the one and unlawful to touch the other will stand for a moment on its feet. It is the special picture that must stand or fall, according as it seem to possess truth or to lack it. Mr. Besant does not, to my sense, light up the subject by intimating that a story must, under penalty of not being a story, consist of "adventures." Why of adventures more than of green spectacles? He mentions a category of impossible things, and among them he places "fiction without adventure." Why without adventure, more than without matrimony, or celibacy, or parturition, or cholera, or hydropathy, or Jansenism? This seems to me to bring the novel back to the hapless little *rôle* of being an artificial, ingenious thing—bring it down from its large, free character of an immense and exquisite correspondence with life. And what *is* adventure, when it comes to that, and by what sign is the listening pupil to recognise it? It is an adventure—an immense one— for me to write this little article; and for a Bostonian nymph to reject an English duke is an adventure only less stirring, I should say, than for an English duke to be rejected by a Bostonian nymph. I see dramas within dramas in that, and innumerable points of view. A psychological reason is, to my imagination, an object adorably pictorial; to catch the tint of its complexion—I feel as if that idea might inspire one to Titianesque efforts. There are few things more exciting to me, in short, than a psychological reason, and yet, I protest, the novel seems to me the most magnificent form of art. I have just been reading, at the same time, the delightful story of *Treasure Island*, by Mr.

Robert Louis Stevenson and, in a manner less consecutive, the last tale from M. Edmond de Goncourt, which is entitled *Chérie*. One of these works treats of murders, mysteries, islands of dreadful renown, hairbreadth escapes, miraculous coincidences and buried doubloons. The other treats of a little French girl who lived in a fine house in Paris, and died of wounded sensibility because no one would marry her. I call *Treasure Island* delightful, because it appears to me to have succeeded wonderfully in what it attempts; and I venture to bestow no epithet upon *Chérie*, which strikes me as having failed deplorably in what it attempts—that is in tracing the development of the moral consciousness of a child. But one of these productions strikes me as exactly as much of a novel as the other, and as having a "story" quite as much. The moral consciousness of a child is as much a part of life as the islands of the Spanish Main, and the one sort of geography seems to me to have those "surprises" of which Mr. Besant speaks quite as much as the other. For myself (since it comes back in the last resort, as I say, to the preference of the individual), the picture of the child's experience has the advantage that I can at successive steps (an immense luxury, near to the "sensual pleasure" of which Mr. Besant's critic in the *Pall Mall* speaks) say Yes or No, as it may be, to what the artist puts before me. l have been a child in fact, but I have been on a quest for a buried treasure only in supposition, and it is a simple accident that with M. de Goncourt I should have for the most part to say No. With George Eliot, when she painted that country with a far other intelligence, I always said Yes.

The most interesting part of Mr. Besant's lecture is unfortunately the briefest passage—his very cursory allusion to the "conscious moral purpose" of the novel. Here again it is not very clear whether he be recording a fact or laying down a principle; it is a great pity that in the latter case he should not have developed his idea. This branch of the subject is of immense importance, and Mr. Besant's few words point to considerations of the widest reach, not to be lightly disposed of. He will have treated the art of fiction but superficially who is not prepared to go every inch of the way that these considerations will carry him. It is for this reason that at the beginning of these remarks I was careful to notify the reader that my reflections on so large a theme have no pretension to be exhaustive. Like Mr. Besant, I have left the question of the morality of the novel till the last, and at the last I find I have used up my space. It is a question surrounded with difficulties, as witness the very first that meets us, in the form of a definite question, on the threshold. Vagueness, in such a discussion, is fatal, and what is the meaning of your morality and your conscious moral purpose? Will you not define your terms and explain how (a novel being a picture) a picture can be either moral or immoral? You wish to paint a moral picture or carve a moral statue: will you not tell us how you would set about it? We are discussing the Art of Fiction; questions of art are questions (in the widest sense) of execution; questions of morality are quite another affair, and will you not let us see how it is that you find it so easy to mix them up? These things are so clear to Mr. Besant that he has deduced from them a law which he sees embodied in English Fiction, and which is "a truly admirable thing and a great cause for congratulation." It is a great cause for congratulation indeed when such thorny problems become as smooth as silk. I may add that in so far as Mr. Besant perceives that in point of fact English Fiction has addressed itself preponderantly to these delicate questions he will appear to many people to have made a vain discovery. They will have been positively struck, on the contrary, with the moral timidity of the usual English novelist; with his (or with her) aversion to face the difficulties with which on every side the treatment of reality bristles. He is apt to be extremely shy (whereas the picture that Mr. Besant draws is a picture of boldness), and the sign of his work, for the most part, is a cautious silence on certain subjects. In the English novel (by which of course I mean the American as well), more than in any other, there is a traditional difference between that which people know and that which they agree to admit that they know, that which they see and that which they speak of, that which they feel to be a part of life and that which they allow to enter into literature. There is the great difference, in short, between what they talk of in conversation and what they talk of in print. The essence of moral energy is to survey the whole field, and I should directly reverse Mr. Besant's remark and say not that the English novel has a purpose, but that it has a diffidence. To what degree a purpose in a work of art is a source of corruption I shall not attempt to inquire; the one that seems to me least dangerous is the purpose of making a perfect work. As for our novel, I may say lastly on this score that as we find it in England to-day it strikes me as addressed in a large degree to "young people," and that this in itself constitutes a presumption that it will be rather shy. There are certain things which it is generally agreed not to discuss, not even to mention, before young people. That is very well, but the absence of discussion is not a symptom of the moral passion. The purpose of the English novel—"a truly admirable thing, and a great cause for congratulation"—strikes me therefore as rather negative.

There is one point at which the moral sense and the artistic sense lie very near together; that is in the light of the very obvious truth that the deepest quality of a work of art will always be the quality of the mind of the producer. In proportion as that intelligence is fine will the novel, the picture, the statue partake of the substance of beauty and truth. To be constituted of such elements is, to my vision, to have purpose enough. No good novel will ever proceed from a superficial mind; that seems to me an axiom which, for the artist in fiction, will cover all needful moral ground: if the youthful aspirant take it to heart it will illuminate for him many of the mysteries of "purpose." There are many other useful things that might be said to him, but I have come to the end of my article, and can only touch them as I pass. The critic in the *Pall Mall Gazette*, whom I have already quoted, draws attention to the danger, in speaking of the art of fiction, of generalising. The danger that he has in mind is rather, I imagine, that of particularising, for there are some comprehensive remarks which, in addition to those embodied in Mr. Besant's suggestive lecture, might without fear of misleading him be addressed to the ingenuous student. I should remind him first of the magnificence of the form that is open to him, which offers to sight so few restrictions and such innumerable opportunities. The other arts, in comparison, appear confined and hampered; the various conditions under which they are exercised are so rigid and definite. But the only condition that I can think of attaching to the composition of the novel is, as I have already said, that it be sincere. This freedom is a splendid privilege, and the first lesson of the young novelist is to learn to be worthy of it. "Enjoy it as it deserves," I should say to him; "take possession of it, explore it to its utmost extent, publish it, rejoice in it. All life belongs to you, and do not listen either to those who would shut you up into corners of it and tell you that it is only here and there that art inhabits, or to those who would persuade you that this heavenly messenger wings her way outside of life altogether, breathing a superfine air, and turning away her head from the truth of things. There is no impression of life, no manner of seeing it and feeling it, to which the plan of the novelist may not offer a place; you have only to remember that talents so dissimilar as those of Alexandre Dumas and Jane Austen, Charles Dickens and Gustave Flaubert have worked in this field with equal glory. Do not think too much about optimism and pessimism; try and catch the colour of life itself. In France to-day we see a prodigious effort (that of Emile Zola, to whose solid and serious work no explorer of the capacity of the novel can allude without respect), we see an extraordinary effort vitiated by a spirit of pessimism on a narrow basis. M. Zola is magnificent, but he strikes an

English reader as ignorant; he has an air of working in the dark; if he had as much light as energy, his results would be of the highest value. As for the aberrations of a shallow optimism, the ground (of English fiction especially) is strewn with their brittle particles as with broken glass. If you must indulge in conclusions, let them have the taste of a wide knowledge. Remember that your first duty is to be as complete as possible—to make as perfect a work. Be generous and delicate and pursue the prize."

At Bolton Street, Henry James in the summer of 1884 replied to Walter Besant's lecture "The Art of Fiction" with his own "The Art of Fiction" which was published in the September number of *Longman's* and was revised for *Partial Portraits* (1888). In 1884, one phase of James' life was over and another was beginning, both professionally and personally. *The Portrait of a Lady* had earned James critical praise as "the first of English-writing novelists" (*Princeton Review* [1884]). But increasingly reviewers were expressing weariness with James' international theme. His reply would be *The Bostonians* and *The Princess Casamassima* (both 1886) which eschew the international theme for the naturalistic dissection of society practiced by the French. "They do the only kind of work, to-day, that I respect," James told Howells (February 21, 1884). James' personal life had been irrevocably altered by the deaths of his parents. Upon returning to London in September of 1883, James was, as Edel and Spilka show, concerned with finding another type of family, a fraternity of fellow writers. "The Art of Fiction" is, among other things, an attempt to foster such a community.

Preeminent among Anglo-American discussions of fiction, "The Art of Fiction" reveals additional richness when read in its historical context. The essay is part of the Victorian period's increasing self-consciousness about the nature of fiction, part of fiction's increasingly tense relations with literary and moral orthodoxies, and part of Henry James' increasingly tense relations with readers.

Victorian self-consciousness about fiction is underrated by James when he says that readers consume novels like pudding. Many of James' ideas were aired and debated in popular periodicals in the years before 1884, as Stang and Graham show. But Spilka and Goode argue persuasively that James was correct in the larger sense which he intended: compared to French discussions of fiction, Anglo-American criticism *was* provincial—moralistic, theme-ridden, antiformalist. By the 1880s, however, things were changing. "The Art of Fiction" is the title of an essay drafted in 1881 by Thomas Hardy and of productions in 1884 by Besant, James, and Andrew Lang. These 1884 works are, in turn, part of a controversy which began in 1882 when William Dean Howells enraged Britain by dismissing the fiction of Dickens as passé and espousing the "new" novel exemplified by Henry James. Also in 1882, Robert Louis Stevenson approached the craft from a very different viewpoint in "A Gossip on Romance." In 1883 Henry Norman contrasted criticism in England with the superior practice in France, Germany, and even America. And in December of 1884, the Besant-Lang-James debate is joined by Stevenson with "A Humble Remonstrance," while *Pall Mall* presents both George Moore's protest against the censorship exercised by booksellers and George Gissing's reply which lays responsibility primarily upon the novelists.

What criticism in 1884 also manifests is that an increased self-consciousness about fiction is part of novelists' larger awareness that their relations with orthodoxy are growing tense. As public outrage, mingled occasionally with critical condescension, greets the advent of such scandalous foreign writers as Flaubert, Zola, and Ibsen, the major English novelists, Meredith, Hardy, Moore, and Gissing, all cross swords with the public. Henry James shares his colleagues' anger.

> What you [Howells] tell me of the success of—'s [this author has never been identified] last novel sickens and almost paralyses me. It seems to me (the book) so contemptibly bad and ignoble that the idea of people reading it in such numbers makes one return upon one's self and ask what is the use of trying to write anything decent or serious for a public so absolutely idiotic. It must be totally wasted. I would rather have produced the basest experiment in the 'naturalism' that is being practiced here than such a piece of sixpenny humbug. Work so shamelessly bad seems to me to dishonour the novelist's art to a degree that is absolutely not to be forgiven; just as its success dishonours the people for whom one supposes one's self to write. Excuse my ferocities. . . . (February 21, 1884)

This is barely two months before Besant makes propriety of subject and tone a precondition for novel writing: "it is, fortunately, not possible in this country for any man to defile and defame humanity and still be called an artist." No wonder James in "The Art of Fiction" singles out the "many people" like Besant for whom "art means rose-coloured window-panes, and selection means picking a bouquet for Mrs. Grundy."

James' anger here is not impersonal or abstract. His concern with the nature of fiction and the freedom of authors grows from personal injury. Mrs. Grundy has hurt *him*. Thus what may seem like James' characterization of critics in general—

> one would say that being good means representing virtuous and aspiring characters . . . another would say that it depends on a "happy ending". . . . Another still would say it means being full of incident and movement. . . . One would hold it [the "artistic" idea] accountable for all the description, another would see it revealed in the absence of sympathy—

185

is in fact a defense against attacks upon himself. Virtuous characters, happy endings, lively incidents, and "sympathy" are, Gard and Goode show, precisely what reviewers found wanting in James' own fiction. The virtuous-happy-lively list also sums up, as Spilka demonstrates, what Howells had dismissed in favor of the complex characters, the open endings, and the psychological orientation which James' fiction epitomized. Besant and Lang are replying to Howells. And James in "The Art of Fiction" is defending the new novel.

James is also, however, trying to keep his defense from being offensive. "The Art of Fiction" is not truculent or outraged, and despite sly moments and devastating understatements, it is not derisive. James is trying to establish a community of discussants, to *persuade* rather than to defeat. (He continues to do so, though with less optimism, in the Prefaces and "The Novel in 'The Ring and the Book'".) 1884 is the year of James' long essay on Matthew Arnold, and in "The Art of Fiction" James is particularly intent upon putting the lessons of Arnold (and Sainte-Beuve) into practice. When James contrasts past critical "dulness" with recent "signs of returning animation," he is applying to fiction Arnold's general view that an "epoch of concentration" was now giving way to an "epoch of expansion." James' insistence that "art lives upon discussion . . . upon the exchange of views" is a virtual paraphrase of Arnold's plea for "free play of mind." James aims for a kind of Arnoldian high seriousness by introducing into the trivialized discussions of Besant and Lang some of criticism's most ancient concerns—the *utile et dulce* question of whether art is "instructive or amusing," and the ontological issue of how formal constructs relate to historical "reality." By insisting upon serious themes, James attempts to effect what Arnold established as the critic's task—that improving of the critical climate which fosters the creative act. "Both Byron and Goethe had a great productive power, but Goethe's was nourished by a great critical effort providing the true materials for it, and Byron's was not" ("The Function of Criticism at the Present Time").

Besides Arnold, the other main influences of James' apprentice years also contribute to "The Art of Fiction." Sainte-Beuve as the premier opponent of dogma sounds in James' rejection of the "rules" formulated bumblingly by Besant. Behind James' discussion of "romance" and "novel" is the immense figure of Balzac. At the center of this discussion is Hawthorne, whose romances reach depths as "real" as any French effort at verisimilitude. And finally there is George Eliot, whose superiority to Edmond de Goncourt is established by James with an affirmation which applies to all these heroes of his youth. "I always said Yes."

Readers of "The Art of Fiction" did not say Yes as volubly and as numerously as James wished. In the month after publication, he told the sole person who had responded directly, T. S. Perry, that

> my poor article has not attracted the smallest attention here & I haven't heard, or seen, an allusion to it. There is almost no care for literary discussion here,—questions of form, of principle, the 'serious' idea of the novel appeals apparently to no one, & they don't understand you when you speak of them. (September 26, 1884).

The silence around "The Art of Fiction" was broken again in December when Stevenson's "A Humble Remonstrance" began a friendship which lasted until the younger man's death and resulted in modifications in the final version of "The Art of Fiction." On the whole, however, James' essay received little attention. McElderry lists only a puzzled note in the *Illustrated London News* 85 (September 13, 1884): 247, and an enthusiastic puff by James' friend Grace Norton in the *Nation* 39 (September 25, 1884): 260–61. In addition there was a parody in *Life*, "How We Do It.—No. 1./By Ennery Jeems (Ne E. J., Junior)" 4 (December 4), pp. 314–15. More encouragingly, the *Boston Daily Advertiser* in 1885 put "The Art of Fiction" to serious use by applying its principles to James' most recent piece of fiction ("New. Publications. The Author of 'Beltraffio'" February 24, p. 3). "The Art of Fiction" continued to be ignored when it appeared in 1888 in *Partial Portraits*. The *Critic* 12 (June 9): 278–79, and the *Literary World* 19 (June 23, July 7): 203, 212, merely mentioned the essay in passing. The *Saturday Review* at least took James' "interesting paper" seriously enough to compare its principles with his practice elsewhere in the volume (65 [May 19]: 610).

Recent commentary on "The Art of Fiction" is of three basic types. Excellent studies of the specific James-Besant situation are provided by Goode's "The art of fiction: Walter Besant and Henry James" in *Tradition and tolerance in nineteenth-century fiction*, ed. David Howard et al. (London: Routledge and Kegan Paul, 1966), pp. 243–81; McElderry's "Henry James's 'The Art of Fiction,'" *Research Studies of the State College of Washington* 25 (1957): 91–100; and Spilka's "Henry James and Walter Besant: 'The Art of Fiction' Controversy," NOVEL 6 (1971): 101–19; rpt. in *Toward a Poetics of Fiction*, ed. Spilka (Bloomington: Indiana University Press, 1977), pp. 190–208. "The Art of Fiction" has been analyzed and placed in the larger context of James' critical oeuvre by several critics, including Daugherty (113–24); Miller, "Henry James: A Theory of Fiction," *Prairie Schooner* 45 (1971–72): 330–56; Todd, "Henry James and the Art of Literary Realism," *Philosophy and Literature* 1 (1976): 79–100; and Wellek, "Henry James's Literary Theory and Criticism," *American Literature* 30 (1958–59): 292–321. A still wider perspective which sees James in the tradition of criticism is provided by Falk's "The Literary Criticism of the Genteel Decades: 1870–1900" in *The Development of American Literary Criticism,* ed. Stovall (Chapel Hill: University of North Carolina Press, 1955), pp. 113–57; Graham's *English Criticism of the Novel, 1865–1900* (London: Oxford University Press, 1965); Hunter's "The Uncritical Attitude" in *Edwardian Fiction* (Cambridge: Harvard University Press, 1982), pp. 35–44; O'Connor's *An Age of Criticism* (Chicago: Regnery, 1952), pp. 58–63; and Stang's *The Theory of the Novel in England, 1850–1870* (New York: Columbia University Press, 1959).

NOTES

165:5. Sir Walter Besant (1836–1901), British novelist, historian of London, and reformer. Besant delivered his lecture on 25 April, 1884. It soon appeared in pamphlet form in both England (Chatto and Windus) and America (Cupples, Upham). It was also published with James' essay in 1884 and 1885 by the latter publisher, and by De Wolfe in 1884. For more on Besant see Boege's "Sir Walter Besant: Novelist" *Nineteenth Century Fiction* 10 (1956): 249–80, 11 (1956): 32–60.

165:17. *discutable:* discussable. Though French words appear throughout James' criticism, the introduction of French here and below ("if I may help myself out with another French word") serves several specific rhetorical purposes. James, as Spilka notes, "was quietly invoking a novel more discussable than the English, a theory more sophisticated" (105). This move is also James' covert introduction into the discussion of a critic who will figure powerfully in his critique of English criticism and culture, Matthew Arnold. Arnold had repeatedly insisted that Britain could profitably imitate the French example of free, nurturing discussion. Finally, James in pledging allegiance to France is insisting upon a superiority where reviewers had found a limitation. They had faulted him as too French in his highly analytic, often dark, and resolutely unsentimental fiction.

165:22. Dickens and Thackeray. "The reference to Thackeray and Dickens is no idle instance here. James's close friend and fellow novelist, William Dean Howells, had courageously roused these spectres in his controversial essay of 1882. 'The art of fiction,' he had then asserted, has 'become a finer art in our day than it was with Dickens and Thackeray. . . . These great men are of the past . . . '; whereas the 'new school . . . which is so largely of the future as well as the present, finds its chief exemplar in Mr. James; it is he who is shaping and directing American fiction at least.' In a letter to Howells, James noted the storm these claims had roused in England: 'articles about you and me are thick as blackberries—we are daily immolated on the altar of Thackeray and Dickens.' [Edel 3: 71] To allay these national gods, and to dissociate himself from Howells' temerity in offending them, James makes his nice distinction between completeness and *naiveté*—and subtly shifts attention from American upstarts to French sophisticates" (Spilka, 105). Gard reprints both the Howells essay and a representatively strident British response.

165:29. within a year or two. James has in mind: Howells' "Henry James, Jr.," *Century*, n.s. 3 (1882): 25–29, and the furor it aroused; Stevenson's "A Gossip on Romance," *Longman's* 1 (1882): 69–79; "The Arabian Nights," *Saturday Review* 54 (November 4, 1882): 609; Mrs. D. M. M. Craik's *Plain Speaking* (1882); Henry Norman's "Theories and Practice of Modern Fiction," *Fortnightly* 40 (1883): 870–86; Trollope's *Autobiography* (1883); Besant's lecture, its appearance in pamphlet form, and reactions to it in Lang's "The Art of Fiction," *Pall Mall Gazette* (April 30, 1884): 1–2; rpt. in *Critic* 4 (1884): 249–50, R. H. Hutton's "Mr. Besant on the Art of Fiction," *Spectator* (May 24, 1884): 674–75; rpt. in *Critic* 4 (1884): 297–98; and Margaret Oliphant's "Three Young Novelists," *Blackwood's* 126 (1884): 296–97, 306.

165:30. era . . . opened. "Epochs of concentration cannot well endure for ever; epochs of expansion, in the due course of things, follow them. Such an epoch of expansion seems to be opening in this country" ("The Function of Criticism at the Present Time").

166:10. Discussion . . . fertilizing. Arnold, after distinguishing between Byron and Goethe, goes on to emphasize the fertilizing priority of critical discussion. "Criticism first; a time of true creative activity, perhaps,— which, as I have said, must inevitably be preceded amongst us by a time of criticism,—hereafter, when criticism has done its work" ("The Function of Criticism at the Present Time").

167:1. analogy. The linking of fiction and painting precedes Besant considerably. Daugherty notes that "Flaubert and his school . . . compared the writing of fiction to painting and," like Besant, "believed that 'precision and exactness' were to be sought in both" (116). Spilka finds the analogy "as early as Bulwer-Lytton" (117).

167:12. history. Confronted with an objection lingering from the eighteenth century, James defends fiction with a version of the argument made originally by Defoe and Fielding. The novel is valuable because it is "true," "real," like history. James sees the novelist as historian in his review of *Middlemarch* and in "Honoré de Balzac," Chapters 3 and 4. He takes the opposite tack and distinguishes between literature and history in the Preface to *The Aspern Papers* and "The Novel in 'The Ring and the Book,'" Chapters 16 and 21.

168:38. virtuous and aspiring characters. In belittling critics who overrate and simplify this component of fiction, James is responding to attacks on his own characterization which began as early as 1869 when *Roundtable* said that "his characters have an air of unreality" (7 [June 27]: 411). The *Nation* in 1871 and 1872 repeated the charge of "unreality" (13 [November 30]: 358; 15 [October 31]: 284), and *Appleton's* in 1875 faulted *Roderick Hudson* for "fail[ing] so utterly in the essential point of impressing us with the objective reality of the people to whom it introduces us" (14 [December 18]: 793). Each of James' subsequent novels in this phase received comparable criticism: *The American* in 1877 (*Literary World* 8 [July]: 29, *Galaxy* 24 [July]: 137–38, *Eclectic*, n.s. 26 [August]: 249–50); *The Europeans* in 1878 (*Spectator* 51 [October 26]: 1334–36) and in 1879 (*Harper's* 58 [January]: 309, *Appleton's*, n.s. 6 [January]: 95, *North American Review* 128 [January]: 101, *Atlantic* 43 [January]: 106–7); *Washington Square* in 1881 (*Atlantic* 47 [May]: 710, *Saturday Review* 51 [March 19]: 372, *Lippincott's* 27 [February]: 214); and *The Portrait of a Lady* in 1881 (*Spectator* 54 [November 26]: 1504, *Saturday Review* 52 [December 3]: 703, 704, *Critic* 1 [December]: 333–34) and in 1882 (*Independent*, 34 [January 19]: 11, *Lippincott's* 29 [February]: 214, *Blackwood's* 131 [March]: 377–81); see also Trevor Creighton's attack on *The Portrait* in *Ethics of Some Modern Novels* (1884).

168:39. "happy ending." As early as 1869, *Roundtable* finds the endings of James' stories "almost always rendered unsatisfactory and faulty" (411). A decade later *The American* was roundly criticized for its ending (*Atlantic* 40 [July 1877]: 108–9, *Nation* 24 [May 31, 1877]: 325–26, *Galaxy* 24 [July 1877]: 135–38 *Appleton's*, n.s. 3 [August 1877]: 189–90, *Eclectic*, n.s. 26 [August 1877]: 249–50, *Scribner's* 14 [July 1877]: 406–7, *British Quarterly* 70 [1879]: 268). See also James' reply to Howells' letter lamenting the ending (March 30, 1877). Again the subsequent novels evoke a similar complaint: *The Europeans* in 1879 (*Scribner's* 17 [January 1879]: 447); *Confidence* in 1880 (*Spectator* 53 [January 10]: 48); *Washington Square* in 1881 (*Spectator* 54 [February 5]: 185, *Saturday Review* 51 [March 19, 1881]: 372); and *The Portrait* in 1881 (*Spectator* 54 [November 26]: 1506) and 1882 (*Dial* 2 [January]: 215, *Lippincott's* 29 [February]: 213–15; *Blackwood's* 131 [March]: 381, *Eclectic* 35 [January]: 281).

168:42. full of incident. James' preference for psychological rather than swashbuckling events was also objected to early on. In 1875 *Appleton's* likened the tales in *The Passionate Pilgrim* to "stories of his in the *Atlantic*, a long time ago": all are "aggravating and unsatisfying things" because they have only "the outline of a plot; nothing complete, vigorous" (13 [February 13, 1875]: 214). By 1879 the *Atlantic* finds that in *The Europeans* "Mr. James has advanced in his art; in *this* story of his there is absolutely no action at all" (43 [January]: 106). *Spectator* 51 (October 26, 1878): 1334–35, *Academy* 14 (1878): 354, *North American Review* 128 (January 1879): 101–6, and *Harper's* 58 (1879): 309, all agreed. *Washington Square* was faulted for its events in 1881 (*Spectator* 185–86), as was *The Portrait* in both 1881 (*Literary World* [12]: 473–74, *Saturday Review* [52]: 703–4) and 1882 (*Nation* [34]: 102–3, *Eclectic* 35 [January]: 281).

169:3. tiresome analysis or "description." James was at times faulted for describing with too great minuteness, but critics worried more about his analytic bent. In 1872 the *Nation* warned about "a danger in the way of the analyst . . . that he may be tempted to make his personages rather with a view to their cutting up interestingly and easily, than with a view to their being men and women capable of being alive" (284). Three years later *Appleton's* found the characters in *Roderick Hudson* "dissected beforehand with a precision and neatness which leaves no opportunity for the spontaneous" (14 [December 18, 1875]: 793). This type of criticism was most in evidence with *The Portrait*: for 1881 see *Athenaeum* 2822 (November 26): 699, and *Critic* 1 (December 3): 333–34; for 1882, *Nation* 34 (February 2): 102–3 and John Nichols' *American Literature: An Historical Sketch, 1620–1880*, p. 389.

169:6. the absence of sympathy. With an insensitivity chillingly prophetic, *Literary World* in 1875 called James' relations to his characters in *A Passionate Pilgrim* "too unsympathetic ever to be popular" (5 [March 1875]: 157). In the same year the *Independent* found that "his cold and heartless tone becomes very tiresome" in *Roderick Hudson* (27 [December 23, 1875]: 8). The same two periodicals agreed about *The American* in 1877, the *Independent* calling it "absolutely cold-blooded" (29 [May 17]: 9), *Literary World* finding the characters "not presented for sympathy but for inspection" (8 [July 1877]: 29). The *Independent* was joined by the *Atlantic* in making a comparable criticism of *The Europeans* (30 [November 21, 1878]: 9; 43 [January 1879]: 7). In its 1882 review of *The Portrait*, the *Critic* complained that James' "scientific . . . realistic, almost materialistic" treatment of life "does not satisfy the heart . . . our author has none of the pathos of Dickens . . . [he is] interesting, but not warming" (2 [January 14]: 1). More harshly, the *Catholic World* called James "unmerciful" (34 [February 1882]: 717), and the *Independent* agreed. "There is no good heart in it [*The Portrait*]" (34 [January 19, 1882]: 1). Besant thus touched a nerve when he descanted upon "modern Sympathy." "It first appeared . . . about a hundred and fifty years ago, when the modern novel came into existence." Inevitably, therefore, fiction "not only requires of its followers, but also creates in readers, that sentiment which is destined to be a most mighty engine in deepening and widening the civilization of the world . . . Sympathy . . . the Enthusiasm of Humanity."

169:34. light and . . . perfection. Arnold in *Culture and Anarchy* defines culture as "*a study of perfection*" and defines the "pursuit of perfection" as "the pursuit of sweetness and light" ("Sweetness and Light"). The ideal of "light" recurs as a touchstone throughout "The Art of Fiction."

170:11. a direct impression of life. James returns to this theme in the Preface to *The Portrait of a Lady*, Chapter 13.

171:35. Mr. Micawber is the colorful paterfamilias who befriends Dickens' David Copperfield.

172:18. a woman of genius. Thackeray's elder daughter, Anne, Lady Ritchie (1837–1919), presents this scene in *The Story of Elizabeth* (1863). Armstrong discusses James' use of the Thackeray scene in *The Phenomenology of Henry James* (Chapel Hill: University of North Carolina Press, 1983), pp. 38–49.

173:4. "one . . . on whom nothing is lost." In espousing a sensitivity which responds to the subtlest intricacies and nuances of the human predicament, James chooses language which parodies Besant's much more mechanical view of the novelist as recording consciousness. "There are places where the production of a note-book would be embarrassing—say, at a dinner party, or a street fight; yet the man who begins to observe will speedily be able to remember everything that he sees and hears until he can find an opportunity to note it down, so that nothing is lost." Then, in 1886, James goes to objectify his ideal of consciousness in Hyacinth Robinson, "a youth on whom nothing was lost" (*The Princess Casamassima*, Chapter 11). And, more than twenty years later, in the Preface to *The Princess*, James (probably unconsciously) continues the attack upon Besant's mechanical version of the noting consciousness by explaining how his "notes" on London, his "working imagination," became both the source of Hyacinth's knowledge of the city and the model of the protagonist's consciousness.

173:7. air of reality (solidity of specification). This equation shows the lingering influence of Balzac and the immediate influence of his heirs, the French naturalists. Although James' concern with the nature of reality derives in part from his family's interest in epistemology, his presentation of the issue in "The Art of Fiction" reflects also his own immediate irritation at reviewers' naiveté. "Nothing so elaborate ever could be real," *Blackwood's* said of the dialogue in *The Portrait* (131 [March 1882]: 383). Little more encouraging was *Lippincott's* faint praise: "the portrait of Miss Archer . . . in all other respects than that of reality is a brilliant success" (29 [February 1882]: 214).

174:18. novel and . . . romance. For James making the opposite argument—distinguishing sharply between these two forms—see the Preface to *The American*, Chapter 12.

174:25. incident . . . character. James expands upon this false distinction in his Preface to *The Portrait of a Lady*, Chapter 13.

175:21. *Blithedale*. James' almost patronizing tone here reflects his repeated refusal to take seriously the dark side of Hawthorne's vision and art. For this and his general discussion of "romance," see "From *Hawthorne*," Chapter 5.

175:36. failure to execute. The apparent contradiction here—James insisting both that writers must be granted their donnée and that some subjects are more remunerative and important than others—was first noticed by McElderry (97) and has been examined at length by McDonald in "The Inconsistencies in Henry James's Aesthetics," *Texas Studies in Literature and Language* 10 (1969): 585–97. For the counterclaim that James is being purposively ambiguous see Falk (134) and Roberts (*The Art of Fiction and Other Essays by Henry James* [New York: Oxford University Press, 1948], pp. xi–xii). Interestingly, Lang seems to catch Besant in something of the same contradiction. Besant, like James, espouses the moral neutrality of the subject and then attacks Zola for the same unclean subjects which James faults in the French novelist.

176:1. a story. *Un Coeur simple* (1877).

176:7. a tale. *Mumu* (written 1852; published 1854).

177:4. Zola. For James' long struggle with Zola's ideas and themes see "Emile Zola," Chapter 20.

177:28. "selection." For the paradoxical need to make selection typical see the Preface to *Roderick Hudson.*

177:31. Mrs. Grundy. In Thomas Morton's play *Speed the Plow* (1798), Dame Ashfield constantly fears the sneers of her neighbor, a Mrs. Grundy. Ashfield's frequent question "What will Mrs. Grundy say?" became proverbial. In the later nineteenth century, "Mrs. Grundy" was often linked with "Mr. Mudie." Charles Edward Mudie (1818–90), whose chain of circulating libraries was the largest in Britain, refused to stock books controversial morally, and thus acted as a censor like Mrs. Grundy. For more on Mudie see Griest's *Mudie's Circulating Library and the Victorian Novel* (Bloomington: Indiana University Press, 1970).

178:22. "school." Having said "there is a school which pretends that there is no need for a story," Besant counters with the claim that "the story is everything."

178:33. the idea and the form. James denies this distinction eloquently in the Preface to *The Awkward Age.* "It helps us ever so happily to see the grave distinction between substance and form in a really wrought work of art signally break down" (p. 313).

178:38. article. James playfully refuses to mention in "The Art of Fiction" his target, the well-known journalist and anthropologist, Andrew Lang (1848–1912), but writes fiercely to Stevenson on July 31, 1888: "Lang, in the D[aily]. N[ews]., every morning, and I believe in a hundred other places, uses his beautiful thin facility to write everything down to the lowest level of philistine twaddle—the view of the old lady round the corner or the clever person at the dinner party." For James' later repsonse to Lang, see note to p. 213, l. 11 of "Guy de Maupassant," Chapter 8, and our commentary on "Criticism," Chapter 9.

179:8. *Margot la Balafrée.* Fortuné-Hippolyte-Auguste Du Boisgobey (1821–91) published this novel in Paris in 1884.

179:9. "Bostonian nymphs." Lang is disparaging here James' own novella, "An International Episode" (1879). Lang's attack was particularly irritating to James because the novella had received chauvinistic criticism from the British upon its publication. James told his family: "So long as one serves up Americans for their entertainment it is all right—but hands off the sacred natives! They are really, I think, thinner-skinned than we are" (January 4, 1879). James' subsequent letter (March 21) in reply to Mrs. Frank H. Hill's negative review in the infamous *Daily News* (March 21, p. 6) is an eloquent defense of his novella and of fiction's freedom generally.

180:2. James' criticism of Goncourt is an attack upon Lang, in at least two ways. Since Lang uses *Chérie* to exemplify the kind of fiction which he thinks Howells is advocating, Lang is equating Goncourt with the novelist whom Howells was actually espousing, Henry James. James' rejection of *Chérie* is an insistence upon the difference between his art and Goncourt's.

James, in turn, by espousing George Eliot at the expense of Goncourt, allies himself with the best of the "old" fiction which Lang in the face of Howells' strictures had sonorously defended—thus largely taking away the distinction between old and new which Lang had used to belittle fiction like James'. Second, by separating Goncourt from Howells, James reveals Lang's inability to make such critical distinctions and thus provides evidence for his larger point—that the British reviewer is incapable of serious criticism generally.

180:24. that country. George Eliot portrayed the consciousness of a young girl in *The Mill on the Floss* (1860) and *Silas Marner* (1861).

180:42. For James' late answer to this question see our commentary on the Prefaces.

181:21. By including America, James implicates one of his Brahmin editors, James Russell Lowell, who insisted that a man should not write what he would forbid his adolescent daughter to read.

181:35. "young people." James is carrying on that critique of prudery in English-language fiction which Dickens had excoriated as "Podsnappery" in *Our Mutual Friend*. "Would it bring a blush to the cheek of the young person" (bk. 1, chap. 11) is a standard which precludes mature examination of life. For this issue in Dickens see Ruth Bernard Yeazell's "Podsnappery, Sexuality, and the English Novel" in *Critical Inquiry* 9 (1982): 339–57. See also Stang's chapter "The Cheek of the Young Person." In 1899 James takes the issue of "things which it is generally agreed not to discuss, nor even to mention, before young people" and makes it the subject of *The Awkward Age*.

182:13. danger . . . of generalizing. Lang had opined: "Hard, hard, it is, to generalize about any art" (2).

182:18. the magnificence of the form. James repeats this testament to the novel in "The Future of the Novel," the Preface to *The Ambassadors*, and "Emile Zola," Chapters 10, 18, and 20.

182:29. corners. James is generalizing from his 1880 attack upon Zola— "Do you call that corner of a pig-sty . . . the *world*?"

TEXTUAL VARIANTS

165:24. be. 1884: is.

165:28. our . . . it. 1884: this was the end of it.

166:28. orthodoxy. 1884: gravity.

166:32. represent. 1884: compete with. James' revision of "compete" in its first three occurrences in the 1884 version of "The Art of Fiction" is made in response to Stevenson's objections in "A Humble Remonstrance." "No art—to use the daring phrase of Mr. James—can successfully 'compete with life'. . . . Life goes before us, infinite in complication. . . . It combines and employs in its manifestation the method and material, not of one art only, but of all the arts. . . . Man's one method, whether he reasons or creates, is to half-shut his eyes against the dazzle and confusion of reality . . . and regard instead a certain figmentary abstraction. . . . Our art is occupied, and bound to be occupied, not so much in making stories true as in making them typical. . . . Life is monstrous, infinite, illogical, abrupt, and poignant; a work of art, in comparison, is neat, finite, self-contained, rational, flowing, and emasculate." Spilka argues convincingly that James meant "compete" in a quite different, ontological sense—the creation of a reality alternate to life but of a comparable intensity (115–17).

166:39. does . . . life. 1884: *does* compete with life.

166:39. it . . . it. 1884: it ceases to compete as the canvas of the painter competes, it.

167:6. Another. The Mahometans. 1884: another. Peculiarities of manner, of execution, that correspond on either side, exist in each of them and contribute to their development. The Mahometans.

167:14. to represent life; it. 1884: to compete with life, as I say; it.

167:30. (the . . .). Added in 1888.

169:14. much of its essence to. 1884: much concerned to.

169:23. character. 1884: substance.

169:24. much. 1884: somewhat.

170:11. a direct. Added in 1888.

170:20. and resemblances. Added in 1888.

170:30. jealous. 1884: deliberate.

171:4. extravagance. 1884: over-statement.

172:28. direct personal. Added in 1888.

172:28. turned out. 1884: evolved.

173:2. rather a. 1884: a rather.

173:9. on. 1884: in.

173:27. manual. 1884: hand-book.

174:9. any. 1884: every.

174:12. shall. 1884: will.

174:16. fabulist. 1884: romancer.

174:24. at will. Added in 1888.

174:26. either. Added in 1888.

175:1. into. . . . [par.] The. 1884: into the interesting and the uninteresting. [par.] The.

175:4. clumsy. Added in 1888.

175:5. their . . . but. 1884: their difficulties, but.

175:21. *Blithedale*. Italics added in 1888.

175:23. name. 1884: word.

175:30. idea, his. 1884: idea, what the French call his.

176:18. remunerative. 1884: substantial.

176:27. prettily. 1884: nicely.

176:29. the pitch. Added in 1888.

176:29. I . . . . Of. 1884: I judge you by what you propose, and you must look out for me there. Of.

176:41. others. . . . They. 1884: others revel in a complete deception. They.

177:28. the. 1884: this.

177:31. window-panes. 1884: windows.

178:1. the . . . life. 1884: the painful.

178:12. a. . . . [par.] Mr. 1884: a vivid sense of reality. [par.] Mr.

178:22. *donnée.* 1884: data.

179:2. theme. 1884: *donnée.*

179:4. an . . . expurgatorius. Added in 1888.

179:8. *Margot la Balafrée.* Italics added in 1888.

180:1. in a manner less consecutive. Added in 1888.

180:9. deplorably. Added in 1888.

180:21. in fact. Added in 1888.

180:21. have . . . and. 1884: have never been on a quest for a buried treasure, and.

180:25. with . . . intelligence. Added in 1888.

180:29. be. 1884: is.

182:3. intelligence is fine. 1884: mind is rich and noble.

182:24. sincere. 1884: interesting.

182:27. publish. 1884: reveal.

182:37. Do not. 1884: Don't.

183:8. and . . . prize. 1884: and then, in the vulgar phrase, go in!

E I G H T

GUY DE MAUPASSANT

T HE FIRST ARTISTS, IN ANY LINE, ARE DOUBTLESS NOT
those whose general ideas about their art are most often on their
lips—those who most abound in precept, apology, and formula and
can best tell us the reasons and the philosophy of things. We know
the first usually by their energetic practice, the constancy with which
they apply their principles, and the serenity with which they leave us
to hunt for their secret in the illustration, the concrete example. None
the less it often happens that a valid artist utters his mystery, flashes
upon us for a moment the light by which he works, shows us the rule
by which he holds it just that he should be measured. This accident is
happiest, I think, when it is soonest over; the shortest explanations of
the products of genius are the best, and there is many a creator of
living figures whose friends, however full of faith in his inspiration,
will do well to pray for him when he sallies forth into the dim wilder-
ness of theory. The doctrine is apt to be so much less inspired than
the work, the work is often so much more intelligent than the doctrine. M. Guy de Maupassant has lately traversed with a firm and
rapid step a literary crisis of this kind; he has clambered safely up the
bank at the further end of the morass. If he has relieved himself in the
preface to *Pierre et Jean*, the last-published of his tales, he has also
rendered a service to his friends; he has not only come home in a
recognisable plight, escaping gross disaster with a success which
even his extreme good sense was far from making in advance a matter
of course, but he has expressed in intelligible terms (that by itself is a
ground of felicitation) his most general idea, his own sense of his
direction. He has arranged, as it were, the light in which he wishes to
sit. If it is a question of attempting, under however many disadvan-
tages, a sketch of him, the critic's business therefore is simplified:
there will be no difficulty in placing him, for he himself has chosen
the spot, he has made the chalk-mark on the floor.

  I may as well say at once that in dissertation M. de Maupassant does not write with his best pen; the philosopher in his composition is perceptibly inferior to the story-teller. I would rather have written half a page of *Boule de Suif* than the whole of the introduction to Flaubert's *Letters to Madame Sand;* and his little disquisition on the novel in general, attached to that particular example of it which he has just put forth,[1] is considerably less to the point than the master-piece which it ushers in. In short, as a commentator M. de Maupassant is slightly common, while as an artist he is wonderfully rare. Of course we must, in judging a writer, take one thing with another, and if I could make up my mind that M. de Maupassant is weak in theory, it would almost make me like him better, render him more approachable, give him the touch of softness that he lacks, and show us a human flaw. The most general quality of the author of *La Maison Tellier* and *Bel-Ami*, the impression that remains last, after the others have been accounted for, is an essential hardness—hardness of form, hardness of nature; and it would put us more at ease to find that if the fact with him (the fact of execution) is so extraordinarily definite and adequate, his explanations, after it, were a little vague and sentimental. But I am not sure that he must even be held foolish to have noticed the race of critics: he is at any rate so much less foolish than several of that fraternity. He has said his say concisely and as if he were saying it once for all. In fine, his readers must be grateful to him for such a passage as that in which he remarks that whereas the public at large very legitimately says to a writer, "Console me, amuse me, terrify me, make me cry, make me dream, or make me think," what the sincere critic says is, "Make me something fine in the form that shall suit you best, according to your temperament." This seems to me to put into a nutshell the whole question of the different classes of fiction, concerning which there has recently been so much discourse. There are simply as many different kinds as there are persons practising the art, for if a picture, a tale, or a novel be a direct impression of life (and that surely constitutes its interest and value), the impression will vary according to the plate that takes it, the particular structure and mixture of the recipient.

I am not sure that I know what M. de Maupassant means when he says, "The critic shall appreciate the result only according to the nature of the effort; he has no right to concern himself with tendencies." The second clause of that observation strikes me as rather in the air, thanks to the vagueness of the last word. But our author adds to the definiteness of his contention when he goes on to say that any

[1]*Pierre et Jean.* Paris: Ollendorff, 1888.

form of the novel is simply a vision of the world from the standpoint of a person constituted after a certain fashion, and that it is therefore absurd to say that there is, for the novelist's use, only one reality of things. This seems to me commendable, not as a flight of metaphysics, hovering over bottomless gulfs of controversy, but, on the contrary, as a just indication of the vanity of certain dogmatisms. The particular way we see the world is our particular illusion about it, says M. de Maupassant, and this illusion fits itself to our organs and senses; our receptive vessel becomes the furniture of *our* little plot of the universal consciousness.

"How childish, moreover, to believe in reality, since we each carry our own in our thought and in our organs. Our eyes, our ears, our sense of smell, of taste, differing from one person to another, create as many truths as there are men upon earth. And our minds, taking instruction from these organs, so diversely impressed, understand, analyse, judge, as if each of us belonged to a different race. Each one of us, therefore, forms for himself an illusion of the world, which is the illusion poetic, or sentimental, or joyous, or melancholy, or unclean, or dismal, according to his nature. And the writer has no other mission than to reproduce faithfully this illusion, with all the contrivances of art that he has learned and has at his command. The illusion of beauty, which is a human convention! The illusion of ugliness, which is a changing opinion! The illusion of truth, which is never immutable! The illusion of the ignoble, which attracts so many! The great artists are those who make humanity accept their particular illusion. Let us, therefore, not get angry with any one theory, since every theory is the generalised expression of a temperament asking itself questions."

What is interesting in this is not that M. de Maupassant happens to hold that we have no universal measure of the truth, but that it is the last word on a question of art from a writer who is rich in experience and has had success in a very rare degree. It is of secondary importance that our impression should be called, or not called, an illusion; what is excellent is that our author has stated more neatly than we have lately seen it done that the value of the artist resides in the clearness with which he gives forth that impression. His particular organism constitutes a *case*, and the critic is intelligent in proportion as he apprehends and enters into that case. To quarrel with it because it is not another, which it could not possibly have been without a wholly different outfit, appears to M. de Maupassant a deplorable waste of time. If this appeal to our disinterestedness may strike some readers as chilling (through their inability to conceive of any other form than the one they like—a limitation excellent for a reader but poor for a judge), the occasion happens to be none of the best for saying so, for M. de Maupassant himself precisely presents all the symptoms of a "case" in the most striking way, and shows us how far the consideration of them may take us. Embracing such an opportunity as this, and giving ourselves to it freely, seems to me indeed to be a course more fruitful in valid conclusions, as well as in entertainment by the way, than the more common method of establishing one's own premises. To make clear to ourselves those of the author of *Pierre et Jean*—those to which he is committed by the very nature of his mind—is an attempt that will both stimulate and repay curiosity. There is no way of looking at his work less dry, less academic, for as we proceed from one of his peculiarities to another, the whole horizon widens, yet without our leaving firm ground, and we see ourselves landed, step by step, in the most general questions—those explanations of things which reside in the race, in the society. Of course there are cases and cases, and it is the salient ones that the disinterested critic is delighted to meet.

What makes M. de Maupassant salient is two facts: the first of which is that his gifts are remarkably strong and definite, and the second that he writes directly *from* them, as it were: holds the fullest, the most uninterrupted—I scarcely know what to call it—the boldest communication with them. A case is poor when the cluster of the artist's sensibilities is small, or they themselves are wanting in keenness, or else when the personage fails to admit them—either through ignorance, or diffidence, or stupidity, or the error of a false ideal—to what may be called a legitimate share in his attempt. It is, I think, among English and American writers that this latter accident is most liable to occur; more than the French we are apt to be misled by some convention or other as to the sort of feeler we *ought* to put forth, forgetting that the best one will be the one that nature happens to have given us. We have doubtless often enough the courage of our opinions (when it befalls that we have opinions), but we have not so constantly that of our perceptions. There is a whole side of our perceptive apparatus that we in fact neglect, and there are probably many among us who would erect this tendency into a duty. M. de Maupassant neglects nothing that he possesses; he cultivates his garden with admirable energy; and if there is a flower you miss from the rich parterre, you may be sure that it could not possibly have been raised, his mind not containing the soil for it. He is plainly of the opinion that the first duty of the artist, and the thing that makes him most useful to his fellow-men, is to master his instrument, whatever it may happen to be.

His own is that of the senses, and it is through them alone, or almost alone, that life appeals to him; it is almost alone by their help that he describes it, that he produces brilliant works. They render him this great assistance because they are evidently, in his constitution, extraordinarily alive; there is scarcely a page in all his twenty volumes that does not testify to their vivacity. Nothing could be further from his thought than to disavow them and to minimise their importance. He accepts them frankly, gratefully, works them, rejoices in them. If he were told that there are many English writers who would be sorry to go with him in this, he would, I imagine, staring, say that that is about what was to have been expected of the Anglo-Saxon race, or even that many of them probably could not go with him if they would. Then he would ask how our authors can be so foolish as to sacrifice such a *moyen*, how they can afford to, and exclaim, "They must be pretty works, those they produce, and give a fine, true, complete account of life, with such omissions, such lacunae!" M. de Maupassant's productions teach us, for instance, that his sense of smell is exceptionally acute—as acute as that of those animals of the field and forest whose subsistence and security depend upon it. It might be thought that he would, as a student of the human race, have found an abnormal development of this faculty embarrassing, scarcely knowing what to do with it, where to place it. But such an apprehension betrays an imperfect conception of his directness and resolution, as well as of his constant economy of means. Nothing whatever prevents him from representing the relations of men and women as largely governed by the scent of the parties. Human life in his pages (would this not be the most general description he would give of it?) appears for the most part as a sort of concert of odours, and his people are perpetually engaged, or he is engaged on their behalf, in sniffing up and distinguishing them, in some pleasant or painful exercise of the nostril. "If everything in life speaks to the nostril, why on earth shouldn't we say so?" I suppose him to inquire; "and what a proof of the empire of poor conventions and hypocrisies, *chez vous autres*, that you should pretend to describe and characterise, and yet take no note (or so little that it comes to the same thing) of that essential sign!"

Not less powerful is his visual sense, the quick, direct discrimination of his eye, which explains the singularly vivid concision of his descriptions. These are never prolonged nor analytic, have nothing of enumeration, of the quality of the observer, who counts the items to be sure he has made up the sum. His eye *selects* unerringly, unscrupulously, almost impudently—catches the particular thing in which the character of the object or the scene resides, and, by expressing it with the artful brevity of a master, leaves a convincing, original picture. If he is inveterately synthetic, he is never more so than in the way he brings this hard, short, intelligent gaze to bear. His vision of the world is for the most part a vision of ugliness, and even when it is not, there is in his easy power to generalise a certain absence of love, a sort of bird's-eye-view contempt. He has none of the superstitions of observation, none of our English indulgences, our tender and often imaginative superficialities. If he glances into a railway carriage bearing its freight into the Parisian suburbs of a summer Sunday, a dozen dreary lives map themselves out in a flash.

> "There were stout ladies in farcical clothes, those middle-class goodwives of the *banlieue* who replace the distinction they don't possess by an irrelevant dignity; gentlemen weary of the office, with sallow faces and twisted bodies, and one of their shoulders a little forced up by perpetual bending at work over a table. Their anxious, joyless faces spoke moreover of domestic worries, incessant needs for money, old hopes finally shattered; for they all belonged to the army of poor threadbare devils who vegetate frugally in a mean little plaster house, with a flower-bed for a garden." . . .

Even in a brighter picture, such as the admirable vignette of the drive of Madame Tellier and her companions, the whole thing is an impression, as painters say nowadays, in which the figures are cheap. The six women at the station clamber into a country cart and go jolting through the Norman landscape to the village.

> "But presently the jerky trot of the nag shook the vehicle so terribly that the chairs began to dance, tossing up the travellers to right, to left, with movements like puppets, scared grimaces, cries of dismay suddenly interrupted by a more violent bump. They clutched the sides of the trap, their bonnets turned over on to their backs, or upon the nose or the shoulder; and the white horse continued to go, thrusting out his head and straightening the little tail, hairless like that of a rat, with which from time to time he whisked his buttocks. Joseph Rivet, with one foot stretched upon the shaft, the other leg bent under him, and his elbows very high, held the reins and emitted from

his throat every moment a kind of cluck which caused the animal to prick up his ears and quicken his pace. On either side of the road the green country stretched away. The colza, in flower, produced in spots a great carpet of undulating yellow, from which there rose a strong, wholesome smell, a smell penetrating and pleasant, carried very far by the breeze. In the tall rye the cornflowers held up their little azure heads, which the women wished to pluck; but M. Rivet refused to stop. Then, in some place, a whole field looked as if it were sprinkled with blood, it was so crowded with poppies. And in the midst of the great level, taking colour in this fashion from the flowers of the soil, the trap passed on with the jog of the white horse, seeming itself to carry a nosegay of richer hues; it disappeared behind the big trees of a farm, to come out again where the foilage stopped and parade afresh through the green and yellow crops, pricked with red or blue, its blazing cartload of women, which receded in the sunshine."

As regards the other sense, the sense *par excellence*, the sense which we scarcely mention in English fiction, and which I am not very sure I shall be allowed to mention in an English periodical, M. de Maupassant speaks for that, and of it, with extraordinary distinctness and authority. To say that it occupies the first place in his picture is to say too little; it covers in truth the whole canvas, and his work is little else but a report of its innumerable manifestations. These manifestations are not, for him, so many incidents of life; they are life itself, they represent the standing answer to any question that we may ask about it. He describes them in detail, with a familiarity and a frankness which leave nothing to be added; I should say with singular truth, if I did not consider that in regard to this article he may be taxed with a certain exaggeration. M. de Maupassant would doubtless affirm that where the empire of the sexual sense is concerned, no exaggeration is possible: nevertheless it may be said that whatever depths may be discovered by those who dig for them, the impression of the human spectacle for him who takes it as it comes has less analogy with that of the monkeys' cage than this admirable writer's account of it. I speak of the human spectacle as we Anglo-Saxons see it—as we Anglo-Saxons pretend we see it, M. de Maupassant would possibly say.

At any rate, I have perhaps touched upon this peculiarity sufficiently to explain my remark that his point of view is almost solely that of the senses. If he is a very interesting case, this makes him also an embarrassing one, embarrassing and mystifying for the moralist. I may as well admit that no writer of the day strikes me as equally so. To find M. de Maupassant a lion in the path—that may seem to some people a singular proof of want of courage; but I think the obstacle will not be made light of by those who have really taken the measure of the animal. We are accustomed to think, we of the English faith, that a cynic is a living advertisement of his errors, especially in proportion as he is a thorough-going one; and M. de Maupassant's cynicism, unrelieved as it is, will not be disposed of off-hand by a critic of a competent literary sense. Such a critic is not slow to perceive, to his no small confusion, that though, judging from usual premises, the author of *Bel-Ami* ought to be a warning, he somehow is not. His baseness, as it pervades him, ought to be written all over him; yet somehow there are there certain aspects—and those commanding, as the house-agents say—in which it is not in the least to be perceived. It is easy to exclaim that if he judges life only from the point of view of the senses, many are the noble and exquisite things that he must leave out. What he leaves out has no claim to get itself considered till after we have done justice to what he takes in. It is this positive side of M. de Maupassant that is most remarkable—the fact that his literary character is so complete and edifying. "Auteur à peu près irréprochable dans un genre qui ne l'est pas," as that excellent critic M. Jules Lemaître says of him, he disturbs us by associating a conscience and a high standard with a temper long synonymous, in our eyes, with an absence of scruples. The situation would be simpler certainly if he were a bad writer; but none the less it is possible, I think, on the whole, to circumvent him, even without attempting to prove that after all he is one.

The latter part of his introduction to *Pierre et Jean* is less felicitous than the beginning, but we learn from it—and this is interesting—that he regards the analytic fashion of telling a story, which has lately begotten in his own country some such remarkable experiments (few votaries as it has attracted among ourselves), as very much less profitable than the simple epic manner which "avoids with care all complicated explanations, all dissertations upon motives, and confines itself to making persons and events pass before our eyes." M. de Maupassant adds that in his view "psychology should be hidden in a book, as it is hidden in reality under the facts of existence. The novel conceived in this manner gains interest, movement, colour, the bustle of life." When it is a question of an artistic process, we must always mistrust very sharp distinctions, for there is surely in every method a little of every other method. It is as difficult to describe an action without glancing at its motive, its moral history, as it is to describe a motive without glancing at its practical consequence. Our history and our fiction are what we do; but it surely is not more easy to determine where what we do begins than to determine where it ends—notoriously a hopeless task. Therefore it would take a very subtle sense to draw a hard and fast line on the borderland of explanation and illustration. If psychology be hidden in life, as, according to M. de Maupassant, it should be in a book, the question immediately comes up, "From whom is it hidden?" From some people, no doubt, but very much less from others; and all depends upon the observer, the nature of one's observation, and one's curiosity. For some people motives, reasons, relations, explanations, are a part of the very surface of the drama, with the footlights beating full upon them. For me an act, an incident, an attitude, may be a sharp, detached, isolated thing, of which I give a full account in saying that in such and such a way it came off. For you it may be hung about with implications, with relations, and conditions as necessary to help you to recognise it as the clothes of your friends are to help you know them in the street. You feel that they would seem strange to you without petticoats and trousers.

M. de Maupassant would probably urge that the right thing is to know, or to guess, how events come to pass, but to say as little about it as possible. There are matters in regard to which he feels the importance of being explicit, but that is not one of them. The contention to which I allude strikes me as rather arbitrary, so difficult is it to put one's finger upon the reason why, for instance, there should be so little mystery about what happened to Christiane Andermatt, in *Mont-Oriol,* when she went to walk on the hills with Paul Brétigny, and so much, say, about the forces that formed her for that gentleman's convenience, or those lying behind any other odd collapse that our author may have related. The rule misleads, and the best rule certainly is the tact of the individual writer, which will adapt itself to the material as the material comes to him. The cause we plead is ever pretty sure to be the cause of our idiosyncrasies, and if M. de Maupassant thinks meanly of "explanations," it is, I suspect, that they come to him in no great affluence. His view of the conduct of man is so simple as scarcely to require them; and indeed so far as they are needed he *is,* virtually, explanatory. He deprecates reference to motives, but there is one, covering an immense ground in his horizon, as I have already hinted, to which he perpetually refers. If the sexual impulse be not a moral antecedent, it is none the less the wire that moves almost all M. de Maupassant's puppets, and as he has not hidden it, I cannot see that he has eliminated analysis or made a sacrifice to discretion. His pages are studded with that particular analysis; he is constantly peeping behind the curtain, telling us what he discovers there. The truth is that the admirable system of simplification which makes his tales so rapid and so concise (especially his shorter ones, for his novels in some degree, I think, suffer from it), strikes us as not in the least a conscious intellectual effort, a selective, comparative process. He tells us all he knows, all he suspects, and if these things take no account of the moral nature of man, it is because he has no window looking in that direction, and not because artistic scruples have compelled him to close it up. The very compact mansion in which he dwells presents on that side a perfectly dead wall.

This is why, if his axiom that you produce the effect of truth better by painting people from the outside than from the inside has a large utility, his example is convincing in a much higher degree. A writer is fortunate when his theory and his limitations so exactly correspond, when his curiosities may be appeased with such precision and promptitude. M. de Maupassant contends that the most that the analytic novelist can do is to put himself—his own peculiarities—into the costume of the figure analysed. This may be true, but if it applies to one manner of representing people who are not ourselves, it applies also to any other manner. It is the limitation, the difficulty of the novelist, to whatever clan or camp he may belong. M. de Maupassant is remarkably objective and impersonal, but he would go too far if he were to entertain the belief that he has kept himself out of his books. They speak of him eloquently, even if it only be to tell us how easy—how easy, given his talent of course—he has found this impersonality. Let us hasten to add that in the case of describing a character it is doubtless more difficult to convey the impression of something that is not one's self (the constant effort, however delusive at bottom, of the novelist), than in the case of describing some object more immediately visible. The operation is more delicate, but that circumstance only increases the beauty of the problem.

On the question of style our author has some excellent remarks; we may be grateful indeed for every one of them, save an odd reflection about the way to "become original" if we happen not to be so. The recipe for this transformation, it would appear, is to sit down in front of a blazing fire, or a tree in a plain, or any object we encounter in the regular way of business, and remain there until the tree, or the fire, or the object, whatever it be, become different for us from all other specimens of the same class. I doubt whether this system would always answer, for surely the resemblance is what we wish to discover, quite as much as the difference, and the best way to preserve it is not to look for something opposed to it. Is not this indication of the road to take to become, as a writer, original touched with the same fallacy as the recommendation about eschewing analysis? It is the only *naïveté* I have encountered in M. de Maupassant's many volumes. The best originality is the most unconscious, and the best way to describe a tree is the way in which it has struck us. "Ah, but we don't always know how it has struck us," the answer to that may be, "and it takes some time and ingenuity—much fasting and prayer—to find out." If we do not know, it probably has not struck us very much: so little indeed that our inquiry had better be relegated to that closed chamber of an artist's meditations, that sacred back kitchen, which no *a priori* rule can light up. The best thing the artist's adviser can do in such a case is to trust him and turn away, to let him fight the matter out with his conscience. And be this said with a full appreciation of the degree in which M. de Maupassant's observations on the whole question of a writer's style, at the point we have come to today, bear the stamp of intelligence and experience. His own style is of so excellent a tradition that the presumption is altogether in favour of what he may have to say.

He feels oppressively, discouragingly, as many another of his countrymen must have felt—for the French have worked their language as no other people have done—the penalty of coming at the end of three centuries of literature, the difficulty of dealing with an instrument of expression so worn by friction, of drawing new sounds from the old familiar pipe. "When we read, so saturated with French writing as we are that our whole body gives us the impression of being a paste made of words, do we ever find a line, a thought, which is not familiar to us, and of which we have not had at least a confused presentiment?" And he adds that the matter is simple enough for the writer who only seeks to amuse the public by means already known; he attempts little, and he produces "with confidence, in the candour of his mediocrity," works which answer no question and leave no trace. It is he who wants to do more than this that has less and less an easy time of it. Everything seems to him to have been done, every effect produced, every combination already made. If he be a man of genius, his trouble is lightened, for mysterious ways are revealed to him, and new combinations spring up for him even after novelty is dead. It is to the simple man of taste and talent, who has only a conscience and a will, that the situation may sometimes well appear desperate; he judges himself as he goes, and he can only go step by step over ground where every step is already a footprint.

If it be a miracle whenever there is a fresh tone, the miracle has been wrought for M. de Maupassant. Or is he simply a man of genius to whom short cuts have been disclosed in the watches of the night? At any rate he has had faith—religion has come to his aid; I mean the religion of his mother tongue, which he has loved well enough to be patient for her sake. He has arrived at the peace which passeth understanding, at a kind of conservative piety. He has taken his stand on simplicity, on a studied sobriety, being persuaded that the deepest science lies in that direction rather than in the multiplication of new terms, and on this subject he delivers himself with superlative wisdom. "There is no need of the queer, complicated, numerous, and Chinese vocabulary which is imposed on us to-day under the name of artistic writing, to fix all the shades of thought; the right way is to distinguish with an extreme clearness all those modifications of the value of a word which come from the place it occupies. Let us have fewer nouns, verbs and adjectives of an almost imperceptible sense, and more different phrases variously constructed, ingeniously cast, full of the science of sound and rhythm. Let us have an excellent general form rather than be collectors of rare terms." M. de Maupassant's practice does not fall below his exhortation (though I must confess that in the foregoing passage he makes use of the detestable expression "stylist," which I have not reproduced). Nothing can exceed the masculine firmness, the quiet force of his own style, in which every phrase is a close sequence, every epithet a paying piece, and the ground is completely cleared of the vague, the ready-made and the second-best. Less than any one to-day does he beat the air; more than any one does he hit out from the shoulder.

II

He has produced a hundred short tales and only four regular novels; but if the tales deserve the first place in any candid appreciation of his talent it is not simply because they are so much the more numerous: they are also more characteristic; they represent him best in his originality, and their brevity, extreme in some cases, does not prevent them from being a collection of masterpieces. (They are very unequal, and I speak of the best.) The little story is but scantily relished in England, where readers take their fiction rather by the volume than by the page, and the novelist's idea is apt to resemble one of those old-fashioned carriages which require a wide court to turn round. In America, where it is associated pre-eminently with Hawthorne's name, with Edgar Poe's, and with that of Mr. Bret Harte, the short tale has had a better fortune. France, however, has been the land of its great prosperity, and M. de Maupassant had from the first the advantage of addressing a public accustomed to catch on, as the modern phrase is, quickly. In some respects, it may be said, he encountered prejudices too friendly, for he found a tradition of indecency ready made to his hand. I say indecency with plainness, though my indication would perhaps please better with another word, for we suffer in English from a lack of roundabout names for the *conte leste*— that element for which the French, with their *grivois,* their *gaillard,* their *égrillard,* their *gaudriole,* have so many convenient synonyms. It is an honoured tradition in France that the little story, in verse or in prose, should be liable to be more or less obscene (I can think only of that alternative epithet), though I hasten to add that among literary forms it does not monopolise the privilege. Our uncleanness is less producible—at any rate it is less produced.

For the last ten years our author has brought forth with regularity these condensed compositions, of which, probably, to an English reader, at a first glance, the most universal sign will be their licentiousness. They really partake of this quality, however, in a very differing degree, and a second glance shows that they may be divided into numerous groups. It is not fair, I think, even to say that what they have most in common is their being extremely *lestes.* What they have most in common is their being extremely strong, and after that their being extremely brutal. A story may be obscene without being brutal, and *vice versâ,* and M. de Maupassant's contempt for those interdictions which are supposed to be made in the interest of good morals is but an incident—a very large one indeed—of his general contempt. A pessimism so great that its alliance with the love of good work, or even with the calculation of the sort of work that pays best in a country of style, is, as I have intimated, the most puzzling of anomalies (for it would seem in the light of such sentiments that nothing is worth anything), this cynical strain is the sign of such gems of narration as *La Maison Tellier, L'Histoire d'une Fille de Ferme, L'Ane, Le Chien, Mademoiselle Fifi, Monsieur Parent, L'Héritage, En Famille, Le Baptême, Le Père Amable.* The author fixes a hard eye on some small spot of human life, usually some ugly, dreary, shabby, sordid one, takes up the particle, and squeezes it either till it grimaces or till it bleeds. Sometimes the grimace is very droll, sometimes the wound is very horrible; but in either case the whole thing is real, observed, noted, and represented, not an invention or a castle in the air. M. de Maupassant sees human life as a terribly ugly business relieved by the comical, but even the comedy is for the most part the comedy of misery, of avidity, of ignorance, helplessness, and grossness. When his laugh is not for these things, it is for the little *saletés* (to use one of his own favourite words) of luxurious life, which are intended to be prettier, but which can scarcely be said to brighten the picture. I like *La Bête à Maître Belhomme, La Ficelle, Le Petit Fût, Le Cas de Madame Luneau, Tribuneaux Rustiques*, and many others of this category much better than his anecdotes of the mutual confidences of his little *marquises* and *baronnes*.

Not counting his novels for the moment, his tales may be divided into the three groups of those which deal with the Norman peasantry, those which deal with the *petit employé* and small shopkeeper, usually in Paris, and the miscellaneous, in which the upper walks of life are represented, and the fantastic, the whimsical, the weird, and even the supernatural, figure as well as the unexpurgated. These last things range from *Le Horla* (which is not a specimen of the author's best vein—the only occasion on which he has the weakness of imitation is when he strikes us as emulating Edgar Poe) to *Miss Harriet*, and from *Boule de Suif* (a triumph) to that almost inconceivable little growl of Anglophobia, *Découverte*—inconceivable I mean in its irresponsibility and ill-nature on the part of a man of M. de Maupassant's distinction; passing by such little perfections as *Petit Soldat, L'Abandonné, Le Collier* (the list is too long for complete enumeration), and such gross imperfections (for it once in a while befalls our author to go woefully astray), as *La Femme de Paul, Châli, Les Sœurs Rondoli*. To these might almost be added as a special category the various forms in which M. de Maupassant relates adventures in railway carriages. Numerous, to his imagination, are the pretexts for enlivening fiction afforded by first, second, and third class compartments; the accidents (which have nothing to do with the conduct of the train) that occur there constitute no inconsiderable part of our earthly transit.

It is surely by his Norman peasant that his tales will live; he knows this worthy as if he had made him, understands him down to the ground, puts him on his feet with a few of the freest, most plastic touches. M. de Maupassant does not admire him, and he is such a master of the subject that it would ill become an outsider to suggest a revision of judgment. He is a part of the contemptible furniture of the world, but on the whole, it would appear, the most grotesque part of it. His caution, his canniness, his natural astuteness, his stinginess, his general grinding sordidness, are as unmistakable as that quaint and brutish dialect in which he expresses himself, and on which our author plays like a virtuoso. It would be impossible to demonstrate with a finer sense of the humour of the thing the fatuities and densities of his ignorance, the bewilderments of his opposed appetites, the overreachings of his caution. His existence has a gay side, but it is apt to be the barbarous gaiety commemorated in *Farce Normande,* an anecdote which, like many of M. de Maupassant's anecdotes, it is easier to refer the reader to than to repeat. If it is most convenient to place *La Maison Tellier* among the tales of the peasantry, there is no doubt that it stands at the head of the list. It is absolutely unadapted to the perusal of ladies and young persons, but it shares this peculiarity with most of its fellows, so that to ignore it on that account would be to imply that we must forswear M. de Maupassant altogether, which is an incongruous and insupportable conclusion. Every good story is of course both a picture and an idea, and the more they are interfused the better the problem is solved. In *La Maison Tellier* they fit each other to perfection; the capacity for sudden innocent delights latent in natures which have lost their innocence is vividly illustrated by the singular scenes to which our acquaintance with Madame and her staff (little as it may be a thing to boast of), successively introduces us. The breadth, the freedom, and brightness of all this give the measure of the author's talent, and of that large, keen way of looking at life which sees the pathetic and the droll, the stuff of which the whole piece is made, in the queerest and humblest patterns. The tone of *La Maison Tellier* and the few compositions which closely resemble it, expresses M. de Maupassant's nearest approach to geniality. Even here, however, it is the geniality of the showman exhilarated by the success with which he feels that he makes his mannikins (and especially his womankins) caper and squeak, and who after the performance tosses them into their box with the irreverence of a practised hand. If the pages of the author of *Bel-Ami* may be searched almost in vain for a manifestation of the sentiment of respect, it is naturally not by Mme. Tellier and her charges that we must look most to see it called forth; but they are among the things that please him most.

Sometimes there is a sorrow, a misery, or even a little heroism, that he handles with a certain tenderness (*Une Vie* is the capital example of this), without insisting on the poor, the ridiculous, or, as he is fond of saying, the bestial side of it. Such an attempt, admirable in its sobriety and delicacy, is the sketch, in *L'Abandonné,* of the old lady and gentleman, Mme. de Cadour and M. d'Apreval, who, staying with the husband of the former at a little watering-place on the Normandy coast, take a long, hot walk on a summer's day, on a straight, white road, into the interior, to catch a clandestine glimpse of a young farmer, their illegitimate son. He has been pensioned, he is ignorant of his origin, and is a commonplace and unconciliatory rustic. They look at him, in his dirty farmyard, and no sign passes between them;

then they turn away and crawl back, in melancholy silence, along the dull French road. The manner in which this dreary little occurrence is related makes it as large as a chapter of history. There is tenderness in *Miss Harriet*, which sets forth how an English old maid, fantastic, hideous, sentimental, and tract-distributing, with a smell of india-rubber, fell in love with an irresistible French painter, and drowned herself in the well because she saw him kissing the maid-servant; but the figure of the lady grazes the farcical. Is it because we know Miss Harriet (if we are not mistaken in the type the author has had in his eye) that we suspect the good spinster was not so weird and desperate, addicted though her class may be, as he says, to "haunting all the *tables d'hôte* in Europe, to spoiling Italy, poisoning Switzerland, making the charming towns of the Mediterranean uninhabitable, carrying everywhere their queer little manias, their *mœurs de vestales pétrifiées*, their indescribable garments, and that odour of india-rubber which makes one think that at night they must be slipped into a case?" What would Miss Harriet have said to M. de Maupassant's friend, the hero of the *Découverte*, who, having married a little Anglaise because he thought she was charming when she spoke broken French, finds she is very flat as she becomes more fluent, and has nothing more urgent than to denounce her to a gentleman he meets on the steamboat, and to relieve his wrath in ejaculations of "Sales Anglais"?

M. de Maupassant evidently knows a great deal about the army of clerks who work under government, but it is a terrible tale that he has to tell of them and of the *petit bourgeois* in general. It is true that he has treated the *petit bourgeois* in *Pierre et Jean* without holding him up to our derision, and the effort has been so fruitful, that we owe to it the work for which, on the whole, in the long list of his successes, we are most thankful. But of *Pierre et Jean*, a production neither comic nor cynical (in the degree, that is, of its predecessors), but serious and fresh, I will speak anon. In *Monsieur Parent, L'Héritage, En Famille, Une Partie de Campagne, Promenade,* and many other pitiless little pieces, the author opens the window wide to his perception of everything mean, narrow, and sordid. The subject is ever the struggle for existence in hard conditions, lighted up simply by more or less *polissonnerie*. Nothing is more striking to an Anglo-Saxon reader than the omission of all the other lights, those with which our imagination, and I think it ought to be said our observation, is familiar, and which our own works of fiction at any rate do not permit us to forget: those of which the most general description is that they spring from a certain mixture of good-humour and piety—piety, I mean, in the civil and domestic sense quite as much as in the religious. The love of sport, the sense of decorum, the necessity for action, the habit of respect, the absence of irony, the pervasiveness of childhood, the expansive tendency of the race, are a few of the qualities (the analysis might, I think, be pushed much further) which ease us off, mitigate our tension and irritation, rescue us from the nervous exasperation which is almost the commonest element of life as depicted by M. de Maupassant. No doubt there is in our literature an immense amount of conventional blinking, and it may be questioned whether pessimistic representation in M. de Maupassant's manner do not follow his particular original more closely than our perpetual quest of pleasantness (does not Mr. Rider Haggard make even his African carnage pleasant?) adheres to the lines of the world we ourselves know.

Fierce indeed is the struggle for existence among even our pious and good-humoured millions, and it is attended with incidents as to which after all little testimony is to be extracted from our literature of fiction. It must never be forgotten that the optimism of that literature is partly the optimism of women and of spinsters; in other words the optimism of ignorance as well as of delicacy. It might be supposed that the French, with their mastery of the *arts d'agrément,* would have more consolations than we, but such is not the account of the matter given by the new generation of painters. To the French we seem superficial, and we are certainly open to the reproach; but none the less even to the infinite majority of readers of good faith there will be a wonderful want of correspondence between the general picture of *Bel-Ami,* of *Mont-Oriol,* of *Une Vie, Yvette* and *En Famille,* and our own vision of reality. It is an old impression of course that the satire of the French has a very different tone from ours; but few English readers will admit that the feeling of life is less in ours than in theirs. The feeling of life is evidently, *de part et d'autre,* a very different thing. If in ours, as the novel illustrates it, there are superficialities, there are also qualities which are far from being negatives and omissions: a large imagination and (is it fatuous to say?) a large experience of the positive kind. Even those of our novelists whose manner is most ironic pity life more and hate it less than M. de Maupassant and his great initiator Flaubert. It comes back I suppose to our good-humour (which may apparently also be an artistic force); at any rate, we have reserves about our shames and our sorrows, indulgences and tolerances about our Philistinism, forbearances about our blows, and a general friendliness of conception about our possibilities, which take the cruelty from our self-derision and operate in the last resort as a sort of tribute to our freedom. There is a horrible, admirable scene in *Monsieur Parent,* which is a capital example of triumphant ugliness.

The harmless gentleman who gives his name to the tale has an abominable wife, one of whose offensive attributes is a lover (unsuspected by her husband), only less impudent than herself. M. Parent comes in from a walk with his little boy, at dinner-time, to encounter suddenly in his abused, dishonoured, deserted home, convincing proof of her misbehaviour. He waits and waits dinner for her, giving her the benefit of every doubt; but when at last she enters, late in the evening, accompanied by the partner of her guilt, there is a tremendous domestic concussion. It is to the peculiar vividness of this scene that I allude, the way we hear it and see it, and its most repulsive details are evoked for us: the sordid confusion, the vulgar noise, the disordered table and ruined dinner, the shrill insolence of the wife, her brazen mendacity, the scared inferiority of the lover, the mere momentary heroics of the weak husband, the scuffle and somersault, the eminently unpoetic justice with which it all ends.

When Thackeray relates how Arthur Pendennis goes home to take pot-luck with the insolvent Newcomes at Boulogne, and how the dreadful Mrs. Mackenzie receives him, and how she makes a scene, when the frugal repast is served, over the diminished mutton-bone, we feel that the notation of that order of misery goes about as far as we can bear it. But this is child's play to the history of M. and Mme. Caravan and their attempt, after the death (or supposed death) of the husband's mother, to transfer to their apartment before the arrival of the other heirs certain miserable little articles of furniture belonging to the deceased, together with the frustration of the manœuvre not only by the grim resurrection of the old woman (which is a sufficiently fantastic item), but by the shock of battle when a married daughter and her husband appear. No one gives us like M. de Maupassant the odious words exchanged on such an occasion as that: no one depicts with so just a hand the feelings of small people about small things. These feelings are very apt to be "fury"; that word is of strikingly frequent occurrence in his pages. L'Héritage is a drama of private life in the little world of the Ministère de la Marine—a world, according to M. de Maupassant, of dreadful little jealousies and ineptitudes. Readers of a robust complexion should learn how the wretched M. Lesable was handled by his wife and her father on his failing to satisfy their just expectations, and how he comported himself in the singular situation thus prepared for him. The story is a model of narration, but it leaves our poor average humanity dangling like a beaten rag.

Where does M. de Maupassant find the great multitude of his detestable women? or where at least does he find the courage to represent them in such colours? Jeanne de Lamare, in Une Vie, receives the outrages of fate with a passive fortitude; and there is something touching in Mme. Roland's *âme tendre de caissière*, as exhibited in *Pierre et Jean*. But for the most part M. de Maupassant's heroines are a mixture of extreme sensuality and extreme mendacity. They are a large element in that general disfigurement, that *illusion de l'ignoble, qui attire tant d'êtres,* which makes the perverse or the stupid side of things the one which strikes him first, which leads him, if he glances at a group of nurses and children sunning themselves in a Parisian square, to notice primarily the *yeux de brute* of the nurses; or if he speaks of the longing for a taste of the country which haunts the shopkeeper fenced in behind his counter, to identify it as the *amour bête de la nature;* or if he has occasion to put the boulevards before us on a summer's evening, to seek his effect in these terms: "The city, as hot as a stew, seemed to sweat in the suffocating night. The drains puffed their pestilential breath from their mouths of granite, and the underground kitchens poured into the streets, through their low windows, the infamous miasmas of their dishwater and old sauces." I do not contest the truth of such indications, I only note the particular selection and their seeming to the writer the most *apropos*.

Is it because of the inadequacy of these indications when applied to the long stretch that M. de Maupassant's novels strike us as less complete, in proportion to the talent expended upon them, than his *contes* and *nouvelles?* I make this invidious distinction in spite of the fact that *Une Vie* (the first of the novels in the order of time) is a remarkably interesting experiment, and that *Pierre et Jean* is, so far as my judgment goes, a faultless production. *Bel-Ami* is full of the bustle and the crudity of life (its energy and expressiveness almost bribe one to like it), but it has the great defect that the physiological explanation of things here too visibly contracts the problem in order to meet it. The world represented is too special, too little inevitable, too much to take or to leave as we like—a world in which every man is a cad and every woman a harlot. M. de Maupassant traces the career of a finished blackguard who succeeds in life through women, and he represents him primarily as succeeding in the profession of journalism. His colleagues and his mistresses are as depraved as himself, greatly to the injury of the ironic idea, for the real force of satire would have come from seeing him engaged and victorious with natures better than his own. It may be remarked that this was the case with the nature of Mme. Walter; but the reply to that is—hardly! Moreover the author's whole treatment of the episode of Mme. Walter is the thing on which his admirers have least to congratulate him. The taste of it is so atrocious, that it is difficult to do justice to the way

215

it is made to stand out. Such an instance as this pleads with irresistible eloquence, as it seems to me, the cause of that salutary diffidence or practical generosity which I mentioned on a preceding page. I know not the English or American novelist who could have written this portion of the history of *Bel-Ami* if he would. But I also find it impossible to conceive a member of that fraternity who would have written it if he could. The subject of *Mont-Oriol* is full of queerness to the English mind. Here again the picture has much more importance than the idea, which is simply that a gentleman, if he happen to be a low animal, is liable to love a lady very much less if she presents him with a pledge of their affection. It need scarcely be said that the lady and gentleman who in M. de Maupassant's pages exemplify this interesting truth are not united in wedlock—that is with each other.

M. de Maupassant tells us that he has imbibed many of his principles from Gustave Flaubert, from the study of his works as well as, formerly, the enjoyment of his words. It is in *Une Vie* that Flaubert's influence is most directly traceable, for the thing has a marked analogy with *L'Education Sentimentale*. That is, it is the presentation of a simple piece of a life (in this case a long piece), a series of observations upon an episode *quelconque,* as the French say, with the minimum of arrangement of the given objects. It is an excellent example of the way the impression of truth may be conveyed by that form, but it would have been a still better one if in his search for the effect of dreariness (the effect of dreariness may be said to be the subject of *Une Vie,* so far as the subject is reducible) the author had not eliminated excessively. He has arranged, as I say, as little as possible; the necessity of a "plot" has in no degree imposed itself upon him, and his effort has been to give the uncomposed, unrounded look of life, with its accidents, its broken rhythm, its queer resemblance to the famous description of "Bradshaw"—a compound of trains that start but don't arrive, and trains that arrive but don't start. It is almost an arrangement of the history of poor Mme. de Lamare to have left so many things out of it, for after all she is described in very few of the relations of life. The principal ones are there certainly; we see her as a daughter, a wife, and a mother, but there is a certain accumulation of secondary experience that marks any passage from youth to old age which is a wholly absent element in M. de Maupassant's narrative, and the suppression of which gives the thing a tinge of the arbitrary. It is in the power of this secondary experience to make a great difference, but nothing makes any difference for Jeanne de Lamare as M. de Maupassant puts her before us. Had she no other points of contact than those he describes?—no friends, no phases, no episodes, no chances, none of the miscellaneous *remplissage* of life? No doubt M. de Maupassant would say that he has had to select, that the most comprehensive enumeration is only a condensation, and that, in accordance with the very just principles enunciated in that preface to which I have perhaps too repeatedly referred, he has sacrificed what is uncharacteristic to what is characteristic. It characterises the career of this French country lady of fifty years ago that its long gray expanse should be seen as peopled with but five or six figures. The essence of the matter is that she was deceived in almost every affection, and that essence is given if the persons who deceived her are given.

The reply is doubtless adequate, and I have only intended my criticism to suggest the degree of my interest. What it really amounts to is that if the subject of this artistic experiment had been the existence of an English lady, even a very dull one, the air of verisimilitude would have demanded that she should have been placed in a denser medium. *Une Vie* may after all be only a testimony to the fact of the melancholy void of the coast of Normandy, even within a moderate drive of a great seaport, under the Restoration and Louis Philippe. It is especially to be recommended to those who are interested in the question of what constitutes a "story," offering as it does the most definite sequences at the same time that it has nothing that corresponds to the usual idea of a plot, and closing with an implication that finds us prepared. The picture again in this case is much more dominant than the idea, unless it be an idea that loneliness and grief are terrible. The picture, at any rate, is full of truthful touches, and the work has the merit and the charm that it is the most delicate of the author's productions and the least hard. In none other has he occupied himself so continuously with so innocent a figure as his soft, bruised heroine; in none other has he paid our poor blind human history the compliment (and this is remarkable, considering the flatness of so much of the particular subject) of finding it so little *bête*. He may think it, here, but comparatively he does not say it. He almost betrays a sense of moral things. Jeanne is absolutely passive, she has no moral spring, no active moral life, none of the edifying attributes of character (it costs her apparently as little as may be in the way of a shock, a complication of feeling, to discover, by letters, after her mother's death, that this lady has not been the virtuous woman she has supposed); but her chronicler has had to handle the immaterial forces of patience and renunciation, and this has given the book a certain purity, in spite of two or three "physiological" passages that come in with violence—a violence the greater as we feel it to be a result of selection. It is very much a mark of M. de Maupassant that on the most striking occasion, with a single exception, on which his picture is not a picture of libertinage it is a picture of unmitigated suffering. Would he suggest that these are the only alternatives?

The exception that I here allude to is for *Pierre et Jean,* which I have left myself small space to speak of. Is it because in this masterly little novel there is a show of those immaterial forces which I just mentioned, and because Pierre Roland is one of the few instances of operative character that can be recalled from so many volumes, that many readers will place M. de Maupassant's latest production altogether at the head of his longer ones? I am not sure, inasmuch as after all the character in question is not extraordinarily distinguished, and the moral problem not presented in much complexity. The case is only relative. Perhaps it is not of importance to fix the reasons of preference in respect to a piece of writing so essentially a work of art and of talent. *Pierre et Jean* is the best of M. de Maupassant's novels mainly because M. de Maupassant has never before been so clever. It is a pleasure to see a mature talent able to renew itself, strike another note, and appear still young. This story suggests the growth of a perception that everything has not been said about the actors on the world's stage when they are represented either as helpless victims or as mere bundles of appetites. There is an air of responsibility about Pierre Roland, the person on whose behalf the tale is mainly told, which almost constitutes a pledge. An inquisitive critic may ask why in this particular case M. de Maupassant should have stuck to the *petit bourgeois,* the circumstances not being such as to typify that class more than another. There are reasons indeed which on reflection are perceptible; it was necessary that his people should be poor, and necessary even that to attenuate Madame Roland's misbehaviour she should have had the excuse of the contracted life of a shopwoman in the Rue Montmartre. Were the inquisitive critic slightly malicious as well, he might suspect the author of a fear that he should seem to give way to the *illusion du beau* if in addition to representing the little group in *Pierre et Jean* as persons of about the normal conscience he had also represented them as of the cultivated class. If they belong to the humble life this belittles and—I am still quoting the supposedly malicious critic—M. de Maupassant *must,* in one way or the other, belittle. To the English reader it will appear, I think, that Pierre and Jean are rather more of the cultivated class than two young Englishmen in the same social position. It belongs to the drama that the struggle of the elder brother—educated, proud, and acute—should be partly with the pettiness of his opportunities. The author's choice of a *milieu,* moreover, will serve to English readers as an example of how much more democratic contemporary French fiction is than that of his own country. The greater part of it—almost all the work of Zola and of Daudet, the best of Flaubert's novels, and the best of those of the brothers De Goncourt—treat of that vast, dim section of society which, lying between those luxurious walks on whose behalf there are easy presuppositions and that darkness of misery which, in addition to being picturesque, brings philanthropy also to the writer's aid, constitutes really, in extent and expressiveness, the substance of any nation. In England, where the fashion of fiction still sets mainly to the country house and the hunting-field, and yet more novels are published than anywhere else in the world, that thick twilight of mediocrity of condition has been little explored. May it yield triumphs in the years to come!

It may seem that I have claimed little for M. de Maupassant, so far as English readers are concerned with him, in saying that after publishing twenty improper volumes he has at last published a twenty-first, which is neither indecent nor cynical. It is not this circumstance that has led me to dedicate so many pages to him, but the circumstance that in producing all the others he yet remained, for those who are interested in these matters, a writer with whom it was impossible not to reckon. This is why I called him, to begin with, so many ineffectual names: a rarity, a "case," an embarrassment, a lion in the path. He is still in the path as I conclude these observations, but I think that in making them we have discovered a legitimate way round. If he is a master of his art and it is discouraging to find what low views are compatible with mastery, there is satisfaction, on the other hand, in learning on what particular condition he holds his strange success. This condition, it seems to me, is that of having totally omitted one of the items of the problem, an omission which has made the problem so much easier that it may almost be described as a short cut to a solution. The question is whether it be a fair cut. M. de Maupassant has simply skipped the whole reflective part of his men and women—that reflective part which governs conduct and produces character. He may say that he does not see it, does not know it; to which the answer is, "So much the better for you, if you wish to describe life without it. The strings you pull are by so much the less numerous, and you can therefore pull those that remain with greater promptitude, consequently with greater firmness, with a greater air of knowledge." Pierre Roland, I repeat, shows a capacity for reflection, but I cannot think who else does, among the thousand figures who compete with him—I mean for reflection addressed to anything higher than the gratification of an instinct. We have an impression that M. d'Apreval and Madame de Cadour reflect, as they trudge back from their mournful excursion, but that indication is not pushed very far. An aptitude for this exercise is a part of disciplined manhood, and disciplined manhood M. de Maupassant has simply not attempted to represent. I can remember no instance in which he sketches any considerable capacity for conduct, and his women betray that capacity as little as his men. I am much mistaken if he has once painted a gentleman, in the English sense of the term. His gentlemen, like Paul Brétigny and Gontran de Ravenel, are guilty of the most extraordinary deflections. For those who are conscious of this element in life, look for it and like it, the gap will appear to be immense. It will lead them to say, "No wonder you have a contempt if that is the way you limit the field. No wonder you judge people roughly if that is the way you see them. Your work, on your premises, remains the admirable thing it is, but is your 'case' not adequately explained?"

The erotic element in M. de Maupassant, about which much more might have been said, seems to me to be explained by the same limitation, and explicable in a similar way wherever else its literature occurs in excess. The carnal side of man appears the most characteristic if you look at it a great deal; and you look at it a great deal if you do not look at the other, at the side by which he reacts against his weaknesses, his defeats. The more you look at the other, the less the whole business to which French novelists have ever appeared to English readers to give a disproportionate place—the business, as I may say, of the senses—will strike you as the only typical one. Is not this the most useful reflection to make in regard to the famous question of the morality, the decency, of the novel? It is the only one, it seems to me, that will meet the case as we find the case to-day. Hard and fast rules, *a priori* restrictions, mere interdictions (you shall not speak of this, you shall not look at that), have surely served their time, and will in the nature of the case never strike an energetic talent as anything but arbitrary. A healthy, living and growing art, full of curiosity and fond of exercise, has an indefeasible mistrust of rigid prohibitions. Let us then leave this magnificent art of the novelist to itself and to its perfect freedom, in the faith that one example is as good as another, and that our fiction will always be decent enough if it be sufficiently general. Let us not be alarmed at this prodigy (though prodigies are alarming) of M. de Maupassant, who is at once so licentious and so impeccable, but gird ourselves up with the conviction that another point of view will yield another perfection.

James' productivity in 1888 was as diverse as it was rich. Besides short stories ("Louisa Pallant," "The Liar," "A London Life," "The Lesson of the Master," "The Patagonia") and novellas (*The Reverberator* and *The Aspern Papers*), there are essays on Stevenson, Loti, and the Goncourts which—especially if we include the December 1887 piece on Emerson—mark a new suppleness in James' discursive prose. No subject in 1888 challenged his critical powers more thoroughly than the author whom he had met first at Flaubert's Sundays in 1875–76 and had hosted in London in 1886, Guy de Maupassant. The emotions which Maupassant evoked, particularly affection and respect, continue strong throughout James' later life, as Edel notes (3: 177). In 1891 James tells Stevenson that "the Frenchmen are passing away— Maupassant dying of locomotor paralysis, the fruit of fabulous habits, I am told. . . . I shall miss him" (October 30). Repeatedly in the *Notebooks*, James invokes the French master's powers of concision—"Oh, spirit of Maupassant, come to my aid!" (March 11, 1888; see also February 2, 1889; February 22, 1891; October 5, 1899). In 1888, James (who had moved from 3 Bolton Street to 34 De Vere Gardens two years before) expressed both affection and respect for Maupassant in an essay published in the *Fortnightly Review* and revised slightly for *Partial Portraits*.

Besides evoking positive emotions, however, Maupassant also challenged and even threatened James, as a lion in the path. Maupassant made especially immediate the issue of literary theory which had been raised in 1884 and not fully resolved in "The Art of Fiction" and "Ivan Turgénieff"—the relation between morality and form. Besant had made things too easy. James needed only to reject Besant's simplistic, a priori moralism and to insist that true morality was inseparable from form. Turgenev also was accommodating; he made form one with a vision of experience which James could sympathize with thoroughly. Only Maupassant was implacable. "He disturbs us by associating a conscience and a high standard with a temper long synonymous, in our eyes, with an absence of scruples."

How would James deal with this issue in 1888? "It is easy to exclaim that if he [Maupassant] judges life only from the point of view of the senses, many are the noble and exquisite things that he must leave out." Since this basically summarizes James' response to Maupassant's limitations, why does he undercut it with "easy" and "exclaim"? Easy exclamations do justice to neither Maupassant nor James. Ignoring the writer's artistry indulges the critic's biases. James, having taken his critical stand at the disinterested place in-between, must give full credit to French practice and take full measure of Anglo-American moralism.

The task of crediting French practice James sets about immediately. Espousing Maupassant's central theoretical tenet—"any form of the novel is simply a vision of the world from the standpoint of a person constituted after a certain fashion"—James pays Maupassant the high compliment of crediting him with an Arnoldian "appeal to our disinterestedness." Then James as "the disinterested critic" draws from Maupassant's theoretical tenet a generalization about critical practice. "His [the artist's] organism constitutes a *case*, and the critic is intelligent in proportion as he apprehends and enters into that case." Now James need only apply this generalization to Maupassant, and justice will be done both to the Frenchman as artist and to himself as critic.

> M. de Maupassant himself precisely presents all the symptoms of a 'case'. . . . Embracing such an opportunity as this . . . seems to me . . . more fruitful in valid conclusions . . . than the more common method of establishing one's own premises.

Criticism oriented to the individual artist is contrasted by James with the rigidity of traditional, a priori practice. "Hard and fast rules, *a priori* restrictions, mere interdictions . . . have surely served their time, and will in the nature of the case never strike an energetic talent as anything but arbitrary." The perennial attractions of a priori criticism ("we have doubtless often enough the courage of our opinions . . . but we have not so constantly that of our perceptions") are particularly tempting when an author like Maupassant threatens received opinions so substantially. "Though, judging from usual premises, the author of *Bel-Ami* ought to be a warning, he somehow is not."

The real critical threat to Maupassant is not from a priori dogmatists but from himself—from inconsistencies between his own theory and practice. Instead of heeding his admonition about the artist as an individual case who will create in an individual way, Maupassant makes rules.

> 'Psychology should be hidden in a book, as it is hidden in reality. . . .'

> The way to become 'original' if we happen not to be so . . . is. . . .

James' reaction is consistent with Maupassant's theory of the individual case.

> 'From whom is it [psychology] hidden?' From some people, no doubt, but very much less from others; and all depends upon the observer.

> The best [most original] way to describe a tree is the way in which it has struck us.

James expressly contrasts Maupassant's rules with individual cases. "The rule [about not discussing motivation] misleads, and the best rule certainly is the tact of the individual writer." Maupassant's rule-making earns from James the same expression, "hard and fast," which he applied to the a priori opponents of the French master. James trusts instead to the individual "artist's meditations, that sacred back kitchen, which no *a priori* rule can light up."

Maupassant proves inconsistent in a second, still more serious way, when James turns from criticism to fiction. Again he looks to Maupassant himself for theory. "A fine, true, complete account" derived from "a direct impression of life" is what fiction should be, according to Maupassant. In his practice, however, "suppression" of "a certain accumulation of secondary experience . . . gives the thing a tinge of the arbitrary." James is referring here to a specific tale, but "suppression" has general importance because it precludes the completeness which is Maupassant's theoretical ideal. Maupassant omits from his fiction not what is out of place there but what he cannot provide, just as his criticism forsakes the latitude indispensable with individual cases and imposes rules which justify the limitations of his own fiction. Incompleteness thus characterizes Maupassant's criticism as well as his art because its rules too strike James "as rather arbitrary."

These strictures about Maupassant's incompleteness are important, but James is at least as concerned with how we experience that incompleteness. Instead of easy exclamations he creates delicate rhetorical structures which require us to appreciate Maupassant's excellence amid his limitations. A scene which is "horrible" is also "admirable." The second half of Maupassant's theoretical essay "is less felicitous . . . but we learn from it." James disputes the contention that Maupassant "has kept himself out of his books" only after James has credited him with being "remarkably objective and impersonal." If we agree that Maupassant generally "contracts the problem in order to meet it," we must also recognize that Maupassant's unquestionable power comes from the same concision. "His tales [are] so rapid and so concise" precisely because of "the admirable system of simplification." Even the word "complete" must be reconsidered under the pressure of Maupassant's peculiar blend of strength and weakness. How can James insist upon all the French master's omissions and still celebrate him as "so complete and edifying"? We come to realize that "complete" can mean two quite different things: complete in terms of what the artist wants to include; and complete in light of all that he might include. If the latter is more admirable, the former allows Maupassant an achievement beyond most writers. "What he leaves out has no claim to get itself considered till after we have done justice to what he takes in."

And even then James is careful. Detailing what exists beyond Maupassant's horizon brings the critic immediately to the Anglo-American world where indignation, complacency, and myopia are perennial responses to French experimentation. To counter smugness, James repeatedly sets up Mrs. Grundy—

> we are accustomed to think, we of the English faith, that a cynic is a living advertisement of his errors. . . .

> it might be thought that he [Maupassant] would . . . have found an abnormal development of this [olfactory] faculty embarrassing—

and then undercuts her on behalf of French heterodoxy.

> M. de Maupassant's cynicism . . . will not be disposed of off-hand by a critic of a competent literary sense.

> But such an apprehension [of the olfactory] betrays an imperfect conception of his directness and resolution.

Later in the essay James insists still more firmly that the Anglo-Saxon alternative to France's limited pessimism is a limited optimism which, "it must never be forgotten[,] . . . is partly the optimism of women and of spinsters." The tyranny of Mrs. Grundy which indicts anything "unadapted to the perusal of ladies and young persons" impedes not only the reception of Maupassant's fiction but also the discussion of that fiction by James. "As regards the other sense, the sense *par excellence*, the sense which we scarcely mention in English fiction, and which I am not very sure I shall be allowed to mention in an English periodical. . . ." That James goes on beyond circumlocution to speak directly of "the sexual sense" is therefore a triumph of Parisian maturity over Puritan fatuity.

As James creates delicate rhetorical structures to enable us to experience the excellences of Maupassant, he works equally hard to make us aware of and to educate us beyond the limitations of Mrs. Grundy.

> For the last ten years our author has brought forth with regularity these condensed compositions, of which, probably, to an English reader, at a first glance, the most universal sign will be their licentiousness. They really partake of this quality, however, in a very differing degree, and a second glance shows that they may be divided into numerous groups. It is not fair, I think, even to say that what they have most in common is their being extremely *lestes*. What they have most in common is their being extremely strong, and after that their being extremely brutal.

What Anglo-American moralizing would dismiss as a single lump of licentiousness, James divides into "numerous groups," and then further separates by denying that licentiousness is their common trait. Readers next discover that what *is* common is not a failing but a virtue, strength, and that the paramount failing is not obscenity but brutality. After we learn that "a story may be obscene without being brutal, and *vice versa*," we have come a long way toward "Maupassant's contempt for those interdictions which are supposed to be made in the interest of good morals." James then continues our moral education by expanding our understanding of the word "moral" itself, as he did with the word "complete."

> He [Maupassant] almost betrays a sense of moral things. Jeanne [in *Une Vie*] . . . has no moral spring, no active moral life . . . but her chronicler has had to handle the immaterial forces of patience and renunciation, and this has given the book a certain purity. . . .

The moral has become not the provincial etiquette of Mrs. Grundy but the transcendent impulses of human consciousness.

It would, of course, be a mistake to overstate James' ultimate distance from Anglo-American values. He ends up, after all, espousing "good-humour and piety" and a long list of qualities (including "the love of sport") whose absence leaves Maupassant's French completeness incomplete. To be in-between, James must express Britain as well as France (like *Partial Portraits* itself which studies both Anglo-American and Continental writers). He confesses, for example, that he shares the very reaction to Maupassant which he has criticized in Anglo-Americans. "Embarrassing and mystifying" is how Maupassant strikes even the disinterested critic. The education in categories and diction which James puts his readers through is required of him as well. "This is why I called him, to begin with, so many ineffectual names: a rarity, a 'case,' an embarrassment, a lion in the path." The tactic by which he insisted upon Maupassant's strengths amid weaknesses is reversed with the Anglo-Saxons. James achieves a convincing advocacy of their values by including a French sense of their limitations.

> To the French we seem superficial, and we are certainly open to the reproach; but none the less. . . . If in ours [the feeling of life], as the novel illustrates it, there are superficialities, there are also qualities which are far from being negatives and omissions: a large imagination and (is it fatuous to say?) a large experience of the positive kind.

A critic who sees that this positive vision involves an "optimism of ignorance as well as of delicacy" has achieved Maupassant's knowledgeability and escaped any indelicacy.

This position in-between is what allows James to resolve the dilemma posed by Maupassant for the Anglo-American consciousness. James can grant the French master's donnée and still fault him *if* the criticism has been made in Maupassant's terms and *after* due recognition of his excellences. "I do not contest the truth of such [unsavory] indications, I only note the particular selection. . . . It [*Une Vie*] is an excellent example of the way the impression of truth may be conveyed by that form, but it would have been a still better one if in his search for the effect of dreariness . . . the author had not eliminated excessively." Confronted by Maupassant's unpleasant data, James responds not by rightously rejecting it as "untrue" or "immoral," but by taking Maupassant's standard of completeness and showing that the unpleasant data which are only part of the truth are being presented by the Frenchman as all of it. James combines M. de Maupassant and Mrs. Grundy, France and England, by defining morality as true completeness. "Fiction will always be decent enough if it be sufficiently general." The critic has in effect had his cake and eaten it too. Disinterestedness is not indifference. Once the critic grants the author's donnée, he is entitled to his own. James saw his task, not as attacking the lion, but as circumventing him in "a legitimate way." He wanted to avoid both the relativism of allowing all subjects equal value and the rejection of any subject a priori. By showing that Maupassant failed in terms of his own donnée, James can generate an a posteriori argument which puts him beyond the lion and on toward an ampler completeness of his own.

Contemporary response to "Guy de Maupassant" indicates that James presented the scandalous author successfully to an apprehensive audience. The *New York Times* called the essay "singularly skillful and thoughtful" (June 10, 1888, p. 12); the *Literary World*, "a triumph of suggestion" (July 17, 1888, p. 212). If anything, James made too little rather than too much of Maupassant's unsavory aspects. The *Atlantic*, while acknowledging "the literary finesse by which the art of Maupassant is substituted for the substance," charged that James had "exceeded the critic's charter and trespassed on the desmene of the partisan" (62 [October 1888]: 567). Like the *New York Tribune* whose headline called James "An Admirer of Art for Art's Sake" (June 17, 1888, p. 10), the *Nation* felt that James' willingness to accept the artist's donnée "leads directly, if it be allowed, to moral indifferentism" (47 [July 26, 1888]: 76). Two other contemporary notes provide important additional insights into the culture's reaction to James' effort. The *Sunday News (and Courier)* of Charleston credited James with starting the Maupassant vogue in America in 1890 (August 24, p. 5). The *Atlantic*, despite its charge of partisanship, concluded that James' "critical work upon French literature, as a whole, is the best accessible to the English reader" and that the essays on Maupassant and Daudet are up to "his earlier, and perhaps more laborious, essays [in *French Poets and Novelists*]" (565).

Admiration for "Guy de Maupassant" has continued among modern writers. See Daugherty (141–43, 169–71) and Edel (3: 176). For bibliographical data about the Maupassant characters and stories mentioned by James, see Steegmuller's *Maupassant: A Lion in the Path* (New York: Random House, 1949) and Lerner's *Guy de Maupassant* (New York: Braziller, 1975).

Notes

197:19. the preface to *Pierre et Jean*. Maupassant published "Le Roman" in *Figaro* on January 7, 1888, one day before the novel's appearance. The essay was so mutilated by editorial excisions that critics and friends including Lemaître complained to Maupassant about "his" incomprehensibility. Maupassant initiated legal proceedings against *Figaro* but withdrew them after a public announcement by the editors.

198:4. Flaubert's *Letters to Madame Sand*. Maupassant provided a prefatory essay for this volume which appeared in 1884.

198:15. hardness. Though Maupassant at his best exhibits an admirable "masculine firmness," he is repeatedly characterized as being too "hard" and as lacking softness. This lack of an androgynous blend of masculine and feminine traits contrasts Maupassant with Turgenev (see our commentary on "Ivan Turgénieff," Chapter 6) and highlights other contrasts between the two authors which emphasize the Frenchman's lack of true completeness. Unlike Turgenev's creative process which integrates head and heart, Maupassant's mode of instinctual analysis is guided by neither: his system of selection is "not in the least a conscious intellectual effort" and his power of generalization displays "a certain absence of love." Moreover, unlike Turgenev, who was both impersonal and personal, Maupassant is only credited with "impersonality."

200:3. reader . . . judge. Maupassant makes this distinction in "Le Roman." "A critic really worthy of the name ought to be an analyst, devoid of preferences or passions. . . . The reader, who looks for no more in a book than that it should satisfy the natural tendencies of his own mind, wants the writer to respond to his predominant taste." Maupassant collapses this distinction in order to protest the incompetence of critics. "But critics, for the most part, are only readers . . . they almost always find fault with us on wrong grounds" (Trans. Clara Dell [New York: P. F. Collier, 1902]). James of course agrees.

200:39. cultivates his garden. Voltaire concludes *Candide* by urging that we forego impossibly heroic tasks and devote our energies to immediate tasks within our powers. " 'We must cultivate our garden.' "

201:17. *moyen.* Means, vehicle.

201:37. *chez vous autres.* That characterize you people.

202:16. *banlieue.* Suburbs.

202:28. as painters say nowadays. For James and impressionism see Winner, *Henry James and the Visual Arts* (Charlottesville: The University Press of Virginia, 1970), Stowell, *Literary Impressionism, James and Chekhov* (Athens: University of Georgia Press, 1980), Kirschke, *Henry James and Impressionism* (Troy, N.Y.: Whitson, 1981).

204:14. house-agents. James is reflecting his experience seeking new quarters in 1885–86. 34 De Vere Gardens offered, among other things, "aspects" excellent and numerous. "A long row of western windows flooded the place with light. An enormous window, with the immensity of London spread below it, provided a place for his desk. . . . All his windows offered a great deal of sky; some looked down upon gardens" (Edel, 3: 159).

204:20. Auteur . . . pas. "An author almost irreproachable in a genre which is not."

204:22. Jules Lemaître (1853–1914), French critic and author of plays and stories. James' quotation is from Lemaître's "Guy de Maupassant" which appeared first in *Revue bleue* and was then collected in the initial volume of Lemaître's *Les Contemporains* (1885). An English version of the essay appeared in a collection of Lemaître essays entitled *Literary Impressions* (1921; rpt. Port Washington, N.Y.: Kennikat Press, 1971). James admired Lemaître for eschewing doctrinal rigidity and espousing Sainte-Beuve's definition of " 'l'esprit critique . . . facile, insinuant, mobile et compréhensif' " (*Les Contempo-rains*, p. 5).

204:30. analytic. James is reintroducing the distinction between stories of character and of plot which Howells had made in 1882 and which had caused such a furor (see our commentary on "The Art of Fiction," Chapter 7). By going on to attest that the analytic method had not attracted many "votaries . . . among ourselves," James is confirming that sense of isolation which increased steadily from 1884. Later in "Guy de Maupassant" James strikes out several times at critics like Besant and Lang who overstress "story" and "plot" at the expense of analysis.

205:3. begins . . . ends. For James' discussion of this issue in the Preface to *Roderick Hudson*, see Chapter 11.

206:36. recipe. Maupassant quoted Flaubert as saying that "if you have originality . . . you must above all things bring it out; if you have not you must acquire it.' " The example of describing the fire and tree is Flaubert's.

209:7. *conte leste*. Risqué tale.

209:8. *grivois*. Cheerily licentious.

gaillard. Risqué.

égrillard. Spicy.

gaudriole. Broad.

211:6. ladies and young persons. For a fuller statement of the complex relationship which James posits between these readers and the state of contemporary fiction in English see "The Future of the Novel," Chapter 10.

212:13. *moeurs de vestales pétrifiés*. Behavior of petrified vestal virgins.

212:35. *polissonnerie*. Depravity.

213:11. Rider Haggard, Sir Henry (1856–1925), author of romances including *King Solomon's Mines* (1886) and *She* (1887). James lamented to Stevenson that "anything so vulgarly brutal [as *She*] should be the thing that succeeds most with the English of today. . . . They seem to me works in which our race and our age make a very vile figure . . ." (August 2 [Edel has dated this letter 1886; the reference to the book version of *She* suggests 1887]). Haggard did not improve his standing in James' eyes by developing a deep friendship with Andrew Lang (see note to p. 178, l. 38 of "The Art of Fiction," Chapter 7, and our commentary on "Criticism,"Chapter 9). Lang disputed the very complaint that James made—Haggard as an index of Britain's impoverished taste—in the very year that James made the complaint. William Watson in the September *Fortnightly* lamented Haggard's popularity ("The Fall of Fiction" 50 [1888]: 324–36); Lang responded in the October *Contemporary* with a rousing defense of Haggard and Britain and a scathing attack upon the critic ("A Dip in Criticism" 54 [1888]: 495–503). Impenitently, Watson repeated his attack upon Haggard and included Lang in the drubbing in the December *Fortnightly* ("Mr. Haggard and His Henchmen" 50 [1888]: 684–88). In 1890 Lang collaborated with Haggard in *The World's Desire*.

213:17. In questioning a female standard for fiction, James is once again setting himself in opposition to Besant, who spoke for orthodoxy when he claimed "that the cultured class of British women—a vast and continually increasing class—are entirely to be trusted" ("Candor in English Fiction," *New Review* 2 [1890]: 8).

213:19. *arts d'agrément*. Social arts.

213:29. *de part et d'autre*. On one side and the other.

213:33. our novelists . . . pity life more and hate it less. James restates here his earlier belief that English writers like Eliot are more forgiving of life than French writers like Balzac and that the heirs of both traditions reflect their lineages.

213:35. initiator. Maupassant apprenticed himself to Flaubert, a lifelong friend of Maupassant's mother.

214:16. Pendennis. *The Newcomes* (1855).

215:2. *âme tendre de caissière*. Cashier's soft heart.

215:5. *illusion de l'ignoble, qui attire tant d'êtres*. The illusion of ignoble things which attracts so many people.

215:9. *yeux de brute*. Animal eyes.

215:11. *amour bête de la nature*. Brute love of nature.

216:16. formerly. Flaubert died suddenly in May of 1880.

216:18. *L'Éducation sentimental* (1869).

216:20. *quelconque*. Commonplace.

216:27. "plot." Maupassant seconds James and Howells in rejecting as old-fashioned that espousal of plot which Besant and Lang continued to make. "This method of construction [producing "an accurate picture of life"], so unlike the old manner which was patent to all, must often mislead the critics. . . . They will not all detect the subtle and secret wires—almost invisibly fine—which certain modern artists use instead of the one string formerly known as the 'plot.'"

216:30. "Bradshaw." George Bradshaw (1801–53), British printer and engraver, began publishing in 1839 a monthly compendium of railroad timetables, *Bradshaw's Railway Guide*. To the erudition of Professor Richard D. Altick we are indebted for the reference to the "famous description" of "Bradshaw." On August 19, 1865, *Punch* presented "The Guide to Bradshaw" which quipped: "After considerable labour, we divide all trains into six classes. . . . The 1st consists of those trains which start and arrive. The 2nd of such as do not start, but arrive. The 3rd of such as *do* start, but *do not* arrive" (64).

217:1. *remplissage*. Filler, details.

217:2. would say. Maupassant did say it. "To tell everything is out of the question. . . . The artist, having chosen his subject, can only select such characteristic details as are of use to it."

218:33. *illusion du beau*. Illusion of the beautiful.

219:11. more novels . . . published. For James' most dire response to the industry of novel production see "Criticism" and "The Future of the Novel," Chapters 9 and 10.

220:32. anything but arbitrary. For James on the distinction between a priori and a posteriori see his July 26, 1899, letter to Mrs. Humphry Ward.

TEXTUAL VARIANTS

197:8. artist . . . shows. 1888 [periodical version]: artist flashes upon us for a moment the light by which he works, utters his mystery and shows.

197:29. in. 1888: about.

198:8. common. 1888: vulgar.

200:23. fullest. 1888: final.

200:27. fails to. 1888: doesn't.

200:41. could not. 1888: couldn't.

205:22. he . . . but. 1888: he goes in, as the phrase is, for saying much, but.

205:40. be. 1888: is.

207:9. do not. 1888: don't.

207:9. has not. 1888: hasn't.

211:1. barbarous. 1888: merciless.

212:20. to . . . on. 1888: to his compatriot on.

217:33. does not. 1888: doesn't.

219:32. be. 1888: is.

219:35. does not. 1888: doesn't.

219:35. does not. 1888: doesn't.

220:23. defeats. 1888: defects.

N I N E

CRITICISM

IF LITERARY CRITICISM MAY BE SAID TO FLOURISH AMONG us at all, it certainly flourishes immensely, for it flows through the periodical press like a river that has burst its dikes. The quantity of it is prodigious, and it is a commodity of which, however the demand may be estimated, the supply will be sure to be in any supposable extremity the last thing to fail us. What strikes the observer above all, in such an affluence, is the unexpected proportion the discourse uttered bears to the objects discoursed of—the paucity of examples, of illustrations and productions, and the deluge of doctrine suspended in the void; the profusion of talk and the contraction of experiment, of what one may call literary conduct. This, indeed, ceases to be an anomaly as soon as we look at the conditions of contemporary journalism. Then we see that these conditions have engendered the practice of "reviewing"—a practice that in general has nothing in common with the art of criticism. Periodical literature is a huge, open mouth which has to be fed—a vessel of immense capacity which has to be filled. It is like a regular train which starts at an advertised hour, but which is free to start only if every seat be occupied. The seats are many, the train is ponderously long, and hence the manufacture of dummies for the seasons when there are not passengers enough. A stuffed manikin is thrust into the empty seat, where it makes a creditable figure till the end of the journey. It looks sufficiently like a passenger, and you know it is not one only when you perceive that it neither says anything nor gets out. The guard attends to it when the train is shunted, blows the cinders from its wooden face and gives a different crook to its elbow, so that it may serve for another run. In this way, in a well-conducted periodical, the blocks of *remplissage* are the dummies of criticism—the recurrent, regulated breakers in the tide of talk. They have a reason for being, and the situation is simpler when we perceive it. It helps to explain the disproportion I just mentioned, as well, in many a case, as the quality of the particular discourse. It helps us to understand that the "organs of public opinion" must be no less copious than punctual, that publicity must maintain its high standard, that ladies and gentlemen may turn an honest penny by the free expenditure of ink. It gives us a glimpse of the high figure presumably reached by all the honest pennies accumulated in the cause, and throws us quite into a glow over the march of civilization and the way we have organized our conveniences. From this point of view it might indeed go far towards making us enthusiastic about our age. What is more calculated to inspire us with a just complacency than the sight of a new and flourishing industry, a fine economy of production? The great business of reviewing has, in its roaring routine, many of the signs of blooming health, many of the features which beguile one into rendering an involuntary homage to successful enterprise.

Yet it is not to be denied that certain captious persons are to be met who are not carried away by the spectacle, who look at it much askance, who see but dimly whither it tends, and who find no aid to vision even in the great light (about itself, its spirit, and its purposes, among other things) that it might have been expected to diffuse. "Is there any such great light at all?" we may imagine the most restless of the sceptics to inquire, "and isn't the effect rather one of a certain kind of pretentious and unprofitable gloom?" The vulgarity, the crudity, the stupidity which this cherished combination of the off-hand review and of our wonderful system of publicity have put into circulation on so vast a scale may be represented, in such a mood, as an unprecedented invention for darkening counsel. The bewildered spirit may ask itself, without speedy answer, What is the function in the life of man of such a periodicity of platitude and irrelevance? Such a spirit will wonder how the life of man survives it, and, above all, what is much more important, how literature resists it; whether, indeed, literature does resist it and is not speedily going down beneath it. The signs of this catastrophe will not in the case we suppose be found too subtle to be pointed out—the failure of distinction, the failure of style, the failure of knowledge, the failure of thought. The case is therefore one for recognizing with dismay that we are paying a tremendous price for the diffusion of penmanship and opportunity; that the multiplication of endowments for chatter may be as fatal as an infectious disease; that literature lives essentially, in the sacred depths of its being, upon example, upon perfection wrought; that, like other sensitive organisms, it is highly susceptible of demoralization, and that nothing is better calculated than irresponsible pedagogy to make it close its ears and lips. To be puerile and untutored

233

about it is to deprive it of air and light, and the consequence of its keeping bad company is that it loses all heart. We may, of course, continue to talk about it long after it has bored itself to death, and there is every appearance that this is mainly the way in which our descendants will hear of it. They will, however, acquiesce in its extinction.

This, I am aware, is a dismal conviction, and I do not pretend to state the case gayly. The most I can say is that there are times and places in which it strikes one as less desperate than at others. One of the places is Paris, and one of the times is some comfortable occasion of being there. The custom of rough-and-ready reviewing is, among the French, much less rooted than with us, and the dignity of criticism is, to my perception, in consequence much higher. The art is felt to be one of the most difficult, the most delicate, the most occasional; and the material on which it is exercised is subject to selection, to restriction. That is, whether or no the French are always right as to what they do notice, they strike me as infallible as to what they don't. They publish hundreds of books which are never noticed at all, and yet they are much neater book-makers than we. It is recognized that such volumes have nothing to say to the critical sense, that they do not belong to literature, and that the possession of the critical sense is exactly what makes it impossible to read them and dreary to discuss them—places them, as a part of critical experience, out of the question. The critical sense, in France, *ne se dérange pas*, as the phrase is, for so little. No one would deny, on the other hand, that when it does set itself in motion it goes further than with us. It handles the subject in general with finer finger-tips. The bluntness of ours, as tactile implements addressed to an exquisite process, is still sometimes surprising, even after frequent exhibition. We blunder in and out of the affair as if it were a railway station—the easiest and most public of the arts. It is in reality the most complicated and the most particular. The critical sense is so far from frequent that it is absolutely rare, and the possession of the cluster of qualities that minister to it is one of the highest distinctions. It is a gift inestimably precious and beautiful; therefore, so far from thinking that it passes overmuch from hand to hand, one knows that one has only to stand by the counter an hour to see that business is done with baser coin. We have too many small school-masters; yet not only do I not question in literature the high utility of criticism, but I should be tempted to say that the part it plays may be the supremely beneficent one when it proceeds from deep sources, from the efficient combination of experience and perception. In this light one sees the critic as the real helper of the artist, a torch-bearing outrider, the interpreter, the brother. The more the tune is noted and the direction observed the more we shall enjoy the convenience of a critical literature. When one thinks of the outfit required for free work in this spirit, one is ready to pay almost any homage to the intelligence that has put it on; and when one considers the noble figure completely equipped—armed *cap-à-pie* in curiosity and sympathy—one falls in love with the apparition. It certainly represents the knight who has knelt through his long vigil and who has the piety of his office. For there is something sacrificial in his function, inasmuch as he offers himself as a general touchstone. To lend himself, to project himself and steep himself, to feel and feel till he understands, and to understand so well that he can say, to have perception at the pitch of passion and expression as embracing as the air, to be infinitely curious and incorrigibly patient, and yet plastic and inflammable and determinable, stooping to conquer and serving to direct—these are fine chances for an active mind, chances to add the idea of independent beauty to the conception of success. Just in proportion as he is sentient and restless, just in proportion as he reacts and reciprocates and penetrates, is the critic a valuable instrument; for in literature assuredly criticism *is* the critic, just as art is the artist; it being assuredly the artist who invented art and the critic who invented criticism, and not the other way round.

And it is with the kinds of criticism exactly as it is with the kinds of art—the best kind, the only kind worth speaking of, is the kind that springs from the liveliest experience. There are a hundred labels and tickets, in all this matter, that have been pasted on from the outside and appear to exist for the convenience of passers-by; but the critic who lives *in* the house, ranging through its innumerable chambers, knows nothing about the bills on the front. He only knows that the more impressions he has the more he is able to record, and that the more he is saturated, poor fellow, the more he can give out. His life, at this rate, is heroic, for it is immensely vicarious. He has to understand for others, to answer for them; he is always under arms. He knows that the whole honor of the matter, for him, besides the success in his own eyes, depends upon his being indefatigably supple, and that is a formidable order. Let me not speak, however, as if his work were a conscious grind, for the sense of effort is easily lost in the enthusiasm of curiosity. Any vocation has its hours of intensity that is so closely connected with life. That of the critic, in literature, is connected doubly, for he deals with life at second-hand as well as at first; that is, he deals with the experience of others, which he resolves into his own, and not of those invented and selected others with whom the novelist makes comfortable terms, but with the uncompromising swarm of authors, the clamorous children of history. He has to make them as vivid and as free as the novelist makes *his* puppets, and yet he has, as the phrase is, to take them as they come. We must be easy with him if the picture, even when the aim has really been to penetrate, is sometimes confused, for there are baffling and there are thankless subjects; and we make everything up to him by the peculiar purity of our esteem when the portrait is really, like the happy portraits of the other art, a text preserved by translation.

Henry James, his old adversary Andrew Lang, and his old friend Edmund Gosse were invited to contribute to a forum on "The Science of Criticism" which the *New Review* featured in May of 1891 as a counterpoint to its forum on "The Science of Fiction" with Besant, Bourget, and Hardy. James, busy at the time with rehearsals for his ill-fated stage versions of *The American*, produced a brief but deeply felt essay which he initially titled after the forum and retitled simply "Criticism" for inclusion in revised form in *Essays in London and Elsewhere* (1893).

Rather than present what readers probably expected and what Lang and Gosse produced, a rehash of previously published ideas, James sent to *New Review* a message quite different from that in "The Art of Fiction." Gone is the conciliatory tone designed to foster a community of discussants. In the seven years since "The Art of Fiction," James had increasingly found isolation rather than communion. His words on criticism had fallen on deaf ears and his innovations in fiction had fallen so stillborn that he had abandoned the novel for the theater. "Criticism" takes aim on imperceptive reviewers and nugatory novelists.

James begins by making an Arnoldian connection between the vitality of criticism and the health of literature, between the mindless industry of contemporary "reviewing" and the flaccid fiction of late-Victorian England. Readers so deadened by both media can be revived only if James can develop formal means of impressing upon them the seriousness of their situation. Since "the vulgarity . . . may be represented . . . as an unprecedented invention for darkening counsel," James must counter with inventions of his own. The chief of these are metaphor and word-play.

The proliferation of criticism is figured first through a metaphor from nature. "It flows . . . like a river that has burst its dikes." But contemporary reviewing is *not* natural, it is a mechanistic aberration which flows "like a regular train." This metaphor then transforms in the amazing sequence which images critics as dummies carried on an endless railroad circuit and concludes with them "blunder[ing] in and out of the affair as if it were a railway station." Since trains are part of the larger process of British industrialization and commercialization, James fits his railroad metaphor into a larger pattern of images. "A new and flourishing industry" is what reviewing has become. Terms like "commodity . . . demand [and] . . . supply . . . great business . . . successful enterprise" proliferate because criticism itself confirms the Philistines' triumph. James has taken the generalization of his friend and mentor John Ruskin—that industrialization alienates the laborer from the product of his labor—and has applied it to criticism. The human is lost amid the mechanical and commercial.

Word-play represents this loss effectively. The humane connotations of words are subsumed by the materialistic, as James provides for readers of "Criticism" an experience analogous to the dehumanization of culture. The "immense capacity" of periodical literature, for example, means not that the art of criticism has a vast capability for excellence, but only that the industry of reviewing has a gross quantity of page space to fill. "The high figure" in reviewing is not a towering genius like Arnold or Sainte-Beuve, but a tower of guineas for Babel's scribblers. A "high standard" marks the "copious," not the elevated. When James refers to British reviewing's "fine economy," the word "economy" does not signify the selectivity of French practice and the word "fine" does not refer to the delicate touch of France's "finer finger-tips." All in all, "what one may call literary conduct" may be so called only if "conduct" no longer connotes true professionalism and if "literary" need not involve real literacy.

James is not, however, so despairing as to see culture entirely co-opted by commerce. He persists in something like Arnold's faith that

> in spite of all that is said about the absorbing and brutalising influence of our passionate material progress, it seems to me indisputable that this progress is likely, though not certain, to lead in the end to an apparition of intellectual life. . . . I grant it is mainly the privilege of faith, at present, to discern this end to our railways, our business, and our fortune-making. ("The Function of Criticism at the Present Time")

James goes beyond castigating reviewers and reaffirms the possibility of true criticism. Metaphors and word-play are again his chief devices. The good critic is figured as the knight "armed" with the Arnoldian virtues of "curiosity" and "sympathy" who "has knelt through his long vigil and who has the piety of his office." The metaphor then expands as an Arnoldian term takes on Christological proportions. Like Jesus who offered himself sacrificially for humankind, the good critic has "something sacrificial in his function, inasmuch as he offers himself as a general touchstone." Redeemed through this act is language itself. Human connotations return to James' diction. "These are fine chances for an active mind, chances to add the idea of independent beauty to the conception of success." Now "success" can again include the noncommercial "beauty" which is "indepen-dent" of the mechanical. And "fine" can reemerge as the excellence available to all the knights of culture.

In the process of affirmation, James elevates criticism beyond what even Arnold argued for. After initially adopting the Arnoldian hierarchy that puts criticism second to literature—James' critic is the "helper of the artist"—James moves toward equality. "Helper" be-gins a dictional sequence which proceeds to "torch-bearing outrider," then to "interpreter," and finally to fraternity, to "brother." Now comes the "knight" metaphor which "one falls in love with." James is not, ultimately, rating criticism as high as literature, but he is insist-ing that both are "art" and derive from the same, the sole creative faculty. "It is with the kinds of criticism exactly as it is with the kinds of art—the best kind, the only kind worth speaking of, is the kind that springs from the liveliest experience." Like the artist, the critic must be "saturated" because criticism, like art, is ultimately a person-al impression of life.

That the critic's task is in at least one respect *more* intricate than the novelist's—"he deals with life at second-hand as well as at first"—is what warrants James' final softening of his strictures upon reviewers. "We must be easy with him if the picture . . . is some-times confused, for there are baffling and there are thankless sub-jects." James is still open to a community of brother critics in arms. He is still four years away from the *Guy Domville* night when they booed him—critics and public—from the stage.

Notes

232:10. contraction of experiment. British fiction by 1891 had further confirmed what James said to Howells in 1884—that only the French were capable of "experiment" and that "the floods of tepid soap and water which under the name of novels are being vomited forth in England, seem to me, by contrast, to do little honour to our race" (February 21).

232:27. *remplissage*. Filler, padding, as of a literary work.

232:31. quality. The other side of the discussion of "quantity."

233:18. light. For this Arnoldian ideal in "The Art of Fiction," see Chapter 7, note to page 169, l. 34.

233:31. going down beneath it. James is less sanguine now than when he discussed fiction's resistence to vulgarization in "The Art of Fiction." "It has been vulgarised, like all other kinds of literature, like everything else to-day, and it has proved more than some kinds accessible to vulgarisation. But there is as much difference as there ever was between a good novel and a bad one . . . and the good subsists and emits its light and stimulates our desire for perfection" (p. 169).

233:34. failure of knowledge . . . thought. James is reconfirming his commitment to Arnold's belief that ideas are the generative force behind all creativity in literature and criticism. "The grand work of literary genius is a work of synthesis and exposition, not of analysis and discovery; its gift lies in the faculty of being happily inspired by a certain intellectual and spiritual atmosphere . . . it must find itself amidst the order of ideas, in order to work freely. . . . To act is so easy, as Goethe says; to think is so hard!" ("The Function of Criticism at the Present Time").

233:39. perfection. For this Arnoldian ideal, see Chapter 7, note to page 169, l. 34.

234:24. *ne se dérange pas.* Does not trouble itself.

235:6. *cap-à-pie.* From head to foot, completely.

235:9. touchstone. James is applying to the critic himself what Arnold asserted about great works of art. "Indeed there can be no more useful help for discovering what poetry belongs to the class of the truly excellent, and can therefore do us most good, than to have always in one's mind lines and expressions of the great masters, and to apply them as a touchstone to other poetry" ("The Study of Poetry"). In James' expression "general touchstone," the adjective also has Arnoldian force since James praised Arnold precisely for being "the *general* critic" (see our commentary on "Matthew Arnold's *Essays in Criticism*," Chapter 1).

235:11. feel till he understands. For the primacy of feeling in Arnold, and for James' espousal of this priority, see our commentary on "Matthew Arnold's *Essays in Criticism*," Chapter 1.

235:13. curious. "It is noticeable that the word *curiosity*, which in other languages is used in a good sense, to mean, as a high and fine quality of man's nature, just this disinterested love of a free play of the mind on all subjects, for its own sake,—it is noticeable, I say, that this word has in our language no sense of the kind, no sense but rather a bad and disparaging one. But criticism, real criticism, is essentially the exercise in this very quality" ("The Function of Criticism at the Present Time").

235:14. stooping to conquer. In Goldsmith's play *She Stoops to Conquer* (1773), Miss Hardcastle, very much a lady, is mistaken by young Marlow for a barmaid and treated accordingly. In the end, however, Miss Hardcastle, denied her station and wealth, prevails over him and is loved for her true natural excellence. Like her, James' good critic must be "plastic" enough to adapt to circumstances. That stooping to conquer is a female trait in Goldsmith and a practice of (largely) male critics in James confirms his belief that the good critic must possess amply those qualities conventionally considered "feminine" (see Introduction).

TEXTUAL VARIANTS

232:3. dikes. 1891: dykes.

232:10. contraction. 1891: poverty.

232:28. breakers in the tide. 1891: billows in the ocean.

233:7. organized. 1891: organised.

233:28. periodicity. 1891: reverberation.

233:35 recognizing. 1891: recognising.

233:40. demoralization. 1891: demoralisation.

233:41. better. . . . We. 1891: better addressed than irresponsible pedagogy to making it lose faith in itself. To talk about it clumsily is to poison the
air it breathes, and the consequence of that sort of taint is that it dwindles and
dies. We.

234:3. has bored itself to death. 1891: is dead.

234:5. it. . . . [par.] This. 1891: it; not, perhaps, that they will much
regret its departure, with *our* report to go by. [par.] This.

234:7. conviction. 1891: impression.

234:8. gayly. 1891: gaily.

234:42. the artist. 1891: mankind.

234:42. the brother. 1891: *par excellence.*

235:1. more. . . . When. 1891: more we have of such the better, though
there will surely always be obstacles enough to our having many. When.

235:6. the apparition. 1891: one's conception.

235:12. expression . . . to. 1891: expression in the form of talent, to.

235:13. patient . . . these. 1891: patient, with the intensely fixed idea of
turning character and genius and history inside out—these.

235:15. fine chances for. 1891: ideas to give.

235:15. mind . . . beauty. 1891: mind a high programme and to add the
element of artistic beauty.

235:17. he . . . is. 1891: he vibrates with intellectual experience, is.

235:24. that. . . . There. 1891: that the most living spirit gives us. There.

235:32. others . . . he. 1891: others and to interpret, and he.

235:33. honor. 1891: honour.

236:6. we . . . the. 1891: we compensate him in the.

236:7. really, like. 1891: really, as it were, like.

236:8. a . . . translation. 1891: a translation into style.

T E N

THE FUTURE OF THE NOVEL

BEGINNINGS, AS WE ALL KNOW, ARE USUALLY SMALL things, but continuations are not always strikingly great ones, and the place occupied in the world by the prolonged prose fable has become, in our time, among the incidents of literature, the most surprising example to be named of swift and extravagant growth, a development beyond the measure of every early appearance. It is a form that has had a fortune so little to have been foretold at its cradle. The germ of the comprehensive epic was more recognisable in the first barbaric chant than that of the novel as we know it to-day in the first anecdote retailed to amuse. It arrived, in truth, the novel, late at self-consciousness; but it has done its utmost ever since to make up for lost opportunities. The flood at present swells and swells, threatening the whole field of letters, as would often seem, with submersion. It plays, in what may be called the passive consciousness of many persons, a part that directly marches with the rapid increase of the multitude able to possess itself in one way and another of the *book*. The book, in the Anglo-Saxon world, is almost everywhere, and it is in the form of the voluminous prose fable that we see it penetrate easiest and farthest. Penetration appears really to be directly aided by mere mass and bulk. There is an immense public, if public be the name, inarticulate, but abysmally absorbent, for which, at its hours of ease, the printed volume has no other association. This public—the public that subscribes, borrows, lends, that picks up in one way and another, sometimes even by purchase—grows and grows each year, and nothing is thus more apparent than that of all the recruits it brings to the book the most numerous by far are those that it brings to the "story."

This number has gained, in our time, an augmentation from three sources in particular, the first of which, indeed, is perhaps but a comprehensive name for the two others. The diffusion of the rudiments, the multiplication of common schools, has had more and more the effect of making readers of women and of the very young. Nothing is so striking in a survey of this field, and nothing to be so much borne in mind, as that the larger part of the great multitude that sustains the teller and the publisher of tales is constituted by boys and girls; by girls in especial, if we apply the term to the later stages of the life of the innumerable women who, under modern arrangements, increasingly fail to marry—fail, apparently, even, largely, to desire to. It is not too much to say of many of these that they live in a great measure by the immediate aid of the novel—confining the question, for the moment, to the fact of consumption alone. The literature, as it may be called for convenience, of children is an industry that occupies by itself a very considerable quarter of the scene. Great fortunes, if not great reputations, are made, we learn, by writing for schoolboys, and the period during which they consume the compound artfully prepared for them appears—as they begin earlier and continue later—to add to itself at both ends. This helps to account for the fact that public libraries, especially those that are private and money-making enterprises, put into circulation more volumes of "stories" than of all other things together of which volumes can be made. The published statistics are extraordinary, and of a sort to engender many kinds of uneasiness. The sort of taste that used to be called "good" has nothing to do with the matter: we are so demonstrably in presence of millions for whom taste is but an obscure, confused, immediate instinct. In the flare of railway bookstalls, in the shop-fronts of most book-sellers, especially the provincial, in the advertisements of the weekly newspapers, and in fifty places besides, this testimony to the general preference triumphs, yielding a good-natured corner at most to a bunch of treatises on athletics or sport, or a patch of theology old and new.

The case is so marked, however, that illustrations easily overflow, and there is no need of forcing doors that stand wide open. What remains is the interesting oddity or mystery—the anomaly that fairly dignifies the whole circumstance with its strangeness: the wonder, in short, that men, women, and children *should* have so much attention to spare for improvisations mainly so arbitrary and frequently so loose. That, at the first blush, fairly leaves us gaping. This great fortune then, since fortune it seems, has been reserved for mere unsupported and unguaranteed history, the *inexpensive* thing, written in the air, the record of what, in any particular case, has *not* been, the account that remains responsible, at best, to "documents" with which we are practically unable to collate it. This is the side of the whole business of fiction on which it can always be challenged, and to

243

that degree that if the general venture had not become in such a manner the admiration of the world it might but too easily have become the derision. It has in truth, I think, never philosophically met the challenge, never found a formula to inscribe on its shield, never defended its position by any better argument than the frank, straight blow: "Why am I not so unprofitable as to be preposterous? Because I can do *that*. There!" And it throws up from time to time some purely practical masterpiece. There is nevertheless an admirable minority of intelligent persons who care not even for the masterpieces, nor see any pressing point in them, for whom the very form itself has, equally at its best and at its worst, been ever a vanity and a mockery. This class, it should be added, is beginning to be visibly augmented by a different circle altogether, the group of the formerly subject, but now estranged, the deceived and bored, those for whom the whole movement too decidedly fails to live up to its possibilities. There are people who have loved the novel, but who actually find themselves drowned in its verbiage, and for whom, even in some of its approved manifestations, it has become a terror they exert every ingenuity, every hypocrisy, to evade. The indifferent and the alienated testify, at any rate, almost as much as the omnivorous, to the reign of the great ambiguity, the enjoyment of which rests, evidently, on a primary need of the mind. The novelist can only fall back on that—on his recognition that man's constant demand for what he has to offer is simply man's general appetite for a *picture*. The novel is of all pictures the most comprehensive and the most elastic. It will stretch anywhere—it will take in absolutely anything. All it needs is a subject and a painter. But for its subject, magnificently, it has the whole human consciousness. And if we are pushed a step farther backward, and asked why the representation should be required when the object represented is itself mostly so accessible, the answer to that appears to be that man combines with his eternal desire for more experience an infinite cunning as to getting his experience as cheaply as possible. He will steal it whenever he can. He likes to live the life of others, yet is well aware of the points at which it may too intolerably resemble his own. The vivid fable, more than anything else, gives him this satisfaction on easy terms, gives him knowledge abundant yet vicarious. It enables him to select, to take and to leave; so that to feel he can afford to neglect it he must have a rare faculty, or great opportunities, for the extension of experience—by thought, by emotion, by energy—at first hand.

Yet it is doubtless not this cause alone that contributes to the contemporary deluge; other circumstances operate, and one of them is probably, in truth, if looked into, something of an abatement of the great fortune we have been called upon to admire. The high prosperity of fiction has marched, very directly, with another "sign of the times," the demoralisation, the vulgarisation of literature in general, the increasing familiarity of all such methods of communication, the making itself supremely felt, as it were, of the presence of the ladies and children—by whom I mean, in other words, the reader irreflective and uncritical. If the novel, in fine, has found itself, socially speaking, at such a rate, the book *par excellence,* so on the other hand the book has in the same degree found itself a thing of small ceremony. So many ways of producing it easily have been discovered that it is by no means the occasional prodigy, for good or for evil, that it was taken for in simpler days, and has therefore suffered a proportionate discredit. Almost any variety is thrown off and taken up, handled, admired, ignored by too many people, and this, precisely, is the point at which the question of its future becomes one with that of the future of the total swarm. How are the generations to face, at all, the monstrous multiplications? Any speculation on the further development of a particular variety is subject to the reserve that the generations may at no distant day be obliged formally to decree, and to execute, great clearings of the deck, great periodical effacements and destructions. It fills, in fact, at moments the expectant ear, as we watch the progress of the ship of civilisation—the huge splash that must mark the response to many an imperative, unanimous "Overboard!" What at least is already very plain is that practically the great majority of volumes printed within a year cease to exist as the hour passes, and give up by that circumstance all claim to a career, to being accounted or provided for. In speaking of the future of the novel we must of course, therefore, be taken as limiting the inquiry to those types that have, for criticism, a present and a past. And it is only superficially that confusion seems here to reign. The fact that in England and in the United States every specimen that sees the light may look for a "review" testifies merely to the point to which, in these countries, literary criticism has sunk. The review is in nine cases out of ten an effort of intelligence as undeveloped as the ineptitude over which it fumbles, and the critical spirit, which knows where it is concerned and where not, is not touched, is still less compromised, by the incident. There are too many reasons why newspapers must live.

So, as regards the tangible type, the end is that in its undefended, its positively exposed state, we continue to accept it, conscious even of a peculiar beauty in an appeal made from a footing so precarious. It throws itself wholly on our generosity, and very often indeed gives us, by the reception it meets, a useful measure of the quality, of the delicacy, of many minds. There is to my sense no work of literary, or of any other, art, that any human being is under the smallest positive obligation to "like." There is no woman—no matter of what loveliness—in the presence of whom it is anything but a man's unchallengeably *own* affair that he is "in love" or out of it. It is not a question of manners; vast is the margin left to individual freedom; and the trap set by the artist occupies no different ground— Robert Louis Stevenson has admirably expressed the analogy—from the offer of her charms by the lady. There only remain infatuations that we envy and emulate. When we do respond to the appeal, when we *are* caught in the trap, we are held and played upon; so that how in the world can there *not* still be a future, however late in the day, for a contrivance possessed of this precious secret? The more we consider it the more we feel that the prose picture can never be at the end of its tether until it loses the sense of what it can do. It can do simply everything, and that is its strength and its life. Its plasticity, its elasticity are infinite; there is no colour, no extension it may not take from the nature of its subject or the temper of its craftsman. It has the extraordinary advantage—a piece of luck scarcely credible—that, while capable of giving an impression of the highest perfection and the rarest finish, it moves in a luxurious independence of rules and restrictions. Think as we may, there is nothing we can mention as a consideration outside itself with which it must square, nothing we can name as one of its peculiar obligations or interdictions. It must, of course, hold our attention and reward it, it must not appeal on false pretences; but these necessities, with which, obviously, disgust and displeasure interfere, are not peculiar to it—all works of art have them in common. For the rest it has so clear a field that if it perishes this will surely be by its fault—by its superficiality, in other words, or its timidity. One almost, for the very love of it, likes to think of its appearing threatened with some such fate, in order to figure the dramatic stroke of its revival under the touch of a life-giving master. The temperament of the artist can do so much for it that our desire for some exemplary felicity fairly demands even the vision of that supreme proof. If we were to linger on this vision long enough, we should doubtless, in fact, be brought to wondering—and still for very loyalty to the form itself—whether our own prospective conditions may not before too long appear to many critics to call for some such happy *coup* on the part of a great artist yet to come.

There would at least be this excuse for such a reverie: that speculation is vain unless we confine it, and that for ourselves the most convenient branch of the question is the state of the industry that makes its appeal to readers of English. From any attempt to measure the career still open to the novel in France I may be excused, in so narrow a compass, for shrinking. The French, as a result of having ridden their horse much harder than we, are at a different stage of the journey, and we have doubtless many of their stretches and baiting-places yet to traverse. But if the range grows shorter from the moment we drop to inductions drawn only from English and American material, I am not sure that the answer comes sooner. I should have at all events—a formidably large order—to plunge into the particulars of the question of the present. If the day *is* approaching when the respite of execution for almost any book is but a matter of mercy, does the English novel of commerce tend to strike us as a production more and more equipped by its high qualities for braving the danger? It would be impossible, I think, to make one's attempt at an answer to that riddle really interesting without bringing into the field many illustrations drawn from individuals—without pointing the moral with names both conspicuous and obscure. Such a freedom would carry us, here, quite too far, and would moreover only encumber the path. There is nothing to prevent our taking for granted all sorts of happy symptoms and splendid promises—so long, of course, I mean, as we keep before us the general truth that the future of fiction is intimately bound up with the future of the society that produces and consumes it. In a society with a great and diffused literary sense the talent at play can only be a less negligible thing than in a society with a literary sense barely discernible. In a world in which criticism is acute and mature such talent will find itself trained, in order successfully to assert itself, to many more kinds of precautionary expertness than in a society in which the art I have named holds an inferior place or makes a sorry figure. A community addicted to reflection and fond of ideas will try experiments with the "story" that will be left untried in a community mainly devoted to travelling and shooting, to pushing trade and playing football. There are many judges, doubtless, who hold that experiments—queer and uncanny things at best—are not necessary to it, that its face has been, once for all, turned in one way, and that it has only to go straight before it. If that is what it is actually doing in England and America the main thing to say about its future would appear to be that this future will in very truth more and more define itself as negligible. For all the while the immense variety of life will stretch away to right and to left, and all the while there may be, on such lines, perpetuation of its great mistake of failing of intelligence. That mistake will be, ever, for the admirable art, the only one really inexcusable, because of being a mistake about, as we may say, its own soul. The form of novel that is stupid on the general question of its freedom is the single form that may, *a priori*, be unhesitatingly pronounced wrong.

The most interesting thing to-day, therefore, among ourselves is the degree in which we may count on seeing a sense of that freedom cultivated and bearing fruit. What else is this, indeed, but one of the most attaching elements in the great drama of our wide English-speaking life! As the novel is at any moment the most immediate and, as it were, admirably *treacherous* picture of actual manners—indirectly as well as directly, and by what it does not touch as well as by what it does—so its present situation, where we are most concerned with it, is exactly a reflection of our social changes and chances, of the signs and portents that lay most traps for most observers, and make up in general what is most "amusing" in the spectacle we offer. Nothing, I may say, for instance, strikes me more as meeting this description than the predicament finally arrived at, for the fictive energy, in consequence of our long and most respectable tradition of making it defer supremely, in the treatment, say, of a delicate case, to the inexperience of the young. The particular knot the coming novelist who shall prefer not simply to beg the question, will have here to untie may represent assuredly the essence of his outlook. By what it shall decide to do in respect to the "young" the great prose fable will, from any serious point of view, practically see itself stand or fall. What is clear is that it has, among us, veritably never chosen—it has, mainly, always obeyed an unreasoning instinct of avoidance in which there has often been much that was felicitous. While society was frank, was free about the incidents and accidents of the human constitution, the novel took the same robust ease as society. The young then were so very young that they were not table-high. But they began to grow, and from the moment their little chins rested on the mahogany, Richardson and Fielding began to go under it. There came into being a mistrust of any but the most guarded treatment of the great relation between men and women, the constant world-renewal, which was the conspicuous sign that whatever the prose picture of life was prepared to take upon itself, it was not prepared to take upon itself not to be superficial. Its position became very much: "There are other things, don't you know? For heaven's sake let *that* one pass!" And to this wonderful propriety of letting it pass the business has been for these so many years—with the consequences we see to-day—largely devoted. These consequences are of many sorts, not a few altogether charming. One of them has been that there is an immense omission in our fiction—which, though many critics will always judge that it has vitiated the whole, others will continue to speak of as signifying but a trifle. One can only talk for one's self, and of the English and American novelists of whom I am fond, I am so superlatively fond that I positively prefer to take them as they are. I cannot so much as imagine Dickens and Scott *without* the "love-making" left, as the phrase is, out. They were, to my perception, absolutely right—from the moment their attention to it could only be perfunctory—practically not to deal with it. In all their work it is, in spite of the number of pleasant sketches of affection gratified or crossed, the element that matters least. Why not therefore assume, it may accordingly be asked, that discriminations which have served their purpose so well in the past will continue not less successfully to meet the case? What will you have better than Scott and Dickens?

Nothing certainly *can* be, it may at least as promptly be replied, and I can imagine no more comfortable prospect than jogging along perpetually with a renewal of such blessings. The difficulty lies in the fact that two of the great conditions have changed. The novel is older, and so are the young. It would seem that everything the young can possibly do for us in the matter has been successfully done. They have kept out one thing after the other, yet there is still a certain completeness we lack, and the curious thing is that it appears to be they themselves who are making the grave discovery. "You have kindly taken," they seem to say to the fiction-mongers, "our education off the hands of our parents and pastors, and that, doubtless, has been very convenient for *them,* and left them free to amuse themselves. But what, all the while, pray, if it is a question of education, have you done with your own? These are directions in which you seem dreadfully untrained, and in which *can* it be as vain as it appears to apply to you for information?" The point is whether, from the moment it is a question of averting discredit, the novel can afford to take things quite so easily as it has, for a good while now, settled down into the way of doing. There are too many sources of interest neglected—whole categories of manners, whole corpuscular classes and provinces, museums of character and condition, unvisited; while it is on the other hand mistakenly taken for granted that safety lies in all the loose and thin material that keeps reappearing in forms at once ready-made and sadly the worse for wear. The simple themselves may finally turn against our simplifications; so that we need not, after all, be more royalist than the king or more childish than the children. It is certain that there is no real health for any art—I am not speaking, of course, of any mere industry—that does not move a step in advance of its farthest follower. It would be curious—really a great comedy—if the renewal were to spring just from the satiety of the very readers for whom the sacrifices have hitherto been supposed to be made. It bears on this that as nothing is more salient in English life today, to fresh eyes, than the revolution taking place in the position and outlook of women—and taking place much more deeply in the quiet than even the noise on the surface demonstrates—so we may very well yet see the female elbow itself, kept in increasing activity by the play of the pen, smash with final resonance the window all this time most superstitiously closed. The particular draught that has been most deprecated will in that case take care of the question of freshness. It is the opinion of some observers that when women do obtain a free hand they will not repay their long debt to the precautionary attitude of men by unlimited consideration for the natural delicacy of the latter.

To admit, then, that the great anodyne can ever totally fail to work, is to imply, in short, that this will only be by some grave fault in some high quarter. Man rejoices in an incomparable faculty for presently mutilating and disfiguring any plaything that has helped create for him the illusion of leisure; nevertheless, so long as life retains its power of projecting itself upon his imagination, he will find the novel work off the impression better than anything he knows. Anything better for the purpose has assuredly yet to be discovered. He will give it up only when life itself too thoroughly disagrees with him. Even then, indeed, may fiction not find a second wind, or a fiftieth, in the very portrayal of that collapse? Till the world is an unpeopled void there will be an image in the mirror. What need more immediately concern us, therefore, is the care of seeing that the image shall continue various and vivid. There is much, frankly, to be said for those who, in spite of all brave pleas, feel it to be considerably menaced, for very little reflection will help to show us how the prospect strikes them. They see the whole business too divorced on the one side from observation and perception, and on the other from the art and taste. They get too little of the first-hand impression, the effort to penetrate—that effort for which the French have the admirable expression to *fouiller*—and still less, if possible, of any science of composition, any architecture, distribution, proportion. It is not a trifle, though indeed it is the concomitant of an edged force, that "mystery" should, to so many of the sharper eyes, have disappeared from the craft, and a facile flatness be, in place of it, in acclaimed possession. But these are, at the worst, even for such of the disconcerted, signs that the novelist, not that the novel, has dropped. So long as there is a subject to be treated, so long will it depend wholly on the treatment to rekindle the fire. Only the ministrant must really approach the altar; for if the novel *is* the treatment, it is the treatment that is essentially what I have called the anodyne.

In the fall of 1899, Henry James purchased Lamb House, the residence in Rye, Sussex, which he had leased since 1897. To make the initial payment, James with startling speed wrote and sold ten short stories, two essays for the *North American Review*, and scenarios for two novels (*The Sense of the Past* and *The Ambassadors*). He also produced for Richard Garnett's *Universal Anthology* the last of his major theoretical essays, "The Future of the Novel."

The gloom which had gathered by the time of "Criticism" had only thickened during the nineties. With his theatrical aspirations booed from the stage, James returned full-time to fiction, reflecting his anguish in tales of beset children (Edel, 4:208–13), expressing his rage in novels of acerbic social commentary, and experimenting with the "divine principle of the Scenario" and the "scenic" method of organization. James as critic persisted in his lonely determination to hold a mirror up to culture. He noted again and again the failure of Anglo-American letters to engage in disinterested discussion. The furor over Ibsen, for example,

> constitutes one of the very few cases of contagious discussion of a matter not political, a question not of mere practice, of which I remember to have felt, in a heavy air, the engaging titillation. In London, in general, I think, the wandering breath of criticism is the stray guest at the big party. . . . literary studies, literary curiosity . . . are the element most absent from the American magazines. ("London" [1897], "American Letter" [1898])

James persisted, in turn, in pointing English-language critics to French practice. "The authors of the English studies appear to labor, in general, under a terror of critical responsibility; the authors of the French, on the contrary, to hunger and thirst for it" ("The Present Literary Situation in France" [1899]).

Critical responsibility is what James accepts in "The Future of the Novel." On the one hand, he confirms cherished positions. The Arnoldian belief that literature can never be healthier than the critical context which nurtures it reappears in the charge that "the review is in nine cases out of ten an effort of intelligence as undeveloped as the ineptitude over which it fumbles"; the Arnoldian insistence upon "ideas" echoes in the definition of contemporary fiction's "great mistake" as a "failing of intelligence." James again attacks the novelistic "timidity" criticized in "The Art of Fiction," again espouses the "experiments" lauded in "Criticism," again contemns the Besant-esque reduction of fiction to the "'story.'" Above all, James continues that lament for the absence of theory which informed "The Art of Fiction"

and its successors. Fiction "has in truth, I think, never philosophically met the challenge [of being only 'unsupported and unguaranteed
history'] . . . never defended its position by any better argument
than the frank, straight blow. . . . [of producing] from time to time
some purely practical masterpiece."

As responsible criticism must go beyond restatement, "The Future of the Novel" avoids any repetition of "Criticism" by altering
both its analysis of the present and its vision of the future. James' new
approach to the present is signaled by his transformation of the dominant metaphor of "Criticism." In 1891, "the flood" became a train
because the mechanization of culture was James' topic. In 1899 he
asks not why the publishing industry churns out reviews but why
human beings crave fiction. He is carrying on Sainte-Beuve's critique
of "industrial literature," but his focus is different. Production is still
an issue because James' subject is again mass culture, but now the
mode of production is schools and the product is readers. James does
not dehumanize literacy and leisure with mechanical metaphors. The
"flood" becomes not a train but a "deluge." As this image, plus
"overflow" and "drowned," indicates, however, James is anything
but sanguine in 1899. Professional rebuffs and personal losses have
encouraged his propensity to disparage today in light of yesterday.
"The sort of taste that used to be called 'good' has nothing to do with
the matter: we are so demonstrably in presence of millions for whom
taste is but an obscure, confused, immediate instinct." Nature's
"flood" becomes nature's "swarm," whose "monstrous multiplications" of readers as well as novels mean that "simpler days" are gone
forever.

James' case against the present leaves him open to three coun-
tercharges—of a reactionary disparagement of humankind, a sexist
deprecation of women, a precipitate dismissal of fiction. He is, finally, innocent on all three counts. Despite nostalgia and nausea, James
remains sufficiently capable of free play of mind that he can find in
the present a sign of hope for the future and can recognize two indications of the timeless in the temporal.

What James finds in the present is freedom, his supreme value.
The very groups which he initially indicts for corrupting literature,
women and young people, are, he goes on to attest, engaged in redemptive rebellion in the nineties. Young people are confronting sexuality in ways which shock their parents and which James portrays in
1899 in *The Awkward Age*. Women are demanding more participation
in the culture and more control over their lives. These rebellions will,
James prophesies, force changes in the novel which assure it a future.

James' initial indictment of women thus derives not from a sexist belief in their fundamental inferiority but from an astute perception of
their miseducation by society. James draws here upon one of the
basic insights of eighteenth- and nineteenth-century fiction: that the
culture's ideal of female "innocence" is in fact an insistence upon
female ignorance. Society treats women like children because many
members of both sexes value "purity" and docility at all costs. This
malformation of woman, and not any limitation innate to her, is what
James is striking at when he joins "ladies and children" together as
"the reader irreflective and uncritical."

His distaste for the perpetual girlhood idealized by society is
augmented, unquestionably, by anxiety at certain features of contemporary feminism: "girls in especial, if we apply the term to the later
stages of the life of innumerable women who, under modern arrangements, increasingly fail to marry—fail, apparently, even, largely, to
desire to." All the commas after the dash reflect an aging man's uneasiness before the coming of new arrangements and the weakening
of old forms. Anxiety cannot, however, override James' lifelong commitment to individual freedom. What he espoused in 1870 in American women—

> I revolt from their [British women's] dreary deathly want
> of—what shall I call it?—Clover Hooper has it—intellec-
> tual grace—Minny Temple has it—moral spontaneity (let-
> ter to William James, March 8)—

he now celebrates in all women who share America's insistence upon
freedom. Repression is finally worse than rebellion to the resilient
critic still capable of looking on with "fresh eyes." James foresees
that, because of "the revolution taking place in the position and outlook of women . . . we may very well yet see the female elbow itself,
kept in increasing activity by the play of the pen, smash with final
resonance the window all this time most superstitiously closed."

In their efforts to save the novel of the future, women and
young people will be assisted by two timeless forces. One is a component of the human psyche, "simply man's general appetite for a *picture*." The other force is what James takes to be a fact of genre. "The
novel is of all pictures the most comprehensive." James can thus face
the present without despairing about the future. What has failed is
the novelist, not the novel or the reader. "Till the world is an unpeopled void there will be an image in the mirror." Readers need only
insist upon high-quality mirrors. Are readers capable of this? In one
of his greatest sentences, James recapitulates the two-part structure of

his essay, acknowledging all limitations to the present and yet continuing to believe in both humankind and fiction. "Man rejoices in an incomparable faculty for presently mutilating and disfiguring any plaything that has helped create for him the illusion of leisure; nevertheless, so long as life retains its power of projecting itself upon his imagination, he will find the novel work off the impression better than anything he knows."

Notes

243:7. fail to marry. James is responding here to two quite different phenomena. Women having difficulty marrying became a major problem in High Victorian England. The "redundancy" question, the fact that male emigration had created a surplus of more than two million women by 1850, was widely discussed. Matters were made worse by economics. An increasingly high standard of living was discouraging bachelors from marrying early. When some young women in the sixties responded with increasingly extreme dress and aggressive behavior which Eliza Lynn Linton attacked in her famous essays on "The Girl of the Period," Henry James responded to Linton's derisive wit by defending young women with humane sympathy. "The attempt to draw an idle smile at the expense of poor girls apprehensive of spinsterhood is . . . not a very creditable one" ("Modern Women," *Nation* 7 [1868]: 333). By 1899 James must confront not only women who cannot marry but also quite another phenomenon—women who don't want to. In late Victorian England women are increasingly questioning the traditional notion that their exclusive, or at least their paramount, goal is wedlock. The advantages of the single life and the attractions of the previously male prerogative of a career (plus the growing pressure for more accommodating divorce laws) are part of the burgeoning "marriage crisis." As James' syntax, punctuation, and the additional connotations of his second "fail . . . to" indicate, he has much more trouble responding sympathetically to this phenomenon.

243:20. published statistics. Sales figures appeared in England throughout the nineties in *Publishers' Circular* and elsewhere, and were widely commented upon. In addition to the standard works on book popularity—Altick's *The English Common Reader* (1957; rpt., Chicago: University of Chicago Press, 1963), Hart's *The Popular Book* (1950; rpt., Berkeley: University of California Press, 1963), Mott's *Golden Multitudes* (1947; rpt., New York: Bowker, 1966)—Jacobson has studied James' fiction specifically in terms of the bestseller in *Henry James and the Mass Market* (University, Alabama: University of Alabama Press, 1983).

243:24. railway bookstalls. William Henry Smith began selling books from stalls in train stations in 1848, and soon had a monopoly over virtually all of England. His standard fare from the mid-fifties through the mid-eighties was cheap reprints known as "yellow backs" after their bright bindings.

248:34. the constant world-renewal. Despite the euphemism, James' insistence that sexuality is the center of human life and must thus be the center of fiction is a firm retort to charges of prudery or worse. Most of James' later fiction focuses upon sexuality, often in its more lurid and bizarre forms. This opening up of subject matter results partly from the freer conditions of the late Victorian marketplace. Edel (4:342–47) and others have suggested that a more personal motive may also be at work. James' "passion" for the sculptor, Hendrik Andersen, may have made him more sympathetic to the sexual toils of his fellow creatures. In "The Novel in 'The Ring and the Book'," Chapter 21, James praises Browning for making sexual relations his primary subject.

249:6. Dickens. The shock-wave of the response to Howells' 1882 essay (see our commentary on "The Art of Fiction," Chapter 7) continues to affect James' criticism. Rather than follow Howells and espouse innovation by attacking the "old" novel of Dickens, James blames Dickens' disregarding of sexuality on the repressiveness of his time. The *fin de siècle* with its greater freedom deserves a new novel. James thus concentrates his attack not upon the limitations of Dickens, but upon those "many judges" today who deride experimentation and consider Dickens' path the only one to follow.

250:6. the quiet. While violent agitations marked feminism at the turn of the century, women less flamboyant were also helping to alter traditional gender patterns. "Domestic feminism" is the term which historians today apply to the wide-scale determination of Victorian women (particularly after mid-century) to gain more control over their lives. See Cott, "Passionlessness: An Interpretation of Victorian Sexual Ideology, 1790–1850," *Signs* 4 (1978): 220–36; Epstein, *The Politics of Domesticity* (Middletown, Conn.: Wesleyan University Press, 1981); Sklar, *Catharine Beecher* (New Haven: Yale University Press, 1973); Smith, "Family Limitation, Birth Control, and Domestic Feminism in Victorian America," in *Clio's Consciousness Raised,* ed. Hartman and Banner (New York: Harper and Row, 1974), pp. 119–36. Various historians today argue that the dramatic decline in the Anglo-American birth rate, particularly at the end of the century, was due in substantial part to women insisting upon limiting family size. How much private discussion of birth control came to James' ears, we can only guess.

250:23. anything better. For other testaments to the novel as "prodigious" form, see "The Art of Fiction" and the Preface to *The Ambassadors,* Chapters 7 and 18.

250:36. *fouiller*. To burrow.

PART THREE

The Master and His Prefaces

E L E V E N

Roderick Hudson

"RODERICK HUDSON" WAS BEGUN IN FLORENCE IN the spring of 1874, designed from the first for serial publication in "The Atlantic Monthly," where it opened in January 1875 and persisted through the year. I yield to the pleasure of placing these circumstances on record, as I shall place others, and as I have yielded to the need of renewing acquaintance with the book after a quarter of a century. This revival of an all but extinct relation with an early work may often produce for an artist, I think, more kinds of interest and emotion than he shall find it easy to express, and yet will light not a little, to his eyes, that veiled face of his Muse which he is condemned for ever and all anxiously to study. The art of representation bristles with questions the very terms of which are difficult to apply and to appreciate; but whatever makes it arduous makes it, for our refreshment, infinite, causes the practice of it, with experience, to spread round us in a widening, not in a narrowing circle. Therefore it is that experience has to organise, for convenience and cheer, some system of observation—for fear, in the admirable immensity, of losing its way. We see it as pausing from time to time to consult its notes, to measure, for guidance, as many aspects and distances as possible, as many steps taken and obstacles mastered and fruits gathered and beauties enjoyed. Everything counts, nothing is superfluous in such a survey; the explorer's note-book strikes me here as endlessly receptive. This accordingly is what I mean by the contributive value—or put it simply as, to one's own sense, the beguiling charm—of the *accessory* facts in a given artistic case. This is why, as one looks back, the private history of any sincere work, however modest its pretensions, looms with its own completeness in the rich, ambiguous aesthetic air, and seems at once to borrow a dignity and to mark, so to say, a station. This is why, reading over, for revision, correction and republication, the volumes here in hand, I find myself, all attentively, in presence of some such recording scroll or engraved commemorative table—from which the "private" character, moreover, quite insists on dropping out. These notes represent, over a considerable course, the continuity of an artist's endeavour, the growth of his whole operative consciousness and, best of all, perhaps, their own tendency to multiply, with the implication, thereby, of a memory much enriched. Addicted to "stories" and inclined to retrospect, he fondly takes, under this backward view, his whole unfolding, his process of production, for a thrilling tale, almost for a wondrous adventure, only asking himself at what stage of remembrance the mark of the relevant will begin to fail. He frankly proposes to take this mark everywhere for granted.

"Roderick Hudson" was my first attempt at a novel, a long fiction with a "complicated" subject, and I recall again the quite uplifted sense with which my idea, such as it was, permitted me at last to put quite out to sea. I had but hugged the shore on sundry previous small occasions; bumping about, to acquire skill, in the shallow waters and sandy coves of the "short story" and master as yet of no vessel constructed to carry a sail. The subject of "Roderick" figured to me vividly this employment of canvas, and I have not forgotten, even after long years, how the blue southern sea seemed to spread immediately before me and the breath of the spice-islands to be already in the breeze. Yet it must even then have begun for me too, the ache of fear, that was to become so familiar, of being unduly tempted and led on by "developments"; which is but the desperate discipline of the question involved in them. They are of the very essence of the novelist's process, and it is by their aid, fundamentally, that his idea takes form and lives; but they impose on him, through the principle of continuity that rides them, a proportionate anxiety. They are the very condition of interest, which languishes and drops without them; the painter's subject consisting ever, obviously, of the related state, to each other, of certain figures and things. To exhibit these relations, once they have all been recognised, is to "treat" his idea, which involves neglecting none of those that directly minister to interest; the degree of that directness remaining meanwhile a matter of highly difficult appreciation, and one on which felicity of form and composition, as a part of the total effect, mercilessly rests. Up to what point is such and such a development *indispensable* to the interest? What is the point beyond which it ceases to be rigorously so? Where, for the complete expression of one's subject, does a particular relation stop—giving way to some other not concerned in that expression?

Really, universally, relations stop nowhere, and the exquisite problem of the artist is eternally but to draw, by a geometry of his own, the circle within which they shall happily *appear* to do so. He is in the perpetual predicament that the continuity of things is the whole matter, for him, of comedy and tragedy; that this continuity is never, by the space of an instant or an inch, broken, and that, to do anything at all, he has at once intensely to consult and intensely to ignore it. All of which will perhaps pass but for a supersubtle way of pointing the plain moral that a young embroiderer of the canvas of life soon began to work in terror, fairly, of the vast expanse of that surface, of the boundless number of its distinct perforations for the needle, and of the tendency inherent in his many-coloured flowers and figures to cover and consume as many as possible of the little holes. The development of the flower, of the figure, involved thus an immense counting of holes and a careful selection among them. That would have been, it seemed to him, a brave enough process, were it not the very nature of the holes so to invite, to solicit, to persuade, to practise positively a thousand lures and deceits. The prime effect of so sustained a system, so prepared a surface, is to lead on and on; while the fascination of following resides, by the same token, in the presumability *somewhere* of a convenient, of a visibly-appointed stopping-place. Art would be easy indeed if, by a fond power disposed to "patronise" it, such conveniences, such simplifications, had been provided. We have, as the case stands, to invent and establish them, to arrive at them by a difficult, dire process of selection and comparison, of surrender and sacrifice. The very meaning of expertness is acquired courage to brace one's self for the cruel crisis from the moment one sees it grimly loom.

"Roderick Hudson" was further, was earnestly pursued during a summer partly spent in the Black Forest and (as I had returned to America early in September) during three months passed near Boston. It is one of the silver threads of the recoverable texture of that embarrassed phase, however, that the book was not finished when it had to begin appearing in monthly fragments: a fact in the light of which I find myself live over again, and quite with wonderment and tenderness, so intimate an experience of difficulty and delay. To have "liked" so much writing it, to have worked out with such conviction the pale embroidery, and yet not, at the end of so many months, to have come through, was clearly still to have fallen short of any facility and any confidence: though the long-drawn process now most appeals to memory, I confess, by this very quality of shy and groping duration. One fact about it indeed outlives all others; the fact that, as the loved Italy was the scene of my fiction—so much more loved than one has ever been able, even after fifty efforts, to say!—and as having had to leave it persisted as an inward ache, so there was soreness in still contriving, after a fashion, to hang about it and in prolonging, from month to month, the illusion of the golden air. Little enough of that medium may the novel, read over to-day, seem to supply; yet half the actual interest lurks for me in the earnest, baffled intention of making it felt. A whole side of the old consciousness, under this mild pressure, flushes up and prevails again; a reminder, ever so penetrating, of the quantity of "evocation" involved in my plan, and of the quantity I must even have supposed myself to achieve. I take the lingering perception of all this, I may add—that is of the various admonitions of the whole reminiscence—for a signal instance of the way a work of art, however small, if but sufficiently sincere, may vivify and even dignify the accidents and incidents of its growth.

I must that winter (which I again like to put on record that I spent in New York) have brought up my last installments in due time, for I recall no haunting anxiety: what I do recall perfectly is the felt pleasure, during those months—and in East Twenty-fifth Street!—of trying, on the other side of the world, still to surround with the appropriate local glow the characters that had combined, to my vision, the previous year in Florence. A benediction, a great advantage, as seemed to me, had so from the first rested on them, and to nurse them along was really to sit again in the high, charming, shabby old room which had originally overarched them and which, in the hot May and June, had looked out, through the slits of cooling shutters, at the rather dusty but ever-romantic glare of Piazza Santa Maria Novella. The house formed the corner (I delight to specify) of Via della Scala, and I fear that what the early chapters of the book most "render" to me to-day is not the umbrageous air of their New England town, but the view of the small cab-stand sleepily disposed—long before the days of strident electric cars—round the rococo obelisk of the Piazza, which is supported on its pedestal, if I remember rightly, by four delightful little elephants. (That, at any rate, is how the object in question, deprecating verification, comes back to me with the clatter of the horse-pails, the discussions, in the intervals of repose under well-drawn hoods, of the unbuttoned *cocchieri*, sons of the most garrulous of races, and the occasional stillness as of the noonday desert.)

Pathetic, as we say, on the other hand, no doubt, to reperusal, the manner in which the evocation, so far as attempted, of the small New England town of my first two chapters, fails of intensity—if intensity, in such a connexion, had been indeed to be looked for. *Could* I verily, by the terms of my little plan, have "gone in" for it at the best, and even though one of these terms was the projection, for my fable,

at the outset, of some more or less vivid antithesis to a state of civilisation providing for "art"? What I wanted, in essence, was the image of
some perfectly humane community which was yet all incapable of
providing for it, and I had to take what my scant experience furnished
me. I remember feeling meanwhile no drawback in this scantness,
but a complete, an exquisite little adequacy, so that the presentation
arrived at would quite have served its purpose, I think, had I not
misled myself into naming my place. To name a place, in fiction, is to
pretend in some degree to represent it—and I speak here of course
but of the use of existing names, the only ones that carry weight. I
wanted one that carried weight—so at least I supposed; but obviously
I was wrong, since my effect lay, so superficially, and could only lie,
in the local *type*, as to which I had my handful of impressions. The
particular local case was another matter, and I was to see again, after
long years, the case into which, all recklessly, the opening passages
of "Roderick Hudson" put their foot. I was to have nothing then, on
the spot, to sustain me but the rather feeble plea that I had not *pretended* so very much to "do" Northampton Mass. The plea was
charmingly allowed, but nothing could have been more to the point
than the way in which, in such a situation, the whole question of the
novelist's "doing," with its eternal wealth, or in other words its eternal torment of interest, once more came up. He embarks, rash adventurer, under the star of "representation," and is pledged thereby to
remember that the art of interesting us in things—once these things
are the right ones for his case—can *only* be the art of representing
them. This relation to them, for invoked interest, involves his accordingly "doing"; and it is for him to settle with his intelligence what
that variable process shall commit him to.

Its fortune rests primarily, beyond doubt, on somebody's having, under suggestion, a *sense* for it—even the reader will do, on occasion, when the writer, as so often happens, completely falls out. The
way in which this sense has been, or has not been, applied constitutes, at all events, in respect to any fiction, the very ground of
critical appreciation. Such appreciation takes account, primarily, of
the thing, in the case, to have *been* done, and I now see what, for the
first and second chapters of "Roderick," that was. It was a peaceful,
rural New England community *quelconque*—it was not, it was under
no necessity of being, Northampton Mass. But one nestled, technically, in those days, and with yearning, in the great shadow of Balzac; his august example, little as the secret might ever be guessed,
towered for me over the scene; so that what was clearer than anything else was how, if it was a question of Saumur, of Limoges, of

Guérande, he "did" Saumur, did Limoges, did Guérande. I remember how, in my feebler fashion, I yearned over the preliminary presentation of my small square patch of the American scene, and yet was not sufficiently on my guard to see how easily his high practice might be delusive for my case. Balzac talked of Nemours and Provins: therefore why shouldn't one, with fond fatuity, talk of almost the only small American *ville de province* of which one had happened to lay up, long before, a pleased vision? The reason was plain: one was not in the least, in one's prudence, emulating his systematic closeness. It didn't confuse the question either that he would verily, after all, addressed as he was to a due density in his material, have found little enough in Northampton Mass. to tackle. He tackled no group of appearances, no presented face of the social organism (conspicuity thus attending it), *but* to make something of it. To name it simply and not in some degree tackle it would have seemed to him an act reflecting on his general course the deepest dishonour. Therefore it was that, as the moral of these many remarks, I "named," under his contagion, when I was really most conscious of not being held to it; and therefore it was, above all, that for all the effect of representation I was to achieve, I might have let the occasion pass. A "fancy" indication would have served my turn—except that I should so have failed perhaps of a pretext for my present insistence.

Since I do insist, at all events, I find this ghostly interest perhaps even more reasserted for me by the questions begotten within the very covers of the book, those that wander and idle there as in some sweet old overtangled walled garden, a safe paradise of self-criticism. Here it is that if there be air for it to breathe at all, the critical question swarms, and here it is, in particular, that one of the happy hours of the painter's long day may strike. I speak of the painter in general and of his relation to the old picture, the work of his hand, that has been lost to sight and that, when found again, is put back on the easel for measure of what time and the weather may, in the interval, have done to it. Has it too fatally faded, has it blackened or "sunk," or otherwise abdicated, or has it only, blest thought, strengthened, for its allotted duration, and taken up, in its degree, poor dear brave thing, some shade of the all appreciable, yet all indescribable grace that we know as pictorial "tone"? The anxious artist has to wipe it over, in the first place, to see; he has to "clean it up," say, or to varnish it anew, or at the least to place it in a light, for any right judgement of its aspect or its worth. But the very uncertainties themselves yield a thrill, and if subject and treatment, working together, have had their felicity, the artist, the prime creator, may find a strange charm in this stage of the connexion. It helps him to live back into a forgotten state, into convictions, credulities too early spent perhaps, it breathes upon the dead reasons of things, buried as they are in the texture of the work, and makes them revive, so that the actual appearances and the old motives fall together once more, and a lesson and a moral and a consecrating final light are somehow disengaged.

All this, I mean of course, if the case will wonderfully take any such pressure, if the work doesn't break down under even such mild overhauling. The author knows well enough how easily that may happen—which he in fact frequently enough sees it do. The old reasons then are too dead to revive; they were not, it is plain, good enough reasons to live. The only possible relation of the present mind to the thing is to dismiss it altogether. On the other hand, when it is not dismissed—as the only detachment is the detachment of aversion—the creative intimacy is reaffirmed, and appreciation, critical apprehension, insists on becoming as active as it can. Who shall say, granted this, where it shall not begin and where it shall consent to end? The painter who passes over his old sunk canvas the wet sponge that shows him what may still come out again makes his criticism essentially active. When having seen, while his momentary glaze remains, that the canvas *has* kept a few buried secrets, he proceeds to repeat the process with due care and with a bottle of varnish and a brush, he is "living back," as I say, to the top of his bent, is taking up the old relation, so workable apparently, yet, and there is nothing logically to stay him from following it all the way. I have felt myself then, on looking over past productions, the painter making use again and again of the tentative wet sponge. The sunk surface has here and there, beyond doubt, refused to respond; the buried secrets, the intentions, are buried too deep to rise again, and were indeed, it would appear, not much worth the burying. Not so, however, when the moistened canvas does obscurely flush and when resort to the varnish-bottle is thereby immediately indicated. The simplest figure for my revision of this present array of earlier, later, larger, smaller, canvases, is to say that I have achieved it by the very aid of the varnish-bottle. It is true of them throughout that, in words I have had occasion to use in another connexion (where too I had revised with a view to "possible amendment of form and enhancement of meaning"), I have "nowhere scrupled to re-write a sentence or a passage on judging it susceptible of a better turn."

To re-read "Roderick Hudson" was to find one remark so promptly and so urgently prescribed that I could at once only take it as

265

pointing almost too stern a moral. It stared me in the face that the time-scheme of the story is quite inadequate, and positively to that degree that the fault but just fails to wreck it. The thing escapes, I conceive, with its life: the effect sought is fortunately more achieved than missed, since the interest of the subject bears down, auspiciously dis-simulates, this particular flaw in the treatment. Everything occurs, none the less, too punctually and moves too fast: Roderick's disin-tegration, a gradual process, and of which the exhibitional interest is exactly that it *is* gradual and occasional, and thereby traceable and watchable, swallows two years in a mouthful, proceeds quite *not* by years, but by weeks and months, and thus renders the whole view the disservice of appearing to present him as a morbidly special case. The very claim of the fable is naturally that he *is* special, that his great gift makes and keeps him highly exceptional; but that is not for a moment supposed to preclude his appearing typical (of the general type) as well; for the fictive hero successfully appeals to us only as an eminent instance, as eminent as we like, of our own conscious kind. My mis-take on Roderick's behalf—and not in the least of conception, but of composition and expression—is that, at the rate at which he falls to pieces, he seems to place himself beyond our understanding and our sympathy. These are not our rates, we say; we ourselves certainly, under like pressure,—for what is it after all?—would make more of a fight. We conceive going to pieces—nothing is easier, since we see people do it, one way or another, all round us; but this young man must either have had less of the principle of development to have had so much of the principle of collapse, or less of the principle of collapse to have had so much of the principle of development. "On the basis of so great a weakness," one hears the reader say, "where was your idea of the interest? On the basis of so great an interest, where is the provi-sion for so much weakness?" One feels indeed, in the light of this challenge, on how much too scantly projected and suggested a field poor Roderick and his large capacity for ruin are made to turn round. It has all begun too soon, as I say, and too simply, and the determinant function attributed to Christina Light, the character of well-nigh sole agent of his catastrophe that this unfortunate young woman has forced upon her, fails to commend itself to our sense of truth and proportion.

It was not, however, that I was at ease on this score even in the first fond good faith of composition; I felt too, all the while, how many more ups and downs, how many more adventures and com-plications my young man would have had to know, how much more experience it would have taken, in short, either to make him go under or to make him triumph. The greater complexity, the superior truth, was all more or less present to me; only the question was, too dreadfully, how make it present to the reader? How boil down so many facts in the alembic, so that the distilled result, the produced appearance, should have intensity, lucidity, brevity, beauty, all the merits required for my effect? How, when it was already so difficult, as I found, to proceed even as I *was* proceeding? It didn't help, alas, it only maddened, to remember that Balzac would have known how, and would have yet asked no additional credit for it. All the difficulty I could dodge still struck me, at any rate, as leaving more than enough; and yet I was already consciously in presence, here, of the most interesting question the artist has to consider. To give the image and the sense of certain things while still keeping them subordinate to his plan, keeping them in relation to matters more immediate and apparent, to give all the sense, in a word, without all the substance or all the surface, and so to summarise and foreshorten, so to make values both rich and sharp, that the mere procession of items and profiles is not only, for the occasion, superseded, but is, for essential quality, almost "compromised"—such a case of delicacy proposes itself at every turn to the painter of life who wishes both to treat his chosen subject and to confine his necessary picture. It is only by doing such things that art becomes exquisite, and it is only by positively becoming exquisite that it keeps clear of becoming vulgar, repudiates the coarse industries that masquerade in its name. This eternal time-question is accordingly, for the novelist, always there and always formidable; always insisting on the *effect* of the great lapse and passage, of the "dark backward and abysm," by the terms of truth, and on the effect of compression, of composition and form, by the terms of literary arrangement. It is really a business to terrify all but stout hearts into abject omission and mutilation, though the terror would indeed be more general were the general consciousness of the difficulty greater. It is not by consciousness of difficulty, in truth, that the story-teller is mostly ridden; so prodigious a number of stories would otherwise scarce get themselves (shall it be called?) "told." None was ever very well told, I think, under the law of mere elimination—inordinately as that device appears in many quarters to be depended on. I remember doing my best not to be reduced to it for "Roderick," at the same time that I did so helplessly and consciously beg a thousand questions. What I clung to as my principle of simplification was the precious truth that I was dealing, after all, essentially with an Action, and that no action, further, was ever made historically vivid without a certain factitious compactness; though this logic indeed opened up horizons and abysses of its own. But into these we must plunge on some other occasion.

It was at any rate under an admonition or two fished out of their depths that I must have tightened my hold of the remedy afforded, such as it was, for the absence of those more adequate illustrations of Roderick's character and history. Since one was dealing with an Action one might borrow a scrap of the Dramatist's all-in-all, his intensity—which the noveslist so often ruefully envies him as a fortune in itself. The amount of illustration I could allow to the grounds of my young man's disaster was unquestionably meagre, but I might perhaps make it lively; I might produce illusion if I should be able to achieve intensity. It was for that I must have tried, I now see, with such art as I could command; but I make out in another quarter above all what really saved me. My subject, all blissfully, in face of difficulties, had defined itself—and this in spite of the title of the book—as not directly, in the least, my young sculptor's adventure. This it had been but indirectly, being all the while in essence and in final effect another man's, his friend's and patron's, view and experience of him. One's luck was to have felt one's subject right—whether instinct or calculation, in those dim days, most served; and the circumstance even amounts perhaps to a little lesson that when this has happily occurred faults may show, faults may disfigure, and yet not upset the work. It remains in equilibrium by having found its centre, the point of command of all the rest. From this centre the subject has been treated, from this centre the interest has spread, and so, whatever else it may do or may not do, the thing has acknowledged a principle of composition and contrives at least to hang together. We see in such a case why it should so hang; we escape that dreariest displeasure it is open to experiments in this general order to inflict, the sense of any hanging-together precluded as by the very terms of the case.

The centre of interest throughout "Roderick" is in Rowland Mallet's consciousness, and the drama is the very drama of that consciousness—which I had of course to make sufficiently acute in order to enable it, like a set and lighted scene, to hold the play. By making it acute, meanwhile, one made its own movement—or rather, strictly, its movement in the particular connexion—interesting; this movement really being quite the stuff of one's thesis. It had, naturally, Rowland's consciousness, not to be *too* acute—which would have disconnected it and made it superhuman: the beautiful little problem was to keep it connected, connected intimately, with the general human exposure, and thereby bedimmed and befooled and bewildered, anxious, restless, fallible, and yet to endow it with such intelligence that the appearances reflected in it, and constituting together there the situation and the "story," should become by that fact intelligible. Discernible from the first the joy of such a "job" as this making of his relation to everything involved a sufficiently limited, a sufficiently pathetic, tragic, comic, ironic, personal state to be thoroughly natural, and yet at the same time a sufficiently clear medium to represent a whole. This whole was to be the sum of what "happened" to him, or in other words his total adventure; but as what happened to him was above all to feel certain things happening to others, to Roderick, to Christina, to Mary Garland, to Mrs. Hudson, to the Cavaliere, to the Prince, so the beauty of the constructional game was to preserve in everything its especial value for *him*. The ironic effect of his having fallen in love with the girl who is herself in love with Roderick, though he is unwitting, at the time, of that secret—the conception of this last irony, I must add, has remained happier than my execution of it; which should logically have involved the reader's being put into position to take more closely home the impression made by Mary Garland. The ground has not been laid for it, and when that is the case one builds all vainly in the air: one patches up one's superstructure, one paints it in the prettiest colours, one hangs fine old tapestry and rare brocade over its window-sills, one flies emblazoned banners from its roof—the building none the less totters and refuses to stand square.

It is not really *worked-in* that Roderick himself could have pledged his faith in such a quarter, much more at such a crisis, before leaving America: and that weakness, clearly, produces a limp in the whole march of the fable. Just so, though there was no reason on earth (unless I except one, presently to be mentioned) why Rowland should *not*, at Northampton, have conceived a passion, or as near an approach to one as he was capable of, for a remarkable young woman there suddenly dawning on his sight, a particular fundamental care was required for the vivification of that possibility. The care, unfortunately, has not been skilfully enough taken, in spite of the later patching-up of the girl's figure. We fail to accept it, on the actual showing, as that of a young person irresistible at any moment, and above all irresistible at a moment of the liveliest *other* preoccupation, as that of the weaver of (even the highly conditioned) spell that the narrative imputes to her. The spell of attraction is cast upon young men by young women in all sorts of ways, and the novel has no more constant office than to remind us of that. But Mary Garland's way doesn't, indubitably, convince us; any more than we are truly convinced, I think, that Rowland's destiny, or say his nature, would have made him accessible at the same hour to two quite distinct commotions, each a very deep one, of his whole personal economy. Rigidly viewed, each of these upheavals of his sensibility must have been exclusive of other upheavals, yet the reader is asked to accept them as working together. They are different vibrations, but the whole sense of the situation depicted is that they should each have been of the strongest, too strong to walk hand in hand. Therefore it is that when, on the ship, under the stars, Roderick suddenly takes his friend into the confidence of his engagement, we instinctively disallow the friend's title to discomfiture. The whole picture presents him as for the time on the mounting wave, exposed highly enough, no doubt, to a hundred discomfitures, but least exposed to that one. The damage to verisimilitude is deep.

The difficulty had been from the first that I required my antithesis—my antithesis to Christina Light, one of the main terms of the subject. One is ridden by the law that antitheses, to be efficient, shall be both direct and complete. Directness seemed to fail unless Mary should be, so to speak, "plain," Christina being essentially so "coloured"; and completeness seemed to fail unless she too should have her potency. She could moreover, by which I mean the antithetic young woman could, perfectly have had it; only success would have been then in the narrator's art to attest it. Christina's own presence and action are, on the other hand, I think, all firm ground; the truth probably being that the ideal antithesis rarely does "come off," and that it has to content itself for the most part with a strong term and a weak term, and even then to feel itself lucky. If one of the terms *is* strong, that perhaps may pass, in the most difficult of the arts, for a triumph. I remember at all events feeling, toward the end of "Roderick," that the Princess Casamassima had been launched, that, wound-up with the right silver key, she would go on a certain time by the motion communicated; thanks to which I knew the pity, the real pang of losing sight of her. I desired as in no other such case I can recall to preserve, to recover the vision; and I have seemed to myself in re-reading the book quite to understand why. The multiplication of touches had produced even more life than the subject required, and that life, in other conditions, in some other prime relation, would still have somehow to be spent. Thus one would watch for her and waylay her at some turn of the road to come—all that was to be needed was to give her time. This I did in fact, meeting her again and taking her up later on.

T W E L V E

The American

"THE AMERICAN," WHICH I HAD BEGUN IN PARIS EARly in the winter of 1875–76, made its first appearance in "The Atlantic Monthly" in June of the latter year and continued there, from month to month, till May of the next. It started on its course while much was still unwritten, and there again come back to me, with this remembrance, the frequent hauntings and alarms of that comparatively early time; the habit of wondering what would happen if anything *should* "happen," if one should break one's arm by an accident or make a long illness or suffer, in body, mind, fortune, any other visitation involving a loss of time. The habit of apprehension became of course in some degree the habit of confidence that one would pull through, that, with opportunity enough, grave interruption never yet *had* descended, and that a special Providence, in short, despite the sad warning of Thackeray's "Denis Duval" and of Mrs. Gaskell's "Wives and Daughters" (that of Stevenson's "Weir of Hermiston" was yet to come) watches over anxious novelists condemned to the economy of serialisation. I make myself out in memory as having at least for many months and in many places given my Providence much to do: so great a variety of scenes of labour, implying all so much renewal of application, glimmer out of the book as I now read it over. And yet as the faded interest of the whole episode becomes again mildly vivid what I seem most to recover is, in its pale spectrality, a degree of joy, an eagerness on behalf of my recital, that must recklessly enough have overridden anxieties of every sort, including any view of inherent difficulties.

I seem to recall no other like connexion in which the case was met, to my measure, by so fond a complacency, in which my subject can have appeared so apt to take care of itself. I see now that I might all the while have taken much better care of it; yet, as I had at the time no sense of neglecting it, neither acute nor rueful solicitude, I can but speculate all vainly to-day on the oddity of my composure. I ask myself indeed if, possibly, recognising after I was launched the danger of an inordinate leak—since the ship has truly a hole in its side more than sufficient to have sunk it—I may not have managed, as a counsel of mere despair, to stop my ears against the noise of waters and *pretend* to myself I was afloat; being indubitably, in any case, at sea, with no harbour of refuge till the end of my serial voyage. If I succeeded at all in that emulation (in another sphere) of the pursued ostrich I must have succeeded altogether; must have buried my head in the sand and there found beatitude. The explanation of my enjoyment of it, no doubt, is that I was more than commonly enamoured of my idea, and that I believed it, so trusted, so imaginatively fostered, not less capable of limping to its goal on three feet than on one. The lameness might be what it would: I clearly, for myself, felt the thing *go*—which is the most a dramatist can ever ask of his drama; and I shall here accordingly indulge myself in speaking first of how, superficially, it did so proceed; explaining then what I mean by its practical dependence on a miracle.

It had come to me, this happy, halting view of an interesting case, abruptly enough, some years before: I recall sharply the felicity of the first glimpse, though I forget the accident of thought that produced it. I recall that I was seated in an American "horse-car" when I found myself, of a sudden, considering with enthusiasm, as the theme of a "story," the situation, in another country and an aristocratic society, of some robust but insidiously beguiled and betrayed, some cruelly wronged, compatriot: the point being in especial that he should suffer at the hands of persons pretending to represent the highest possible civilisation and to be of an order in every way superior to his own. What would he "do" in that predicament, how would he right himself, or how, failing a remedy, would he conduct himself under his wrong? This would be the question involved, and I remember well how, having entered the horse-car without a dream of it, I was presently to leave that vehicle in full possession of my answer. He would behave in the most interesting manner—it would all depend on that: stricken, smarting, sore, he would arrive at his just vindication and then would fail of all triumphantly and all vulgarly enjoying it. He would hold his revenge and cherish it and feel its sweetness, and then in the very act of forcing it home would sacrifice it in disgust. He would let them go, in short, his haughty contemners, even while feeling them, with joy, in his power, and he would obey, in so doing, one of the large and easy impulses *generally* characteristic of his type. He wouldn't "forgive"—that would have, in the case, no application; he would simply turn, at the supreme moment, away, the bitterness of his personal loss yielding to the very force of his aversion. All he would have at the end would be therefore just the moral convenience, indeed the moral necessity, of his practical, but quite unappreciated, magnanimity; and one's last view of him would be that of a strong man indifferent to his strength and too wrapped in fine, too wrapped above all in *other* and intenser, reflexions for the assertion of his "rights." This last point was of the essence and constituted in fact the subject: there would be no subject at all, obviously,—or simply the commonest of the common,—if my gentleman should enjoy his advantage. I was charmed with my idea, which would take, however, much working out; and precisely because it had so much to give, I think, must I have dropped it for the time into the deep well of unconscious cerebration: not without the hope, doubtless, that it might eventually emerge from that reservoir, as one had already known the buried treasure to come to light, with a firm iridescent surface and a notable increase of weight.

This resurrection then took place in Paris, where I was at the moment living, and in December 1875; my good fortune being apparently that Paris had ever so promptly offered me, and with an immediate directness at which I now marvel (since I had come back there, after earlier visitations, but a few weeks before), everything that was needed to make my conception concrete. I seem again at this distant day to see it become so quickly and easily, quite as if filling itself with life in that air. The objectivity it had wanted it promptly put on, and if the questions had been, with the usual intensity, for my hero and his crisis—the whole formidable list, the who? the what? the where? the when? the why? the how?—they gathered their answers in the cold shadow of the Arc de Triomphe, for fine reasons, very much as if they had been plucking spring flowers for the weaving of a frolic garland. I saw from one day to another my particular cluster of circumstances, with the life of the splendid city playing up in it like a flashing fountain in a marble basin. The very splendour seemed somehow to witness and intervene; it was important for the effect of my friend's discomfiture that it should take place on a high and lighted stage, and that his original ambition, the project exposing him, should have sprung from beautiful and noble suggestions—those that, at certain hours and under certain impressions, we feel the many-tinted medium by the Seine irresistibly to communicate. It was all charmingly simple, this conception, and the current must have gushed, full and clear, to my imagination, from the moment Christopher Newman rose before me, on a perfect day of the divine Paris spring, in the great gilded Salon Carré of the Louvre. Under this strong contagion of the place he would, by the happiest of hazards, meet his old comrade, now initiated and domiciled; after which the rest would go of itself. If he was to be wronged he would be wronged with just that conspicuity, with his felicity at just that pitch and with the highest aggravation of the general effect of misery mocked at. Great and gilded the whole trap set, in fine, for his wary freshness and into which it would blunder upon its fate. I have, I confess, no memory of a disturbing doubt; once the man himself was imaged to me (and *that* germination is a process almost always untraceable) he must have walked into the situation as by taking a pass-key from his pocket.

But what then meanwhile would be the affront one would see him as most feeling? The affront of course done him as a lover; and yet not that done by his mistress herself, since injuries of this order are the stalest stuff of romance. I was not to have him jilted, any more than I was to have him successfully vindictive: both his wrong and his right would have been in these cases of too vulgar a type. I doubtless even then felt that the conception of Paris as the consecrated scene of rash infatuations and bold bad treacheries belongs, in the Anglo-Saxon imagination, to the infancy of art. The right renovation of any such theme as *that* would place it in Boston or at Cleveland, at Hartford or at Utica—give it some local connexion in which we had not already had so much of it. No, I should make my heroine herself, if heroine there was to be, an equal victim—just as Romeo was not less the sport of fate for not having been interestedly sacrificed by Juliet; and to this end I had but to imagine "great people" again, imagine my hero confronted and involved with them, and impute to them, with a fine free hand, the arrogance and cruelty, the tortuous behaviour, in given conditions, of which great people have been historically so often capable. But as this was the light in which they were to show, so the essence of the matter would be that he should at the right moment find them in his power, and so the situation would reach its highest interest with the question of his utilisation of that knowledge. It would be here, in the possession and application of his power, that he would come out strong and would so deeply appeal to our sympathy. Here above all it really was, however, that my conception unfurled, with the best conscience in the world, the emblazoned flag of romance; which venerable ensign it had, though quite unwittingly, from the first and at every point sported in perfect good faith. I had been plotting arch-romance without knowing it, just as I began to write it that December day without recognising it and just as I all serenely and blissfully pursued the process from month to month and from place to place; just as I now, in short, reading the book over,

274

find it yields me no interest and no reward comparable to the fond perception of this truth.

The thing is consistently, consummately—and I would fain really make bold to say charmingly—romantic; and all without intention, presumption, hesitation, contrition. The effect is equally undesigned and unabashed, and I lose myself, at this late hour, I am bound to add, in a certain sad envy of the free play of so much unchallenged instinct. One would like to woo back such hours of fine precipitation. They represent to the critical sense which the exercise of one's *whole* faculty has, with time, so inevitably and so thoroughly waked up, the happiest season of surrender to the invoked muse and the projected fable: the season of images so free and confident and ready that they brush questions aside and disport themselves, like the artless schoolboys of Gray's beautiful Ode, in all the ecstasy of the ignorance attending them. The time doubtless comes soon enough when questions, as I call them, rule the roost and when the little victim, to adjust Gray's term again to the creature of frolic fancy, doesn't dare propose a gambol till they have all (like a board of trustees discussing a new outlay) sat on the possibly scandalous case. I somehow feel, accordingly, that it was lucky to have sacrificed on this particular altar while one still could; though it is perhaps droll—in a yet higher degree—to have done so not simply because one was guileless, but even quite under the conviction, in a general way, that, since no "rendering" of any object and no painting of any picture can take effect without some form of reference and control, so these guarantees could but reside in a high probity of observation. I must decidedly have supposed, all the while, that I was acutely observing—and with a blest absence of wonder at its being so easy. Let me certainly at present rejoice in that absence; for I ask myself how without it I could have written "The American."

Was it indeed meanwhile my excellent conscience that kept the charm as unbroken as it appears to me, in rich retrospect, to have remained?—or is it that I suffer the mere influence of remembered, of associated places and hours, all acute impressions, to palm itself off as the sign of a finer confidence than I could justly claim? It is a pleasure to perceive how again and again the shrunken depths of old work yet permit themselves to be sounded or—even if rather terrible the image—"dragged": the long pole of memory stirs and rummages the bottom, and we fish up such fragments and relics of the submerged life and the extinct consciousness as tempt us to piece them together. My windows looked into the Rue de Luxembourg—since then meagrely re-named Rue Cambon—and the particular light Pari-

275

sian click of the small cab-horse on the clear asphalt, with its sharpness of detonation between the high houses, makes for the faded
page to-day a sort of interlineation of sound. This sound rises to a
martial clatter at the moment a troop of cuirassiers charges down the
narrow street, each morning, to file, directly opposite my house,
through the plain portal of the barracks occupying part of the vast
domain attached in a rearward manner to one of the Ministères that
front on the Place Vendôme; an expanse marked, along a considerable stretch of the street, by one of those high painted and admin-
istratively-placarded garden walls that form deep, vague, recurrent
notes in the organic vastness of the city. I have but to re-read ten lines
to recall my daily effort not to waste time in hanging over the win-
dow-bar for a sight of the cavalry the hard music of whose hoofs so
directly and thrillingly appealed; an effort that inveterately failed—
and a trivial circumstance now dignified, to my imagination, I may
add, by the fact that the fruits of this weakness, the various items of
the vivid picture, so constantly recaptured, must have been in themselves suggestive and inspiring, must have been rich strains, in their
way, of the great Paris harmony. I have ever, in general, found it
difficult to write of places under too immediate an impression—the
impression that prevents standing off and allows neither space nor
time for perspective. The image has had for the most part to be dim if
the reflexion was to be, as is proper for a reflexion, both sharp and
quiet: one has a horror, I think, artistically, of agitated reflexions.

Perhaps that is why the novel, after all, was to achieve, as it went
on, no great—certainly no very direct—transfusion of the immense
overhanging presence. It had to save as it could its own life, to keep
tight hold of the tenuous silver thread, the one hope for which was that
it shouldn't be tangled or clipped. This earnest grasp of the silver
thread was doubtless an easier business in other places—though as I
remount the stream of composition I see it faintly coloured again: with
the bright protection of the Normandy coast (I worked away a few
weeks at Etretat); with the stronger glow of southernmost France,
breaking in during a stay at Bayonne; then with the fine historic and
other "psychic" substance of Saint-Germain-en-Laye, a purple patch
of terraced October before returning to Paris. There comes after that
the memory of a last brief intense invocation of the enclosing scene, of
the pious effort to unwind my tangle, with a firm hand, in the very
light (that light of high, narrowish French windows in old rooms, the
light somehow, as one always feels, of "style" itself) that had quickened my original vision. I was to pass over to London that autumn;
which was a reason the more for considering the matter—the matter of

Newman's final predicament—with due intensity: to let a loose end dangle over into alien air would so fix upon the whole, I strenuously felt, the dishonour of piecemeal composition. Therefore I strove to finish—first in a small dusky hotel of the Rive Gauche, where, though the windows again were high, the days were dim and the crepuscular court, domestic, intimate, "quaint," testified to ancient manners almost as if it had been that of Balzac's Maison Vauquer in "Le Père Goriot": and then once more in the Rue de Luxembourg, where a black-framed Empire portrait-medallion, suspended in the centre of each white panel of my almost noble old salon, made the coolest, discreetest, most measured decoration, and where, through casements open to the last mildness of the year, a belated Saint Martin's summer, the tale was taken up afresh by the charming light click and clatter, that sound as of the thin, quick, quite feminine surface-breathing of Paris, the shortest of rhythms for so huge an organism.

I shall not tell whether I did there bring my book to a close—and indeed I shrink, for myself, from putting the question to the test of memory. I follow it so far, the old urgent ingenious business, and then I lose sight of it: from which I infer—all exact recovery of the matter failing—that I did not in the event drag over the Channel a lengthening chain; which would have been detestable. I reduce to the absurd perhaps, however, by that small subjective issue, any undue measure of the interest of this insistent recovery of what I have called attendant facts. There always has been, for the valid work of art, a history—though mainly inviting, doubtless, but to the curious critic, for whom such things grow up and are formed very much in the manner of attaching young lives and characters, those conspicuous cases of happy development as to which evidence and anecdote are always in order. The development indeed must be certain to have been happy, the life sincere, the character fine: the work of art, to create or repay critical curiosity, must in short have been very "valid" indeed. Yet there is on the other hand no mathematical measure of that importance—it may be a matter of widely-varying appreciation; and I am willing to grant, assuredly, that this interest, in a given relation, will nowhere so effectually kindle as on the artist's own part. And I am afraid that after all even his best excuse for it must remain the highly personal plea—the joy of living over, as a chapter of experience, the particular intellectual adventure. Here lurks an immense homage to the general privilege of the artist, to that constructive, that creative passion—portentous words, but they are convenient—the exercise of which finds so many an occasion for appearing to him the highest of human fortunes, the rarest boon of the gods. He values it, all sublimely and perhaps a little fatuously, for itself—as the great extension, great beyond all others, of experience and of consciousness; with the toil and trouble a mere sun-cast shadow that falls, shifts and vanishes, the result of his living in so large a light. On the constant nameless felicity of this Robert Louis Stevenson has, in an admirable passage and as in so many other connexions, said the right word: that the partaker of the "life of art" who repines at the absence of the rewards, as they are called, of the pursuit might surely be better occupied. Much rather should he endlessly wonder at his not having to pay half his substance for his luxurious immersion. He enjoys it, so to speak, without a tax; the effort of labour involved, the torment of expression, of which we have heard in our time so much, being after all but the last refinement of his privilege. It may leave him weary and worn; but how, after his fashion, he will have lived! As if one were to expect at once freedom and ease! That silly safety is but the sign of bondage and forfeiture. Who can imagine free selection—which is the beautiful, terrible *whole* of art—without free difficulty? This is the very franchise of the city and high ambition of the citizen. The vision of the difficulty, as one looks back, bathes one's course in a golden glow by which the very objects along the road are transfigured and glorified; so that one exhibits them to other eyes with an elation possibly presumptuous.

Since I accuse myself at all events of these complacencies I take advantage of them to repeat that I value, in my retrospect, nothing so much as the lively light on the romantic property of my subject that I had not expected to encounter. If in "The American" I invoked the romantic association without malice prepense, yet with a production of the romantic effect that is for myself unmistakeable, the occasion is of the best perhaps for penetrating a little the obscurity of that principle. By what art or mystery, what craft of selection, omission or commission, does a given picture of life appear to us to surround its theme, its figures and images, with the air of romance while another picture close beside it may affect us as steeping the whole matter in the element of reality? It is a question, no doubt, on the painter's part, very much more of perceived effect, effect *after* the fact, than of conscious design—though indeed I have ever failed to see how a coherent picture of anything is producible save by a complex of fine measurements. The cause of the deflexion, in one pronounced sense or the other, must lie deep, however; so that for the most part we recognise the character of our interest only after the particular magic, as I say, has thoroughly operated—and then in truth but if we be a bit critically minded, if we find our pleasure, that is, in these intimate appreciations (for which, as

278

I am well aware, ninety-nine readers in a hundred have no use whatever). The determining condition would at any rate seem so latent that one may well doubt if the full artistic consciousness ever reaches it; leaving the matter thus a case, ever, not of an author's plotting and planning and calculating, but just of his feeling and seeing, of his conceiving, in a word, and of his thereby inevitably expressing himself, under the influence of one value or the other. These values represent different sorts and degrees of the communicable thrill, and I doubt if any novelist, for instance, ever proposed to commit himself to one kind or the other with as little mitigation as we are sometimes able to find for him. The interest is greatest—the interest of his genius, I mean, and of his general wealth—when he commits himself in both directions; not quite at the same time or to the same effect, of course, but by some need of performing his whole possible revolution, by the law of some rich passion in him for extremes.

Of the men of largest responding imagination before the human scene, of Scott, of Balzac, even of the coarse, comprehensive, prodigious Zola, we feel, I think, that the deflexion toward either quarter has never taken place; that neither the nature of the man's faculty nor the nature of his experience has ever quite determined it. His current remains therefore extraordinarily rich and mixed, washing us successively with the warm wave of the near and familiar and the tonic shock, as may be, of the far and strange. (In making which opposition I suggest not that the strange and the far are at all necessarily romantic: they happen to be simply the unknown, which is quite a different matter. The real represents to my perception the things we cannot possibly *not* know, sooner or later, in one way or another; it being but one of the accidents of our hampered state, and one of the incidents of their quantity and number, that particular instances have not yet come our way. The romantic stands, on the other hand, for the things that, with all the facilities in the world, all the wealth and all the courage and all the wit and all the adventure, we never *can* directly know; the things that can reach us only through the beautiful circuit and subterfuge of our thought and our desire.) There have been, I gather, many definitions of romance, as a matter indispensably of boats, or of caravans, or of tigers, or of "historical characters," or of ghosts, or of forgers, or of detectives, or of beautiful wicked women, or of pistols and knives, but they appear for the most part reducible to the idea of the facing of danger, the acceptance of great risks for the fascination, the very love, of their uncertainty, the joy of success if possible and of battle in any case. This would be a fine formula if it bore examination; but it strikes me as weak and inadequate, as by no means covering the true ground and yet as landing us in strange confusions.

The panting pursuit of danger is the pursuit of life itself, in which danger awaits us possibly at every step and faces us at every turn; so that the dream of an intenser experience easily becomes rather some vision of a sublime security like that enjoyed on the flowery plains of heaven, where we may conceive ourselves proceeding in ecstasy from one prodigious phase and form of it to another. And if it be insisted that the measure of the type is then in the *appreciation* of danger—the sign of our projection of the real being the smallness of its dangers, and that of our projection of the romantic the hugeness, the mark of the distinction being in short, as they say of collars and gloves and shoes, the size and "number" of the danger—this discrimination again surely fails, since it makes our difference not a difference of kind, which is what we want, but a difference only of degree, and subject by that condition to the indignity of a sliding scale and a shifting measure. There are immense and flagrant dangers that are but sordid and squalid ones, as we feel, tainting with their quality the very defiances they provoke; while there are common and covert ones, that "look like nothing" and that can be but inwardly and occultly dealt with, which involve the sharpest hazards to life and honour and the highest instant decisions and intrepidities of action. It is an arbitrary stamp that keeps these latter prosaic and makes the former heroic; and yet I should still less subscribe to a mere "subjective" division—I mean one that would place the difference wholly in the temper of the imperilled agent. It would be impossible to have a more romantic temper than Flaubert's Madame Bovary, and yet nothing less resembles a romance than the record of her adventures. To classify it by that aspect—the definition of the spirit that happens to animate her—is like settling the question (as I have seen it witlessly settled) by the presence or absence of "costume." Where again then does costume begin or end?—save with the "run" of one or another sort of play? We must reserve vague labels for artless mixtures.

The only *general* attribute of projected romance that I can see, the only one that fits all its cases, is the fact of the kind of experience with which it deals—experience liberated, so to speak; experience disengaged, disembroiled, disencumbered, exempt from the conditions that we usually know to attach to it and, if we wish so to put the matter, drag upon it, and operating in a medium which relieves it, in a particular interest, of the inconvenience of a *related*, a measurable state, a state subject to all our vulgar communities. The greatest intensity may so be arrived at evidently—when the sacrifice of community, of the "related" sides of situations, has not been too rash. It must to this end not flagrantly betray itself; we must even be kept if possible, for our illusion, from suspecting any sacrifice at all. The balloon of experience is in fact of course tied to the earth, and under that necessity we swing, thanks to a rope of remarkable length, in the more or less commodious car of the imagination; but it is by the rope we know where we are, and from the moment that cable is cut we are at large and unrelated: we only swing apart from the globe—though remaining as exhilarated, naturally, as we like, especially when all goes well. The art of the romancer is, "for the fun of it," insidiously to cut the cable, to cut it without our detecting him. What I have recognised then in "The American," much to my surprise and after long years, is that the experience here represented is the disconnected and uncontrolled experience—uncontrolled by our general sense of "the way things happen"—which romance alone more or less successfully palms off on us. It is a case of Newman's own intimate experience all, that being my subject, the thread of which, from beginning to end, is not once exchanged, however momentarily, for any other thread; and the experience of others concerning us, and concerning him, only so far as it touches him and as he recognises, feels or divines it. There is our general sense of the way things happen—it abides with us indefeasibly, as readers of fiction, from the moment we demand that our fiction shall be intelligible; and there is our particular sense of the way they don't happen, which is liable to wake up unless reflexion and criticism, in us, have been skilfully and successfully drugged. There are drugs enough, clearly—it is all a question of applying them with tact; in which case the way things don't happen may be artfully made to pass for the way things do.

Amusing and even touching to me, I profess, at this time of day, the ingenuity (worthy, with whatever lapses, of a better cause) with which, on behalf of Newman's adventure, this hocus-pocus is attempted: the value of the instance not being diminished either, surely, by its having been attempted in such evident good faith. Yes, all is romantic to my actual vision here, and not least so, I hasten to add, the fabulous felicity of my candour. The way things happen is frankly not the way in which they are represented as having happened, in Paris, to my hero: the situation I had conceived only saddled me with that for want of my invention of something better. The great house of Bellegarde, in a word, would, I now feel, given the circumstances, given the *whole* of the ground, have comported itself in a manner as different as possible from the manner to which my narrative commits it; of which truth, moreover, I am by no means sure that, in spite of what I have called my serenity, I had not all the while an uneasy suspicion. I had dug in my path, alas, a hole into which I was destined to fall. I was so possessed of my idea that Newman should be ill-used—which was the essence of my subject—that I attached too scant an importance to its fashion of coming about. Almost any fashion would serve, I appear to have assumed, that would give me my main chance for him; a matter depending not so much on the particular trick played him as on the interesting face presented by him to *any* damnable trick. So where I part company with *terra-firma* is in making that projected, that performed outrage so much more showy, dramatically speaking, than sound. Had I patched it up to a greater apparent soundness my own trick, artistically speaking, would have been played; I should have cut the cable without my reader's suspecting it. I doubtless at the time, I repeat, believed I had taken my precautions; but truly they should have been greater, to impart the air of truth to the attitude—that is first to the pomp and circumstance, and second to the queer falsity—of the Bellegardes.

They would positively have jumped then, the Bellegardes, at my rich and easy American, and not have "minded" in the least any drawback—especially as, after all, given the pleasant palette from which I have painted him, there were few drawbacks to mind. My subject imposed on me a group of closely-allied persons animated by immense pretensions—which was all very well, which might be full of the promise of interest: only of interest felt most of all in the light of comedy and of irony. This, better understood, would have dwelt in the idea not in the least of their not finding Newman good enough for their alliance and thence being ready to sacrifice him, but in that of their taking with alacrity everything he could give them, only asking for more and more, and then adjusting their pretensions and their pride to it with all the comfort in life. Such accommodation of the theory of a noble indifference to the practice of a deep avidity is the real note of policy in forlorn aristocracies—and I meant of course that the Bellegardes should be virtually forlorn. The perversion of truth is by no means, I think, in the displayed acuteness of their remembrance of "who" and "what" they are, or at any rate take themselves for; since it is the misfortune of all insistence on "worldly" advantages—and the situation of such people bristles at the best (by which I mean under whatever invocation of a superficial simplicity) with emphasis, accent, assumption—to produce at times an effect of grossness. The picture of their tergiversation, at all events, however it may originally have seemed to me to hang together, has taken on this rococo appearance precisely because their preferred course, a thousand times preferred, would have been to haul him and his fortune into their boat under cover of night perhaps, in any case as quietly and with as little bumping and splashing as possible, and there accommodate him with the very safest and the most convenient seat. Given Newman, given the fact that the thing constitutes itself organically as *his* adventure, that too might very well be a situation and a subject: only it wouldn't have been the theme of "The American" as the book stands, the theme to which I was from so early pledged. Since I had wanted a "wrong" this other turn might even have been arranged to give me *that*, might even have been arranged to meet my requirement that somebody or something should be "in his power" so delightfully; and with the signal effect, after all, of "defining" everything. (It is as difficult, I said above, to trace the dividing-line between the real and the romantic as to plant a milestone between north and south; but I am not sure an infallible sign of the latter is not this rank vegetation of the "power" of bad people that good get into, or *vice versa*. It is so rarely, alas, into *our* power that any one gets!)

It is difficult for me to-day to believe that I had not, as my work went on, *some* shade of the rueful sense of my affront to verisimilitude; yet I catch the memory at least of no great sharpness, no true critical anguish, of remorse: an anomaly the reason of which in fact now glimmers interestingly out. My concern, as I saw it, was to make and to keep Newman consistent; the picture of his consistency was all my undertaking, and the memory of *that* infatuation perfectly abides with me. He was to be the lighted figure, the others—even doubtless to an excessive degree the woman who is made the agent of his discomfiture—were to be the obscured; by which I should largely get the very effect most to be invoked, that of a generous nature engaged with forces, with difficulties and dangers, that it but half understands. If Newman was attaching enough, I must have argued, his tangle would be sensible enough; for the interest of everything is all that it is *his* vision, *his* conception, *his* interpretation: at the window of his wide, quite sufficiently wide, consciousness we are seated, from that admirable position we "assist." He therefore supremely matters; all the rest matters only as he feels it, treats it, meets it. A beautiful infatuation this, always, I think, the intensity of the creative effort to get into the skin of the creature; the act of personal possession of one being by another at its completest—and with the high enhancement, ever, that it is, by the same stroke, the effort of the artist to preserve for his subject that unity, and for his use of it (in other words for the interest he desires to excite) that effect of a *centre*, which most economise its value. Its value is most discussable when that economy has most operated; the content and the "importance" of a work of art are in fine wholly dependent on its *being* one: outside of which all prate of its representative character, its meaning and its bearing, its morality and humanity, are an impudent thing. Strong in that character, which is the condition of its really bearing witness at all, it is strong every way. So much remains true then on behalf of my instinct of multiplying the fine touches by which Newman should live and communicate life; and yet I still ask myself, I confess, what I can have made of "life," in my picture, at such a juncture as the interval offered as elapsing between my hero's first accepted state and the nuptial rites that are to crown it. Nothing here is in truth "offered"— everything is evaded, and the effect of this, I recognise, is of the oddest. His relation to Madame de Cintré takes a great stride, but the author appears to view that but as a signal for letting it severely alone.

I have been stupefied, in so thoroughly revising the book, to find, on turning a page, that the light in which he is presented immediately after Madame de Bellegarde has conspicuously introduced him to all her circle as her daughter's husband-to-be is that of an evening at the opera quite alone; as if he wouldn't surely spend his leisure, and especially those hours of it, with his intended. Instinctively, from that moment, one would have seen them intimately and, for one's interest, beautifully together; with some illustration of the beauty incumbent on the author. The truth was that at this point the author, all gracelessly, could but hold his breath and pass; lingering was too difficult—he had made for himself a crushing complication. Since Madame de Cintré was after all to "back out" every touch in the picture of her apparent loyalty would add to her eventual shame. She had acted in clear good faith, but how could I give the *detail* of an attitude, on her part, of which the foundation was yet so weak? I preferred, as the minor evil, to shirk the attempt—at the cost evidently of a signal loss of "charm"; and with this lady, altogether, I recognise, a light plank, too light a plank, is laid for the reader over a dark "psychological" abyss. The delicate clue to her conduct is never definitely placed in his hand: I must have liked verily to think it *was* delicate and to flatter myself it was to be felt with finger-tips rather than heavily tugged at. Here then, at any rate, is the romantic *tout craché*—the fine flower of Newman's experience blooming in a medium "cut off" and shut up to itself. I don't for a moment pronounce any spell proceeding from it necessarily the less workable, to a rejoicing ingenuity, for that; beguile the reader's suspicion of *his* being shut up, transform it for *him* into a positive illusion of the largest liberty, and the success will ever be proportionate to the chance. Only all this gave me, I make out, a great deal to look to, and I was perhaps wrong in thinking that Newman by himself, and for any occasional extra inch or so I might smuggle into his measurements, would see me through my wood. Anything more liberated and disconnected, to re-peat my terms, than his prompt general profession, before the Tri-strams, of aspiring to a "great" marriage, for example, could surely not well be imagined. I had to take that over with the rest of him and fit it in—I had indeed to exclude the outer air. Still, I find on re-perusal that I have been able to breathe at least in my aching void; so that, clinging to my hero as to a tall, protective, good-natured elder brother in a rough place, I leave the record to stand or fall by his more or less convincing image.

The Portrait of a Lady

"THE PORTRAIT OF A LADY" WAS, LIKE "RODERICK Hudson," begun in Florence, during three months spent there in the spring of 1879. Like "Roderick" and like "The American," it had been designed for publication in "The Atlantic Monthly," where it began to appear in 1880. It differed from its two predecessors, however, in finding a course also open to it, from month to month, in "Macmillan's Magazine"; which was to be for me one of the last occasions of simultaneous "serialisation" in the two countries that the changing conditions of literary intercourse between England and the United States had up to then left unaltered. It is a long novel, and I was long in writing it; I remember being again much occupied with it, the following year, during a stay of several weeks made in Venice. I had rooms on Riva Schiavoni, at the top of a house near the passage leading off to San Zaccaria; the waterside life, the wondrous lagoon spread before me, and the ceaseless human chatter of Venice came in at my windows, to which I seem to myself to have been constantly driven, in the fruitless fidget of composition, as if to see whether, out in the blue channel, the ship of some right suggestion, of some better phrase, of the next happy twist of my subject, the next true touch for my canvas, mightn't come into sight. But I recall vividly enough that the response most elicited, in general, to these restless appeals was the rather grim admonition that romantic and historic sites, such as the land of Italy abounds in, offer the artist a questionable aid to concentration when they themselves are not to be the subject of it. They are too rich in their own life and too charged with their own meanings merely to help him out with a lame phrase; they draw him away from his small question to their own greater ones; so that, after a little, he feels, while thus yearning toward them in his difficulty, as if he were asking an army of glorious veterans to help him to arrest a peddler who has given him the wrong change.

There are pages of the book which, in the reading over, have seemed to make me see again the bristling curve of the wide Riva, the large colour-spots of the balconied houses and the repeated undulation of the little hunchbacked bridges, marked by the rise and drop again, with the wave, of foreshortened clicking pedestrians. The Venetian footfall and the Venetian cry—all talk there, wherever uttered, having the pitch of a call across the water—come in once more at the window, renewing one's old impression of the delighted senses and the divided, frustrated mind. How can places that speak *in general* so to the imagination not give it, at the moment, the particular thing it wants? I recollect again and again, in beautiful places, dropping into that wonderment. The real truth is, I think, that they express, under this appeal, only too much—more than, in the given case, one has use for; so that one finds one's self working less congruously, after all, so far as the surrounding picture is concerned, than in presence of the moderate and the neutral, to which we may lend something of the light of our vision. Such a place as Venice is too proud for such charities; Venice doesn't borrow, she but all magnificently gives. We profit by that enormously, but to do so we must either be quite off duty or be on it in her service alone. Such, and so rueful, are these reminiscences; though on the whole, no doubt, one's book, and one's "literary effort" at large, were to be the better for them. Strangely fertilising, in the long run, does a wasted effort of attention often prove. It all depends on *how* the attention has been cheated, has been squandered. There are high-handed insolent frauds, and there are insidious sneaking ones. And there is, I fear, even on the most designing artist's part, always witless enough good faith, always anxious enough desire, to fail to guard him against their deceits.

Trying to recover here, for recognition, the germ of my idea, I see that it must have consisted not at all in any conceit of a "plot," nefarious name, in any flash, upon the fancy, of a set of relations, or in any one of those situations that, by a logic of their own, immediately fall, for the fabulist, into movement, into a march or a rush, a patter of quick steps; but altogether in the sense of a single character, the character and aspect of a particular engaging young woman, to which all the usual elements of a "subject," certainly of a setting, were to need to be superadded. Quite as interesting as the young woman herself, at her best, do I find, I must again repeat, this projection of memory upon the whole matter of the growth, in one's imagination, of some such apology for a motive. These are the fascinations of the fabulist's art, these lurking forces of expansion, these necessities of upspringing in the seed, these beautiful determinations, on the part of the idea entertained, to grow as tall as possible, to push into the light and the air and thickly flower there; and, quite as much, these fine possibilities of recovering, from some good standpoint on the ground gained, the intimate history of the business—of retracing and reconstructing its steps and stages. I have always fondly remembered a remark that I heard fall years ago from the lips of Ivan Turgenieff in regard to his own experience of the usual origin of the fictive picture. It began for him almost always with the vision of some person or persons, who hovered before him, soliciting him, as the active or passive figure, interesting him and appealing to him just as they were and by what they were. He saw them, in that fashion, as *disponibles*, saw them subject to the chances, the complications of existence, and saw them vividly, but then had to find for them the right relations, those that would most bring them out; to imagine, to invent and select and piece together the situations most useful and favourable to the sense of the creatures themselves, the complications they would be most likely to produce and to feel.

"To arrive at these things is to arrive at my 'story,'" he said, "and that's the way I look for it. The result is that I'm often accused of not having 'story' enough. I seem to myself to have as much as I need—to show my people, to exhibit their relations with each other; for that is all my measure. If I watch them long enough I see them come together, I see them *placed*, I see them engaged in this or that act and in this or that difficulty. How they look and move and speak and behave, always in the setting I have found for them, is my account of them—of which I dare say, alas, *que cela manque souvent d'architecture.* But I would rather, I think, have too little architecture than too much—when there's danger of its interfering with my measure of the truth. The French of course like more of it than I give—having by their own genius such a hand for it; and indeed one must give all one can. As for the origin of one's wind-blown germs themselves, who shall say, as you ask, where *they* come from? We have to go too far back, too far behind, to say. Isn't it all we can say that they come from every quarter of heaven, that they are *there* at almost any turn of the road? They accumulate, and we are always picking them over, selecting among them. They are the breath of life—by which I mean that life, in its own way, breathes them upon us. They are so, in a manner prescribed and imposed—floated into our minds by the current of life. That reduces to imbecility the vain critic's quarrel, so often, with one's subject, when he hasn't the wit to accept it. Will he point out then which other it should properly have been?—his office being, essentially *to* point out. *Il en serait bien embarrassé.* Ah, when he points out what I've done or failed to do with it, that's another matter: there he's on his ground. I give him up my 'architecture,'" my distinguished friend concluded, "as much as he will."

So this beautiful genius, and I recall with comfort the gratitude I drew from his reference to the intensity of suggestion that may reside in the stray figure, the unattached character, the image *en disponsibilité*. It gave me higher warrant than I seemed then to have met for just that blest habit of one's own imagination, the trick of investing some conceived or encountered individual, some brace or group of individuals, with the germinal property and authority. I was myself so much more antecedently conscious of my figures than of their setting—a too preliminary, a preferential interest in which struck me as in general such a putting of the cart before the horse. I might envy, though I couldn't emulate, the imaginative writer so constituted as to see his fable first and to make out its agents afterwards: I could think so little of any fable that didn't need its agents positively to launch it; I could think so little of any situation that didn't depend for its interest on the nature of the persons situated, and thereby on their way of taking it. There are methods of so-called presentation, I believe— among novelists who have appeared to flourish—that offer the situation as indifferent to that support; but I have not lost the sense of the value for me, at the time, of the admirable Russian's testimony to my not needing, all superstitiously, to try and perform any such gymnastic. Other echoes from the same source linger with me, I confess, as unfadingly—if it be not all indeed one much-embracing echo. It was impossible after that not to read, for one's uses, high lucidity into the tormented and disfigured and bemuddled question of the objective value, and even quite into that of the critical appreciation, of "subject" in the novel.

One had had from an early time, for that matter, the instinct of the right estimate of such values and of its reducing to the inane the dull dispute over the "immoral" subject and the moral. Recognising so promptly the one measure of the worth of a given subject, the question about it that, rightly answered, disposes of all others—is it valid, in a word, is it genuine, is it sincere, the result of some direct impression or perception of life?—I had found small edification, mostly, in a critical pretension that had neglected from the first all delimitation of ground and all definition of terms. The air of my earlier time shows, to memory, as darkened, all round, with that vanity—unless the difference to-day be just in one's own final impatience, the lapse of one's attention. There is, I think, no more nutritive or suggestive truth in this connexion than that of the perfect dependence of the "moral" sense of a work of art on the amount of felt life concerned in producing it. The question comes back thus, obviously, to the kind and the degree of the artist's prime sensibility, which is the soil out of which his subject springs. The quality and capacity of that soil, its ability to "grow" with due freshness and straightness any vision of life, represents, strongly or weakly, the projected morality. That element is but another name for the more or less close connexion of the subject with some mark made on the intelligence, with some sincere experience. By which, at the same time, of course, one is far from contending that this enveloping air of the artist's humanity—which gives the last touch to the worth of the work— is not a widely and wondrously varying element; being on one occasion a rich and magnificent medium and on another a comparatively poor and ungenerous one. Here we get exactly the high price of the novel as a literary form—its power not only, while preserving that form with closeness, to range through all the differences of the individual relation to its general subject-matter, all the varieties of outlook on life, of disposition to reflect and project, created by conditions that are never the same from man to man (or, so far as that goes, from man to woman), but positively to appear more true to its character in proportion as it strains, or tends to burst, with a latent extravagance, its mould.

The house of fiction has in short not one window, but a million— a number of possible windows not to be reckoned, rather; every one of which has been pierced, or is still pierceable, in its vast front, by the need of the individual vision and by the pressure of the individual will. These apertures, of dissimilar shape and size, hang so, all together, over the human scene that we might have expected of them a greater sameness of report than we find. They are but windows at the best, mere holes in a dead wall, disconnected, perched aloft; they are not hinged doors opening straight upon life. But they have this mark of their own that at each of them stands a figure with a pair of eyes, or at least with a field-glass, which forms, again and again, for observation, a unique instrument, insuring to the person making use of it an impression distinct from every other. He and his neighbours are watching the same show, but one seeing more where the other sees less, one seeing black where the other sees white, one seeing big where the other sees small, one seeing coarse where the other sees fine. And so on, and so on; there is fortunately no saying on what, for the particular pair of eyes, the window may *not* open; "fortunately" by reason, precisely, of this incalculability of range. The spreading field, the human scene, is the "choice of subject"; the pierced aperture, either broad or balconied or slit-like and low-browed, is the "literary form"; but they are, singly or together, as nothing without the posted presence of the watcher—without, in other words, the consciousness of the artist. Tell me what the artist is, and I will tell you of what he has *been* conscious. Thereby I shall express to you at once his boundless freedom and his "moral" reference.

All this is a long way round, however, for my word about my dim first move toward "The Portrait," which was exactly my grasp of a single character—an acquisition I had made, moreover, after a fashion not here to be retraced. Enough that I was, as seemed to me, in complete possession of it, that I had been so for a long time, that this had made it familiar and yet had not blurred its charm, and that, all urgently, all tormentingly, I saw it in motion and, so to speak, in transit. This amounts to saying that I saw it as bent upon its fate— some fate or other; *which,* among the possibilities, being precisely the question. Thus I had my vivid individual—vivid, so strangely, in spite of being still at large, not confined by the conditions, not engaged in the tangle, to which we look for much of the impress that constitutes an identity. If the apparition was still all to be placed how came it to be vivid?—since we puzzle such quantities out, mostly, just by the business of placing them. One could answer such a question beautifully, doubtless, if one could do so subtle, if not so monstrous, a thing as to write the history of the growth of one's imagination. One would describe then what, at a given time, had extraordinarily happened to it, and one would so, for instance, be in a position to tell, with an approach to clearness, how, under favour of occasion, it had been able to take over (take over straight from life) such and such a constituted, animated figure or form. The figure has to that extent, as you see, *been* placed—placed in the imagination that detains it, preserves, protects, enjoys it, conscious of its presence in the dusky, crowded, heterogeneous back-shop of the mind very much as a wary dealer in precious odds and ends, competent to make an "advance" on rare objects confided to him, is conscious of the rare little "piece" left in deposit by the reduced, mysterious lady of title or the speculative amateur, and which is already there to disclose its merit afresh as soon as a key shall have clicked in a cupboard-door.

That may be, I recognise, a somewhat superfine analogy for the particular "value" I here speak of, the image of the young feminine nature that I had had for so considerable a time all curiously at my disposal; but it appears to fond memory quite to fit the fact—with the recall, in addition, of my pious desire but to place my treasure right. I quite remind myself thus of the dealer resigned not to "realise," resigned to keeping the precious object locked up indefinitely rather than commit it, at no matter what price, to vulgar hands. For there *are* dealers in these forms and figures and treasures capable of that refinement. The point is, however, that this single small corner-stone, the conception of a certain young woman affronting her destiny, had begun with being all my outfit for the large building of "The Portrait of a Lady." It came to be a square and spacious house—or has at least seemed so to me in this going over it again; but, such as it is, it had to be put up round my young woman while she stood there in perfect isolation. That is to me, artistically speaking, the circumstance of interest; for I have lost myself once more, I confess, in the curiosity of analysing the structure. By what process of logical accretion was this slight "personality," the mere slim shade of an intelligent but presumptuous girl, to find itself endowed with the high attributes of a Subject?—and indeed by what thinness, at the best, would such a subject not be vitiated? Millions of presumptuous girls, intelligent or not intelligent, daily affront their destiny, and what is it open to their destiny to *be*, at the most, that we should make an ado about it? The novel is of its very nature an "ado," an ado about something, and the larger the form it takes the greater of course the ado. Therefore, consciously, that was what one was in for—for positively organising an ado about Isabel Archer.

One looked it well in the face, I seem to remember, this extravagance; and with the effect precisely of recognising the charm of the problem. Challenge any such problem with any intelligence, and you immediately see how full it is of substance; the wonder being, all the while, as we look at the world, how absolutely, how inordinately, the Isabel Archers, and even much smaller female fry, insist on mattering. George Eliot has admirably noted it—"In these frail vessels is borne onward through the ages the treasure of human affection." In "Romeo and Juliet" Juliet has to be important, just as, in "Adam Bede" and "The Mill on the Floss" and "Middlemarch" and "Daniel Deronda," Hetty Sorrel and Maggie Tulliver and Rosamond Vincy and Gwendolen Harleth have to be; with that much of firm ground, that much of bracing air, at the disposal all the while of their feet and their lungs. They are typical, none the less, of a class difficult, in the individual case, to make a centre of interest; so difficult in fact that many an expert painter, as for instance Dickens and Walter Scott, as for instance even, in the main, so subtle a hand as that of R. L. Stevenson, has preferred to leave the task unattempted. There are in fact writers as to whom we make out that their refuge from this is to assume it to be not worth their attempting; by which pusillanimity in truth their honour is scantly saved. It is never an attestation of a value, or even of our imperfect sense of one, it is never a tribute to any truth at all, that we shall represent that value badly. It never makes up, artistically, for an artist's dim feeling about a thing that he shall "do" the thing as ill as possible. There are better ways than that, the best of all of which is to begin with less stupidity.

It may be answered meanwhile, in regard to Shakespeare's and to George Eliot's testimony, that their concession to the "importance" of their Juliets and Cleopatras and Portias (even with Portia as the very type and model of the young person intelligent and presumptuous) and to that of their Hettys and Maggies and Rosamonds and Gwendolens, suffers the abatement that these slimnesses are, when figuring as the main props of the theme, never suffered to be sole ministers of its appeal, but have their inadequacy eked out with comic relief and underplots, as the playwrights say, when not with murders and battles and the great mutations of the world. If they are shown as "mattering" as much as they could possibly pretend to, the proof of it is in a hundred other persons, made of much stouter stuff, and each involved moreover in a hundred relations which matter to *them* concomitantly with that one. Cleopatra matters, beyond bounds, to Antony, but his colleagues, his antagonists, the state of Rome and the impending battle also prodigiously matter; Portia matters to Antonio, and to Shylock, and to the Prince of Morocco, to the fifty aspiring princes, but for these gentry there are other lively concerns; for Antonio, notably, there are Shylock and Bassanio and his lost ventures and the extremity of his predicament. This extremity indeed, by the same token, matters to Portia—though its doing so becomes of interest all by the fact that Portia matters to *us*. That she does so, at any rate, and that almost everything comes round to it again, supports my contention as to this fine example of the value recognised in the mere young thing. (I say "mere" young thing because I guess that even Shakespeare, preoccupied mainly though he may have been with the passions of princes, would scarce have pretended to found the best of his appeal for her on her high social position.) It is an example exactly of the deep difficulty braved—the difficulty of making George Eliot's "frail vessel," if not the all-in-all for our attention, at least the clearest of the call.

Now to see deep difficulty braved is at any time, for the really addicted artist, to feel almost even as a pang the beautiful incentive, and to feel it verily in such sort as to wish the danger intensified. The difficulty most worth tackling can only be for him, in these conditions, the greatest the case permits of. So I remember feeling here (in presence, always, that is, of the particular uncertainty of my ground), that there would be one way better than another—oh, ever so much better than any other!—of making it fight out its battle. The frail vessel, that charged with George Eliot's "treasure," and thereby of such importance to those who curiously approach it, has likewise possibilities of importance to itself, possibilities which permit of treatment and in fact peculiarly require it from the moment they are considered at all. There is always the escape from any close account of the weak agent of such spells by using as a bridge for evasion, for retreat and flight, the view of her relation to those surrounding her. Make it predominantly a view of *their* relation and the trick is played: you give the general sense of her effect, and you give it, so far as the raising on it of a superstructure goes, with the maximum of ease. Well, I recall perfectly how little, in my now quite established connexion, the maximum of ease appealed to me, and how I seemed to get rid of it by an honest transposition of the weights in the two scales. "Place the centre of the subject in the young woman's own consciousness," I said to myself, "and you get as interesting and as beautiful a difficulty as you could wish. Stick to *that*—for the centre; put the heaviest weight into *that* scale, which will be so largely the scale of her relation to herself. Make her only interested enough, at the same time, in the things that are not herself, and this relation needn't fear to be too limited. Place meanwhile in the other scale the lighter weight (which is usually the one that tips the balance of interest): press least hard, in short, on the consciousness of your heroine's satellites, especially the male; make it an interest contributive only to the greater one. See, at all events, what can be done in this way. What better field could there be for a due ingenuity? The girl hovers, inextinguishable, as a charming creature, and the job will be to translate her into the highest terms of that formula, and as nearly as possible moreover into *all* of them. To depend upon her and her little concerns wholly to see you through will necessitate, remember, your really 'doing' her."

So far I reasoned, and it took nothing less than that technical rigour, I now easily see, to inspire me with the right confidence for erecting on such a plot of ground the neat and careful and proportioned pile of bricks that arches over it and that was thus to form, constructionally speaking, a literary monument. Such is the aspect that to-day "The Portrait" wears for me: a structure reared with an "architectural" competence, as Turgenieff would have said, that makes it, to the author's own sense, the most proportioned of his productions after "The Ambassadors"—which was to follow it so many years later and which has, no doubt, as superior roundness.

On one thing I was determined; that, though I should clearly have to pile brick upon brick for the creation of an interest, I would leave no pretext for saying that anything is out of line, scale or perspective. I would build large—in fine embossed vaults and painted arches, as who should say, and yet never let it appear that the chequered pavement, the ground under the reader's feet, fails to stretch at every point to the base of the walls. That precautionary spirit, on re-perusal of the book, is the old note that most touches me: it testifies so, for my own ear, to the anxiety of my provision for the reader's amusement. I felt, in view of the possible limitations of my subject, that no such provision could be excessive, and the development of the latter was simply the general form of that earnest quest. And I find indeed that this is the only account I can give myself of the evolution of the fable: it is all under the head thus named that I conceive the needful accretion as having taken place, the right complications as having started. It was naturally of the essence that the young woman should be herself complex; that was rudimentary—or was at any rate the light in which Isabel Archer had originally dawned. It went, however, but a certain way, and other lights, contending, conflicting lights, and of as many different colours, if possible, as the rockets, the Roman candles and Catherine-wheels of a "pyrotechnic display," would be employable to attest that she was. I had, no doubt, a groping instinct for the right complications, since I am quite unable to track the footsteps of those that constitute, as the case stands, the general situation exhibited. They are there, for what they are worth, and as numerous as might be; but my memory, I confess, is a blank as to how and whence they came.

I seem to myself to have waked up one morning in possession of them—of Ralph Touchett and his parents, of Madame Merle, of Gilbert Osmond and his daughter and his sister, of Lord Warburton, Caspar Goodwood and Miss Stackpole, the definite array of contributions to Isabel Archer's history. I recognised them, I knew them, they were the numbered pieces of my puzzle, the concrete terms of my "plot." It was as if they had simply, by an impulse of their own, floated into my ken, and all in response to my primary question: "Well, what will she *do*?" Their answer seemed to be that if I would trust them they would show me; on which, with an urgent appeal to them to make it at least as interesting as they could, I trusted them. They were like the group of attendants and entertainers who come down by train when people in the country give a party; they represented the contract for carrying the party on. That was an excellent relation with them—a possible one even with so broken a reed (from her slightness of cohesion) as Henrietta Stackpole. It is a familiar truth to the novelist, at the strenuous hour, that, as certain elements in any work are of the essence, so others are only of the form; that as this or that character, this or that disposition of the material, belongs to the subject directly, so to speak, so this or that other belongs to it but indirectly—belongs intimately to the treatment. This is a truth, however, of which he rarely gets the benefit—since it could be assured to him, really, but by criticism based upon perception, criticism which is too little of this world. He must not think of benefits, moreover, I freely recognise, for that way dishonour lies: he has, that is, but one to think of—the benefit, whatever it may be, involved in his having cast a spell upon the simpler, the very simplest, forms of attention. This is all he is entitled to; he is entitled to nothing, he is bound to admit, that can come to him, from the reader, as a result on the latter's part of any act of reflexion or discrimination. He may *enjoy* this finer tribute—that is another affair, but on condition only of taking it as a gratuity "thrown in," a mere miraculous windfall, the fruit of a tree he may not pretend to have shaken. Against reflexion, against discrimination, in his interest, all earth and air conspire; wherefore it is that, as I say, he must in many a case have schooled himself, from the first, to work but for a "living wage." The living wage is the reader's grant of the least possible quantity of attention required for consciousness of a "spell." The occasional charming "tip" is an act of his intelligence over and beyond this, a golden apple, for the writer's lap, straight from the wind-stirred tree. The artist may of course, in wanton moods, dream of some Paradise (for art) where the direct appeal to the intelligence might be legalised; for to such extravagances as these his yearning mind can scarce hope ever completely to close itself. The most he can do is to remember they *are* extravagances.

All of which is perhaps but a gracefully devious way of saying that Henrietta Stackpole was a good example, in "The Portrait," of the truth to which I just adverted—as good an example as I could name were it not that Maria Gostrey, in "The Ambassadors," then in the bosom of time, may be mentioned as a better. Each of these persons is but wheels to the coach; neither belongs to the body of that vehicle, or is for a moment accommodated with a seat inside. There the subject alone is ensconced, in the form of its "hero and heroine," and of the privileged high officials, say, who ride with the king and queen. There are reasons why one would have liked this to be felt, as in general one would like almost anything to be felt, in one's work, that one has one's self contributively felt. We have seen, however, how idle is that pretension, which I should be sorry to make too much of. Maria Gostrey and Miss Stackpole then are cases, each, of the light *ficelle*, not of the true agent; they may run beside the coach "for all they are worth," they may cling to it till they are out of breath (as poor Miss Stackpole all so visibly does), but neither, all the while, so much as gets her foot on the step, neither ceases for a moment to tread the dusty road. Put it even that they are like the fishwives who helped to bring back to Paris from Versailles, on that most ominous day of the first half of the French Revolution, the carriage of the royal family. The only thing is that I may well be asked, I acknowledge, why then, in the present fiction, I have suffered Henrietta (of whom we have indubitably too much) so officiously, so strangely, so almost inexplicably, to pervade. I will presently say what I can for that anomaly—and in the most conciliatory fashion.

A point I wish still more to make is that if my relation of confidence with the actors in my drama who *were*, unlike Miss Stackpole, true agents, was an excellent one to have arrived at, there still remained my relation with the reader, which was another affair altogether and as to which I felt no one to be trusted but myself. That solicitude was to be accordingly expressed in the artful patience with which, as I have said, I piled brick upon brick. The bricks, for the whole counting-over—putting for bricks little touches and inventions and enhancements by the way—affect me in truth as well-nigh innumerable and as ever so scrupulously fitted together and packed-in. It is an effect of detail, of the minutest; though, if one were in this connexion to say all, one would express the hope that the general, the ampler air of the modest monument still survives. I do at least seem to catch the key to a part of this abundance of small anxious, ingenious illustration as I recollect putting my finger, in my young woman's interest, on the most obvious of her predicates. "What will she 'do'? Why, the first thing she'll do will be to come to Europe; which in fact will form, and all inevitably, no small part of her principal adventure. Coming to Europe is even for the 'frail vessels,' in this wonderful age, a mild adventure; but what is truer than that on one side— the side of their independence of flood and field, of the moving accident, of battle and murder and sudden death—her adventures are to be mild? Without her sense of them, her sense *for* them, as one may say, they are next to nothing at all; but isn't the beauty and the difficulty just in showing their mystic conversion by that sense, conversion into the stuff of drama or, even more delightful word still, of 'story'?" It was all as clear, my contention, as a silver bell. Two very good instances, I think, of this effect of conversion, two cases of the rare chemistry, are the pages in which Isabel, coming into the drawing-room at Gardencourt, coming in from a wet walk or whatever, that rainy afternoon, finds Madame Merle in possession of the place, Madame Merle seated, all absorbed but all serene, at the piano, and deeply recognises, in the striking of such an hour, in the presence there, among the gathering shades, of this personage, of whom a moment before she had never so much as heard, a turning-point in her life. It is dreadful to have too much, for any artistic demonstration, to dot one's i's and insist on one's intentions, and I am not eager to do it now; but the question here was that of producing the maximum of intensity with the minimum of strain.

The interest was to be raised to its pitch and yet the elements to be kept in their key; so that, should the whole thing duly impress, I might show what an "exciting" inward life may do for the person leading it even while it remains perfectly normal. And I cannot think of a more consistent application of that ideal unless it be in the long statement, just beyond the middle of the book, of my young woman's extraordinary meditative vigil on the occasion that was to become for her such a landmark. Reduced to its essence, it is but the vigil of searching criticism; but it throws the action further forward than twenty "incidents" might have done. It was designed to have all the vivacity of incident and all the economy of picture. She sits up, by her dying fire, far into the night, under the spell of recognitions on which she finds the last sharpness suddenly wait. It is a representation simply of her motionlessly *seeing*, and an attempt withal to make the mere still lucidity of her act as "interesting" as the surprise of a caravan or the identification of a pirate. It represents, for that matter, one of the identifications dear to the novelist, and even indispensable to him; but it all goes on without her being approached by another person and without her leaving her chair. It is obviously the best thing in the book, but it is only a supreme illustration of the general plan. As to Henrietta, my apology for whom I just left incomplete, she exemplifies, I fear, in her superabundance, not an element of my plan, but only an excess of my zeal. So early was to begin my tendency to *overtreat*, rather than undertreat (when there was choice or danger) my subject. (Many members of my craft, I gather, are far from agreeing with me, but I have always held overtreating the minor disservice.) "Treating" that of "The Portrait" amounted to never forgetting, by any lapse, that the thing was under a special obligation to be amusing. There was the danger of the noted "thinness"—which was to be averted, tooth and nail, by cultivation of the lively. That is at least how I see it to-day. Henrietta must have been at that time a part of my wonderful notion of the lively. And then there was another matter. I had, within the few preceding years, come to live in London, and the "international" light lay, in those days, to my sense, thick and rich upon the scene. It was the light in which so much of the picture hung. But that *is* another matter. There is really too much to say.

The Awkward Age

I RECALL WITH PERFECT EASE THE IDEA IN WHICH "THE Awkward Age" had its origin, but re-perusal gives me pause in respect to naming it. This composition, as it stands, makes, to my vision—and will have made perhaps still more to that of its readers— so considerable a mass beside the germ sunk in it and still possibly distinguishable, that I am half-moved to leave my small secret undivulged. I shall encounter, I think, in the course of this copious commentary, no better example, and none on behalf of which I shall venture to invite more interest, of the quite incalculable tendency of a mere grain of subject-matter to expand and develop and cover the ground when conditions happen to favour it. I say all, surely, when I speak of the thing as planned, in perfect good faith, for brevity, for levity, for simplicity, for jocosity, in fine, and for an accommodating irony. I invoked, for my protection, the spirit of the lightest comedy, but "The Awkward Age" was to belong, in the event, to a group of productions, here re-introduced, which have in common, to their author's eyes, the endearing sign that they asserted in each case an unforeseen principle of growth. They were projected as small things, yet had finally to be provided for as comparative monsters. That is my own title for them, though I should perhaps resent it if applied by another critic—above all in the case of the piece before us, the careful measure of which I have just freshly taken. The result of this consideration has been in the first place to render sharp for me again the interest of the whole process thus illustrated, and in the second quite to place me on unexpectedly good terms with the work itself. As I scan my list I encounter none the "history" of which embodies a greater number of curious truths—or of truths at least by which I find contemplation more enlivened. The thing done and dismissed has ever, at the best, for the ambitious workman, a trick of looking dead, if not buried, so that he almost throbs with ecstasy when, on an anxious review, the flush of life reappears. It is verily on recognising that flush on a whole side of "The Awkward Age" that I brand it all, but ever so tenderly, as monstrous—which is but my way of noting the *quantity* of finish it stows away. Since I speak so undauntedly, when need is, of the value of composition, I shall not beat about the bush to claim for these pages the maximum of that advantage. If such a feat be possible in this field as really taking a lesson from one's own adventure I feel I have now not failed of it—to so much more demonstration of my profit than I can hope to carry through do I find myself urged. Thus it is that, still with a remnant of self-respect, or at least of sanity, one may turn to complacency, one may linger with pride. Let my pride provoke a frown till I justify it; which—though with more matters to be noted here than I have room for—I shall accordingly proceed to do.

Yet I must first make a brave face, no doubt, and present in its native humility my scant but quite ponderable germ. The seed sprouted in that vast nursery of sharp appeals and concrete images which calls itself, for blest convenience, London; it fell even into the order of the minor "social phenomena" with which, as fruit for the observer, that mightiest of the trees of suggestion bristles. It was not, no doubt, a fine purple peach, but it might pass for a round ripe plum, the note one had inevitably had to take of the difference made in certain friendly houses and for certain flourishing mothers by the sometimes dreaded, often delayed, but never fully arrested coming to the forefront of some vague slip of a daughter. For such mild revolutions as these not, to one's imagination, to remain mild one had had, I dare say, to be infinitely addicted to "noticing"; under the rule of that secret vice or that unfair advantage, at any rate, the "sitting downstairs," from a given date, of the merciless maiden previously perched aloft could easily be felt as a crisis. This crisis, and the sense for it in those whom it most concerns, has to confess itself courageously the prime propulsive force of "The Awkward Age." Such a matter might well make a scant show for a "thick book," and no thick book, but just a quite charmingly thin one, was in fact originally dreamt of. For its proposed scale the little idea seemed happy—happy, that is, above all in having come very straight; but its proposed scale was the limit of a small square canvas. One had been present again and again at the exhibition I refer to—which is what I mean by the "coming straight" of this particular London impression; yet one was (and through fallibilities that after all had their sweetness, so that one would on the whole rather have kept them than parted with them) still capable of so false a measurement. When I think indeed of those of my many false measurements that have resulted, after much anguish, in decent symmetries, I find the whole case, I profess, a theme for the philosopher. The little ideas one wouldn't have treated save for the design of keeping them small, the developed situations that one would never with malice prepense have undertaken, the long stories that had thoroughly meant to be short, the short subjects that had underhandedly plotted to be long, the hypocrisy of modest beginnings, the audacity of misplaced middles, the triumph of intentions never entertained—with these patches, as I look about, I see my experience paved: an experience to which nothing is wanting save, I confess, some grasp of its final lesson.

This lesson would, if operative, surely provide some law for the recognition, the determination in advance, of the just limits and the just extent of the situation, *any* situation, that appeals, and that yet, by the presumable, the helpful law of situations, must have its reserves as well as its promises. The storyteller considers it because it promises, and undertakes it, often, just because also making out, as he believes, where the promise conveniently drops. The promise, for instance, of the case I have just named, the case of the account to be taken, in a circle of free talk, of a new and innocent, a wholly unacclimatised presence, as to which such accommodations have never had to come up, might well have appeared as limited as it was lively; and if these pages were not before us to register my illusion I should never have made a braver claim for it. They themselves admonish me, however, in fifty interesting ways, and they especially emphasise that truth of the vanity of the *a priori* test of what an *idée-mère* may have to give. The truth is that what a happy thought has to give depends immensely on the general turn of the mind capable of it, and on the fact that its loyal entertainer, cultivating fondly its possible relations and extensions, the bright efflorescence latent in it, but having to take other things in their order too, is terribly at the mercy of his mind. That organ has only to exhale, in its degree, a fostering tropic air in order to produce complications almost beyond reckoning. The trap laid for his superficial convenience resides in the fact that, though the relations of a human figure or a social occurrence are what make such objects interesting, they also make them, to the same tune, difficult to isolate, to surround with the sharp black line, to frame in the square, the circle, the charming oval, that helps any arrangements of objects to become a picture. The storyteller has but to have been condemned by nature to a liberally amused and beguiled, a richly sophisticated, view of relations and a fine inquisitive speculative sense for them, to find himself at moments flounder in a deep warm jungle. These are the moments at which he recalls ruefully that the great merit of such and such a small case, the merit for his particular advised use, had been precisely in the smallness.

I may say at once that this had seemed to me, under the first flush of recognition, the good mark for the pretty notion of the "free circle" put about by having, of a sudden, an ingenuous mind and a pair of limpid searching eyes to count with. Half the attraction was in the current actuality of the thing: repeatedly, right and left, as I have said, one had seen such a drama constituted, and always to the effect of proposing to the interested view one of those questions that are of the essence of drama: what will happen, who suffer, who not suffer, what turn be determined, what crisis created, what issue found? There had of course to be, as a basis, the free circle, but this was material of that admirable order with which the good London never leaves its true lover and believer long unprovided. One could count them on one's fingers (an abundant allowance), the liberal firesides beyond the wide glow of which, in a comparative dimness, female adolescence hovered and waited. The wide glow was bright, was favourable to "real" talk, to play of mind, to an explicit interest in life, a due demonstration of the interest by persons qualified to feel it: all of which meant frankness and ease, the perfection, almost as it were, of intercourse, and a tone as far as possible removed from that of the nursery and the schoolroom—as far as possible removed even, no doubt, in its appealing "modernity," from that of supposedly privileged scenes of conversation twenty years ago. The charm was, with a hundred other things, in the freedom—the freedom menaced by the inevitable irruption of the ingenuous mind; whereby, if the freedom should be sacrificed, what would truly *become* of the charm? The charm might be figured as dear to members of the circle consciously contributing to it, but it was none the less true that some sacrifice in some quarter would have to be made, and what meditator worth his salt could fail to hold his breath while waiting on the event? The ingenuous mind might, it was true, be suppressed altogether, the general disconcertment averted either by some master-stroke of diplomacy or some rude simplification; yet these were ugly matters, and in the examples before one's eyes nothing ugly, nothing harsh or crude, had flourished. A girl might be married off the day after her irruption, or better still the day before it, to remove her from the sphere of the play of mind; but these were exactly not crudities, and even then, at the worst, an interval had to be bridged. "The Awkward Age" is precisely a study of one of these curtailed or extended periods of tension and apprehension, an account of the manner in which the resented interference with ancient liberties came to be in a particular instance dealt with.

I note once again that I had not escaped seeing it actually and traceably dealt with—after (I admit) a good deal of friendly suspense; also with the nature and degree of the "sacrifice" left very much to one's appreciation. In circles highly civilised the great things, the real things, the hard, the cruel and even the tender things, the true elements of any tension and true facts of any crisis, have ever, for the outsider's, for the critic's use, to be translated into terms—terms in the distinguished name of which, terms for the right employment of which, more than one situation of the type I glance at had struck me as all irresistibly appealing. There appeared in fact at moments no end to the things they said, the suggestions into which they flowered; one of these latter in especial arriving at the highest intensity. Putting vividly before one the perfect system on which the awkward age is handled in most other European societies, it threw again into relief the inveterate English trick of the so morally well-meant and so intellectually helpless compromise. We live notoriously, as I suppose every age lives, in an "epoch of transition"; but it may still be said of the French for instance, I assume, that their social scheme absolutely provides against awkwardness. That is it would be, by this scheme, so infinitely awkward, so awkward beyond any patching-up, for the hovering female young to be conceived as present at "good" talk, that their presence is, theoretically at least, not permitted till their youth has been promptly corrected by marriage—in which case they have ceased to be merely young. The better the talk prevailing in any circle, accordingly, the more organised, the more complete, the element of precaution and exclusion. Talk—giving the term a wide application—is one thing, and a proper inexperience another; and it has never occurred to a logical people that the interest of the greater, the general, need be sacrificed to that of the less, the particular. Such sacrifices strike them as gratuitous and barbarous, as cruel above all to the social intelligence; also as perfectly preventable by wise arrangement. Nothing comes home more, on the other hand, to the observer of English manners than the very moderate degree in which wise arrangement, in the French sense of a scientific economy, has ever been invoked; a fact indeed largely explaining the great interest of their incoherence, their heterogeneity, their wild abundance. The French, all analytically, have conceived of fifty different proprieties, meeting fifty different cases, whereas the English mind, less intensely at work, has never conceived but of one—the grand propriety, for every case, it should in fairness be said, of just being English. As practice, however, has always to be a looser thing than theory, so no application of that rigour has been possible in the London world without a thousand departures from the grim ideal.

The American theory, if I may "drag it in," would be, I think, that talk should never become "better" than the female young, either actually or constructively present, are minded to allow it. *That* system involves as little compromise as the French; it has been absolutely simple, and the beauty of its success shines out in every record of our conditions of intercourse—premising always our "basic" assumption that the female young read the newspapers. The English theory may be in itself almost as simple, but different and much more complex forces have ruled the application of it; so much does the goodness of talk depend on what there may be to talk about. There are more things in London, I think, than anywhere in the world; hence the charm of the dramatic struggle reflected in my book, the struggle somehow to fit propriety into a smooth general case which is really all the while bristling and crumbling into fierce particular ones. The circle surrounding Mrs. Brookenham, in my pages, is of course nothing if not a particular, even a "peculiar" one—and its rather vain effort (the vanity, the real inexpertness, being precisely part of my tale) is toward the courage of that condition. It has cropped up in a social order where individual appreciations of propriety have not been formally allowed for, in spite of their having very often quite rudely and violently and insolently, rather of course than insidiously, flourished; so that as the matter stands, rightly or wrongly, Nanda's retarded, but eventually none the less real, incorporation means virtually Nanda's exposure. It means this, that is, and many things beside—means them for Nanda herself and, with a various intensity, for the other participants in the action; but what it particularly means, surely, is the failure of successful arrangement and the very moral, sharply pointed, of the fruits of compromise. It is compromise that has suffered her to be in question at all, and that has condemned the freedom of the circle to be self-conscious, compunctious, on the whole much more timid than brave—the consequent muddle, if the term be not too gross, representing meanwhile a great inconvenience for life, but, as I found myself feeling, an immense promise, a much greater one than on the "foreign" showing, for the painted picture of life. Beyond which let me add that here immediately is a prime specimen of the way in which the obscurer, the lurking relations of a motive apparently simple, always in wait for their spring, may by seizing their chance for it send simplicity flying. Poor Nanda's little case, and her mother's, and Mr. Longdon's and Vanderbank's and Mitchy's, to say nothing of that of the others, has only to catch a reflected light from over the Channel in order to double at once its appeal to the imagination. (I am considering all these matters, I need scarce say, only as they are concerned with that faculty. With a relation *not* imaginative to his material the storyteller has nothing whatever to do.)

It exactly happened moreover that my own material here was to profit in a particular way by that extension of view. My idea was to be treated with light irony—it would be light and ironical or it would be nothing; so that I asked myself, naturally, what might be the least solemn form to give it, among recognised and familiar forms. The question thus at once arose: What form so familiar, so recognised among alert readers, as that in which the ingenious and inexhaustible, the charming philosophic "Gyp" casts most of her social studies? Gyp had long struck me as mistress, in her levity, of one of the happiest of forms—the only objection to my use of which was a certain extraordinary benightedness on the part of the Anglo-Saxon reader. One had noted this reader as perverse and inconsequent in respect to the absorption of "dialogue"—observed the "public for fiction" consume it, in certain connexions, on the scale and with the smack of lips that mark the consumption of bread-and-jam by a children's school-feast, consume it even at the theatre, so far as our theatre ever vouchsafes it, and yet as flagrantly reject it when served, so to speak, *au naturel.* One had seen good solid slices of fiction, well endued, one might surely have thought, with this easiest of lubrications, deplored by editor and publisher as positively not, for the general gullet as known to *them,* made adequately "slick." " 'Dialogue,' always 'dialogue'!" I had seemed from far back to hear them mostly cry: "We can't have too much of it, we can't have enough of it, and no excess of it, in the form of no matter what savourless dilution, or what boneless dispersion, ever began to injure a book so much as even the very scantest claim put in for form and substance." This wisdom had always been in one's ears; but it had at the same time been equally in one's eyes that really constructive dialogue, dialogue organic and dramatic, speaking for itself, representing and embodying substance and form, is among us an uncanny and abhorrent thing, not to be dealt with on any terms. A comedy or a tragedy may run for a thousand nights without prompting twenty persons in London or in New York to desire that view of its text which is so desired in Paris, as soon as a play begins to loom at all large, that the number of copies of the printed piece in circulation far exceeds at last the number of performances. But as with the printed piece our own public, infatuated as it may be with the theatre, refuses all commerce—though indeed this can't but be, without cynicism, very much through the infirmity the piece, *if* printed, would reveal—so the same horror seems to attach to any typographic hint of the proscribed playbook or any insidious plea for it. The immense oddity resides in the almost exclusively typographic order of the offence. An English, an American Gyp would typographically offend, and that would be the end of her. *There* gloomed at me my warning, as well as shone at me my provocation, in respect to the example of this delightful writer. I might emulate her, since I presumptuously would, but dishonour would await me if, proposing to treat the different faces of my subject in the most completely instituted colloquial form, I should evoke the figure and affirm the presence of participants by the repeated and prefixed name rather than by the recurrent and *affixed* "said he" and "said she." All I have space to go into here—much as the funny fact I refer to might seem to invite us to dance hand in hand round it—is that I was at any rate duly admonished, that I took my measures accordingly, and that the manner in which I took them has lived again for me ever so arrestingly, so amusingly, on re-examination of the book.

But that I did, positively and seriously—ah so seriously!—emulate the levity of Gyp and, by the same token, of that hardiest of flowers fostered in her school, M. Henri Lavedan, is a contribution to the history of "The Awkward Age" that I shall obviously have had to brace myself in order to make. Vivid enough to me the expression of face of any kindest of critics, even, moved to declare that he would never in the least have suspected it. Let me say at once, in extenuation of the too respectful distance at which I may thus have appeared to follow my model, that my first care *had* to be the covering of my tracks—lest I truly should be caught in the act of arranging, of organising dialogue to "speak for itself." What I now see to have happened is that I organised and arranged but too well—too well, I mean, for any betrayal of the Gyp taint, however faded and feeble. The trouble appears to have been that while I on the one hand exorcised the baleful association, I succeeded in rousing on nobody's part a sense of any other association whatever, or of my having cast myself into any conceivable or calculable form. My private inspiration had been in the Gyp plan (artfully dissimulated, for dear life, and applied with the very subtlest consistency, but none the less kept in secret view); yet I was to fail to make out in the event that the book succeeded in producing the impression of *any* plan on any person. No hint of that sort of success, or of any critical perception at all in relation to the business, has ever come my way; in spite of which when I speak, as just

307

above, of what was to "happen" under the law of my ingenious labour, I fairly lose myself in the vision of a hundred bright phenomena. Some of these incidents I must treat myself to naming, for they are among the best I shall have on any occasion to retail. But I must first give the measure of the degree in which they were mere matters of the study. This composition had originally appeared in "Harper's Weekly" during the autumn of 1898 and the first weeks of the winter, and the volume containing it was published that spring. I had meanwhile been absent from England, and it was not till my return, some time later, that I had from my publisher any news of our venture. But the news then met at a stroke all my curiosity: "I'm sorry to say the book has done nothing to speak of; I've never in all my experience seen one treated with more general and complete disrespect." There was thus to be nothing left me for fond subsequent reference—of which I doubtless give even now so adequate an illustration—save the rich reward of the singular interest attaching to the very intimacies of the effort.

It comes back to me, the whole "job," as wonderfully amusing and delightfully difficult from the first; since amusement deeply abides, I think, in any artistic attempt the basis and groundwork of which are conscious of a particular firmness. On that hard fine floor the element of execution feels it may more or less confidently *dance*; in which case puzzling questions, sharp obstacles, dangers of detail, may come up for it by the dozen without breaking its heart or shaking its nerve. It is the difficulty produced by the loose foundation or the vague scheme that breaks the heart—when a luckless fatuity has over-persuaded an author of the "saving" virtue of treatment. Being "treated" is never, in a workable idea, a mere passive condition, and I hold no subject ever susceptible of help that isn't, like the embarrassed man of our proverbial wisdom, first of all able to help itself. I was thus to have here an envious glimpse, in carrying my design through, of that artistic rage and that artistic felicity which I have ever supposed to be intensest and highest, the confidence of the dramatist strong in the sense of his postulate. The dramatist has verily to *build*, is committed to architecture, to construction at any cost; to driving in deep his vertical supports and laying across and firmly fixing his horizontal, his resting pieces—at the risk of no matter what vibration from the tap of his master-hammer. This makes the active value of his basis immense, enabling him, with his flanks protected, to advance undistractedly, even if not at all carelessly, into the comparative fairyland of the mere minor anxiety. In other words his scheme *holds*, and as he feels this in spite of noted strains and under repeated tests, so he keeps his face to the day. I rejoiced, by that same token, to feel *my* scheme hold, and even a little ruefully watched it give me much more than I had ventured to hope. For I promptly found my conceived arrangement of my material open the door wide to ingenuity. I remember that in sketching my project for the conductors of the periodical I have named I drew on a sheet of paper—and possibly with an effect of the cabalistic, it now comes over me, that even anxious amplification may have but vainly attenuated—the neat figure of a circle consisting of a number of small rounds disposed at equal distance about a central object. The central object was my situation, my subject in itself, to which the thing would owe its title, and the small rounds represented so many distinct lamps, as I liked to call them, the function of each of which would be to light with all due intensity one of its aspects. I had divided it, didn't they see? into aspects—uncanny as the little term might sound (though not for a moment did I suggest we should use it for the public), and by that sign we would conquer.

They "saw," all genially and generously—for I must add that I had made, to the best of my recollection, no morbid scruple of not blabbing about Gyp and her strange incitement. I the more boldly held my tongue over this that the more I, by my intelligence, lived in my arrangement and moved about in it, the more I sank into satisfaction. It was clearly to work to a charm and, during this process—by calling at every step for an exquisite management—"to haunt, to startle and waylay." Each of my "lamps" would be the light of a single "social occasion" in the history and intercourse of the characters concerned, and would bring out to the full the latent colour of the scene in question and cause it to illustrate, to the last drop, its bearing on my theme. I revelled in this notion of the Occasion as a thing by itself, really and completely a scenic thing, and could scarce name it, while crouching amid the thick arcana of my plan, with a large enough O. The beauty of the conception was in this approximation of the respective divisions of my form to the successive Acts of a Play— as to which it was more than ever a case for charmed capitals. The divine distinction of the act of a play—and a greater than any other it easily succeeds in arriving at—was, I reasoned, in its special, its guarded objectivity. This objectivity, in turn, when achieving its ideal, came from the imposed absence of that "going behind," to compass explanations and amplifications, to drag out odds and ends from the "mere" storyteller's great property-shop of aids to illusion: a resource under denial of which it was equally perplexing and delightful, for a change, to proceed. Everything, for that matter, becomes interesting from the moment it has closely to consider, for full effect positively to bestride, the law of its kind. "Kinds" are the very life of literature, and truth and strength come from the complete recognition of them, from abounding to the utmost in their respective senses and sinking deep into their consistency. I myself have scarcely to plead the cause of "going behind," which is right and beautiful and fruitful in its place and order; but as the confusion of kinds is the inelegance of letters and the stultification of values, so to renounce that line utterly and do something quite different instead may become in another connexion the true course and the vehicle of effect. Something in the very nature, in the fine rigour, of this special sacrifice (which is capable of affecting the form-lover, I think, as really more of a projected form than any other) lends it moreover a coercive charm; a charm that grows in proportion as the appeal to it tests and stretches and strains it, puts it powerfully to the touch. To make the presented occasion tell all its story itself, remain shut up in its own presence and yet on that patch of staked-out ground become thoroughly interesting and remain thoroughly clear, is a process not remarkable, no doubt, so long as a very light weight is laid on it, but difficult enough to challenge and inspire great adroitness so soon as the elements to be dealt with begin at all to "size up."

The disdainers of the contemporary drama deny, obviously, with all promptness, that the matter to be expressed by its means— richly and successfully expressed that is—*can* loom with any largeness; since from the moment it does one of the conditions breaks down. The process simply collapses under pressure, they contend, proves its weakness as quickly as the office laid on it ceases to be simple. "Remember," they say to the dramatist, "that you have to be, supremely, three things: you have to be true to your form, you have to be interesting, you have to be clear. You have in other words to prove yourself adequate to taking a heavy weight. But we defy you really to conform to your conditions with any but a light one. Make the thing you have to convey, make the picture you have to paint, at all rich and complex, and you cease to be clear. Remain clear—and with the clearness required by the infantine intelligence of any public consenting to see a play—and what becomes of the 'importance' of your subject? If it's important by any other critical measure than the little foot-rule the 'produced' piece has to conform to, it is predestined to be a muddle. When it has escaped being a muddle the note it has succeeded in striking at the furthest will be recognised as one of those that are called high but by the courtesy, by the intellectual provinciality, of theatrical criticism, which, as we can see for ourselves any morning, is—well, an abyss even deeper than the theatre itself. Don't attempt to crush us with Dumas and Ibsen, for such values are from any informed and enlightened point of view, that is measured by other high values, literary, critical, philosophic, of the most moderate order. Ibsen and Dumas are precisely cases of men, men in their degree, in their poor theatrical straight-jacket, speculative, who have *had* to renounce the finer thing for the coarser, the thick, in short, for the thin and the curious for the self-evident. What earthly intellectual distinction, what 'prestige' of achievement, would have attached to the substance of such things as 'Denise,' as 'Monsieur Alphonse,' as 'Francillon' (and we take the Dumas of the supposedly subtler period) in any other form? What virtues of the same order would have attached to 'The Pillars of Society,' to 'An Enemy of the People,' to 'Ghosts,' to 'Rosmersholm' (or taking also Ibsen's 'subtler period') to 'John Gabriel Borkmann,' to 'The Master-Builder'? Ibsen is in fact wonderfully a case in point, since from the moment he's clear, from the moment he's 'amusing,' it's on the footing of a thesis as simple and superficial as that of 'A Doll's House'—while from the moment he's by apparent intention comprehensive and searching it's on the footing of an effect as confused and obscure as 'The Wild Duck.' From which you easily see *all* the conditions can't be met. The dramatist has to choose but those he's most capable of, and by that choice he's known."

So the objector concludes, and never surely without great profit from his having been "drawn." His apparent triumph—if it be even apparent—still leaves, it will be noted, convenient cover for retort in the riddled face of the opposite stronghold. The last word in these cases is for nobody who can't pretend to an *absolute* test. The terms here used, obviously, are matters of appreciation, and there is no short cut to proof (luckily for us all round) either that "Monsieur Alphonse" develops itself on the highest plane of irony or that "Ghosts" simplifies almost to excruciation. If "John Gabriel Borkmann" is but a pennyworth of effect as to a character we can imagine much more amply presented, and if "Hedda Gabler" makes an appeal enfeebled by remarkable vagueness, there is by the nature of the case no catching the convinced, or call him the deluded, spectator or reader in the act of a mistake. He is to be caught at the worst in the act of attention, of the very greatest attention, and that is all, as a precious preliminary at least, that the playwright asks of him, besides being all the very divinest poet can get. I remember rejoicing as much to remark this, after getting launched in "The Awkward Age," as if I were in fact constructing a play; just as I may doubtless appear now not less anxious to keep the philosophy of the dramatist's course before me than if I belonged to his order. I felt, certainly, the support he feels, I participated in his technical amusement, I tasted to the full the bitter-sweetness of his draught—the beauty and the difficulty (to harp again on that string) of escaping poverty *even though* the references in one's action can only be, with intensity, to each other, to things exactly on the same plane of exhibition with themselves. Exhibition may mean in a "story" twenty different ways, fifty excursions, alternatives, excrescences, and the novel, as largely practised in English, is the perfect paradise of the loose end. The play consents to the logic of but one way, mathematically right, and with the loose end as gross an impertinence on its surface, and as grave a dishonour, as the dangle of a snippet of silk or wool on the right side of a tapestry. We are shut up wholly to cross-relations, relations all within the action itself; no part of which is related to anything but some other part—save of course by the relation of the total to life. And, after invoking the protection of Gyp, I saw the point of my game all in the problem of keeping these conditioned relations crystalline at the same time that I should, in emulation of life, consent to their being numerous and fine and characteristic of the London world (as the London world was in this quarter and that to be deciphered). All of which was to make in the event for complications.

I see now of course how far, with my complications, I got away from Gyp; but I see to-day so much else too that this particular deflexion from simplicity makes scarce a figure among the others; after having once served its purpose, I mean, of lighting my original imitative innocence. For I recognise in especial, with a waking vibration of that interest in which, as I say, the plan of the book is embalmed for me, that my subject was probably condemned in advance to appreciable, or more exactly perhaps to almost preposterously appreciative, over-treatment. It places itself for me thus in a group of small productions exhibiting this perversity, representations of conceived cases in which my process has been to pump the case gaspingly dry, dry not only of superfluous moisture, but absolutely (for I have encountered the charge) of breatheable air. I may note, in fine, that coming back to the pages before us with a strong impression of their recording, to my shame, that disaster, even to the extent of its disqualifying them for decent reappearance, I have found the adventure taking, to my relief, quite another turn, and have lost myself in the wonder of what "over-treatment" may, in the detail of its desperate ingenuity, consist of. The revived interest I speak of has been therefore that of following critically, from page to page, even as the red Indian tracks in the forest the pale-face, the footsteps of the systematic loyalty I was able to achieve. The amusement of this *constatation* is, as I have hinted, in the detail of the matter, and the detail is so dense, the texture of the figured and smoothed tapestry so close, that the genius of Gyp herself, muse of general looseness, would certainly, once warned, have uttered the first disavowal of my homage. But what has occurred meanwhile is that this high consistency has itself, so to speak, constituted an exhibition, and that an important artistic truth has seemed to me thereby lighted. We brushed against that truth just now in our glance at the denial of expansibility to any idea the mould of the "stage-play" may hope to express without cracking and bursting; and we bear in mind at the same time that the picture of Nanda Brookenham's situation, though perhaps seeming to a careless eye so to wander and sprawl, yet presents itself on absolutely scenic lines, and that each of these scenes in itself, and each as related to each and to all of its companions, abides without a moment's deflexion by the principle of the stage-play.

In doing this then it does more—it helps us ever so happily to see the grave distinction between substance and form in a really wrought work of art signally break down. I hold it impossible to say, before "The Awkward Age," where one of these elements ends and the other begins: I have been unable at least myself, on re-examination, to mark any such joint or seam, to see the two *discharged* offices as separate. They are separate before the fact, but the sacrament of execution indissolubly marries them, and the marriage, like any other marriage, has only to be a "true" one for the scandal of a breach not to show. The thing "done," artistically, is a fusion, or it has not *been* done—in which case of course the artist may be, and all deservedly, pelted with any fragment of his botch the critic shall choose to pick up. But his ground once conquered, in this particular field, he knows nothing of fragments and may say in all security: "Detach one if you can. You can analyse in *your* way, oh yes—to relate, to report, to explain; but you can't disintegrate my synthesis; you can't resolve the elements of my whole into different responsible agents or find your way at all (for your own fell purpose). My mixture has only to be perfect literally to bewilder you—you are lost in the tangle of the forest. Prove this value, this effect, in the air of the whole result, to be of my subject, and that other value, other effect, to be of my treatment, prove that I haven't so shaken them together as the conjurer I profess to be *must* consummately shake, and I consent but to parade as before a booth at the fair." The exemplary closeness of "The Awkward Age" even affects me, on re-perusal, I confess, as treasure quite instinctively and foreseeingly laid up against my present opportunity for these remarks. I have been positively struck by the quantity of meaning and the number of intentions, the extent of *ground for in-*

terest, as I may call it, that I have succeeded in working scenically, yet without loss of sharpness, clearness or "atmosphere," into each of my illuminating Occasions—where, at certain junctures, the due preservation of all these values took, in the familiar phrase, a good deal of doing.

I should have liked just here to re-examine with the reader some of the positively most artful passages I have in mind—such as the hour of Mr. Longdon's beautiful and, as it were, mystic attempt at a compact with Vanderbank, late at night, in the billiard-room of the country-house at which they are staying; such as the other nocturnal passage, under Mr. Longdon's roof, between Vanderbank and Mitchy, where the conduct of so much fine meaning, so many flares of the exhibitory torch through the labyrinth of mere immediate appearances, mere familiar allusions, is successfully and safely effected; such as the whole array of the terms of presentation that are made to serve, all systematically, yet without a gap anywhere, for the presentation, throughout, of a Mitchy "subtle" no less than concrete and concrete no less than deprived of that officious explanation which we know as "going behind"; such as, briefly, the general service of co-ordination and vivification rendered, on lines of ferocious, of really quite heroic compression, by the picture of the assembled group at Mrs. Grendon's, where the "cross-references" of the action are as thick as the green leaves of a garden, but none the less, as they have scenically to be, counted and disposed, weighted with responsibility. Were I minded to use in this connexion a "loud" word—and the critic in general hates loud words as a man of taste may hate loud colours— I should speak of the composition of the chapters entitled "Tishy Grendon," with all the pieces of the game on the table together and each unconfusedly and contributively placed, as triumphantly scientific. I must properly remind myself, rather, that the better lesson of my retrospect would seem to be really a supreme revision of the question of what it may be for a subject to suffer, to call it suffering, by over-treatment. Bowed down so long by the inference that its product had in this case proved such a betrayal, my artistic conscience meets the relief of having to recognise truly here no traces of suffering. The thing carries itself to my maturer and gratified sense as with every symptom of soundness, an insolence of health and joy. And from this precisely I deduce my moral; which is to the effect that, since our only way, in general, of knowing that we have had too much of anything is by *feeling* that too much: so, by the same token, when we don't feel the excess (and I am contending, mind, that in "The Awkward Age" the multiplicity yields to the order) how do we know that the measure

314

not recorded, the notch not reached, does represent adequacy or satiety? The mere feeling helps us for certain degrees of congestion, but for exact science, that is for the criticism of "fine" art, we want the notation. The notation, however, is what we lack, and the verdict of the mere feeling is liable to fluctuate. In other words an imputed defect is never, at the worst, disengageable, or other than matter for appreciation—to come back to my claim for that felicity of the dramatist's case that his synthetic "whole" *is* his form, the only one we have to do with. I like to profit in his company by the fact that if our art has certainly, for the impression it produces, to defer to the rise and fall, in the critical temperature, of the telltale mercury, it still hasn't to reckon with the engraved thermometer-face.

What Maisie Knew

I RECOGNISE AGAIN, FOR THE FIRST OF THESE THREE Tales, another instance of the growth of the "great oak" from the little acorn; since "What Maisie Knew" is at least a tree that spreads beyond any provision its small germ might on a first handling have appeared likely to make for it. The accidental mention had been made to me of the manner in which the situation of some luckless child of a divorced couple was affected, under my informant's eyes, by the re-marriage of one of its parents—I forget which; so that, thanks to the limited desire for its company expressed by the step-parent, the law of its little life, its being entertained in rotation by its father and its mother, wouldn't easily prevail. Whereas each of these persons had at first vindictively desired to keep it from the other, so at present the re-married relative sought now rather to be rid of it—that is to leave it as much as possible, and beyond the appointed times and seasons, on the hands of the adversary; which malpractice, resented by the latter as bad faith, would of course be repaid and avenged by an equal treachery. The wretched infant was thus to find itself practically dis-owned, rebounding from racquet to racquet like a tennis-ball or a shuttlecock. This figure could but touch the fancy to the quick and strike one as the beginning of a story—a story commanding a great choice of developments. I recollect, however, promptly thinking that for a proper symmetry the second parent should marry too—which in the case named to me indeed would probably soon occur, and was in any case what the ideal of the situation required. The second step-parent would have but to be correspondingly incommoded by obliga-tions to the offspring of a hated predecessor for the misfortune of the little victim to become altogether exemplary. The business would ac-cordingly be sad enough, yet I am not sure its possibility of interest would so much have appealed to me had I not soon felt that the ugly facts, so stated or conceived, by no means constituted the whole appeal.

The light of an imagination touched by them couldn't help therefore projecting a further ray, thanks to which it became rather quaintly clear that, not less than the chance of misery and of a degraded state, the chance of happiness and of an improved state might be here involved for the child, round about whom the complexity of life would thus turn to fineness, to richness—and indeed would have but so to turn for the small creature to be steeped in security and ease. Sketchily clustered even, these elements gave out the vague pictorial glow which forms the first appeal of a living "subject" to the painter's consciousness; but the glimmer became intense as I proceeded to a further analysis. The further analysis is for that matter almost always the torch of rapture and victory, as the artist's firm hand grasps and plays it—I mean, naturally, of the smothered rapture and the obscure victory, enjoyed and celebrated not in the street but before some innermost shrine; the odds being a hundred to one, in almost any connexion, that it doesn't arrive by any easy first process at the *best* residuum of truth. That was the charm, sensibly, of the picture thus at first confusedly showing; the elements so couldn't but flush, to their very surface, with some deeper depth of irony than the mere obvious. It lurked in the crude postulate like a buried scent; the more the attention hovered the more aware it became of the fragrance. To which I may add that the more I scratched the surface and penetrated, the more potent, to the intellectual nostril, became this virtue. At last, accordingly, the residuum, as I have called it, reached, I was in presence of the red dramatic spark that glowed at the core of my vision and that, as I gently blew upon it, burned higher and clearer. This precious particle was the *full* ironic truth—the most interesting item to be read into the child's situation. For satisfaction of the mind, in other words, the small expanding consciousness would have to be saved, have to become presentable as a register of impressions; and saved by the experience of certain advantages, by some enjoyed profit and some achieved confidence, rather than coarsened, blurred, sterilised, by ignorance and pain. This better state, in the young life, would reside in the exercise of a function other than that of disconcerting the selfishness of its parents—which was all that had on the face of the matter seemed reserved to it in the way of criticism applied to their rupture. The early relation would be exchanged for a later; instead of simply submitting to the inherited tie and the imposed complication, of suffering from them, our little wonder-working agent would create, without design, quite fresh elements of this order—contribute, that is, to the formation of a fresh tie, from which it would then (and for all the world as if through a small demonic foresight) proceed to derive great profit.

This is but to say that the light in which the vision so readily grew to a wholeness was that of a second marriage on both sides; the father having, in the freedom of divorce, but to take another wife, as well as the mother, under a like licence, another husband, for the case to begin, at least, to stand beautifully on its feet. There would be thus a perfect logic for what might come—come even with the mere attribution of a certain sensibility (if but a mere relative fineness) to either of the new parties. Say the prime cause making for the ultimate attempt to shirk on one side or the other, and better still if on both, a due share of the decreed burden should have been, after all, in each progenitor, a constitutional inaptitude of *any* burden, and a base intolerance of it: we should thus get a motive not requiring, but happily dispensing with, too particular a perversity in the step-parents. The child seen as creating by the fact of its forlornness a relation between its step-parents, the more intimate the better, dramatically speaking; the child, by the mere appeal of neglectedness and the mere consciousness of relief, weaving about, with the best faith in the world, the close web of sophistication; the child becoming a centre and pretext for a fresh system of misbehaviour, a system moreover of a nature to spread and ramify: *there* would be the "full" irony, there the promising theme into which the hint I had originally picked up would logically flower. No themes are so human as those that reflect for us, out of the confusion of life, the close connexion of bliss and bale, of the things that help with the things that hurt, so dangling before us for ever that bright hard medal, of so strange an alloy, one face of which is somebody's right and ease and the other somebody's pain and wrong. To live with all intensity and perplexity and felicity in its terribly mixed little world would thus be the part of my interesting small mortal; bringing people together who would be at least more correctly separate; keeping people separate who would be at least more correctly together; flourishing, to a degree, at the cost of many conventions and proprieties, even decencies; really keeping the torch of virtue alive in an air tending infinitely to smother it; really in short making confusion worse confounded by drawing some stray fragrance of an ideal across the scent of selfishness, by sowing on barren strands, through the mere fact of presence, the seed of the moral life.

All this would be to say, I at once recognised, that my light vessel of consciousness, swaying in such a draught, couldn't be with verisimilitude a rude little boy; since, beyond the fact that little boys are never so "present," the sensibility of the female young is indubitably, for early youth, the greater, and my plan would call, on the part of my protagonist, for "no end" of sensibility. I might impute that amount of it without extravagance to a slip of a girl whose faculties should have been well shaken up; but I should have so to depend on its action to keep my story clear that I must be able to show it in all assurance as naturally intense. To this end I should have of course to suppose for my heroine dispositions originally promising, but above all I should have to invest her with perceptions easily and almost infinitely quickened. So handsomely fitted out, yet not in a manner too grossly to affront probability, she might well see me through the whole course of my design; which design, more and more attractive as I turned it over, and dignified by the most delightful difficulty, would be to make and to keep her so limited consciousness the very field of my picture while at the same time guarding with care the integrity of the objects represented. With the charm of this possibility, therefore, the project for "Maisie" rounded itself and loomed large—any subject looming large, for that matter, I am bound to add, from the moment one is ridden by the law of entire expression. I have already elsewhere noted, I think, that the memory of my own work preserves for me no theme that, at some moment or other of its development, and always only waiting for the right connexion or chance, hasn't signally refused to remain humble, even (or perhaps all the more resentfully) when fondly selected for its conscious and hopeless humility. Once "out," like a house-dog of a temper above confinement, it defies the mere whistle, it roams, it hunts, it seeks out and "sees" life; it can be brought back but by hand and then only to take its futile thrashing. It wasn't at any rate for an idea seen in the light I here glance at not to have due warrant of its value— how could the value of a scheme so finely workable *not* be great? The one presented register of the whole complexity would be the play of the child's confused and obscure notation of it, and yet the whole, as I say, should be unmistakeably, should be honourably there, seen through the faint intelligence, or at the least attested by the imponderable presence, and still advertising its sense.

I recall that my first view of this neat possibility was as the attaching problem of the picture restricted (while yet achieving, as I say, completeness and coherency) to what the child might be conceived to have *understood*—to have been able to interpret and appreciate. Further reflexion and experiment showed me my subject strangled in that extreme of rigour. The infant mind would at the best leave great gaps and voids; so that with a systematic surface possibly beyond reproach we should nevertheless fail of clearness of sense. I should have to stretch the matter to what my wondering witness materially and inevitably *saw*; a great deal of which quantity she either wouldn't understand at all or would quite misunderstand—and on those lines, only on those, my task would be prettily cut out. To that then I settled—to the question of giving it *all*, the whole situation surrounding her, but of giving it only through the occasions and connexions of her proximity and her attention; only as it might pass before her and appeal to her, as it might touch her and affect her, for better or worse, for perceptive gain or perceptive loss: so that we fellow witnesses, we not more invited but only more expert critics, should feel in strong possession of it. This would be, to begin with, a plan of absolutely definite and measurable application—that in itself always a mark of beauty; and I have been interested to find on reperusal of the work that some such controlling grace successfully rules it. Nothing could be more "done," I think, in the light of its happiest intention; and this in spite of an appearance that at moments obscures my consistency. Small children have many more perceptions than they have terms to translate them; their vision is at any moment much richer, their apprehension even constantly stronger, than their prompt, their at all producible, vocabulary. Amusing therefore as it might at the first blush have seemed to restrict myself in this case to the terms as well as to the experience, it became at once plain that such an attempt would fail. Maisie's terms accordingly play their part—since her simpler conclusions quite depend on them; but our own commentary constantly attends and amplifies. This it is that on occasion, doubtless, seems to represent us as going so "behind" the facts of her spectacle as to exaggerate the activity of her relation to them. The difference here is but of a shade: it is her relation, her activity of spirit, that determines all our own concern—we simply take advantage of these things better than she herself. Only, even though it is her interest that mainly makes matters interesting for us, we inevitably note this in figures that are not yet at her command and that are nevertheless required whenever those aspects about her and those parts of her experience that she understands darken off into others that she rather tormentedly misses. All of which gave me a high firm logic to observe; supplied the force for which the straightener of almost any tangle is grateful while he labours, the sense of pulling at threads intrinsically worth it—strong enough and fine enough and entire enough.

Of course, beyond this, was another and well-nigh equal charm—equal in spite of its being almost independent of the acute constructional, the endless expressional question. This was the quite different question of the particular kind of truth of resistance I might be able to impute to my central figure—*some* intensity, some continuity of resistance being naturally of the essence of the subject. Successfully to resist (to resist, that is, the strain of observation and the assault of experience) what would that be, on the part of so young a person, but to remain fresh, and still fresh, and to have even a freshness to communicate?—the case being with Maisie to the end that she treats her friends to the rich little spectacle of objects embalmed in her wonder. She wonders, in other words, to the end, to the death—the death of her childhood, properly speaking; after which (with the inevitable shift, sooner or later, of her point of view) her situation will change and become another affair, subject to other measurements and with a new centre altogether. The particular reaction that will have led her to that point, and that it has been of an exquisite interest to study in her, will have spent itself; there will be another scale, another perspective, another horizon. Our business meanwhile therefore is to extract from her current reaction whatever it may be worth; and for that matter we recognise in it the highest exhibitional virtue. Truly, I reflect, if the theme had had no other beauty it would still have had this rare and distinguished one of its so expressing the variety of the child's values. She is not only the extraordinary "ironic centre" I have already noted; she has the wonderful importance of shedding a light far beyond any reach of her comprehension; of lending to poorer persons and things, by the mere fact of their being involved with her and by the special scale she creates for them, a precious element of dignity. I lose myself, truly, in appreciation of my theme on noting what she does by her "freshness" for appearances in themselves vulgar and empty enough. They become, as she deals with them, the stuff of poetry and tragedy and art; she has simply to wonder, as I say, about them, and they begin to have meanings, aspects, solidities, connexions—connexions with the "universal!"—that they could scarce have hoped for. Ida Farange alone, so to speak, or Beale alone, that is either of them otherwise connected—what intensity, what "objectivity" (the most developed degree of *being* anyhow thinkable for them) would they have? How would they repay at all the favour of our attention?

Maisie makes them portentous all by the play of her good faith, makes her mother above all, to my vision—unless I have wholly failed to render it—concrete, immense and awful, so that we get, for our profit, and get by an economy of process interesting in itself, the thoroughly pictured creature, the striking figured symbol. At two points in particular, I seem to recognise, we enjoy at its maximum this effect of associational magic. The passage in which her father's terms of intercourse with the insinuating but so strange and unattractive lady whom he has had the detestable levity to whisk her off to see late at night, is a signal example of the all but incalculable way in which interest may be constituted. The facts involved are that Beale Farange is ignoble, that the friend to whom he introduces his daughter is deplorable, and that from the commerce of the two, *as* the two merely, we would fain avert our heads. Yet the thing has but to become a part of the child's bewilderment for these small sterilities to drop from it and for the *scene* to emerge and prevail—vivid, special, wrought hard, to the hardness of the unforgettable; the scene that is exactly what Beale and Ida and Mrs. Cuddon, and even Sir Claude and Mrs. Beale, would never for a moment have succeeded in making their scant unredeemed importances—namely *appreciable*. I find another instance in the episode of Maisie's unprepared encounter, while walking in the Park with Sir Claude, of her mother and that beguiled attendant of her mother, the encouraging, the appealing "Captain," to whom this lady contrives to commit her for twenty minutes while she herself deals with the second husband. The human substance here would have seemed in advance well-nigh too poor for conversion, the three "mature" figures of too short a radiation, too stupid (*so* stupid it was for Sir Claude to have married Ida!) too vain, too thin, for any clear application; but promptly, immediately, the child's own importance, spreading and contagiously acting, has determined the *total* value otherwise. Nothing of course, meanwhile, is an older story to the observer of manners and the painter of life than the grotesque finality with which such terms as "painful," "unpleasant" and "disgusting" are often applied to his results; to that degree, in truth, that the free use of them as weightily conclusive again and again re-enforces his estimate of the critical sense of circles in which they artlessly flourish. Of course under that superstition I was punctually to have had read to me the lesson that the "mixing-up" of a child with anything unpleasant confessed itself an aggravation of the unpleasantness, and that nothing could well be more disgusting than to attribute to Maisie so intimate an "acquaintance" with the gross immoralities surrounding her.

The only thing to say of such lucidities is that, however one may have "discounted" in advance, and as once for all, their general radiance, one is disappointed if the hour for them, in the particular connexion, doesn't strike—they so keep before us elements with which even the most sedate philosopher must always reckon. The painter of life has indeed work cut out for him when a considerable part of life offers itself in the guise of that sapience. The effort really to see and really to represent is no idle business in face of the *constant* force that makes for muddlement. The great thing is indeed that the muddled state too is one of the very sharpest of the realities, that it also has colour and form and character, has often in fact a broad and rich comicality, many of the signs and values of the appreciable. Thus it was to be, for example, I might gather, that the very principle of Maisie's appeal, her undestroyed freshness, in other words that vivacity of intelligence by which she indeed does vibrate in the infected air, indeed does flourish in her immoral world, may pass for a barren and senseless thing, or at best a negligible one. For nobody to whom life at large is *easily* interesting do the finer, the shyer, the more anxious small vibrations, fine and shy and anxious with the passion that precedes knowledge, succeed in being negligible: which is doubtless one of many reasons why the passage between the child and the kindly, friendly, ugly gentleman who, seated with her in Kensington Gardens under a spreading tree, positively answers to her for her mother as no one has ever answered, and so stirs her, filially and morally, as she has never been stirred, throws into highest relief, to my sense at least, the side on which the subject is strong, and becomes the type-passage—other advantages certainly aiding, as I may say—for the expression of its beauty. The active, contributive close-circling wonder, as I have called it, in which the child's identity is guarded and preserved, and which makes her case remarkable exactly by the weight of the tax on it, provides distinction for her, provides vitality and variety, through the operation of the tax—which would have done comparatively little for us hadn't it been monstrous. A pity for us surely to have been deprived of this just reflexion. "Maisie" is of 1907.

I pass by, for the moment, the second of these compositions, finding in the third, which again deals with the experience of a very young person, a connexion more immediate; and this even at the risk of seeming to undermine my remark of a few pages back as to the comparative sensibility of the sexes. My urchin of "The Pupil" (1891) has sensibility in abundance, it would seem—and yet preserves in spite of it, I judge, his strong little male quality. But there are fifty things to say here; which indeed rush upon me within my present close limits in such a cloud as to demand much clearance. This is perhaps indeed but the aftersense of the assault made on my mind, as I perfectly recall, by every aspect of the original vision, which struck me as abounding in aspects. It lives again for me, this vision, as it first alighted; though the inimitable prime flutter, the air as of an ineffable sign made by the immediate beat of the wings of the poised figure of fancy that has just settled, is one of those guarantees of value that can never be re-captured. The sign has been made to the seer only—it is *his* queer affair; of which any report to others, not as yet involved, has but the same effect of flatness as attends, amid a group fathered under the canopy of night, any stray allusion to a shooting star. The miracle, since miracle it seems, is all for the candid exclaimer. The miracle for the author of "The Pupil," at any rate, was when, years ago, one summer day, in a very hot Italian railway-carriage, which stopped and dawdled everywhere, favouring conversation, a friend with whom I shared it, a doctor of medicine who had come from a far country to settle in Florence, happened to speak to me of a wonderful American family, an odd adventurous, extravagant band, of high but rather unauthenticated pretensions, the most interesting member of which was a small boy, acute and precocious, afflicted with a heart of weak action, but beautifully intelligent, who saw their prowling precarious life exactly as it was, and measured and judged it, and measured and judged *them,* all round, ever so quaintly; presenting himself in short as an extraordinary little person. Here was more than enough for a summer's day even in old Italy—here was a thumping windfall. No process and no steps intervened: I *saw*, on the spot, little Morgan Moreen, I saw all the rest of the Moreens; I felt, to the last delicacy, the nature of my young friend's relation with them (he had become at once my young friend) and, by the same stroke, to its uttermost fine throb, the subjection to *him* of the beguiled, bewildered, defrauded, unremunerated, yet after all richly repaid youth who would to a certainty, under stress of compassion, embark with the tribe on tutorship, and whose edifying connexion with it would be my leading document.

This must serve as my account of the origin of "The Pupil": it will commend itself, I feel, to all imaginative and projective persons who have had—and what imaginative and projective person hasn't?—any like experience of the suddenly-determined *absolute* of perception. The whole cluster of items forming the image is on these occasions born at once; the parts are not pieced together, they conspire and interdepend; but what it really comes to, no doubt, is that at a simple touch an old latent and dormant impression, a buried germ, implanted by experience and then forgotten, flashes to the surface as a fish, with a single "squirm," rises to the baited hook, and there meets instantly the vivifying ray. I remember at all events having no doubt of anything or anyone here; the vision kept to the end its ease and its charm; it worked itself out with confidence. These are minor matters when the question is of minor results; yet almost any assured and downright imaginative

act is—granted the sort of record in which I here indulge—worth
fondly commemorating. One cherishes, after the fact, any proved case
of the independent life of the imagination; above all if by that faculty
one has been appointed mainly to live. We are then *never* detached
from the question of what it may out of simple charity do for us.
Besides which, in relation to the poor Moreens, innumerable notes, as
I have intimated, all equally urging their relevance, press here to the
front. The general adventure of the little composition itself—for singular things were to happen to it, though among such importunities
not the most worth noting now—would be, occasion favouring, a
thing to live over; moving as one did, roundabout it, in I scarce know
what thick and coloured air of slightly tarnished anecdote, of dim
association, of casual confused romance; a compound defying analysis, but truly, for the social chronicler, any student in especial of the
copious "cosmopolite" legend, a boundless and tangled, but highly
explorable, garden. Why, somehow—these were the intensifying
questions—did one see the Moreens, whom I place at Nice, at Venice,
in Paris, as of the special essence of the little old miscellaneous cosmopolite Florence, the Florence of other, of irrecoverable years, the
restless yet withal so convenient scene of a society that has passed
away for ever with all its faded ghosts and fragile relics; immaterial
presences that have quite ceased to revisit (trust an old romancer's, an
old pious observer's fine sense to have made sure of it!) walks and
prospects once sacred and shaded, but now laid bare, gaping wide,
despoiled of their past and unfriendly to any appreciation of it?—
through which the unconscious Barbarians troop with the regularity
and passivity of "supplies," or other promiscuous goods, prepaid and
forwarded.

They had nothing to do, the dear Moreens, with this dreadful
period, any more than I, as occupied and charmed with them, was
humiliatingly subject to it; we were, all together, of a better romantic
age and faith; we referred ourselves, with our highest complacency,
to the classic years of the great Americano-European legend; the
years of limited communication, of monstrous and unattenuated contrast, of prodigious and unrecorded adventure. The comparatively
brief but infinitely rich "cycle" of romance embedded in the earlier,
the very early American reactions and returns (mediæval in the sense
of being, at most, of the mid-century), what does it resemble to-day
but a gold-mine overgrown and smothered, dislocated, and no longer
workable?—all for want of the right indications for sounding, the
right implements for digging, doubtless even of the right workmen,
those with the right tradition and "feeling," for the job. The most

extraordinary things appear to have happened, during that golden age, in the "old" countries—in Asia and Africa as well as in Europe— to the candid children of the West, things admirably incongruous and incredible; but no story of all the list was to find its just interpreter, and nothing is now more probable than that every key to interpretation has been lost. The modern reporter's big brushes, attached to broom-handles that match the height of his sky-scrapers, would sadly besmear the fine parchment of our missing record. We were to lose, clearly, at any rate, a vast body of precious anecdote, a long gallery of wonderful portraits, an array of the oddest possible figures in the oddest possible attitudes. The Moreens were of the family then of the great unstudied precursors—poor and shabby members, no doubt; dim and superseded types. I must add indeed that, such as they were, or as they may at present incoherently appear, I don't pretend really to have "done" them; all I have given in "The Pupil" is little Morgan's troubled vision of them as reflected in the vision, also troubled enough, of his devoted friend. The manner of the thing may thus illustrate the author's incorrigible taste for gradations and superpositions of effect; his love, when it is a question of a picture, of anything that makes for proportion and perspective, that contributes to a view of *all* the dimensions. Addicted to seeing "through"—one thing through another, accordingly, and still other things through *that*—he takes, too greedily perhaps, on any errand, as many things as possible by the way. It is after this fashion that he incurs the stigma of labouring uncannily for a certain fulness of truth—truth diffused, distributed and, as it were, atmospheric.

The second in order of these fictions speaks for itself, I think, so frankly as scarce to suffer further expatiation. Its origin is written upon it large, and the idea it puts into play so abides in one of the commonest and most taken-for-granted of London impressions that some such experimentally-figured situation as that of "In the Cage" must again and again have flowered (granted the grain of observation) in generous minds. It had become for me, at any rate, an old story by the time (1898) I cast it into this particular form. The postal-telegraph office in general, and above all the small local office of one's immediate neighbourhood, scene of the transaction of so much of one's daily business, haunt of one's needs and one's duties, of one's labours and one's patiences, almost of one's rewards and one's disappointments, one's joys and one's sorrows, had ever had, to my sense, so much of London to give out, so much of its huge perpetual story to tell, that any momentary wait there seemed to take place in a strong social draught, the stiffest possible breeze of the human comedy. One had of course in these connexions one's especial resort, the office nearest one's own door, where one had come to enjoy in a manner the fruits of frequentation and the amenities of intercourse. So had grown up, for speculation—prone as one's mind had ever been to that form of waste—the question of what it might "mean," wherever the admirable service was installed, for confined and cramped and yet considerably tutored young officials of either sex to be made so free, intellectually, of a range of experience otherwise quite closed to them. This wonderment, once the spark was kindled, became an amusement, or an obsession, like another; though falling indeed, at the best, no doubt, but into that deepest abyss of all the wonderments that break out for the student of great cities. From the moment that he *is* a student, this most beset of critics, his danger is inevitably of imputing to too many others, right and left, the critical impulse and the acuter vision—so very long may it take him to learn that the mass of mankind are banded, probably by the sanest of instincts, to defend themselves to the death against any such vitiation of their simplicity. To criticise is to appreciate, to appropriate, to take intellectual possession, to establish in fine a relation with the criticised thing and make it one's own. The large intellectual appetite projects itself thus on many things, while the small—not better advised, but unconscious of need for advice—projects itself on few.

Admirable thus its economic instinct; it is curious of nothing that it hasn't vital use for. You may starve in London, it is clear, without discovering a use for any theory of the more equal division of victuals—which is moreover exactly what it would appear that thousands of the non-speculative annually do. Their example is much to the point, in the light of all the barren trouble they are saved; but somehow, after all, it gives no pause to the "artist," to the morbid, imagination. That rash, that idle faculty continues to abound in questions, and to supply answers to as many of them as possible; all of which makes a great occupation for idleness. To the fantastic scale on which this last-named state may, in favoring conditions, organise itself, to the activities it may practise when the favouring conditions happen to crop up in Mayfair or in Kensington, our portrayal of the caged telegraphist may well appear a proper little monument. The composition before us tells in fact clearly enough, it seems to me, the story of its growth; and relevance will probably be found in any moral it may pluck—by which I mean any moral the impulse to have framed it may pluck—from the vice of reading rank subtleties into simple souls and reckless expenditure into thrifty ones. The matter comes back again, I fear, but to the author's irrepressible and insatiable, his extravagant and immoral, interest in personal character and in the "nature" of a mind, of almost any mind the heaving little sea of his subject may cast up—as to which these remarks have already, in other connexions, recorded his apology: all without prejudice to such shrines and stations of penance as still shall enliven our way. The range of wonderment attributed in our tale to the young woman employed at Cocker's differs little in essence from the speculative thread on which the pearls of Maisie's experience, in this same volume—pearls of so strange an iridescence—are mostly strung. She wonders, putting it simply, very much as Morgan Moreen wonders; and they all wonder, for that matter, very much after the fashion of our portentous little Hyacinth of "The Princess Casamassima," tainted to the core, as we have seen him, with the trick of mental reaction on the things about him and fairly staggering under the appropriations, as I have called them, that he owes to the critical spirit. He collapses, poor Hyacinth, like a thief at night, overcharged with treasures of reflexion and spoils of passion of which he can give, in his poverty and obscurity, no honest account.

It is much in this manner, we see on analysis, that Morgan Moreen breaks down—his burden indeed not so heavy, but his strength so much less formed. The two little spirits of maidens, in the group, bear up, oddly enough, beyond those of their brothers; but the just remark for each of these small exhibited lives is of course that, in the longer or the shorter piece, they are actively, are luxuriously, lived. The luxury is that of the number of their moral vibrations, well-nigh unrestricted—not that of an account at the grocer's: whatever it be, at any rate, it makes them, as examples and "cases," rare. My brooding telegraphist may be in fact, on her ground of ingenuity, scarcely more thinkable than desirable; yet if I have made her but a libel, up and down the city, on an estimable class, I feel it still something to have admonished that class, even though obscurely enough, of neglected interests and undivined occasions. My central spirit, in the anecdote, is, for verisimilitude, I grant, too ardent a focus of divination; but without this excess the phenomena detailed would have lacked their principle of cohesion. The action of the drama is simply the girl's "subjective" adventure—that of her quite definitely winged intelligence; just as the catastrophe, just as the solution, depends on her winged wit. Why, however, should I explain further—for a case that, modestly as it would seem to present itself, has yet already whirled us so far? A course of incident complicated by the intervention of winged wit—which is here, as I say, confessed to—would be generally expected, I judge, to commit me to the explanation of everything.

But from that undertaking I shrink, and take refuge instead, for an instant, in a much looser privilege.

If I speak, as just above, of the *action* embodied, each time, in these so "quiet" recitals, it is under renewed recognition of the inveterate instinct with which they keep conforming to the "scenic" law. They demean themselves for all the world—they quite insist on it, that is, whenever they have a chance—as little constituted dramas, little exhibitions founded on the logic of the "scene," the unit of the scene, the general scenic consistency, and knowing little more than that. To read them over has been to find them on this ground never at fault. The process repeats and renews itself, moving in the light it has once for all adopted. These finer idiosyncracies of a literary form seem to be regarded as outside the scope of criticism—small reference to them do I remember ever to have met; such surprises of re-perusal, such recoveries of old fundamental intention, such moments of almost ruefully independent discrimination, would doubtless in that case not have waylaid my steps. Going over the pages here placed together has been for me, at all events, quite to watch the scenic system at play. The treatment by "scene," regularly, quite rhythmically recurs; the intervals between, the massing of the elements to a different effect and by a quite other law, remain, in this fashion, all preparative, just as the scenic occasions in themselves become, at a given moment, illustrative, each of the agents, true to its function, taking up the theme from the other very much as the fiddles, in an orchestra, may take it up from the cornets and flutes, or the wind-instruments take it up from the violins. The point, however, is that the scenic passages are *wholly* and logically scenic, having for their rule of beauty the principle of the "conduct," the organic development, of a scene—the entire succession of values that flower and bear fruit on ground solidly laid for them. The great advantage for the total effect is that we feel, with the definite alternation, how the theme *is* being treated. That is we feel it when, in such tangled connexions, we happen to care. I shouldn't really go on as if this were the case with many readers.

The Aspern Papers

I NOT ONLY RECOVER WITH EASE, BUT I DELIGHT TO RE-
call the first impulse given to the idea of "The Aspern Papers."
It is at the same time true that my present mention of it may perhaps
too effectually dispose of any complacent claim to my having "found"
the situation. Not that I quite know indeed what situations the seeking
fabulist does "find"; he seeks them enough assuredly, but his discoveries are, like those of the navigator, the chemist, the biologist, scarce
more than alert recognitions. He *comes upon* the interesting thing as
Columbus came upon the isle of San Salvador, because he had moved
in the right direction for it—also because he knew, with the encounter,
what "making land" then and there represented. Nature had so
placed it, to profit—if as profit we may measure the matter!—by his
fine unrest, just as history, "literary history" we in this connexion call
it, had in an out-of-the-way corner of the great garden of life thrown off
a curious flower that I was to feel worth gathering as soon as I saw it. I
got wind of my positive fact, I followed the scent. It was in Florence
years ago; which is precisely, of the whole matter, what I like most to
remember. The air of the old-time Italy invests it, a mixture that on the
faintest invitation I rejoice again to inhale—and this in spite of the
mere cold renewal, ever, of the infirm side of that felicity, the sense, in
the whole element, of things too numerous, too deep, too obscure, too
strange, or even simply too beautiful, for any ease of intellectual relation. One must pay one's self largely with words, I think, one must
induce almost any "Italian subject" to *make believe* it gives up its secret,
in order to keep at all on working—or call them perhaps rather playing—terms with the general impression. We entertain it thus, the
impression, by the aid of a merciful convention which resembles the
fashion of our intercourse with Iberians or Orientals whose form of
courtesy places everything they have at our disposal. We thank them
and call upon them, but without acting on their professions. The offer
has been too large and our assurance is too small; we peep at most into

two or three of the chambers of their hospitality, with the rest of the case stretching beyond our ken and escaping our penetration. The pious fiction suffices; we have entered, we have seen, we are charmed. So, right and left, in Italy—before the great historic complexity at least—penetration fails; we scratch at the extensive surface, we meet the perfunctory smile, we hang about in the golden air. But we exaggerate our gathered values only if we are eminently witless. It is fortunately the exhibition in all the world before which, as admirers, we can most remain superficial without feeling silly.

All of which I note, however, perhaps with too scant relevance to the inexhaustible charm of Roman and Florentine memories. Off the ground, at a distance, our fond indifference to being "silly" grows fonder still; the working convention, as I have called it—the convention of the real revelations and surrenders on one side and the real immersions and appreciations on the other—has not only nothing to keep it down, but every glimpse of contrast, every pang of exile and every nostalgic twinge to keep it up. These latter haunting presences in fact, let me note, almost reduce at first to a mere blurred, sad, scarcely consolable vision this present revisiting, re-appropriating impulse. There are parts of one's past, evidently, that bask consentingly and serenely enough in the light of other days—which is but the intensity of thought; and there are other parts that take it as with agitation and pain, a troubled consciousness that heaves as with the disorder of drinking it deeply in. So it is at any rate, fairly in too thick and rich a retrospect, that I see my old Venice of "The Aspern Papers," that I see the still earlier one of Jeffrey Aspern himself, and that I see even the comparatively recent Florence that was to drop into my ear the solicitation of these things. I would fain "lay it on" thick for the very love of them—that at least I may profess; and, with the ground of this desire frankly admitted, something that somehow makes, in the whole story, for a romantic harmony. I have had occasion in the course of these remarks to define my sense of the romantic, and am glad to encounter again here an instance of that virtue as I understand it. I shall presently say why this small case so ranges itself, but must first refer more exactly to the thrill of appreciation it was immediately to excite in me. I saw it somehow at the very first blush as romantic—for the use, of course I mean, I should certainly have had to make of it—that Jane Clairmont, the half-sister of Mary Godwin, Shelley's second wife and for a while the intimate friend of Byron and the mother of his daughter Allegra, should have been living on in Florence, where she had long lived, up to our own day, and that in fact, had I happened to hear of her but a little sooner, I might have seen her in the flesh. The question of whether I should have wished to do so was another matter—the question of whether I shouldn't have preferred to keep her preciously unseen, to run no risk, in other words, by too rude a choice, of depreciating that romance-value which, as I say, it was instantly inevitable to attach (through association above all, with another signal circumstance) to her long survival.

I had luckily not had to deal with the difficult option; difficult in such a case by reason of that odd law which somehow always makes the minimum of valid suggestion serve the man of imagination better than the maximum. The historian, essentially, wants more documents than he can really use; the dramatist only wants more liberties than he can really take. Nothing, fortunately, however, had, as the case stood, depended on my delicacy; I might have "looked up" Miss Clairmont in previous years had I been earlier informed—the silence about her seemed full of the "irony of fate"; but I felt myself more concerned with the mere strong fact of her having testified for the reality and the closeness of our relation to the past than with any question of the particular sort of person I might have flattered myself I "found." I had certainly at the very least been saved the undue simplicity of pretending to read meanings into things absolutely sealed and beyond test or proof—to tap a fount of waters that couldn't possibly not have run dry. The thrill of learning that she had "overlapped," and by so much, and the wonder of my having doubtless at several earlier seasons passed again and again, all unknowing, the door of her house, where she sat above, within call and in her habit as she lived, these things gave me all I wanted; I seem to remember in fact that my more or less immediately recognising that I positively oughtn't—"for anything to come of it"— to have wanted more. I saw, quickly, how something might come of it *thus*; whereas a fine instinct told me that the effect of a nearer view of the case (the case of the overlapping) would probably have had to be quite differently calculable. It was really with another item of knowledge, however, that I measured the mistake I should have made in waking up sooner to the question of opportunity. That item consisted of the action taken on the premises by a person who *had* waked up in time, and the legend of whose consequent adventure, as a few spoken words put it before me, at once kindled a flame. This gentleman, an American of long ago, an ardent Shelleyite, a singularly marked figure and himself in the highest degree a subject for a free sketch—I had known him a little, but there is not a reflected glint of him in "The Aspern Papers"—was named to me as having made interest with Miss Clairmont to be accepted as a lodger on the calculation that she would have Shelley documents for which, in the possibly not remote event of

332

her death, he would thus enjoy priority of chance to treat with her representatives. He had at any rate, according to the legend, become, on earnest Shelley grounds, her yearning, though also her highly diplomatic, *pensionnaire*—but without gathering, as was to befall, the fruit of his design.

Legend here dropped to another key; it remained in a manner interesting, but became of my ear a trifle coarse, or at least rather vague and obscure. It mentioned a younger female relative of the ancient woman as a person who, for a queer climax, had had to be dealt with; it flickered so for a moment and then, as a light, to my great relief, quite went out. It had flickered indeed but at the best— yet had flickered enough to give me my "facts," bare facts of intimation; which, scant handful though they were, were more distinct and more numerous than I mostly *like* facts: like them, that is, as we say of an etcher's progressive subject, in an early "state." Nine tenths of the artist's interest in them is that of what he shall add to them and how he shall turn them. Mine, however, in the connexion I speak of, had fortunately got away from me, and quite of their own movement, in time not to crush me. So it was, at all events, that my imagination preserved power to react under the mere essential charm—that, I mean, of a final scene of the rich dim Shelley drama played out in the very theatre of our own "modernity." This was the beauty that appealed to me; there had been, so to speak, a forward continuity, from the actual man, the divine poet, on; and the curious, the ingenious, the admirable thing would be to throw it backward again, to compress—squeezing it hard!—the connexion that had drawn itself out, and convert so the stretched relation into a value of nearness on our own part. In short I saw my chance as admirable, and one reason, when the direction is right, may serve as well as fifty; but if I "took over," as I say, everything that was of the essence, I stayed my hand for the rest. The Italian side of the legend closely clung; if only because the so possible terms of my Juliana's life in the Italy of other days could make conceivable for her the fortunate privacy, the long uninvaded and uninterviewed state on which I represent her situation as founded. Yes, a surviving unexploited unparagraphed Juliana was up to a quarter of a century since still supposeable—as much so as any such buried treasure, any such grave unprofaned, would defy probability now. And then the case had the air of the past just in the degree in which that air, I confess, most appeals to me—when the region over which it hangs is far enough away without being too far.

I delight in a palpable imaginable *visitable* past—in the nearer distances and the clearer mysteries, the marks and signs of a world we may reach over to as by making a long arm we grasp an object at the other end of our own table. The table is the one, the common expanse, and where we lean, so stretching, we find it firm and continuous. That, to my imagination, is the past fragrant of all, or of almost all, the poetry of the thing outlived and lost and gone, and yet in which the precious element of closeness, telling so of connexions but tasting so of differences, remains appreciable. With more moves back the element of the appreciable shrinks—just as the charm of looking over a garden-wall into another garden breaks down when successions of walls appear. The other gardens, those still beyond, may be there, but even by use of our longest ladder we are baffled and bewildered—the view is mainly a view of barriers. The one partition makes the place we have wondered about *other*, both richly and recogniseably so; but who shall pretend to impute an effect of composition to the twenty? We are divided of course between liking to feel the past strange and liking to feel it familiar; the difficulty is, for intensity, to catch it at the moment when the scales of the balance hang with the right evenness. I say for intensity, for we may profit by them in other aspects enough if we are content to measure or to feel loosely. It would take me too far, however, to tell why the particular afternoon light that I thus call intense rests clearer to my sense on the Byronic age, as I conveniently name it, than on periods more protected by the "dignity" of history. With the times beyond, intrinsically more "strange," the tender grace, for the backward vision, has faded, the afternoon darkened; for any time nearer to us the special effect hasn't begun. So there, to put the matter crudely, is the appeal I fondly recognise, an appeal residing doubtless more in the "special effect," in some deep associational force, than in a virtue more intrinsic. I am afraid I must add, since I allow myself so much to fantasticate, that the impulse had more than once taken me to project the Byronic age and the afternoon light across the great sea, to see in short whether association would carry so far and what the young century might pass for on that side of the modern world where it was not only itself so irremediably youngest, but was bound up with youth in everything else. There was a refinement of curiosity in this imputation of a golden strangeness to American social facts—though I cannot pretend, I fear, that there was any greater wisdom.

Since what it had come to then was, harmlessly enough, cultivating a sense of the past under that close protection, it was natural, it was fond and filial, to wonder if a few of the distilled drops mightn't be gathered from some vision of, say, "old" New York. Would that human congeries, to aid obligingly in the production of a fable, be conceivable as "taking" the afternoon light with the right happy slant?—or could a recogniseable reflexion of the Byronic age, in other words, be picked up on the banks of the Hudson? (Only just there, beyond the great sea, if anywhere: in no other connexion would the question so much as raise its head. I admit that Jeffrey Aspern isn't even feebly localised, but I *thought* New York as I projected him.) It was "amusing," in any case, always, to try experiments; and the experiment for the right *transposition* of my Juliana would be to fit her out with an immortalising poet as transposed as herself. Delicacy had demanded, I felt, that my appropriation of the Florentine legend should purge it, first of all, of references too obvious; so that, to begin with, I shifted the scene of the adventure. Juliana, as I saw her, was thinkable only in Byronic and more or less immediately post-Byronic Italy; but there were conditions in which she was ideally arrangeable, as happened, especially in respect to the later time and the long undetected survival; there being absolutely no refinement of the mouldy rococo, in human or whatever other form, that you may not disembark at the dislocated water-steps of almost any decayed monument of Venetian greatness in auspicious quest of. It was a question, in fine, of covering one's tracks—though with no great elaboration I am bound to admit; and I felt I couldn't cover mine more than in postulating a comparative American Byron to match an American Miss Clairmont—she as absolute as she would. I scarce know whether best to say for this device to-day that it cost me little or that it cost me much; it was "cheap" or expensive according to the degree of verisimilitude artfully obtained. If that degree appears *nil* the "art," such as it was, is wasted, and my remembrance of the contention, on the part of a highly critical friend who at that time and later on often had my ear, that it had been simply foredoomed to be wasted, puts before me the passage in the private history of "The Aspern Papers" that I now find, I confess, most interesting. I comfort myself for the needful brevity of a present glance at it by the sense that the general question involved, under criticism, can't but come up for us again at higher pressure.

My friend's argument bore then—at the time and afterward—on my vicious practice, as he maintained, of postulating for the purpose of my fable celebrities who not only *hadn't* existed in the conditions I imputed to them, but who for the most part (and in no case more markedly than in that of Jeffrey Aspern) couldn't possibly have done so. The stricture was to apply itself to a whole group of short fictions in which I had, with whatever ingenuity, assigned to several so-called eminent figures positions absolutely unthinkable in our actual encompassing air, an air definitely unfavourable to certain forms of eminence. It was vicious, my critic contended, to flourish forth on one's page "great people," public persons, who shouldn't more or less square with our quite definite and calculable array of such notabilities; and by this rule I was heavily incriminated. The rule demanded that the "public person" portrayed should be at least of the tradition, of the general complexion, of the face-value, exactly, of some past or present producible counterfoil. Mere private figures, under one's hand, might correspond with nobody, it being of their essence to be but narrowly known; the represented state of being conspicuous, on the other hand, involved before anything else a recognition—and none of my eminent folk were recogniseable. It was all very well for instance to have put one's self at such pains for Miriam Rooth in "The Tragic Muse"; but *there* was misapplied zeal, there a case of pitiful waste, crying aloud to be denounced. Miriam is offered not as a young person passing unnoticed by her age—like the Biddy Dormers and Julia Dallows, say, of the same book, but as a high rarity, a time-figure of the scope inevitably attended by other commemorations. Where on earth would be then Miriam's inscribed "counterfoil," and in what conditions of the contemporary English theatre, in what conditions of criticism, of appreciation, under what conceivable Anglo-Saxon star, might we take an artistic value of this order either for produced or for recognised? We are, as a "public," chalk-marked by nothing, more unmistakeably, than by the truth that we know nothing of such values—any more than, as my friend was to impress on me, we are susceptible of consciousness of such others (these in the sphere of literary eminence) as my Neil Paraday in "The Death of the Lion," as my Hugh Vereker in "The Figure in the Carpet," as my Ralph Limbert, above all, in "The Next Time," as sundry unprecedented and unmatched heroes and martyrs of the artistic ideal, in short, elsewhere exemplified in my pages. We shall come to these objects of animadversion in another hour, when I shall have no difficulty in producing the defence I found for them—since, obviously, I hadn't cast them into the world *all* naked and ashamed; and I deal for the moment but with the stigma in general as Jeffrey Aspern carries it.

The charge being that I foist upon our early American annals a distinguished presence for which they yield me absolutely no warrant—"Where, within them, gracious heaven, were we to look for so much as an approach to the social elements of habitat and climate of birds of that note and plumage?"—I find his link with reality then just in the tone of the picture wrought round him. What was the tone but exactly, but exquisitely, calculated, the harmless hocus-pocus under cover of which we might suppose him to have existed? This tone is the tone, artistically speaking, of "amusement," the current floating that precious influence home quite as one of those high tides watched by the smugglers of old might, in case of their boat's being boarded, be trusted to wash far up the strand the cask of foreign liquor expertly committed to it. If through our lean prime Western period no dim and charming ghost of an adventurous lyric genius might by a stretch of fancy flit, if the time was really too hard to "take," in the light form proposed, the elegant reflexion, then so much the worse for the time—it was all one could say! The retort to that of course was that such a plea represented no "link" with reality—which was what was under discussion—but only a link, and flimsy enough too, with the deepest depths of the artificial: the restrictive truth exactly contended for, which may embody my critic's last word rather of course than my own. My own, so far as I shall pretend in that especial connexion to report it, was that one's warrant, in such a case, hangs essentially on the question of whether or no the false element imputed would have borne that test of further development which so exposes the wrong and so consecrates the right. My last word was, heaven forgive me, that, occasion favouring, I could have perfectly "worked out" Jeffrey Aspern. The boast remains indeed to be verified when we shall arrive at the other challenged cases.

That particular challenge at least "The Turn of the Screw" doesn't incur; and this perfectly independent and irresponsible little fiction rejoices, beyond any rival on a like ground, in a conscious provision of prompt retort to the sharpest question that may be addressed to it. For it has the small strength—if I shouldn't say rather the unattackable ease—of a perfect homogeneity, of being, to the very last grain of its virtue, all of a kind; the very kind, as happens, least apt to be baited by earnest criticism, the only sort of criticism of which account need be taken. To have handled again this so full-blown flower of high fancy is to be led back by it to easy and happy recognitions. Let the first of these be that of the starting-point itself—the sense, all charming again, of the circle, one winter afternoon, round the hall-fire of a grave old country-house where (for all the world as if to resolve itself promptly and obligingly into convertible, into "literary" stuff) the talk turned, on I forget what homely pretext, to apparitions and night-fears, to the marked and sad drop in the general supply, and still more in the general quality, of such commodities. The good, the really effective and heart-shaking ghost-stories (roughly so to term them) appeared all to have been told, and neither new crop nor new type in any quarter awaited us. The new type indeed, the mere modern "psychical" case, washed clean of all queerness as by exposure to a flowing laboratory tap, and equipped with credentials vouching for this—the new type clearly promised little, for the more it was respectably certified the less it seemed of a nature to rouse the dear old sacred terror. Thus it was, I remember, that amid our lament for a beautiful lost form, our distinguished host expressed the wish that he might but have recovered for us one of the scantest of fragments of this form at its best. He had never forgotten the impression made on him as a young man by the withheld glimpse, as it were, of a dreadful matter that had been reported years before, and with as few particulars, to a lady with whom he had youthfully talked. The story would have been thrilling could she but have found herself in better possession of it, dealing as it did with a couple of small children in an out-of-the way place, to whom the spirits of certain "bad" servants, dead in the employ of the house, were believed to have appeared with the design of "getting hold" of them. This was all, but there had been more, which my friend's old converser had lost the thread of: she could only assure him of the wonder of the allegations as she had anciently heard them made. He himself could give us but this shadow of a shadow—my own appreciation of which, I need scarcely say, was exactly wrapped up in that thinness. On the surface there wasn't much, but another grain, none the less, would have spoiled the precious pinch addressed to its end as neatly as some modicum extracted from an old silver snuff-box and held between finger and thumb. I was to remember the haunted children and the prowling servile spirits as a "value," of the disquieting sort, in all conscience sufficient; so that when, after an interval, I was asked for something seasonable by the promoters of a periodical dealing in the time-honoured Christmas-tide toy, I bethought myself at once of the vividest little note for sinister romance that I had ever jotted down.

Such was the private source of "The Turn of the Screw"; and I wondered, I confess, why so fine a germ, gleaming there in the wayside dust of life, had never been deftly picked up. The thing had for me the immense merit of allowing the imagination absolute freedom of hand, of inviting it to act on a perfectly clear field, with no "outside" control involved, no pattern of the usual or the true or the terrible "pleasant" (save always of course the high pleasantry of one's very form) to consort with. This makes in fact the charm of my second reference, that I find here a perfect example of an exercise of the imagination unassisted, unassociated—playing the game, making the score, in the phrase of our sporting day, off its own bat. To what degree the game was worth playing I needn't attempt to say: the exercise I have noted strikes me now, I confess, as the interesting thing, the imaginative faculty acting with the *whole* of the case on its hands. The exhibition involved is in other words a fairy-tale pure and simple—save indeed as to its springing not from an artless and measureless, but from a conscious and cultivated credulity. Yet the fairy-tale belongs mainly to either of two classes, the short and sharp and single, charged more or less with the compactness of anecdote (as to which left the familiars of our childhood, Cinderella and Blue-Beard and Hop o' my Thumb and Little Red Riding Hood and many of the gems of the Brothers Grimm directly testify), or else the long and loose, the copious, the various, the endless, where, dramatically speaking, roundness is quite sacrificed—sacrificed to fulness, sacrificed to exuberance, if one will: witness at hazard almost any one of the Arabian Nights. The charm of all these things for the distracted modern mind is in the clear field of experience, as I call it, over which we are thus led to roam; an annexed but independent world in which nothing is right save as we rightly imagine it. We have to do *that*, and we do it happily for the short spurt and in the smaller piece, achieving so perhaps beauty and lucidity; we flounder, we lose breath, on the other hand—that is we fail, not of continuity, but of an agreeable unity, of the "roundness" in which beauty and lucidity largely reside—when we go in, as they say, for great lengths and breadths. And this, oddly enough, not because "keeping it up" isn't abundantly within the compass of the imagination appealed to in certain conditions, but because the finer interest depends just on *how* it is kept up.

Nothing is so easy as improvisation, the running on and on of invention; it is sadly compromised, however, from the moment its stream breaks bounds and gets into flood. Then the waters may spread indeed, gathering houses and herds and crops and cities into their arms and wrenching off, for our amusement, the whole face of the land—only violating by the same stroke our sense of the course and the channel, which is our sense of the uses of a stream and the virtue of a story. Improvisation, as in the Arabian Nights, may keep on terms with encountered objects by sweeping them in and floating them on its breast; but the great effect it so loses—that of keeping on terms with itself. This is ever, I intimate, the hard thing for the fairy-tale; but by just so much as it struck me as hard did it in "The Turn of the Screw" affect me as irresistibly prescribed. To improvise with extreme freedom and yet at the same time without the possibility of ravage, without the hint of a flood; to keep the stream, in a word, on something like ideal terms with itself: that was here my definite business. The thing was to aim at absolute singleness, clearness and roundness, and yet to depend on an imagination working freely, working (call it) with extravagance; by which law it wouldn't be thinkable except as free and wouldn't be amusing except as controlled. The merit of the tale, as it stands, is accordingly, I judge, that it has struggled successfully with its dangers. It is an excursion into chaos while remaining, like Blue-Beard and Cinderella, but an anecdote—though an anecdote amplified and highly emphasised and returning upon itself; as, for that matter, Cinderella and Blue-Beard return. I need scarcely add after this that it is a piece of ingenuity pure and simple, of cold artistic calculation, an *amusette* to catch those not easily caught (the "fun" of the capture of the merely witless being ever but small), the jaded, the disillusioned, the fastidious. Otherwise expressed, the study is of a conceived "tone," the tone of suspected and felt trouble, of an inordinate and incalculable sort—the tone of tragic, yet of exquisite, mystification. To knead the subject of my young friend's, the supposititious narrator's, mystification thick, and yet strain the expression of it so clear and fine that beauty would result: no side of the matter so revives for me as that endeavour. Indeed if the artistic value of such an experiment be measured by the intellectual echoes it may again, long after, set in motion, the case would make in favour of this little firm fantasy—which I seem to see draw behind it today a train of associations. I ought doubtless to blush for thus confessing them so numerous that I can but pick among them for reference. I recall for instance a reproach made me by a reader capable evidently, for the time, of some attention, but not quite capable of enough, who complained that I hadn't sufficiently "characterised" my young woman engaged in her labyrinth; hadn't endowed her with signs and marks, features and humours, hadn't in a word invited her to deal with her own mystery as well as with that of Peter Quint, Miss Jessel and the hapless children. I remember well, whatever the absurdity of its now coming back to me, my reply to that criticism—under which one's artistic, one's ironic heart shook for the instant almost to breaking. "You indulge in that stricture at your ease, and I don't mind confiding to you that—strange as it may appear!—one has to choose ever so delicately among one's difficulties, attaching one's self to the greatest, bearing hard on those and intelligently neglecting the others. If one attempts to tackle them all one is certain to deal completely with none; whereas the effectual dealing with a few casts a blest golden haze under cover of which, like wanton mocking goddesses in clouds, the others find prudent to retire. It was 'déjà très-joli,' in 'The Turn of the Screw,' please believe, the general proposition of our young woman's keeping crystalline her record of so many intense anomalies and obscurities—by which I don't of course mean her explanation of them, a different matter; and I saw no way, I feebly grant (fighting, at the best too, periodically, for every grudged inch of my space) to exhibit her in relations other than those; one of which, precisely, would have been her relation to her own nature. We have surely as much of her own nature as we can swallow in watching it reflect her anxieties and inductions. It constitutes no little of a character indeed, in such conditions, for a young person, as she says, 'privately bred,' that she is able to make her particular credible statement of such strange matters. She has 'authority,' which is a good deal to have given her, and I couldn't have arrived at so much had I clumsily tried for more."

For which truth I claim part of the charm latent on occasion in the extracted reasons of beautiful things—putting for the beautiful always, in a work of art, the close, the curious, the deep. Let me place above all, however, under the protection of that presence the side by which this fiction appeals most to consideration: its choice of its way of meeting its gravest difficulty. There were difficulties not so grave: I had for instance simply to renounce all attempt to keep the kind and degree of impression I wished to produce on terms with the to-day so copious psychical record of cases of apparitions. Different signs and circumstances, in the reports, mark these cases; different things are done—though on the whole very little appears to be—by the persons appearing; the point is, however, that some things are never done at all: this negative quantity is large—certain reserves and proprieties and immobilities consistently impose themselves. Recorded and attested "ghosts" are in other words as little expressive, as little dramatic, above all as little continuous and conscious and responsive, as is consistent with their taking the trouble—and an immense trouble they find it, we gather—to appear at all. Wonderful and interesting therefore at a given moment, they are inconceivable figures in an *action*—and "The Turn of the Screw" was an action, desperately, or it was nothing. I had to decide in fine between having my apparitions correct and having my story "good"—that is producing my impression of the dreadful, my designed horror. Good ghosts, speaking by book, make poor subjects, and it was clear that from the first my hovering prowling blighting presences, my pair of abnormal agents, would have to depart altogether from the rules. They would be agents in fact; there would be laid on them the dire duty of causing the situation to reek with the air of Evil. Their desire and their ability to do so, visibly measuring meanwhile their effect, together with their observed and described success—this was exactly my central idea; so that, briefly, I cast my lot with pure romance, the appearances conforming to the true type being so little romantic.

This is to say, I recognise again, that Peter Quint and Miss Jessel are not "ghosts" at all, as we now know the ghost, but goblins, elves, imps, demons as loosely constructed as those of the old trials for witchcraft; if not, more pleasingly, fairies of the legendary order, wooing their victims forth to see them dance under the moon. Not indeed that I suggest their reducibility to any form of the pleasing pure and simple; they please at the best but through having helped me to express my subject all directly and intensely. Here it was—in the use made of them—that I felt a high degree of art really required; and here it is that, on reading the tale over, I find my precautions justified. The essence of the matter was the villainy of motive in the evoked predatory creatures; so that the result would be ignoble—by which I mean would be trivial—were this element of evil but feebly or inanely suggested. Thus arose on behalf of my idea the lively interest of a possible suggestion and process of *adumbration*; the question of how best to convey that sense of the depths of the sinister without which my fable would so woefully limp. Portentous evil—how was I to save that, as an intention on the part of my demon-spirits, from the drop, the comparative vulgarity, inevitably attending, throughout the whole range of possible brief illustration, the offered example, the imputed vice, the cited act, the limited deplorable presentable instance? To bring the bad dead back to life for a second round of badness is to warrant them as indeed prodigious, and to become hence as shy of specifications as of a waiting anti-climax. One had seen, in fiction, some grand form of wrong-doing, or better still of wrong-being, imputed, seen it promised and announced as by the hot breath of the Pit—and then, all lamentably, shrink to the compass of some particular brutality, some particular immorality, some particular infamy portrayed: with the result, alas, of the demonstration's falling sadly short. If *my* bad things, for "The Turn of the Screw," I felt, should succumb to this danger, if they shouldn't seem sufficiently bad, there would be nothing for me but to hang my artistic head lower than I had ever known occasion to do.

The view of that discomfort and the fear of that dishonour, it accordingly must have been, that struck the proper light for my right, though by no means easy, short cut. What, in the last analysis, had I to give the sense of? Of their being, the haunting pair, capable, as the phrase is, of everything—that is of exerting, in respect to the children, the very worst action small victims so conditioned might be conceived as subject to. What would *be* then, on reflexion, this utmost conceivability?—a question to which the answer all admirably came. There is for such a case no eligible *absolute* of the wrong; it remains relative to fifty other elements, a matter of appreciation, speculation, imagination—these things moreover quite exactly in the light of the spectator's, the critic's, the reader's experience. Only make the reader's general vision of evil intense enough, I said to myself—and that already is a charming job—and his own experience, his own imagination, his own sympathy (with the children) and horror (of their false friends) will supply him quite sufficiently with all the particulars. Make him *think* the evil, make him think it for himself, and you are released from weak specifications. This ingenuity I took pains—as indeed great pains were required—to apply; and with a success apparently beyond my liveliest hope. Droll enough at the same time, I must add, some of the evidence—even when most convincing—of this success. How can I feel my calculation to have failed, my wrought suggestion not to have worked, that is, on my being assailed, as has befallen me, with the charge of a monstrous emphasis, the charge of all indecently expatiating? There is not only from beginning to end of the matter not an inch of expatiation, but my values are positively all blanks save so far as an excited horror, a promoted pity, a created expertness—on which punctual effects of strong causes no writer can ever fail to plume himself—proceed to read into them more or less fantastic figures. Of high interest to the author meanwhile—and by the same stroke a theme for the moralist—the artless resentful reaction of the entertained person who has abounded in the sense of the situation. He visits his abundance, morally, on the artist—who has but clung to an ideal of faultlessness. Such indeed, for this latter, are some of the observations by which the prolonged strain of that clinging may be enlivened!

I arrive with "The Liar" (1888) and "The Two Faces" (1900) at the first members of the considerable group of shorter, of shortest tales here republished; though I should perhaps place quite in the forefront "The Chaperon" and "The Pupil," at which we have already glanced. I am conscious of much to say of these numerous small productions as a family—a family indeed quite organised as such, with its proper representatives, its "heads," its subdivisions and its branches, its poor relations perhaps not least: its unmistakeable train of poor relations in fact, the very poorer, the poorest of whom I am, in family parlance, for this formal appearance in society, "cutting" without a scruple. These repudiated members, some of them, for that matter, well-nourished and substantial presences enough, with their compromising rustiness plausibly, almost touchingly dissimulated, I fondly figure as standing wistful but excluded, after the fashion of the outer fringe of the connected whom there are not carriages enough to convey from the church—whether (for we have our choice of similes) to the wedding-feast or to the interment! Great for me from far back had been the interest of the whole "question of the short story," roundabout which our age has, for lamentable reasons, heard so vain a babble; but I foresee occasions yet to come when it will abundantly waylay me. Then it will insist on presenting itself but in too many lights. Little else perhaps meanwhile is more relevant as to "The Liar" than the small fact of its having, when its hour came, quite especially conformed to that custom of shooting straight from the planted seed, of responding at once to the touched spring, of which my fond appeal here to "origins" and evolutions so depicts the sway. When it shall come to fitting, historically, anything like *all* my small children of fancy with their pair of progenitors, and all my reproductive unions with their inevitable fruit, I shall seem to offer my backward consciousness in the image of a shell charged and recharged by the Fates with some patent and infallible explosive. Never would there seem to have been a pretence to such economy of ammunition!

However this may be, I come back, for "The Liar," as for so many of its fellows, to holding my personal experience, poor thing though it may have been, immediately accountable. For by what else in the world but by fatal design had I been placed at dinner one autumn evening of old London days face to face with a gentleman, met for the first time, though favourably known to me by name and fame, in whom I recognised the most unbridled colloquial romancer the "joy of life" had ever found occasion to envy? Under what other conceivable coercion had I been invited to reckon, through the evening, with the type, with the character, with the countenance, of this magnificent master's wife, who, veracious, serene and charming, yet not once meeting straight the eyes of one of us, did her duty by each, and by her husband most of all, without so much as, in the vulgar phrase, turning a hair? It was long ago, but I have never, to this hour, forgotten the evening itself—embalmed for me now in an old-time sweetness beyond any aspect of my reproduction. I made but a fifth person, the other couple our host and hostess; between whom and one of the company, while we listened to the woven wonders of a summer holiday, the exploits of a salamander, among Mediterranean isles, were exchanged, dimly and discreetly, ever so guardedly, but all expressively, imperceptible lingering looks. It was exquisite, it *could* but

344

become, inevitably, some "short story" or other, which it clearly pre-fitted as the hand the glove. I must reserve "The Two Faces" till I come to speak of the thrilling question of the poor painter's tormented acceptance, in advance, of the scanted canvas; of the writer's rueful hopeful assent to the conditions known to him as "too little room to turn round." Of the liveliest interest then—or so at least I could luckily always project the case—to see how he may nevertheless, in the event, effectively manœuvre. The value of "The Two Faces"—by reason of which I have not hesitated to gather it in—is thus peculiarly an economic one. It may conceal rather than exhale its intense little principle of calculation; but the neat evolution, as I call it, the example of the turn of the *whole* coach and pair in the contracted court, without the "spill" of a single passenger or the derangement of a single parcel, is only in three or four cases (where the coach is fuller still) more appreciable.

The Wings of the Dove

"THE WINGS OF THE DOVE," PUBLISHED IN 1902, REPRE-
sents to my memory a very old—if I shouldn't perhaps
rather say a very young—motive; I can scarce remember the time
when the situation on which this long-drawn fiction mainly rests was
not vividly present to me. The idea, reduced to its essence, is that of a
young person conscious of a great capacity for life, but early stricken
and doomed, condemned to die under short respite, while also enamoured of the world; aware moreover of the condemnation and passionately desiring to "put in" before extinction as many of the finer
vibrations as possible, and so achieve, however briefly and brokenly,
the sense of having lived. Long had I turned it over, standing off from
it, yet coming back to it; convinced of what might be done with it, yet
seeing the theme as formidable. The image so figured would be, at
best, but half the matter; the rest would be all the picture of the struggle involved, the adventure brought about, the gain recorded or the
loss incurred, the precious experience somehow compassed. These
things, I had from the first felt, would require much working-out; that
indeed was the case with most things worth working at all; yet there
are subjects and subjects, and this one seemed particularly to bristle.
It was formed, I judged, to make the wary adventurer walk round
and round it—it had in fact a charm that invited and mystified alike
that attention; not being somehow what one thought of as a "frank"
subject, after the fashion of some, with its elements well in view and
its whole character in its face. It stood there with secrets and compartments, with possible treacheries and traps; it might have a great deal
to give, but would probably ask for equal services in return, and
would collect this debt to the last shilling. It involved, to begin with,
the placing in the strongest light a person infirm and ill—a case sure
to prove difficult and to require much handling; though giving perhaps, with other matters, one of those chances for good taste, possibly even for the play of the very best in the world, that are not only

always to be invoked and cultivated, but that are absolutely to be jumped at from the moment they make a sign.

Yes then, the case prescribed for its central figure a sick young woman, at the whole course of whose disintegration and the whole ordeal of whose consciousness one would have quite honestly to assist. The expression of her state and that of one's intimate relation to it might therefore well need to be discreet and ingenious; a reflexion that fortunately grew and grew, however, in proportion as I focussed my image—roundabout which, as it persisted, I repeat, the interesting possibilities and the attaching wonderments, not to say the insoluble mysteries, thickened apace. Why had one to look so straight in the face and so closely to cross-question that idea of making one's protagonist "sick"?—as if to be menaced with death or danger hadn't been from time immemorial, for heroine or hero, the very shortest of all cuts to the interesting state. Why should a figure be disqualified for a central position by the particular circumstance that might most quicken, that might crown with a fine intensity, its liability to many accidents, its consciousness of all relations? This circumstance, true enough, might disqualify it for many activities—even though we should have imputed to it the unsurpassable activity of passionate, of inspired resistance. This last fact was the real issue, for the way grew straight from the moment one recognised that the poet essentially *can't* be concerned with the act of dying. Let him deal with the sickest of the sick, it is still by the act of living that they appeal to him, and appeal the more as the conditions plot against them and prescribe the battle. The process of life gives way fighting, and often may so shine out on the lost ground as in no other connexion. One had had moreover, as a various chronicler, one's secondary physical weaklings and failures, one's accessory invalids—introduced with a complacency that made light of criticism. To Ralph Touchett in "The Portrait of a Lady," for instance, his deplorable state of health was not only no drawback; I had clearly been right in counting it, for any happy effect he should produce, a positive good mark, a direct aid to pleasantness and vividness. The reason of this moreover could never in the world have been his fact of sex; since men, among the mortally afflicted, suffer on the whole more overtly and more grossly than women, and resist with a ruder, an inferior strategy. I had thus to take *that* anomaly for what it was worth, and I give it here but as one of the ambiguities amid which my subject ended by making itself at home and seating itself quite in confidence.

With the clearness I have just noted, accordingly, the last thing in the world it proposed to itself was to be the record predominantly of a collapse. I don't mean to say that my offered victim was not present to my imagination, constantly, as dragged by a greater force than any she herself could exert; she had been given me from far back as contesting every inch of the road, as catching at every object the grasp of which might make for delay, as clutching these things to the last moment of her strength. Such an attitude and such movements, the passion they expressed and the success they in fact represented, what were they in truth but the soul of drama?—which is the portrayal, as we know, of a catastrophe determined in spite of oppositions. My young woman would *herself* be the opposition—to the catastrophe announced by the associated Fates, powers conspiring to a sinister end and, with their command of means, finally achieving it, yet in such straits really to *stifle* the sacred spark that, obviously, a creature so animated, an adversary so subtle, couldn't but be felt worthy, under whatever weaknesses, of the foreground and the limelight. She would meanwhile wish, moreover, all along, to live for particular things, she would found her struggle on particular human interests, which would inevitably determine, in respect to her, the attitude of other persons, persons affected in such a manner as to make them part of the action. If her impulse to wrest from her shrinking hour still as much of the fruit of life as possible, if this longing can take effect only by the aid of others, their participation (appealed to, entangled and coerced as they find themselves) becomes their drama too—that of their promoting her illusion, under her importunity, for reasons, for interests and advantages, from motives and points of view, of their own. Some of these promptings, evidently, would be of the highest order—others doubtless mightn't; but they would make up together, for her, contributively, her sum of experience, represent to her somehow, in good faith or in bad, what she should have *known*. Somehow, too, at such a rate, one would see the persons subject to them drawn in as by some pool of a Lorelei—see them terrified and tempted and charmed; bribed away, it may even be, from more prescribed and natural orbits, inheriting from their connexion with her strange difficulties and still stranger opportunities, confronted with rare questions and called upon for new discriminations. Thus the scheme of her situation would, in a comprehensive way, see itself constituted; the rest of the interest would be in the number and nature of the particulars. Strong among these, naturally, the need that life should, apart from her infirmity, present itself to our young woman as quite dazzlingly liveable, and that if the great pang for her is in what she must give up we shall appreciate it the more from the sight of all she has.

One would see her then as possessed of all things, all but the single most precious assurance; freedom and money and a mobile mind and personal charm, the power to interest and attach; attributes, each one, enhancing the value of a future. From the moment his imagination began to deal with her at close quarters, in fact, nothing could more engage her designer than to work out the detail of her perfect rightness for her part; nothing above all more solicit him than to recognise fifty reasons for her national and social status. She should be the last fine flower—blooming alone, for the fullest attestation of her freedom—of an "old" New York stem; the happy congruities thus preserved for her being matters, however, that I may not now go into, and this even though the fine association that shall yet elsewhere await me is of a sort, at the best, rather to defy than to encourage exact expression. There goes with it, for the heroine of "The Wings of the Dove," a strong and special implication of liberty, liberty of action, of choice, of appreciation, of contact—proceeding from sources that provide better for large independence, I think, than any other conditions in the world—and this would be in particular what we should feel ourselves deeply concerned with. I had from far back mentally projected a certain sort of young American as more the "heir of all the ages" than any other young person whatever (and precisely on those grounds I have just glanced at but to pass them by for the moment); so that here was a chance to confer on some such figure a supremely touching value. To be the heir of all the ages only to know yourself, as that consciousness should deepen, balked of your inheritance, would be to play the part, it struck me, or at least to arrive at the type, in the light on the whole the most becoming. Otherwise, truly, what a perilous part to play *out*—what a suspicion of "swagger" in positively attempting it! So at least I could reason—so I even think I *had* to—to keep my subject to a decent compactness. For already, from an early stage, it had begun richly to people itself: the difficulty was to see whom the situation I had primarily projected might, by this, that or the other turn, *not* draw in. My business was to watch its turns as the fond parent watches a child perched, for its first riding-lesson, in the saddle; yet its interest, I had all the while to recall, was just in its making, on such a scale, for developments.

What one had discerned, at all events, from an early stage, was that a young person so devoted and exposed, a creature with her security hanging so by a hair, couldn't but fall somehow into some abysmal trap—this being, dramatically speaking, what such a situation most naturally implied and imposed. Didn't the truth and a great part of the interest also reside in the appearance that she would constitute for others (given her passionate yearning to live while she might) a complication as great as any they might constitute for herself?—which is what I mean when I speak of such matters as "natural." They would be as natural, these tragic, pathetic, ironic, these indeed for the most part sinister, liabilities, to her living associates, as they could be to herself as prime subject. If her story was to consist, as it could so little help doing, of her being let in, as we say, for this, that and the other irreducible anxiety, how could she not have put a premium on the acquisition, by any close sharer of her life, of a consciousness similarly embarrassed? I have named the Rhine-maiden, but our young friend's existence would create rather, all round her, very much that whirlpool movement of the waters produced by the sinking of a big vessel or the failure of a great business; when we figure to ourselves the strong narrowing eddies, the immense force of suction, the general engulfment that, for any neighbouring object, makes immersion inevitable. I need scarce say, however, that in spite of these communities of doom I saw the main dramatic complication much more prepared *for* my vessel of sensibility than by her—the work of other hands (though with her own imbued too, after all, in the measure of their never not being, in some direction, generous and extravagant, and thereby provoking).

The great point was, at all events, that if in a predicament she was to be, accordingly, it would be of the essence to create the predicament promptly and build it up solidly, so that it should have for us as much as possible its ominous air of awaiting her. That reflexion I found, betimes, not less inspiring than urgent; one begins so, in such a business, by looking about for one's compositional key, unable as one can only be to move till one has found it. To start without it is to pretend to enter the train and, still more, to remain in one's seat, without a ticket. Well—in the steady light and for the continued charm of these verifications—I had secured my ticket over the tolerably long line laid down for "The Wings of the Dove" from the moment I had noted that there could be no full presentation of Milly Theale as *engaged* with elements amid which she was to draw her breath in such pain, should not the elements have been, with all solicitude, duly prefigured. If one had seen that her stricken state was but half her case, the correlative half being the state of others as affected by her (they too should have a "case," bless them, quite as much as she!) then I was free to choose, as it were, the half with which I should begin. If, as I had fondly noted, the little world determined for her was to "bristle"—I delighted in the term!—with meanings, so, by the same token, could I but make my medal hang free, its obverse and its reverse, its face and its back, would beautifully become optional for the spectator. I somehow wanted them correspondingly embossed, wanted them inscribed and figured with an equal salience; yet it was none the less visibly my "key," as I have said, that though my regenerate young New Yorker, and what might depend on her, should form my centre, my circumference was every whit as treatable. Therefore I must trust myself to know when to proceed from the one and when from the other. Preparatively and, as it were, yearningly—given the whole ground—one began, in the event, with the outer ring, approaching the centre thus by narrowing circumvallations. There, full-blown, accordingly, from one hour to the other, rose one's process—for which there remained all the while so many amusing formulae.

The medal *did* hang free—I felt this perfectly, I remember, from the moment I had comfortably laid the ground provided in my first Book, ground from which Milly is superficially so absent. I scarce remember perhaps a case—I like even with this public grossness to insist on it—in which the curiosity of "beginning far back," as far back as possible, and even of going, to the same tune, far "behind," that is behind the face of the subject, was to assert itself with less scruple. The free hand, in this connexion, was above all agreeable— the hand the freedom of which I owed to the fact that the work had ignominiously failed, in advance, of all power to see itself "serialised." This failure had repeatedly waited, for me, upon shorter fictions; but the considerable production we here discuss was (as "The Golden Bowl" was to be, two or three years later) born, not otherwise than a little bewilderedly, into a world of periodicals and editors, of roaring "successes" in fine, amid which it was well-nigh unnotedly to lose itself. There is fortunately something bracing, ever, in the alpine chill, that of some high icy *arête*, shed by the cold editorial shoulder; sour grapes may at moments fairly intoxicate and the story-teller worth his salt rejoice to feel again how many accommodations he can practise. Those addressed to "conditions of publication" have in a degree their interesting, or at least their provoking, side; but their charm is qualified by the fact that the prescriptions here spring from a soil often wholly alien to the ground of the work itself. They are almost always the fruit of another air altogether and conceived in a light liable to represent *within* the circle of the work itself little else than darkness. Still, when not too blighting, they often operate as a tax on ingenuity—that ingenuity of the expert craftsman which likes to be taxed very much to the same tune to which a well-bred horse likes to be saddled. The best and finest ingenuities, nevertheless, with all respect to that truth, are apt to be, not one's compromises, but one's fullest conformities, and I well remember, in the case before us, the pleasure of feeling my divisions, my proportions and general rhythm, rest all on permanent rather than in any degree on momentary proprieties. It was enough for my alternations, thus, that they were good in themselves; it was in fact so much for them that I really think any further account of the constitution of the book reduces itself to a just notation of the law they followed.

There was the "fun," to begin with, of establishing one's successive centres—of fixing them so exactly that the portions of the subject commanded by them as by happy points of view, and accordingly treated from them, would constitute, so to speak, sufficiently solid *blocks* of wrought material, squared to the sharp edge, as to have weight and mass and carrying power; to make for construction, that is, to conduce to effect and to provide for beauty. Such a block, obviously, is the whole preliminary presentation of Kate Croy, which, from the first, I recall, absolutely declined to enact itself save in terms of amplitude. Terms of amplitude, terms of atmosphere, those terms, and those terms only, in which images assert their fulness and roundness, their power to revolve, so that they have sides and backs, parts in the shade as true as parts in the sun—these were plainly to be my conditions, right and left, and I was so far from overrating the amount of expression the whole thing, as I saw and felt it, would require, that to retrace the way at present is, alas, more than anything else, but to mark the gaps and the lapses, to miss, one by one, the intentions that, with the best will in the world, were not to fructify. I have just said that the process of the general attempt is described from the moment the "blocks" are numbered, and that would be a true enough picture of my plan. Yet one's plan, alas, is one thing and one's result another; so that I am perhaps nearer the point in saying that this last strikes me at present as most characterised by the happy features that *were*, under my first and most blest illusion, to have contributed to it. I meet them all, as I renew acquaintance, I mourn for them all as I remount the stream, the absent values, the palpable voids, the missing links, the mocking shadows, that reflect, taken together, the early bloom of one's good faith. Such cases are of course far from abnormal—so far from it that some acute mind ought surely to have worked out by this time the "law" of the degree in which the artist's energy fairly depends on his fallibility. How much and how often, and in what connexions and with what almost infinite variety, must he be a dupe, that of his prime object, to be at all measurably a master, that of his actual substitute for it—or in other words at all appreciably to exist? He places, after an earnest survey, the piers of his bridge—he has at least sound-ed deep enough, heaven knows, for their brave position; yet the bridge spans the stream, after the fact, in apparently complete independence of these properties, the principal grace of the original design. *They* were an illusion, for their necessary hour; but the span itself, whether of a single arch or of many, seems by the oddest chance in the world to be a reality; since, actually, the rueful builder, passing under it, sees figures and hears sounds above: he makes out, with his heart in his throat, that it bears and is positively being "used."

The building-up of Kate Croy's consciousness to the capacity for the load little by little to be laid on it was, by way of example, to have been a matter of as many hundred close-packed bricks as there are actually poor dozens. The image of her so compromised and compro-mising father was all effectively to have pervaded her life, was in a certain particular way to have tampered with her spring; by which I mean that the shame and the irritation and the depression, the gener-al poisonous influence of him, were to have been *shown*, with a truth beyond the compass even of one's most emphasised "word of hon-our" for it, to do these things. But where do we find him, at this time of day, save in a beggarly scene or two which scarce arrives at the dignity of functional reference? He but "looks in," poor beautiful daz-zling, damning apparition that he was to have been; he sees his place so taken, his company so little missed, that, cocking again that fine form of hat which has yielded him for so long his one effective cover, he turns away with a whistle of indifference that nobly misrepresents the deepest disappointment of his life. One's poor word of honour has *had* to pass muster for the show. Every one, in short, was to have enjoyed so much better a chance that, like stars of the theatre conde-scending to oblige, they have had to take small parts, to content themselves with minor identities, in order to come on at all. I haven't the heart now, I confess, to adduce the detail of so many lapsed im-portances; the explanation of most of which, after all, I take to have been in the crudity of a truth beating full upon me through these reconsiderations, the odd inveteracy with which picture, at almost any turn, is jealous of drama, and drama (though on the whole with a greater patience, I think) suspicious of picture. Between them, no doubt, they do much for the theme; yet each baffles insidiously the other's ideal and eats round the edges of its position; each is too ready to say "I can take the thing for 'done' only when done in *my* way." The residuum of comfort for the witness of these broils is of course meanwhile in the convenient reflexion, invented for him in the twi-light of time and the infancy of art by the Angel, not to say by the

Demon, of Compromise, that nothing is so easy to "do" as not to be thankful for almost any stray help in its getting done. It wasn't, after this fashion, by making good one's dream of Lionel Croy that my structure was to stand on its feet—any more than it was by letting him go that I was to be left irretrievably lamenting. The who and the what, the how and the why, the whence and the whither of Merton Densher, these, no less, were quantities and attributes that should have danced about him with the antique grace of nymphs and fauns circling round a bland Hermes and crowning him with flowers. One's main anxiety, for each one's agents, is that the air of each shall be *given*; but what does the whole thing become, after all, as one goes, but a series of sad places at which the hand of generosity has been cautioned and stayed? The young man's situation, personal, professional, social, was to have been so decanted for us that we should get all the taste; we were to have been penetrated with Mrs. Lowder, by the same token, saturated with her presence, her "personality," and felt all her weight in the scale. We were to have revelled in Mrs. Stringham, my heroine's attendant friend, her fairly choral Bostonian, a subject for innumerable touches, and in an extended and above all an *animated* reflexion of Milly Theale's experience of English society; just as the strength and sense of the situation in Venice, for other gathered friends, was to have come to us in a deeper draught out of a larger cup, and just as the pattern of Densher's final position and fullest consciousness there was to have been marked in fine stitches, all silk and gold, all pink and silver, that have had to remain, alas, but entwined upon the reel.

It isn't, no doubt, however—to recover, after all, our critical balance—that the pattern didn't, for each compartment, get itself somehow wrought, and that we mightn't thus, piece by piece, opportunity offering, trace it over and study it. The thing has doubtless, as a whole, the advantage that each piece is true to its pattern, and that while it pretends to make no simple statement it yet never lets go its scheme of clearness. Applications of this scheme are continuous and exemplary enough, though I scarce leave myself room to glance at them. The clearness is obtained in Book First—or otherwise, as I have said, in the first "piece," each Book having its subordinate and contributive pattern—through the associated consciousness of my two prime young persons, for whom I early recognised that I should have to consent, under stress, to a practical *fusion* of consciousness. It is into the young woman's "ken" that Merton Densher is represented as swimming; but her mind is not here, rigorously, the one reflector. There are occasions when it plays this part, just as there are others when his plays it, and an intelligible plan consists naturally not a little in fixing such occasions and making them, on one side and the other, sufficient to themselves. Do I sometimes in fact forfeit the advantage of that distinctness? Do I ever abandon one centre for another after the former has been postulated? From the moment we proceed by "centres"—and I have never, I confess, embraced the logic of any superior process—they must *be*, each, as a basis, selected and fixed; after which it is that, in the high interest of economy of treatment, they determine and rule. There is no economy of treatment without an adopted, a related point of view, and though I understand, under certain degrees of pressure, a represented community of vision between several parties to the action when it makes for concentration, I understand no breaking-up of the register, no sacrifice of the recording consistency, that doesn't rather scatter and weaken. In this truth resides the secret of the discriminated occasion—that aspect of the subject which we have our noted choice of treating either as picture or scenically, but which is apt, I think, to show its fullest worth in the Scene. Beautiful exceedingly, for that matter, those occasions or parts of an occasion when the boundary line between picture and scene bears a little the weight of the double pressure.

Such would be the case, I can't but surmise, for the long passage that forms here before us the opening of Book Fourth, where all the offered life centres, to intensity, in the disclosure of Milly's single throbbing consciousness, but where, for a due rendering, everything has to be brought to a head. This passage, the view of her introduction to Mrs. Lowder's circle, has its mate, for illustration, later on in the book and at a crisis for which the occasion submits to another rule. My registers or "reflectors," as I so conveniently name them (burnished indeed as they generally are by the intelligence, the curiosity, the passion, the force of the moment, whatever it be, directing them), work, as we have seen, in arranged alternation; so that in the second connexion I here glance at it is Kate Croy who is, "for all she is worth," turned on. She is turned on largely at Venice, where the appearances, rich and obscure and portentous (another word I rejoice in) as they have by that time become and altogether exquisite as they remain, are treated almost wholly through her vision of them and Densher's (as to the lucid interplay of which conspiring and conflicting agents there would be a great deal to say). It is in Kate's consciousness that at the stage in question the drama is brought to a head, and the occasion on which, in the splendid saloon of poor Milly's hired palace, she takes the measure of her friend's festal evening, squares itself to the same synthetic firmness as the compact constructional block inserted by the scene at Lancaster Gate. Milly's situation ceases at a given moment to be "renderable" in terms closer than those supplied by Kate's intelligence, or, in a richer degree, by Densher's, or, for one fond hour, by poor Mrs. Stringham's (since to that sole brief futility is this last participant, crowned by my original plan with the quaintest functions, in fact reduced); just as Kate's relation with Densher and Densher's with Kate have ceased previously, and are then to cease again, to be projected for us, so far as Milly is concerned with them, on any more responsible plate than that of the latter's admirable anxiety. It is as if, for these aspects, the impersonal plate—in other words the poor author's comparatively cold affirmation or thin guarantee—had felt itself a figure of attestation at once too gross and too bloodless, likely to affect us as an abuse of privilege when not as an abuse of knowledge.

Heaven forbid, we say to ourselves during almost the whole Venetian climax, heaven forbid we should "know" anything more of our ravaged sister than what Densher darkly pieces together, or than what Kate Croy pays, heroically, it must be owned, at the hour of her visit alone to Densher's lodging, for her superior handling and her dire profanation of. For we have time, while this passage lasts, to turn round critically; we have time to recognise intentions and proprieties; we have time to catch glimpses of an economy of composition, as I put it, interesting in itself: all in spite of the author's scarce more than half-dissimulated despair at the inveterate displacement of his general centre. "The Wings of the Dove" happens to offer perhaps the most striking example I may cite (though with public penance for it already performed) of my regular failure to keep the appointed halves of my whole equal. Here the makeshift middle—for which the best I can say is that it's always rueful and never impudent—reigns with even more than its customary contrition, though passing itself off perhaps too with more than its usual craft. Nowhere, I seem to recall, had the need of dissimulation been felt so as anguish; nowhere had I condemmed a luckless theme to complete its revolution, burdened with the accumulation of its difficulties, the difficulties that grow with a theme's development, in quarters so cramped. Of course, as every novelist knows, it is difficulty that inspires; only, for that perfection of charm, it must have been difficulty inherent and congenital, and not difficulty "caught" by the wrong frequentations. The latter half, that is the false and deformed half, of "The Wings" would verily, I think, form a signal object-lesson for a literary critic bent on improving his occasion to the profit of the budding artist. This whole corner of the picture bristles with "dodges"—such as he should feel himself all committed to recognise and denounce—for disguising the reduced scale of the exhibition, for foreshortening at any cost, for imparting to patches the value of presences, for dressing objects in an *air* as of the dimensions they can't possibly have. Thus he would have his free hand for pointing out what a tangled web we weave when—well, when, through our mislaying or otherwise trifling with our blest pair of compasses, we have to produce the illusion of mass without the illusion of extent. *There* is a job quite to the measure of most of our monitors—and with the interest for them well enhanced by the preliminary cunning quest for the spot where deformity has begun.

I recognise meanwhile, throughout the long earlier reach of the book, not only no deformities but, I think, a positively close and felicitous application of method, the preserved consistencies of which, often illusive, but never really lapsing, it would be of a certain diversion, and might be of some profit, to follow. The author's accepted task at the outset has been to suggest with force the nature of the tie formed between the two young persons first introduced—to give the full impression of its peculiar worried and baffled, yet clinging and confident, ardour. The picture constituted, so far as may be, is that of a pair of natures well-nigh consumed by a sense of their intimate affinity and congruity, the reciprocity of their desire, and thus passionately impatient of barriers and delays, yet with qualities of intelligence and character that they are meanwhile extraordinarily able to draw upon for the enrichment of their relation, the extension of their prospect and the support of their "game." They are far from a common couple, Merton Densher and Kate Croy, as befits the remarkable fashion in which fortune was to waylay and opportunity was to distinguish them—the whole strange truth of their response to which opening involves also, in its order, no vulgar art of exhibition; but what they have most to tell us is that, all unconsciously and with the best faith in the world, all by mere force of the terms of their superior passion combined with their superior diplomacy, they are laying a trap for the great innocence to come. If I like, as I have confessed, the "portentous" look, I was perhaps never to set so high a value on it as for all this prompt provision of forces unwittingly waiting to close round my eager heroine (to the eventual deep chill of her eagerness) as the result of her mere lifting of a latch. Infinitely interesting to have built up the relation of the others to the point at which its aching restlessness, its need to affirm itself otherwise than by an exasperated patience, meets as with instinctive relief and recognition the possibilities shining out of Milly Theale. Infinitely interesting to have prepared and organised, correspondingly, that young woman's precipitations and liabilities, to have constructed, for Drama essentially to take possession, the whole bright house of her exposure.

These references, however, reflect too little of the detail of the treatment imposed; such a detail as I for instance get hold of in the fact of Densher's interview with Mrs. Lowder before he goes to America. It forms, in this preliminary picture, the one patch not strictly seen over Kate Croy's shoulder; though it's notable that immediately after, at the first possible moment, we surrender again to our major convenience, as it happens to be at the time, that of our drawing breath through the young woman's lungs. Once more, in other words, before we know it, Densher's direct vision of the scene at Lancaster Gate is replaced by her apprehension, her contributive assimilation, of his experience: it melts back into that accumulation, which we have been, as it were, saving up. Does my apparent deviation here count accordingly as a muddle?—one of the muddles ever blooming so thick in any soil that fails to grow reasons and determinants. No, distinctly not; for I had definitely opened the door, as attention of perusal of the first two Books will show, to the subjective community of my young pair. (Attention of perusal, I thus confess by the way, is what I at every point, as well as here, absolutely invoke and take for granted; a truth I avail myself of this occasion to note once for all—in the interest of that variety of ideal reigning, I gather, in the connexion. The enjoyment of a work of art, the acceptance of an irresistible illusion, constituting, to my sense, our highest experience of "luxury," the luxury is not greatest, by my consequent measure, when the work asks for as little attention as possible. It is greatest, it is delightfully, divinely great, when we feel the surface, like the thick ice of the skater's pond, bear without cracking the strongest pressure we throw on it. The sound of the crack one may recognise, but never surely to call it a luxury.) That I had scarce availed myself of the privilege of seeing with Densher's eyes is another matter; the point is that I had intelligently marked my possible, my occasional need of it. So, at all events, the constructional "block" of the first two Books compactly forms itself. A new block, all of the squarest and not a little of the smoothest, begins with the Third—by which I mean of course a new mass of interest governed from a new centre. Here again I make prudent *provision*—to be sure to keep my centre strong. It dwells mainly, we at once see, in the depths of Milly Theale's "case," where, close beside it, however, we meet a supplementary reflector, that of the lucid even though so quivering spirit of her dedicated friend.

The more or less associated consciousness of the two women

deals thus, unequally, with the next presented face of the subject— deals with it to the exclusion of the dealing of others; and if, for a highly particular moment, I allot to Mrs. Stringham the responsibility of the direct appeal to us, it is again, charming to relate, on behalf of that play of the portentous which I cherish so as a "value" and am accordingly for ever setting in motion. There is an hour of evening, on the alpine height, at which it becomes of the last importance that our young woman should testify eminently in this direction. But as I was to find it long since of a blest wisdom that no expense should be incurred or met, in any corner of picture of mine, without some concrete image of the account kept of it, that is of its being organically re-economised, so under that dispensation Mrs. Stringham has to register the transaction. Book Fifth is a new block mainly in its provision of a new set of occasions, which readopt, for their order, the previous centre, Milly's now almost full-blown consciousness. At my game, with renewed zest, of driving portents home, I have by this time all the choice of those that are to brush that surface with a dark wing. They are used, to our profit, on an elastic but a definite system; by which I mean that having to sound here and there a little deep, as a test, for my basis of method, I find it everywhere obstinately present. It draws the "occasion" into tune and keeps it so, to repeat my tiresome term; my nearest approach to muddlement is to have sometimes—but not too often—to break my occasions small. Some of them succeed in remaining ample and in really aspiring then to the higher, the sustained lucidity. The whole actual centre of the work, resting on a misplaced pivot and lodged in Book Fifth, pretends to a long reach, or at any rate to the larger foreshortening—though bringing home to me, on reperusal, what I find striking, charming and curious, the author's instinct everywhere for the *indirect* presentation of his main image. I note how, again and again, I go but a little way with the direct—that is with the straight exhibition of Milly; it resorts for relief, this process, whenever it can, to some kinder, some merciful indirection: all as if to approach her circuitously, deal with her at second hand, as an unspotted princess is ever dealt with; the pressure all round her kept easy for her, the sounds, the movements regulated, the forms and ambiguities made charming. All of which proceeds, obviously, from her painter's tenderness of imagination about her, which reduces him to watching her, as it were, through the successive windows of other people's interest in her. So, if we talk of princesses, do the balconies opposite the palace gates, do the coigns of vantage and respect enjoyed for a fee, rake from afar the mystic figure in the gilded coach as it comes forth into the great *place*. But my use of windows and balconies is doubtless at best an extravagance by itself, and as to what there may be to note, of this and other super-subtleties, other arch-refinements, of tact and taste, of design and instinct, in "The Wings of the Dove," I become conscious of overstepping my space without having brought the full quantity to light. The failure leaves me with a burden of residuary comment of which I yet boldly hope elsewhere to discharge myself.

E I G H T E E N
The Ambassadors

NOTHING IS MORE EASY THAN TO STATE THE SUBJECT OF "The Ambassadors," which first appeared in twelve numbers of *The North American Review* (1903) and was published as a whole the same year. The situation involved is gathered up betimes, that is in the second chapter of Book Fifth, for the reader's benefit, into as few words as possible—planted or "sunk," stiffly and saliently, in the centre of the current, almost perhaps to the obstruction of traffic. Never can a composition of this sort have sprung straighter from a dropped grain of suggestion, and never can that grain, developed, overgrown and smothered, have yet lurked more in the mass as an independent particle. The whole case, in fine, is in Lambert Strether's irrepressible outbreak to little Bilham on the Sunday afternoon in Gloriani's garden, the candour with which he yields, for his young friend's enlightenment, to the charming admonition of that crisis. The idea of the tale resides indeed in the very fact that an hour of such unprecedented ease should have been felt by him *as* a crisis, and he is at pains to express it for us as neatly as we could desire. The remarks to which he thus gives utterance contain the essence of "The Ambassadors," his fingers close, before he has done, round the stem of the full-blown flower; which, after that fashion, he continues officiously to present to us. "Live all you can; it's a mistake not to. It doesn't so much matter what you do in particular so long as you have your life. If you haven't had that what *have* you had? I'm too old—too old at any rate for what I see. What one loses one loses; make no mistake about that. Still, we have the illusion of freedom; therefore don't, like me to-day, be without the memory of that illusion. I was either, at the right time, too stupid or too intelligent to have it, and now I'm a case of reaction against the mistake. Do what you like so long as you don't make it. For it *was* a mistake. Live, live!" Such is the gist of Strether's appeal to the impressed youth, whom he likes and whom he desires to befriend; the word "mistake" occurs several times, it will be seen, in the course of his remarks—which gives the measure of the signal warning he feels attached to his case. He has accordingly missed too much, though perhaps after all constitutionally qualified for a better part, and he wakes up to it in conditions that press the spring of a terrible question. *Would* there yet perhaps be time for reparation?—reparation, that is, for the injury done his character; for the affront, he is quite ready to say, so stupidly put upon it and in which he has even himself had so clumsy a hand? The answer to which is that he now at all events *sees;* so that the business of my tale and the march of my action, not to say the precious moral of everything, is just my demonstration of this process of vision.

Nothing can exceed the closeness with which the whole fits again into its germ. That had been given me bodily, as usual, by the spoken word, for I was to take the image over exactly as I happened to have met it. A friend had repeated to me, with great appreciation, a thing or two said to him by a man of distinction, much his senior, and to which a sense akin to that of Strether's melancholy eloquence might be imputed—said as chance would have, and so easily might, in Paris, and in a charming old garden attached to a house of art, and on a Sunday afternoon of summer, many persons of great interest being present. The observation there listened to and gathered up had contained part of the "note" that I was to recognise on the spot as to my purpose—had contained in fact the greater part; the rest was in the place and the time and the scene they sketched: these constituents clustered and combined to give me further support, to give me what I may call the note absolute. There it stands, accordingly, full in the tideway; driven in, with hard taps, like some strong stake for the noose of a cable, the swirl of the current roundabout it. What amplified the hint to more than the bulk of hints in general was the gift with it of the old Paris garden, for in that token were sealed up values infinitely precious. There was of course the seal to break and each item of the packet to count over and handle and estimate; but somehow, in the light of the hint, all the elements of a situation of the sort most to my taste were there. I could even remember no occasion on which, so confronted, I had found it of a livelier interest to take stock, in this fashion, of suggested wealth. For I think, verily, that there are degrees of merit in subjects—in spite of the fact that to treat even one of the most ambiguous with due decency we must for the time, for the feverish and prejudiced hour, at least figure its merit and its dignity as *possibly* absolute. What it comes to, doubtless, is that even among the supremely good—since with such alone is it one's theory of one's honour to be concerned—there is an ideal *beauty* of goodness the invoked action of which is to raise the artistic faith to its maximum. Then truly, I hold, one's theme may be said to shine, and that of "The Ambassadors," I confess, wore this glow for me from beginning to end. Fortunately thus I am able to estimate this as, frankly, quite the best, "all round," of all my productions; any failure of that justification would have made such an extreme of complacency publicly fatuous.

I recall then in this connexion no moment of subjective intermittence, never one of those alarms as for a suspected hollow beneath one's feet, a felt ingratitude in the scheme adopted, under which confidence fails and opportunity seems but to mock. If the motive of "The Wings of the Dove," as I have noted, was to worry me at moments by a sealing-up of its face—though without prejudice to its again, of a sudden, fairly grimacing with expression—so in this other business I had absolute conviction and constant clearness to deal with; it had been a frank proposition, the whole bunch of data, installed on my premises like a monotony of fine weather. (The order of composition, in these things, I may mention, was reversed by the order of publication; the earlier written of the two books having appeared as the later.) Even under the weight of my hero's years I could feel my postulate firm; even under the strain of the difference between those of Madame de Vionnet and those of Chad Newsome, a difference liable to be denounced as shocking, I could still feel it serene. Nothing resisted, nothing betrayed, I seem to make out, in this full and sound sense of the matter; it shed from any side I could turn it to the same golden glow. I rejoiced in the promise of a hero so mature, who would give me thereby the more to bite into—since it's only into thickened motive and accumulated character, I think, that the painter of life bites more than a little. My poor friend should have accumulated character, certainly; or rather would be quite naturally and handsomely possessed of it, in the sense that he would have, and would always have felt he had, imagination galore, and that this yet wouldn't have wrecked him. It was immeasurable, the opportunity to "do" a man of imagination, for if *there* mightn't be a chance to "bite," where in the world might it be? This personage of course, so enriched, wouldn't give me, for his type, imagination in *predominance* or as his prime faculty, nor should I, in view of other matters, have found that convenient. So particular a luxury—some occasion, that is, for study of the high gift in *supreme* command of a case or of a career—would still doubtless come on the day I should be ready to pay for it; and till then might, as from far back, remain hung up well in view and just out of reach. The comparative case meanwhile would serve—it was only on the minor scale that I had treated myself even to comparative cases.

I was to hasten to add however that, happy stopgaps as the minor scale had thus yielded, the instance in hand should enjoy the advantage of the full range of the major; since most immediately to the point was the question of that *supplement* of situation logically involved in our gentleman's impulse to deliver himself in the Paris garden on the Sunday afternoon—or if not involved by strict logic then all ideally and enchantingly implied in it. (I say "ideally," because I need scarce mention that for development, for expression of its maximum, my glimmering story was, at the earliest stage, to have nipped the thread of connexion with the possibilities of the actual reported speaker. *He* remains but the happiest of accidents; his actualities, all too definite, precluded any range of possibilities; it had only been his charming office to project upon that wide field of the artist's vision—which hangs there ever in place like the white sheet suspended for the figures of a child's magic-lantern—a more fantastic and more moveable shadow.) No privilege of the teller of tales and the handler of puppets is more delightful, or has more of the suspense and the thrill of a game of difficulty breathlessly played, than just this business of looking for the unseen and the occult, in a scheme half-grasped, by the light or, so to speak, by the clinging scent, of the gage already in hand. No dreadful old pursuit of the hidden slave with bloodhounds and the rag of association can ever, for "excitement," I judge, have bettered it at its best. For the dramatist always, by the very law of his genius, believes not only in a possible right issue from the rightly-conceived tight place; he does much more than this—he believes, irresistibly, in the necessary, the precious "tightness" of the place (whatever the issue) on the strength of any respectable hint. It being thus the respectable hint that I had with such avidity picked up, what would be the story to which it would most inevitably form the centre? It is part of the charm attendant on such questions that the "story," with the omens true, as I say, puts on from this stage the authenticity of concrete existence. It then *is*, essentially—it begins to be, though it may more or less obscurely lurk; so that the point is not in the least what to make of it, but only, very delightfully and very damnably, where to put one's hand on it.

In which truth resides surely much of the interest of that admirable mixture for salutary application which we know as art. Art deals with what we see, it must first contribute full-handed that ingredient; it plucks its material, otherwise expressed, in the garden of life—which material elsewhere grown is stale and uneatable. But it has no sooner done this than it has to take account of a *process*—from which

only when it's the basest of the servants of man, incurring igno-
minious dismissal with no "character," does it, and whether under
some muddled pretext of morality or on any other, pusillanimously
edge away. The process, that of the expression, the literal squeezing-
out, of value is another affair—with which the happy luck of mere
finding has little to do. The joys of finding, at this stage, are pretty
well over; that quest of the subject as a whole by "matching," as the
ladies say at the shops, the big piece with the snippet, having ended,
we assume, with a capture. The subject is found, and if the problem is
then transferred to the ground of what to do with it the field opens
out for any amount of doing. This is precisely the infusion that, as I
submit, completes the strong mixture. It is on the other hand the part
of the business that can least be likened to the chase with horn and
hound. It's all a sedentary part—involves as much ciphering, of sorts,
as would merit the highest salary paid to a chief accountant. Not,
however, that the chief accountant hasn't *his* gleams of bliss; for the
felicity, or at least the equilibrium, of the artist's state dwells less,
surely, in the further delightful complications he can smuggle in than
in those he succeeds in keeping out. He sows his seed at the risk of
too thick a crop; wherefore yet again, like the gentlemen who audit
ledgers, he must keep his head at any price. In consequence of all
which, for the interest of the matter, I might seem here to have my
choice of narrating my "hunt" for Lambert Strether, of describing the
capture of the shadow projected by my friend's anecdote, or of reporting on the occurrences subsequent to that triumph. But I had
probably best attempt a little to glance in each direction; since it
comes to me again and again, over this licentious record, that one's
bag of adventures, conceived or conceivable, has been only half-emp-
tied by the mere telling of one's story. It depends so on what one
means by that equivocal quantity. There is the story of one's hero,
and then, thanks to the intimate connexion of things, the story of
one's story itself. I blush to confess it, but if one's a dramatist one's a
dramatist, and the latter imbroglio is liable on occasion to strike me as
really the more objective of the two.

The philosophy imputed to him in that beautiful outbreak, the
hour there, amid such happy provision, striking for him, would have
been then, on behalf of my man of imagination, to be logically and, as
the artless craft of comedy has it, "led up" to; the probable course to
such a goal, the goal of so conscious a predicament, would have in
short to be finely calculated. Where has he come from and why has he
come, what is he doing (as we Anglo-Saxons, and we only, say, in our
foredoomed clutch of exotic aids to expression) in that *galère?* To an-

swer these questions plausibly, to answer them as under cross-examination in the witness-box by counsel for the prosecution, in other words satisfactorily to account for Strether and for his "peculiar tone," was to possess myself of the entire fabric. At the same time the clue to its whereabouts would lie in a certain *principle* of probability: he wouldn't have indulged in his peculiar tone without a reason; it would take a felt predicament or a false position to give him so ironic an accent. One hadn't been noting "tones" all one's life without recognising when one heard it the voice of the false position. The dear man in the Paris garden was then admirably and unmistakeably *in* one—which was no small point gained; what next accordingly concerned us was the determination of *this* identity. One could only go by probabilities, but there was the advantage that the most general of the probabilities were virtual certainties. Possessed of our friend's nationality, to start with, there was a general probability in his narrower localism; which, for that matter, one had really but to keep under the lens for an hour to see it give up its secrets. He would have issued, our rueful worthy, from the very heart of New England—at the heels of which matter of course a perfect train of secrets tumbled for me into the light. They had to be sifted and sorted, and I shall not reproduce the detail of that process; but unmistakeably they were all there, and it was but a question, auspiciously, of picking among them. What the "position" would infallibly be, and why, on his hands, it had turned "false"—these inductive steps could only be as rapid as they were distinct. I accounted for everything—and "everything" had by this time become the most promising quantity—by the view that he had come to Paris in some state of mind which was literally undergoing, as a result of new and unexpected assaults and infusions, a change almost from hour to hour. He had come with a view that might have been figured by a clear green liquid, say, in a neat glass phial; and the liquid, once poured into the open cup of *application*, once exposed to the action of another air, had begun to turn from green to red, or whatever, and might, for all he knew, be on its way to purple, to black, to yellow. At the still wilder extremes represented perhaps, for all he could say to the contrary, by a variability so violent, he would at first, naturally, but have gazed in surprise and alarm; whereby the *situation* clearly would spring from the play of wildness and the development of extremes. I saw in a moment that, should this development proceed both with force and logic, my "story" would leave nothing to be desired. There is always, of course, for the story-teller, the irresistible determinant and the incalculable advantage of his interest in the story *as such*; it is ever, obviously, overwhelmingly, the prime and precious thing (as other than this I have never been able to see it); as to which what makes for it, with whatever headlong energy, may be said to pale before the energy with which it simply makes for itself. It rejoices, none the less, at its best to seem to offer itself in a light, to seem to know, and with the very last knowledge, what it's about—liable as it yet is at moments to be caught by us with its tongue in its cheek and absolutely no warrant but its splendid impudence. Let us grant then that the impudence is always there—there, so to speak, for grace and effect and *allure;* there, above all, because the Story is just the spoiled child of art, and because, as we are always disappointed when the pampered don't "play up," we like it, to that extent, to look all its character. It probably does so, in truth, even when we most flatter ourselves that we negotiate with it by treaty.

All of which, again, is but to say that the *steps,* for my fable, placed themselves with a prompt and, as it were, functional as-surance—an air quite as of readiness to have dispensed with logic had I been in fact too stupid for my clue. Never, positively, none the less, as the links multiplied, had I felt less stupid than for the deter-mination of poor Strether's errand and for the apprehension of his issue. These things continued to fall together, as by the neat action of their own weight and form, even while their commentator scratched his head about them; he easily sees now that they were always well in advance of him. As the case completed itself he had in fact, from a good way behind, to catch up with them, breathless and a little flur-ried, as he best could. *The* false position, for our belated man of the world—belated because he had endeavoured so long to escape being one, and now at last had really to face his doom—the false position for him, I say, was obviously to have presented himself at the gate of that boundless menagerie primed with a moral scheme of the most approved pattern which was yet framed to break down on any ap-proach to vivid facts; that is to any at all liberal appreciation of them. There would have been of course the case of the Strether prepared, wherever presenting himself, only to judge and to feel meanly; but *he* would have moved for me, I confess, enveloped in no legend what-ever. The actual man's note, from the first of our seeing it struck, is the note of discrimination, just as his drama is to become, under stress, the drama of discrimination. It would have been his blest imagination, we have seen, that had already helped him to discrimi-nate; the element that was for so much of the pleasure of my cutting thick, as I have intimated, into his intellectual, into his moral sub-stance. Yet here it was, at the same time, just here, that a shade for a moment fell across the scene.

There was the dreadful little old tradition, one of the platitudes of the human comedy, that people's moral scheme *does* break down in Paris; that nothing is more frequently observed; that hundreds of thousands of more or less hypocritical or more or less cynical persons annually visit the place for the sake of the probable catastrophe, and that I came late in the day to work myself up about it. There was in fine the *trivial* association, one of the vulgarest in the world; but which gave me pause no longer, I think, simply because its vulgarity is so advertised. The revolution performed by Strether under the influence of the most interesting of great cities was to have nothing to do with any *bêtise* of the imputably "tempted" state; he was to be thrown forward, rather, thrown quite with violence, upon his lifelong trick of intense reflexion: which friendly test indeed was to bring him out, through winding passages, through alternations of darkness and light, very much *in* Paris, but with the surrounding scene itself a minor matter, a mere symbol for more things than had been dreamt of in the philosophy of Woollett. Another surrounding scene would have done as well for our show could it have represented a place in which Strether's errand was likely to lie and his crisis to await him. The *likely* place had the great merit of sparing me preparations; there would have been too many involved—not at all impossibilities, only rather worrying and delaying difficulties—in positing elsewhere Chad Newsome's interesting relation, his so interesting complexity of relations. Strether's appointed stage, in fine, could be but Chad's most luckily selected one. The young man had gone in, as they say, for circumjacent charm; and where he would have found it, by the turn of his mind, most "authentic," was where his earnest friend's analysis would most find *him;* as well as where, for that matter, the former's whole analytic faculty would be led such a wonderful dance.

"The Ambassadors" had been, all conveniently, "arranged for"; its first appearance was from month to month, in the *North American Review* during 1903, and I had been open from far back to any pleasant provocation for ingenuity that might reside in one's actively adopting—so as to make it, in its way, a small compositional law—recurrent breaks and resumptions. I had made up my mind here regularly to exploit and enjoy these often rather rude jolts—having found, as I believed, an admirable way to it; yet every question of form and pressure, I easily remember, paled in the light of the major propriety, recognised as soon as really weighed; that of employing but one centre and keeping it all within my hero's compass. The thing was to be so much this worthy's intimate adventure that even the projection of his consciousness upon it from beginning to end without intermission or deviation would probably still leave a part of its value for him, and *a fortiori* for ourselves, unexpressed. I might, however, express every grain of it that there would be room for—on condition of contriving a splendid particular economy. Other persons in no small number were to people the scene, and each with his or her axe to grind, his or her situation to treat, his or her coherency not to fail of, his or her relation to my leading motive, in a word, to establish and carry on. But Strether's sense of these things, and Strether's only, should avail me for showing them; I should know them but through his more or less groping knowledge of them, since his very gropings would figure among his most interesting motions, and a full observance of the rich rigour I speak of would give me more of the effect I should be most "after" than all other possible observances together. It would give me a large unity, and that in turn would crown me with the grace to which the enlightened story-teller will at any time, for his interest, sacrifice if need be all other graces whatever. I refer of course to the grace of intensity, which there are ways of signally achieving and ways of signally missing—as we see it, all round us, helplessly and woefully missed. Not that it isn't, on the other hand, a virtue eminently subject to appreciation—there being no strict, no absolute measure of it; so that one may hear it acclaimed where it has quite escaped one's perception, and see it unnoticed where one has gratefully hailed it. After all of which I am not sure, either, that the immense amusement of the whole cluster of difficulties so arrayed may not operate, for the fond fabulist, when judicious not less than fond, as his best of determinants. That charming principle is always there, at all events, to keep interest fresh: it is a principle, we remember, essentially ravenous, without scruple and without mercy, appeased with no cheap nor easy nourishment. It enjoys the costly sacrifice and rejoices thereby in the very odour of difficulty—even as ogres, with their "Fee-faw-fum!" rejoice in the smell of the blood of Englishmen.

Thus it was, at all events, that the ultimate, though after all so speedy, definition of my gentleman's job—his coming out, all solemnly appointed and deputed, to "save" Chad, and his then finding the young man so disobligingly and, at first, so bewilderingly not lost that a new issue altogether, in the connexion, prodigiously faces them, which has to be dealt with in a new light—promised as many calls on ingenuity and on the higher branches of the compositional art as one could possibly desire. Again and yet again, as, from book to book, I proceed with my survey, I find no source of interest equal to this verification after the fact, as I may call it, and the more in detail the better, of the scheme of consistency "gone in" for. As always—

since the charm never fails—the retracing of the process from point to point brings back the old illusion. The old intentions bloom again and flower—in spite of all the blossoms they were to have dropped by the way. This is the charm, as I say, of adventure *transposed*—the thrilling ups and downs, the intricate ins and outs of the compositional problem, made after such a fashion admirably objective, becoming the question at issue and keeping the author's heart in his mouth. Such an element, for instance, as his intention that Mrs. Newsome, away off with her finger on the pulse of Massachusetts, should yet be no less intensely than circuitously present through the whole thing, should be no less felt as to be reckoned with than the most direct exhibition, the finest portrayal at first hand could make her, such a sign of artistic good faith, I say, once it's unmistakeably there, takes on again an actuality not too much impaired by the comparative dimness of the particular success. Cherished intention too inevitably acts and operates, in the book, about fifty times as little as I had fondly dreamt it might; but that scarce spoils for me the pleasure of recognising the fifty ways in which I had sought to provide for it. The mere charm of seeing such an idea constituent, in its degree; the fineness of the measures taken—a real extension, if successful, of the very terms and possibilities of representation and figuration—such things alone were, after this fashion, inspiring, such things alone were a gage of the probable success of that dissimulated calculation with which the whole effort was to square. But oh the cares begotten, none the less, of that same "judicious" sacrifice to a particular form of interest! One's work should have composition, because composition alone is positive beauty; but all the while—apart from one's inevitable consciousness too of the dire paucity of readers ever recognising or ever missing positive beauty—how, as to the cheap and easy, at every turn, how, as to immediacy and facility, and even as to the commoner vivacity, positive beauty might have to be sweated for and paid for! Once achieved and installed it may always be trusted to make the poor seeker feel he would have blushed to the roots of his hair for failing of it; yet, how, as its virtue can be essentially but the virtue of the whole, the wayside traps set in the interest of muddlement and pleading but the cause of the moment of the particular bit in itself, have to be kicked out of the path! All the sophistications in life, for example, might have appeared to muster on behalf of the menace—the menace to a bright variety—involved in Strether's having all the subjective "say," as it were, to himself.

Had I, meanwhile, made him at once hero and historian, endowed him with the romantic privilege of the "first person"—the darkest abyss of romance this, inveterately, when enjoyed on the grand scale—variety, and many other queer matters as well, might have been smuggled in by a back door. Suffice it, to be brief, that the first person, in the long piece, is a form foredoomed to looseness, and that looseness, never much my affair, had never been so little so as on this particular occasion. All of which reflexions flocked to the standard from the moment—a very early one—the question of how to keep my form amusing while sticking so close to my central figure and constantly taking its pattern from him had to be faced. He arrives (arrives at Chester) as for the dreadful purpose of giving his creator "no end" to tell about him—before which rigorous mission the serenest of creators might well have quailed. I was far from the serenest; I was more than agitated enough to reflect that, grimly deprived of one alternative or one substitute for "telling," I must address myself tooth and nail to another. I couldn't, save by implication, make other persons tell *each other* about him—blest resource, blest necessity, of the drama, which reaches its effects of unity, all remarkably, by paths absolutely opposite to the paths of the novel: with other persons, save as they were primarily *his* persons (not he primarily but one of theirs), I had simply nothing to do. I had relations for him none the less, by the mercy of Providence, quite as much as if my exhibition *was* to be a muddle; if I could only by implication and a show of consequence make other persons tell each other about him, I could at least make him tell *them* whatever in the world he must; and could so, by the same token—which was a further luxury thrown in—see straight into the deep differences between what that could do for me, or at all events for *him*, and the large ease of "autobiography." It may be asked why, if one so keeps to one's hero, one shouldn't make a single mouthful of "method," shouldn't throw the reins on his neck and, letting them flap there as free as in "Gil Blas" or in "David Copperfield," equip him with the double privilege of subject and object—a course that has at least the merit of brushing away questions at a sweep. The answer to which is, I think, that one makes that surrender only if one is prepared *not* to make certain precious discriminations.

The "first person" then, so employed, is addressed by the author directly to ourselves, his possible readers, whom he has to reckon with, at the best, by our English tradition, so loosely and vaguely after all, so little respectfully, on so scant a presumption of exposure to criticism. Strether, on the other hand, encaged and provided for as "The Ambassadors" encages and provides, has to keep in view proprieties much stiffer and more salutary than any our straight and credulous gape are likely to bring home to him, has exhibitional con-

371

ditions to meet, in a word, that forbid the terrible *fluidity* of self-reve-
lation. I may seem not to better the case for my discrimination if I say
that, for my first care, I had thus inevitably to set him up a confidant
or two, to wave away with energy the custom of the seated mass of
explanation after the fact, the inserted block of merely referential narrative, which flourishes so, to the shame of the modern impatience,
on the serried page of Balzac, but which seems simply to appal our
actual, our general weaker, digestion. "Harking back to make up"
took at any rate more doing, as the phrase is, not only than the reader
of to-day demands, but than he will tolerate at any price any call upon
him either to understand or remotely to measure; and for the beauty
of the thing when done the current editorial mind in particular appears wholly without sense. It is not, however, primarily for either of
these reasons, whatever their weight, that Strether's friend Waymarsh is so keenly clutched at, on the threshold of the book, or that
no less a pounce is made on Maria Gostrey—without even the pretext, either, of *her* being, in essence, Strether's friend. She is the reader's friend much rather—in consequence of dispositions that make
him so eminently require one; and she acts in that capacity, and *really*
in that capacity alone, with exemplary devotion, from beginning to
end of the book. She is an enrolled, a direct, aid to lucidity; she is in
fine, to tear off her mask, the most unmitigated and abandoned of
ficelles. Half the dramatist's art, as we well know—since if we don't
it's not the fault of the proofs that lie scattered about us—is in the use
of *ficelles*; by which I mean in a deep dissimulation of his dependence
on them. Waymarsh only to a slighter degree belongs, in the whole
business, less to my subject than to my treatment of it; the interesting
proof, in these connexions, being that one has but to take one's subject for the stuff of drama to interweave with enthusiasm as many
Gostreys as need be.

The material of "The Ambassadors," conforming in this respect
exactly to that of "The Wings of the Dove," published just before it, is
taken absolutely for the stuff of drama; so that, availing myself of the
opportunity given me by this edition for some prefatory remarks on
the latter work, I had mainly to make on its behalf the point of its scenic
consistency. It disguises that virtue, in the oddest way in the world, by
just *looking*, as we turn its pages, as little scenic as possible; but it
sharply divides itself, just as the composition before us does, into the
parts that prepare, that tend in fact to over-prepare, for scenes, and the
parts, or otherwise into the scenes, that justify and crown the preparation. It may definitely be said, I think, that everything in it that is not
scene (not, I of course mean, complete and functional scene, treating

all the submitted matter, as by logical start, logical turn, and logical finish) is discriminated preparation, is the fusion and synthesis of picture. These alternations propose themselves all recogniseably, I think, from an early stage, as the very form and figure of "The Ambassadors"; so that, to repeat, such an agent as Miss Gostrey, pre-engaged at a high salary, but waits in the draughty wing with her shawl and her smelling-salts. Her function speaks at once for itself, and by the time she has dined with Strether in London and gone to a play with him her intervention as a *ficelle* is, I hold, expertly justified. Thanks to it we have treated scenically, and scenically alone, the whole lumpish question of Strether's "past," which has seen us more happily on the way than anything else could have done; we have strained to a high lucidity and vivacity (or at least we hope we have) certain indispensable facts; we have seen our two or three immediate friends all conveniently and profitably in "action"; to say nothing of our beginning to descry others, of a remoter intensity, getting into motion, even if a bit vaguely as yet, for our further enrichment. Let my first point be here that the scene in question, that in which the whole situation at Woollett and the complex forces that have propelled my hero to where this lively extractor of his value and distiller of his essence awaits him, is normal and entire, is really an excellent *standard* scene; copious, comprehensive, and accordingly never short, but with its office as definite as that of the hammer on the gong of the clock, the office of expressing *all that is in* the hour.

The *"ficelle"* character of the subordinate party is as artfully dissimulated, throughout, as may be, and to that extent that, with the seams or joints of Maria Gostrey's ostensible connectedness taken particular carē of, duly smoothed over, that is, and anxiously kept from showing as "pieced on," this figure doubtless achieves, after a fashion, something of the dignity of a prime idea: which circumstance but shows us afresh how many quite incalculable but none the less clear sources of enjoyment for the infatuated artist, how many copious springs of our never-to-be-slighted "fun" for the reader and critic susceptible of contagion, may sound their incidental plash as soon as an artistic process begins to enjoy free development. Exquisite—in illustration of this—the mere interest and amusement of such at once "creative" and critical questions as how and where and why to make Miss Gostrey's false connexion carry itself, under a due high polish, as a real one. Nowhere is it more of an artful expedient for mere consistency of form, to mention a case, than in the last "scene" of the book, where its function is to give or to add nothing whatever, but only to express as vividly as possible certain things quite other than itself and that are of the already fixed and appointed measure. Since, however, all art is *expression,* and is thereby vividness, one was to find the door open here to any amount of delightful dissimulation. These verily are the refinements and ecstasies of method—amid which, or certainly under the influence of any exhilarated demonstration of which, one must keep one's head and not lose one's way. To cultivate an adequate intelligence for them and to make that sense operative is positively to find a charm in any produced ambiguity of appearance that is not by the same stroke, and all helplessly, an ambiguity of sense. To project imaginatively, for my hero, a relation that has nothing to do with the matter (the matter of my subject) but has everything to do with the manner (the manner of my presentation of the same) and yet to treat it, at close quarters and for fully economic expression's possible sake, as if it were important and essential—to do that sort of thing and yet muddle nothing may easily become, as one goes, a signally attaching proposition; even though it all remains but part and parcel, I hasten to recognise, of the merely general and related question of expressional curiosity and expressional decency.

I am moved to add after so much insistence on the scenic side of my labour that I have found the steps of re-perusal almost as much waylaid here by quite another style of effort in the same signal interest—or have in other words not failed to note how, even so associated and so discriminated, the finest proprieties and charms of the non-scenic may, under the right hand for them, still keep their intelligibility and assert their office. Infinitely suggestive such an observation as this last on the whole delightful head, where representation is concerned, of possible variety, of effective expressional change and contrast. One would like, at such an hour as this, for critical licence, to go into the matter of the noted inevitable deviation (from too fond an original vision) that the exquisite treachery even of the straightest execution may ever be trusted to inflict even on the most mature plan—the case being that, though one's last reconsidered production always seems to bristle with that particular evidence, "The Ambassadors" would place a flood of such light at my service. I must attach to my final remark here a different import; noting in the other connexion I just glanced at that such passages as that of my hero's first encounter with Chad Newsome, absolute attestations of the non-scenic form though they be, yet lay the firmest hand too—so far at least as intention goes—on representational effect. To report at all closely and completely of what "passes" on a given occasion is inevitably to become more or less scenic; and yet in the instance I allude to, *with* the conveyance, expressional curiosity and expressional decency are sought and arrived at under quite another law. The true inwardness of this may be at bottom but that one of the suffered treacheries has consisted precisely, for Chad's whole figure and presence, of a direct presentability diminished and compromised—despoiled, that is, of its *proportional* advantage; so that, in a word, the whole economy of his author's relation to him has at important points to be redetermined. The book, however, critically viewed, is touchingly full of these disguised and repaired losses, these insidious recoveries, these intensely redemptive consistencies. The pages in which Mamie Pocock gives her appointed and, I can't but think, duly felt lift to the whole action by the so inscrutably-applied side-stroke or short-cut of our just watching, and as quite at an angle of vision as yet untried, her single hour of suspense in the hotel salon, in our partaking of her concentrated study of the sense of matters bearing on her own case, all the bright warm Paris afternoon, from the balcony that overlooks the Tuileries garden—these are as marked an example of the representational virtue that insists here and there on being, for the charm of opposition and renewal, other than the scenic. It wouldn't take much to make me further argue that from an equal play of such oppositions the book gathers an intensity that fairly adds to the dramatic—though the latter is supposed to be the sum of all intensities; or that has at any rate nothing to fear from juxtaposition with it. I consciously fail to shrink in fact from that extravagance—I risk it, rather, for the sake of the moral involved; which is not that the particular production before us exhausts the interesting questions it raises, but that the Novel remains still, under the right persuasion, the most independent, most elastic, most prodigious of literary forms.

The Golden Bowl

$\mathbf{A}$ MONG MANY MATTERS THROWN INTO RELIEF BY A RE-
freshed acquaintance with "The Golden Bowl" what perhaps
most stands out for me is the still marked inveteracy of a certain indirect and oblique view of my presented action; unless indeed I make
up my mind to call this mode of treatment, on the contrary, any superficial appearance notwithstanding, the very straightest and closest
possible. I have already betrayed, as an accepted habit, and even to
extravagance commented on, my preference for dealing with my subject-matter, for "seeing my story," through the opportunity and the
sensibility of some more or less detached, some not strictly involved,
though thoroughly interested and intelligent, witness or reporter,
some person who contributes to the case mainly a certain amount of
criticism and interpretation of it. Again and again, on review, the
shorter things in especial that I have gathered into this Series have
ranged themselves not as my own impersonal account of the affair in
hand, but as my account of somebody's impression of it—the terms
of this person's access to it and estimate of it contributing thus by
some fine little law to intensification of interest. The somebody is
often, among my shorter tales I recognise, but an unnamed, unintroduced and (save by right of intrinsic wit) unwarranted participant,
the impersonal author's concrete deputy or delegate, a convenient
substitute or apologist for the creative power otherwise so veiled and
disembodied. My instinct appears repeatedly to have been that to
arrive at the facts retailed and the figures introduced by the given
help of some other conscious and confessed agent is essentially to
find the whole business—that is, as I say, its effective interest—enriched *by the way*. I have in other words constantly inclined to the idea
of the particular attaching case *plus* some near individual view of it;
that nearness quite having thus to become an imagined observer's, a
projected, charmed painter's or poet's—however avowed the
"minor" quality in the latter—close and sensitive contact with it.

376

Anything, in short, I now reflect, must always have seemed to me better—better for the process and the effect of representation, my irrepressible ideal—than the mere muffled majesty of irresponsible "authorship." Beset constantly with the sense that the painter of the picture or the chanter of the ballad (whatever we may call him) can never be responsible *enough*, and for every inch of his surface and note of his song, I track my uncontrollable footsteps, right and left, after the fact, while they take their quick turn, even on stealthiest tiptoe, toward the point of view that, within the compass, will give me most instead of least to answer for.

I am aware of having glanced a good deal already in the direction of this embarrassed truth—which I give for what it is worth; but I feel it come home to me afresh on recognising that the manner in which it betrays itself may be one of the liveliest sources of amusement in "The Golden Bowl." It's not that the muffled majesty of authorship doesn't here *ostensibly* reign; but I catch myself again shaking it off and disavowing the pretence of it while I get down into the arena and do my best to live and breathe and rub shoulders and converse with the persons engaged in the struggle that provides for the others in the circling tiers the entertainment of the great game. There is no other participant, of course, than each of the real, the deeply involved and immersed and more or less bleeding participants; but I nevertheless affect myself as having held my system fast and fondly, with one hand at least, by the manner in which the whole thing remains subject to the register, ever so closely kept, of the consciousness of but two of the characters. The Prince, in the first half of the book, virtually sees and knows and makes out, virtually represents to himself everything that concerns us—very nearly (though he doesn't speak in the first person) after the fashion of other reporters and critics of other situations. Having a consciousness highly susceptible of registration, he thus makes us see the things that may most interest us reflected in it as in the clean glass held up to so many of the "short stories" of our long list; and yet after all never a whit to the prejudice of his being just as consistently a foredoomed, entangled, embarrassed agent in the general imbroglio, actor in the offered play. The function of the Princess, in the remainder, matches exactly with his; the register of *her* consciousness is as closely kept—as closely, say, not only as his own, but as that (to cite examples) either of the intelligent but quite unindividualised witness of the destruction of "The Aspern Papers," or of the all-noting heroine of "The Spoils of Poynton," highly individualised *though* highly intelligent; the Princess, in fine, in addition to feeling everything she has to, and to playing her part just in that proportion, duplicates, as it were, her value and becomes a compositional resource, and of the finest order, as well as a value intrinsic. So it is that the admirably-endowed pair, between them, as I retrace their fortune and my own method, point again for me the moral of the endless interest, endless worth for "delight," of the compositional contribution. Their chronicle strikes me as quite of the stuff to keep us from forgetting that absolutely *no* refinement of ingenuity or of precaution need be dreamed of as wasted in that most exquisite of all good causes the appeal to variety, the appeal to incalculability, the appeal to a high refinement and a handsome wholeness of effect.

There are other things I might remark here, despite its perhaps seeming a general connexion that I have elsewhere sufficiently shown as suggestive; but I have other matter in hand and I take a moment only to meet a possible objection—should any reader be so far solicitous or even attentive—to what I have just said. It may be noted, that is, that the Prince, in the volume over which he nominally presides, is represented as in comprehensive cognition only of those aspects as to which Mrs. Assingham doesn't functionally—perhaps all too officiously, as the reader may sometimes feel it—supersede him. This disparity in my plan is, however, but superficial; the thing abides rigidly by its law of showing Maggie Verver at first through her suitor's and her husband's exhibitory vision of her, and of then showing the Prince, with at least an equal intensity, through his wife's; the advantage thus being that these attributions of experience display the sentient subjects themselves at the same time and by the same stroke with the nearest possible approach to a desirable vividness. It is the Prince who opens the door to half our light upon Maggie, just as it is she who opens it to half our light upon himself; the rest of our impression, in either case, coming straight from the very motion with which that act is performed. We see Charlotte also at first, and we see Adam Verver, let alone our seeing Mrs. Assingham, and every one and every thing else, but as they are visible in the Prince's interest, so to speak—by which I mean of course in the interest of his being himself handed over to us. With a like consistency we see the same persons and things again but as Maggie's interest, *her* exhibitional charm, determines the view. In making which remark, with its apparently so limited enumeration of my elements, I naturally am brought up against the fact of the fundamental fewness of these latter—of the fact that my large demand is made for a group of agents who may be counted on the fingers of one hand. We see very few persons in "The Golden Bowl," but the scheme of the book, to make up for that, is that we shall really see about as much of them as a coherent literary form permits. That was my problem, so to speak, and my *gageure*—to play the small handful of values really for all they were worth—and to work my system, my particular propriety of appeal, particular degree of pressure on the spring of interest, for all that this specific ingenuity itself might be. To have a scheme and a view of its dignity is of course congruously to work it out, and the "amusement" of the chronicle in question—by which, once more, I always mean the gathered cluster of all the *kinds* of interest—was exactly to see what a consummate application of such sincerities would give.

So much for some only of the suggestions of re-perusal here— since, all the while, I feel myself awaited by a pair of appeals really more pressing than either of those just met; a minor and a major appeal, as I may call them: the former of which I take first. I have so thoroughly "gone into" things, in an expository way, on the ground covered by this collection of my writings, that I should still judge it superficial to have spoken no word for so salient a feature of our Edition as the couple of dozen decorative "illustrations." This series of frontispieces contribute less to ornament, I recognise, than if Mr. Alvin Langdon Coburn's beautiful photographs, which they reproduce, had had to suffer less reduction; but of those that have suffered least the beauty, to my sense, remains great, and I indulge at any rate in this glance at our general intention for the sake of the small page of history thereby added to my already voluminous, yet on the whole so unabashed, memoranda. I should in fact be tempted here, but for lack of space, by the very question itself at large—that question of the general acceptability of illustration coming up sooner or later, in these days, for the author of any text putting forward illustrative claims (that is producing an effect of illustration) by its own intrinsic virtue and so finding itself elbowed, on that ground, by another and a competitive process. The essence of any representational work is of course to bristle with immediate images; and I, for one, should have looked much askance at the proposal, on the part of my associates in the whole business, to graft or "grow," at whatever point, a picture by another hand on my own picture—this being always, to my sense, a lawless incident. Which remark reflects heavily, of course, on the "picture-book" quality that contemporary English and American prose appears more and more destined, by the conditions of publication, to consent, however grudgingly, to see imputed to it. But a moment's thought points the moral of the danger.

Anything that relieves responsible prose of the duty of being, while placed before us, good enough, interesting enough and, if the question be of picture, pictorial enough, above all *in itself*, does it the worst of services, and may well inspire in the lover of literature certain lively questions as to the future of that institution. That one should, as an author, reduce one's reader, "artistically" inclined, to such a state of hallucination by the images one has evoked as doesn't permit him to rest till he has noted or recorded them, set up some semblance of them in his own other medium, by his own other art—nothing could better consort than *that*, I naturally allow, with the desire or the pretension to cast a literary spell. Charming, that is, for the projector and creator of figures and scenes that are as nought from the moment they fail to become more or less visible appearances, charming for this manipulator of aspects to see such power as he may possess approved and registered by the springing of such fruit from his seed. His own garden, however, remains one thing, and the garden he has prompted the cultivation of at other hands becomes quite another; which means that the frame of one's own work no more provides place for such a plot than we expect flesh and fish to be served on the same platter. One welcomes illustration, in other words, with pride and joy; but also with the emphatic view that, might one's "literary jealousy" be duly deferred to, it would quite stand off and on its own feet and thus, as a separate and independent subject of publication, carrying its text in its spirit, just as that text correspondingly carries the plastic possibility, become a still more glorious tribute. So far my invidious distinction between the writer's "frame" and the draughtsman's; and if in spite of it I could still make place for the idea of a contribution of value by Mr. A. L. Coburn to each of these volumes—and a contribution in as different a "medium" as possible—this was just because the proposed photographic studies were to seek the way, which they have happily found, I think, not to keep, or to pretend to keep, anything like dramatic step with their suggestive matter. This would quite have disqualified them, to my rigour; but they were "all right," in the so analytic modern critical phrase, through their discreetly disavowing emulation. Nothing in fact could more have amused the author than the opportunity of a hunt for a series of reproducible subjects—such moreover as might best consort with photography—the reference of which to Novel or Tale should exactly be *not* competitive and obvious, should on the contrary plead its case with some shyness, that of images always confessing themselves mere optical symbols or echoes, expressions of no particular thing in the text, but only of the type or idea of this or that thing. They were to remain at the most small pictures of our "set" stage with the actors left out; and what was above all interesting was that they were first to be constituted.

This involved an amusing search which I would fain more fully commemorate; since it took, to a great degree, and rather unexpectedly and incalculably, the vastly, though but incidentally, instructive form of an enquiry into the street-scenery of London; a field yielding a ripe harvest of treasure from the moment I held up to it, in my fellow artist's company, the light of our fond idea—the idea, that is, of the aspect of things or the combination of objects that might, by a latent virtue in it, speak for its connexion with something in the book, and yet at the same time speak enough for its odd or interesting self. It will be noticed that our series of frontispieces, while doing all justice to our need, largely consists in a "rendering" of certain inanimate characteristics of London streets; the ability of which to suffice to this furnishing forth of my Volumes ministered alike to surprise and convenience. Even at the cost of inconsistency of attitude in the matter of the "grafted" image, I should have been tempted, I confess, by the mere pleasure of exploration, abounding as the business at once began to do in those prizes of curiosity for which the London-lover is at any time ready to "back" the prodigious city. It wasn't always that I straightway found, with my fellow searcher, what we were looking for, but that the looking itself so often flooded with light the question of what a "subject," what "character," what a saving sense in things, is and isn't; and that when our quest was rewarded, it was, I make bold to say, rewarded in perfection. On the question, for instance, of the proper preliminary compliment to the first volume of "The Golden Bowl" we easily felt that nothing would so serve as a view of the small shop in which the Bowl is first encountered.

The problem thus was thrilling, for though the small shop was but a shop of the mind, of the author's projected world, in which objects are primarily related to each other, and therefore not "taken from" a particular establishment anywhere, only an image distilled and intensified, as it were, from a drop of the essence of such establishments in general, our need (since the picture was, as I have said, also completely to speak for itself) prescribed a concrete, independent, vivid instance, the instance that should oblige us by the marvel of an accidental rightness. It might so easily be wrong—by the act of being at all. It would have to be in the first place what London and chance and an extreme improbability should have made it, and then it would have to let us truthfully read into it the Prince's and Charlotte's and the Princess's visits. It of course on these terms long evaded us, but all the while really without prejudice to our fond confidence that, as London ends by giving one absolutely everything one asks, so it awaited us somewhere. It awaited us in fact—but I check myself; nothing, I find now, would induce me to say where. Just so, to conclude, it was equally obvious that for the second volume of the same fiction nothing would so nobly serve as some generalised vision of Portland Place. Both our limit and the very extent of our occasion, however, lay in the fact that, unlike wanton designers, we had, not to "create" but simply to recognise—recognise, that is, with the last fineness. The thing was to induce the vision of Portland Place *to* generalise itself. This is precisely, however, the fashion after which the prodigious city, as I have called it, does on occasion meet halfway those forms of intelligence of it that *it* recognises. All of which meant that at a given moment the great featureless Philistine vista would itself perform a miracle, would become interesting, for a splendid atmospheric hour, as only London knows how; and that our business would be then to understand. But my record of that lesson takes me too far.

So much for some only of the suggestions of re-perusal, and some of those of re-representation here, since, all the while, I feel myself awaited by an occasion more urgent than any of these. To reread in their order my final things, all of comparatively recent date, has been to become aware of my putting the process through, for the latter end of my series (as well as, throughout, for most of its later constituents) quite in the same terms as the apparent and actual, the contemporary terms; to become aware in other words that the march of my present attention coincides sufficiently with the march of my original expression; that my apprehension fits, more concretely stated, without an effort or a struggle, certainly without bewilderment or anguish, into the innumerable places prepared for it. As the historian of the matter sees and speaks, so my intelligence of it, as a reader, meets him halfway, passive, receptive, appreciative, often even grateful; unconscious, quite blissfully, of any bar to intercourse, any disparity of sense between us. Into his very footprints the responsive, the imaginative steps of the docile reader that I consentingly become for him all comfortably sink; his vision, superimposed on my own as an image in cut paper is applied to a sharp shadow on a wall, matches, at every point, without excess or deficiency. This truth throws into relief for me the very different dance that the taking in hand of my earlier productions was to lead me; the quite other kind of consciousness proceeding from *that* return. Nothing in my whole renewal of attention to these things, to almost any instance of my work previous to some dozen years ago, was more evident than that no such active, appreciative process could take place on the mere palpable lines of expression—thanks to the so frequent lapse of harmony between my present mode of motion and that to which the existing footprints were due. It was, all sensibly, as if the clear matter being still there, even as a shining expanse of snow spread over a plain, my exploring tread, for application to it, had quite unlearned the old pace and found itself naturally falling into another, which might sometimes indeed more or less agree with the original tracks, but might most often, or very nearly, break the surface in other places. What was thus predominantly interesting to note, at all events, was the high spontaneity of these deviations and differences, which became thus things not of choice, but of immediate and perfect necessity: necessity to the end of dealing with the quantities in question at all.

No march, accordingly, I was soon enough aware, could possibly be more confident and free than this infinitely interesting and amusing *act* of re-appropriation; shaking off all shackles of theory, unattended, as was speedily to appear, with humiliating uncertainties, and almost as enlivening, or at least as momentous, as, to a philosophic mind, a sudden large apprehension of the Absolute. What indeed could be more delightful than to enjoy a sense of the absolute in such easy conditions? The deviations and differences might of course not have broken out at all, but from the moment they began so naturally to multiply they became, as I say, my very terms of cognition. The question of the "revision" of existing work had loomed large for me, had seemed even at moments to bristle with difficulties; but that phase of anxiety, I was rejoicingly to learn, belonged all but to the state of postponed experience or to that of a prolonged and fatalistic indifference. Since to get and to keep finished and dismissed work well behind one, and to have as little to say to it and about it as possible, had been for years one's only law, so, during that flat interregnum, involving, as who should say, the very cultivation of unacquaintedness, creeping superstitions as to what it might really have been had time to grow up and flourish. Not least among these rioted doubtless the fond fear that any tidying-up of the uncanny brood, any removal of accumulated dust, any washing off wizened faces, or straightening of grizzled locks, or twitching, to a better effect, of superannuated garments, might let one in, as the phrase is, for expensive renovations. I make use here of the figure of age and infirmity, but in point of fact I had rather viewed the reappearance of the first-born of my progeny—a reappearance unimaginable save to some inheritance of brighter and more congruous material form, of stored-up braveries of type and margin and ample page, of general dignity and attitude, than had mostly waited on their respective casual cradles— as a descent of awkward infants from the nursery to the drawing-room under the kind appeal of enquiring, of possibly interested, visitors. I had accordingly taken for granted the common decencies of such a case—the responsible glance of some power above from one nursling to another, the rapid flash of an anxious needle, the not imperceptible effect of a certain audible splash of soap-and-water; all in consideration of the searching radiance of drawing-room lamps as compared with nursery candles. But it had been all the while present to me that from the moment a stitch should be taken or a hair-brush applied the *principle* of my making my brood more presentable under the nobler illumination would be accepted and established, and it was there complications might await me. I am afraid I had at stray moments wasted time in wondering what discrimination against the freedom of the needle and the sponge would be able to describe itself as not arbitrary. For it to confess to that taint would be of course to write itself detestable.

"Hands off altogether on the nurse's part!" was, as a merely barbarous injunction, strictly conceivable; but only in the light of the truth that it had never taken effect in any fair and stately, in any not vulgarly irresponsible re-issue of anything. Therefore it was easy to see that any such apologetic suppression as that of the "altogether," any such admission as that of a single dab of the soap, left the door very much ajar. Any request that an indulgent objector to drawing-room discipline, to the purification, in other words, of innocent childhood, should kindly measure out then the appropriate amount of ablutional fluid for the whole case, would, on twenty grounds, indubitably leave that invoked judge gaping. I had none the less, I repeat, as muddled moments, seemed to see myself confusedly invoke him; thanks to my but too naturally not being able to forecast the perfect grace with which an answer to all my questions was meanwhile awaiting me. To expose the case frankly to a test—in other words to begin to re-read—was at once to get nearer all its elements and so, as by the next felicity, feel it purged of every doubt. It was the nervous postponement of that respectful approach that I spoke of just now as, in the connexion, my waste of time. This felt awkwardness sprang, as I was at a given moment to perceive, from my too abject acceptance of the grand air with which the term Revision had somehow, to my imagination, carried itself—and from my frivolous failure to analyse the content of the word. To revise is to see, or to look over, again— which means in the case of a written thing neither more nor less than to re-read it. I had attached to it, in a brooding spirit, the idea of re-writing—with which it was to have in the event, for my *conscious* play of mind, almost nothing in common. I had thought of re-writing as so difficult, and even so absurd, as to be impossible—having also indeed, for that matter, thought of re-reading in the same light. But the felicity under the test was that where I had thus ruefully prefigured two efforts there proved to be but one—and this an effort but at the first blush. What re-writing might be was to remain—it has remained for me to this hour—a mystery. On the other hand the act of revision, the act of seeing it again, caused whatever I looked at on any page to flower before me as into the only terms that honourably expressed it; and the "revised" element in the present Edition is accordingly these terms, these rigid conditions of re-perusal, registered; so many close notes, as who should say, on the particular vision of the matter itself that experience had at last made the only possible one.

What it would be really interesting, and I dare say admirably difficult, to go into would be the very history of this effect of experience; the history, in other words, of the growth of the immense array of terms, perceptional and expressional, that, after the fashion I have indicated, in sentence, passage and page, simply looked over the heads of the standing terms—or perhaps rather, like alert winged creatures, perched on those diminished summits and aspired to a clearer air. What it comes back to, for the maturer mind—granting of course, to begin with, a mind accessible to questions of such an order—is this attaching speculative interest of the matter, or in vulgar parlance the inordinate intellectual "sport" of it: the how and the whence and the why these intenser lights of experience come into being and insist on shining. The interest of the question is attaching, as I say, because really half the artist's life seems involved in it—or doubtless, to speak more justly, the whole of his life intellectual. The "old" matter is there, re-accepted, re-tasted, exquisitely re-assimilated and re-enjoyed—believed in, to be brief, with the same "old" grateful faith (since wherever the faith, in a particular case, has become aware of a twinge of doubt I have simply concluded against the matter itself and left it out); yet for due testimony, for re-assertion of value, perforating as by some strange and fine, some latent and gathered force, a myriad more adequate channels. It is over the fact of such a phenomenon and its so possibly rich little history that I am moved just fondly to linger—and for the reason I glanced at above, that to do so is in a manner to retrace the whole growth of one's "taste," as our fathers used to say: a blessed comprehensive name for many of the things deepest in us. The "taste" of the poet is, at bottom and so far as the poet in him prevails over everything else, his active sense of life: in accordance with which truth to keep one's hand on it is to hold the silver clue to the whole labyrinth of his consciousness. He feels this himself, good man—he recognises an attached importance—whenever he feels that consciousness bristle with the notes, as I have called them, of consenting re-perusal; as has again and again publicly befallen him, to our no small edification, on occasions within recent view. It has befallen him most frequently, I recognise, when the supersessive terms of his expression have happened to be verse; but that doesn't in the least isolate his case, since it is clear to the most limited intelligence that the title we give him is the only title of *general* application and convenience for those who passionately cultivate the image of life and the art, on the whole so beneficial, of projecting it. The seer and speaker under the descent of the god is the "poet," whatever his form, and he ceases to be one only when his form, whatever else it may nominally or superficially or vulgarly be, is unworthy of the god: in which event, we promptly submit, he isn't worth talking of at all. He becomes so worth it, and the god so adopts him, and so confirms his charming office and name, in the degree in which his impulse and passion are general and comprehensive—a definitional provision for them that makes but a mouthful of so minor a distinction, in the fields of light, as that between verse and prose.

The circumstance that the poets then, and the more charming ones, *have* in a number of instances, with existing matter in hand, "registered" their renewals of vision, attests quite enough the attraction deeply working whenever the mind is, as I have said, accessible—accessible, that is, to the finer appeal of accumulated "good stuff" and to the interest of taking it in hand at all. For myself, I am prompted to note, the "taking" has been to my consciousness, through the whole procession of this re-issue, the least part of the affair: under the first touch of the spring my hands were to feel themselves full; so much more did it become a question, on the part of the accumulated good stuff, of seeming insistently to give and give. I have alluded indeed to certain lapses of that munificence—or at least to certain connexions in which I found myself declining to receive again on *any* terms; but for the rest the sense of receiving has borne me company without a break; a luxury making for its sole condition that I should intelligently attend. The blest good stuff, sitting up, in its myriad forms, so touchingly responsive to new care of any sort whatever, seemed to pass with me a delightful bargain, and in the fewest possible words. "Actively believe in us and then you'll see!"— it wasn't more complicated than that, and yet was to become as thrilling as if conditioned on depth within depth. I saw therefore what I saw, and what these numerous pages record, I trust, with clearness; though one element of fascination tended all the while to rule the business—a fascination, at each stage of my journey, on the noted score of that so shifting and uneven character of the tracks of my original passage. This by itself introduced the charm of suspense: what would the operative terms, in the given case, prove, under criticism, to have been—a series of waiting satisfactions or an array of waiting misfits? The misfits had but to be positive and concordant, in the special intenser light, to represent together (as the two sides of a coin show different legends) just so many effective felicities and substitutes. But I couldn't at all, in general, forecast these chances and changes and proportions; they could but show for what they were as I went; criticism after the fact was to find in them arrests and surprises, emotions alike of disappointment and of elation: all of which means, obviously, that the whole thing was a *living* affair.

The rate at which new readings, new conductors of sense interposed, to make any total sense at all right, became, to this wonderful tune, the very record and mirror of the general adventure of one's intelligence; so that one at all times quite marvelled at the fair reach, the very length of arm, of such a developed difference of measure as to what might and what mightn't constitute, all round, a due decency of "rendering." What I have been most aware of asking myself, however, is how writers, on such occasions of "revision," arrive at that successful resistance to the confident assault of the new reading which appears in the great majority of examples to have marked their course. The term that superlatively, that finally "renders," is a flower that blooms by a beautiful law of its own (the fiftieth part of a second often so sufficing it) in the very heart of the gathered sheaf; it is *there* already, at any moment, almost before one can either miss or suspect it—so that in short we shall never guess, I think, the working secret of the revisionist for whom its colour and scent stir the air but as immediately to be assimilated. Failing our divination, too, we shall apparently not otherwise learn, for the simple reason that no revisionist I can recall has ever been communicative. "People don't do such things," we remember to have heard it, in this connexion, declared; in other words they don't really re-read—no, not *really;* at least they do so to the effect either of seeing the buried, the latent life of a past composition vibrate, at renewal of touch, into no activity and break through its settled and "sunk" surface at no point whatever—on which conclusion, I hasten to add, the situation remains simple and their responsibility may lie down beside their work even as the lion beside the lamb; or else they

387

have in advance and on system stopped their ears, their eyes and even their very noses. This latter heroic policy I find myself glancing at, however, to wonder in what particular cases—failing, as I say, all the really confessed—it can have been applied. The actual non-revision-ists (on any terms) are of course numerous enough, and with plenty to say for themselves; their faith, clearly, is great, their lot serene and their peace, above all, equally protected and undisturbed. But the tantalising image of the revisionist who isn't one, the partial, the piece-meal revisionist, inconsequent and insincere, this obscure and decid-edly *louche* personage hovers before me mainly, I think, but to chal-lenge my belief. Where have we met him, when it comes to that, in the walks of interesting prose literature, and why assume that we *have* to believe in him before we are absolutely forced?

If I turn for relief and contrast to some image of his opposite I at once encounter it, and with a completeness that leaves nothing to be desired, on any "old" ground, in presence of any "old" life, in the vast example of Balzac. He (and these things, as we know, grew be-hind him at an extraordinary rate) re-assaulted by supersessive terms, re-penetrated by finer channels, never had on the one hand seen or said all or had on the other ceased to press forward. His case has equal mass and authority—and beneath its protecting shade, at any rate, I move for the brief remainder of these remarks. We owe to the never-extinct operation of his sensibility, we have but meanwhile to recall, our greatest exhibition of felt finalities, our richest and hugest inheritance of imaginative prose. That by itself might intensify for me the interest of this general question of the reviving and reacting vi-sion—didn't my very own lucky experience, all so publicly incurred, give me, as my reader may easily make out, quite enough to think of. I almost lose myself, it may perhaps seem to him, in that obscure quantity; obscure doubtless because of its consisting of the manifold delicate things, the shy and illusive, the inscrutable, the indefinable, that minister to deep and quite confident processes of change. It is enough, in any event, to be both beguiled and mystified by evolu-tions so near home, without sounding strange and probably even more abysmal waters. Since, however, an agreeable flurry and an im-perfect presence of mind might, on the former ground, still be such a source of refreshment, so the constant refrain humming through the agitation, "If only one *could* re-write, if only one *could* do better justice to the patches of crude surface, the poor morsels of consciously-de-cent matter that catch one's eye with their rueful reproach for old stupidities of touch!"—so that yearning reflexion, I say, was to have its superlative as well as its positive moments. It was to reach its max-imum, no doubt, over many of the sorry businesses of "The Ameri-can," for instance, where, given the elements and the essence, the long-stored grievance of the subject bristling with a sense of over-prolonged exposure in a garment misfitted, a garment cheaply em-broidered and unworthy of it, thereby most proportionately sounded their plaint. This sharpness of appeal, the claim for exemplary damages, or at least for poetic justice, was reduced to nothing, on the other hand, in presence of the altogether better literary manners of "The Ambassadors" and "The Golden Bowl"—a list I might much extend by the mention of several shorter pieces.

Inevitably, in such a case as that of "The American," and scarce less indeed in those of "The Portrait of a Lady" and "The Princess Casamassima," each of these efforts so redolent of good intentions baffled by a treacherous vehicle, an expertness too retarded, I could but dream the whole thing over as I went—as I read; and, bathing it, so to speak, in that medium, hope that, some still newer and shrewder critic's intelligence subtly operating, I shouldn't have breathed upon the old catastrophes and accidents, the old wounds and mutilations and disfigurements, wholly in vain. The same is true of the possible effect of this process of re-dreaming on many of these gathered com-positions, shorter and longer; I have prayed that the finer air of the better form may sufficiently seem to hang about them and gild them over—at least for readers, however few, at all *curious* of questions of air and form. Nothing even at this point, and in these quite final remarks, I confess, could strike me as more pertinent than—with a great wealth of margin—to attempt to scatter here a few gleams of the light in which some of my visions have all sturdily and complacently repeated and others have, according to their kind and law, all joyously and blushingly renewed themselves. These have doubtless both been ways of remaining unshamed; though, for myself, on the whole, as I seem to make out, the interest of the watched renewal has been livelier than that of the accepted repetition. What has the affair been at the worst, I am most moved to ask, but an earnest invitation to the reader to dream again in my company and in the interest of his own larger absorption of my sense? The prime consequence on one's own part of re-perusal is a sense for ever so many more of the shining silver fish afloat in the deep sea of one's endeavour than the net of widest casting could pretend to gather in; an author's common courtesy dictating thus the best general course for making that sense contagious—so beautifully tangled a web, when not so glorious a crown, does he weave by having at heart, and by cherishing there, the confidence he has invited or imagined. There is then absolutely no release to his pledged honour on the question of repaying that confidence.

The ideally handsome way is for him to multiply in any given connexion all the possible sources of entertainment—or, more grossly expressing it again, to intensify his whole chance of pleasure. (It all comes back to that, to my and your "fun"—if we but allow the term its full extension; to the production of which no humblest question involved, even to that of the shade of a cadence or the position of a comma, is not richly pertinent.) We have but to think a moment of such a matter as the play of *representational* values, those that make it a part, and an important part, of our taking offered things in that we should take them as aspects and visibilities—take them to the utmost as appearances, images, figures, objects, so many important, so many contributive items of the furniture of the world—in order to feel immediately the effect of such a condition at every turn of our adventure and every point of the representative surface. One has but to open the door to any forces of exhibition at all worthy of the name in order to see the imaging and qualifying agency called at once into play and put on its mettle. We may traverse acres of pretended exhibitory prose from which the touch that directly evokes and finely presents, the touch that operates for closeness and for charm, for conviction and illusion, for communication, in a word, is unsurpassably absent. All of which but means of course that the reader is, in the common phrase, "sold"—even when, poor passive spirit, systematically bewildered and bamboozled on the article of his dues, he may be but dimly aware of it. He has by the same token and for the most part, I fear, a scarce quicker sensibility on other heads, least of all perhaps on such a matter as his really quite swindled state when the pledge given for his true beguilement fails to ensure him that fullest experience of his pleasure which waits but on a direct reading *out* of the addressed appeal. It is scarce necessary to note that the highest test of any literary form conceived in the light of "poetry"—to apply that term in its largest literary sense—hangs back unpardonably from its office when it fails to lend itself to *vivâ-voce* treatment. We talk here, naturally, not of non-poetic forms, but of those whose highest bid is addressed to the imagination, to the spiritual and the aesthetic vision, the mind led captive by a charm and a spell, an incalculable art. The essential property of such a form as that is to give out its finest and most numerous secrets, and to give them out most gratefully, under the closest pressure—which is of course the pressure of the attention articulately *sounded*. Let it reward as much as it will and can the soundless, the "quiet" reading, it still deplorably "muffs" its chance and its success, still trifles with the roused appetite to which it can never honestly be indifferent, by not having so arranged itself as to owe the flower of its effect to the act and process of apprehension that so beautifully asks most from it. It then infallibly, and not less beautifully, most responds; for I have nowhere found vindicated the queer thesis that the right values of interesting prose depend all on withheld tests—that is on its being, for very pity and shame, but skimmed and scanted, shuffled and mumbled. Gustave Flaubert has somewhere in this connexion an excellent word—to the effect that any imaged prose that fails to be richly rewarding in return for a competent utterance ranks itself as wrong through not being "in the conditions of life." The more we remain in *them*, all round, the more pleasure we dispense; the moral of which is—and there would be fifty other pertinent things to say about this—that I have found revision intensify at every step my impulse intimately to answer, by my light, to those conditions.

All of which amounts doubtless but to saying that as the whole conduct of life consists of things done, which do other things in their turn, just so our behaviour and its fruits are essentially one and continuous and persistent and unquenchable, so the act has its way of abiding and showing and testifying, and so, among our innumerable acts, are no arbitrary, no senseless separations. The more we are capable of acting the less gropingly we plead such differences; whereby, with any capability, we recognise betimes that to "put" things is very exactly and responsibly and interminably to do them. Our expression of them, and the terms on which we understand that, belong as nearly to our conduct and our life as every other feature of our freedom; these things yield in fact some of its most exquisite material to the religion of doing. More than that, our literary deeds enjoy this marked advantage over many of our acts, that, though they go forth into the world and stray even in the desert, they don't to the same extent lose themselves; their attachment and reference to us, however strained, needn't necessarily lapse—while of the tie that binds us to *them* we may make almost anything we like. We are condemned, in other words, whether we will or no, to abandon and outlive, to forget and disown and hand over to desolation, many vital or social performances—if only because the traces, records, connexions, the very memorials we would fain preserve, are practically impossible to rescue for that purpose from the general mixture. We give them up even when we wouldn't—it is not a question of choice. Not so on the other hand our really "done" things of this superior and more appreciable

order—which leave us indeed all licence of disconnexion and disavowal, but positively impose on us no such necessity. Our relation
to them is essentially traceable, and in that fact abides, we feel, the
incomparable luxury of the artist. It rests altogether with himself not
to break with his values, not to "give away" his importances. Not to *be*
disconnected, for the tradition of behaviour, he has but to feel that he
is not; by his lightest touch the whole chain of relation and responsibility is reconstituted. Thus if he is always doing he can scarce, by his
own measure, ever have done. All of which means for him conduct
with a vengeance, since it is conduct minutely and publicly attested.
Our noted behaviour at large may show for ragged, because it perpetually escapes our control; we have again and again to consent to
its appearing in undress—that is in no state to brook criticism. But on
all the ground to which the pretension of performance by a series of
exquisite laws may apply there reigns one sovereign truth—which
decrees that, as art is nothing if not exemplary, care nothing if not
active, finish nothing if not consistent, the proved error is the base
apologetic deed, the helpless regret is the barren commentary, and
"connexions" are employable for finer purposes than mere
gaping contrition.

Just over two weeks after returning to England from his 1904–5 visit to America, James wrote to Scribner's "to arrange for a handsome 'definitive edition' of the greater number of my novels and tales" (Memorandum to Charles Scribner's Sons, July 30, 1905). Such an edition had been under discussion with various publishers since 1900. James, now in his sixties, had completed the last of his major novels, *The Golden Bowl* and was the acknowledged living Master of prose fiction. "He is *par excellence* the American novelist. . . . He is the representative cosmopolitan novelist, also," Scribner's prospectus for the edition announced (Edel, 5: 324). Between 1905 and 1909, the years during which he undertook the New York Edition, he wrote *The American Scene*, "Julia Bride," "The Jolly Corner," "The Velvet Glove," "Mora Montravers," "Crapy Cornelia," "The Bench of Desolation," a series of articles on American women for *Harper's Bazaar*, a chapter for Harper's *The Whole Family: A Novel by Twelve Authors*; revised and collected his travel writings into *English Hours* and *Italian Hours*; and rewrote several fictions into plays: "The Covering End" (which had started out as the drama *Summersoft*) became the three-act *The High Bid; The Other House* returned to its original dramatic form; and "Owen Wingrave" became *The Saloon*.

The work of defining himself as a novelist through the New York Edition is itself an extraordinary literary effort. Having started with the Balzacian model of an *édition définitive*, James makes the form his own: he re-presents his oeuvre, analytically confronting the body of his work at the same time that he makes it new.

In his memorandum to Scribner's, James is very clear about the nature of the edition. It is to be at once inclusive and selective: all of the "principal novels—that is with the possible exception of one" (*The Bostonians*) are to be collected, but James wishes to "sift and select" and rearrange his shorter writings. "My impression is that my shorter things will gain in significance and importance, very considerably, by a fresh grouping or classification, a placing together, from series to series, of those that will help each other, those that will conduce to something of a common effect." James' fictions will also be made fresh by revision: "My idea is, further, to revise everything carefully, and *to re-touch*, as to expression, turn of sentence, and the question of surface generally, wherever this may strike me as really required." Revision will result, as James says in a letter to Scribner's on June 12, 1906, in "benefit not only for myself, but for the public at large." *Portrait*, for example, will receive "a new lease of such life as it may still generally aspire to." The originality and importance of this newly arranged, newly written edition will be underscored, James explains in the memorandum, by a series of prefaces. "Lastly, I desire to furnish each book, whether consisting of a single fiction, or of several minor ones, with a freely colloquial and even, perhaps, as I may say, confidential preface or introduction, representing, in a manner, the history of the work or the group, representing more particularly, perhaps, a frank critical talk about its subject, its origin, its place in the whole artistic chain, and embodying, in short, whatever of interest there may be to be said about it." The prefaces will themselves be fresh because James has, as he says, "never committed myself in print in any way, even so much as by three lines to a newspaper, on the subject of anything I have written, and I feel as if I should come to this part of the business with a certain freshness of appetite and effect." Finally, James' works "will gain rather than lose by enjoying for the first time . . . a form and appearance, a dignity and beauty of outward aspect, that may seem to bespeak consideration for them as a matter of course. Their being thus presented, in fine, as fair and shapely will contribute, to my mind, to their coming legitimately into a 'chance' that has been hitherto rather withheld from them, and for which they have long and patiently waited."

What James describes to Scribner's is "a new and more honorable presentation" of his writings. His emphasis on the edition's newness is, no doubt, partly a justification of this publishing venture. Yet James' closely pondered description (he suggests not only the number and size of the volumes, but the word count for the prefaces) indicates that he wants to obtain for his work the careful, serious attention that it had not yet received. Arranging for the edition was difficult partly because, despite James' position as Master of prose fiction, his books had not been selling well (see our commentary on "Criticism," Chapter 9). The New York Edition is meant to create a critically sophisticated audience of readers, the first of whom will be James himself as he re-reads his works. As first reader James is an exemplar; the Prefaces which describe his confrontations with his fictions are, as James' famous 1908 letter to Howells makes clear, "a sort of plea for Criticism, for Discrimination, for Appreciation . . . " (August 17, 1908, *The Letters of Henry James*, vol. 2, ed. Lubbock [New York: Charles Scribner's Sons, 1920]). The search for a critical community that began with "The Art of Fiction" is now focused on the reader.

James' comment to Howells is even more telling when we consider its context. Wearied by his long work on the Prefaces, James wrote "This staleness of sensibility, in connection with them, blocks out for the hour every aspect but that of their being all done, and of their perhaps helping the Edition to sell two or three copies more! They will have represented much labour to this latter end—though in that they will have differed indeed from no other of their fellow manifestations (in general) whatever; and the resemblance will be even increased if the two or three copies *don't*, in the form of an extra figure or two, mingle with my withered laurels. They are, in general, a sort of plea for Criticism, for Discrimination, for Appreciation on other than infantile lines—as against the so almost universal Anglo-Saxon absence of these things; which tends so, in our general trade, it seems to me, to break the heart. . . . They ought, collected together, none the less, to form a sort of comprehensive manual or *vademecum* for aspirants in our arduous profession."

The letter to Howells also reveals James' pragmatism, both as to the saleability of his writing'and as to the craft that produced it, a pragmatism that recurs throughout the Prefaces. The theory of fiction that James propounds is always based upon analysis of specific reading and writing experiences. As Beerbohm's famous 1915 cartoon of the critical confrontation between the older and younger Jameses illustrates, James is in two places at once in the New York Edition. And this doubling is spatial as well as temporal: Not only does the Master recall the younger man's experiences, but James also occupies two positions in relation to the text; he is reader and writer. In the Preface to *The Golden Bowl* James describes the process of re-reading or "revision" as that of a man following his own footsteps in the snow, sometimes matching his original tread, sometimes creating a new path (p. 383). James finds himself surprised at the freedom with which he re-encounters his work "No march . . . could possibly be more confident and free than this infinitely interesting and amusing *act* of re-appropriation; shaking off all shackles of theory" (Preface to *The Golden Bowl*, p. 383). In this wide-ranging walk through his works, James freely follows his 1884 declaration that "*a priori*" standards must be rejected in favor of a flexible engagement with'the text: "The only obligation to which in advance we may hold a novel, without incurring the accusation of being arbitrary, is that it be interesting" ("The Art of Fiction," p. 170).

But, where does this practical, a posteriori approach leave the reader who seeks to follow James through his fiction?

At the center of attention. James is "addicted to seeing through," not only the consciousnesses of his characters, but the eyes of his audience. As writer, he is constantly concerned with what will interest and convince his readers. At the same time, his judgments about what will interest and convince are based on his experience as reader. The intimacy of this writer-reader relationship is illustrated in the Preface to *The Golden Bowl* when James explains that he has not re-written but revised his fiction—seen it again, re-read it. "What has the affair been at the worst, I am most moved to ask, but an earnest invitation to the reader to dream again in my company and in the interest of his own larger absorption of my sense?" (p. 389) James' double identity is rather astonishingly demonstrated in his earlier description of how we read romance. "There is our general sense of the way things happen—it abides with us indefeasibly, as readers of fiction, from the moment that we demand that our fiction shall be intelligible; and there is our particular sense of the way they don't happen, which is liable to wake up unless reflexion and criticism, in us, have been skilfully and successfully drugged" (Preface to *The American*, p. 281). What is remarkable here is that James is both drugged and druggist. The "really addicted artist," as he calls himself in the Preface to *The Portrait of a Lady* (p. 293), pushes for an equally addicted reader to share the delightfully demanding work of fiction: "The enjoyment of a work of art, the acceptance of an irresistable illusion, constituting, to my sense, our highest experience of 'luxury,' the luxury is not greatest, by my consequent measure, when the work asks for as little attention as possible. It is greatest, it is delightfully, divinely great, when we feel the surface, like the thick ice of the skater's pond, bear without cracking the strongest pressure we throw on it" (Preface to *The Wings of the Dove*, p. 358). In reading, as in writing, "difficulty" provides the necessary firm surface.

Unfortunately, as James repeatedly reminds himself, most readers work on fiction not at all (See James' earlier complaints about readers in "Criticism" and "The Future of the Novel," Chapters 9 and 10). The Prefaces illustrate again and again that James is his own best reader. *The Awkward Age's* dramatic structure and use of dialogue remain unnoticed until he points them out. " . . . I was to fail to make out in the event that the book succeeded in producing the impression of *any* plan on any person. No hint of that sort of success, or of any critical perception at all in relation to the business, has ever come my way; in spite of which when I speak, as just above, of what was to 'happen' under the law of my ingenious labour, I fairly lose myself in the vision of a hundred bright phenomena" (Preface to *The Awkward Age*, pp. 307–8). Caught up in admiring how *Maisie's* careful structure makes us feel "the theme *is* being treated," James reminds himself: "That is we feel it when, in such tangled connexions, we happen to care. I shouldn't really go on as if this were the case with many readers" (Preface to *What Maisie Knew*, p. 329).

Even if readers care enough to judge what they read, they use uncritical, a priori standards. In contrast, James, expecting *The Awkward Age* to prove a case of "over-treatment," instead finds himself wondering what over-treatment might be. Reading the novel helps us to see "the grave distinction between substance and form in a really wrought work of art signally break down" (Preface to *The Awkward Age*, p. 313). "Over-treatment" becomes a meaningless term because the completed novel's subject cannot be separated from its treatment. "And" James concludes, "from this precisely I deduce my moral," we can only judge by results, by the *"feeling"* the novel produces (Preface to *The Awkward Age*, p. 314). In its dependence upon the individual consciousness of the reader and the specific nature of the text, this "moral" pointedly does not provide a uniform, easily applied standard of judgment.

What James' "moral" does is illustrate how the reader's role doubles the writer's: fiction ends where it begins—with "felt life." The topic of fictional sources is generally broached in the Prefaces by James' personal recollections of the circumstances under which a work was written. In beginning with the artist, James is exploring the claim of "The Art of Fiction" (p. 175), that "We must grant the artist his subject, his idea, his *donnée*." Since the artist's task is that "of wondering and, with all achievable adroitness, of causing to wonder . . . " (Preface to "The Altar of the Dead"), the choice of subject depends upon the sensibility of the individual artist. "[O]ne never really chooses one's general range of vision—the experience from which ideas and themes and suggestions spring. . . . The subject thus pressed upon the artist is the necessity of his case and the fruit of his consciousness . . . " (Preface to "Lady Barbarina"). The image of the house of fiction in the preface to *The Portrait of a Lady* shows how "the 'choice of subject' " and "the 'literary form' " are "as nothing without the posted presence of the watcher. . . " (pp. 290–91). Fiction's sources must include the artist's consciousness.

This deep connection between the artist and his or her work—stressed in "Guy de Maupassant" and "Emile Zola" (Chapters 8 and 20)—makes "vanity of the *a priori* test of what an *idée mère* may have to give (Preface to *The Awkward Age*, p. 302). "The Beast in the Jungle" has its origins in James' "attested predeliction for poor sensitive gentlemen"; the germ for "The Altar of the Dead" lies in the interest in "the lost Dead" that he shares (albeit on a lesser scale) with his protagonist (Preface to "The Altar of the Dead"). To decide beforehand that certain subjects are immoral is to fail to recognize the natures of both morality and art. In "The Art of Fiction" (p. 181) James asked,

"You wish to paint a moral picture or carve a moral statue: will you not tell us how you would set about it?" Bolstered by Turgenev's example, he responds twenty years later by positing "the perfect dependence of the 'moral' sense of a work of art on the amount of felt life concerned in producing it" (Preface to *The Portrait of a Lady*, pp. 289–90).

Selecting a subject is, however, also a formal, technical task. For James, the "germ" of fiction is inevitably of "inveterate minuteness. . . . its virtue is all in its needlelike quality, the power to penetrate as finely as possible. The fineness it is that communicates the virus of suggestion. . . " (Preface to *The Spoils of Poynton*). The diffidence that he describes in the Preface to *The Aspern Papers* about seeing Jane Clairmont is an affirmation of "that odd law which somehow always makes the minimum of valid suggestion serve the man of imagination better than the maximum" (p. 332). "Life being all inclusion and confusion," it often provides too much material; art is "all discrimination and selection" (Preface to *The Spoils of Poynton*). The artist must not present life, but *represent* it through the creation of forms. "Art deals with what we see . . . it plucks its material, otherwise expressed, in the garden of life. . . . But it has no sooner done this than it has to take account of a *process*. . . . that of the expression, the literal squeezing-out of value . . ." (Preface to *The Ambassadors*, pp. 364–65).

Formal structures therefore pervade the Prefaces: circles, houses, and picture frames; the "system," "geometry," "plan," "arrangement," and "composition" of the work of art. As James shows in the Preface to *Roderick Hudson*, the construction of such forms is made difficult by the fact that the artist's subject, the relations among people and things, is boundless: "Really, universally, relations stop nowhere" (p. 260). The writer must avoid what James calls in the Preface to *The Awkward Age*, "The trap laid for his superficial convenience . . . though the relations of a human figure or a social occurrence are what make such objects interesting, they also make them, to the same tune, difficult to isolate, to surround with the sharp black line, to frame in the square, the circle, the charming oval, that helps any arrangement of objects to become a picture" (Preface to *The Awkward Age*, p. 302). Structuring fiction formally will allow the writer to avoid formless "large loose baggy monsters" (Preface to *The Tragic Muse*). Yet drawing lines is difficult not only because life's complexity is interesting but also because the interested artist has so active an imagination. The writer's delicately balanced task is "To improvise with extreme freedom and yet at the same time without the possibility of ravage. . . . to aim at absolute singleness, clearness and roundness, and yet to depend on an imagination working freely . . . " (Preface to *The Aspern Papers*, pp. 339–40).

One of the problems entailed in drawing the circle of representation is that while fiction cannot present every moment in time, "the law of mere elimination" makes for sketchy and uninteresting art. Instead, the writer must "give all the sense, in a word, without all the substance or all the surface" (Preface to *Roderick Hudson*, p. 267). Time should be represented through summary and foreshortening, "the art of figuring synthetically, a compactness into which the imagination may cut thick, as into the rich density of wedding-cake" (Preface to *The Tragic Muse*).

Another way to draw the circle is to use a center of consciousness as a "principle of composition." By centering the events of a fiction in the consciousness of a character, James, who is "[A]ddicted to seeing 'through,'" is able to order and dramatize them (Preface to *What Maisie Knew*, p. 326). Further, compositional benefits accrue even when the consciousness remains anonymous, as James makes clear in the Preface to *The Golden Bowl*. And the structural use of the central consciousness has other benefits as well: Fictions filtered through an observer's mind are "enriched *by the way*" (Preface to *The Golden Bowl*, p. 376).

Throughout the Prefaces, James confronts the problem of creating the limited yet acute consciousness that will best organize and reveal his subject, exploring "that provision for interest which consists in placing advantageously, placing right in the middle of the light, the most polished of possible mirrors of the subject" (Preface to *The Princess Casamassima*). This mirroring mind cannot be "*too* acute" without seeming "disconnected" and "super-human" (Preface to *Roderick Hudson*, p. 268). But neither can its limitations be too severe; a fool's point of view, James argues in the Preface to *The Princess Casamassima*, can never be central.

Even when the central consciousness is fine, there are problems of limitation. What makes the "frail vessel" of Isabel Archer's mind important enough to warrant our attention? James argues that, just as the artist's vision animates what are otherwise "mere holes in a dead wall" of the house of fiction, Isabel's sensibility transforms her "mild adventure" into a "drama" as engrossing as "battle and murder and sudden death" (Preface to *The Portrait of a Lady*, p. 297). Isabel gains importance because James, like George Eliot, shows the protagonists "adventures and their history—the author's subject matter all—as determined by their feelings and the nature of their minds. Their emotions, their stirred intelligence, their moral consciousness, become thus, by sufficiently charmed perusal, our own very adventure" (Preface to *The Princess Casamassima*). The result is the situation described in the Preface to *The Spoils of Poynton*: "a subject residing in somebody's excited and concentrated feeling about something—both the something and the somebody being of course as important as possible—has more beauty to give out than under any other style of pressure."

Maisie's childish consciousness allows James to analyze the limited center still further. Just as he dismisses the possibility of a fool as a central consciousness, he rejects the idea of limiting his narrative to what Maisie comprehends. At the same time he avoids the danger described in the Preface to *The Princess Casamassima*, that of "filling too full any supposed and above all any obviously limited vessel of consciousness," by not making Maisie understand more than befits her character. James shows that Maisie's limitations are, in fact, the very terms of narrative. "It seems probable that if we were never bewildered there would never be a story to tell about us . . . " (Preface to *The Princess Casamassima*). At the same time that Maisie's innocent wonder makes the events of the novel into "the stuff of poetry and tragedy and art," her bewilderment creates the book's ironic structure: "our own commentary constantly attends and amplifies . . . we simply take advantage of these things better than she herself" (Preface to *What Maisie Knew*, pp. 321, 320).

The Preface to *The Ambassadors* focuses, not on the limited consciousness per se, but on the limitations imposed upon a narrative when it is restricted to a single point of view. The danger is that unity may be achieved at the expense of variety. "[E]mploying but one centre and keeping it all within my hero's compass" gives James "a large unity" and "the grace of intensity"; yet there is a "menace to a bright variety—involved in Strether's having all the subjective 'say,' as it were, to himself" (p. 368–70). A more varied unity might be obtained by writing *The Ambassadors* in the first person, but "the first person, in the long piece, is a form foredoomed to looseness"; for James, Strether's point of view is useful only when "encaged and provided for" (Preface to *The Ambassadors*, p. 371).

A more structured source of variety is the use of multiple centers of consciousness. Such a solution presents the artist with the structural task "of establishing one's successive centres—of fixing them so exactly that the portions of the subject commanded by them as by happy points of view, and accordingly treated from them, would constitute, so to speak, sufficiently solid *blocks* of wrought material, squared to the sharp edge, as to have weight and mass and carrying power; to make for construction, that is, to conduce to effect and to provide for beauty" (Preface to *The Wings of the Dove*, p. 352). In *The Golden Bowl* each of the two main characters is at once "a foredoomed, entangled, embarrassed agent in the general imbroglio" and "the clean glass held up" to reflect the other (Preface to *The Golden Bowl*, p. 377).

James also uses the term "center" to describe the subjects of his fictions. These central subjects may be centers of consciousness as well. Thus in the Preface to *Portrait*, Isabel is described as a figure surrounded by satellites. Similarly, in the Preface to *The Wings of the Dove*, Milly is imaged as the Lorelei or whirlpool at the center of the novel. However, James emphasizes circumference, not center, in his analysis of *Wings* because the novel's central situation—Milly's life-and-death struggle—is, as we have seen, largely treated indirectly "through the successive windows of other people's interest in her" (Preface to *The Wings of the Dove*, p. 359). Sketching the composition of *The Awkward Age*, James again describes a figure circled by lesser entities, but that figure is, instead of a character, James' subject, the awkward situation of the novel. And, rather than being elucidated by surrounding characters, the various aspects of *The Awkward Age*'s situation are lit by a series of social occasions or scenes.

The use of scenes as fictional structures is, like the center of consciousness, a topic in nearly all of the Prefaces. "Dramatise it, dramatise it!'" James admonishes himself repeatedly. In the Preface to *The Awkward Age*, the novel which draws most heavily on his theater experiences of the 90s, James focuses on the role of the dramatic in fiction. The "current actuality" of *The Awkward Age*'s situation, the uncertainty of "what will happen," is naturally dramatic (p. 303). The clear-cut demands that dramatic structures make on the artist—writing in dialogue, which must be disguised in the English novel; being "shut up wholly to cross-relations"; keeping those relations clear yet complex—restrict James, yet provide him with a "hard fine floor" on which "the element of execution feels it may more or less confidently dance . . . " (Preface to *The Awkward Age*, pp. 312, 308). James yields, "luxuriously," as he says in the Preface to *The Tragic Muse*, to the "charm of the scenic consistency, the consistency of the multiplication of *aspects*, that of making them amusingly various. . . ."

Structuring the divisions of his novel like "acts of a play" implies, for James, a certain objectivity, an avoidance of "going behind." "No character in a play (any play not a mere monologue) has, for the right expression of the thing, a *usurping consciousness*" (Preface to *The Tragic Muse*).

Pleased as he is with this program for *The Awkward Age,* James does not decree an ironclad literary law against going behind. As he wrote to Mrs. Humphry Ward on July 26, 1899, far from advocating "one general 'hard and fast rule of presentation,'" he pragmatically maintains that there are as many "'rules'" as there are subjects, "each of them imposed, artistically, by the particular case. . . ." James goes on to describe his own varied practice: "I 'go behind' right and left in "The Princess Casamassima," "The Bostonians," "The Tragic Muse," just as I do the same but singly in "The American" and "Maisie," and just as I do it consistently *never at all* (save for a false and limited *appearance,* here and there, of doing it a *little,* which I haven't time to explain) in "The Awkward Age."

This practical flexibility can be seen in the Preface to *The Wings of the Dove* where James distinguishes between "scene" and "picture." Throughout his life, James, who wrote widely on the visual arts, compares literary with pictorial representation. However, he uses "picture" here in a more specific, technical sense. Pictures are told, the work of narration; scenes are "shown" or dramatized by the characters' interactions or consciousnesses. James tends to favor the scenic in the Prefaces, as in the Preface to *The Ambassadors* when he shows how using Maria Gostrey as a *ficelle* permits him "to wave away with energy the custom of the seated mass of explanation after the fact, the inserted block of merely referential narrative"; Strether confides the information that we need to know to this "reader's friend" (p. 372). Yet while James laments his failure to fully dramatize *Wings* because of picture and scene's mutual jealousy, he also makes a case in the Preface to *The Ambassadors* for "the finest proprieties and charms of the non-scenic" and argues that an alternation between picture and scene can provide a strong structure: "[*The Wings of the Dove*] sharply divides itself, just as the composition before us does, into the parts that prepare, that tend in fact to over-prepare, for the scenes, and the part, or otherwise into the scenes, that justify and crown the preparation" (p. 372).

The results of such over-preparation can be, as it is in *The Tragic Muse* and *The Wings of the Dove,* a misplaced middle: "in very few of my productions, to my eye, *has* the organic centre succeeded in getting into proper position. . . . the infirmity I speak of, for example, has been always but the direct and immediate fruit of a positive excess of foresight, the overdone desire to provide for future need and lay up heavenly treasure against the demands of my climax. . . . The first half of a fiction insists ever on figuring to me as the stage or theatre for the second half . . ." (Preface to *The Tragic Muse*). Here, the very failure to form a fiction properly is attributable to James' scrupulous attention to form.

The Prefaces' constant emphasis on form is, however, accompanied from the beginning by a regard for life, for verisimilitude. The antithesis between Mary Garland and Christina Light helps structure *Roderick Hudson*, yet too strict a dichotomy damages realism. Next to Christina Light, Mary Garland seems too colorless to be believably attractive. Even "special" characters like Roderick must also be "typical" enough to receive our understanding and sympathy. "[The] painter of life who wishes both to treat his chosen subject and to confine his necessary picture" must balance the demands of life and art (Preface to *Roderick Hudson*, p. 267).

These demands weigh differently in different genres. In 1884, James, bent on establishing that all fiction should be held to the same standard of execution, observes "The novel and the romance, the novel of incident and that of character—these clumsy separations appear to me to have been made by critics and readers for their own convenience, and to help them out of their occasional queer predicaments, but to have little reality or interest for the producer . . . " ("The Art of Fiction," p. 175). However, twenty years later, faced with the queer predicament of criticizing and reading his own productions, James recognizes that different "kinds" of fictions are executed differently. He therefore attempts to discover the distinctions between fictional genres. In the Preface to *The American* he distinguishes realism from romance. As he analyzes the nature of this phenomenon, James discards definitions based on traditional trappings ("the strange and the far . . . a matter indispensably of boats, or of caravans, or of tigers, or of 'historical characters,'" etc.) or on either quantitative distinctions (romantic situations are those seen as *more* dangerous than real ones) or "'subjective'" ones (distinctions made according to the temper of the subject or protagonist) (pp. 279–80). Realism and romance differ in *kind*. The real is what "we cannot possibly *not* know"; the romantic, "we never *can* directly know" (Preface to *The American*, p. 279). Thus James turns away from the "facts" in the Preface to *The Aspern Papers:* to keep Jane Clairmont "preciously unseen" is "to run no risk of . . . of depreciating that romance-value . . . " (p. 332). James pursues the factual germ for "The Aspern Papers" as an artist rather than as an historian; he expands upon it imaginatively rather than augmenting it through research.

However, even "experience disengaged, disembroiled, disencumbered" must *appear* to be tied to earth (Preface to *The American*, p. 280). James delights in the romance of the "palpable imaginable *visita-*

ble past" of *The Aspern Papers*, an era which is *"other*, both richly and recogniseably so," because it allows us to balance our "liking to feel the past strange and liking to feel it familiar" (pp. 333–34). In such a setting "the way things don't happen may be artfully made to pass for the way things do" (Preface to *The American*, p. 281).

To the claim that fictions like *The Aspern Papers* which deal with public figures *must* be strictly bound by "the way things happen," that they should be written as realistic romans à clef, the Master replies that such stories are, in fact, lessons in reality. "If the life about us for the last thirty years refuses warrant for these examples, then so much the worse for that life. . . . I can't tell you, no, who it is I 'aimed at' in the story of Henry St. George. . . . But I none the less maintain his situation to have been in *essence* an observed reality . . ." (Preface to "The Lesson of the Master"). Challenges to his representation of London in *The Princess Casamassima* from those whose "knowledge" is greater are answered similarly. "Yet knowledge, after all, of what? My vision of the aspects I more or less fortunately rendered *was*, exactly, my knowledge. If I made my appearances live, what was this but the utmost one could do with them?" (Preface to *The Princess Casamassima*). Even the claims of verisimilitude must be understood in context of the artist's consciousness.

The way things happen is less of a problem in the "pure romance" of "The Turn of the Screw" since James argues that fairytales treat "an annexed but independent world in which nothing is right save as we rightly imagine it" (Preface to *The Aspern Papers*, pp. 342, 339). "The Turn of the Screw" has "the immense merit of allowing the imagination absolute freedom of hand, of inviting it to act on a perfectly clear field, with no 'outside' control involved, no pattern of the usual or the true or the terrible 'pleasant' (save always of course the high pleasantry of one's very form) to consort with" (Preface to *The Aspern Papers*, p. 338). Free of the usual demands of fictional verisimilitude, the artist need only be true to his form. Faced with the choice of creating factually accurate ghosts or constructing a "good" story, James chooses the latter. To make his story "good," he must make his ghosts "bad." Here, as throughout the Prefaces, James chooses what works. And what works differs for different kinds of fiction.

The New York Edition was initially published in a limited special issue of 156 copies. There was a first printing of 1,500 for volumes 1–10; 1,000 for 11–23.

It failed financially. Not only did the edition not sell well, James had not realized how the complicated copyright arrangements necessary to its publication would cut into his profits. His letters to his literary agent, James B. Pinker, on October 20 and 23, 1908 describe James' "hour of shock" at his earnings (the first of these, an unpublished letter located at Yale, is quoted by Anesko, who gives a thorough description of these arrangements).

Critical reaction to the edition by James' contemporaries was sparse. In general, critics praised the Prefaces (although some saw them as eloquent but unoriginal restatements of James' earlier criticism). Among the articles that dealt directly with the Prefaces were: Schuyler, *New York Times* 13 (January 11, 1908): 13–15; Hale, "The Rejuvenation of Henry James," *Dial* 44 (March 16, 1908): 174–76; *New York Tribune Weekly Review* (April 5, 1908): 6–7; Lubbock, "The Novels of Henry James," *Times Literary Supplement* 391 (July 8, 1909): 249–50; Marsh, "Henry James: Auto-Critic," *Bookman* 30 (October 1909): 138–43; Gretton, "Mr. Henry James and His Prefaces," *Contemporary* 101 (January 1912): 69–78. Most reviewers, however, dealt largely, and often harshly, with the revisions. James himself praised Lubbock's "admirable and exquisite article" in a letter to Howard Sturgis on July 11, 1909. But his response to Edmund Gosse's thoughtful letter on the edition was more characteristic of how the Master felt that his work had yet again failed to find an intelligent readership. James wrote on August 25, 1915, that although he was "touched" by what Gosse had written, such efforts "on behalf of my poor old rather truncated edition, in fact, entirely frustrate one—which has the grotesque likeness for me of a sort of miniature Ozymandias of Egypt ('look on my *works*, ye mighty, and despair!')—round which the lone and level sands stretch further away than ever. . . . That Edition has been, from the point of view of profit either to the publishers or to myself, practically a complete failure; vulgarly speaking it doesn't sell. . . . I remain at my age (which you know), and after my long career, utterly, insurmountably, unsaleable. . . . The edition is from that point of view really a monument (like Ozymandias) which never had the least intelligent critical justice done it—or any sort of critical attention at all paid it—and the artistic problem involved in my scheme was a deep and exquisite one, and moreover was, as I held, very effectively solved. Only it took such time—*and* such taste—in other words such aesthetic light. No more commercially thankless job of the literary order was (Prefaces and all—*they* of a thanklessness!) accordingly ever achieved."

Despite James' pessimism, the Prefaces clearly have changed the way his fiction is read, as their widespread use in James scholarship testifies. However, criticism that deals with the Prefaces as a whole is less extensive. Blackmur's essay, "The Critical Prefaces," *Hound and Horn* 7 (April–May): 444–77 (reprinted as the introduction to *The Art of the Novel* (New York: Charles Scribner's Sons, 1934]), remains invaluable, and Anesko's " 'Friction with the Market': The Publication of Henry James's New York Edition," *New England Quarterly* 56 (September 1983): 354–81, has recently provided much useful information. Other treatments of the Prefaces include: Aiken, review of *The Art of the Novel: Critical Prefaces,* in *Criterion* 14 (July 1935): 313–15; rpt. in *A Reviewer's ABC* (New York: Meridian Books, 1958); Blasing, "The Story of the Stories: Henry James's Prefaces as Autobiography," in *Approaches to Victorian Autobiography,* ed. Landow (Athens, Ohio: Ohio University Press, 1979), pp. 311–32; Burgess, "The Seeds of Art: Henry James's *Donnée,*" *Literature and Psychology* 13 (Summer 1963): 67–73; Edel (5: 330–33); *Prefaces of Henry James* (Paris: Jouve, 1931); "The Architecture of the New York Edition," *New England Quarterly* 24 (June 1951): 169–78; Franklin, *An Index to Henry James's Prefaces to the New York Edition* (Charlottesville: Bibliographical Society of the University of Virginia, 1966); Goetz, "Criticism and Autobiography in James's Prefaces," *American Literature* 51 (1979): 333–48; Kappeler, "Reader and Critic writ large," in *Writing and Reading in Henry James* (New York: Columbia University Press, 1980), pp. 174–90; Leavis, "Henry James," *Scrutiny* 5 (March 1937): 398–417; Leitch, "The Editor as Hero: Henry James and the New York Edition," *Henry James Review* 3 (Fall 1981): 24–32; Lewis, Foreword, *The Art of the Novel* (Boston: Northeastern University Press, 1984); Smith, "The Quest of Beauty," in *Forces in American Criticism* (New York: Harcourt, Brace, 1939), pp. 185–228.

Notes to *Roderick Hudson*

259:2. serial publication in "The Atlantic Monthly." Scribner's had asked James to write a serial in 1874, but James managed to get Howells at the *Atlantic* to offer him more money. He therefore began *Roderick Hudson* for the *Atlantic* at 10 Piazza Santa Maria Novela in Florence.

260:12. my first attempt at a novel. James' first novel was actually *Watch and Ward,* serialized in the *Atlantic* 28 (August–December 1871) and published, after revision, in book form in 1878. James never reprinted it again and commonly referred to *Roderick Hudson* as his first novel.

261:28. summer partly spent in the Black Forest. James stayed at the Hotel Royal in Baden-Baden.

261:29. three months passed near Boston. James was living at his parents' home, 20 Quincy Street, Cambridge.

262:15. James' address in New York was 11 East Twenty-fifth Street.

263:1. state of civilisation providing for "art". Returning to his American artist of 1875, James reiterates his complaint in *Hawthorne* (1879) about the thin environment that America provides for art. See Chapter 5. See also James' comments about Jeffrey Aspern as an American artist in the Preface to *The Aspern Papers,* Chapter 16.

263:37. *quelconque.* any.

263:39. the great shadow of Balzac. See our commentary to "Honoré de Balzac," Chapter 4.

265:9. such mild overhauling. James had revised *Roderick Hudson* twice, for the American book version and the English edition. For discussions of James' revision of the novel for the New York Edition, see: Altick, "The Spirit of Scholarship," in *The Art of Literary Research* (New York: W. W. Norton, 1963), p. 15; Bercovitch, "The Revision of Rowland Mallett," *Nineteenth Century Fiction* 24 (September 1969): 210–21; Harvitt, "How Henry James Revised *Roderick Hudson*: A Study in Style," *PMLA* 39 (March 1924): 203–27; Havens' reply to Harvitt, *PMLA* 40 (June 1925): 433–34; Maxwell, "The Revision of *Roderick Hudson*," *English Studies* 45 (June 1964): 239; McIntyre, "The Later Manner of Mr. Henry James," *PMLA* 27 (1912): 354–71; Putt Editorial Note, *Roderick Hudson* (Baltimore: Penguin Publishers, 1969), pp. 5–7; Ray, "The Importance of Original Editions," in *Nineteenth Century English Books* (Urbana: University of Illinois Press, 1952), p. 22; Tintner, "Henry James's Salome and the Arts of the *Fin de Siècle*," *Markham Review* 5 (1975): 5–10; Tintner, "*Roderick Hudson*: A Centennial Reading," *Henry James Review* 2 (Spring 1981): 172–98.

265:39. "nowhere . . . turn." In volume 2 of the Library of America edition of James' criticism, Edel identifies this as a quote from the introductory note to *English Hours* (1905).

267:16. foreshorten. In the Preface to "Daisy Miller," James describes foreshortening as "the particular economic device for which one must have a name and which has in its single blessedness and its determined pitch, I think, a higher price than twenty other clustered loosenesses; and just because full-fed statement, just because the picture of as many of the conditions as possible made and kept proportionate, just because the surface iridescent, even in the short piece, by what is beneath it and what throbs and gleams through, are things all conducive to the only compactness that has a charm, to the only spareness that has a force, to the only simplicity that has a grace— those, in each order, that produce the *rich* effect."

267:24. coarse industries. James here continues the critique of literature as industry that he makes in "Criticism" and "The Future of the Novel," Chapters 9 and 10.

267:27. "dark backward and abysm." *The Tempest,* I, 2, l. 50.

268:3. on some other occasion. For example, the Preface to *The Awkward Age,* Chapter 14.

270:39. meeting her again and taking her up later on. Christina Light reappears as the title character in *The Princess Casamassima* (1886). In the Preface to that novel, James is distrustful of this reappearance: "my sense of a really expressed character is that it shall have originally so tasted of the ordeal of service as to feel no disposition to yield again to the strain. Why should the Princess of the climax of 'Roderick Hudson' still have made her desire felt, unless in fact to testify that she had not been—for what she was—completely recorded?" Another *Roderick Hudson* character, the artist Gloriani, also reappears in a later novel, *The Ambassadors*.

Notes to *The American*

271:1. begun in Paris. James began writing *The American* at 29 Rue de Luxembourg in November 1875. He had originally proposed the project to *Galaxy*, thinking that Howells at the *Atlantic* would not follow *Roderick Hudson* so closely with another serial.

271:14. the sad warning. *Denis Duval, Wives and Daughters*, (first published in *Cornhill Magazine* in March–June, 1864, and August 1864–January 1866, respectively), and *Weir of Hermiston* (*Cosmopolis*, January–April, 1896) were all left unfinished by their authors' untimely deaths. James wrote an essay on "Winchelsea, Rye, and *Denis Duval*," reviewed *Wives and Daughters*, and said of *Weir of Hermiston* in his 1900 review of Stevenson's letters: "Among prose fragments it stands quite alone, with the particular grace and sanctity of mutilation worn by the marble morsels of masterwork in another art."

272:23. in another country and an aristocratic society. That James, "seated in an American 'horse-car,' " is inspired to locate his American businessman in Europe makes sense in light of his confession in the Preface to *The Reverberator*: "before the American business-man, as I have been prompt to declare, I was absolutely and irredeemably helpless, with no fibre of my intelligence responding to his mystery. No approach I could make to him on his 'business side' really got near it. This is where I was fatally incompetent. . . ."

273:42. The Salon Carré of the Louvre is the setting for the opening scene in *The American*.

274:17. the conception of Paris. In the Preface to *The Ambassadors*, James again describes himself as determined to avoid a clichéd Parisian melodrama: "There was the dreadful little old tradition, one of the platitudes of the human comedy, that people's moral scheme *does* break down in Paris . . . and that I came late in the day to work myself up about it" (p. 368).

274:36. the emblazoned flag of romance. Studies of James and romance include: Beach, *The Method of Henry James*, rev. ed. (Philadelphia: Albert Saifer, 1954); Blackmur, Introduction, *The American* (New York: Dell, 1960), pp. 5–13; Chase, "James on the Novel vs. the Romance," *The American Novel and Its Tradition* (Garden City, New York: Doubleday Anchor Books, 1957), pp. 117–37; Daugherty (chaps. 7, 8); Knox, "Romance and Fable in James's *The American*," *Anglia* 83 (1965): 308–23 (rpt. in Stafford, ed., *Merrill Studies in "The American"* [Columbus, Ohio: Merrill, 1971]); Porte, "James," in *The Romance in America* (Middletown, Conn.: Wesleyan University Press, 1969), pp.

193–226; Tytell, "Henry James and the Romance," *Markham Review* 5 (May 1969): 1–2.

274:39. plotting arch-romance without knowing it. At the time of its writing James had regarded *The American* as a realistic novel and repeatedly defended its unhappy ending with appeals to verisimilitude. Responding on March 30, 1877, to Howells' criticisms, James argued that marrying Claire de Cintré to Newman would have been "throwing a rather vulgar sop to readers who don't really know the world and who don't measure the merit of a novel by its correspondence to the same." The grounds of James' defense reveal his early attraction to French realism, an attraction that, as his 1879 judgment of Hawthorne illustrates, fostered his ambivalence towards romance. See "From *Hawthorne*," Chapter 5. On happy endings, see "The Art of Fiction," p. 168 and note 168:39.

275:14. Gray's beautiful Ode. "Ode on a Distant Prospect of Eton College," by Thomas Gray (1716–1771), ends: "where ignorance is bliss, / 'Tis folly to be wise."

277:4. small dusky hotel of the Rive Gauche. After returning from the summer trip that included the visits to Etretat and Bayonne mentioned above, James stayed at the Hôtel Lorraine, Rue de Beaune, the residence of his friend James Russell Lowell when Lowell was in Paris. The stay at the Hôtel Lorraine actually came *before* James' trip to Saint-Germain-en-Laye.

277:7. Balzac's Maison Vauquer in "Le Père Goriot." In "Honoré de Balzac," p. 75, James says: "We, for our part, have always found Balzac's houses and rooms extremely interesting; we often prefer his places to his people." He goes on to describe the Maison Vauquer as "the best of all" Balzac's houses.

277:8. once more in the Rue de Luxembourg. James finished *The American* in a different apartment at No. 29 and then left for England on December 10, 1876.

279:17. the coarse, comprehensive, prodigious Zola. See "Emile Zola," Chapter 20.

283:32. the window of his wide . . . consciousness. In the Preface to *The Portrait of a Lady*, pp. 290–91, James uses the metaphor of the window to describe the individual vision of the artist.

284:15. so thoroughly revising the book. Although *The American* is the second volume in the New York Edition, James revised it third, after *Roderick Hudson* and *The Portrait of a Lady*. In the Preface to *The Golden Bowl*, James describes *The American* as a "subject bristling with a sense of over-prolonged exposure in a garment misfitted, a garment cheaply embroidered and unworthy of it. . ." (p. 389). Thus, its revision was substantive as well as stylistic. Edel calls *The American* "the most rewritten of all the novels" (5: 327), and many critics have studied James' revisions of the novel. See: Blackmur, Introduction, *The American* (New York: Dell, 1960), pp. 5–13; Bosanquet, " 'The Revised Version,' " *The Little Review* 5 (August 1918): 56–62; Butterfield, "*The American*," in *The Air of Reality: New Essays on Henry James*, ed. Goode (London: Methuen, 1972), pp. 5–35; Gettmann, "Henry James's Revision of *The*

American," *American Literature* 16 (January 1945): 279–95; Herrick, "A Visit to Henry James," *Yale Review*, n.s. 12 (July 1923): 724–41; n.s. 13 (October 1923), 206–8; Pearce, Introduction, *The American* (Boston: Houghton Mifflin, 1962), pp. v–xxv (rpt. as "Henry James and His *American*," in *Historicism Once More* [Princeton: Princeton University Press, 1969], p. 240–60); Reynolds, "Henry James's New Christopher Newman," *Studies in the Novel* 5 (Winter 1973): 457–68; Schulz, "The Bellegardes' Feud with Christopher Newman: A Study of Henry James's Revision of *The American*," *American Literature* 27 (March 1955): 42–55; Stafford, "The Ending of James's *The American*: A Defense of the Early Version," *Nineteenth Century Fiction* 18 (June 1963): 86–89 (rpt. in *Merrill Studies in "The American"* [Columbus, Ohio: Merrill, 1971], pp. 104–7); Tintner, "Balzac's *La Comédie humaine* in Henry James's *The American*," *Revue de Littérature Comparée*, 54 (1980), 101–4; Traschen, "An American in Paris," *American Literature* 26 (March 1954): 67–77; Traschen, "Henry James and the Art of Revision," *Philological Quarterly* 35 (January 1956): 39–47; Traschen, "James's Revisions of the Love Affair in *The American*," *New England Quarterly* 29 (March 1956): 43–62; Tuttleton, "Rereading *The American*: A Century Since," *Henry James Review* 1 (Winter 1980): 139–53; Watkins, "Christopher Newman's Final Instinct," *Nineteenth Century Fiction* 12 (June 1957): 85–88; Wyatt, "Modernity and Paternity: James's *The American*," in *Prodigal Sons: A Study in Authorship and Authority* (Baltimore: Johns Hopkins University Press, 1980): 1–25.

284:36. *tout craché.* very image.

Notes to *The Portrait of a Lady*

286:2. begun in Florence. Writing to Howells on June 17, 1879, James spoke of how "a certain novel about a Europeanizing heroine . . . begun sometime since, has remained an aching fragment." He took up that fragment at the end of April 1880 at the Hotel de l'Arno in Florence. *Portrait* was finished in the summer of 1881 at 4161 Riva degli Schiavoni in Venice. It was published in *Macmillan's Magazine* from October 1880 through November 1881 and in the *Atlantic Monthly* from November 1880 through December 1881.

287:29. any conceit of a "plot". On novels of plot vs. novels of character, see "Ivan Turgénieff" and "The Art of Fiction," Chapters 6 and 7.

288:5. a remark that I heard. James is recalling a visit to Turgenev described in a letter to William James on February 8, 1876: [Turgenev] "said he had never *invented* anything or any one. Everything in his stories comes from some figure he has seen. . . . To his sense all the interest, the beauty, the poetry, the strangeness, etc., are there, *in* the people and things. . . ."

288:10. *disponibles.* at one's disposal; available.

288:25. *que cela manque souvent d'architecture.* it is often lacking architecture.

288:41. *Il en serait bien embarrassé.* He would be quite embarassed by it.

289:5. *en disponibilité.* unattached, in availability.

289:31. dull dispute over the "immoral" subject and the moral. See "The Art of Fiction," "Guy de Maupassant," and "Emile Zola." Chapter 7, 8, and 20.

290:1. felt life. On the connections between art and life, see "Sainte-Beuve," "The Art of Fiction," and the Preface to *The Golden Bowl,* Chapters 2, 7, and 19. James also argues that criticism is grounded in feeling. See his review of Arnold's *Essays in Criticism,* "Saint-Beuve," and "Criticism," Chapters 1, 2, and 9.

292:28. George Eliot has admirably noted it. *Daniel Deronda,* chap. 11: "In these delicate vessels is borne onward through the ages the treasure of human affections."

294:41. after *The Ambassadors.* See the Preface to *The Ambassadors,* p. 363.

297:2. *ficelle.* thread; (theat.) stage-trick; (fig.) dodge. For the discussion of another *ficelle,* see the Preface to *The Ambassadors,* Chapter 18.

297:30. to come to Europe. Discussing American unawareness of Europe in the last decades of the nineteenth century in the Preface to *The Reverberator,* James describes "certain of the women, the younger, the youngest, those of whom least might at the best have been expected, and in the interest of whose 'success' their share of the characteristic blankness underwent what one might call a sea-change. Conscious of so few things in the world, these unprecedented creatures—since that is what it came to for them—were least of all conscious of deficiencies and dangers; so that, the grace of youth and innocence and freshness aiding, their negatives were converted and became in certain relations lively positives and values."

297:39. into the stuff of drama. From at least as early as "The Art of Fiction," James recognizes that ordinary life is capable of drama: "It is an incident for a woman to stand up with her hand resting on a table and look out at you in a certain way . . ." (p. 174).

298:25. as "interesting" as the surprise of a caravan or the identification of a pirate. In *The Golden Bowl* (XXIV, 5, II), Maggie Verver finds that "the straight vindictive view . . . figured nothing nearer to experience than a wild eastern caravan, looming into view with crude colours in the sun, fierce pipes in the air, high spears against the sky, all a thrill, a natural joy to mingle with, but turning off short before it reached her and plunging into other defiles."

299:2. "international" light. Writing to Howells on October 24, 1876, James forecasted: "My novel is to be an *Americana*—the adventures in Europe of a female Newman. . . ." He discusses the period during which the "international" light shone strongest for him primarily in the Prefaces to *The Spoils of Poynton, The Reverberator,* and "Lady Barbarina." In the latter, he distinguishes those works that are essentially "international" and those "in which the work is by no means merely addressed to the illustration of it." "Lady Barbarina" and "The International Episode" belong to the first category; *The Wings of the Dove* and *The Golden Bowl* to the second. The light faded because of a change in international relations, "a new scale of relations altogether, a state of things from which *emphasised* internationalism has either quite dropped or is well on its way to drop." James lists *Portrait* as one of those novels that depends upon this newly "achieved social fusion." James' turning from the international theme was also a response to negative criticism. See our commentary to "The Art of Fiction," Chapter 7.

Notes to *The Awkward Age*

300:29. a trick of looking dead . . . the flush of life. See the Preface to *Roderick Hudson,* Chapter 11, for another description of this revival.

302:7. misplaced middles. See the Preface to *The Wings of the Dove,* Chapter 17.

302:33. The trap laid for his superficial convenience. "Any real art of representation is, I make out, a controlled and guarded acceptance, in fact a perfect economic mastery, of that conflict: the general sense of the expansive, the explosive principle in one's material thoroughly noted, adroitly allowed to flush and colour and animate the disputed value, but with its other appetites and treacheries, its characteristic space-hunger and space-cunning, kept down" (Preface to "Daisy Miller").

303:19. play of mind. James finds the free play of mind, which Arnold sets as the ideal for the critic, culturally realized in London society itself. His comment below about living in an "epoch of transition" also echoes Arnold's contention that the high Victorian period was self-consciously transitional.

305:11. the female young read. For how James felt that focusing on this audience injured the novel, see "The Future of the Novel," Chapter 10.

306:14. "Gyp". pseudonym of Marie-Antoinette de Riquetti de Mirabeau, comtesse de Martel de Janville (1850–1932), French author of novels and sketches of society life.

307:22. M. Henri Lavedan (1859–1940), French dramatist of Parisian manners.

309:23. "to haunt, to startle and waylay." James quotes l. 10 of Wordsworth's "She was a Phantom of Delight."

309:32. successive Acts of a Play. James' theater experiences in the 90s had brought him to realize drama's importance to the novel. "Has a *part* of all this wasted passion and squandered time (of the last 5 years) been simply the precious lesson, taught me in that roundabout and devious, that cruelly expensive, way, *of the singular value for a narrative plan too* of the (I don't know *what* adequately to call it) divine principle of the Scenario? . . . the divine principle in question is a key that, working in the same *general* way fits the complicated chambers of *both* the dramatic and the narrative lock . . ." (*N*, February 14, 1895).

310:21. disdainers of the contemporary drama. Edel (4: 30–31) argues that the problems with drama that James describes here actually reflect "his own difficulties with the stage" rather than the views of other critics.

311:1. Dumas and Ibsen. Alexandre Dumas (Dumas *fils*) (1824–95),

French novelist and playwright who specialized in drama set in the present. *Denise* (1885), *Monsieur Alphonse* (1873), *Francillon* (1887). Henrik Ibsen (1828–1906), Norwegian poet and playwright, a pioneer in modern, realistic, prose drama. *Pillars of Society* (1877), *An Enemy of the People* (1882), *Ghosts* (1881), *Rosmersholm* (1886), *John Gabriel Borkmann* (1896), *The Master Builder* (1892), *A Doll's House* (1879), *The Wild Duck* (1884). On Dumas and James, see: Cargill, *The Novels of Henry James* (New York: Macmillan, 1961); Daugherty, pp. 176–78; Dunbar, "A Source for Roderick Hudson," *Modern Language Notes* 63 (May 1948): 303–10; Grover, "Henry James and the Theme of the Adventuress," *Revue de Littérature Comparée* 47 (October–December 1973): 586–96; Habegger, "'The Siege of London': Henry James and the *Pièce Bien Faite*," *Modern Fiction Studies* 15 (Summer 1969): 219–30; Larson, "The Drama Criticism of Henry James," *Yale/Theatre* 4 (1973): 103–9; Maguire, "James and Dumas, fils," *Modern Drama* 10 (May 1967): 34–42. On Ibsen and James: Cromer, "James and Ibsen," *Comparative Literature* 25 (Spring 1973): 114–27; Cargill; Daugherty; Edel (3, 4, 5); Introduction, *The Other House* (London: Rupert Hart-Davis, 1948); Edwards, "Henry James and Ibsen," *American Literature* 24 (May 1952): 208–23; Egan, *Henry James: The Ibsen Years* (London: Vision Press, 1972); Griggs, "The Novel in *John Gabriel Borkman* [sic]: Henry James's *The Ambassadors*," *Henry James Review* 1 (Spring 1980): 211–18; Larson; Robins, *Theatre and Friendship* (New York: G. P. Putnam's Sons, 1932).

Notes to *What Maisie Knew*

316:2. the "great oak" from the little acorn. James describes *The Awkward Age* as "the best example" of this phenomenon. See Chapter 14.

316:5. The accidental mention. James describes this event in his notebook entry for November 12, 1892: "Two days ago, at dinner at James Bryce's, Mrs. Ashton, Mrs. Bryce's sister, mentioned to me a situation that she had known of, of which it immediately struck me that something might be made in a tale. A child (boy or girl would do, but I see a girl, which would make it different from *The Pupil*) was *divided* by its parents in consequence of their being divorced." James describes *both* parents as remarrying in this entry, as he will in the novel itself. There is an extensive discussion of *Maisie* in the *Notebooks*. In addition to the above, see the entries for August 26, 1893; December 22, 1895; September 22, 1896; October 26, 1896; December 21, 1896.

318:27. that bright hard medal. In the Preface to *The Wings of the Dove* James uses a similar image to describe how that story is simultaneously concerned with Milly's "case" and the "case" of those who are affected by her. See pp. 350–51.

319:19. elsewhere noted. See the Preface to *Roderick Hudson*, Chapter 11.

320:12. a plan of absolutely definite and measurable application. "The artist is free, surely, to adopt any [plan] he fancies, provided it *be* a plan and he adopt it intelligently . . ." (Preface to *The Spoils of Poynton*).

324:10. a doctor of medicine. In 1890, James traveled in Italy with William Wilberforce Baldwin, an American physician who had treated him for jaundice in 1887. William and Alice James and Constance Fenimore Woolson were among Baldwin's patients.

325:37. the very early American reactions and returns. On "the international theme," see note 299:2 to the Preface to *The Portrait of a Lady*.

326:6. the modern reporter's big brushes . . . the height of his skyscrapers. Both images are central to James' lament about the deterioration of American culture in *The American Scene* (1907).

329:5. the "scenic" law. In a notebook entry for December 21, 1896, James said of *Maisie* "I realise—none too soon—that the *scenic* method is my absolute, my imperative, my *only* salvation. The *march of action* is the thing for me to, more and more, *attach* myself to: it is the only thing that really, for *me*, at least, will *produire* L'OEUVRE, and L'OEUVRE is, before God, what I'm going in for. Well, the scenic scheme is the only one that *I* can trust, with my tendencies, to stick to the march of an action. How reading Ibsen's splendid *John Gabriel* a day or two ago (in proof) brought that, FINALLY AND FOR-EVER, home to me!" On the scenic in fiction, see the Prefaces to *The Awkward Age* and *The Wings of the Dove*, Chapters 14 and 17.

Notes to *The Aspern Papers*

331:31. occasion . . . to define my sense of the romantic. See the Preface to *The American*, Chapter 12.

332:10. The historian . . . the dramatist. On the distinction between literature and history, see "The Novel in *The Ring and the Book*," Chapter 21. On the novel as history, see "The Art of Fiction," Chapter 7, and James' review of *Middlemarch*, Chapter 3.

332:35. the legend of whose consequent adventure. James' notebook entry for January 12, 1887, recounts the legend. "Hamilton (V.L.'s brother) told me a curious thing of Capt. Silsbee—the Boston art-critic and Shelley-worshipper; that is of a curious adventure of his. Miss Claremont [sic], Byron's *ci-devant* mistress (the mother of Allegra) was living, until lately, here in Florence, at a great age, 80 or thereabouts, and with her lived her niece, a younger Miss Claremont—of about 50. Silsbee knew that they had interesting papers—letters of Shelley's and Byron's—he had known it for a long time and cherished the idea of getting hold of them. To this end he laid the plan of going to lodge with the Misses Claremont—hoping that the old lady in view of her great age and failing condition would die while he was there, so that he might then put his hand upon the documents, which she hugged close in life. He carried out this scheme—and things *se passèrent* as he had expected. The old woman *did* die—and then he approached the younger one—the old maid of 50—on the subject of his desires. Her answer was—'I will give you all the letters if you marry me!' H. says that Silsbee *court encore*." Matthiessen and

Murdock suggest that "Hamilton (V.L.'s brother)" was Vernon Lee's half-brother, Eugene Lee-Hamilton.

333:41. palpable imaginable *visitable* past. In "The Novel in *The Ring and the Book*," p. 470, James describes "Italy of the eve of the eighteenth century" as "beautiful . . . because of the quantity of romantic and esthetic tradition from a more romantic and esthetic age still visibly, palpably, in solution there. . . ."

334:8. the charm of looking over a garden wall. Cf. Ralph Pendrel's vision of the past in *The Sense of the Past* (Book Second): "No man, he well believed, could ever so much have wanted to look behind and still behind—to scale the high wall into which the successive years, each a squared block, pile themselves in our rear and look over as nearly as possible with the eye of sense into, unless it should rather be called out of, the vast prison yard." Also see Edel (5: 366–67) for an account of how William James embarrassed Henry by spying on G. K. Chesterton over a garden wall.

335:4. isn't even feebly localised. On geographic localization, see the Preface to *Roderick Hudson*, Chapter 11.

336:31. these objects of animadversion in another hour. In the Preface to "The Lesson of the Master," James replies to the friend who asks him where he has "found" these characters: " 'If the life about us for the last thirty years refuses warrant for these examples, then so much the worse for that life. The *constatation* would be so deplorable that instead of making it we must dodge it: there are decencies that in the name of the general self-respect we must take for granted, there's a kind of rudimentary intellectual honour to which we must, in the interest of civilisation, at least pretend.' "

336:37. absolutely no warrant. On the thinness of the American artistic environment, see "From *Hawthorne*," and the Preface to *Roderick Hudson*, Chapters 5 and 11.

338:1. "psychical" case. On James' involvement with the Society for Psychical Research, see Sheppard, *Henry James and "The Turn of the Screw"* (Bungay, Suffolk: Aukland University Press, Oxford University Press, 1974), and Banta, *Henry James and the Occult* (Bloomington: Indiana University Press, 1972).

338:29. time-honoured Christmas-tide toy. James refers to the English custom of telling ghost stories at Christmas.

339:4. a fairy-tale pure and simple. In the Preface to "The Altar of the Dead," James explains "It may seem odd, in a search for the amusing, to try to steer wide of the silly by hugging close the 'supernatural'; but one man's amusement is at the best (we have surely long had to recognise) another's desolation; and I am prepared with the confession that the 'ghost-story,' as we for convenience call it, has ever been for me the most possible form of the fairy-tale. It enjoys, to my eyes, this honour by being so much the neatest—neat with that neatness without which *representation*, and therewith beauty, drops. One's working of the spell is of course—decently and effectively—but by the represented thing, and the grace of the more or less closely represented state is the measure of any success. . . ."

339:10. Hop o' my Thumb. In a letter to Elizabeth Jordan on May 3, 1907, reproduced in part in her *Favorite Fairy Tales: The Childhood Choice of Representative Men and Women* (1907), James described his early reaction to this tale: "However, I *had* thrilled by the nursery fire, over a fat little Boys'—or perhaps Children's Own Book which contained all the 'regular' fairy-tales, dear to that generation—an enormous number, amid which I recall 'Hop o' my Thumb,' *Le Petit Poucet*, as my small romance of yearning predilection. I seem to remember that story in some other particularly thrilling and haunting form, with a picture of the old woodcutter and his wife sitting at night in the glow of the fire and the depths of the wood and plotting for the mislaying of their brood; a very dreadful and romantic image of a strange far-off world in which the enchanting heroism of the small boy, smaller than one's self, who had in that crisis gained immortality, gave one's fond fancy the most attaching of possible companions. There was no boy one had ever heard of one would have given so much to know—and one focussed him as a tiny brown mite much more vividly and saliently, in the picture, at the great moment, than any of the terrible big people by whom he was surrounded. It is the vague memory of this sense of him as some small precious object, like a lost gem, or a rare and beautiful insect on which one might inadvertently tread, or might find under the sofa or behind the window-curtain, that leads me to think of Hop-o'-my-Thumb as my earliest and sweetest and most repeated cupful at the fount of fiction."

341:1. 'déjà très-joli'. already very pretty, very neat.

342:1. visibly measuring meanwhile their effect. "The extraordinary is most extraordinary in that it happens to you and me, and it's of value (of value for others) but so far as visibly brought home to us" (Preface to "The Altar of the Dead").

343:41. "cutting" without a scruple. Edel (5: 323) notes that "of the 108 short stories he had written up to this time, only 66 found their way into the definitive edition." See Anesko for a discussion of how James' selections for the New York Edition were responses to "friction with the market."

344:7. the whole "question of the short story". James discusses this question in the Preface to "The Author of Beltraffio": "I undertook the brevity, so often undertaken on a like scale before, and again arrived at it by the innumerable repeated chemical reductions and condensations that tend to make of the very short story, as I risk again noting, like the hard, shining sonnet, one of the most indestructible, forms of composition in general use." The more flexible version of this costly form, the *nouvelle,* is discussed in the Preface to "The Lesson of the Master." The short story was first treated seriously as a genre in the 1880s by, among others, Brander Matthews, whose "Philosophy of the Short-story" appeared in *Lippincott's Magazine* 10, n.s. 22 (October 1885): 366–74.

344:23. my personal experience. See James' notebook entry for June 19, 1884, where he seems to indicate that Daudet's *Numa Roumestan* (1881) was actually the source of his inspiration.

Notes to *The Wings of the Dove*

346:2. a very old . . . motive. Sandeen, *"The Wings of the Dove* and *The Portrait of a Lady:* A Study of James's Later Phase," *PMLA* 69 (December 1954): 1060–75, was perhaps the first to formally connect Milly Theale and Minnie Temple. A notebook entry for November 3, 1894, contains James' first scenario for the novel.

346:20. to make the wary adventurer walk round and round it. . . . It stood there with secrets and compartments. This description recalls Maggie Verver's circuit around the pagoda in *The Golden Bowl* (XXIV, 4, I): "This situation had been occupying, for months and months, the very centre of the garden of her life, but it had reared itself there like some strange, tall tower of ivory, or perhaps some wonderful, but outlandish pagoda, a structure plated with hard bright porcelain, coloured and figured and adorned, at the overhanging eaves with silver bells that tinkled, ever so charmingly, when stirred by chance airs. She had walked round and round it. . . . The great decorated surface had remained consistently impenetrable and inscrutable." See also "The Novel in *The Ring and the Book,"* p. 460.

347:18. This circumstance . . . might disqualify it for many activities. James confronts a similar problem in the Preface to *The Portrait of a Lady,* Chapter 13.

348:31. Lorelei is a Rhine River siren who lures sailors to their deaths on the rock whose name she bears. In the nineteenth century, she was the subject of poems by, among others, Heinrich Heine and an opera by Max Bruch.

349:2. freedom and money and a mobile mind and personal charm, the power to interest and attach. James echoes Ralph Touchett's argument in chapter 18 of *The Portrait of a Lady* for dividing his patrimony with Isabel: "I call people rich when they are able to gratify their imagination. Isabel has a great deal of imagination."

350:42. my medal hang free. In the Preface to *What Maisie Knew,* James uses the image of a medal to describe "the close connexion of bliss and bale . . . " (p. 318).

351:19. going . . . "behind". On "going behind," see our commentary on the Prefaces, pp. 401–2.

351:27. a world of . . . roaring "successes". For James on literature as industry, see "Criticism" and "The Future of the Novel," Chapters 9 and 10. For James' response to the phenomenon of "best-sellers," see Jacobson, *Henry James and the Mass Market* (Birmingham: University of Alabama Press, 1983).

351:30. *arête.* ridge.

351:40. that ingenuity of the expert craftsman which likes to be taxed. See the Preface to *The Awkward Age,* Chapter 14, on the "delightfully difficult."

355:20. weight of the double pressure. The Preface to *The Ambassadors,* Chapter 18, discusses how the alternation of picture and scene can be useful.

356:28. the makeshift middle. See our commentary on the Prefaces, p. 402.

359:40. coigns of vantage and respect. In *The Wings of the Dove* (II, 7, III), James describes Milly and Kate as characters "in a Maeterlinck play . . . we have positively the image, in the delicate dusk, of the figures so associated and yet so opposed, so mutually watchful: that of the angular pale princess, ostrich-plumed, black-robed, hung about with amulets, reminders, relics, mainly seated, mainly still, and that of the upright restless slow-circling lady of her court who exchanges with her, across the black water streaked with evening gleams, fitful questions and answers."

Notes to *The Ambassadors*

361:9. a dropped grain of suggestion. James describes that grain for the first time in a notebook entry for October 31, 1895: "I was struck last evening with something that Jonathan Sturges, who has been staying here 10 days, mentioned to me: it was only 10 words, but I seemed, as usual, to catch a glimpse of a *sujet de nouvelle* in it. We were talking of W. D. H. [William Dean Howells] and of his having seen him during a short and interrupted stay H. had made 18 months ago in Paris—called away—back to America, when he had just come—at the end of 10 days by the news of the death—or illness—of his father. He had scarcely been in Paris, ever, in former days, and he had come there to see his domiciled and initiated son, who was at the Beaux Arts. Virtually in the evening, as it were, of life, it was all new to him; all, all, all. Sturges said he seemed sad—rather brooding; and I asked him what gave him (Sturges) that impression. 'Oh—somewhere—I forget, when I was with him—he laid his hand on my shoulder and said *à propos* of some remark of mine: 'Oh, you are young, you are young—be glad of it: be glad of it and *live*. Live all you can: it's a mistake not to. It doesn't so much matter what you do—but live. This place makes it all come over me. I see it now. I haven't done so—and now I'm old. It's too late. It has gone past me—I've lost it. You have time. You are young. Live!" I amplify and improve a little—but that was the tone. It touches me—I can see him—I can hear him. Immediately, of course—as everything, thank God, does—it suggests a little situation." The entry continues at some length. James later wrote up a detailed "project" of some 20,000 words for the novel, which is included in the *Notebooks*. See also James' letter to Howells on August 10, 1901.

362:30. the old Paris garden. In the letter to Howells cited above, James identifies the garden as James McNeill Whistler's.

362:36. there are degrees of merit in subjects. As in "The Art of Fiction" and "Guy de Maupassant," Chapters 7 and 8, James balances the need to grant the artist his or her subject against the varying merits of subjects.

363:17. The order of composition . . . was reversed by the order of publication. It took James quite some time to get *The Ambassadors* published (the *North American Review* serialized the novel from January to December of 1903).

Harper's reader, H. M. Alden, had rejected James' 20,000 word "project" for the novel, saying "We ought to do better." See *N*, pp. 370–72.

363:34. a man of imagination. In the Preface to *The Princess Casamassima*, James insists "At the same time I confess I never see the *leading* interest of any human hazard but in a consciousness (on the part of the moved and moving creature) subject to fine intensification and wide enlargement."

364:12. the actual reported speaker. In the Preface to "The Lesson of the Master," James glances at "the so interesting question . . . of the story-teller's 'real person' or actual contemporary transplanted and exhibited." He argues that "We can surely account for nothing in the novelist's work that hasn't passed through the crucible of his imagination, hasn't, in that perpetually simmering cauldron his intellectual *pot-au-feu*, been reduced to savoury fusion. . . . Its final savour has been constituted, but its prime identity destroyed. . . ." Of Strether, James decided, "I can't make him a novelist—too like W. D. H., and too generally *invraisemblable*" (*N*, October 31, 1895). In both the notebook entry and the novel James does stick to "the actual" by making Strether the editor of a magazine (Howells edited the *Atlantic Monthly* from 1866 to 1871).

364:13. his actualities, all too definite. In the Preface to *The Aspern Papers*, Chapter 16, James explains that *missing* his chance to see Jane Clairmont freed him to write the novella.

365:42. *galère*. literally, (slave) galley; fig., bad, unpleasant position.

367:29. moral scheme . . . framed to break down. In "Guy de Maupassant," and "Emile Zola," Chapters 8 and 20, James shows how moral schemes are critically inadequate to deal with recent French fiction. In discussing Strether here, James describes his own development away from critical moralism.

368:10. *bêtise*. stupidity.

369:16. grace of intensity. In the Preface to *The Princess Casamassima*, James maintains that "Intimacy with a man's specific behaviour, with his given case, is desperately certain to make us see it as a whole—in which even arbitrary limitations of our vision lose whatever beauty they may on occasion have pretended to. What a man thinks and what he feels are the history and the character of what he does; on all of which things the logic of intensity rests. Without intensity where is vividness, and without vividness where is presentability?"

370:26. composition alone is positive beauty. The Preface to *The Tragic Muse* argues that "A picture without composition slights its most precious chance for beauty, and is moreover not composed at all unless the painter knows *how* that principle of health and safety, working as an absolutely unpremeditated art, has prevailed."

371:31. as in "Gil Blas" or in "David Copperfield". Lesage's picaresque romance, *Gil Blas de Santillane* (1715–35), and Dicken's semi-autobiographical *David Copperfield* (1849–50) are first-person narratives.

372:24. *ficelles*: threads; (theat.) stage-tricks; (fig.) dodges. For the discussion of another *ficelle*, see the Preface to *The Portrait of a Lady*, Chapter 13.

372:42. everything in it that is not scene . . . is . . . picture. On the distinction between picture and scene, see the Preface to *The Wings of the Dove*, Chapter 17; on the scenic, see especially the Preface to *The Awkward Age*, Chapter 14.

375:27. most independent, most elastic, most prodigious of literary forms. See "The Art of Fiction," "The Future of the Novel," "Emile Zola," Chapters 7, 10, and 20.

Notes to *The Golden Bowl*

376:7. an accepted habit . . . for "seeing my story," through. James' most famous formulation of this habit is given in the Preface to *What Maisie Knew:* "Addicted to seeing 'through'—one thing through another, accordingly, and still other things through *that*—he takes, too greedily perhaps, on any errand, as many things as possible by the way" (p. 326).

377:32. reflected in it as in the clean glass. James uses the same image in the Preface to *The Princess Casamassima:* "I should even like to give myself the pleasure of retracing from one of my own productions to another the play of a like instinctive disposition, of catching in the fact, at one point after another, from 'Roderick Hudson' to 'The Golden Bowl,' that provision for interest which consists in placing advantageously, placing right in the middle of the light, the most polished of possible mirrors of the subject."

378:13. a general connexion that I have elsewhere sufficiently shown as suggestive. James discusses the center of consciousness in nearly all of the Prefaces (See index).

379:2. *gageure:* wager, stake; something which seems impossible to do.

379:19. Mr. Alvin Langdon Coburn's beautiful photographs. In a letter to Scribner's on June 12, 1906, James wrote: "I spent yesterday afternoon in being again 'artistically' photographed here on my own premises by a young American expert, A. L. Coburn, who had already done me in London, but without satisfactory success, and who came down from town for an earnest second attack. He is quite the best person going, here, I think, and this time I hope for good results; which he promises within ten days, when I will promptly send you the best." James then went on to discuss the problems of illustrating the New York Edition. "It consists, this difficulty, in our really not wanting at all the common black-and-white drawing, of the magazine sort (and of however much character or cleverness); and wanting instead some scene, object or locality, and associated with some one or other of the tales in the volume, both consummately photographed and consummately reproduced." For further discussions of Coburn's work with James, see James' letters to him on October 2, December 6, December 7, and 9, 1906, as well as Bogardus, *Pictures and Texts: Henry James, A. L. Coburn, and New Ways of Seeing in Literary Culture* (Ann Arbor: UMI Research Press, 1984); Coburn, *Alvin Langdon Coburn, Photographer: An Autobiography* (New York: Frederick A. Praeger, 1966); Edel (5: 334–38); Firebaugh, "Coburn: Henry James's Photographer," *American Quarterly* 7 (Fall 1955): 215–33; and Higgins, "Photographic Aperture: Coburn's Frontispieces to James's New York Edition," *American Literature* 53 (1982): 661–75.

383:6. expanse of snow. In volume 2 of the Library of America edition of James' criticism, Edel traces this phrase to a remark Daudet made to James about Turgenev: "How I used to envy the calm serenity of Turgenev, working in a field and in a language the white snow of which had so few footprints."

383:25. The question of the "revision". On August 7, 1905, James responded to Robert Herrick's remonstrations at the idea of revision by noting that extensive "retouching" would be limited to a few novels, but nonetheless insisting "in essence I shouldn't have planned the edition at all unless I had felt close revision—wherever seeming called for—to be an indispensable part of it." He wrote to his brother William on October 18, 1907, describing the uniqueness of the prefaces and continued "What I am doing in the way of revision is equally 'unique'—but overwhelmingly enlightened, inevitable and interesting; any judgment *a priori* (or even subsequently) to the contrary being simply fifteenth-rate!" The scholarship on James' revisions is too voluminous to list here, but two important studies are an early essay, McIntyre, "The Later Manner of Mr. Henry James," *PMLA* 27 n.s., 20 (1912): 354–71, and Matthiessen, "The Painter's Sponge and Varnish Bottle," in *Henry James: The Major Phase* (New York: Oxford University Press, 1944). For a recent essay that finds nearly all previous scholarship inadequate, see Parker, "Henry James 'In the Wood': Sequence and Significances of his Literary Labors, 1905–1907," *Nineteenth Century Fiction* 38 (March 1984): 492–513. For specific studies of James' revisions of two early novels, see our notes to the Prefaces to *Roderick Hudson* and *The American,* Chapters 11 and 12.

383:29. keep finished and dismissed work well behind one. On December 5, 1887, James responded to Robert Louis Stevenson's comments on *Roderick Hudson:* "(in whom, at best, as in all my past and shuffled off emanations and efforts, my interest is of the slenderest). . . . Besides, directly my productions are finished, or at least thrust out to earn their living, they seem to *me* dead. They dwindle when weaned—removed from the parental breast, and only flourish, a little, while imbibing the milk of my plastic care."

385:41. "taste." See our commentary on "Emile Zola," Chapter 20.

388:10. *louche.* dubious, equivocal, suspicious.

388:17. vast example of Balzac. See "Honoré de Balzac," p. 66.

391:9. Gustave Flaubert . . . utterance. In his 1893 essay "Gustave Flaubert," James commented, "But if subjects were made for style (as to which Flaubert had a rigid theory: the idea was good enough if the expression was), so style was made for the ear, the last court of appeal, the supreme touchstone of perfection." James himself had been composing orally since 1896.

391:25. to "put" things is very exactly and responsibly and interminably to do them. In a now famous letter to H. G. Wells on July 15, 1915, James held to the belief that art and life are not opposed, and defended himself from Wells' attack in *Boon:* "Of course for myself I live, live intensely and am fed by life, and my value, whatever it be, is in my own kind of expression of that. Therefore I am pulled up to wonder by the fact that for you my kind (my sort of sense of expression and sort of sense of life alike) doesn't exist; and that wonder is, I admit, a disconcerting comment on my idea of the various appreciability of our addiction to the novel and of all the personal and intellectual history, sympathy and curiosity, behind the given example of it. It is when that history and curiosity have been determined in the way most different from my own that I myself want to get at them—precisely *for* the extension of life, which is the novel's best gift. . . . I . . . hold your distinction between a form that is (like) painting and a form that is (like) architecture for wholly null and void. There is no sense in which architecture is aesthetically 'for use' that doesn't leave any other art whatever exactly as much so; and so far from that of literature being irrelevant to the literary report upon life, and to its being made as interesting as possible, I regard it as relevant in a degree that leaves everything else behind. It is art that *makes* life, makes interest, makes importance, for our consideration and application of these things, and I know of no substitute whatever for the force and beauty of its process." On the connections between art and life, see also "Sainte-Beuve," "The Art of Fiction," and the Preface to *The Portrait of a Lady,* Chapters 2, 7, and 13. On the relations between criticism and life, see "Matthew Arnold's *Essays in Criticism,*" Saint-Beuve," and "Criticism," Chapters 1, 2, and 9.

PART FOUR

GENIUS IN OLD AGE

T W E N T Y

EMILE ZOLA

IF IT BE TRUE THAT THE CRITICAL SPIRIT TO-DAY, IN PRES-
ence of the rising tide of prose fiction, a watery waste out of which
old standards and landmarks are seen barely to emerge, like chim-
neys and the tops of trees in a country under flood—if it be true that
the anxious observer, with the water up to his chin, finds himself
asking for the *reason* of the strange phenomenon, for its warrant and
title, so we likewise make out that these credentials rather fail to float
on the surface. We live in a world of wanton and importunate fable,
we breathe its air and consume its fruits; yet who shall say that we are
able, when invited, to account for our preferring it so largely to the
world of fact? To do so would be to make some adequate statement of
the good the product in question does us. What does it do for our life,
our mind, our manners, our morals—what does it do that history,
poetry, philosophy may not do, as well or better, to warn, to comfort
and command the countless thousands for whom and by whom it
comes into being? We seem too often left with our riddle on our
hands. The lame conclusion on which we retreat is that "stories" are
multiplied, circulated, paid for, on the scale of the present hour, simply because people "like" them. As to why people *should* like anything so loose and mean as the preponderant mass of the "output,"
so little indebted for the magic of its action to any mystery in the
making, is more than the actual state of our perceptions enables us to
say.

This bewilderment might be our last word if it were not for the
occasional occurrence of accidents especially appointed to straighten
out a little our tangle. We are reminded that if the unnatural prosperity of the wanton fable cannot be adequately explained, it can at
least be illustrated with a sharpness that is practically an argument.
An abstract solution failing we encounter it in the concrete. We catch
in short a new impression or, to speak more truly, recover an old one.
It was always there to be had, but we ourselves throw off an oblivion,

an indifference for which there are plenty of excuses. We become conscious, for our profit, of a *case,* and we see that our mystification came from the way cases had appeared for so long to fail us. None of the shapeless forms about us for the time had attained to the dignity of one. The one I am now conceiving as suddenly effective—for which I fear I must have been regarding it as somewhat in eclipse—is that of Émile Zola, whom, as a manifestation of the sort we are considering, three or four striking facts have lately combined to render more objective and, so to speak, more massive. His close connection with the most resounding of recent public quarrels; his premature and disastrous death; above all, at the moment I write, the appearance of his last-finished novel, bequeathed to his huge public from beyond the grave—these rapid events have thrust him forward and made him loom abruptly larger; much as if our pedestrian critic, treading the dusty highway, had turned a sharp corner.

It is not assuredly that Zola has ever been veiled or unapparent; he had, on the contrary, been digging his field these thirty years, and for all passers to see, with an industry that kept him, after the fashion of one of the grand grim sowers or reapers of his brother of the brush, or at least of the canvas, Jean-François Millet, duskily outlined against the sky. He was there in the landscape of labour—he had always been; but he was there as a big natural or pictorial feature, a spreading tree, a battered tower, a lumpish round-shouldered useful hayrick, confounded with the air and the weather, the rain and the shine, the day and the dusk, merged more or less, as it were, in the play of the elements themselves. We had got used to him, and, thanks in a measure just to this stoutness of his presence, to the long regularity of his performance, had come to notice him hardly more than the dwellers in the marketplace notice the quarters struck by the town-clock. On top of all accordingly, for our skeptical mood, the sense of his work—a sense determined afresh by the strange climax of his personal history—rings out almost with violence as a reply to our wonder. It is as if an earthquake or some other rude interference had shaken from the town-clock a note of such unusual depth as to compel attention. We therefore once more give heed, and the result of this is that we feel ourselves after a little probably as much enlightened as we can hope ever to be. We have worked round to the so marked and impressive anomaly of the adoption of the futile art by one of the stoutest minds and stoutest characters of time. This extraordinarily robust worker has found it good enough for him, and if the fact is, as I say, anomalous, we are doubtless helped to conclude that by its anomalies, in future, the bankrupt business, as we are so often moved to pronounce it, will most recover credit.

What is at all events striking for us, critically speaking, is that, in the midst of the dishonour it has gradually harvested by triumphant vulgarity of practice, its pliancy and applicability can still plead for themselves. The curious contradiction stands forth for our relief—the circumstance that thirty years ago a young man of extraordinary brain and indomitable purpose, wishing to give the measure of these endowments in a piece of work supremely solid, conceived and sat down to Les Rougon-Macquart rather than to an equal task in physics, mathematics, politics or economics. He saw his undertaking, thanks to his patience and courage, practically to a close; so that it is exactly neither of the so-called constructive sciences that happens to have had the benefit, intellectually speaking, of one of the few most constructive achievements of our time. There then, provisionally at least, we touch bottom; we get a glimpse of the pliancy and variety, the ideal of vividness, on behalf of which our equivocal form may appeal to a strong head. In the name of what ideal on its own side, however, does the strong head yield to the appeal? What is the logic of its so deeply committing itself? Zola's case seems to tell us, as it tells us other things. The logic is in its huge freedom of adjustment to the temperament of the worker, which it carries, so to say, as no other vehicle can do. It expresses fully and directly the whole man, and big as he may be it can still be big enough for him without becoming false to its type. We see this truth made strong, from beginning to end, in Zola's work; we see the temperament, we see the whole man, with his size and all his marks, stored and packed away in the huge hold of Les Rougon-Macquart as a cargo is packed away on a ship. His personality is the thing that finally pervades and prevails, just as so often on a vessel the presence of the cargo makes itself felt for the assaulted senses. What has most come home to me in reading him over is that a scheme of fiction so conducted is in fact a capacious vessel. It can carry anything—with art and force in the stowage; nothing in this case will sink it. And it is the only form for which such a claim can be made. All others have to confess to a smaller scope—to selection, to exclusion, to the danger of distortion, explosion, combustion. The novel has nothing to fear but sailing too light. It will take aboard all we bring in good faith to the dock.

An intense vision of this truth must have been Zola's comfort from the earliest time—the years, immediately following the crash of the Empire, during which he settled himself to the tremendous task he had mapped out. No finer act of courage and confidence, I think, is recorded in the history of letters. The critic in sympathy with him returns again and again to the great wonder of it, in which something so strange is mixed with something so august. Entertained and carried out almost from the threshold of manhood, the high project, the work of a lifetime, announces beforehand its inevitable weakness and yet speaks in the same voice for its admirable, its almost unimaginable strength. The strength was in the young man's very person—in his character, his will, his passion, his fighting temper, his aggressive lips, his squared shoulders (when he "sat up") and overweening confidence; his weakness was in that inexperience of life from which he proposed not to suffer, from which he in fact suffered on the surface remarkably little, and from which he was never to suspect, I judge, that he had suffered at all. I may mention for the interest of it that, meeting him during his first short visit to London—made several years before his stay in England during the Dreyfus trial—I received a direct impression of him that was more informing than any previous study. I had seen him a little, in Paris, years before that, when this impression was a perceptible promise, and I was now to perceive how time had made it good. It consisted, simply stated, in his fairly bristling with the betrayal that nothing whatever had happened to him in life but to write Les Rougon-Macquart. It was even for that matter almost more as if Les Rougon-Macquart had written *him*, written him as he stood and sat, as he looked and spoke, as the long, concentrated, merciless effort had made and stamped and left him. Something very fundamental was to happen to him in due course, it is true, shaking him to his base; fate was not wholly to cheat him of an independent evolution. Recalling him from this London hour one strongly felt during the famous "Affair" that his outbreak in connection with it was the act of a man with arrears of personal history to make up, the act of a spirit for which life, or for which at any rate freedom, had been too much postponed, treating itself at last to a luxury of experience.

I welcomed the general impression at all events—I intimately entertained it; it represented so many things, it suggested, just as it was, such a lesson. You could neither have everything nor be everything—you had to choose; you could not at once sit firm at your job and wander through space inviting initiations. The author of Les Rougon-Macquart had had all those, certainly, that this wonderful company could bring him; but I can scarce express how it was implied in him that his time had been fruitfully passed with *them* alone. His artistic evolution struck one thus as, in spite of its magnitude, singularly simple, and evidence of the simplicity seems further offered by his last production, of which we have just come into possession. "Vérité" truly does give the measure, makes the author's high maturity join hands with his youth, marks the rigid straightness of his course from point to point. He had seen his horizon and his fixed goal from the first, and no cross-scent, no new distance, no blue gap in the hills to right or to left ever tempted him to stray. "Vérité," of which I shall have more to say, is in fact, as a moral finality and the crown of an edifice, one of the strangest possible performances. Machine-minted and made good by an immense expertness, it yet makes us ask how, for disinterested observation and perception, the writer had used so much time and so much acquisition, and how he can all along have handled so much material without some larger subjective consequence. We really rub our eyes in other words to see so great an intellectual adventure as Les Rougon-Macquart come to its end in deep desert sand. Difficult truly to read, because showing him at last almost completely a prey to the danger that had for a long time more and more dogged his steps, the danger of the mechanical all confident and triumphant, the book is nevertheless full of interest for a reader desirous to penetrate. It speaks with more distinctness of the author's temperament, tone and manner than if, like several of his volumes, it achieved or enjoyed a successful life of its own. Its heavy completeness, with all this, as of some prodigiously neat, strong and complicated scaffolding constructed by a firm of builders for the erection of a house whose foundations refuse to bear it and that is unable therefore to rise—its very betrayal of a method and a habit more than adequate, on past occasions, to similar ends, carries us back to the original rare exhibition, the grand assurance and grand patience with which the system was launched.

If it topples over, the system, by its own weight in these last applications of it, that only makes the history of its prolonged success the more curious and, speaking for myself, the spectacle of its origin more attaching. Readers of my generation will remember well the publication of "La Conquête de Plassans" and the portent, indefinable but irresistible, after perusal of the volume, conveyed in the general rubric under which it was a first instalment, Natural and Social History of a Family under the Second Empire. It squared itself there at its ease, the announcement, from the first, and we were to learn promptly enough what a fund of life it masked. It was like the mouth of a cave with a signboard hung above, or better still perhaps like the big booth at a fair with the name of the show across the flapping canvas. One strange animal after another stepped forth into the light, each in its way a monster bristling and spotted, each a curiosity of that "natural history" in the name of which we were addressed, though it was doubtless not till the issue of "L'Assommoir" that the true type of the monstrous seemed to be reached. The enterprise, for those who had attention, was even at a distance impressive, and the nearer the critic gets to it retrospectively the more so it becomes. The pyramid had been planned and the site staked out, but the young builder stood there, in his sturdy strength, with no equipment save his two hands and, as we may say, his wheelbarrow and his trowel. His pile of material—of stone, brick and rubble or whatever—was of the smallest, but this he apparently felt as the least of his difficulties. Poor, uninstructed, unacquainted, unintroduced, he set up his subject wholly from the outside, proposing to himself wonderfully to get into it, into its depths, as he went.

If we imagine him asking himself what he knew of the "social" life of the second Empire to start with, we imagine him also answering in all honesty: "I have my eyes and my ears—I have all my senses: I have what I've seen and heard, what I've smelled and tasted and touched. And then I've my curiosity and my pertinacity; I've libraries, books, newspapers, witnesses, the material from step to step, of an *enquête*. And then I've my genius—that is, my imagination, my passion, my sensibility to life. Lastly I've my method, and that will be half the battle. Best of all perhaps even, I've plentiful lack of doubt." Of the absence in him of a doubt, indeed of his inability, once his direction taken, to entertain so much as the shadow of one, "Vérité" is a positive monument—which again represents in this way the unity of his tone and the meeting of his extremes. If we remember that his design was nothing if not architectural, that a "majestic whole," a great balanced façade, with all its orders and parts, that a singleness of mass and a unity of effect, in fine, were before him from the first, his notion of picking up his bricks as he proceeded becomes, in operation, heroic. It is not in the least as a record of failure for him that I note this particular fact of the growth of the long series as on the whole the liveliest interest it has to offer. "I don't know my subject, but I must live into it; I don't know life, but I must learn it as I work"—that attitude and programme represent, to my sense, a drama more intense on the worker's own part than any of the dramas he was to invent and put before us.

It was the fortune, it was in a manner the doom, of Les Rougon-Macquart to deal with things almost always in gregarious form, to be a picture of *numbers*, of classes, crowds, confusions, movements, industries—and this for a reason of which it will be interesting to attempt some account. The individual life is, if not wholly absent, reflected in coarse and common, in generalised terms; whereby we arrive precisely at the oddity just named, the circumstance that, looking out somewhere, and often woefully athirst, for the taste of fineness, we find it not in the fruits of our author's fancy, but in a different matter altogether. We get it in the very history of his effort, the image itself of his lifelong process, comparatively so personal, so spiritual even, and, through all its patience and pain, of a quality so much more distinguished than the qualities he succeeds in attributing to his figures even when he most aims at distinction. There can be no question in these narrow limits of my taking the successive volumes one by one—all the more that our sense of the exhibition is as little as possible an impression of parts and books, of particular "plots" and persons. It produces the effect of a mass of imagery in which shades are sacrificed, the effect of character and passion in the lump or by the ton. The fullest, the most characteristic episodes affect us like a sounding chorus or procession, as with a hubbub of voices and a multitudinous tread of feet. The setter of the mass into motion, he himself, in the crowd, figures best, with whatever queer idiosyncrasies, excrescences and gaps, a being of a substance akin to our own. Taking him as we must, I repeat, for quite heroic, the interest of detail in him is the interest of his struggle at every point with his problem.

The sense for crowds and processions, for the gross and the general, was largely the *result* of this predicament, of the disproportion between his scheme and his material—though it was certainly also in part an effect of his particular turn of mind. What the reader easily discerns in him is the sturdy resolution with which breadth and energy supply the place of penetration. He rests to his utmost on his documents, devours and assimilates them, makes them yield him extraordinary appearances of life; but in his way he too improvises in the grand manner, the manner of Walter Scott and of Dumas the elder. We feel that he *has* to improvise for his moral and social world, the world as to which vision and opportunity must come, if they are to come at all, unhurried and unhustled—must take their own time, helped undoubtedly more or less by blue-books, reports and interviews, by inquiries "on the spot," but never wholly replaced by such substitutes without a general disfigurement. Vision and opportunity reside in a personal sense and a personal history, and no short cut to them in the interest of plausible fiction has ever been discovered. The short cut, it is not too much to say, was with Zola the subject of constant ingenious experiment, and it is largely to this source, I surmise, that we owe the celebrated element of his grossness. He was *obliged* to be gross, on his system, or neglect to his cost an invaluable aid to representation, as well as one that apparently struck him as lying close at hand; and I cannot withhold my frank admiration from the courage and consistency with which he faced his need.

His general subject in the last analysis was the nature of man; in dealing with which he took up, obviously, the harp of most numerous strings. His business was to make these strings sound true, and there were none that he did not, so far as his general economy permitted, persistently try. What happened then was that many—say about half, and these, as I have noted, the most silvered, the most golden—refused to give out their music. They would only sound false, since (as with all his earnestness he must have felt) he could command them, through want of skill, of practice, of ear, to none of the right harmony. What therefore was more natural than that, still splendidly bent on producing his illusion, he should throw himself on the strings he might thump with effect, and should work them, as our phrase is, for all they were worth? The nature of man, he had plentiful warrant for holding, is an extraordinary mixture, but the great thing was to represent a sufficient part of it to show that it was solidly, palpably, commonly the nature. With this preoccupation he doubtless fell into extravagance—there was clearly so much to lead him on. The coarser side of his subject, based on the community of all the instincts, was for instance the more practicable side, a sphere the vision of which required but the general human, scarcely more than the plain physical, initiation, and dispensed thereby conveniently enough with special introductions or revelations. A free entry into this sphere was undoubtedly compatible with a youthful career as hampered right and left even as Zola's own.

He was in prompt possession thus of the range of sympathy that he *could* cultivate, though it must be added that the complete exercise of that sympathy might have encountered an obstacle that would somewhat undermine his advantage. Our friend might have found himself able, in other words, to pay to the instinctive, as I have called it, only such tribute as protesting taste (his own dose of it) permitted. Yet there it was again that fortune and his temperament served him. Taste as he knew it, taste as his own constitution supplied it, proved to have nothing to say to the matter. His own dose of the precious elixir had no perceptible regulating power. Paradoxical as the remark may sound, this accident was positively to operate as one of his greatest felicities. There are parts of his work, those dealing with romantic or poetic elements, in which the inactivity of the principle in question is sufficiently hurtful; but it surely should not be described as hurtful to such pictures as "Le Ventre de Paris," as "L'Assommoir," as "Germinal." The conception on which each of these productions rests is that of a world with which taste has nothing to do, and though the act of representation may be justly held, as an artistic act, to involve its presence, the discrimination would probably have been in fact, given the particular illusion sought, more detrimental than the deficiency. There was a great outcry, as we all remember, over the rank materialism of "L'Assommoir," but who cannot see to-day how much a milder infusion of it would have told against the close embrace of the subject aimed at? "L'Assommoir" is the nature of man—but not his finer, nobler, cleaner or more cultivated nature; it is the image of his free instincts, the better and the worse, the better struggling as they can, gasping for light and air, the worse making themselves at home in darkness, ignorance and poverty. The whole handling makes for emphasis and scale, and it is not to be measured how, as a picture of conditions, the thing would have suffered from timidity. The qualification of the painter was precisely his stoutness of stomach, and we scarce exceed in saying that to have taken in and given out again less of the infected air would, with such a resource, have meant the waste of a faculty.

I may add in this connection moreover that refinement of intention did on occasion and after a fashion of its own unmistakably preside at these experiments; making the remark in order to have done once for all with a feature of Zola's literary physiognomy that appears to have attached the gaze of many persons to the exclusion of every other. There are judges in these matters so perversely preoccupied that for them to see anywhere the "improper" is for them straightway to cease to see anything else. The said improper, looming supremely large and casting all the varieties of the proper quite into the shade, suffers thus in their consciousness a much greater extension than it ever claimed, and this consciousness becomes, for the edification of many and the information of a few, a colossal reflector and record of it. Much may be said, in relation to some of the possibilities of the nature of man, of the nature in especial of the "people," on the defect of our author's sense of proportion. But the sense of proportion of many of those he has scandalised would take us further yet. I recall at all events as relevant—for it comes under a very attaching general head—two occasions of long ago, two Sunday afternoons in Paris, on which I found the question of intention very curiously lighted. Several men of letters of a group in which almost every member either had arrived at renown or was well on his way to it, were assembled under the roof of the most distinguished of their number, where they exchanged free confidences on current work, on plans and ambitions, in a manner full of interest for one never previously privileged to see artistic conviction, artistic passion (at least on the literary ground) so systematic and so articulate. "Well, I on my side," I remember Zola's saying, "am engaged on a book, a study of the *mœurs* of the people, for which I am making a collection of all the 'bad words,' the *gros mots,* of the language, those with which the vocabulary of the people, those with which their familiar talk, bristles." I was struck with the tone in which he made the announcement—without bravado and without apology, as an interesting idea that had come to him and that he was working, really to arrive at character and particular truth, with all his conscience; just as I was struck with the unqualified interest that his plan excited. It was *on* a plan that he was working—formidably, almost grimly, as his fatigued face showed; and the whole consideration of this interesting element partook of the general seriousness.

But there comes back to me also as a companion-piece to this another day, after some interval, on which the interest was excited by the fact that the work for love of which the brave license had been taken was actually under the ban of the daily newspaper that had engaged to "serialise" it. Publication had definitively ceased. The thing had run a part of its course, but it had outrun the courage of editors and the curiosity of subscribers—that stout curiosity to which it had evidently in such good faith been addressed. The chorus of contempt for the ways of such people, their pusillanimity, their superficiality, vulgarity, intellectual platitude, was the striking note on this occasion; for the journal impugned had declined to proceed and the serial, broken off, been obliged, if I am not mistaken, to seek the hospitality of other columns, secured indeed with no great difficulty. The composition so qualified for future fame was none other, as I was later to learn, than "L'Assommoir"; and my reminiscence has perhaps no greater point than in connecting itself with a matter always dear to the critical spirit, especially when the latter has not too completely elbowed out the romantic—the matter of the "origins," the early consciousness, early steps, early tribulations, early obscurity, as so often happens, of productions finally crowned by time.

Their greatness is for the most part a thing that has originally begun so small; and this impression is particularly strong when we have been in any degree present, so to speak, at the birth. The course of the matter is apt to tend preponderantly in that case to enrich our stores of irony. In the eventual conquest of consideration by an abused book we recognise, in other terms, a drama of romantic interest, a drama often with large comic no less than with fine pathetic interweavings. It may of course be said in this particular connection that "L'Assommoir" had not been one of the literary things that creep humbly into the world. Its "success" may be cited as almost insolently prompt, and the fact remains true if the idea of success be restricted, after the inveterate fashion, to the idea of circulation. What remains truer still, however, is that for the critical spirit circulation mostly matters not the least little bit, and it is of the success with which the history of Gervaise and Coupeau nestles in *that* capacious bosom, even as the just man sleeps in Abraham's, that I here speak. But it is a point I may better refer to a moment hence.

Though a summary study of Zola need not too anxiously concern itself with book after book—always with a partial exception from this remark for "L'Assommoir"—groups and varieties none the less exist in the huge series, aids to discrimination without which no measure of the presiding genius is possible. These divisions range themselves to my sight, roughly speaking, however, as scarce more than three in number—I mean if the ten volumes of the Œuvres Critiques and the Théâtre be left out of account. The critical volumes in especial abound in the characteristic, as they were also a wondrous addition to his sum of achievement during his most strenuous years. But I am forced not to consider them. The two groups constituted after the close of Les Rougon-Macquart—"Les Trois Villes" and the incomplete "Quatre Évangiles"—distribute themselves easily among the three types, or, to speak more exactly, stand together under one of the three. This one, so comprehensive as to be the author's main exhibition, includes to my sense all his best volumes—to the point in fact of producing an effect of distinct inferiority for those outside of it, which are, luckily for his general credit, the less numerous. It is so inveterately pointed out in any allusion to him that one shrinks, in repeating it, from sounding flat; but as he was admirably equipped from the start for the evocation of number and quantity, so those of his social pictures that most easily surpass the others are those in which appearances, the appearances familiar to him, are at once most magnified and most multiplied.

To make his characters swarm, and to make the great central thing they swarm about "as large as life," portentously, heroically big, that was the task he set himself very nearly from the first, that was the secret he triumphantly mastered. Add that the big central thing was always some highly representative institution or industry of the France of his time, some seated Moloch of custom, of commerce, of faith, lending itself to portrayal through its abuses and excesses, its idol-face and great devouring mouth, and we embrace the main lines of his attack. In "Le Ventre de Paris" he had dealt with the life of the huge Halles, the general markets and their supply, the personal forces, personal situations, passions, involved in (strangest of all subjects) the alimentation of the monstrous city, the city whose victualling occupies so inordinately much of its consciousness. Paris richly gorged, Paris sublime and indifferent in her assurance (so all unlike poor Oliver's) of "more," figures here the theme itself, lies across the scene like some vast ruminant creature breathing in a cloud of parasites. The book was the first of the long series to show the full freedom of the author's hand, though "La Curée" had already been symptomatic. This freedom, after an interval, broke out on a much bigger scale in "L'Assommoir," in "Au Bonheur des Dames," in "Germinal," in "La Bête Humaine," in "L'Argent," in "La Débâcle," and then again, though more mechanically and with much of the glory gone, in the more or less wasted energy of "Lourdes," "Rome," "Paris," of "Fécondité," "Travail" and "Vérité."

"Au Bonheur des Dames" handles the colossal modern shop, traces the growth of such an organisation as the Bon Marché or the Magasin-du-Louvre, sounds the abysses of its inner life, marshals its population, its hierarchy of clerks, counters, departments, divisions and sub-divisions, plunges into the labyrinth of the mutual relations of its staff, and above all traces its ravage amid the smaller fry of the trade, of all the trades, pictures these latter gasping for breath in an air pumped clean by its mighty lungs. "Germinal" revolves about the coal-mines of Flemish France, with the subterranean world of the pits for its central presence, just as "La Bête Humaine" has for its protagonist a great railway and "L'Argent" presents in terms of human passion—mainly of human baseness—the fury of the Bourse and the monster of Credit. "La Débâcle" takes up with extraordinary breadth the first act of the Franco-Prussian war, the collapse at Sedan, and the titles of the six volumes of The Three Cities and the Four Gospels sufficiently explain them. I may mention, however, for the last lucidity, that among these "Fécondité" manipulates, with an amazing misapprehension of means to ends, of remedies to ills, no less thickly peopled a theme than that of the decline in the French birth-rate, and that "Vérité" presents a fictive equivalent of the Dreyfus case, with a vast and elaborate picture of the battle in France between lay and clerical instruction. I may even further mention, to clear the ground, that with the close of Les Rougon-Macquart the diminution of freshness in the author's energy, the diminution of intensity and, in short, of quality, becomes such as to render sadly difficult a happy life with some of the later volumes. Happiness of the purest strain never indeed, in old absorptions of Zola, quite sat at the feast; but there was mostly a measure of coercion, a spell without a charm. From these last-named productions of the climax everything strikes me as absent but quantity ("Vérité," for instance, is, with the possible exception of "Nana," the longest of the list); though indeed there is something impressive in the way his quantity represents his patience.

There are efforts here at stout perusal that, frankly, I have been unable to carry through, and I should verily like, in connection with the vanity of these, to dispose on the spot of the sufficiently strange phenomenon constituted by what I have called the climax. It embodies in fact an immense anomaly; it casts back over Zola's prime and his middle years the queerest grey light of eclipse. Nothing moreover—nothing "literary"—was ever so odd as in this matter the whole turn of the case, the consummation so logical yet so unexpected. Writers have grown old and withered and failed; they have grown weak and sad; they have lost heart, lost ability, yielded in one way or another—the possible ways being so numerous—to the cruelty of time. But the singular doom of this genius, and which began to multiply its symptoms ten years before his death, was to find, with life, at fifty, still rich in him, strength only to undermine all the "authority" he had gathered. He had not grown old and he had not grown feeble; he had only grown all too wrongly insistent, setting himself to wreck, poetically, his so massive identity—to wreck it in the very waters in which he had formally arrayed his victorious fleet. (I say "poetically" on purpose to give him the just benefit of all the beauty of his power.) The process of the disaster, so full of the effect, though so without the intention, of perversity, is difficult to trace in a few words; it may best be indicated by an example or two of its action.

The example that perhaps most comes home to me is again connected with a personal reminiscence. In the course of some talk that I had with him during his first visit to England I happened to ask him what opportunity to travel (if any) his immense application had ever left him, and whether in particular he had been able to see Italy, a country from which I had either just returned or which I was luckily—not having the Natural History of a Family on my hands—about to revisit. "All I've done, alas," he replied, "was, the other year, in the course of a little journey to the south, to my own *pays*—all that has been possible was then to make a little dash as far as Genoa, a matter of only a few days." "Le Docteur Pascal," the conclusion of Les Rougon-Macquart, had appeared shortly before, and it further befell that I asked him what plans he had for the future, now that, still *dans la force de l'âge*, he had so cleared the ground. I shall never forget the fine promptitude of his answer—"Oh, I shall begin at once Les Trois Villes." "And which cities are they to be?" The reply was finer still—"Lourdes, Paris, Rome."

It was splendid for confidence and cheer, but it left me, I fear, more or less gaping, and it was to give me afterwards the key, critically speaking, to many a mystery. It struck me as breathing to an almost tragic degree the fatuity of those in whom the gods stimulate that vice to their ruin. He was an honest man—he had always bristled with it at every pore; but no artistic reverse was inconceivable for an adventurer who, stating in one breath that his knowledge of Italy consisted of a few days spent at Genoa, was ready to declare in the next that he had planned, on a scale, a picture of Rome. It flooded his career, to my sense, with light; it showed how he had marched from subject to subject and had "got up" each in turn—showing also how consummately he had reduced such getting-up to an artifice. He had success and a rare impunity behind him, but nothing would now be so interesting as to see if he could again play the trick. One would leave him, and welcome, Lourdes and Paris—he had already dealt, on a scale, with his own country and people. But was the adored Rome also to be his on such terms, the Rome he was already giving away before possessing an inch of it? One thought of one's own frequentations, saturations—a history of long years, and of how the effect of them had somehow been but to make the subject too august. Was *he* to find it easy through a visit of a month or two with "introductions" and a Baedeker?

It was not indeed that the Baedeker and the introductions didn't show, to my sense, at that hour, as extremely suggestive; they were positively a part of the light struck out by his announcement. They defined the system on which he had brought Les Rougon-Macquart safely into port. He had had his Baedeker and his introductions for "Germinal," for "L'Assommoir," for "L'Argent," for "La Débâcle," for "Au Bonheur des Dames"; which advantages, which researches, had clearly been all the more in character for being documentary, extractive, a matter of *renseignements,* published or private, even when most mixed with personal impressions snatched, with *enquêtes sur les lieux,* with facts obtained from the best authorities, proud and happy to co-operate in so famous a connection. That was, as we say, all right, all the more that the process, to my imagination, became vivid and was wonderfully reflected back from its fruits. There *were* the fruits—so it hadn't been presumptuous. Presumption, however, was now to begin, and what omen mightn't there be in its beginning with such complacency? Well, time would show—as time in due course effectually did. "Rome," as the second volume of The Three Cities, appeared with high punctuality a year or two later; and the interesting question, an occasion really for the moralist, was by that time not to recognise in it the mere triumph of a mechanical art, a "receipt" applied with the skill of long practice, but to do much more than this—that is really to give a name to the particular shade of blindness that could constitute a trap for so great an artistic intelligence. The presumptuous volume, without sweetness, without antecedents, superficial and violent, has the minimum instead of the maximum of *value*; so that it betrayed or "gave away" just in this degree the state of mind on the author's part responsible for its inflated hollowness. To put one's finger on the state of mind was to find out accordingly what was, as we say, the matter with him.

It seemed to me, I remember, that I found out as never before when, in its turn, "Fécondité" began the work of crowning the edifice. "Fécondité" is physiological, whereas "Rome" is not, whereas "Vérité" likewise is not; yet these three productions joined hands at a given moment to fit into the lock of the mystery the key of my meditation. They came to the same thing, to the extent of permitting me to read into them together the same precious lesson. This lesson may not, barely stated, sound remarkable; yet without being in possession of it I should have ventured on none of these remarks. "The matter with Zola then, so far as it goes, was that, as the imagination of the artist is in the best cases not only clarified but intensified by his equal possession of Taste (deserving here if ever the old-fashioned honour of a capital) so when he has lucklessly never inherited that auxiliary blessing the imagination itself inevitably breaks down as a consequence. There is simply no limit, in fine, to the misfortune of being tasteless; it does not merely disfigure the surface and the fringe of your performance—it eats back into the very heart and enfeebles the sources of life. When you have no taste you have no discretion, which is the conscience of taste, and when you have no discretion you perpetrate books like "Rome," which are without intellectual modesty, books like "Fécondité," which are without a sense of the ridiculous, books like "Vérité," which are without the finer vision of human experience.

It is marked that in each of these examples the deficiency has been directly fatal. No stranger doom was ever appointed for a man so plainly desiring only to be just than the absurdity of not resting till he had buried the felicity of his past, such as it was, under a great flat leaden slab. "Vérité" is a plea for science, as science, to Zola, is *all* truth, the mention of any other kind being mere imbecility; and the simplification of the human picture to which his negations and exasperations have here conducted him was not, even when all had been said, credible in advance. The result is amazing when we consider that the finer observation is the supposed basis of all such work. It is not that even here the author has not a queer idealism of his own; this idealism is on the contrary so present as to show positively for the falsest of his simplifications. In "Fécondité" it becomes grotesque, makes of the book the most muscular mistake of *sense* probably ever committed. Where was the judgment of which experience is supposed to be the guarantee when the perpetrator could persuade himself that the lesson he wished in these pages to convey could be made immediate and direct, chalked, with loud taps and a still louder commentary, the sexes and generations all convoked, on the blackboard of the "family sentiment?"

I have mentioned, however, all this time but one of his categories. The second consists of such things as "La Fortune des Rougon" and "La Curée," as "Eugène Rougon" and even "Nana," as "Pot-Bouille," as "L'Œuvre" and "La Joie de Vivre." These volumes may rank as social pictures in the narrowest sense, studies, comprehensively speaking, of the manners, the morals, the miseries—for it mainly comes to that—of a bourgeoisie grossly materialised. They deal with the life of individuals in the liberal professions and with that of political and social adventures, and offer the personal character and career, more or less detached, as the centre of interest. "La Curée" is an evocation, violent and "romantic," of the extravagant appetites, the fever of the senses, supposedly fostered, for its ruin, by the hapless second Empire, upon which general ills and turpitudes at large were at one time so freely and conveniently fathered. "Eugène Rougon" carries out this view in the high colour of a political portrait, not other than scandalous, for which one of the ministerial *âmes damnées* of Napoleon III., M. Rouher, is reputed, I know not how justly, to have sat. "Nana," attaching itself by a hundred strings to a prearranged table of kinships, heredities, transmissions, is the vast crowded *epos* of the daughter of the people filled with poisoned blood and sacrificed as well as sacrificing on the altar of luxury and lust; the panorama of such a "progress" as Hogarth would more definitely have named—the progress across the high plateau of "pleasure" and down the facile descent on the other side. "Nana" is truly a monument to Zola's patience; the subject being so ungrateful, so formidably special, that the multiplication of illustrative detail, the plunge into pestilent depths, represents a kind of technical intrepidity.

There are other plunges, into different sorts of darkness; of which the esthetic, even the scientific, even the ironic motive fairly escapes us—explorations of stagnant pools like that of "La Joie de Vivre," as to which, granting the nature of the curiosity and the substance laboured in, the patience is again prodigious, but which make us wonder what pearl of philosophy, of suggestion or just of homely recognition, the general picture, as of rats dying in a hole, has to offer. Our various senses, sight, smell, sound, touch, are, as with Zola always, more or less convinced; but when the particular effect upon each of these is added to the effect upon the others the mind still remains bewilderedly unconscious of any use for the total. I am not sure indeed that the case is in this respect better with the productions of the third order—"La Faute de l'Abbé Mouret," "Une Page d'Amour," "Le Rêve," "Le Docteur Pascal"—in which the appeal is more directly, is in fact quite earnestly, to the moral vision; so much, on such ground, was to depend precisely on those discriminations in which the writer is least at home. The volumes whose names I have just quoted are his express tribute to the "ideal," to the select and the charming—fair fruits of invention intended to remove from the mouth so far as possible the bitterness of the ugly things in which so much of the rest of his work had been condemned to consist. The subjects in question then are "idyllic" and the treatment poetic, concerned essentially to please on the largest lines and involving at every turn that salutary need. They are matters of conscious delicacy, and nothing might interest us more than to see what, in the shock of the potent forces enlisted, becomes of this shy element. Nothing might interest us more, literally, and might positively affect us more, even very nearly to tears, though indeed sometimes also to smiles, than to see the constructor of Les Rougon-Macquart trying, "for all he is worth," to be fine with fineness, finely tender, finely true—trying to be, as it is called, distinguished—in face of constitutional hindrance.

The effort is admirably honest, the tug at his subject splendidly strong; but the consequences remain of the strangest, and we get the impression that—as representing discriminations unattainable—they are somehow the price he paid. "Le Docteur Pascal," for instance, which winds up the long chronicle on the romantic note, on the note of invoked beauty, in order to sweeten, as it were, the total draught— "Le Docteur Pascal," treating of the erotic ardour entertained for each other by an uncle and his niece, leaves us amazed at such a conception of beauty, such an application of romance, such an estimate of sweetness, a sacrifice to poetry and passion so little in order. Of course, we definitely remind ourselves, the whole long chronicle is explicitly a scheme, solidly set up and intricately worked out, lighted, according to the author's pretension, by "science," high, dry and clear, and with each part involved and necessitated in all the other parts, each block of the edifice, each "morceau de vie," *physiologically* determined by previous combinations. "How can I help it," we hear the builder of the pyramid ask, "if experience (by which alone I proceed) shows me certain plain results—if, holding up the torch of my famous 'experimental method,' I find it stare me in the face that the union of certain types, the conflux of certain strains of blood, the intermarriage, in a word, of certain families, produces nervous conditions, conditions temperamental, psychical and pathological, in which nieces *have* to fall in love with uncles and uncles with nieces? Observation and imagination, for any picture of life," he as audibly adds, "know no light but science, and are false to all intellectual decency, false to their own honour, when they fear it, dodge it, darken it. To pretend to any other guide or law is mere base humbug."

That is very well, and the value, in a hundred ways, of a mass of production conceived in such a spirit can never (when robust execution has followed) be small. But the formula really sees us no further. It offers a definition which is no definition. "Science" is soon said—the whole thing depends on the ground so covered. Science accepts surely *all* our consciousness of life; even, rather, the latter closes maternally round it—so that, becoming thus a force within us, not a force outside, it exists, it illuminates only as we apply it. We do emphatically apply it in art. But Zola would apparently hold that it much more applies *us*. On the showing of many of his volumes then it makes but a dim use of us, and this we should still consider the case even were we sure that the article offered us in the majestic name is absolutely at one with its own pretension. This confidence we can on too many grounds never have. The matter is one of appreciation, and when an artist answers for science who answers for the artist—who at the least answers for art? Thus it is with the mistakes that affect us, I say, as Zola's penalties. We are reminded by them that the game of art has, as the phrase is, to be played. It may not with any sure felicity for the result be both taken and left. If you insist on the common you must submit to the common; if you discriminate, on the contrary, you must, however invidious your discriminations may be called, trust to them to see you through.

To the common then Zola, often with splendid results, inordinately sacrifices, and this fact of its overwhelming him is what I have called his paying for it. In "L'Assommoir," in "Germinal," in "La Débâcle," productions in which he must most survive, the sacrifice is ordered and fruitful, for the subject and the treatment harmonise and work together. He describes what he best feels, and feels it more and more as it naturally comes to him—quite, if I may allow myself the image, as we zoologically see some mighty animal, a beast of a corrugated hide and a portentous snout, soaking with joy in the warm ooze of an African riverside. In these cases everything matches, and "science," we may be permitted to believe, has had little hand in the business. The author's perceptions go straight, and the subject, grateful and responsive, gives itself wholly up. It is no longer a case of an uncertain smoky torch, but of a personal vision, the vision of genius, springing from an inward source. Of this genius "L'Assommoir" is the most extraordinary record. It contains, with the two companions I have given it, all the best of Zola, and the three books together are solid ground—or would be could I now so take them—for a study of the particulars of his power. His strongest marks and features abound in them; "L'Assommoir" above all is (not least in respect to its bold free linguistic reach, already glanced at) completely genial, while his misadventures, his unequipped and delusive pursuit of the life of the spirit and the tone of culture, are almost completely absent.

It is a singular sight enough this of a producer of illusions whose interest for us is so independent of our pleasure or at least of our complacency—who touches us deeply even while he most "puts us off," who makes us care for his ugliness and yet himself at the same time pitilessly (pitilessly, that is, for *us*) makes a mock of it, who fills us with a sense of the rich which is none the less never the rare. Gervaise, the most immediately "felt," I cannot but think, of all his characters, is a lame washerwoman, loose and gluttonous, without will, without any principle of cohesion, the sport of every wind that assaults her exposed life, and who, rolling from one gross mistake to another, finds her end in misery, drink and despair. But her career, as presented, has fairly the largeness that, throughout the chronicle, we feel as epic, and the intensity of her creator's vision of it and of the dense sordid life hanging about it is one of the great things the modern novel has been able to do. It has done nothing more completely constitutive and of a tone so rich and full and sustained. The tone of "L'Assommoir" is, for mere "keeping up," unsurpassable, a vast deep steady tide on which every object represented is triumphantly borne. It never shrinks nor flows thin, and nothing for an instant drops, dips or catches; the high-water mark of sincerity, of the genial, as I have called it, is unfailingly kept.

For the artist in the same general "line" such a production has an interest almost inexpressible, a mystery as to origin and growth over which he fondly but rather vainly bends. How after all does it so get itself *done?*—the "done" being admirably the sign and crown of it. The light of the richer mind has been elsewhere, as I have sufficiently hinted, frequent enough, but nothing truly in all fiction was ever built so strong or made so dense as here. Needless to say there are a thousand things with more charm in their truth, with more beguilement of every sort, more prettiness of pathos, more innocence of drollery, for the spectator's sense of truth. But I doubt if there has ever been a more totally *represented* world, anything more founded and established, more provided for all round, more organised and carried on. It is a world practically workable, with every part as functional as every other, and with the parts all chosen for direct mutual aid. Let it not be said either that the equal constitution of parts makes for repletion or excess; the air circulates and the subject blooms; deadness comes in these matters only when the right parts are absent and there is vain beating of the air in their place—the refuge of the fumbler incapable of the thing "done" at all.

The mystery I speak of, for the reader who reflects as he goes, is the wonder of the scale and energy of Zola's assimilations. This wonder besets us above all throughout the three books I have placed first. How, all sedentary and "scientific," did he get so *near*? By what art, inscrutable, immeasurable, indefatigable, did he arrange to make of his documents, in these connections, a use so vivified? Say he was "near" the subject of "L'Assommoir" in imagination, in more or less familiar impression, in temperament and humour, he could not after all have been near it in personal experience, and the copious personalism of the picture, not to say its frank animalism, yet remains its note and its strength. When the note had been struck in a thousand forms we had, by multiplication, as a kind of cumulative consequence, the finished and rounded book; just as we had the same result by the same process in "Germinal." It is not of course that multiplication and accumulation, the extraordinary pair of legs on which he walks, are easily or directly consistent with his projecting himself morally; this immense diffusion, with its appropriation of everything it meets, affects us on the contrary as perpetually delaying access to what we may call the private world, the world of the individual. Yet since the individual—for it so happens—is simple and shallow our author's dealings with him, as met and measured, maintain their resemblance to those of the lusty bee who succeeds in plumping for an instant, of a summer morning, into every flower-cup of the garden.

Grant—and the generalisation may be emphatic—that the shallow and the simple are *all* the population of his richest and most crowded pictures, and that his "psychology," in a psychologic age, remains thereby comparatively coarse, grant this and we but get another view of the miracle. We see enough of the superficial among novelists at large, assuredly, without deriving from it, as we derive from Zola at his best, the concomitant impression of the solid. It is in general—I mean among the novelists at large—the impression of the *cheap*, which the author of Les Rougon-Macquart, honest man, never faithless for a moment to his own stiff standard, manages to spare us even in the prolonged sandstorm of "Vérité." The Common is another matter; it is one of the forms of the superficial—pervading and consecrating all things in such a book as "Germinal"—and it only adds to the number of our critical questions. How in the world is it made, this deplorable democratic malodorous Common, so strange and so interesting? How is it taught to receive into its loins the stuff of the epic and still, in spite of that association with poetry, never depart from its nature? It is in the great lusty game he plays with the shallow and the simple that Zola's mastery resides, and we see of course that when values are small it takes innumerable items and combinations to make up the sum. In "L'Assommoir" and in "Germinal," to some extent even in "La Débâcle," the values are all, morally, personally, of the lowest—the highest is poor Gervaise herself, richly human in her generosities and follies—yet each is as distinct as a brass-headed nail.

What we come back to accordingly is the unprecedented case of such a combination of parts. Painters, of great schools, often of great talent, have responded liberally on canvas to the appeal of ugly things, of Spanish beggars, squalid and dusty-footed, of martyred saints or other convulsed sufferers, tortured and bleeding, of boors and louts soaking a Dutch proboscis in perpetual beer; but we had never before had to reckon with so literary a treatment of the mean and vulgar. When we others of the Anglo-Saxon race are vulgar we are, handsomely and with the best conscience in the world, vulgar all through, too vulgar to be in any degree literary, and too much so therefore to be critically reckoned with at all. The French are different—they separate their sympathies, multiply their possibilities, observe their shades, remain more or less outside of their worst disasters. They mostly contrive to get the *idea*, in however dead a faint, down into the lifeboat. They may lose sight of the stars, but they save in some such fashion as that their intellectual souls. Zola's own reply to all puzzlements would have been, at any rate, I take it, a straight summary of his inveterate professional habits. "It is all very simple— I produce, roughly speaking, a volume a year, and of this time some five months go to preparation, to special study. In the other months, with all my *cadres* established, I write the book. And I can hardly say which part of the job is stiffest."

The story was not more wonderful for him than that, nor the job more complex; which is why we must say of his whole process and its results that they constitute together perhaps the most extraordinary *imitation* of observation that we possess. Balzac appealed to "science" and proceeded by her aid; Balzac had *cadres* enough and a tabulated world, rubrics, relationships and genealogies; but Balzac affects us in spite of everything as personally overtaken by life, as fairly hunted and run to earth by it. He strikes us as struggling and all but submerged, as beating over the scene such a pair of wings as were not soon again to be wielded by any visitor of his general air and as had not at all events attached themselves to Zola's rounded shoulders. His bequest is in consequence immeasurably more interesting, yet who shall declare that his adventure was in its greatness more successful? Zola "pulled it off," as we say, supremely, in that he never but once found himself obliged to quit, to our vision, his magnificent treadmill of the pigeonholed and documented—the region we may qualify as that of experience by imitation. His splendid economy saw him through, he laboured to the end within sight of his notes and his charts.

The extraordinary thing, however, is that on the single occasion when, publicly—as his whole manifestation was public—life did swoop down on him, the effect of the visitation was quite perversely other than might have been looked for. His courage in the Dreyfus connection testified admirably to his ability to live for himself and out of the order of his volumes—little indeed as living at all might have seemed a question for one exposed, when his crisis was at its height and he was found guilty of "insulting" the powers that were, to be literally torn to pieces in the precincts of the Palace of Justice. Our point is that nothing was ever so odd as that these great moments should appear to have been wasted, when all was said, for his creative intelligence. "Vérité," as I have intimated, the production in which they might most have been reflected, is a production unrenewed and unrefreshed by them, spreads before us as somehow flatter and greyer, not richer and more relieved, by reason of them. They really arrived, I surmise, too late in the day; the imagination they might have vivified was already fatigued and spent.

I must not moreover appear to say that the power to evoke and present has not even on the dead level of "Vérité" its occasional minor revenges. There are passages, whole pages, of the old full-bodied sort, pictures that elsewhere in the series would in all likelihood have seemed abundantly convincing. Their misfortune is to have been discounted by our intensified, our finally fatal sense of the *procédé*. Quarrelling with all conventions, defiant of them in general, Zola was yet inevitably to set up his own group of them—as, for that matter, without a sufficient collection, without their aid in simplifying and making possible, how could he ever have seen his big ship into port? Art welcomes them, feeds upon them always; no sort of form is practicable without them. It is only a question of what particular ones we use—to wage war on certain others and to arrive at particular forms. The convention of the blameless being, the thoroughly "scientific" creature possessed impeccably of all truth and serving as the mouthpiece of it and of the author's highest complacencies, this character is for instance a convention inveterate and indispensable, without whom the "sympathetic" side of the work could never have been achieved. Marc in "Vérité," Pierre Froment in "Lourdes" and in "Rome," the wondrous representatives of the principle of reproduction in "Fécondité," the exemplary painter of "L'Œuvre," sublime in his modernity and paternity, the patient Jean Macquart of "La Débâcle," whose patience is as guaranteed as the exactitude of a well-made watch, the supremely enlightened Docteur Pascal even, as I recall him, all amorous nepotism but all virtue too and all beauty of life—such figures show us the reasonable and the good not merely in the white light of the old George Sand novel and its improved moralities, but almost in that of our childhood's nursery and schoolroom, that of the moral tale of Miss Edgeworth and Mr. Thomas Day.

Yet let not these restrictions be my last word. I had intended, under the effect of a reperusal of "La Débâcle," "Germinal" and "L'Assommoir," to make no discriminations that should not be in our hero's favour. The long-drawn incident of the marriage of Gervaise and Cadet-Cassis and that of the Homeric birthday feast later on in the laundress's workshop, each treated from beginning to end and in every item of their coarse comedy and humanity, still show the unprecedented breadth by which they originally made us stare, still abound in the particular kind and degree of vividness that helped them, when they appeared, to mark a date in the portrayal of manners. Nothing had then been so sustained and at every moment of its grotesque and pitiful existence lived into as the nuptial day of the Coupeau pair in especial, their fantastic processional pilgrimage through the streets of Paris in the rain, their bedraggled exploration of the halls of the Louvre museum, lost as in the labyrinth of Crete, and their arrival at last, ravenous and exasperated, at the *guinguette* where they sup at so much a head, each paying, and where we sit down with them in the grease and the perspiration and succumb, half in sympathy, half in shame, to their monstrous pleasantries, acerbities and miseries. I have said enough of the mechanical in Zola; here in truth is, given the elements, almost insupportably the sense of life. That effect is equally in the historic chapter of the strike of the miners in "Germinal," another of those illustrative episodes, viewed as great passages to be "rendered," for which our author established altogether a new measure and standard of handling, a new energy and veracity, something since which the old trivialities and poverties of treatment of such aspects have become incompatible, for the novelist, with either rudimentary intelligence or rudimentary self-respect.

As for "La Débâcle," finally, it takes its place with Tolstoï's very much more universal but very much less composed and condensed epic as an incomparably human picture of war. I have been re-reading it, I confess, with a certain timidity, the dread of perhaps impairing the deep impression received at the time of its appearance. I recall the effect it then produced on me as a really luxurious act of submission. It was early in the summer; I was in an old Italian town; the heat was oppressive, and one could but recline, in the lightest garments, in a great dim room and give one's self up. I like to think of the conditions and the emotion, which melt for me together into the memory I fear to imperil. I remember that in the glow of my admiration there was not a reserve I had ever made that I was not ready to take back. As an application of the author's system and his supreme faculty, as a triumph of what these things could do for him, how could such a performance be surpassed? The long, complex, horrific, pathetic battle, embraced, mastered, with every crash of its squadrons, every pulse of its thunder and blood resolved for us, by reflection, by communication from two of the humblest and obscurest of the military units, into immediate vision and contact, into deep human thrills of terror and pity—this bristling centre of the book was such a piece of "doing" (to come back to our word) as could only shut our mouths. That doubtless is why a generous critic, nursing the sensation, may desire to drop for a farewell no term into the other scale. That our author was clearly great at congruous subjects—this may well be our conclusion. If the others, subjects of the private and intimate order, gave him more or less inevitably "away," they yet left him the great distinction that the more he could be promiscuous and collective, the more even he could (to repeat my imputation) illustrate our large natural allowance of health, heartiness and grossness, the more he could strike us as penetrating and true. It was a distinction not easy to win and that his name is not likely soon to lose.

In 1902 James disposed of the lease on 34 De Vere Gardens, making official what had been fact since 1899—that Lamb House was his permanent residence. James did, however, return to London for the winter months each year. From his room at the Reform Club in 1902–3, James wrote the fourth of his new essays on French masters. It was, as Edel notes, as though James were updating *French Poets and Novelists*, retracing in his sixtieth year the ground surveyed a quarter century before (5: 163). Sand, Balzac, and Flaubert had recently been reassessed in light of their whole careers, their overall achievement. Now came Zola's turn. James had discussed the Frenchman's "unclean" subjects in 1876, had reviewed *Nana* in 1880, and would contrast him with Balzac in 1905. But 1903 is the paramount essay. Death had suddenly cut Zola off amidst his labors, and James, as in the Turgenev appreciation, needed to put the life into perspective. "Émile Zola" appeared in the *Atlantic Monthly* in 1903 and was revised for *Notes on Novelists* in 1914.

The evolution away from moralistic criticism which James' essays of the 1880s showed continues into the twentieth century. Now he expressly reprimands readers who attack Zola righteously. "There are judges in these matters so perversely preoccupied that for them to see anywhere the 'improper' is for them straightway to cease to see anything else." James undertakes quite a different enterprise—"to make some adequate statement of the good the product in question does us." The good critic defines "the good" in functional rather than normative terms, and he sees the moral now as only one aspect of life, an aspect emphatically distinct from the moralistic. "What does it do for our life, our mind, our manners, our morals . . . to warn, to comfort and command . . . ?"

Asking the proper questions puts James beyond moralistic critics, but he must be careful that in answering the questions he does not lapse back into moralism. One way to avoid rigidity is to keep on questioning. Feeling initially "left with our riddle on our hands," James near the end of the essay remains full of "wonder . . . [at] the scale and energy of Zola's assimilations. . . . How, all sedentary and 'scientific,' did he get so *near*? By what art . . . ?" A provisional answer lies in the distinction between the cheap and the Common, but rather than fostering complacency this answer "only adds to the number of our critical questions."

Questions contribute to a sense of fluidity, but truly free play of mind derives from a more complex source, an epistemological position delicately defined.

> If the unnatural prosperity of the wanton fable cannot be
> adequately explained, it can at least be illustrated with a
> sharpness that is practically an argument. An abstract solu-
> tion failing we encounter it in the concrete. We catch in
> short a new impression. . . .

The mind, when baffled, must neither settle for an "abstract solution" nor forgo "argument" altogether. An "impression" is a bona
fide source of truth because "'genius,'" as James has Zola attest, *is*
"'imagination . . . sensibility to life.'" Throughout the essay, James
contrasts his recurrent term "impression" with the rigid, cerebral alternative adopted by Zola—"system . . . system . . . system . . . 'receipt' . . . lesson . . . blackboard . . . formula . . . system."

Even if James as reader manages to follow the traces of his impressions, however, how does he as critic convey impressions in a
print medium intractably static? Even if an impression is not a system, in other words, isn't a sentence a formula? James in his late
essays brings to unprecedented suppleness a technique he began developing a quarter-century before—argument by image. He expresses his initial bafflement and discouragement pictorially:

> If it be true that the critical spirit to-day, in presence of the
> rising tide of prose fiction, a watery waste out of which old
> standards and landmarks are seen barely to emerge, like
> chimneys and the tops of trees in a country under
> flood. . . .

Once the salutary impression is caught, once Zola as a "case" is sight-
ed, the initial images cannot rigidify into any formulaic allegory because James immediately begins transforming them.

> He was there in the landscape of labour—he had always
> been . . . a spreading tree, a battered tower. . . .

In this striking move James acknowledges that his initial despair was
more a quality of his outlook than a response warranted by actual
conditions. He was forgetting what he had believed for decades—
that the novel would endure, and that Zola was an enduring practi-
tioner. Instead of despairing at the floodtide of transitory failures,
James need only focus on the enduring features, and consolation is
ensured. Zola the battered tower becomes the clock-tower which can
be shaken but not toppled. "A note of such unusual depth as to compel attention" is what Zola provides us. And depth is exactly what
our bafflement requires, for the "credentials" by which we seek to
explain the tide of recent fiction had previously "fail[ed] to float on
the surface."

Granted that images are fluid enough to suggest impressions, what is to prevent the image from rigidifying into a systematic allegory as the impression hardens into a system? James takes his initial image of the landscape aflood and develops it in various ways which reflect the complexity of Zola. The Frenchman's architectural aspect as battered tower and clock-tower transforms into a "cave" and a "booth," then into a "pyramid," then into a "monument" stoutly "architectural." A second, quite different type of salvation appears when Zola is imaged as a "vessel" which survives the floodtide of vulgarity by floating atop it. He is, first, the cargo within the ship Rougon-Macquart; next the admiral who had "arrayed his victorious fleet" and then "wreck[ed] it." James proceeds to concentrate upon the success by which Zola as captain "had brought Les Rougon-Macquart safely into port." The most successful of the Rougon-Macquart novels, *L'Assommoir*, becomes the water itself, "a vast deep steady tide. . . . the high-water mark of sincerity." Even when disaster strikes, Zola, like all French (as opposed to Anglo-American) talents "contrive[s] to get the *idea*, in however dead a faint, down into the lifeboat." And, in keeping with his determination to focus finally upon the positive, James returns at the end to Zola as captain seeing "his big ship into port."

The very fact that the images never become systematic allegory, that they are carefully prevented from fitting into one, finally coherent picture—the ship cannot be the water, the cargo cannot be the captain—requires us to recognize the disparate nature of James' subject. Zola is both a master and a failure. His strength is represented by his "squared shoulders," but initially he was imaged as a "round-shouldered" hayrick. How, in turn, can a round-shouldered hayrick be also a "spreading tree"? For the same reason that James presented first Zola's "squared shoulders" and then added "(when he 'sat up')." Zola's tremendous energy is set off against an equally salient fact—his "fatigued face," his "diminution of freshness," his genius "fatigued and spent." James' capacity to see both sides of his subject is what allows him to do full justice in 1903 to Zola whom he found quite problematic earlier. In 1876 James, having defined Zola as "the most thoroughgoing of the little band of the out-and-out realists," went on to say that "unfortunately the real, for him, means exclusively the unclean" (*Parisian Sketches*, 135). In 1880, James took the same line. "On what authority does M. Zola represent nature to us as a combination of the cesspool and the house of prostitution?" ("*Nana*"). James' development by 1903 is reflected graphically in the transformation of an 1880 image:

> he [Zola] presents us with his decoction of 'nature' in a vessel unfit for the purpose, a receptacle lamentably, fatally in need of scouring.

> What has most come home to me in reading him over is that a scheme of fiction so conducted is in fact a capacious vessel.

The 1880 move from "vessel" to "receptacle" is no development, no revelation of the subject's diverse nature and the perceiver's complex response. Vessel is simply the container of James' indignation, whereas the metaphorical possibilities of vessel as sailing ship allow James in 1903, as we have seen, to do justice to a subject now recognized as tremendous in its intricacy. Death has put Zola in the ultimate perspective, so that James now concentrates on the mortal rather than the moralistic, upon the man's enormous achievement. "Heroic" is now the recurrent epithet, "sympathy" the recurrent response. As "the generous critic," James finds Zola "attaching. . . . impressive" and expresses "frank admiration."

Even an awareness of death, however, cannot prevent the critic from seeing both sides of the subject. Using the technique perfected in the 1888 Maupassant essay, James recognizes limitations amid excellences. "Splendid . . . but . . . . honest . . . but. . . ." Having acknowledged all that Zola's "science," his careful study and detailed notebooks, has enabled him to do, James, again as in the essay on Maupassant, uses the French master's own standards to define his limitations. "Science accepts, surely, *all* our consciousness of life." If, then, Zola in the name of science *excludes* much of life, even the generous critic cannot accept his system. James is being particularly fair-minded here because the standard of completeness operated in Zola's favor when he was compared to Anglo-American practitioners in 1880.

> In England or the United States . . . the story-teller's art is almost exclusively feminine, is mainly in the hands of timid (even when very accomplished) women, whose acquaintance with life is severely restricted. . . . M. Zola would probably decline to take *au sérieux* any work produced under such unnatural conditions. Half of life is a sealed book to young unmarried ladies, and how can a novel be worth anything that deals with only half of life?

In turn, if Zola leaves out the other half of life which the Anglo-American novel features—James calls it in 1880 "a deeper, more delicate

452

perception of the play of character and the state of the soul"—Zola cannot complain that his science is judged unfairly.

Another comparison further locates Zola's blend of strength and weakness. In light of the "cheap" fiction produced in 1903, Zola is solid and admirable. But the very condition upon which Zola gives James encouragement about the novel—his enduring presence as a contemporary writer—means that Zola will partake of the weakness of the contemporary literary scene. Taste has "nothing to say" to Zola, for example, because he is one with an era which James defined in "The Future of the Novel" as having "nothing to do" with taste. In an age when quantity has replaced quality, Zola does not escape unscathed when James praises him for being "admirably equipped, from the start, for the evocation of number and quantity." And in an age given to "fable" rather than "fact," Zola is again undermined when James praises him for having produced "perhaps the most extraordinary *imitation* of experience that we possess."

James' stance in-between precludes our overstating the extent of his development in old age, as Roberts, for example, does when he says that "James is no longer the avowed moralist. . . . Zola's coarseness of vision . . . is consistently referred to an esthetic criterion, never for a moment to a moral one." The word "moral" and its derivatives recur at least seven times in the essay. More important, James' argument, despite all its fluidity, is less immune than he suggests to the charm of the "receipt," to the consolation of an all-explaining proposition, to a

> precious lesson. This lesson may not, barely stated, sound remarkable; yet without being in possession of it I should have ventured on none of these remarks. "The matter with" Zola then, so far as it goes, was that, as the imagination of the artist is in the best cases not only clarified but intensified by his equal possession of Taste (deserving here if ever the old-fashioned honour of a capital), so, when he has lucklessly never inherited that auxiliary blessing the imagination itself inevitably breaks down as a consequence.

Particularly important here is the word "old." It contrasts with the ostensibly ever-new "impressions" which constitute, as we have seen, the driving force of James' criticism. The saving impression announced early in the essay is "a new impression or, to speak more truly . . . an old one." The old truths remain true. Taste may have nothing to do with Zola's art or contemporary life, but it remains the standard by which James judges both. As the still-faithful heir of Arnold and Sainte-Beuve, James remains capable of "disinterested observation" and "curiosity," but as their heir he speaks out for consciousness in an age of commerce. James' later criticism is not devoid of moral "lessons," but these lessons derive their force not from any propositional formulation, any appeal to conventional truth, but from the capacity of images to make experiential the intricacy of the truth espoused. This criticism persists in traditional standards even as it demonstrates beyond any prose of the time a fluidity of style and mental process which reflects the era of pragmatic philosophy and modern physics.

Critical reception of *Notes on Novelists* was highly favorable. (See *New Republic* 1 [November 21, 1914]: 26–28; *Athenaeum* [November 7, 1914): 471–72; *Saturday Review* 118 [November 7, 1914]: 488–89; *Independent* 80 [November 16, 1914]: 243; *Yale Review*, n.s. 4 [April 1915]: 608–11.) The Zola essay was singled out by the *Bookman* as "a more mature and more elaborate consideration" than the *Nana* review (40 [December 1914]: 460). The *Dial* locates the Zola essay, along with those on Flaubert, Balzac, and Sand, as "fascinating examples of the critical and the appreciative working in full and conscious harmony" (57 [November 1, 1914]: 332). For recent critics of "Émile Zola," see Daughtery (184–86), Edel (5: 498), Field's " 'Nervous Anglo-Saxon Apprehensions': Henry James and the French," *French-American Review* 5 (1981): 5–6,9, and Roberts (109–11).

NOTES

425:1. critical spirit . . . prose fiction. As in so many of his critical essays, James insists here upon the Arnoldian link between the state of art and the vitality of criticism.

426:10. the most resounding . . . quarrels. In 1894, Captain Alfred Dreyfus, a Jewish officer of unblemished record, was courtmartialed for conveying military secrets to the Germans. For the next three years, evidence of Dreyfus' innocence and indications of a military coverup surfaced in increasingly convincing amounts. Finally, Zola, early in 1898, published in *L'Aurore* his famous *J'accuse* letter to the president of the French Republic, charging the government with malfeasance. Zola was tried for libel, and found guilty; he fled to England. James followed the controversy closely, proclaiming Zola's act "one of the most courageous things ever done and an immense honour to our too-puling corporation" (Edel, 5: 274).

426:10. his premature . . . death. On September 29, 1902, Zola at the age of 62 died of carbon-monoxide poisoning due to a blocked chimney in his home.

426:12. his last-finished novel. *Vérité* (1903).

426:20. Jean-François Millet (1814–75), French painter of the Barbizon school, most famous for his monumental compositions of peasants in the fields ("The Sower," "The Reapers," "The Gleaners," "The Man with a Hoe").

427:34. only form. James gives comparable praise to the novel's amplitude in "The Art of Fiction," "The Future of the Novel," and the Preface to *The Ambassadors*, Chapters 7, 10, and 18.

427:40. the crash of the Empire. France's humiliating defeat by the Germans in the Franco-Prussian War (1870–71) brought down the Second Empire of Napoleon Bonaparte's nephew, Louis Napoleon, and inaugurated the Third Republic. Zola details the disaster in *La Débâcle* (1892).

428:1. act of courage. James sees Balzac's life in a comparable terms ("Honoré de Balzac," Chapter 4).

428:15. first short visit to London. In September of 1893, James and Zola renewed an aquaintance begun at Flaubert's Sundays in 1876 (see our commentary on "Ivan Turgénieff," Chapter 6, and James' reminiscence below) and fostered by James' trip to Paris in 1884.

429:5. his horizon. The limited horizon of Parisians is insisted upon by James repeatedly. See our commentary on "Matthew Arnold's *Essays in Criticism*" and "Ivan Turgénieff," Chapters 1 and 6.

429:34. "La Conquête de Plassans" (1874).

430:21. *enquête*. Investigation.

431:34. blue-books. These extended explanations of government policy were bound in blue covers.

433:37. two Sunday afternoons. Edel speculates that the first of these two visits to Flaubert's rooms may have been on December 12, 1875; the second "was in mid-January of 1876, about a month after the first" (2: 214, 216).

436:7. poor Oliver's. In Dickens' *Oliver Twist* (1837–38), the title character is so ill-fed at the workhouse that he asks pathetically for "more" gruel.

437:37. *pays*. The region from which one comes.

437:42. *dans la force de l'âge*. In the prime of life.

438:34. *renseignements*. Information, particulars.

438:35. *enquêtes sur les lieux*. Investigations on the spot.

439:25. Taste. James had already associated "taste" with the past in "The Future of the Novel" and in the Preface to *The Golden Bowl*, Chapters 10 and 19.

440:30. *âmes damnées*. Damned souls.

440:34. *epos*. Epic.

440:36. William Hogarth (1697–1764), English painter and engraver. One of his famous series of engravings was "The Harlot's Progress."

445:6. The *cheap*. James had been indicting the age for its commitment to quantity over quality since at least 1884. See "The Art of Fiction," "Criticism," and "The Future of the Novel," Chapters 7, 9, and 10.

445:33. The French are different. Though the French, as usual in James' comparisons between them and the Anglo-Saxons, are held up as superior here, James believed that the decline of the Anglo-American novel was paralleled by a general decline in French fiction. "It is distinctly when we come to the novelists [of France] . . . that we remain rather persistently more aware of what has gone than of what is left. There is in this quarter, evidently, a distinct chill in the air" ("The Present Literary Situation in France" [1899]).

446:7. *cadres*. Plans, outline.

447:2. *procédé*. Method.

447:9. convention. James makes the same criticism of Zola's brother-radical, Maupassant—that what presents itself as shocking is finally drearily stereotypic.

447:24. Maria Edgeworth (1767–1849), English novelist and educator whose admonitory tales remained popular throughout the nineteenth century, as James himself attests. He singles out *Parent's Assistant* as "admirable" and overall judges her "productions . . . still well worth reading" ("Hayward's Essays," *Nation* 27 [1878]: 403).

Thomas Day (1748–89), English barrister and author of works of moral and social reform.

447:40. *guinguette*. Suburban tavern, inn.

448:11. Tolstoi's . . . epic. *War and Peace* (1869). James' famous statement in the Preface to *The Tragic Muse* that Tolstoy's novels are "large loose baggy monsters" sums up his general belief that the Russian novelist was deficient on the side of form, though admirably redolent of life. In his 1896 essay "Ivan Turgénieff," James characterized Tolstoy as "a monster harnessed to his great subject—all human life!—as an elephant might be harnessed . . . not to a carriage, but to a coach-house. . . . his example for others [is] dire."

TEXTUAL VARIANTS

425:4. country under flood. 1903: flooded land.

425:20. mean. 1903: cheap.

425:30. truly, recover. 1903: truly, we recover.

425:31. we ourselves throw off. 1903: we throw off, ourselves.

426:2. mystification . . . way. 1903: mystification was in the way.

426:6. have . . . it. 1903: have looked on it.

426:13. thrust him forward. 1903: made him more evident.

426:17. these. 1903: for.

426:27. just. Added 1914.

426:27. stoutness of. 1903: stoutness, precisely, of.

426:36. enlightened. 1903: answered.

426:38. futile. 1903: "cheap."

427:11. or. Added 1914.

427:12. that . . . neither. 1903: that, precisely, it is neither.

427:37. aboard. Added 1914.

427:38. dock. 1903: wharf.

429:10. made good. 1903: solidified.

429:15. Rougon-Macquart . . . desert. 1903: Rougon-Macquart terminate in unmistakable desert.

429:22. it . . . successful. 1903: it had a really successful.

429:28. exhibition. 1903: phenomenon.

429:37. It . . . announcement. 1903: It loomed large, the announcement.

430:3. issue. 1903: appearance.

430:11. this. 1903: that.

430:21. my passion. Added 1914.

430:23. I've. . . . of. 1903: I've an incomparable absence of doubt." Of
the paucity of his doubts indeed, of.

430:29. a singleness of mass and. Added 1914.

430:30. were. 1903: was.

430:33. as . . . it. 1903: as the liveliest interest, on the whole, it.

431:34. undoubtedly. 1903: doubtless.

432:13. harmony. 1903: felicity.

432:15. might. 1903: *could*.

432:20. was. . . . The. 1903: was so much, obviously, to encourage him.
The.

433:8. have . . . of. 1903: have weakened the whole strong treatment
of.

433:16. stoutness. 1903: strength.

433:18. have . . . air. 1903: have captured less of the air.

434:6. *mots*, of. 1903: *mots*, words of.

434:10. and particular truth. Added 1914.

434:14. element. 1903: feature.

434:18. for love. 1903: on behalf.

434:26. impugned. 1903: in question.

434:38. course of the matter. 1903: history.

435:9. here speak. 1903: am speaking.

435:10. point . . . moment. 1903: point on which I can speak better a
moment.

435:15. divisions . . . roughly. 1903: divisions seem to me, roughly.

435:16. as. Added 1914.

435:17. I mean. 1903: that is.

435:21. not to consider. 1903: to neglect.

435:26. exhibition. 1903: achievement.

436:4. alimentation. 1903: nutrition.

436:22. staff. 1903: personnel.

436:27. "L'Argent". . . . "La Débâcle." 1903: L'Argent makes supremely personal and "intimate" the fury of the Bourse and the money-mar-
ket. La Débâcle.

436:29. extraordinary breadth. 1903: magnificently.

436:34. less . . . than. 1903: less populous a subject than.

437:8. carry through. 1903: make.

437:8. verily like. 1903: like in fact.

437:11. in fact. 1903: truly.

437:14. turn of the case. 1903: history.

437:18. began . . . ten. 1903: began, for that matter, to threaten ten.

437:22. all too wrongly. 1903: mortally.

437:22. setting. 1903: set.

437:35. on my hands. 1903: to count with.

438:7. those. . . . He. 1903: those whom the gods ruin through their blindness. He.

438:21. possessing. 1903: having acquired.

438:33. clearly been. 1903: been, clearly.

438:34. extractive. 1903: bibliographic.

438:37. happy. . . . That. 1903: happy, in so famous a connection, to cooperate. That.

438:39. and. Added 1914.

438:42. complacency. 1903: serenity.

439:1. did. "Rome,". 1903: did how. Rome.

439:6. this . . . to. 1903: this—really to give a name, that is, to.

439:11. its inflated hollowness. 1903: it.

439:20. same precious lesson. 1903: most precious of lessons.

439:23. was. 1903: is.

440:8. muscular. 1903: energetic.

440:19. narrowest. 1903: narrower.

440:21. bourgeoisie grossly materialised. 1903: grossly materialized *bourgeoisie.*

440:33. is the vast. 1903: in the large.

440:41. intrepidity. 1903: heroism.

441:3. laboured. 1903: worked.

441:10. case . . . better. 1903: case in this respect is better.

441:14. moral vision. 1903: mind.

441:17. select. 1903: romantic.

441:28. be . . . trying. 1903: be delicate, trying to be finely tender, trying.

441:39. sweetness, a. 1903: sweetness, so eccentric a.

442:20. on. . . . Science. 1903: on what is meant by it. Science.

442:24. apply it in art. 1903: in art, apply it.

442:26. but. Added 1914.

442:29. The . . . of. 1903: The thing is a matter of.

442:33. may not. 1903: cannot

443:6. had. Added 1914.

443:11. is the. 1903: is, to my sense, the.

443:18. life of the spirit. 1903: intimate and fine.

443:20. this. 1903: that.

443:23. at the same time. Added 1914.

443:24. makes a mock of. 1903: plays with.

443:33. is one. 1903: is to my sense one.

444:5. dense. 1903: solid.

444:11. functional. 1903: as much done.

444:13. constitution. 1903: doing.

444:14. comes . . . when. 1903: comes only, in these matters, when.

444:17. thing "done". 1903: "doing."

444:18. reader . . . is. 1903: reader capable of observation, is.

444:27. not to say its frank animalism. Added 1914.

444:37. since. 1903: as.

444:38. met and measured. 1903: frankly met.

445:2. but get. 1903: get but.

445:7. man . . . manages. 1903: man, full, after all, of his own delicacies, manages.

445:15. that. 1903: this.

445:23. the . . . combination. 1903: the rare phenomenon of the combination.

445:24. of parts. 1903: of the rider's parts.

445:29. mean and. Added 1914.

445:33. critically reckoned with. 1903: reckoned with, critically.

445:34. multiply their possibilities, observe their shades. Added 1914.

445:39. straight. 1903: simple.

446:1. hardly. 1903: hardest.

446:6. observation. 1903: experience.

446:16. we. 1903: I.

446:25. connection. 1903: matter.

446:31. when. 1903: after all.

446:36. really arrived. 1903: arrived, really.

447:6. form is. 1903: form, at least, is.

447:28. long-drawn. 1903: prolonged.

448:4. That effect. 1903: It.

448:4. strike of the miners. 1903: miners' strike.

448:6. for. 1903: as to.

448:8. something since. 1903: something, absolutely, since.

448:9. aspects. 1903: occasions.

448:14. it, I. 1903: it, but with, I.

448:23. and his. 1903: and of his.

448:26. embraced. 1903: captured.

448:30. was . . . (to. 1903: was "done" (to.

448:34. conclusion. 1903: last.

448:38. my. 1903: any.

448:38. imputation) . . . the. 1903: imputation—common, the.

TWENTY-ONE

THE NOVEL IN
The Ring and the Book

IF ON SUCH AN OCCASION AS THIS—EVEN WITH OUR NAT-
ural impulse to shake ourselves free of reserves—some sharp
choice between the dozen different aspects of one of the most copious
of our poets becomes a prime necessity, though remaining at the same
time a great difficulty, so in respect to the most voluminous of his
works the admirer is promptly held up, as we have come to call it; finds
himself almost baffled by alternatives. "The Ring and the Book" is so
vast and so essentially gothic a structure, spreading and soaring and
branching at such a rate, covering such ground, putting forth such
pinnacles and towers and brave excrescences, planting its transepts
and chapels and porticos, its clustered hugeness or inordinate
muchness, that with any first approach we but walk vaguely and
slowly, rather bewilderedly, round and round it, wondering at what
point we had best attempt such entrance as will save our steps and
light our uncertainty, most enable us to reach our personal chair, our
indicated chapel or shrine, when once within. For it is to be granted
that to this inner view the likeness of the literary monument to one of
the great religious gives way a little, sustains itself less than in the first,
the affronting mass; unless we simply figure ourselves, under the
great roof, looking about us through a splendid thickness and dimness
of air, an accumulation of spiritual presences or unprofaned mysteries,
that makes our impression heavily general—general only—and leaves
us helpless for reporting on particulars. The particulars for our purpose have thus their identity much rather in certain features of the
twenty faces—either of one or of another of these—that the structure
turns to the outer day and that we can, as it were, sit down before and
consider at our comparative ease. I say comparative advisedly, for I
cling to the dear old tradition that Browning is "difficult"—which we
were all brought up on and which I think we should, especially on a
rich retrospective day like this, with the atmosphere of his great career
settling upon us as much as possible, feel it a shock to see break down

in too many places at once. Selecting my ground, by your kind invitation, for sticking in and planting before you, to flourish so far as it shall, my little sprig of bay, I have of course tried to measure the quantity of ease with which our material may on that noted spot allow itself to be treated. There are innumerable things in "The Ring and the Book"—as the comprehensive image I began with makes it needless I should say; and I have been above all appealed to by the possibility that one of these, pursued for a while through the labyrinth, but at last overtaken and then more or less confessing its identity, might have yielded up its best essence as a grateful theme under some fine strong economy of *prose* treatment. So here you have me talking at once of prose and seeking that connection to help out my case.

From far back, from my first reading of these volumes, which took place at the time of their disclosure to the world, when I was a fairly young person, the sense, almost the pang, of the novel they might have constituted sprang sharply from them; so that I was to go on through the years almost irreverently, all but quite profanely if you will, thinking of the great loose and uncontrolled composition, the great heavy-hanging cluster of related but unreconciled parts, as a fiction of the so-called historic type, that is as a suggested study of the manners and conditions from which our own have more or less traceably issued, just tragically spoiled—or as a work of art, in other words, smothered in the producing. To which I hasten to add my consciousness of the scant degree in which such a fresh start from our author's documents, such a reprojection of them, wonderful documents as they can only have been, may claim a critical basis. Conceive me as simply astride of my different fancy, my other dream, of the matter—which bolted with me, as I have said, at the first alarm.

Browning worked in this connection literally *upon* documents; no page of his long story is more vivid and splendid than that of his find of the Book in the litter of a market-stall in Florence and the swoop of practised perception with which he caught up in it a treasure. Here was a subject stated to the last ounce of its weight, a living and breathing record of facts pitiful and terrible, a mass of matter bristling with revelations and yet at the same time wrapped over with layer upon layer of contemporary appreciation; which appreciation, in its turn, was a part of the wealth to be appreciated. What our great master saw was his situation founded, seated there in positively packed and congested significance, though by just so much as it was charged with meanings and values were those things undeveloped and unexpressed. They looked up at him, even in that first flush and from their market-stall, and said to him, in their compressed compass, as with the muffled rumble of a slow-coming earthquake, "Express us, express us, immortalise us as we'll immortalise *you!*"—so that the terms of the understanding were so far cogent and clear. It was an understanding, on their side, with the poet; and since that poet had produced "Men and Women," "Dramatic Lyrics," "Dramatis Personæ" and sundry plays—we needn't even foist on him "Sordello"—he could but understand in his own way. That way would have had to be quite some other, we fully see, had he been by habit and profession not just the lyric, epic, dramatic commentator, the extractor, to whatever essential potency and redundancy, of the moral of the fable, but the very fabulist himself, the inventor and projector, layer down of the postulate and digger of the foundation. I doubt if we have a precedent for this energy of appropriation of a deposit of *stated* matter, a block of sense already in position and requiring not to be shaped and squared and caused any further to solidify, but rather to suffer disintegration, be pulled apart, melted down, hammered, by the most characteristic of the poet's processes, to powder—dust of gold and silver, let us say. He was to apply to it his favourite system—that of looking at his subject from the point of view of a curiosity almost sublime in its freedom, yet almost homely in its method, and of smuggling as many more points of view together into that one as the fancy might take him to smuggle, on a scale on which even he had never before applied it; this with a courage and a confidence that, in presence of all the conditions, conditions many of them arduous and arid and thankless even to defiance, we can only pronounce splendid, and of which the issue was to be of a proportioned monstrous magnificence.

The one definite forecast for this product would have been that it should figure for its producer as a poem—as if he had simply said, "I embark at any rate for the Golden Isles"; everything else was of the pure incalculable, the frank voyage of adventure. To what extent the Golden Isles were in fact to be reached is a matter we needn't pretend, I think, absolutely to determine; let us feel for ourselves and as we will about it—either see our adventurer, disembarked bag and baggage and in possession, plant his flag on the highest eminence within his circle of sea, or, on the other hand, but watch him approach and beat back a little, tack and turn and stand off, always fairly in sight of land, catching rare glimpses and meeting strange airs, but not quite achieving the final *coup* that annexes the group. He returns to us under either view all scented and salted with his measure of contact, and that for the moment is enough for us—more than enough for me at any rate, engaged for your beguilement in this practical relation of snuffing up what he brings. He brings, however one puts it, a detailed report, which is but another word for a story; and it is with his story, his offered, not his borrowed one—a very different matter—that I am concerned. We are probably most of us so aware of its general content that if I sum this up I may do so briefly. The Book of the Florentine rubbish-heap is the full account (as full accounts were conceived in those days) of the trial before the Roman courts, with inquiries and judgments by the Tuscan authorities intermixed, of a certain Count Guido Franceschini of Arezzo, decapitated, in company with four con-federates—these latter hanged—on February 22, 1698, for the murder of his young wife Pompilia Comparini and her ostensible parents, Pietro and Violante of that ilk.

The circumstances leading to this climax were primarily his mar-riage to Pompilia, some years before, in Rome—she being then but in her thirteenth year—under the impression, fostered in him by the elder pair, that she was their own child and on this head heiress to moneys settled on them from of old in the event of their having a child. They had in fact had none, and had, in substitution, invented, so to speak, Pompilia, the luckless base-born baby of a woman of lamenta-ble character easily induced to part with her for cash. They bring up the hapless creature as their daughter, and as their daughter they marry her, in Rome, to the middle-aged and impecunious Count Guido, a rapacious and unscrupulous fortune-seeker by whose superior social position, as we say, dreadfully *decaduto* though he be, they are dazzled out of all circumspection. The girl, innocent, ignorant, bewildered, scared and purely passive, is taken home by her husband to Arezzo, where she is at first attended by Pietro and Violante and where the direst disappointment await the three. Count Guido proves the basest of men and his home a place of terror and of torture, from which at the age of seventeen, and shortly prior to her giving birth to an heir to the house, such as it is, she is rescued by a pitying witness of her misery, Canon Caponsacchi, a man of the world and adorning it, yet in holy orders, as men of the world in Italy might then be, who clandestinely helps her, at peril of both their lives, back to Rome, and of whom it is attested that he has had no other relation with her but this of dis-tinguished and all-disinterested friend in need. The pretended parents have at an early stage thrown up their benighted game, fleeing from the rigour of their dupe's domestic rule, disclosing to him vindictively the part they have played and the consequent failure of any profit to him through his wife, and leaving him in turn to wreak his spite, which has become infernal, on the wretched Pompilia. He pursues her to Rome, on her eventual flight, and overtakes her, with her companion, just outside the gates; but having, by the aid of the local powers, reachieved possession of her, he contents himself for the time with procuring her sequestration in a convent, from which, however, she is presently allowed to emerge in view of the near birth of her child. She rejoins Pietro and Violante, devoted to her, oddly enough, through all their folly and fatuity; and under their roof, in a lonely Roman suburb, her child comes into the world. Her husband meanwhile, hearing of her release, gives way afresh to the fury that had not at the climax of his former pursuit taken full effect; he recruits a band of four of his young tenants or farm-labourers and makes his way, armed, like his companions, with knives, to the door behind which three of the parties to all the wrong done him, as he holds, then lurk. He pronounces, after knocking and waiting, the name of Caponsacchi; upon which, as the door opens, Violante presents herself. He stabs her to death on the spot with repeated blows—like her companions she is off her guard; and he throws himself on each of these with equal murderous effect. Pietro, crying for mercy, falls second beneath him; after which he attacks his wife, whom he literally hacks to death. She survives, by a miracle, long enough, in spite of all her wounds, to testify; which testimony, as may be imagined, is not the least precious part of the case. Justice is on the whole, though deprecated and delayed, what we call satisfactory; the last word is for the Pope in person, Innocent XII. Pignatelli, at whose deliberation, lone and supreme, on Browning's page, we splendidly assist; and Count Guido and his accomplices, bloodless as to the act though these appear to have been, meet their discriminated doom.

That is the bundle of facts, accompanied with the bundle of proceedings, legal, ecclesiastical, diplomatic and other, *on* the facts, that our author, of a summer's day, made prize of; but our general temptation, as I say—out of which springs this question of the other values of character and effect, the other completeness of picture and drama, that the confused whole might have had for us—is a distinctly different thing. The difference consists, you see, to begin with, in the very breath of our poet's genius, already, and so inordinately, at play on them from the first of our knowing them. And it consists in the second place of such an extracted sense of the whole, which becomes, after the most extraordinary fashion, bigger by the extraction, immeasurably bigger than even the most cumulative weight of the mere crude evidence, that our choice of how to take it all is in a manner determined for us: we can only take it as tremendously interesting, interesting not only in itself but with the great added interest, the dignity and authority and beauty, of Browning's general perception of it. We can't not accept this, and little enough on the whole do we want not to: it sees us, with its tremendous push, that of its poetic, esthetic, historic, psychologic shoulder (one scarce knows how to name it), so far on our way. Yet all the while we are in presence not at all of an achieved form, but of a mere preparation for one, though on the hugest scale; so that, you see, we are no more than decently attentive with our question: "Which of them all, of the various methods of casting the wondrously mixed metal, is he, as he goes, preparing?" Well, as he keeps giving and giving, in immeasurable plenty, it is in our selection from it all and our picking it over that we seek, and to whatever various and unequal effect find, our account. He works over his vast material, and we then work *him* over, though not availing ourselves, to this end, of a grain he himself doesn't somehow give us; and there we are.

I admit that my faith in my particular contention would be a degree firmer and fonder if there didn't glimmer through our poet's splendid hocus-pocus just the hint of one of those flaws that sometimes deform the fair face of a subject otherwise generally appealing or promising—of such a subject in especial as may have been submitted to us, possibly even with the pretension to impose it, in too complete a shape. The idea but half hinted—when it is a very good one—is apt to contain the germ of happier fruit than the freight of the whole branch, waved at us or dropped into our lap, very often proves. This happens when we take over, as the phrase is, established data, take them over from existing records and under some involved obligation to take them as they stand. That drawback rests heavily for instance on the so-called historic fiction—so beautiful a case it is of a muddlement of terms—and is just one of the eminent reasons why the embarrassed Muse of that form, pulled up again and again, and the more often the fine intelligence invokes her, by the need of a superior harmony which shall be after all but a superior truth, catches up her flurried skirts and makes her saving dash for some gap in the hedge of romance. Now the flaw on this so intensely expressive face, that of the general *donnée* of the fate of Pompilia, is that amid the variety of forces at play about her the unity of the situation isn't, by one of those large straight ideal gestures on the part of the Muse, handed to us at a stroke. The question of the whereabouts of the unity of a group of data subject to be wrought together into a thing of art, the question in other words of the point at which the various implications of interest, no matter how many, *most* converge and interfuse, becomes always, by my sense of the affair, quite the first to be answered; for according to the answer shapes and fills itself the very vessel of that beauty—the beauty, exactly, *of* interest, of maximum interest, which is the ultimate extract of any collocation of facts, any picture of life, and the finest aspect of any artistic work. Call a novel a picture of life as much as we will; call it, according to one of our recent fashions, a slice, or even a chunk, even a "bloody" chunk, of life, a rough excision from that substance as superficially cut and as summarily served as possible, it still fails to escape this exposure to appreciation, or in other words to criticism, that it has had to be selected, selected under some sense for something; and the unity of the exhibition should meet us, does meet us if the work be done, at the point at which that sense is most patent. If the slice or the chunk, or whatever we call it, if *it* isn't "done," as we say—and as it so often declines to be—the work itself of course isn't likely to be; and there we may dismiss it.

The first thing we do is to cast about for some centre in our field; seeing that, for such a purpose as ours, the subject might very nearly go a-begging with none more definite than the author has provided for it. I find that centre in the embracing consciousness of Caponsacchi, which, coming to the rescue of our question of treatment, of our search for a point of control, practically saves everything, and shows itself moreover the only thing that *can* save. The more we ask of any other part of our picture that it shall exercise a comprehensive function, the more we see that particular part inadequate; as inadequate even in the extraordinarily magnified range of spirit and reach of intelligence of the atrocious Franceschini as in the sublime passivity and plasticity of the childish Pompilia, educated to the last point though she be indeed by suffering, but otherwise so untaught that she can neither read nor write. The magnified state is in this work still more than elsewhere the note of the intelligence, of any and every faculty of thought, imputed by our poet to his creatures; and it takes a great mind, one of the greatest, we may at once say, to make these persons express and confess themselves to such an effect of intellectual splendour. He resorts primarily to *their* sense, their sense of themselves and of everything else they know, to exhibit them, and has for this purpose to keep them, and to keep them persistently and inexhaustibly, under the fixed lens of his prodigious vision. He thus makes out in them boundless treasures of truth—truth even when it happens to be, as in the case of Count Guido, but a shining wealth of constitutional falsity. Of the extent to which he may after this fashion unlimitedly draw upon them his exposure of Count Guido, which goes on and on, though partly, I admit, by repeating itself, is a wondrous example. It is not too much to say of Pompilia—Pompilia pierced with twenty wounds, Pompilia on her death-bed, Pompilia but seventeen years old and but a fortnight a mother—that she *acquires* an intellectual splendour just by the fact of the vast covering charity of imagination with which her recording, our commemorated, avenger, never so as in this case an avenger of the wronged beautiful things of life, hangs over and breathes upon her. We see her come out to him, and the extremely remarkable thing is that we see it, on the whole, without doubting that it might just have been. Nothing could thus be more interesting, however it may at moments and in places puzzle us, than the impunity, on our poet's part, of most of these overstretchings of proportion, these violations of the immediate appearance. Browning is deep down below the immediate with the first step of his approach; he has vaulted over the gate, is already far afield and never, so long as we watch him, has occasion to fall back. We wonder, for, after all, the real is his quest, the very ideal of the real, the real most finely mixed with life, which *is* in the last analysis the ideal; and we know, with our dimmer vision, no such reality as a Franceschini fighting for his life, fighting for the vindication of his baseness, embodying his squalor, with an audacity of wit, an intensity of colour, a variety of speculation and illustration, that represent well-nigh the maximum play of the human mind. It is in like sort scarce too much to say of the exquisite Pompilia that on her part intelligence and expression are disengaged to a point at which the angels may well begin to envy her; and all again without our once wincing so far as our consistently liking to see and hear and believe is concerned. Caponsacchi regales us, of course, with the rarest fruit of a great character, a great culture and a great case; but Caponsacchi is acceptedly and naturally, needfully and illustratively, splendid. He *is* the soul of man at its finest—having passed through the smoky fires of life and emerging clear and high. Greatest of all the spirits exhibited, however, is that of the more than octogenarian Pope, at whose brooding, pondering, solitary vigil, by the end of a hard grey winter day in the great bleak waiting Vatican—"in the plain closet where he does such work"—we assist as intimately as at every other step of the case, and on whose grand meditation we heavily hang. But the Pope strikes us at first—though indeed perhaps only at first—as too high above the whole connection functionally and historically for us to place him within it dramatically. Our novel faces provisionally the question of dispensing with him, as it dispenses with the amazing, bristling, all too indulgently presented Roman advocates on either side of the case, who combine to put together the most formidable monument we possess to Browning's active curiosity and the liveliest proof of his almost unlimited power to give on his readers' nerves without giving on his own.

What remains with us all this time, none the less, is the effect of magnification, the exposure of each of these figures, in its degree, to that iridescent wash of personality, of temper and faculty, that our author ladles out to them, as the copious share of each, from his own great reservoir of spiritual health, and which makes us, as I have noted, seek the reason of a perpetual anomaly. Why, bristling so with references to *him* rather than with references to each other or to any accompanying set of circumstances, do they still establish more truth and beauty than they sacrifice, do they still, according to their chance, help to make "The Ring and the Book" a great living thing, a great objective mass? I brushed by the answer a moment ago, I think, in speaking of the development in Pompilia of the resource of expression, which brings us round, it seems to me, to the justification of Browning's method. To express his inner self—his outward was a different affair!—and to express it utterly, even if no matter how, was clearly, for his own measure and consciousness of that inner self, to *be* poetic; and the solution of all the deviations and disparities or, speaking critically, monstrosities, in the mingled tissue of this work, is the fact that whether or no by such convulsions of soul and sense life got delivered for him, the garment of life (which for him was poetry and poetry alone) got disposed in its due and adequate multitudinous folds. We move with him but in images and references and vast and far correspondences; we eat but of strange compounds and drink but of rare distillations; and very soon, after a course of this, we feel ourselves, however much or however little to our advantage we may on occasion pronounce it, in the world of Expression at any cost. That, essentially, *is* the world of poetry—which in the cases known to our experience where it seems to us to differ from Browning's world does so but through this latter's having been, by the vigour and violence, the bold familiarity, of his grasp and pull at it, moved several degrees nearer us, so to speak, than any other of the same general sort with which we are acquainted; so that, intellectually, we back away from it a little, back down before it, again and again, as we try to get off from a picture or a group or a view which is too much *upon* us and thereby out of focus. Browning is "upon" us, straighter upon us always, somehow, than anyone else of his race; and we thus recoil, we push our chair back, from the table he so tremendously spreads, just to see a little better what is on it. This makes a relation with him that it is difficult to express; as if he came up against us, each time, on the same side of the street and not on the other side, across the way, where we mostly see the poets elegantly walk, and where we greet them without danger of concussion. It is on this same side, as I call it,

468

on *our* side, on the other hand, that I rather see our encounter with the novelists taking place; we being, as it were, more mixed with them, or they at least, by their desire and necessity, more mixed with us, and our brush of them, in their minor frenzy, a comparatively muffled encounter.

We have in the whole thing, at any rate, the element of action which is at the same time constant picture, and the element of picture which is at the same time constant action; and with a fusion, as the mass moves, that is none the less effective, none the less thick and complete, from our not owing it in the least to an artful economy. Another force pushes its way through the waste and rules the scene, making wrong things right and right things a hundred times more so—that breath of Browning's own particular matchless Italy which takes us full in the face and remains from the first the felt rich coloured air in which we live. The quantity of that atmosphere that he had to give out is like nothing else in English poetry, any more than in English prose, that I recall; and since I am taking these liberties with him, let me take one too, a little, with the fruit of another genius shining at us here in association—with that great placed and timed prose fiction which we owe to George Eliot and in which *her* projection of the stage and scenery is so different a matter. Curious enough this difference where so many things make for identity—the quantity of talent, the quantity of knowledge, the high equality (or almost) of culture and curiosity, not to say of "spiritual life." Each writer drags along a far-sweeping train, though indeed Browning's spreads so considerably furthest; but his stirs us, to my vision, a perfect cloud of gold-dust, while hers, in "Romola," by contrast, leaves the air about as clear, about as white, and withal about as cold, as before she had benevolently entered it. This straight saturation of our author's, this prime assimilation of the elements for which the name of Italy stands, is a single splendid case, however; I can think of no second one that is not below it—if we take it as supremely expressed in those of his lyrics and shorter dramatic monologues that it has most helped to inspire. The Rome and Tuscany of the early 'fifties had become for him so at once a medium, a bath of the senses and perceptions, into which he could sink, in which he could unlimitedly soak, that wherever he might be touched afterwards he gave out some effect of that immersion. This places him to my mind quite apart, makes the rest of our poetic record of a similar experience comparatively pale and abstract. Shelley and Swinburne—to name only his compeers—are, I know, a part of the record; but the author of "Men and Women," of "Pippa Passes," of certain of the Dramatic Lyrics and other scattered felicities, not only expresses and reflects the matter; he fairly, he heatedly, if I may use such a term, exudes and perspires it. Shelley, let us say in the connection, is a light and Swinburne, let us say, a sound; Browning alone of them all is a temperature. We feel it, we are in it at a plunge, with the very first pages of the thing before us; to which, I confess, we surrender with a momentum drawn from fifty of their predecessors, pages not less sovereign, elsewhere.

The old Florence of the late spring closes round us; the hand of Italy is at once, with the recital of the old-world litter of Piazza San Lorenzo, with that of the great glare and of the great shadow-masses, heavy upon us, heavy with that strange weight, that mixed pressure, which is somehow, to the imagination, at once a caress and a menace. Our poet kicks up on the spot and at short notice what I have called his cloud of gold-dust. I can but speak for myself at least—something that I want to feel both as historic and esthetic truth, both as pictorial and moral interest, something that will repay my fancy tenfold if I can but feel it, hovers before me, and I say to myself that, whether or no a great poem is to come off, I will be hanged if one of the vividest of all stories and one of the sharpest of all impressions doesn't. I beckon these things on, I follow them up, I so desire and need them that I of course, by my imaginative collaboration, contribute to them—from the moment, that is, of my finding myself really in relation to the great points. On the other hand, as certainly, it has taken the author of the first volume, and of the two admirable chapters of the same— since I can't call them cantos—entitled respectively "Half-Rome" and "The Other Half-Rome," to put me in relation; where it is that he keeps me more and more, letting the closeness of my state, it must be owned, occasionally drop, letting the finer call on me even, for bad quarters-of-an-hour, considerably languish, but starting up before me again in vivid authority if I really presume to droop or stray. He takes his wilful way with me, but I make it my own, picking over and over as I have said, like some lingering talking pedlar's client, his great unloosed pack; and thus it is that by the time I am settled with Pompilia at Arezzo I have lived into all the conditions. They press upon me close, those wonderful dreadful beautiful particulars of the Italy of the eve of the eighteenth century—Browning himself moving about, darting hither and thither in them, at his mighty ease: beautiful, I say, because of the quantity of romantic and esthetic tradition from a more romantic and esthetic age still visibly, palpably, in solution there; and wonderful and dreadful through something of a similar tissue of matchless and ruthless consistencies and immoralities. I make to my hand, as this infatuated reader, *my* Italy of the eve of the eighteenth century—a vast painted and gilded rococo shell roofing over a scenic, an amazingly figured and furnished earth, but shutting out almost the whole of our own dearly-bought, rudely-recovered spiritual sky. You see I have this right, all the while, if I recognise my suggested material, which keeps coming and coming in the measure of my need, and my duty to which *is* to recognise it, and as handsomely and actively as possible. The great thing is that I have such a group of figures moving across so constituted a scene—figures so typical, so salient, so reeking with the old-world character, so impressed all over with its manners and its morals, and so predestined, we see, to this particular horrid little drama. And let me not be charged with giving it away, the idea of the latent prose fiction, by calling it little and horrid; let me not—for with my contention I can't possibly afford to— appear to agree with those who speak of the Franceschini-Comparini case as a mere vulgar criminal anecdote.

It might have been such but for two reasons—counting only the principal ones; one of these our fact that we see it so, I repeat, in Browning's inordinately-coloured light, and the other—which is indeed perhaps but another face of the same—that, with whatever limitations, it gives us in the rarest manner three characters of the first importance. I hold three a great many; I could have done with it almost, I think, if there had been but one or two; our rich provision shows you at any rate what I mean by speaking of our author's performance as above all a preparation for something. Deeply he felt that with the three—the three built up at us each with an equal genial rage of reiterative touches—there couldn't eventually not be something done (artistically done, I mean) if someone would only do it. There they are in their old yellow Arezzo, that miniature milder Florence, as sleepy to my recollection as a little English cathedral city clustered about a Close, but dreaming not so peacefully nor so innocently; there is the great fretted fabric of the Church on which they are all swarming and grovelling, yet after their fashion interesting parasites, from the high and dry old Archbishop, meanly wise or ignobly edifying, to whom Pompilia resorts in her woe and who practically pushes her away with a shuffling velvet foot; down through the couple of Franceschini cadets, Canon Girolamo and Abate Paul, mere minions, fairly in the verminous degree, of the overgrown order or too-rank organism; down to Count Guido himself and to Canon Caponsacchi, who have taken the tonsure at the outset of their careers, but none too strictly the vows, and who lead their lives under some strangest profanest pervertedest clerical category. There have been before this the Roman preliminaries, the career of the queer Comparini, the adoption, the assumption of the parentship, of the ill-starred little girl, with the sordid cynicism of her marriage out of hand, conveying her presumptive little fortune, her poor handful of even less than contingent cash, to hungry middle-aged Count Guido's stale "rank"; the many-toned note or turbid harmony of all of which recurs to us in the vivid image of the pieties and paganisms of San Lorenzo in Lucina, that banal little church in the old upper Corso—banal, that is, at the worst, with the rare Roman *banalité;* bravely banal, or banal with style—that we have all passed with a sense of its reprieve to our sight-seeing, and where the bleeding bodies of the still-breathing Pompilia and her extinct companions are laid out on the greasy marble of the altar-steps. To glance at these things, however, is fairly to be tangled, and at once, in the author's complexity of suggestion, to which our own thick-coming fancies respond in no less a measure; so that I have already missed my time to so much even as name properly the tremendous little chapter we should have devoted to the Franceschini interior as revealed at last to Comparini eyes; the sinister scene or ragged ruin of the Aretine "palace," where pride and penury and, at once, rabid resentment show their teeth in the dark and the void, and where Pompilia's inspired little character, clear silver hardened, effectually beaten and battered, to steel, begins to shine at the blackness with a light that fairly outfaces at last the gleam of wolfish fangs—the character that draws from Guido, in his, alas, too boundless harangue of the fourth volume, some of the sharpest specifications into which that extraordinary desert, that indescribable waste of intellectual life, as I have hinted at its being, from time to time flowers.

> "None of your abnegation of revenge!
> Fly at me frank, tug where I tear again!
> Away with the empty stare! Be holy still,
> And stupid ever! Occupy your patch
> Of private snow that's somewhere in what world
> May now be growing icy round your head,
> And aguish at your foot-print—freeze not me!"

I have spoken of the enveloping consciousness—or call it just the struggling, emerging, comparing, at last intensely living conscience—of Caponsacchi as the indicated centre of our situation or determinant of our form, in the matter of the excellent novel; and know of course what such an indication lets me in for, responsibly speaking, in the way of a rearrangement of relations, in the way of liberties taken. To lift our subject out of the sphere of anecdote and place it in the sphere of drama, liberally considered, to give it dignity by extracting its finest importance, causing its parts to flower together into some splendid special sense, we supply it with a large lucid reflector, which we find only, as I have already noted, in that mind and soul concerned in the business that have at once the highest sensibility and the highest capacity, or that are, as we may call it, most admirably agitated. There is the awkward fact, the objector may say, that by our record the mind and soul in question are not concerned till a given hour, when many things have already happened and the climax is almost in sight; to which we reply, at our ease, that we simply don't suffer that fact to be awkward. From the moment I am taking liberties I suffer *no* awkwardness; I should be very helpless, quite without resource and without vision, if I did. I said it to begin with: Browning works the whole thing over—the whole thing as originally given him—and we work *him;* helpfully, artfully, boldly, which is our whole blest basis. We therefore turn Caponsacchi on earlier, ever so much earlier; turn him on, with a brave ingenuity, from the very first—that is in Rome if need be; place him there in the field, at once recipient and agent, vaguely conscious and with splendid brooding apprehension, awaiting the adventure of his life, awaiting his call, his real call (the others have been such vain shows and hollow stopgaps), awaiting, in fine, his terrible great fortune. His direct connection with Pompilia begins certainly at Arezzo, only after she has been some time hideously mismated and has suffered all but her direst extremity—that is of the essence; we *take* it; it's all right. But his indirect participation is another affair, and we get it—at a magnificent stroke—by the fact that his view of Franceschini, his fellow-Aretine sordidly "on the make," his measure of undesired, indeed of quite execrated contact with him, brushed against in the motley hungry Roman traffic, where and while that sinister soul snuffs about on the very vague or the very foul scent of *his* fortune, may begin whenever we like. We have only to have it begin right, only to make it, on the part of two men, a relation of strong irritated perception and restless righteous convinced instinct in the one nature and of equally instinctive hate and envy, jealousy and latent fear, on the other, to see the indirect connection, the one with Pompilia, as I say, throw across our page as portentous a shadow as we need. Then we get Caponsacchi as a recipient up to the brim—as an agent, a predestined one, up to the hilt. I can scarce begin to tell you what I see him give, as we say, or how his sentient and observational life, his fine reactions in presence of such a creature as Guido, such a social type and image and lurid light, as it were, make him comparatively a modern man, breathed upon, to that deep and interesting agitation I have mentioned, by more forces than he yet reckons or knows the names of.

The direct relation—always to Pompilia—is made, at Arezzo, as we know, by Franceschini himself; preparing his own doom, in the false light of his debased wit, by creating an appearance of hidden dealing between his wife and the priest which shall, as promptly as he likes—if he but work it right—compromise and overwhelm them. The particular deepest damnation he conceives for his weaker, his weakest victim is that she shall take the cleric Caponsacchi for her lover, he indubitably willing—to Guido's apprehension; and that her castigation at his hands for this, sufficiently proved upon her, shall be the last luxury of his own baseness. He forges infernally, though grossly enough, an imputed correspondence between them, a series of love-letters, scandalous scrawls, of the last erotic intensity; which we in the event see solemnly weighed by his fatuous judges, all fatuous save the grave old Pope, in the scale of Pompilia's guilt and responsibility. It is this atrocity that at the *dénouement* damns Guido himself most, or well-nigh; but if it fails and recoils, as all his calculations do—it is only his rush of passion that doesn't miss—this is by the fact exactly that, as we have seen, his wife and her friend are, for our perfect persuasion, characters of the deepest dye. There, if you please, is the finest side of our subject; such sides come up, such sides flare out upon us, when we get such characters in such embroilments. Admire with me therefore our felicity in this first-class value of Browning's beautiful critical genial vision of his Caponsacchi—vision of him as the tried and tempered and illuminated *man*, a great round smooth, though as yet but little worn gold-piece, an embossed and figured ducat or sequin of the period, placed by the poet in my hand. He gives me that value to spend for him, spend on all the strange old experience, old sights and sounds and stuffs, of the old stored Italy—so we have at least the wit to spend it to high advantage; which is just what I mean by our taking the liberties we spoke of. I see such bits we can get with it; but the difficulty is that I see so many more things than I can have even dreamed of giving you a hint of. I see the Arezzo life and the Arezzo crisis with every "i" dotted and every circumstance presented; and when Guido takes his wife, as a possible trap for her, to the theatre—the theatre of old Arezzo: share with me the tattered vision and inhale the musty air!—I am well in range of Pompilia, the tragically exquisite, in her box, with her husband not there for the hour but posted elsewhere; I look at her in fact over Caponsacchi's shoulder and that of his brother-canon Conti, while this light character, a vivid recruit to our company, manages to toss into her lap, and as coming in guise of overture from his smitten friend, "a papertwist of comfits." There is a particular famous occasion at the theatre in a work of more or less contemporary fiction—at a petty provincial theatre which isn't even, as you might think, the place where Pendennis had his first glimpse of Miss Fotheringay. The evening at the Rouen playhouse of Flaubert's "Madame Bovary" has a relief not elsewhere equalled—it is the most *done* visit to the play in all literature—but, though "doing" is now so woefully out of favour, my idea would be to give it here a precious *pendant;* which connection, silly Canon Conti, the old fripperies and levities, the whole queer picture and show of manners, is handed over to us, expressly, as inapt for poetic illustration.

What is equally apt for poetic or for the other, indeed, is the thing for which we feel "The Ring and the Book" preponderantly done—it is at least what comes out clearest, comes out as straightest and strongest and finest, from Browning's genius—the exhibition of the great constringent relation between man and woman at once at its maximum and as the relation most worth while in life for either party; an exhibition forming quite the main substance of our author's message. He has dealt, in his immense variety and vivacity, with other relations, but on this he has thrown his most living weight; it remains the thing of which his own rich experience most convincingly spoke to him. He has testified to it as charged to the brim with the burden of the senses, and has testified to it as almost too clarified, too liberated and sublimated, for traceable application or fair record; he has figured it as never too much either of the flesh or of the spirit for him, so long as the possibility of both of these is in each, but always and ever as the thing absolutely most worth while. It is in the highest and rarest degree clarified and disengaged for Caponsacchi and Pompilia; but what their history most concludes to is how ineffably it was, whatever happened, worth while. Worth while most then for them or for us is the question? Well, let us say worth while assuredly for us, in this noble exercise of our imagination. Which accordingly shows us what we, for all our prose basis, would have found, to repeat my term once more, prepared for us. There isn't a detail of their panting flight to Rome over the autumn Apennines—the long hours when they melt together only *not* to meet—that doesn't positively plead for our perfect prose transcript. And if it be said that the mere massacre at the final end is a lapse to passivity from the high plane, for our pair of protagonists, of constructive, of heroic vision, this is not a blur from the time everything that happens happens most effectively to Caponsacchi's life. Pompilia's is taken, but she is none the less given; and it is in his consciousness and experience that she most intensely flowers—with all her jubilation for doing so. So that *he* contains the whole—unless indeed after all the Pope does, the Pope whom I was leaving out as too transcendent for *our* version. Unless, unless, further and further, I see what I have at this late moment no right to; see, as the very end and splendid climax of all, Caponsacchi sent for to the Vatican and admitted alone to the Papal presence. *There* is a scene if we will; and in the mere mutual confrontation, brief, silent, searching, recognising, consecrating, almost as august on the one part as on the other. It rounds us off; but you will think I stray too far. I have wanted, alas, to say such still other fond fine things—it being of our poet's great nature to prompt them at every step—that I almost feel I have missed half my points; which will doubtless therefore show you these remarks in their nakedness. Take them and my particular contention as a pretext and a minor affair if you will only feel them at the same time as at the worst a restless refinement of homage. It has been easy in many another case to run to earth the stray prime fancy, the original anecdote or artless tale, from which a great imaginative work, starting off after meeting it, has sprung and rebounded again and soared; and perhaps it is right and happy and final that one should have faltered in attempting by a converse curiosity to clip off or tie back the wings that once have spread. You will agree with me none the less, I feel, that Browning's great generous wings are over us still and even now, more than ever now; and also that they shake down on us his blessing.

After his long last visit to America (August 1910–July 1911), and the death of his brother, William, Henry James returned briefly to Lamb House, only to find that country life now seemed too solitary. He spent the winter and early spring of 1912 at the Reform Club; work on *A Small Boy and Others* and *Notes of a Son and Brother* was done in Theodora Bosanquet's flat at 10 Lawrence Street in Chelsea. Lamb House was loaned to Henry's nephew Billy for a honeymoon residence until James returned to the country in June for a summer filled with visitors and visiting.

"The Novel in *The Ring and the Book*" resulted from Edmund Gosse's invitation to speak with the British playwright Arthur Wing Pinero (1855–1934) at the Browning centenary on May 7, 1912. James had known Browning's poetry since about 1860, when John La Farge had "revealed" the works of the poet whose *Men and Women* already lay upon his parents' book-table (*A*, 291). He had met Browning at numerous social events over the years, had lived a few buildings away from the poet at De Vere Gardens, and had written at least one short story, "The Private Life," inspired by Browning's life. James' other critical pieces on Browning are an extremely negative review of "The Inn Album" (1876) and an essay memorializing the poet's interment in Westminster Abbey ("Browning in Westminster Abbey" [1890]).

Accepting Gosse's invitation, James weighed two quite different topics: "I shall make up my distracted mind between two things: a shy at the subject (as who should say) 'The Browning of One's Youth'; or, quite differently, a go at '*The Ring and the Book* as a Novel' (or perhaps better 'The Novel in *The Ring and the Book*'). I predominate toward the latter" (February 5, 1912). The latter earned James a prolonged ovation.

It was a time for commemorations. Although James often expressed ambivalence about such events, formal recognitions of literary fellowship took on new importance in his later years. On June 26 he received an honorary Doctor of Letters degree from Oxford (Harvard had honored him similarly in the spring of 1911). That same spring, James wrote a letter in celebration of Howells' seventy-fifth birthday, a public tribute to an intimacy at once professional and personal. "My debt to you began well-nigh half a century ago in the most personal way possible, and then kept growing and growing with your own admirable growth. . . . This benefit was that you held out your open editorial hand to me at the time I began to write . . . with a frankness and sweetness that was really the making of me, the making of the confidence that required help and sympathy. . . . I mean that you talked to me and listened to me. . . ." ("A letter to Mr. Howells" [1912]). Howells constituted, for James, a literary community. The importance of such literary sharing is further highlighted by a letter written on March 20, 1912, in which James attempts to persuade H. G. Wells to accept his election as Fellow of the Royal Society of Literature. "I have no greater affinity with associations and academies than you *a priori;* and yet I find myself glad to have done the simple, civil, social *easiest* thing in accepting my election—touched by the amenity and geniality of the thought that we shall probably *make something* collectively—in addition to what we may make individually." Having striven for a critical community in the essays of the 80s and 90s and attempted to train, by example, a community of readers in the Prefaces, James focuses in 1912 on writers.

What "The Novel in *The Ring and the Book*" makes clear is that the focus on writers is, in fact, a way of connecting writer, reader, and critic. As in the Howells letter, James shows these connections to be intimate and personal. His talk is a description of his personal reactions to the Browning whom he finds on *"our* side" of the street. Rather than a distanced, respectful "shy" at "The Browning of One's Youth," the mature novelist takes a friendly "go" at reading his fellow writer critically and, in doing so, recreating the writing process.

James' reencounter with *The Ring and the Book* closely resembles his "revision" of his own fiction in the Prefaces (see, in particular, the Preface to *The Golden Bowl,* Chapter 19) and is typical of his reading practice in his later years. As he explained to Mrs. Humphry Ward on July 26, 1899, his criticisms of her *Eleanor* result from "giving way to my irresistible need of wondering how, *given* the subject, one could best work one's self into the presence of it. And, lo and behold, the subject isn't (of course, in so scant a show and brief a piece) 'given' at all—I have doubtless simply, with violence and mutilation *stolen* it. It is of the nature of that violence that I'm a wretched person to *read* a novel—I begin so quickly and concomitantly, *for myself,* to write it rather—even before I know clearly what it's about! The novel I can *only* read, I can't read at all!" (See also his letter to Mrs. W. K. Clifford on May 18, 1912.)

The Ring and the Book's rich accessibility to such imaginative reading and rereading is precisely what James in 1876 had missed in *The Inn Album,* which he called "unavailable": "A poem with so many presumptions in its favor as such an authorship carries with it is a thing to make some intellectual use of, to care for, to remember, to return to, to linger over, to become intimate with. But we can as little imagine a reader (who has not the misfortune to be a reviewer) addressing himself more than once to the perusal of 'The Inn Album,' as we can fancy cultivating for conversational purposes the society of a person afflicted with a grievous impediment of speech." Even Browning's burial offered more opportunities for intellectual intimacy: James opens "Browning in Westminster Abbey" by declaring that the occasion must prompt Browning's admirers to imaginative speculation about how the poet himself would have described it.

The difference between James' harshness about *The Inn Album* and his praise of *The Ring and the Book* stems less from a change in his judgment of Browning than from the nature of the specific poems. In an early description of how he reads poetry, James gives an almost uncannily accurate characterization of "The Novel in *The Ring and the Book.*" In a September 1, 1875, letter to Edmund Clarence Stedman, who had complimented him on a Tennyson review, James wrote: "I know poets and poetry only as an irredeemable proser! . . . I quite sympathise with you in your wonder that Browning should have never felt the intellectual comfort of 'a few grave, rigid laws.' But Browning's badness I have never professed to understand. I limit myself to vastly enjoying his goodness."

That James reads poetry as a proser does not mean he praises Browning's work for being prose-like. He complained of *The Inn Album,* "It is not lyrical, for there is not a phrase which in any degree does the office of the poetry that comes lawfully into the world—chants itself, images itself, or lingers in the memory"; in 1890, he called Browning "a poet without a lyre." What reading as a proser does mean can be seen in "The Novel in *The Ring and the Book*" where James rewrites a poem *into* a prose fiction. As James' metaphor of the Gothic cathedral makes clear, this is only one of innumerable ways to read Browning's vast, varied poem. James' position as a fiction writer reveals a particular point of personal access, one that "will save our steps and light our uncertainty, most enable us to reach our personal chair, our indicated chapel or shrine, when once within."

James uses a second, telling metaphor to describe the adventure of writing, an adventure upon which both Browning and he embark in the course of the essay. As in the Prefaces, James is fascinated by the story of the writer's story. Browning's discovery of the Book is one such "story"; his embarkation with it for the Golden Isles of poetry is another. And James' encounter with the poem, and thus with Browning, is also an adventure. Having discovered his point of entry into the poem, James describes himself as a explorer "sticking in and planting before you, to flourish so far as it shall, my little sprig of bay. . . ." He stakes his artistic claim to the subject that his point of view has revealed to him and figures himself as victor.

Not only is point of view central to the discovery of the novel in *The Ring and the Book*, it is also basic to that fiction's structure. James' own use of point of view has been traced back to Browning (see below). However, *The Ring and the Book's* intricate multiple perspectives are, for James, "unreconciled." His contention that Canon Caponsacchi's particular angle of perception should structure the narrative is best understood in context of his distinction between how the historian and the literary artist treat their raw materials, a distinction highlighted in this case by the voluminous data of "the Book." They begin with very different attitudes. "The historian, essentially, wants more documents than he can really use; the dramatist only wants more liberties than he can really take" (Preface to *The Aspern Papers*, p. 332). The literary artist's greater liberty even includes the freedom to avoid facts. In the Preface to *The Ambassadors*, James makes it clear that the germ for his novel came from an incident in Howells' life and makes it just as clear that that life, as a whole, can only restrict his inspiration " . . . I need scarce mention that for development, for expression of its maximum, my glimmering story was, at the earliest stage, to have nipped the thread of connexion with the possibilities of the actual reported speaker. *He* remains but the happiest of accidents; his actualities, all too definite, precluded any range of possibilities . . ." (p. 364). *The Ambassadors* is not Howells' biography.

Browning's situation in *The Ring and the Book* differs in that, like writers of "historic fiction," he must incorporate a huge body of "established data." Nonetheless James maintains that even these artists must select and arrange. Comparing Browning's position to that of the naturalists who claim to write the fictional history of their own times, James insists that a slice of life is just that. As he argues in "The New Novel" (1914): "the principle of selection having been involved at the worst or the least, one would suppose, in any approach whatever to the loaf of life with the *arrière-pensée* of a slice. There being no question of a slice upon which the further question of where and how to cut it does not wait, the office of method, the idea of choice and comparison, have occupied the ground from the first. This makes clear, to a moment's reflection, that there can be no such thing as an amorphous slice, and that any waving aside of inquiry as to the sense and value of a chunk of matter has to reckon with the simple truth of its having been *born* of naught else but measured excision. . . . How can a slice of life be anything but illustrational of the loaf, and how

can illustration not immediately bristle with every sign of the extracted and related state? The relation is at once to what the thing comes
from and to what it waits upon—which last is our act of recognition."

Such selection allows, paradoxically, for artistic expansion.
Browning's "bundle of facts" and documents becomes "bigger by the
extraction, immeasurably bigger than even the most cumulative
weight of the mere crude evidence." This paradox is figured in the
Preface to "The Spoils of Poynton" by a double metaphor: the artist's
starting point is described as both a nugget mined out of the crude
material of life and the spreading "virus of suggestion."

Despite the principles of selection that James elaborates for his
own *Ring and the Book,* he locates the strength of Browning's poem
precisely in the poet's *failure* to restrict himself to a central consciousness. Browning's *Ring and the Book* is just that—Browning's.
The poet's curiosity makes him turn the lens of his vision upon all of
the poem's many characters, coloring them with his "iridescent wash
of personality." What James calls in 1890 "the all-touching, all-trying
spirit" of Browning's work is, in fact, an expression of the poet's "inner self." His work is intimate, not only in that it is, like all poetry,
"Expression at any cost," but also in that it forces us into an intimacy
with Browning.

James' description of how Browning is " 'upon' " us offers a further explanation for why James reads *The Ring and the Book* as a novel.
The poetic Master is almost too novelistic for, and thus too nearly a
threat to, the prose Master. James' ambivalence about *The Ring and the
Book*—he never reveals whether Browning reaches the Golden Isles—
may be partly accounted for by the need to "back away," to "get off
from," to refocus; to assert, in other words, his own point of view, to
write his own *Ring and the Book.*

The intimate force of Browning's personality may, at times,
threaten James, but it is also necessary to him. In 1890 he argued that
Browning's "individualism" introduced modernity into the hallowed
literary community of Westminster Abbey: "The tradition of the poetic character as something high, detached, and simple . . . is one that
Browning has broken at every turn. . . ." James suggests that Browning will make Westminster more comfortable for other moderns
(perhaps planting an earlier bay sprig). And the comfort of a literary
sharing with Browning is obvious by the end of "The Novel in *The
Ring and the Book*" where James, in the familiar, private voice of the
Notebooks—"Unless, unless, further and further"—seems to work
out his reading before the audience. Browning's "vast covering charity of imagination" spreads its wings not only over his characters but

also over his readers. Like Milly Theale, his virtue lies in its effects upon others. "The Novel in *The Ring and the Book*" is truly a tribute to Browning in that, as James says repeatedly, we do as he does. In reading, we write. Although he disclaims "The Novel in *The Ring and the Book*" as criticism, it has the critical effect that James describes in "The New Novel." "The effect, if not the prime office, of criticism is to make our absorption and our enjoyment of the things that feed the mind as aware of itself as possible, since that awareness quickens the mental demand, which thus in turn wanders further and further for pasture."

For reviews of *Notes on Novelists,* see our commentary on "Emile Zola," p. 454. Among these, the *Saturday Review* singled out the Browning essay as an example of James' admirable personal, "English" method of criticism: "He simply sets out to describe faithfully the effect Browning has upon himself. His enterprise depends for its interest, like most English critical enterprises, less upon the author being discussed than upon the critics discussing him" (p. 488).

The fullest treatment of the two writers, Posnock's *Henry James and the Problem of Robert Browning* (Athens: University of Georgia Press, 1985), analyzes James' literary and personal anxiety at Browning's influence. For other discussions, see: Bargainnier, "Browning, James and 'The Private Life,'" *Studies in Short Fiction* 14 (1977): 151–58; Buckler, "Rereading Henry James Rereading Robert Browning: 'The Novel in *The Ring and the Book,*'" *Henry James Review* 5 (Winter 1984): 135–45; D'Avanzo, "James's 'Maud-Evelyn': Source, Allusion, and Meaning," *Iowa English Yearbook* 13 (Fall 1968): 24–33; Davies, *Browning and the Modern Novel* (Hull: University of Hull Publications, 1962), pp. 3–27; Drew, *The Poetry of Robert Browning* (London: Metheun, 1970), pp. 385–96; Edel (3: 274–77; 5: 465–69); Empet, "James' *Portrait of a Lady* and Browning's 'My Last Duchess': A Comparison," *DeKalb Literary Arts Journal* 13, nos. 1–2 (1978–79): 79–84; Lind, "James's 'The Private Life' and Browning," *American Literature* 23 (November 1951): 315–22; B. Melchiori, *Browning's Poetry of Reticence* (New York: Barnes and Noble, 1968), pp. 190–95; G. Melchiori, "Browning e Henry James," in *Friendship's Garland,* vol. 2, ed. Gabrieli (Roma: Edizioni di Storia e Letteratura, 1966), pp. 143–80; Monteiro, "Henry James and the Lessons of *Sordello,*" *Western Humanities Review* 31 (1977): 69–78; Ross, "Henry James' 'Half Man': The Legacy of Browning in 'The Madonna of the Future'," *Browning Institute Studies* 2 (1974): 25–42; Solimine, "Henry James, William Wetmore Story, and Friend: A Noble Mistake?" *Studies in Browning and His Circle* 8, no. 1 (1980): 57–61; Wadman, "W. W. Story *and His Friends:* Henry James's Portrait of Robert Browning," *Yearbook of English Studies* 11 (1981): 210–18.

NOTES

460:12. we but walk . . . round and round it. James uses similar images both in the Preface to *The Wings of the Dove*, p. 346, and in *The Golden Bowl*, see 346:20.

460:28. "difficult." The "tradition of Browning as 'difficult' " led in the 1880s to the formation of Browning societies for the discussion of his poems. In his review of *The Inn Album*, James complains "His thought knows no simple stage—at the very moment of its birth it is a terribly complicated affair. We frankly confess, at the risk of being accused of deplorable levity of mind, that we have found this want of clearness of explanation, of continuity, of at least superficial verisimilitude, of the smooth, the easy, the agreeable, quite fatal to our enjoyment of 'The Inn Album'. It is all too argumentative, too curious and recondite."

461:13. my first reading of these volumes. *The Ring and the Book* was first published in 1868–69. On March 8, 1870, Henry wrote to William James that "During the past month I have been tasting lightly of the pleasure [of reading] among other things Browning's Ring and Book, in honor of Italy. . . . Browning decidedly gains in interest tho' he loses in a certain mystery and (so to speak) infinitude, after a visit to Italy."

461:15. the novel they might have constituted. Altick and Loucks, *Browning's Roman Murder Story* (Chicago: University of Chicago Press, 1968), p. 14, show that Browning did, in fact, offer the material to several novelists—Miss Ogle, W. C. Cartwright, Trollope—as well as to Tennyson.

461:18. the great loose and uncontrolled composition. James' description here resembles his characterization of Victorian fiction's "large loose baggy monsters" in the Preface to *The Tragic Muse*. James is also echoing his earlier criticism of *The Inn Album*: "That Mr. Browning knows he 'neglects the form,' and does not particularly care, does not very much help matters; it only deepens the reader's sense of the graceless and thankless and altogether unavailable character of the poem." His judgment that *The Ring and the Book* is formless has been directly challenged by a number of Browning scholars. See, for example, Altick and Loucks, including their useful bibliographical note.

461:20. fiction of the so-called historic type. James addresses this topic as early as 1867. See "Historical Novels," *Nation*, 5 (August 15, 1867), 126–27. For discussion of the affinities and distinctions between literature and history, see James' review of *Middlemarch*, "The Art of Fiction," and the Preface to *The Aspern Papers*, Chapters 3, 7, and 16.

461:30. his find of the Book. See *The Ring and the Book*, ll. 32–82.

462:4. "Men and Women" (1855), "Dramatic Lyrics" (1842), "Dramatis Personae" (1864), "Sordello" (1840).

462:13. a deposit of *stated* matter. In the Preface to *The Spoils of Poynton,* James states: "Strange and attaching, certainly, the consistency with which the first thing to be done for the communicated and seized idea is to reduce almost to nought the form, the air as of a mere disjoined and lacerated lump of life, in which we may have happened to meet it."

463:23. *decaduto.* decayed.

466:4. slice . . . of life. This is a translation of the phrase *tranche de vie* which the French playwright Jean Jullien (1854–1919) applied to naturalist writing. James' argument for the principle of artistic selection is based on the distinction made in the Preface to *The Spoils of Poynton:* "Life being all inclusion and confusion, and art being all discrimination and selection. . . ."

466:14. centre. James' fullest discussion of the centre is in the Prefaces (see index).

466:32. *their* sense. James' admiration for George Eliot has a similar basis, as he explains in the Preface to *The Princess Casamassima:* "I have for example a weakness of sympathy with that constant effort of George Eliot's which plays through Adam Bede and Felix Holt and Tito Melema, through Daniel Deronda and through Lydgate in 'Middlemarch,' through Maggie Tulliver, through Romola, through Dorothea Brooke and Gwendolen Harleth; the effort to show their adventures and their history—the author's subject-matter all—as determined by their feelings and the nature of their minds." See also our commentary on James' review of *Middlemarch.*

467:20. on her part intelligence and expression are disengaged. In the Preface to *What Maisie Knew,* James justifies a similar disengagement in "In the Cage." "My central spirit, in the anecdote, is for verisimilitude, I grant, too ardent a focus of divination; but without this excess the phenomena detailed would have lacked their principle of cohesion" (p. 328).

468:14. his outward was a different affair. James explores what he sees as the curious split between Browning the poet and Browning the social lion in the short story "The Private Life" (See *N*, July 27 and August 3, 1891). He also repeatedly remarks this split in his letters. For example, he writes to his mother on January 31, 1877, "(I forgot to say that after Smalley's dinner I had a long talk with Browning, who, personally, is no more like to *Paracelsus* than I to Hercules, but is a great gossip and a very 'sympathetic' easy creature.)" Similarly, James comments to Howells on March 30, 1877, "Browning is a great chatterer but no *Sordello* at all."

469:6. the element of action which is at the same time constant picture. For a distinction between picture and action or drama, see the Preface to *The Wings of the Dove,* Chapter 17.

469:13. Browning's own particular matchless Italy. In "From A Roman Notebook" in *Italian Hours,* James' January 30 entry describes "A drive the other day with a friend to Villa Madama, on the side of Monte Mario; a place like a page out of one of Browning's richest evocations of this clime and civilisation. Wondrous in its haunting melancholy, it might have inspired half 'The Ring and the Book' at a stroke. What a grim commentary on history such a scene—what an irony of the past!" On Browning in Italy, see also James' *William Wetmore Story and His Friends* (1903).

469:27. "Romola." James never wrote a piece devoted exclusively to *Romola*, but he mentions the novel in nearly all of his essays on George Eliot. In "The Life of George Eliot" (1885), he comments, "A twentieth part of the erudition would have sufficed, would have given us the feeling and colour of the time, if there had been more of the breath of the Florentine streets, more of the faculty of optical evocation, a greater saturation of the senses with the elements of the adorable little city. The difficulty with the book, for the most part, is that it is not Italian; it has always seemed to me the most Germanic of the author's productions." See also James' mentions of *Romola* in his review of *Middlemarch,* Chapter 3.

470:2. Shelley . . . is a light and Swinburne . . . a sound. Edel notes that James' audience responded to this comparison with "a great stir and a great flutter" (5: 466). James' earlier description of Shelley's house at Lerici in "Italy Revisited" in *Italian Hours* emphasizes the scene's light: " . . . I remember few episodes of Italian travel more sympathetic, as they have it here, than that perfect autumn afternoon; the half-hour's station on the little battered terrace of the villa; the climb to the singularly felicitous old castle that hangs above Lerici; the meditative lounge, in the fading light, on the vine-decked platform that looked out toward the sunset and the darkening mountains and, far below, upon the quiet sea, beyond which the pale-faced tragic villa stared up at the brightening moon." His 1875 review of Swinburne's *Essays and Studies,* while it does not deal with Italy, does describe Swinburne's writing in terms of sound: "His style . . . is always listening to itself—always turning its head over its shoulders to see its train flowing behind it. The train shimmers and tumbles in a very gorgeous fashion, but the rustle of its embroidery is fatally importunate."

470:39. age still visibly, palpably, in solution there. Speaking of Italy in the time of Shelley, James says in the Preface to *The Aspern Papers,* "I delight in a palpable imaginable *visitable* past—in the nearer distances and the clearer mysteries, the marks and signs of a world we may reach over to as by making a long arm we grasp an object at the other end of our own table" (pp. 333–34).

473:3. a large lucid reflector. James uses the term "reflector" throughout the Prefaces to describe the mirroring qualities of the center of consciousness. For example, in the Preface to *The Wings of the Dove,* James speaks of "My registers or 'reflectors,' as I so conveniently name them (burnished indeed as they generally are by the intelligence, the curiosity, the passion, the force of the moment, whatever it be, directing them)" (p. 355). Also, see index.

475:18. the great constringent relation between man and woman. Intimacy is even the *topic* of Browning's poetry, as James recognized in "Browning in Westminster Abbey" (1890): "If Browning had spoken for us in no other way, he ought to have been made sure of, tamed, and chained as a classic, on account of the extraordinary beauty of his treatment of the special relation between man and woman." In "The Future of the Novel," James describes how the nineteenth century's "mistrust of any but the most guarded treatment of the great relation between men and women, the constant world-renewal" makes literature run the risk of superficiality (p. 248).

475:23. his own rich experience. For another discussion of how art depends upon the artist's experience of "felt life," see the Preface to *The Portrait of a Lady*, Chapter 13. James also argues that criticism is grounded in feeling. See "Arnold's *Essays in Criticism*," "Saint-Beuve," and "Criticism," Chapters 1, 2, and 9.

TEXTUAL VARIANTS

James' address to the Royal Society was printed in the *Transactions of the Royal Society of Literature*, 2d series, 31, pt. 4 (1912): 269–98. He revised the speech for publication in the *Quarterly Review* 217 (July 1912): 68–87. Some minor alterations were made when James collected the essay in *Notes on Novelists* in 1914. Variants listed are between the first and last versions of the essay.

460:12. muchness . . . that. 1912: muchness (to put the effect at once most plainly and most expressively), that.

460:15. us . . . to. 1912: us, in a word, to.

461:10. essence . . . under. 1912: essence (as a grateful theme, of course I mean) under.

461:41. in. 1912: at.

462:19. a . . . and. 1912: a sort of sublime curiosity, and.

462:23. and . . . confidence. 1912: and confidence.

462:35. circle. 1912: ring.

462:36. turn. 1912: circle.

462:42. however. 1912: anyhow.

463:9. on . . . 1698. 1912: on the 22nd of February, 1698.

463:10. ostensible. 1912: adopted.

463:12. were. 1912: had been.

463:24. bewildered . . . purely. 1912: bewildered and scared, is purely.

463:27. disappointment. 1912: disappointments.

463:42. local powers. 1912: authorities.

464:15. equal. 1912: equally.

464:42. We . . . accept. 1912: We cannot accept.

465:1. want . . . to. 1912: want to.

465:1. tremendous. 1912: prodigious.

465:2. psychologic . . . so. 1912: psychologic (one scarce knows what to call it) shoulder, so.

465:10. effect . . . find. 1912: effect we find.

465:14–466:13. I . . . it. Added in revision.

466:14. do . . . is. 1912: do then is.

466:24. atrocious. 1912: infernal.

466:35. fixed. 1912: huge.

466:35. his . . . prodigious. 1912: his own prodigious.

466:37. a. 1912: the.

467:7. might . . . . Nothing. 1912: might have been so. Nothing.

467:33. Pope . . . too. 1912: Pope is too.

467:36. novel . . . with. 1912: Novel—which please believe me I still keep before me!—dispenses with.

468:29. this. 1912: the.

468:38. This. 1912: That.

469:5. encounter. 1912: matter.

470:3. Swinburne. . . . a. 1912: Swinburne is a.

470:4. alone . . . is. 1912: alone is.

470:18. is . . . to. 1912: is going to.

470:18. I will. 1912: I'll.

471:8. across . . . scene. 1912: across a so constituted scene.

471:38. Canon. 1912: Count.

471:39. but . . . the. 1912: but not the.

472:9. have . . . with. 1912: have passed, but with.

472:24. specifications. 1912: characterisations.

472:26. have . . . from. 1912: have called it from.

472:34. me!'' . . . I. 1912:

Or elsewhere:

> "She could play off her sex's armoury,
> Entreat, reproach, be female to my male,
> Try all the shrieking doubles of the hare,
> And yield fair sport so: but the tactics change,
> The hare stands stock-still to enrage the hound!
>
> .   .   .
>
> This self-possession to the uttermost,
> How does it differ in aught save degree
> From the terrible patience of God?''

But I find myself, too unresistingly, quoting, and so, frankly, as I cannot justify some of my positions here by another example or two, I must cut short as to what I should have liked to add for that shaft further to be sunk into the dense deposit of social decay forming Count Guido's domestic life; the shaft so soon widening out to his awful mother, evoked for us in our author's single sufficing line:

"The gaunt grey nightmare in the furthest smoke."

The mere use of "furthest" there somehow makes the image! But other single lines glance at us, more flower-like, all along, out of the rank vegetation; such as:

"Fragment of record very strong and old."

Or such as:

"Those old odd corners of an empty heart."

Or such as:

"Leave that live passion, come be dead with me."

And even these already take me too far, or would if I didn't feel it really important just to put in, for your brief attention, the page or two representing to my sense the highest watermark of our author's imagination here; representing not, like too many others, mere imaginative motion, but real imaginative life. Taken from Caponsacchi's address in the second volume it consists of his superb visionary dismissal and disposal of Guido; which let me just preface, however, by the latter's own splendid howl, when at the end of his prodigious final interview with justice, an interview, as given us, all on his own side and involving, well-nigh, a complete conspectus of human history, the man, with the officers of the law at the door and the red scaffold in view, breaks out in the concrete truth of his weakness and terror and his cry, first, to his judges, "Hold me from them! I am yours." And then, frantically, wonderfully:

"I am the Grand-duke's—No, I am the Pope's!
Abate—Cardinal—Christ—Maria—God . . .
Pompilia, will you let them murder me?"

I have pronounced them all splendid contentious minds; so that the return there, at a jump, to alarmed nature, to passion and pain as we more easily, that is less loquaciously, know them, has again no less a value at Caponsacchi's broken climax of his magnificent plea—"I do but play with an imagined life"—when he drops suddenly straight down from magnanimous speculative heights to his personal sense of the reality:

"O great, just, good God! Miserable me!"

However, the great passage I allude to has everything.

"Let us go away—leave Guido all alone
Back on the world again that knows him now!
I think he will be found (indulged so far!)
Not to die so much as slide out of life,
Pushed by the general horror and common hate
Low, lower—left o' the very ledge of things,
I seem to see him catch convulsively
One by one at all honest forms of life,
At reason, order, decency and use—
To cramp him and get foothold by at least;
And still they disengage them from his clutch.
'What, you are he then had Pompilia once
And so forewent her? Take not up with us!'
And thus I see him slowly and surely edged
Of all the table-land whence life upsprings
Aspiring to be immortality,

As the snake, hatched on hill-top by mischance,
Despite his wriggling, slips, slides, slidders down
Hillside, lies low and prostrate on the smooth
Level of the outer place, lapsed in the vale:
So I lose Guido in the loneliness,
Silence and dusk, till at the doleful end,
At the horizontal line, creation's verge,
From what just is to absolute nothingness—
Lo, what is this he meets, strains onward still?
What other man deep further in the fate,
Who, turning at the prize of a footfall
To flatter him and promise fellowship,
Discovers in the act a frightful face—
Judas, made monstrous by much solitude!
The two are at one now! Let them love their love
That bites and claws like hate, or hate their hate
That mops and mows and makes as it were love!
There, let them each tear each in devil's-fun,
Or fondle this the other while malice aches—
Both teach, both learn detestability!
Kiss him the kiss, Iscariot! Pay that back,
That smatch o' the slaver blistering on your lip—
By the better trick, the insult he spared Christ—
Lure him the lure o' the letters, Aretine!
Lick him o'er slimy-smooth with jelly filth
O' the verse-and-prose pollution in love's guise!
The cockatrice is with the basilisk!
There let them grapple, denizen's o' the dark,
Foes or friends, but indissolubly bound,
In their one spot out of the ken of God
Or care of man, for ever and ever more!"

I.

473:28. undesired . . . quite. 1912: undesired, of, indeed, quite.
474:23. come. 1912: comes.
476:11. It . . . homage. Added in revision.
476:25. and. 1912: as.

BIBLIOGRAPHY OF HENRY JAMES'
CRITICISM OF FICTION

We have chosen James' texts which are primarily or importantly on fiction. We give initial publication information and republication by James in collections printed during his lifetime. We have included essays on poets when that poet wrote fiction to which James makes sustained reference, as in the case of Gautier and de Musset. Our subcategories do not of course contain all texts equally smoothly; "Essays on Groups of Works" contain references to various authors who can be looked up in the index. Only one posthumous anthology besides *The Art of the Novel* is included, *Parisian Sketches*, because the alternative, citing from the *New York Tribune*, makes access to these essays nearly impossible.

1: Books of Criticism

French Poets and Novelists. London: Macmillan, 1878.
Hawthorne. London: Macmillan, 1879.
The Art of Fiction (with Walter Besant). Boston: Cupples, Upham, 1884.
Partial Portraits. London and New York: Harper and Brothers, 1893.
Essays in London and Elsewhere. New York: Harper and Brothers, 1893.
The Question of Our Speech / The Lesson of Balzac: Two Lectures. Boston and New York: Houghton, Mifflin, 1905.
Notes on Novelists with Some Other Notes. New York: Charles Scribner's Sons, 1914.
The Art of the Novel: Critical Prefaces. New York: Charles Scribner's Sons, 1934.
Parisian Sketches: Letters to the New York Tribune, 1875–1876, ed. Leon Edel and Ilse Dusoir Lind. London: Rupert Hart-Davis, 1958.

2: Essays on Criticism

"The Art of Fiction," *Longman's Magazine* 4 (September 1884): 502–21; revised for *Partial Portraits*.
"Letter to the Summer School at Deerfield," *New York Tribune* (August 4, 1889): Sec. 2, p. 10; rpt. as "The Modern Novel" in *The Author* 1 (August 15, 1889): 116.
"Note on Literary Form," *The Art of Authorship: Literary Reminiscences, Methods of Work, and Advice to Young Beginners,* comp. and ed. G. Bainton. New York: D. Appleton, 1890. P. 208.

"The Science of Criticism," *New Review* 4 (May 1891): 398–402; revised for "Criticism" in *Essays in London and Elsewhere*.

"American Letter" [the reading public], *Literature* 2 (March 26, 1898): 356–58.

"American Letter" [the quantity of present fiction], *Literature* 2 (April 9, 1898): 422–23.

"American Letter" [the critic in America], *Literature* 2 (May 21, 1898): 593–94.

"The Future of the Novel," *The Universal Anthology*, ed. Richard Garnett. New York: Merrill and Baker, 1901. Vol. 28, pp. xiii–xxiv.

"The Younger Generation," *The Times Literary Supplement*, no. 635 (March 19, 1914): 133–34; no. 637 (April 2, 1914): 157–58; revised, and retitled, as "The New Novel, 1914," for *Notes on Novelists with Some Other Notes*.

"The Founding of the *Nation*: Recollection of the 'Fairies' That Attended Its Birth," *The Nation* 101 (July 8, 1915): 44–45.

3: Essays on Individual Critics

MATTHEW ARNOLD

[*Essays in Criticism*], *North American Review* 101 (July 1865): 206–13.

"Matthew Arnold," *English Illustrated Magazine* 1 (January 1884): 241–46.

GEORGE H. CALVERT

[*Essays—Aesthetical*], *The Nation* 20 (June 3, 1875): 383.

MR. AND MRS. JAMES T. FIELDS

"Mr. and Mrs. Fields," *Cornhill Magazine* n.s. 39 (July 1915): 29–43; rpt. as "Mr. and Mrs. James T. Fields," *Atlantic Monthly*, 116 (July 1915): 21–31.

ABRAHAM HAYWARD

"Hayward's Essays," *The Nation* 27 (December 26, 1878): 402–3.

T. L. KINGTON-OLIPHANT

"*The Duke and the Scholar, and Other Essays*," *The Nation* 21 (September 30, 1875): 216.

JAMES RUSSELL LOWELL

"James Russell Lowell," *Atlantic Monthly* 69 (January 1892): 35–50; revised for *Essays in London and Elsewhere*.

"James Russell Lowell," *Library of the World's Best Literature*, ed. Charles Dudley Warner. New York: R. S. Peale and J. A. Hill, 1896. Vol. 16: 9229–37.

CHARLES DE MAZADE

["La Littérature et nos Désastres"], *The Nation* 21 (December 30, 1875): 419.

CHARLES AUGUSTIN SAINTE-BEUVE

"Sainte-Beuve's Portraits," *The Nation* 6 (June 4, 1868): 454–55.

"Sainte-Beuve's First Articles," *The Nation* 20 (February 18, 1875): 117–18.
"Sainte-Beuve's English Portraits," *The Nation* 20 (April 15, 1875): 261–62.
"Sainte-Beuve," *North American Review* 130 (January 1880): 51–68; revised for *American Literary Criticism*, ed. William M. Payne. New York: Longmans, Green, 1904. Pp. 299–318.

EDMOND SCHERER

"A French Critic," *The Nation* 1 (October 12, 1865): 468–70.
"Scherer's Literary Studies," *The Nation* 22 (April 6, 1876): 233.

NASSAU W. SENIOR

[*Essays on Fiction*], *North American Review* 99 (October 1864): 580–87.

GEORGE BARNETT SMITH

[*Poets and Novelists: A Series of Literary Studies*], *The Nation* 21 (December 30, 1875): 422–23.

HIPPOLYTE-ADOLPHE TAINE

"Taine's English Literature," *Atlantic Monthly* 29 (April 1872): 469–72.

JULIUS RODENBERG

[*England, Literary and Social, From A German Point of View*], *The Nation* 22 (March 16, 1876): 182.

4: ESSAYS ON INDIVIDUAL NOVELISTS

LOUISA M. ALCOTT

"Moods," *North American Review* 101 (July 1865): 276–81.
[*Eight Cousins: Or The Aunthill*], *The Nation* 21 (October 14, 1875): 250–51.

CHARLES WOLCOTT BALESTIER

"Wolcott Balestier," Introduction to *The Average Woman* by Wolcott Balestier. New York: United States Book Co., 1892. Pp. 11–34; rpt. in *Cosmopolitan Magazine* 13 (May 1892): 43–47.

HONORÉ DE BALZAC

"Honoré de Balzac," *The Galaxy* 20 (December 1875): 814–36; revised for *French Poets and Novelists*.
"The Letters of Honoré de Balzac," *The Galaxy* 23 (February 1877): 183–95; revised, and retitled, as "Balzac's Letters," for *French Poets and Novelists*.
"Honoré de Balzac," Introduction to *The Two Young Brides* by Honoré de Balzac. New York: D. Appleton, 1902. Pp. v–xliii; revised, and retitled, as "Honoré de Balzac, 1902," for *Notes on Novelists with Some Other Notes*.
"The Lesson of Balzac," *Atlantic Monthly* 96 (August 1905): 166–80; revised for *The Question of Our Speech/ The Lesson of Balzac: Two Lectures*. Boston: Houghton, Mifflin, 1905.

"Balzac," *The Times Literary Supplement*, no. 597 (June 19, 1913): 261–63; revised, and retitled, as "Honoré de Balzac, 1913," for *Notes on Novelists with Some Other Notes*.

WILLIAM BLACK

[Review of number two of *The Portrait: A Weekly Photograph and Memoir*], *The Nation* 24 (March 22, 1877): 177.
[*Macleod of Dare*], *The Nation* 27 (December 19, 1878): 387–88.

MARY ELIZABETH BRADDON

"Miss Braddon," *The Nation* 1 (November 9, 1865): 593–94.

ROBERT BROWNING

"The Novel in *The Ring and the Book*," *Transactions of the Royal Society of Literature in Commemoration of the Centenary of the Birth of Robert Browning*, 2nd series, vol. 31, pt. 4 (1912): 269–98; rpt. in *Browning's Centenary*, ed. Edmund Gosse and others. London: Asher, 1912. Pp. 21–50; revised for *Quarterly Review* 217 (July 1912): 68–87; revised again, and retitled, as "The Novel in *The Ring and the Book*, 1912," for *Notes on Novelists with Some Other Notes*.

JOHN BURROUGHS

[*Winter Sunshine*], *The Nation* 22 (January 27, 1876): 66.

MRS. E. R. CHARLES

"The Schönberg-Cotta Family," *The Nation* 1 (September 14, 1865): 344–45.
"Winifred Bertram and the World She Lived In," *The Nation* 2 (February 1, 1866): 147–48.

VICTOR CHERBULIEZ

"Meta Holdenis," *North American Review* 17 (October 1873): 461–68.
[*Miss Rovel*], *The Nation* 20 (June 3, 1875): 381.

HUBERT CRACKANTHORPE

"Hubert Crackanthorpe," Introduction to *Last Studies* by Hubert Crackanthorpe. London: William Heinemann, 1897. Pp. xi–xxiii.

MRS. D. M. M. CRAIK

"A Noble Life," *The Nation* 2 (March 1, 1866): 276.

GABRIELE D'ANNUNZIO

"Gabriele D'Annunzio," *Quarterly Review* 199 (April 1904): 383–419; revised, and retitled, as "Gabriele D'Annunzio, 1902," for *Notes on Novelists with Some Other Notes*.

BIBLIOGRAPHY

ALPHONSE DAUDET

"Alphonse Daudet," *Atlantic Monthly* 49 (June 1882): 846–51.

"Alphonse Daudet," *Century Magazine* 26 (August 1883): 498–509; revised for *Partial Portraits.*

"Port Tarascon: The Last Adventures of the Illustrious Tartarin," translation and translator's preface by Henry James. *Harper's New Monthly Magazine* 81 (June–November 1890): 3–25, 166–85, 327–40, 521–37, 683–99, 937–55.

"Alphonse Daudet," *Literature* 1 (December 25, 1897): 306–7.

XIMENES DOUDAN

"M. Doudan's New Volumes," *The Nation* 26 (January 24, 1878): 64–65.

REBECCA HARDING DAVIS

"Waiting for the Verdict," *The Nation* 5 (November 21, 1867): 410–11.

"Dallas Galbraith," *The Nation* 7 (October 22, 1868): 330–31.

JOHN WILLIAM DE FOREST

[*Honest John Vane: A Story*], *The Nation* 19 (December 31, 1874): 441–42.

CHARLES DICKENS

"Our Mutual Friend," *The Nation* 1 (December 21, 1865): 786–87.

BENJAMIN DISRAELI

[*Lothair*], *Atlantic Monthly* 26 (August 1870): 249–51.

GUSTAVE DROZ

[*Around a Spring*], *Atlantic Monthly* 28 (August 1871): 248–51.

ALEXANDRE DUMAS, FILS

"The Last French Novel," *The Nation* 3 (October 11, 1866): 286–88.

GEORGE ELIOT

"Felix Holt, The Radical," *The Nation* 3 (August 16, 1866): 127–28.

"The Novels of George Eliot," *Atlantic Monthly* 18 (October 1866): 479–92.

"Middlemarch," *The Galaxy* 15 (March 1873): 424–28.

[*Daniel Deronda*], *The Nation* 22 (February 24, 1876): 131.

"Daniel Deronda: A Conversation," *Atlantic Monthly* 38 (December 1876): 684–94; revised for *Partial Portraits.*

[Newly published tales], *The Nation* 26 (April 25, 1878): 277.

"George Eliot's Life," *Atlantic Monthly* 55 (May 1885): 668–78; revised, and retitled, as "The Life of George Eliot," for *Partial Portraits.*

FRANCIS ELLIOT

[*The Italians: A Novel*], The Nation 21 (August 12, 1875): 107.

OCTAVE FEUILLET

"Camors: Or Life Under The New Empire," The Nation 7 (July 30, 1868): 91–93.
[Les Amours de Philippe], The Nation 25 (November 15, 1877): 306.

GUSTAVE FLAUBERT

"Flaubert's Temptation of Saint Anthony," The Nation 18 (June 4, 1874): 365–66.
"Gustave Flaubert," Macmillan's Magazine 67 (March 1893): 332–43; revised for Essays in London and Elsewhere.
"Gustave Flaubert," Introduction to Madame Bovary by Gustave Flaubert. New York: D. Appleton, 1902. Pp. v–xliii; revised for Notes on Novelists with Some Other Notes.

JULIA CONSTANCE FLETCHER [GEORGE FLEMING]

[Kismet], The Nation 24 (June 7, 1877): 341.
[Mirage], The Nation 26 (March 7, 1878): 172–73.

ELIZABETH GASKELL

"Wives and Daughters: A Novel," The Nation 2 (February 22, 1866): 246–47.

THÉOPHILE GAUTIER

[Théâtre de Théophile Gautier: Mystères, Comédies, et Ballets], North American Review 116 (April 1873): 310–29; revised, and retitled, as "Théophile Gautier," for French Poets and Novelists.

JOSEPH ARTHUR GOBINEAU

"Gobineau's Nouvelles Asiatiques," The Nation 23 (December 7, 1876): 344–45.

JOHANN WOLFGANG VON GOETHE

[Wilhelm Meister's Apprenticeship and Travels], North American Review 101 (July 1865): 281–85.

OLIVER GOLDSMITH

Introduction to The Vicar of Wakefield by Oliver Goldsmith. New York: The Century Co., 1900. Pp. xi–xx.

EDMOND DE GONCOURT

[La Fille Elisa], The Nation 24 (May 10, 1877): 280.
"The Journal of the Brothers de Goncourt," Fortnightly Review 50 (October 1888): 501–20; revised for Essays in London and Elsewhere.

THOMAS HARDY

"Far From the Madding Crowd," The Nation 19 (December 24, 1874): 423–24.

HENRY HARLAND

"The Story-Teller At Large: Mr. Henry Harland," Fortnightly Review 69 (April 1898): 650–54.

BIBLIOGRAPHY

JULIAN HAWTHORNE

[*Idolatry: A Romance*], *Atlantic Monthly* 34 (December 1874): 746–48.
[*Garth*], *The Nation* 24 (June 21, 1877): 369.

NATHANIEL HAWTHORNE

"Nathaniel Hawthorne," *Library of the World's Best Literature*, ed. Charles
 Dudley Warner. New York: R. S. Peale and J. A. Hill, 1896. Vol. 12:
 7053–61.
"Hawthorne's French and Italian Journals," *The Nation* 14 (March 14, 1872):
 172–73.
"Letter to the Hon. Robert S. Rantoul, President of the Essex Institute," *The
 Proceedings in Commemoration of the One Hundredth Anniversary of the Birth
 of Nathaniel Hawthorne*. Salem, Mass.: The Essex Institute, 1904. Pp. 55–
 62.

WILLIAM DEAN HOWELLS

[*A Foregone Conclusion*], *North American Review* 120 (January 1875): 207–14.
"Howells's *Foregone Conclusion*," *The Nation* 20 (January 7, 1875): 12–13.
"William Dean Howells," *Harper's Weekly* 30 (June 19, 1886): 394–95.
"A Letter to Mr. Howells," *North American Review* 195 (April 1912): 558–62.

VICTOR HUGO

"Victor Hugo's Last Novel," *The Nation* 2 (April 12, 1866): 466–68.
"Victor Hugo's *Ninety-Three*," *The Nation* 18 (April 9, 1874): 238–39.

CHARLES KINGSLEY

"*Hereward*," *The Nation* 2 (January 25, 1866): 115–16.
[Charles Kingsley], *The Nation* 20 (January 28, 1875): 61.
"Charles Kingsley's Life and Letters," *The Nation* 24 (January 25, 1877): 60–61.

HENRY KINGSLEY

"The Noble School of Fiction," *The Nation* 1 (July 6, 1865): 21–23.

RUDYARD KIPLING

Introduction to *Mine Own People*, by Rudyard Kipling. New York: United
 States Book Co., 1891. Pp. [vii]–xxvi.
Introduction to *Soldiers Three*, by Rudyard Kipling. London: Heinemann and
 Balastier, 1891. Pp. [i] –xxi.

HORACE DE LAGARDIE

[French Novels and French Life], *The Nation* 24 (March 29, 1877): 194–95.

PIERRE LOTI

"Pierre Loti," *Fortnightly Review* 49 (May 1888): 647–64; revised for *Essays in
 London and Elsewhere*.

"Pierre Loti," Introduction to *Impressions,* by Pierre Loti. New York: Brentano's, 1900. Pp. [1]–21.

ANNE E. MANNING

"Historical Novels," *The Nation* 5 (August 15, 1867): 126–27.

DAVID MASSON

"Professor Masson's Essays," *The Nation* 20 (February 18, 1875): 114–15.

GUY DE MAUPASSANT

"Guy de Maupassant," *Fortnightly Review* 49 (March 1888): 364–86; revised for *Partial Portraits.*

"Guy de Maupassant," *Harper's Weekly* 33 (October 19, 1889) 834–35; also published as Introduction to *The Odd Number, Thirteen Tales* by Guy de Maupassant. New York: Harper and Brothers, 1889. Pp. [vii]–xvii.

PROSPER MÉRIMÉE

[*Dernières Nouvelles*], *The Nation* 18 (February 12, 1874): 111.

"The Letters of Prosper Mérimée," *The Independent* 26 (April 9, 1874): 9–10; revised, and retitled, as "Mérimée's Letters," for *French Poets and Novelists.*

[*Lettres à une autre Inconnue*], *The Nation* 22 (January 27, 1876): 67–68.

"Prosper Mérimée," *Literature* 3 (July 23, 1898): 66–68.

ALFRED DE MUSSET

"Selections from de Musset," *Atlantic Monthly* 26 (September 1870): 379–81.

"Alfred de Musset," *The Galaxy* 23 (June 1877): 790–802; revised for *French Poets and Novelists.*

LAURENCE OLIPHANT

"*The Tender Recollections of Irene Macgillicuddy,*" *The Nation* 26 (May 30, 1878): 357.

OUIDA [MARIE LOUISE DE LA RAMÉE]

[*Signa: A Story*], *The Nation* 21 (July 1, 1875): 11.

JAMES PAYN

"The Late James Payn," *Illustrated London News* 112 (April 9, 1898): 500.

GEORGE SAND

"George Sand's *Mademoiselle Merguem,*" *The Nation* 7 (July 16, 1868): 52–53.

"George Sand," *New York Tribune* (July 22, 1876), p. 3; rpt. in *Parisian Sketches.*

[M. Taine's Letter on George Sand], *The Nation* 23 (July 27, 1876): 61.

"George Sand," *The Galaxy* 24 (July 1877): 45–61; revised for *French Poets and Novelists.*

"*Dernières Pages,*" *The Nation* 25 (October 25, 1877): 259–60.

"She and He: Recent Documents," *The Yellow Book* 12 (January 1897): 15–38 [on the friendship of George Sand and Alfred de Musset]; revised, and retitled, as "George Sand, 1897," for *Notes on Novelists with Some Other Notes.*

"George Sand: The New Life," *North American Review* 174 (April 1902): 536–54; revised, and retitled, as "George Sand, 1899," for *Notes on Novelists with Some Other Notes.*

"George Sand," *Quarterly Review* 220 (April 1914): 315–38; revised, and retitled, as "George Sand, 1914," for *Notes on Novelists with Some Other Notes.*

JULES SANDEAU

"Jean de Thommeray: Le Colonel Evrard," The Nation 18 (February 5, 1874): 95.

HENRY D. SEDLEY

"Marian Rooke," The Nation 2 (February 22, 1866): 247–48.

MRS. A. M. C. SEEMULLER

[*Emily Chester: A Novel*], *North American Review* 100 (January 1865): 279–84.
"Opportunity," *The Nation* 5 (December 5, 1867): 449–50.

MATHILDE SERAO

"Mathilde Serao," *North American Review* 172 (March 1901): 367–80; revised, and retitled, as "Mathilde Serao, 1902," for *Notes on Novelists with Some Other Notes.*

HARRIET E. PRESCOTT SPOFFARD

[*Azarian: an Episode*], *North American Review* 100 (January 1865): 268–77.

STENDAHL [MARIE-HENRI BEYLE]

"Henry Beyle," *The Nation* 19 (September 17, 1874): 187–89.

ROBERT LOUIS STEVENSON

"Robert Louis Stevenson," *Century Magazine* 35 (April 1888): 868–79; revised for *Partial Portraits.*

"The Letters of Robert Louis Stevenson," *North American Review* 170 (January 1900): 61–77; revised, and retitled, as "Robert Louis Stevenson, 1894," for *Notes on Novelists with Some Other Notes.*

ELIZABETH STODDARD

Two Men: A Novel. In James Kraft, "An Unpublished Review by Henry James," *Studies in Bibliography* 20 (1967): 267–73.

HARRIET BEECHER STOWE

[*We and Our Neighbors: Records of an Unfashionable Street*], *The Nation* 21 (July 22, 1875): 61.

BAYARD TAYLOR

"Autobiography in Fiction—An Unpublished Review by Henry James," *Harvard Library Bulletin* 11 (1957): 245–47.

WILLIAM MAKEPEACE THACKERAY

"Thackerayana: Notes and Anecdotes," *The Nation* 21 (December 9, 1875): 376.

"Winchelsea, Rye, and *Denis Duval*," *Scribner's Magazine* 29 (January 1901): 44–53; revised for *English Hours*.

ANTHONY TROLLOPE

"Miss Mackenzie," *The Nation* 1 (July 13, 1865): 51–52.

"Can You Forgive Her?" *The Nation* 1 (September 28, 1865): 409–10.

"The Belton Estate," *The Nation* 2 (January 4, 1866): 21–22.

"Linda Tressel," *The Nation* 6 (June 18, 1868): 494–95.

"Anthony Trollope," *Century Magazine* 26 (July 1883): 384–95; revised for *Partial Portraits*.

T. ADOLPHUS TROLLOPE

[*Lindisfarn Chase: A Novel*], *North American Review* 100 (January 1865): 277–78.

IVAN TURGENEV

[*Frühlingsfluthen. Ein König Lear des Dorfes. Zwei Novellen*], *North American Review* 118 (April 1874): 326–56; revised, and retitled, as "Ivan Turgénieff," for *French Poets and Novelists*.

[A Turgenev poem], *The Nation* 23 (October 5, 1876): 213.

"Ivan Turgnef's New Novel," *The Nation* 24 (April 26, 1877): 252–53.

"Ivan Turgénieff," *Atlantic Monthly* 53 (January 1884): 42–55; revised for *Partial Portraits*.

"Ivan Turgénieff," *Library of the World's Best Literature*, ed. Charles Dudley Warner. New York: R. S. Peale and J. A. Hill, 1896. Vol. 25: 15057–62.

MRS. HUMPHRY WARD

"Mrs. Humphry Ward," *English Illustrated Magazine* 9 (February 1892): 399–401; revised for *Essays in London and Elsewhere*.

ADELINE DUTTON WHITNEY

[*The Gayworthys: a Story of Threads and Thrums*], *North American Review* 101 (October 1865): 619–22.

CONSTANCE FENIMORE WOOLSON

"Miss Constance Fenimore Woolson," *Harper's Weekly* 31 (February 12, 1887): 114–15; revised, and retitled, as "Miss Woolson" for *Partial Portraits*.

WALTER WYCKOFF

[*The Workers*], *Literature* 2 (April 23, 1898): 484.

EMILE ZOLA

[*Une Page d'Amour*], *The Nation* 26 (May 30, 1878): 361–62.
"*Nana,*" *The Parisian* 48 (February 26, 1880): 9.
"Mr. Henry James on *Nana,*" in *Nana: A Realistic Novel* by Emile Zola. London: Vizetelly, 1884. Pp. [xiv]–xv.
"Emile Zola," *Atlantic Monthly* 92 (August 1903): 193–210; revised for *Notes on Novelists with Some Other Notes.*

5: Essays on Various Topics

"[Vicomte Henri de Bornier's] *La Fille de Roland,* [Alphonse Daudet's] *Fromont Jeune et Risler Aine,* and [H. Wallon's] *Jeanne d'Arc,*" *The Galaxy* 20 (August 1875): 276–80.
"New Novels," *The Nation* 21 (September 23, 1875): 201–3 [Anne Tackeray, Margaret Oliphant, Mrs. T. Erskine, Mrs. C. Denkin, André Theuriet, Gustave Droz, L. B. Walford].
"Recent Novels," *The Nation* 22 (January 13, 1876): 32–34 [Frank Lee Benedict, Charles H. Doe, Annie Edwards, George Sand, Octave Feuillet].
"The Minor French Novelists," *The Galaxy* 21 (February 1876): 219–33; revised, and retitled, as "Charles de Bernard and Gustave Flaubert," for *French Poets and Novelists.*
"Parisian Festivity," *New York Tribune* (May 13, 1876): 2:cols. 1–3; rpt. in *Parisian Sketches* [C. A. Sainte-Beuve, Emile Zola].
"Parisian Topics," *New York Tribune* (July 1, 1876), 3:col. 1–2; rpt. in *Parisian Sketches* [Ximenes Doudan, George Sand].
"An American and An English Novel," *The Nation* 23 (December 21, 1876): 372–73 [Helen Hunt Jackson, Rhoda Broughton].
"An Animated Conversation," *Scribner's Magazine* 5 (March 1889): 371–84; revised for *Essays in London and Elsewhere* [the current literary market].
"London," *Harper's Weekly* 41 (February 6, 1897): 134–35 [state of criticism, Mrs. Edward Ridley, Clement Shorter's *Charlotte Brontë and Her Circle*].
"London," *Harper's Weekly* 41 (July 31, 1897): 754 [theory, George Gissing, Pierre Loti]; revised, and retitled, as "London Notes, July 1897," for *Notes on Novelists with Some Other Notes.*
"London," *Harper's Weekly* 41 (August 21, 1897): 834 [state of criticism, Paul Bourget lecture on Flaubert, Margaret Oliphant]; revised, and retitled, as "London Notes, August 1897," for *Notes on Novelists with Some Other Notes.*
"American Letter," *Literature* 2 (April 9, 1898): 422–42 [Gertrude Atherton, Henry Garland].
"American Letter," *Literature* 2 (April 30, 1898): 511–12 [criticism, Winston Churchill, Gertrude Atherton, Bret Harte].
"American Letter," *Literature* 2 (May 7, 1898): 541–42 [the war and literature: George Cary Eggleston, Paul Leicester Ford].
"American Letter," *Literature* 2 (May 28, 1898): 620–21. [military novels: Robert W. Chambers, J. A. Altsheler, Captain Charles King].

"American Letter," *Literature* 2 (June 11, 1898): 676–78 [criticism of American magazines, John Jay Chapman's essays on Stevenson and others].

"American Letter," *Literature* 3 (July 9, 1898): 17–19 [the novel of dialect: Charles Egbert Craddock, Miss Sarah Barnwell Elliot, William Dean Howells, Mary Wilkins].

"The Present Literary Situation in France," *North American Review* 169 (October 1899): 488–500 [state of criticism, Emile Zola, Paul Bourget].

INDEX

About, Edmond, 132, 156

Aesthetics, morality v., 39–41

Alden, H. M., 418n

"Altar of the Dead, The," Preface to, 397, 415n, 416n

Altick, Richard D., 230n, 483n

Ambassadors, The, 252, 296–97, 389, 408n, 411n; filling out the story of, 364–69; first-person narrative in, 370–71; as James' best production, 363; Lambert Strether as central consciousness in, 363, 368–69, 371–72, 418n; Maria Gostrey as *ficelle* in, 372–74; origin of the story of, 361–62, 418n; Paris setting of, 368; the scenic method in, 372–75; subordinate characters as dramatic devices in, 372–73

Ambassadors, The, Preface to, 194, 256n, 398, 400, 402, 408n, 411n, 417n, 455n, 480

America. *See* United States

American, The, 125, 190n, 191n, 237, 286, 389, 402, 421n; Christoper Newman as central consciousness in, 281; James' re-reading of, 274–75, 276; origin of the story of, 272–73; Paris and, 273, 275–76, 277; realism and, 278–79, 409n; revision of, 388–89; as romance, 274–75, 278–85, 408n, 409n

American, The, Preface to, 127, 396, 403–4, 414n

"American Letter," 252

American Scene, The, 393, 414n

Americans. *See* Anglo-Saxons, the; United States

Ampère, André-Marie, 30, 42n

Anderson, Hendrik, 256n

Anesko, Michael W., 405, 416n

Anglo-Saxons, the (including Anglo-Americans) (*see also* British, the; United States): Anglo-American v. French criticism, 252; Anglo-American v. French writers, 200, 201, 203, 216, 230n, 247; decline in birth rate among, 256n; feminine story-tellers predominate among, 452; reaction to Maupassant, 212–13, 216, 224–25, 226; as readers averse to dialogue, 306–7

Architecture: the novel and, 288–89, 294, 308; novelists as architects, 288, 294–95, 422, 451; Zola and, 451

Aristotle, 69

Arnold, Matthew, 93; connection between vital criticism and healthy literature, 186, 237, 252, 454n; controversy in England over, 11–15, 22n; *Culture and Anarchy*, 191n; disinterestedness of the critic, 2, 14–15; faith in the future, 238; free play of mind and, 2, 412n; great masters as touchstones of criticism for, 235, 240n; on the high Victorian as a transitional period, 20–21, 412n; on ideas and creativity in literature and criticism, 240n, 252; in-betweenness of, 19–20; James as disciple of, 186, 188n, 237–39, 239n, 252, 453–54; James disinterested as critic of, 19–21; James on *Essays in Criticism*, 11–18; versus James on place of critic vis-à-vis literature, 239; James' relationship with, 19, 21; as one who sticks to his subject, 17; and Philis-

503

Arnold, Matthew (*continued*)
tines, 15, 96n; "practical" criticism and, 16–17; Sainte-Beuve v., 20–21, 40; sentiment and, 13, 20; style of, 11–13; sympathetic spirit of, 12
"[Arnold's] *Essays in Criticism*," 58n, 130n, 411n, 422n, 486n
Art: Andrew Lang and the art of fiction, 184, 186, 193n, 229n, 230n, 237; Anglo-Saxons v. French on novel as a work of, 157n; "competing" with life, 194–95; critic as equal of artist, 234–35, 238; discussion good for, 165–66, 186, 188n, 189n; and experience, 235–36; "felt life" as a source of, 289–90, 397, 411n, 486n; and life, 41n, 166, 382–92, 397, 403–4, 421n, 486n; life v., 41n, 166; Protestantism and, 168; theory and, 197–98; theory v. practice in, 197, 222–23; Turgenev on morality and, 138–39; Turgenev's nature as poetic v. artistic, 137; United States as thin environment for, 108–9, 336–37, 407n, 415n
"Art of Fiction, The," 5–6, 41, 56, 58n, 130n, 154, 157n, 158n, 229n, 237, 239n, 252, 256n, 394, 395, 397–98, 403, 409n, 410n, 411n, 414n, 420n, 422n, 455n, 483n; "Criticism" v., 237
Aspern Papers, The, 221, 377, 403–4; alteration of the Florence legend for, 334–36; development of the story of, 334–35; Jeffrey Aspern as American Byron, 335; origin of the story of, 330, 331–33; as romance, 331–32; verisimilitude in, 335; the visitable past in, 333–35, 414n
Aspern Papers, The, Preface to, 58n, 130n, 189n, 398–99, 403, 404, 407n, 419n, 480, 483n, 485n
Auden, W. H., 4
Austen, Jane, 53, 58n, 182
"Author of Beltraffio, The," Preface to, 416n
Awkward Age, The, 193n, 253, 396, 397, 401–2, 413n; central object of, 309; dialogue in, 306–7; disrespectful reception of, 308; French v. English manners regarding coming of age, 304–5; "Gyp" and, 306–7, 309, 312–13, 412n; London and, 301, 303, 305; ori-

gin of the story of, 300–301; overtreatment in, 312–15, 397; as scenic, 308–15, 401–2, 412n; unforeseen growth of a grain of subject-matter in, 300–303
Awkward Age, The, Preface to, 396, 397, 398, 401, 407n, 414n, 417n, 419n

Bacon, Francis, 69
Baldwin, William Wilberforce, 324, 413n
Balzac, Honoré de: admiration for duplicity and dissimulation in, 74; on Catholic Church, 71–72; Charles de Bernard and, 82, 97n; charm of, 90, 92; *La Comédie Humaine*, 61–62, 64, 66–68, 81, 85, 88, 90, 93; and Comte, 68, 96n; conservatism of, 69; contradictions in, 69, 89; and Dickens, 77; *Edition définitive* and, 91, 393; estimate of, by the French, 59–60; expertise of, 267; explanation and referential narrative in, 372; forgiveness and, 230n; form and content in, 145; French characteristics of his plan for *La Comédie Humaine*, 68; French irony and contempt in, 56, 80–82, 96; French manners and morals as portrayed by, 103; George Eliot v., 56, 61, 73; grandiose plan of *La Comédie Humaine*, 66–68; hatred of the bourgeois and provincial in, 81; and Hawthorne, 95n, 130n; James' changing estimate of, 91–93; kindliness of, 69; lack of travel of, 62–63; lingering influence of, 96, 192n; maturation of, 61, 65–66; monarchism of, 71, 72; money as subject of novels of, 62; morality and, 71–72, 73–74, 92; Paris as world and universe of, 62; pedigree of, 63; *Le Père Goriot*, 82–84, 277, 409n; personal finances of, 60, 61–62; as philosophic novelist, 69; philosophy of, 68–69; portraits of people by, 77–89; portraits of places by, 75–77, 277, 409n; portraits of women by, 84–88; portraits of young gentlemen by, 88–89; as portrayer of virtue and vice, 70; preparatory research for novels by, 64; productivity of, 64–65; reassessment of, 449; religion in, 71–72; revision and, 388; Sainte-Beuve and, 28, 35, 36,

59, 94n; Shakespeare and, 82–83, 90, 92; snobbishness of, 87–88; as social novelist, 61, 64; as spontaneous v. reflective writer, 70–71; style of, 89–90; and Rabelais, 70; Thackeray v. (Taine on), 94n; this-worldliness of, 73–74, 89; and Trollope, 65; truth in, 72–73; and Turgenev, 77–78; as two writers in one, 70–71

Baudelaire, Charles: and Sainte-Beuve, 32–33, 35, 36–37, 39, 41; James' low estimate of, 41; "Les Fleurs du Mal," 32

"Beast in the Jungle, The," 397

Beerbohm, Max, 395

"Bench of Desolation, The," 393

Bernard, Charles de, 82, 97n

Bersot, Ernest, 30–32

Besant, Walter, 165–93 seriatim, 221, 229n, 230n, 237

Blackmur, R. P., 406

Bosanquet, Theodora, 477

Bossuet, Jacques-Bénigne, 14, 22n, 31, 42n

Bostonians, The, 125, 184, 393, 402

Boswell, James 59

Bourget, Paul, 237

Bradshaw, George, 230n

British, the (*see also* Anglo-Saxons, the): their attitude towards the cynic, 204; chauvinistic criticism of James' "An International Episode" by, 193n; Continental thinkers v., 11, 14, 16, 22n; controversy over Arnold among, 11–15, 22n; decorum of, 52; English and American writers v. the French, 200, 201, 203, 216, 230n, 247; English fiction, 181, 224; the English novel, 57, 165–66; English novelists as failing to appreciate form, 57; English v. French criticism, 152, 234, 252; English v. French fiction, 213, 218–19, 220, 239n, 247; English v. French imagination, 68; English v. French manners, young lady's coming of age, 304; flaccid fiction of late-Victorian England, 237; George Eliot as an *English* writer, 56, 80–81, 96; James between French and, 225–26; no demand for printed versions of plays, 306; reaction to Maupassant's short tales, 209; reception of the short tale, 208; Sainte-Beuve as French, not English, in temperament, 46; small-mindedness of, 16; superiority of English sympathy to French, 56; theory and the English novel, 165; Turgenev and the English language, 136; Turgenev and English literature, 136–37; Turgenev and English people, 158; Victorian self-consciousness about fiction, 184; view of French irony and caricature, 80, 96n; Zola and the English reader, 182–83, 219

"Browning in Westminster Abbey," 477, 479, 485n

Browning, Robert, 6; charity of imagination in, 467, 476, 481–82; "difficulty" of, 460, 483n; *The Inn Album*, 478–79, 483n; James' relationship with, 477; literature as adventure for, 462, 479–80; neglect of form by, 483n; as poet v. as social lion, 484n; and point of view, 480, 481; as portrayer of the special relation between men and women, 485n; *The Ring and the Book*, 6, 460–76; and Trollope, 483n

Bruch, Max, 417n

Bryce, James 413n

Bullock, William Henry, 158n

Bulwer-Lytton, Edward, 189n

"Bundle of Letters, A," 125

Bunyan, John, 114

Byron, 61, 186, 189n, 331, 414n

Camp, Maxime du, 138n

Cartwright, W. C., 483n

Center, as subject or topic of a work, 268, 273, 281–83, 294, 309, 401

Center of consciousness, 259, 268–69, 281, 283, 294, 318–23, 328, 363, 368–69, 371–72, 409n, 418n, 420n, 466, 472–73, 481, 484n; first-person narrative, 370–71, 400, 419n; "going behind," 309, 351, 402, 417n; mirror, 250, 254, 420n; multiple centers of consciousness, 400–401; reflector, 355, 485n

"Chaperon, The," 343

Character(s): children as, 318–19, 320, 328, 338, 400; drawn from real persons, 335–36, 364, 419n; incident v., 174–75, 192n; "mystic conversion" of a

Character(s) (*continued*)
quiet character into the stuff of drama, 297–98; plot v., 173–74,. 185–86, 287–89, 294–95, 410n; public persons as, 335–36, 404; a single character as the subject of fiction, 368–69, 400; special, 266, 403; women as central, 292–94; writer's sympathy with his, 169, 191n; young people as, 293–94, 347–51

Charles Scribner's Sons, 393–94

Chateaubriand, François-René de, 28, 42n

Chesterton, G. K., 415n

Children: as characters, 318–19, 320, 328, 338, 400; perception v. vocabulary of, 320, 400; as protagonists, 318–19; as readers, 243

Clairmont, Jane, 331–33, 398, 403, 414n, 419n

Clifford, Mrs. W. K., 478

Coburn, Alvin Langdon, 378–82, 420n

Colet, Louise, 32

Community: of critics, 186, 237, 239, 478; of readers, 394, 478; of writers, 184, 239, 477–78

Comte, Auguste, 68, 96n

Confidence, 125

Cousin, Victor, 28, 32, 42n

"Covering End, The," 393

"Crapy Cornelia," 393

Creativity in literature and criticism, 240n, 247, 252

Critic: community of critics, 186, 237, 239, 478; as equal of artist, 234–35, 238; "feeling [his] way," 154; as helper of artist, 234, 239; James' defense against his critics, 189–91nn; located between historian and philosopher, 2; Maupassant as, 197–208; phases of James' career as a, 5–6; sacrificial function, 235, 238; as touchstone, 240n

Criticism: androgyny and, 3, 26, 153; Anglo-American v. Continental 11, 14, 16, 22n, 152, 234, 252; creativity in, 240n, 247, 252; dignity of, among the French, 234; discussion as good for art, 165–66; 186, 188n, 189n; disinterestedness and, 2, 14–15; experience and, 235–36; feminine qualities and, 240n; free play of mind and, 2, 4, 412n; freedom as first

condition of, 2; Goethe and, 2n, 31, 186n, 189n; great masters as touchstones of, 235, 240n; grounded in feeling, 486n; history v., 2–3; ideas and creativity in, 240n, 247, 252; in-betweenness and, 2–4, 19–20, 41; industrialization and, 237–38; as an industry, 233, 237–38, 253; James on, 232–36; James' output of, 4–5; judging a novelist on execution alone, 170, 175, 176, 181, 226–27; life and, 382–92, 422n; literature v., 239; New York Edition as plea for, 394–95; oriented to the individual artist, 222; philosophy v., 2–3; practical, 16–17, 19; proliferation of, 232–34, 237; "reviewing" v. 232–33, 237–38, 245; Sainte-Beuve on truth in, 28–32; and superstition that fiction is wicked, 166–67; vital, and healthy literature, 237, 247, 252, 454n; vulgarization of, 233

"Criticism," 6, 193n, 230n, 252, 253, 396, 407n, 411n, 417n, 422n, 455n, 486n; "The Art of Fiction" v., 237; "The Future of the Novel" v., 252, 253

Curiosity, 165–66, 454

"Daisy Miller," 39, 128

"Daisy Miller," Preface to, 407n, 412n

Darwin, Charles, 54

Daudet, Alphonse, 138n, 219, 416n, 421n

Daugherty, Sarah B., 8, 21, 189n; on "The Art of Fiction," 188; on Dumas and James, 413n; on "Emile Zola," 454; on George Eliot and James, 57; on Hawthorne and James, 128–29; on Ibsen and James, 413n; on James and romance, 408n; on Maupassant and James, 227; on Turgenev and James, 155

Day, Thomas, 447, 456n

"Death of the Lion, The," 336

Defoe, Daniel, 189n

Delacroix, Eugène, 20

Delorme, Joseph, 35, 43n

"Diary of a Man of Fifty," 125

Dialogue, 65, 82, 306–7, 434

Dickens, Charles, 158n, 191n, 455n; characterizations by, 53, 58n, 77, 146, 292; disregard of sexuality by, 249, 256n;

and first-person narrative, 371, 419n; and the novel, 165, 182, 188n; *Our Mutual Friend*, 194n; and Podsnappery, 194n; and Turgenev, 146; Howells on, 184, 188n

Difficulty, 358, 396; Browning and, 460, 483n; as novelist's inspiration, 356; in reading as in writing, 396

Disinterestedness (*see also* In-betweenness): as critical ideal, 2; James and, 19–21, 39, 221–22, 226, 454

Donnée, 41, 83, 175, 192n, 226–27, 362, 397–98, 418n, 465

Drama (*see also* Scene): *The Ambassadors* and, 372–75; in consciousness, 268–69, 355; demand for text of a long-running play in England, France, and U.S., 306; James turning some of his works into plays, 393; "mystic conversion" of a quiet character into the stuff of, 297–98; and the novelist, 268, 303, 308–15, 329, 401, 412n, 414n; scene v. picture, 353, 372–73, 419n; scenes as fictional structures, 401

Dreyfus, Alfred, 446, 454n

Du Boisgobey, Fortuné-Hippolyte-Auguste, 193n

Dumas, Alexandre (fils), 35, 65, 182, 412n

Dumas, Alexandre (père), 431

Dupanloup, Félix-Antoine-Philibert, 31, 42n

Durousov, Princess, 157n

Dutch picture, 76, 96n

Edel, Leon, 97n, 393, 407n, 415n, 421n, 485n; on *The American*, 409n; on Balzac's *Édition définitive* and James' New York Edition, 95n; collection of James' letters by, 7; collection of James' literary criticism by, 4; on James and Balzac, 92–93; on James and a community of writers, 184; on James and A. L. Coburn, 420n; on James and George Eliot, 57; on James and Hawthorne, 129; on James and Hendrik Andersen, 256n; on James and Ibsen, 413n; on James and Maupassant, 221, 227; on James' "Emile Zola," 454; on James' essays on French masters, 449; on

James' prefaces, 406; on James' problems with drama, 412n; on James' short stories, 416n; on James vis-à-vis Arnold and Sainte-Beuve, 21; on *The Portrait of a Lady*, 55; on the year 1879 for James, 125; on Turgenev's response to James' fiction, 156n

Edgeworth, Maria, 447, 456n

Eliot, George, 194n, 230n; *Adam Bede*, 292; Austen and, 53, 58n; Balzac v., 56, 61, 73; "brain" combined with observation in, 54, 56, 57n; v. Browning as portrayer of Italy, 469, 485n; v. Charles Reade, 58n; combination of realism and idealism in, 54; consciousness as basis of story in, 399, 484n; *Daniel Deronda*, 55–56, 292, 411n; depictions of men and women by, 49; too much detail in, 48, 50, 56; echo of Darwin and Huxley in, 54; as an *English* writer, 56, 80–81, 96; as failing to see importance of form, 56; Fielding v., 54; frail vessels in, 292, 293, 294, 411n; James on *Middlemarch*, 48–54; James' relationship with, 55; James' tribute to, 57; late starter as novelist, 61; *Middlemarch*, 6, 292, 483n, 485n; *The Mill on the Floss*, 55, 80–81, 292; and "new school" of fiction, 125; pedantry of, 56; psychological penetration of, 52; *Romola*, 48, 52, 54, 56, 469, 485n; *Silas Marner*, 54; superiority to Edmond de Goncourt of, 186–87, 193n; sympathetic treatment of characters by, 54, 56

Eliot, T. S., 125–26

Emerson, Ralph Waldo, 131n

"Emile Zola," 6, 129n, 157n, 193n, 194n, 397, 409n, 411n, 419n, 420n

England, the English. *See* British, the

English Hours, 393

European v. American culture, 1

Europeans, The, 190n, 191n

Experience (*see also* Life): art and, 177–78, 235–36; writing from, 172–73, 289–90

Fairy-tales, 339–40, 415n

Felix Holt, the Radical, 56

Feminism (*see also* Sexuality; Women), 85, 97, 253–34, 256n

Feydeau, Ernest: and Sainte-Beuve, 35, 36, 37, 39, 41, 42n; *Sylvie*, 41, 42n
Ficelle, 297, 372–74, 402, 411n, 419n
Fiction (*see also* Literature; Novel; Short story); Andrew Lang and the art of, 184, 186, 193n, 229n, 230n, 237; as bound up with society, 247–48; democratic nature of contemporary French, 218–19; English, 181, 224; English v. French, 213, 218–19, 220, 239n, 247; flaccid fiction of late-Victorian England, 237; George Eliot and "new school" of, 125; historical, 461, 465, 480; as history, 465, 480; house of, 290–91, 397, 399; Howells on "new school" of, 125, 184, 188n, 193n, 230; importance of architecture in French, 288; James' defense against critics of his, 189–91nn.; "laws" of, 170–73; morality in, 180–82, 221, 224–25, 226, 289, 397–98, 419n, 449; as one of the *fine* arts, 167–68; pietism in Anglo-Saxon, 212–13; proliferation of, 242, 425; scene in, 372–75, 401, 414n; single character as subject of, 368–69, 400; Stevenson and the difficult in, 278; theory of, 252–53; Turgenev's response to James', 156n; vulgarization of, 239n, 245, 253; as wicked, 166–67; Zola's, as picture of numbers, not individuals, 430–32
Fielding, Henry, 51, 89, 189n, 248
"Figure in the Carpet, The," 336
First-person narrative. *See* Center of consciousness
Flaubert, Gustave, 182, 227n; on expression, 391, 421n; failure of, 147, 176; as "initiator" of Maupassant, 213, 216; *Madame Bovary*, 146, 147, 475; public reaction to, 185; reassessment of, 449; Sainte-Beuve and, 35; as testifying to the manners and morals of the French, 103; and Turgenev, 134, 137, 146–47, 152, 156n, 158n, 176
Fontanes, Christine de, 29–30
Fontanes, Louis de, 29, 31, 42n
Form, 398; anecdote, 472; antitheses, 270; Balzac and, 145; Browning and, 483n; consistency, 283–84; Edmond de Goncourt and, 137; English novelists and,

57; essence v., 296; foreshortening, 267, 288, 357, 359, 399, 407n, 422n; George Eliot and, 56; importance of architecture in French fiction, 288; life v., 260–61; misplaced middle, 356, 402–3, 417n; novel as a literary, 179, 182, 194n, 254, 290, 375, 420n, 455n; novelist as architect, 422n; overtreatment, 298, 312–15, 397; plan, 413n; selecting a subject, 398; Thackeray on, 165; Turgenev and, 137; unforeseen growth of a germ of subject-matter, 300–303
France. *See* French, the
Free play of mind, 186, 253; Arnold and, 2, 412n; criticism and, 2, 4, 412n
Freedom, 169–70, 175–76, 182, 185, 220, 246–48, 253–54, 339–40
French, the: and argument over literature, 46n; Balzac as a Frenchman, 56, 68, 80–82, 96; British view of French irony and caricature, 80, 96n; decline of the French novel, 455n; demand for text of a long-running play, 306; democratic nature of contemporary French fiction, 218–19; dignity of criticism among, 234; their estimate of Balzac, 59–60; French v. Anglo-American criticism, 152, 234, 252; French v. Anglo-American writers, 200, 201, 203, 216, 230n, 247; French v. Anglo-Saxons on novel as a work of art, 157n; French v. English and American writers, 200, 201, 203, 216, 230n, 247; French v. English criticism, 152, 234, 252; French v. English ideas of fiction, 213, 218–19, 220, 239n, 247; French v. English imagination, 68; French v. English manners, young lady coming of age, 304; high importance of architecture in French fiction, 288; how they treat their great literary figures, 59; Howells on *French Poets and Novelists*, 93; influence on Arnold, 12; irony and contempt among, 56, 80, 96n; James between English and, 225–26; James' essays on French masters, 449; James' sympathy with French language and culture, 188n; literary argument and, 46n; literary tradition of, 207; manners and morals of, 103; Maupassant and

French tradition, 207; morality among, 103; morality and French fiction, 419n; party passion and, 27, 28; reception of the short tale, 208–9; Sainte-Beuve as evaluated by the, 26–28, 41n; Sainte-Beuve as French, not English, in temperament, 46; Sainte-Beuve's Gallic imagination, 39–41, 47; superiority of English mind to the French, 56; Turgenev and the French language, 136; Turgenev and French realistic literature, 137–38; view of French irony and caricature, 80, 96n

"French Critic, A," 2–3, 20–21, 40

French Poets and Novelists, 39, 93, 449

"Frühlingsfluthen. . . ," 156n

"Function of Criticism at the Present Time, The," 22n, 189n, 238, 240n

"Future of the Novel, The," 6, 194n, 230n, 396, 407n, 412n, 417n, 420n, 453, 455n, 486n; "Criticism" v., 252, 253

Gaskell, Mrs. Elizabeth: *Wives and Daughters*, 271, 408n

Gautier, Théophile, 36, 59, 95n

Gavarni (Sulpice-Guillaume Chevalier), 36, 43n

Gibbon, Edward, 167

Gide, André, 157n

Girardin, Emile de, 36, 43n

Gissing, George, 5, 184, 185

Godkin, Edwin Lawrence, 19

Godwin, Mary, 331

Goethe: on the common, 14; and criticism, 2n, 31, 186, 189n; disinterestedness and, 2; and his native soil, 63; Sante-Beuve on, 2n; on thought v. action, 240n

Golden Bowl, The, 351, 389, 393, 411n, 417n; central consciousness in, 376–79; indirect presentation in, 376–79; London and, 381–82; revision of, 382–92; use of photographs with, in the N.Y. Edition, 379–82, 420n

Golden Bowl, The, Preface to, 41n, 395, 396, 399, 401, 409n, 411n, 455n, 478

Goldsmith, Oliver: *She Stoops to Conquer*, 54, 240n

Goncourt, Edmond de, 43n: *Chérie*, 179–80, 193n; as democratic, 219; and form,

137; George Eliot v., 186–87; as modern, 35

Goncourt, Jules de, 35, 43n, 219, 221

Goode, John, 2, 184, 187

Gosse, Edmund, 125, 237, 405, 477

Gozlan, Léon, 60, 62, 64, 95n

Graham, Kenneth, 184, 188

Gray, Thomas, 275, 409n

Grundy, Mrs., 185, 193n, 224–25, 226

Guérin, Eugenie de, 11, 14, 22n

Guérin, Maurice de, 11, 14, 22n

Guizot, François-Pierre-Guillaume, 65, 95n

Guy Domville, 239

"Guy de Maupassant," 6, 129n, 157n, 193n, 397, 411n, 419n

"Gyp" (Marie-Antoinette de Riquetti de Mirabeau, comtesse de Martel de Janville), 306–7, 309, 312–13, 412n

Haggard, Henry Rider, 213, 229n

Hallam, Henry, 65, 95n

Hardy, Thomas, 5, 184, 185, 237

Harte, Bret, 208

Hawthorne, 7, 39, 407n, 409n, 415n: reception of, 128

Hawthorne, Nathaniel: allegory in, 114–16; *American Note-Books*, 108, 129n; as American writer, 101–2; and Balzac, 95n, 130n; *The Blithedale Romance*, 127; and the deeper psychology, 125; democratic feeling in, 109–10; *English Note-Books*, 104, 129n; fancy and imagination in, 113–14; historical coloring weak in, 118, 127; imagination in, 113–14, 117–18, 120, 121, 124, 127; influence on James, 125–26; James as biographer of, 126–28; James' refusal to take seriously the dark side of, 128, 192n; as a man of fancy, 113, 119; *The Marble Faun (Transformation)*, preface to, 108, 130n; morality in, 115–16, 117, 118, 124, 127; note-books, 107–8, 110, 123, 129n; as an observer of small things, 107; period of incubation for, 103–6; as a pessimist, 112–13; neither philosopher nor historian, 103; Poe on, 115; productivity of, 101; Puritan conscience and, 111–13, 118; and realism, 103, 127; and romance, 125, 127; *The*

Hawthorne, Nathaniel (*continued*)
 Scarlet Letter, 116–24, 127; and the
 short tale, 208; simple life of, 101; as
 springing from the soil of New England, 95n, 101–2, 104–5, 110, 126,
 127; style of, 122–24; symbolism over
 realism in, 118, 122
"Hayward's Essays," 456n
Hegel, Georg Friedrich Wilhelm, 69
Heine, Heinrich, 11, 18, 22n, 417n
Herrick, Robert, 421n
High Bid, The, 393
Hill, Mrs. Frank H., 193n
"Historical Novels," 483
History: artist v. historian, 403; critic and
 philosopher v. historian, 2–3; fiction
 as, 465, 480, 483n; Hawthorne and,
 103, 118, 127; literature v., 54, 58n,
 167, 465, 480–81, 483n; novel as, 58n,
 167, 189n
Hogarth, William, 96n, 440, 445n
Homer, 18, 23n
"Honoré de Balzac," 56, 58n, 129n, 130n,
 131n, 189n, 421n, 455n
"Hop o' my Thumb," 339, 415n
House of fiction, 290–91, 397, 399
Howells, William Dean, 185, 189n, 239n,
 394–95, 410n, 411n, 484n; and *The Ambassadors*, 418n, 419n; and the *Atlantic
 Monthly*, 406n, 408n, 419n; on Dickens,
 184, 188n; on *French Poets and Novelists*,
 93; on Hawthorne, 128; James' public
 tribute to, 477–78; and Jonathan
 Sturges, 418n; on living life to the fullest, 418n; Maupassant and, 230n; on
 "new school" of fiction, 125, 184,
 188n, 193n, 230; on stories of character
 v. stories of plot, 229n; style of, 125
Hugo, Victor, 28, 35, 61, 159
Humboldt, Alexander von, 64, 95n
Huxley, T. H., 54, 58n

Ibsen, Henrik, 185, 252, 412n; *A Doll's
 House*, 311; *Ghosts*, 311; *Hedda Gabler*,
 311; *John Gabriel Borkmann*, 311; *Monsieur Alphonse*, 311; *The Wild Duck*, 311
Ideas, in literature and criticism, 240n,
 247, 252
Illustration (*see also* Picture): word-pic-
 ture v., 379–80

Imagination, 404, 450; Browning and,
 467, 476, 481–82; English v. French, 68;
 Hawthorne and, 113–14, 117–18, 120,
 121, 124, 127; Sainte-Beuve's Gallic,
 39–41, 47
In-betweenness: defined by James, 2–4;
 exemplified by James, 19, 41, 152–53,
 221–22, 225–26, 453
Industrialization: effects on culture, 237–
 38; and literature, 407n, 455n
Industry: criticism as an, 233, 237–38,
 253; fiction as an, 247; literature as an,
 267, 407n; Sainte-Beuve on "industrial
 literature," 253
Intensity, 268, 369, 419n
"International Episode, An," 125, 193n,
 411n
International theme, 184, 299, 411n, 414n
"In the Cage," 326–28, 484n
Irving, Washington, 125
Italian Hours, 393, 484n, 485n
Italy: Browning's *The Ring and the Book*
 and, 469–72, 474; Browning v. George
 Eliot on, 469, 485n; Florence, 259, 262,
 286, 330–31; James on the difficulty of
 working in Venice, 286–87; Rome, 331,
 437–39; Venice, 286–87, 331; Zola and,
 249–50, 253–54, 437–39
"Ivan Turgénieff," 410n, 456n
Ivory Tower, The, 4

Jacobson, Marcia, 255n
James, Alice (sister), 131n, 414n
James, Billy (nephew), 477
James, Henry (*see also* titles of individual
 works): able to transcend nationality,
 1; advice to the young novelist by,
 182–83; as *the* American novelist, 393;
 as androgynous, 3; Beerbohm cartoon
 of, 395; defense against critics of his
 own fiction, 189–91nn; as New Yorker,
 4; older v. younger, 395; phases of his
 critical career, 5–6; phases of his life,
 184; poetry and, 479; as both reader
 and writer, 395–97; as reader, 478;
 short stories in New York Edition,
 416n
James (Sr.), Henry, 150, 156n, 184
James, William (brother), 3, 156n, 414n,
 415n, 421n, 477, 483n

Johnson, Samuel, 62, 95n
"Jolly Corner, The," 393
Jordan, Elizabeth, 415n
Joubert, Joseph, 11, 22n
"Julia Bride," 393
Jullien, Jean, 484n

Keats, John, 61

"Lady Barbarina," 411n
"Lady Barbarina," Preface to, 397, 411n
La Farge, John, 477
La Harpe, Jean-François de, 31, 42n
Lamartine, Alphonse de, 28, 35, 61, 95n
Lang, Andrew: and the art of fiction,
     184, 186, 193n, 229n, 230n, 237; on
     Haggard, 229n; on James, 193n
Lathrop, George Parson, 103, 106–7,
     129n
Lavedan, Henri, 307, 412n
Lee, Vernon, 414n
Lee-Hamilton, Eugene, 414n
Lemaître, Jules, 204, 228n
Lesage, 419n; Gil Blas, 371
"Lesson of Balzac, The," 92, 130n
"Lesson of the Master, The," 221
"Lesson of the Master, The," Preface to,
     404, 415n, 416n, 419n
"Letters of Eugène Delacroix, The" 20
"Liar, The," 221, 343–45
Life (see also Experience): and art, 41n,
     166, 177–78, 382–92, 397, 403–4, 421n,
     486n; art v., 41n, 166; criticism and,
     382–92, 422n; "felt life" as a source of
     art, 289–90, 397, 411n, 486n; fiction
     and, 172–73; novel's representation of,
     166, 169–70; slice of, 466; society and
     fiction 247–48
"Life of George Eliot, The," 485n
Linton, Eliza Lynn, 255n
"Literary Influence of the Academies,
     The," 22n
Literature (see also Fiction; Novel; Short
     story): as adventure for Browning, 462,
     479–80; argument over, among the
     French, 46n; creativity in, 240n, 247,
     252; criticism v., 239; French tradition
     in, 207; great figures of, treatment by
     the French, 59; history v., 54, 58n, 167,
     465, 480–81, 483n; ideas and creativity

in, 240n, 247, 252; industrialization
     and, 407n, 455n; as an industry, 267,
     351, 407n, 417n; Sainte-Beuve as liter-
     ary man par excellence, 24–25; Sainte-
     Beuve's critique of "industrial," 253;
     Turgenev and English, 136–37;
     Turgenev and French realistic, 137–38;
     vital criticism and healthy, 237, 247,
     252, 454n; vulgarization of, 245; and
     the vulgarization of criticism, 233;
     women's changing social role and bet-
     ter, 250, 253–54, 256n
Littré, Emile, 31, 42n
Lockhart, John Gibson, 59, 119–20, 131n;
     Adam Blair, 119–20, 131n
"London," 252
"London Life, A," 221
Lorelei, 348, 350, 401, 417n
Loti, Pierre, 221
Loucks, James F., 483n
"Louisa Pallant," 221
Lowell, James Russell, 93, 130n, 409n;
     The Biglow Papers, 130n
Lucretius, 32, 42n

Macaulay, Thomas Babington, 167
Maeterlinck, Maurice, 417n
Mathilde, the Princess, 24, 32
"Matthew Arnold," 19–20, 40
Matthews, Brander, 93
Matthiessen, F. O., 414n, 421n
Maupassant, Guy de, 6, 41, 96n, 157n;
     L'Abandonné, 211–12; Anglo-American
     consciousness and, 226; Anglo-Saxon
     reaction to the short tales of, 212–13;
     Bel-Ami, 215–16; better as an artist
     than as a commentator, 197–98; his
     characters have no reflective side, 219–
     20; his characters too exclusively erot-
     ic, 220; as critic, 197–208; as cynic, 204,
     215; his failure, 226–27; as feeling the
     weight of French tradition, 207;
     L'Héritage, 214; on illusion v. reality in
     novels, 199; incompleteness of, 223–
     24, 226, 228n; inconsistencies between
     theory and practice in, 222–24; and
     James, 221; James' disinterestedness in
     criticism of, 226; as a lion in the path,
     204, 219, 226; La Maison Tellier, 202–3,
     211; making the most of his consider-

Maupassant, Guy de (*continued*)
able gifts, 200; masculine quality of,
208, 228n; *Miss Harriet*, 212; *Monsieur
Parent*, 213–14; *Mont-Oriol*, 216; and
morality, 203, 217, 224–25, 226; perceiving life through the senses, 201–3,
204; *Pierre et Jean*, 197, 204, 212, 215,
218, 227n; and plot, 216, 217; portrayal
of the Norman peasant by, 210–12;
powers of concision of, 221; on psychology and the novel, 204–6; and
sense of sight, 201–3; and sense of
smell, 201; and sexual sense, 203, 205–
6, 220, 224; his short tales, 208; and the
ugliness of life, 209, 215, 216; *Une Vie*,
216–17, 225, 226; women in, 214–15;
and Zola in James' eyes, 456n
Maurois, André, 94n
McIntyre, Clara, 421n
Meredith, George, 185
Mesmer, Friedrich Anton, 96n
Micawber, Mr., 171, 191n
Middle Years, The, 55
Millet, Jean-François, 426, 455
Mirror. *See* Center of consciousness
"*Modern Women*," 255n
Montégut, Emile, 112–13, 118, 131n
Moore, George, 5, 184, 185
"Mora Montravers," 393
Morality: aesthetics v., 39–41; art and,
397–98; Balzac and, 71–72, 73–74, 92;
"dull dispute" over, 289, 410n; in fic-
tion, 168–69, 171, 180–82, 221, 224–25,
226, 289, 397–98, 419n, 449; among the
French, 103; and French fiction, 419n;
Hawthorne and, 115–16, 117, 118, 124,
127; James' fiction and, 185–86;
Maupassant and, 203, 217, 224–25,
226; Paris and, 368; pietism in Anglo-
Saxon fiction, 212–13; prudery, 181,
194n, 224–25; as true completeness,
226; Zola and, 453–54
Morton, Thomas, 193n
"Mr. and Mrs. James T. Fields," 19
Mudie, Charles Edward, 193n
Murdock, Kenneth, 414n
Musset, Alfred de, 36, 61, 95n

Napoleon, Louis, 455
"New Novel, The," 6, 480, 482

New York Edition: as *édition définitive*,
393; effect on James criticism of, 405–6;
financial result of, 404; James' prefaces
for, 393–95; photographs and, 379–82;
quotations from, 7; revision for, 382–
92, 393, 395, 421n
"Next Time, The," 336
Norton, Grace, 187
Notebooks of Henry James, The, 130n, 412n,
413n, 416n, 417n, 418n, 419n, 481,
484n
Notes of a Son and Brother, 477
Notes on Novelists, 482, 486
Novel(s) (*see also* Fiction; Literature): Anglo-Saxons v. the French on novel as a
work of art, 157n; architecture and the,
288–89, 294, 308; "best-sellers," 351,
417n; decline of French, 455n; Dickens
and the, 165, 182, 188n; the English,
57, 165–66; the good, 168–76, 185, 449;
historical, 465, 480; as history, 58n,
167, 189n; illusion v. reality in, 199; as
a literary form, 179, 182, 194n, 254,
290, 375, 420n, 455n; money as subject
of Balzac's, 62; the new, 184, 186,
256n; preparatory research for Balzac's, 64; and the principle of
selection, 480–81; psychology and the,
204–6; *Roderick Hudson* as James' first,
260, 406n; and romance, 175, 192n;
same character in more than one, 67–
68, 96n; short story v., 466; as slice of
life, 466; Stevenson on the, 184, 189n;
"story," 178–80; Thackeray on the
form of the, 165; vulgarization of, 169;
young people's changing view of sexuality and the future of the, 249–50,
253–54; Zola and the, 177, 435–37
"Novel in *The Ring and the Book*, The," 6,
58n, 130n, 186, 189n, 256n, 414n
Novelist(s) (*see also* individual novelists):
age of maturity for, 61; as architects,
288, 294–95, 422n, 451; difficulty as inspiration for the, 356; drama and the,
268, 303, 308–15, 329, 401, 412n, 414n;
James' advice to young, 182–83; James
as *the* American, 393; judging on execution alone, 170, 175, 176, 181, 226–
27; as painters, 49, 57n, 167, 189n,
260–61, 264, 265, 267, 275, 278, 317,

322, 345, 402, 422n; painters v., 167, 168, 189n; philosophers and, 167; poets v., 61
Novella (*see also* Short story), 193n
"Novels of George Eliot, The," 58n

Ogle, Miss Annie, 483n
Optimism, 182–83, 224
Other House, The, 393
"Owen Wingrave," 393
Ozymandias, 405

Painter(s). *See* Novelist(s)
Paris, 62; and *The American*, 273, 275–76, 277; Balzac and, 62; melodrama and, 368, 408n; morality and, 368; as setting for *The Ambassadors*, 368; Turgenev and, 132, 134, 137–38, 140–42, 143, 148, 150, 155
Parisian Sketches, 451
Parker, Hershel, 421n
Partial Portraits, 150, 184, 221, 225
Passionate Pilgrim, A, 190n, 191n
Past: representation of the, 167; the visitable, 333–35, 414n
"Patagonia, The," 221
Payne, William M., 39
Pendrel, Ralph, 415n
"Pension Beaurepas, The," 125
Perry, Thomas Sargent, letters of James to, 1, 19, 129n, 187
Pessimism, 182–83, 224
Philosopher: critic a compromise between historian and, 2; novelist and, 167
Philosophy: Balzac and, 68–69; criticism v., 2–3; Hawthorne and, 103
Picture (*see also* Dutch picture; Illustration): 96n; man's appetite for a, 244, 254; narrative segment v. dramatic scene, 353, 402; novelist as painter, 49, 57n, 167, 189n, 260–61, 264, 265, 267, 275, 278, 317, 322, 345, 402, 422n; novelist v. painter, 167, 168, 189n
Pindar, 14
Pinero, Arthur Wing, 477
Pinker, James B., 405
Plato, 69
Plot: character v., 173–74, 185–86, 287–89, 294–95, 403, 410n; psychology v., 179–80, 190n; story v., 217

Poe, Edgar Allen, 115, 208
Poetry, James and, 479
Poets: age of maturity for, 61; novelists v., 61
Portrait of a Lady, The, 39, 41n, 55, 125, 184, 190n, 191n, 192n, 347, 389, 393, 409n, 411n, 417n; and central female characters in other writers, 292–93; character v. plot in, 287–89, 294–95; creation of subordinate characters in, 295; difficulty of working in Venice on, 286–87; Henrietta Stackpole as *ficelle*, 296–97, 298; international theme, 299; Isabel Archer as central consciousness in, 294; "mystic conversion" of a quiet character into the stuff of drama, 297–98, 411n; origin of the story of, 287, 292; structure of, 294–95, 297
Portrait of a Lady, The, Preface to, 41n, 55, 396, 398, 399, 401, 409n, 414n, 417n, 419n, 422n, 486n
"Present Literary Situation in France, The," 252, 456n
Princess Casamassima The, 184, 192n, 328, 389, 402, 404, 407n
Princess Casamassima, The, Preface to, 399–400, 404, 418n, 419n, 420n, 484n
"Private Life, The," 477, 484n
Psychology: George Eliot and, 52; Hawthorne and the deeper, 125; Maupassant and, 204–6; plot v., 179–80, 190n; Zola and, 445
"Pupil, The," 324–26, 343, 413n

Quixote, Don, 171

Rabelais, François, 70
Ralston, W. R. S., 156n
Reade, Charles, 51, 58n
Reader(s): James as a, 395–97, 478; James' complaints about, 396; James' relationship with his, 395–97; women and children, 243
Realism (*see also* Verisimilitude): air of reality, 173, 192n; and *The Ambassadors*, 278–79, 409n; Balzac and, 64, 192n; in George Eliot, 54; in Hawthorne, 103, 118, 122, 127; novel and, 166, 171–72; novel as slice of life, 466; romance and, 278–79, 403–4, 409n; romanticism v., 409n; in Turgenev, 146

Reflector. *See* Center of consciousness
Renan, Ernest, 19, 31, 42n, 156n; on Turgenev, 132
Re-reading: *The American*, 274–75, 276; Browning's *The Ring and the Book*, 478; *The Golden Bowl*, 382–92, 395; *The Portrait of a Lady*, 286–87; *Roderick Hudson*, 259–60, 264–66
Reverberator, The, 221
Reverberator, The, Preface to, 411n
Revision, 259, 264–65, 284, 382–92, 393–95, 407n, 409n, 421n
Richardson, Samuel, 248
Ritchie, Lady Anne, 191n
Roberts, Morris, 8, 57, 192n, 453; on Balzac and James, 94; on James' "Emile Zola," 454; on James in old age, 453
Roderick Hudson, 19, 125, 190n, 191n, 193n, 286, 403, 409n; antitheses in, 270; Balzac and the sense of place and, 263–64; center of interest in, 268; central consciousness in, 268–69; inadequacy of time-scheme of, 266–68; as James' first novel, 260, 406n; James' re-reading of, 259–60, 264–65; revision of, 259, 264–65, 407n; Roderick Hudson as special character in, 266; verisimilitude in, 269–70
Roderick Hudson, Preface to, 130n, 398, 399, 403, 412n, 413n, 415n
Romance: *The American* as, 274–75, 278–85, 408n, 409n; *The Aspern Papers* as, 331–32; defined, 279–81; in Hawthorne, 125, 127; historic fiction and, 465; James' ambivalence towards, 409n; James and, 408n; novel and, 175, 192n; realism and, 278–79, 409n; realism v., 403–4; *The Turn of the Screw* as, 342
Romantic, the, 274–75, 278–85, 331–32, 342, 414n; Sainte-Beuve and the romantic tradition, 35–36; Sand and the romantic tradition, 137
Rousseau, Theodore, 140
Ruskin, John, 237–38

Sainte-Beuve, Charles-Augustin: able to transcend nationality, 37; as androgynous, 3, 26; Arnold v., 20–21, 40; and Balzac, 28, 35, 36, 59, 94n; and Baudelaire, 32–33, 35, 36–37, 39, 41; on Christian mythology, 34; as combination of scholar and man of the world, 3, 25–26; as compared to Scherer by James, 40; critique of "industrial literature" by, 253; on the death of his heart, 34; and Delorme, 43n; as evaluated by the French, 26–28, 41n; and Feydeau, 36; as French rather than English in temperament, 46; Gallic imagination of, 39–41, 47; on Gavarni, 36; and George Sand, 35, 36; James as follower of, 186, 188n, 453–54; James on his collected letters, 24–38; letter to Christine de Fontanes of, 29–30; letter to Ernest Bersot of, 30–32; letter to Louise Colet of, 32; letter to the Princess Mathilde of, 32; and liberty, 28, 30; as a literary rather than a philosophical talent, 40, 130n; as the literary man par excellence, 24–25; as a model for emulation, 1; on modern drama, 35–36; and "modern" writers, 35; as opponent of dogma, 186; personal finances of, 33; remarkable combination of qualities in, 25–26; and romantic tradition, 35–36; on truth in criticism, 28–32; and Zola, 35, 37–38
"Sainte-Beuve," 3, 130n, 411n, 422n, 486n
"Sainte-Beuve's English Portraits," 3, 40–41
"Sainte-Beuve's First Articles," 40
Saintsbury, George, 93
Saloon, The, 393
Sand, George: age of maturity of, 61; Balzac v., 65; James' essay on, 93; reassessment of, 449; and romantic tradition, 137; Sainte-Beuve and, 35, 36; Zola v., 447
Sandeen, Ernest, 416n
Scene (*see also* Drama): in *The Ambassadors*, 372–75; in *The Awkward Age*, 308–15, 401–2, 412n; in fiction, 252, 372–75, 401, 414n; narrative segment v. dramatic, 353, 402; picture v., 353, 372–73, 419n; in *What Maisie Knew*, 329, 414n; in *The Wings of the Dove*, 353, 372
Scherer, Edmond, 37, 43n; on Balzac, 59,

95n; compared to Sainte-Beuve by James, 40

"Scherer's Literary Studies," 40

Scott, Sir Walter, 61, 63, 148, 249, 292, 431

Selection, 177, 193n, 217, 259–61, 302–3

Sense of the Past, The, 252

Sexuality (*see also* Characters; Feminism; Women): Balzac and, 84–88; in Browning's *The Ring and the Book,* 475, 485–86; Dickens and, 249, 256n; James on, 248–49, 253–54, 256n, 452; and James' portrayal of young people, 269; Maupassant and, 203, 205–6, 220, 224; young people, changing view of among, 249–50, 253–54

Shakespeare: and Balzac, 82–83, 90, 92; Charles Reade and, 58n; intermissions and lapses in, 69; *King Lear* and Balzac's *Le Père Goriot,* 82–83; and his native soil, 63; *Romeo and Juliet,* 292; strong women characters in, 293

Shelley, Percy Bysshe: age of maturity of, 61; Browning and Swinburne v., 469–70, 485n; letters of, held by the Misses Clairmont, 331–33, 414n

Short story: James on, 344, 416n; in New York Edition, 416n; novel v., 260; reception in England, France, and the United States, 208–9

Silsbee, Captain, 332, 414n

Slice of life, 466

Small Boy and Others, A, 477

Smith, Seba, 130n

Smith, William Henry, 255n

Soulié, Frédéric, 36, 43n

Spenser, Edmund, 114

Spilka, Mark, 184, 188n, 189n

Spinoza, Baruch, 11, 22n

Spoils of Poynton, The, 377

Spoils of Poynton, The, Preface to, 398, 400, 411n, 413n, 481, 484n

Staël, Madame Germaine de, 30

Stang, Richard, 184

Stedman, Edmund Clarence, 479

Stephen, Leslie, 125

Stephens, Fitz-James, 22n

Stevenson, Robert Louis, 5, 193n, 221, 229n, 246, 271, 421n; on art "competing" with life, 194–95; and the difficult

in fiction, 278; James' relationship with, 187; on the novel, 184, 189n; and strong female characters, 292; *Treasure Island,* 179–80; *Weir of Hermiston,* 271, 408n

"Story," 178, 180, 217, 260, 288

Stowe, Harriet Beecher: *Uncle Tom's Cabin,* 2

Sturges, Jonathan, 418n

Sturgis, Howard, 405

Subject. *See* Center, as subject or topic of a work

Sue, Eugène, 36, 43n

Summersoft, 393

Supernatural, the, 337, 341–42, 415n

Swinburne, A. C., 469–70, 485n; *Essays and Studies,* 485n

Symonds, J. A., 125

Tacitus, 14

Taine, Hippolyte-Adolphe, 3, 37, 43n; on Balzac, 59, 68–69, 85–86, 87, 90, 94n; comparison of Balzac and Thackeray by, 94n

Tennyson, Alfred, 97n, 479, 483n

Thackeray, William Makepeace: age of maturity of, 61; daughter of, Lady Anne Ritchie, 191n; *Denis Duval,* 271, 408n; and the form of the novel, 165; and misery, 214; portrayal of women by, 51–52, 87; same figure in more than one novel of, 67–68, 96n; serialization and, 271; Taine on Balzac v., 94n; Howells on, 188n

Theory: and art, 197–98, 222–23; and the English novel, 165; of fiction, 252–53

Tolstoy, Leo, 448, 456n

Tragic Muse, The, 336, 402

Tragic Muse, The, Preface to, 57n, 398, 399, 401, 402, 419n, 483n

Trilling, Lionel, 128

Trollope, Anthony, 125; *Autobiography,* 157n; Balzac v., 65; Browning and, 483n; and making believe, 167; same figure in more than one novel of, 68, 96n; work habits of, 142, 157n

Turgenev, Ivan, 221, 294; "aristocratic temperament" of (James on), 135, 153–54, 156n; as androgynous, 139, 153, 156; Balzac v., 77–78; as combination

Turgenev, Ivan (*continued*)
of observer and poet, 146; constructing
a story from memorable individuals
encountered, 288–89; Daudet to James
on, 421n; and England, 147–48; and
the English language, 136; and English
literature, 136–37; and Flaubert, 134,
137, 146–47, 152, 156n, 158n; and
form, 137; and the French language,
136; and French realistic literature,
137–38; importance of characters v.
plot in, 144–45; individuality v. impersonality in, 133; as never inventing,
410n; James' changing estimate of, 150,
153–55; James' "distancing" in his appreciation of, 151–52; James'
relationship with, 150–53, 155; James'
similarity to, 153; and the keeping of
appointments, 143, 150; living quarters
at Bougival, 148; living quarters in
Paris, 140–42; masculinity of, 139, 153,
156n; modesty of, 134–35; on morality
and art, 138–39; natural goodness of,
135, 143, 149; and Paris, 132, 134, 137–
39, 140, 143, 148, 150, 155; and Pauline
Viardot, 140, 157, 158n; personal finances of, 142–43; poetic v. artistic
nature in, 137; realism of, 146; Renan
on impersonality of, 132; and the Russian language, 133; Russianness of,
132–33, 139, 141–42, 149; similarity between James and, 153; his tale about a
serf and a lap-dog, 176; *A Sportsman's
Notebook* (*Memoirs of a Sportsman*), 142,
154, 157n; as talker, 133, 138, 143–44;
young Russian protégés of, 140–41;
and Zola, 138, 152
Turn of the Screw, The, 337–43, 404; as anecdote, 340; central idea of, 341–42;
difficulty in, 341; evil in, 341–43; as
fairy tale, 339; indirect presentation in,
340–41; origin of the story of, 338; as
romance, 342; supernatural in, 337–38
"Two Faces, The," 343, 345

United States (*see also* Anglo-Saxons,
the): appreciation of *Middlemarch* in,
54; culture of, v. European culture, 1;
demand for text of a long-running play
in, 306; deterioration of culture, 414n;

Hawthorne as an American writer,
101–2; lack of awareness of Europe in,
411n; reception of the short tale in,
208; social position of the writer in,
105, 130n; thin environment for art,
108–9, 336–37, 407n, 415n; young
lady's coming of age in, 305

"Velvet Glove, The," 393
Verisimilitude (*see also* Realism), 186, 270,
283, 318, 335, 403, 404, 409n
Viardot-Garcia, Pauline, 140, 157n, 158n
Villemain, Abel-François, 28, 32, 42n
Voltaire, 228n

Waggoner, Hyatt, 128
Walpole, Robert, 89, 97n
Ward, Mrs. Humphry, 230n, 402, 478
Washington Square, 4, 130n, 190n
Watson, William, 229n
Wells, H. G., 421n, 478
What Maisie Knew, 402; boy or girl as protagonist, 318–19; central consciousness
in, 318–23, 328; child's perception v.
child's vocabulary, 320; genesis and
development of the story of, 316–23;
and immorality, 322–23; ironic center
of, 321–22; and *In the Cage*, 326–28;
and *The Pupil*, 324–26; the scenic method and, 329, 414n; verisimilitude in,
318
What Maisie Knew, Preface to, 396, 399,
400, 417n, 420n, 484n
Whistler, James McNeill, 418n
William Wetmore Story and His Friends, 485n
Wings of the Dove, The, 372, 402, 411n;
challenge of having a sick protagonist,
346–47, 350–51; not designed to be a
popular success, 351–52; difficulty as
the novelist's inspiration, 356; flawed
presentation of characters in, 352–53;
foreshortening in, 359; misplaced middle in, 356, 402; Molly Theale as
center, 348–51, 358; origin of the story
of, 346, 416n; picture v. scene in, 353;
scenic consistency of, 372; successive
centers in, 352–55
Wings of the Dove, The, Preface to, 57n,
396, 400–401, 402, 413n, 414n, 419n,
484n, 485n

Women (*see also* Feminism; Sexuality): Anglo-American women as story-tellers, 452; in Balzac, 84–88, 91, 97n; in Browning, 485n; as central characters, 293–94; changing social role leading to better literature, 250, 253–54, 256n; coming of age in France, England, and America, 304–5; feminine qualities in criticism, 240n; in George Eliot, 49, 292, 293, 294; not marrying in Victorian England, 243, 255n; in Maupassant, 214–15; as readers, 243; in Thackeray, 51–52, 87

Wonder, 323, 328, 397

Woolson, Constance Fenimore, 414n

Wordsworth, William, 37, 145, 158n, 412n

Young people: changing view of sexuality among, and the future of the novel, 249–50, 253–54; James' advice to young novelists, 182–83; James' portrayal of, 269; James as young and old, 395; portraits of young gentlemen by Balzac, 88–89; Russian protégés of Turgenev, 140–41; young lady's coming of age, 301, 303–5

Zhukovsky, Paul, 157n

Zola, Emile, 6, 41, 138n, 193n, 194n; as architect, 451; *L'Argent*, 436, 457; *L'Assommoir*, 430–47 passim; *La Bête Humaine*, 436; *Au Bonheur des Dames*, 436; *La Conquête de Plassans*, 429, 455n; *La Débâcle*, 436, 442, 447, 448, 455n; as democratic, 219; "Le Docteur Pascal," 441–42; and Dreyfus, 446, 454n; and the English reader, 182–83, 219; *Fécondité*, 436, 439; his fiction as a picture of numbers, not of individuals, 430–32; *Germinal*, 436, 442, 444, 447, 448; institutions as "central thing" of his novels, 435–37; James' changing estimate of, 451; *La Joie de Vivre*, 441; and Les Rougon-Macquart, 427, 429, 430, 435, 436, 445; as both master and failure, 451, 452–53; morality and, 453–54; and the nature of man, 432, 433; on the novel, 177; personality reflected in his work, 427–28; psychology and, 445; public reaction to, 138, 185; *Quatre Evangiles*, 435; *Rome*, 439; Sainte-Beuve and, 35, 37–38; scale of his creations, 444, 446, 448; and science, 439–40, 442, 452–53; as short on experience of life, 428, 430, 431; solid and serious work of, 182; sordid detail v. whole in, 440–42; system v. impressions in, 450; taste and, 177, 432–33, 439, 453; as testifying to the manners and morals of the French, 103; *Thérèse Raquin*, 37; *Les Trois Villes*, 433, 437–39; Turgenev on, 152; *Vérité*, 429, 430, 436, 437, 439, 445, 446–47; writing about Rome without knowing it, 437–39